The Cold War and After

EXPANDED EDITION

International Security Readers

Strategy and Nuclear Deterrence (1984)

Military Strategy and the Origins of the First World War (1985)

Conventional Forces and American Defense Policy (1986)

The Star Wars Controversy (1986)

Naval Strategy and National Security (1988)

Military Strategy and the Origins of the First World War, rev. and
  exp. ed. (1991)

—published by Princeton University Press

Soviet Military Policy (1989)

Conventional Forces and American Defense Policy, rev. ed. (1989)

Nuclear Diplomacy and Crisis Management (1990)

The Cold War and After: Prospects for Peace (1991)

America's Strategy in a Changing World (1992)

The Cold War and After: Prospects for Peace, exp. ed. (1993)

—published by The MIT Press

The Cold War and After

Prospects for Peace

EXPANDED EDITION

AN *International Security* READER

EDITED BY

Sean M. Lynn-Jones
and Steven E. Miller

THE MIT PRESS
CAMBRIDGE, MASSACHUSETTS
LONDON, ENGLAND

Third printing, 1994

The contents of this book were first published in *International Security* (ISSN 0162-2889), a publication of The MIT Press under the sponsorship of the Center for Science and International Affairs at Harvard University. Except as otherwise noted, copyright in each article is owned jointly by the President and Fellows of Harvard College and of the Massachusetts Institute of Technology.

John Lewis Gaddis, "The Long Peace: Elements of Stability in the Postwar International System," *IS* 10, no. 4 (Spring 1986) © 1986 by John Lewis Gaddis. Reprinted with permission of the author. John Mueller, "The Essential Irrelevance of Nuclear Weapons: Stability in the Postwar World," *IS* 13, no. 2 (Fall 1988); Robert Jervis, "The Political Effects of Nuclear Weapons: A Comment," *IS* 13, no. 2 (Fall 1988); Carl Kaysen, "Is War Obsolete? A Review Essay," *IS* 14, no. 4 (Spring 1990); Jack Snyder, "Averting Anarchy in the New Europe," *IS* 14, no. 4 (Spring 1990); John J. Mearsheimer, "Back to the Future: Instability in Europe After the Cold War," *IS* 15, no. 1 (Summer 1990); Stephen Van Evera, "Primed for Peace: Europe After the Cold War," *IS* 15, no. 3 (Winter 1990/91); Christopher Layne, "The Unipolar Illusion: Why New Great Powers Will Rise," *IS* 17, no. 4 (Spring 1993); Robert Jervis, "International Primacy, Is the Game Worth the Candle?," *IS* 17, no. 4 (Spring 1993); Samuel P. Huntington, "Why International Primacy Matters," *IS* 17, no. 4 (Spring 1993); John Lewis Gaddis, "International Relations Theory and the End of the Cold War," *IS* 17, no. 3 (Winter 1992/93).

Selection and preface, copyright © 1993 by the President and Fellows of Harvard College and of the Massachusetts Institute of Technology.

ISBN 0-262-62088-X

Library of Congress Catalog Card Number 93-77977

Contents

The Contributors

SEAN M. LYNN-JONES is an Adjunct Research Fellow at the Center for Science and International Affairs, Harvard University, and Consulting Editor of *International Security*. He was the journal's Managing Editor, 1987–91.

STEVEN E. MILLER is Editor of *International Security* and Director of Studies at the Center for Science and International Affairs, Harvard University.

JOHN LEWIS GADDIS is Distinguished Professor of History and Director of the Contemporary History Institute at Ohio University.

JOHN MUELLER is Professor of Political Science at the University of Rochester.

ROBERT JERVIS is Adlai E. Stevenson Professor of International Relations at Columbia University and a member of its Institute of War and Peace Studies.

CARL KAYSEN is David W. Skinner Professor of Political Economy in the Program on Science, Technology, and Society at the Massachusetts Institute of Technology.

JACK SNYDER is Professor of Political Science at Columbia University.

JOHN J. MEARSHEIMER is Professor of Political Science at the University of Chicago.

STEPHEN VAN EVERA is Assistant Professor of Political Science at the Massachusetts Institute of Technology.

CHRISTOPHER LAYNE teaches international politics at UCLA.

SAMUEL P. HUNTINGTON is Eaton Professor of the Science of Government at Harvard University, where he is Director of the John M. Olin Institute for Strategic Studies.

Acknowledgments

The editors gratefully acknowledge the assistance that has made this book possible. A deep debt is owed to all those at the Center for Science and International Affairs (CSIA), Harvard University, who have played an editorial role at *International Security*. Teresa Pelton Johnson and Stephen L. Stillwell, jr., were indispensable to the preparation of the contents for publication. We thank John Lewis Gaddis for granting permission to reprint his article, "The Long Peace," here. Special thanks go to Julia Slater and Karen Motley at CSIA and to Patrice Baer and Sally Gregg at MIT Press for their invaluable help in preparing the volume for publication.

Preface | Sean M. Lynn-Jones and Steven E. Miller

The first edition of *The Cold War and After* appeared in March of 1991, amid unprecedented upheaval in the post-1945 international order. The authors of the essays collected in that volume applied prominent theories of international relations to explain why the Cold War was a "long peace" and to predict whether the future will be as stable. Although none of the authors who made predictions in the first edition of this book foresaw the immediate demise of the Soviet Union, they did argue, among other things, that the Soviet Union would eventually collapse, that post–Cold War Europe would be less stable than Cold War Europe, and that ethnic and national conflicts would plague the Balkans and the former Soviet Union.

This expanded edition includes all the essays that were in the original edition, as well as four new ones that extend the effort to anticipate and assess the implications of the end of the Cold War. None of the original essays has been edited or updated. Because they address fundamental questions about the character of post–Cold War international politics, and because the real-life answers to those questions will emerge only over a period of years, these essays remain timely and relevant. Readers can judge for themselves how the predictions offered in these essays have fared so far.

The first edition of this volume was published because it was clear that an important era in world politics was coming to an end. During the Cold War, the world's great powers enjoyed an uneasy peace. For all its costs in terms of tension and tyranny, the Cold War was a remarkably stable era in world history. Despite frequent crises and harsh rhetoric, the United States and the Soviet Union avoided armed conflict with one another. Europe, which had decimated itself in two bloody and catastrophic world wars in the first forty-five years of the twentieth century, suffered only limited and brief wars in Hungary and Cyprus, as well as intermittent terrorist violence. Conflicts raged outside Europe, but even these wars rarely involved major powers and remained limited compared to the two world wars.

The dramatic events of 1989–91 brought the long postwar era to a close. The collapse of the Soviet Empire in East Central Europe ended the division of Europe and restored democracy to countries that had been ruled by

International Security, Winter 1992/93 (Vol. 17, No. 3)
© 1993 by the President and Fellows of Harvard College and of the Massachusetts Institute of Technology.

communist parties for over forty years. Communism collapsed in the Soviet Union, and that country splintered into fifteen newly independent states. These momentous changes were accompanied by perceptions of a shift in the structure of world power. Many observers argue that the bipolar world dominated by the two superpowers will be replaced by a new multipolar system in which a united Germany, an economically vital Japan, and a populous China will join the top ranks of the leading powers. Others claim that the new world will be unipolar, with the United States the only super-power.

Will this new world be at least as peaceful as the old? Why was the Cold War era so remarkably stable? Has war become obsolete? Is there still a need to worry about the traditional security problems that have dominated inter-national politics? What kind of international system will the future bring? What will be the distinguishing features of the new international order? The essays in this book attempt to address these fundamental questions.

Several central themes run through this volume. First, there is the question whether the most important causes of war are to be found in the configu-ration of the international system or within the domestic political orders of states. Some observers, particularly realist theorists of international politics, emphasize the importance of systemic causes and claim, for example, that bipolar international systems are less prone to war than multipolar ones; others argue the opposite. Another school of thought finds many causes of war at the level of the state. In particular, the argument that democracies tend to be peace-loving has inspired considerable research and debate. All of these arguments have obvious relevance to the emerging post–Cold War international system.

Second, the role of nuclear weapons in the postwar world has been a central question. Have nuclear weapons maintained peace by eliminating incentives to start wars? Or have they put the world on a hair-trigger footing in which enormous destruction could result from the slightest miscalculation or mistake? In the absence of nuclear war, there can, of course, be no empirical resolution of such questions, but the importance of preventing nuclear war requires a continuing search for answers.

Third, how do international economic relations affect the prospects for peace? The classic nineteenth-century liberal argument that economic inter-dependence breeds peace is widely discredited as an oversimplification. Lib-eral theories of international cooperation now go beyond interdependence in explaining how international regimes and institutions can affect the probability of war. In addition, changes in the primary means of production—from agricultural to industrial, and then to post-industrial—may alter the incentives for war.

The first four essays collected here (Gaddis, Mueller, Jervis, and Kaysen) begin by analyzing the sources of the post-1945 peace. They then turn to a consideration of whether nuclear weapons or other factors have prevented war. The next three essays (Snyder, Mearsheimer, Van Evera) debate whether the new world will see war or peace, and offer different prescriptions for preventing a return to chaos. The subsequent three essays (Layne, Jervis, and Huntington) focus on America's predominance in the aftermath of the collapse of the Soviet Union: Is U.S. primacy sustainable, desirable, and beneficial? The final essay (Gaddis) explores why so many theories and theorists failed to predict the end of the Cold War.

John Lewis Gaddis's "The Long Peace" explores the reasons why the United States and the Soviet Union kept the Cold War from becoming a shooting war. Gaddis suggests that the bipolar distribution of power in the international system helped to preserve stability. This structure was simple enough that it did not require sophisticated leadership to maintain it. Alliance patterns after 1945 thus were remarkably stable. Even defections to opposing alliance systems, such as those of China (twice) and Cuba, did not have much effect on the basic distribution of power, because each of the two major poles was in a position to defend itself without allies. The United States and the Soviet Union also were economically independent; they were geographically remote and did not depend on one another for trade or resources in any important way. This independence eliminated potential sources of conflict.

Gaddis also considers arguments at the state level, noting that claims that capitalist (or Marxist) states are innately aggressive and expansionist do not seem to fit the pattern of Cold War politics. He recognizes that the democratic American system of government often has made U.S. foreign policy erratic, but that the resulting deficiencies have not made the United States more likely to risk war. Both superpowers moderated their ideologies during the Cold War. Systemic imperatives apparently triumphed over domestic sources of instability.

Nuclear weapons have provided an additional source of stability. As Gaddis points out, before the nuclear age statesmen could optimistically contemplate how their countries would gain from war. The clear threat of nuclear destruction makes optimistic miscalculation far more difficult and induces a healthy degree of caution.

Gaddis suggests that another technological revolution—the development of the reconnaissance satellite—may have been almost as important as the advent of nuclear weapons. Sophisticated satellite monitoring gives states a better idea of their opponents' capabilities and reduces the risk of surprise attacks. Further, it has made verification of arms control agreements possible.

The United States and the Soviet Union also developed largely tacit "rules of the game" to manage their rivalry during the Cold War. Gaddis proposes the following list, based on the observable pattern of U.S.-Soviet behavior: (1) Respect spheres of influence; (2) Avoid direct military confrontation; (3) Use nuclear weapons only as an ultimate resort; (4) Prefer predictable anomaly (e.g., West Berlin, Cuba) over unpredictable rationality; and (5) Do not seek to undermine the other side's leadership.

Writing in 1986, Gaddis notes that the most important test for the Soviet-American relationship may come when one or both of the superpowers faces the prospect of its own decline. Under such conditions, Gaddis suggests that the preservation of stability may require great powers to recognize that they have a stake in the survival of their rivals.

Like Gaddis, John Mueller in his "The Essential Irrelevance of Nuclear Weapons" finds redundant sources of stability in the postwar world. He argues that nuclear weapons may have enhanced this stability, but even in their absence the United States and the Soviet Union almost certainly would have avoided a major war. Mueller contends that nuclear weapons influenced public debates and defense budgets, but that they have had far less impact on the course of world affairs since World War II than have non-nuclear factors. The memory of the Second World War, superpower contentment with the status quo, the cautious, pragmatic nature of Soviet ideology, and fears of escalation to a major conventional conflict would have sufficed to deter World War III without the added prudence engendered by nuclear weapons. Alliance patterns and crisis behavior also would have been similar in the absence of nuclear weapons.

Mueller argues that the stability of the postwar world is part of a long-term trend away from war among the major developed countries. He claims that the idea of war has lost its legitimacy in the developed world. Before 1914, war was considered an acceptable, even glorious, instrument of state policy. Its proponents declared that war could be spiritually elevating and a necessary means of moral purification. Since the First World War, however, war has been regarded as repugnant and futile. World War II—an aberration brought on by Adolf Hitler—reinforced these lessons. Since 1945 there have been virtually no international or civil wars among the advanced industrialized countries. Mueller thus concludes that war in the developed world is obsolescent, like dueling, slavery, and other once-fashionable or accepted practices.

The next two essays challenge Mueller's arguments in different ways. Robert Jervis's "The Political Effects of Nuclear Weapons" responds to Mueller by arguing that nuclear weapons have had unique political effects because they ensure that all parties to a conflict face the threat of enormous and rapid destruction. These effects are qualitatively different from those of conventional warfare. Jervis thus suggests that the stability of the postwar world cannot be attributed to conventional deterrence alone. He agrees, however, with Mueller's argument that nonmilitary dimensions of deterrence must be taken into account to explain postwar stability. Jervis nonetheless concludes that satisfaction with the status quo is not enough to prevent major war and that nuclear weapons are necessary to make mutual security more feasible.

In "Is War Obsolete?" Carl Kaysen presents a broader challenge to Mueller's thesis. He begins by reviewing Mueller's book, *Retreat from Doomsday*, which presents an extended version of the argument that war is obsolescent. Kaysen suggests that Mueller is wrong to conclude that war has become "subrationally unthinkable." Kaysen agrees, however, with Mueller's central claim that war is becoming increasingly unlikely among advanced industrialized countries. But he argues that a complete account of why war is becoming obsolescent must go beyond Mueller's analysis of attitudes toward war to consider the changing political and economic calculus of war.

The bulk of Kaysen's essay is devoted to his explanation of why war is no longer politically or economically profitable for developed countries. Kaysen examines six centuries of social, political, and economic changes that have influenced the likelihood of war among major powers. According to Kaysen, war was profitable from the ninth to the fifteenth centuries for traditional European agricultural societies because it was relatively easy to seize and control land without destroying its productive energies. Warrior elites waged wars, which had little impact on most of the population. This basic pattern remained unchanged through the eighteenth century. Despite the growth of cities and commerce, war still paid, and ruling elites still made the decisions for war. In the nineteenth century, the industrial revolution ushered in an era of large-scale manufacturing in which capital assumed greater economic importance than land, thereby increasing the scale and cost of war. War entailed larger economic burdens, and the difficulty of organizing a hostile population for continued production in an industrial society reduced the probable economic benefits of war. The gradual spread of democracy changed the basis of political legitimacy. Publics generally sought increased economic welfare, which could not be obtained through war. Attitudes took time to catch up to these changes in society, economy, and polity, but the wars of the twentieth century removed hereditary elites and provided ample evidence that war no longer pays. Far from being irrelevant, the development of nuclear weapons has reinforced these conclusions. Although Kaysen recognizes that domestic violence may continue and that wars may rage between nonindustrialized countries, he concludes that Europe can be transformed without war.

After the revolutions of 1989, it appeared that Kaysen's guarded optimism about the new Europe was more than justified. A relatively peaceful transition to democracy was underway in Poland, Hungary, and Czechoslovakia, and possibly in Romania and Bulgaria. Even Stalinist Albania underwent political change. The essays by Jack Snyder, John Mearsheimer, and Stephen Van Evera focus on the prospects for peace in the new Europe.

Jack Snyder's "Averting Anarchy in the New Europe" examines the impact of the transformation of Central and Eastern European polities on European stability after the Cold War.[1] Snyder begins by examining two widely-held perspectives on the collapse of the communist order in Central and Eastern Europe. The first, liberal end-of-history optimism, holds that liberal, market-oriented, democratic regimes in the former Soviet bloc will keep Europe peaceful, because democratic governments virtually never go to war with one another. According to Snyder, the flaw in this vision of the future is that democratic regimes may not flourish in all the former communist countries of Eastern and Central Europe.

The second perspective, which Snyder calls Hobbesian pessimism, argues that domestic political orders are irrelevant to war and peace. In this realist view, the bipolar division of Europe has been the decisive factor in averting conflict since 1945. Without the co-hegemonic rule of the two superpowers,

---

1. Snyder's article, which appeared in the Spring 1990 issue of *International Security*, was written in the midst of rapid political changes in Central and Eastern Europe. The version published here was updated in several places to take into account recent events as of fall 1990.

a multipolar Europe would revert to the warlike patterns of politics that caused the two world wars. Insecurity also would fuel nationalism and militarism, especially in the former Soviet bloc. But, as Snyder notes, realism offers few prescriptions for the dangers it predicts.

Snyder's own perspective, neo-liberal institutionalism, grows out of concern that the gap between political participation and political institutions in the emerging democracies of East Central Europe will lead to praetorian patterns of politics, in which nationalist demagogy will emerge to threaten international stability. Imperial Japan and Wilhelmine Germany are the two leading examples of this type of state in the twentieth century. To head off the development of praetorian regimes, Snyder recommends integrating Eastern and Central Europe's new regimes into the existing institutional framework of the European Community. This proposal is not based on the belief that economic interdependence will ensure peace, but on the hope that international economic regimes will create an environment in which democratic regimes can emerge and flourish in Eastern and Central Europe. Changes at the international level thus would influence events at the state level to reduce the likelihood of war in the new Europe. Such a strategy of institution-building, Snyder argues, can avert the potential anarchy that could accompany the transformation of the Soviet bloc.

In "Back to the Future," John Mearsheimer presents a pessimistic vision of Europe's future. Mearsheimer adopts a realist position, and contends that Europe has enjoyed peace for the past forty-five years because bipolar systems tend to be stable, because war is less likely when there is a rough equality between the two leading states of a system, and because the presence of thousands of nuclear weapons has induced general caution. The end of the Cold War and the withdrawal of Soviet and American armed forces from Europe, he argues, will result in a devolution to multipolarity in Europe—and a new era of wars and major crises may erupt on that continent. Following other realists, Mearsheimer argues that the absence of central governance in international politics ensures that states compete for security and periodically go to war. Major crises and wars are much more likely in a multipolar system because potential aggressors confront uncertain alliances and thus are not deterred. These uncertainties and complexities of multipolarity contributed to the outbreak of both world wars. In a bipolar system, like the one that has existed in Europe since 1945, the major powers confront more certain opposition and war is less likely. The rough equality of the United States and the Soviet Union enhanced the stabilizing effects of bipolarity, because neither power was able to entertain hopes of achieving preponderance.

The effects of bipolarity have been supplemented in Europe by the presence of thousands of nuclear weapons, which make escalation and destruction even more certain. If Washington and Moscow were to withdraw their nuclear weapons from Europe, Mearsheimer argues, many European countries might seek nuclear weapons, with potentially destabilizing effects.

Mearsheimer examines three alternative explanations of Europe's long peace and finds them wanting. First, he argues that Mueller's claim that the idea of war is obsolescent is wishful thinking. There is little evidence that European attitudes toward war have changed. If any war could have made war unthinkable, it was World War I. But Europe went to war on an even greater scale only two decades after the guns of the Great War fell silent. Even if European attitudes have turned against war, public opinion could shift again, particularly if manipulated by a clever leader.

What Mearsheimer calls economic liberalism is a second theory of peace that he finds deficient. This theory suggests that the growth of European institutions, economic interdependence, and international regimes has stabilized post-1945 Europe and will continue to do so even after the bipolar division of Europe ends. Mearsheimer contends that this theory fails to take into account the extent to which security concerns prevent economic cooperation. States are not motivated solely by a desire for prosperity. They fear the relative economic gains other states may achieve through cooperation and thus prefer independent strategies. Moreover, economic ties actually can build frictions. The historical record shows that economic interdependence did not prevent wars in Europe before 1945. The postwar economic integration has been made possible by the stability of the Cold War. Mearsheimer suggests that it will dissolve with the passing of the bipolar order.

Third, Mearsheimer also finds the theory that democracies do not go to war with one another unpersuasive. He suggests that even democratic states cannot transcend the anarchic logic of the international system. Although the historical record suggests that democracies do not fight one another, Mearsheimer argues that there have been too few democracies to draw firm conclusions and that other factors—such as the unity imposed by a common German or Soviet threat—can explain the absence of wars between democracies. In any event, some states in the new Europe may not be democracies, rendering this theory irrelevant.

To preserve peace in Europe, Mearsheimer recommends that the United States maintain troops in Europe, limit proliferation so that Germany acquires nuclear weapons but other European states do not, and take steps to prevent a resurgence of hypernationalism.[2]

Stephen Van Evera's "Primed for Peace" offers a more optimistic outlook on Europe's future. According to Van Evera, the principal causes of Europe's major wars have vanished or are vanishing. At the international level, the dominance of the offense over the defense has disappeared with the deployment of nuclear weapons, the lasting commitment of the United States to Europe, and the growth of knowledge-based economies that cannot flourish under the heel of a conqueror.

Domestic changes in European states have had an even more decisive impact. The decline of social stratification and the rise of democracy have removed elites with incentives to purvey nationalist myths. Democratization also has eliminated the dangers of militarism, which can breed war because military organizations have numerous incentives to propagandize in ways that encourage war. Most of these changes cannot be quickly reversed.

Van Evera argues that Snyder and Mearsheimer have false fears about the new Europe. Snyder is wrong because praetorianism will not emerge in Central and Eastern Europe. It is a disease of highly stratified societies and thus it will not take root in the leveled polities of the post-communist states. Mearsheimer places too much faith in the theory of bipolarity. The effects of multipolarity and bipolarity are essentially indeterminate; other factors determine the probability of war.

Van Evera also asks whether the new united Germany will follow the aggressive path of Hitler's Reich and the Kaiser's German Empire. He gives the reassuring reply that the new Germany poses no threat to European stability. Germany is now thoroughly democratized, its civil-military relations are a model for the rest of Europe, and it understands its past in a way that makes future aggression unlikely.

---

2. Mearsheimer's article provoked widespread discussion and debate. For critical perspectives, and Mearsheimer's replies, see the letters from Stanley Hoffmann and Robert O. Keohane in "Correspondence: Back to the Future, Part II: International Relations Theory and Post–Cold War Europe," *International Security*, Vol. 15, No. 2 (Fall 1990), pp. 191–199; and from Bruce M. Russett and Thomas Risse-Kappen in "Correspondence: Back to the Future, Part III: Realism and the Realities of European Security," *International Security*, Vol. 15, No. 3 (Winter 1990/91), pp. 216–222.

The real danger in the new Europe, according to Van Evera, lies in the potential turmoil that could accompany the collapse of the Soviet Empire and the Soviet Union itself. In Eastern and Central Europe long-buried national and ethnic conflicts, as well as many boundary disputes, seethed under the surface of Soviet suppression. Withdrawing Soviet troops could be like lifting the lid off Pandora's box.

In addition to transforming the international and domestic politics of Europe, the end of the Cold War and the collapse of the Soviet Union changed the structure of the global international system. Some analysts claimed that the United States was the only surviving superpower and the world was unipolar. The essays by Layne, Jervis, and Huntington assess the existence and implications of apparent unipolarity.

In "The Unipolar Illusion," Christopher Layne explores in detail the implications of America's predominant international position in the aftermath of the Cold War. He argues that a "strategy of predominance," aimed at perpetuating the singular status of the United States in the new international order, is unlikely to succeed and could be counterproductive. The reason, Layne suggests, is that both theory and history indicate that "unipolar moments" are fleeting: new great powers inevitably rise to challenge the power and standing of the hegemon.

The theoretical underpinnings of this argument are grounded in realism. Layne notes that differential growth rates result over time in substantial shifts in relative power—shifts that are usually reflected in the conduct of international diplomacy and eventually in the structure of the international system. He emphasizes also the structural incentives for states that have the potential to do so to seek great power status, and the tendency for other states to attempt to balance against the power of the hegemon, even if the hegemon is relatively benign. In the post–Cold War era, Layne argues, these factors will act to erode U.S. predominance. He augments this theoretical argument with historical evidence that leads to the same conclusion: both French hegemony in the late seventeenth century and British hegemony in the mid-nineteenth century were completely undermined within a few decades. In Layne's view, just as earlier unipolar moments were temporary, so too will American hegemony wither with the passage of time.

Layne believes that the United States is mistakenly pursuing a strategy of preponderance, attempting to preserve its "benign hegemony." The inevitable rise of new great powers—notably Germany and Japan—dooms this approach to failure, and the aggressive quest to preserve primacy could provoke and hasten the unavoidable challenges to U.S. power. Layne advocates instead an approach that combines focus on correcting internal sources of relative decline with an international strategy that takes multipolarity as its starting point. A multipolar world can be difficult and potentially dangerous, and Layne refuses to dismiss entirely the possibility even of great power war. But if multipolarity is inescapable, as Layne asserts, then the United States must adapt to it. Accordingly, he urges that U.S. strategy focus first on preserving its interests during the transition from the unipolar to the multipolar world, and secondly on maximizing U.S. prospects in a multipolar world.

While Christopher Layne questions the sustainability of U.S. primacy, Robert Jervis and Samuel Huntington debate its value. In "International Primacy: Is the Game Worth the Candle?" Jervis raises doubts about the necessity and desirability of primacy. He notes that the quest for primacy was important—and unavoidable—when the possibility of war made concerns about relative gains central on the external agendas of states. But Jervis does not accept that this is necessarily true in a post–Cold War environment in which war among the leading states seems very unlikely. Nor does he believe that primacy remains a key in the competition for economic well-being. Rather, he foresees a world marked by low security threats and high degrees of cooperation among the major powers, and hence, "the stakes and the intensity of the competition will be much lower than was the case when international politics was infused with deep concerns for survival and security." Jervis also considers the argument that U.S. primacy is desirable because its leadership is necessary to maintain international order on behalf of all actors in the system—a "non-competitive" rationale for primacy. He concedes the merits of this argument, but concludes that on balance it is better if other major powers share the costs and risks of preserving order. Hence, in Jervis's view, the case for seeking or preserving primacy is weak.

Samuel Huntington, on the other hand, argues that primacy remains centrally important in international politics. Primacy, he explains, has to do with which state has the greatest influence in "shaping decisions affecting the world," and he believes that it is self-evident that this matters greatly. Huntington agrees that war among major powers has become unlikely, but rejects the idea that primacy is now unimportant as a consequence. Rather, the contest for primacy has shifted into the economic realm, where intense conflicts of interest remain among the major powers. He illustrates this proposition by examining U.S. relations with Japan. In his view, Tokyo is a formidable challenger to the United States and has adopted a "strategy of economic warfare" to advance its cause in the struggle for economic primacy. The Japanese drive to prevail economically can harm U.S. interests and well-being in a variety of ways, and therefore, Huntington argues, the United States should regard Japan as a rival for the same reason it regarded the Soviet Union as a rival: Japan is "a major threat to its primacy in a crucial arena of power." Should Japan prevail, key economic decisions affecting the U.S. economy will be made in Tokyo; Americans, he suggests, rightly prefer that these decisions continue to be taken in Washington. In this fundamental sense, primacy matters.

In addition, Huntington champions the world order rationale for U.S. primacy that Jervis considers but does not embrace. In Huntington's argument, only the United States possesses the power and the values to support a prosperous, increasingly democratic, and stable international order. "A world without U.S. primacy will be a world with more violence and disorder and less democracy and economic growth." Thus, U.S. primacy matters not only for American power and well-being, but also to the broader international community. The value of primacy, Huntington concludes, is not doubtful but crucial.

In the final essay in this collection, "International Relations Theory and the End of the Cold War," John Lewis Gaddis assesses the performance of theoretical approaches to international relations in anticipating the events that together comprised the end of the Cold War. Gaddis's tale is one of failure: "Very few of our theoretical approaches to the study of international relations came anywhere close to forecasting any of these developments. One might as well have relied upon stargazers, readers of entrails, and other 'pre-scientific' methods for all the good our 'scientific' methods did." He sustains this conclusion by examining three bodies of theory: behavioralist, structural, and evolutionary. He surveys the methods, the main findings, and the key works of each approach, noting their contributions but appraising their shortcomings in forecasting the end of the Cold War. Gaddis does not shy away from the severe judgments that follow logically from his analysis; he concludes, for example, that "the behavioralist approach has produced neither theory, nor forecasts, nor usable policy recommendations." And he suggests that this failure calls into question the value of these bodies of theory, which proved either irrelevant or wrong in anticipating the end of the Cold War; what good are theories that fail to account for reality? Gaddis ends by arguing that efforts to fashion theories of international relations may have been derailed by an excessive embrace of an obsolescent version of the scientific method and that this relatively sterile methodology supplanted the judgment, values, intuition, imagination, and other more impressionistic approaches that, however unrigorous they may appear to a social scientist, may more fully account for the complexities of human behavior.

The passing of the Cold War has swept away many of the familiar and convenient frameworks of analysis and categories of thought about international politics. Scholars and policymakers alike are unanchored from previous intellectual moorings, and the certainties of the past have given way to the ambiguities of the present. As a result, now prominent on the agenda are much more fundamental questions about the future of the international system and about the role of the United States in that system. Where not so long ago we debated the technicalities of nuclear modernization in Europe and the details of strategic arms control agreements, today we contend over the sources of peace and stability in world politics, over the likely character of the emerging international order, and over the purposes of American power. The new agenda is more difficult and daunting, but also more important, more interesting, and more exciting. We believe that this volume contains essays that contribute to the now urgent struggle to explain the world that has passed and to apprehend the world that is to come.

The Long Peace | *John Lewis Gaddis*

Elements of Stability in the Postwar International System

I should like to begin this essay with a fable. Once upon a time, there was a great war that involved the slaughter of millions upon millions of people. When, after years of fighting, one side finally prevailed over the other and the war ended, everyone said that it must go down in history as the last great war ever fought. To that end, the victorious nations sent all of their wisest men to a great peace conference, where they were given the task of drawing up a settlement that would be so carefully designed, so unquestionably fair to all concerned, that it would eliminate war as a phenomenon of human existence. Unfortunately, that settlement lasted only twenty years.

There followed yet another great war involving the slaughter of millions upon millions of people. When, after years of fighting, one side finally prevailed over the other and the war ended, everyone said that it must go down in history as the last great war ever fought. To everyone's horror, though, the victors in that conflict immediately fell to quarreling among themselves, with the result that no peace conference ever took place. Within a few years each of the major victors had come to regard each other, and not their former enemies, as the principal threat to their survival; each sought to ensure that survival by developing weapons capable, at least in theory, of ending the survival of everyone on earth. Paradoxically, that arrangement lasted twice as long as the first one, and as the fable ended showed no signs of coming apart anytime soon.

It is, of course, just a fable, and as a general rule one ought not to take fables too seriously. There are times, though, when fables can illuminate reality more sharply than conventional forms of explanation are able to do, and this may well be one of them. For it is the case that the post-World War II system of international relations, which nobody designed or even thought could last for very long, which was based not upon the dictates of morality

This paper was presented, in a slightly different form, at the Nobel Institute Symposium on "The Study of War and Peace," Noresund, Norway, June 1985, and is to appear in Öyvind Österud, ed., *Studies of War and Peace*, to be published by the Norwegian University Press in 1986. I am grateful as well to Stanley Hoffmann, Robert Jervis, and Uwe Nerlich for providing opportunities to discuss this paper before seminars conducted by them, and to Ole Holsti, Harold Molineu, and Joseph S. Nye, Jr., for helpful suggestions.

John Lewis Gaddis is Distinguished Professor of History at Ohio University.

International Security, Spring 1986 (Vol. 10, No. 4)

and justice but rather upon an arbitrary and strikingly artificial division of the world into spheres of influence, and which incorporated within it some of the most bitter and persistent antagonisms short of war in modern history, has now survived twice as long as the far more carefully designed World War I settlement, has approximately equaled in longevity the great 19th century international systems of Metternich and Bismarck, and unlike those earlier systems after four decades of existence shows no perceptible signs of disintegration. It is, or ought to be, enough to make one think.

To be sure, the term "peace" is not the first one that comes to mind when one recalls the history of the past forty years. That period, after all, has seen the greatest accumulation of armaments the world has ever known, a whole series of protracted and devastating limited wars, an abundance of revolutionary, ethnic, religious, and civil violence, as well as some of the deepest and most intractable ideological rivalries in human experience. Nor have those more ancient scourges—famine, disease, poverty, injustice—by any means disappeared from the face of the earth. Is it not stretching things a bit, one might well ask, to take the moral and spiritual desert in which the nations of the world conduct their affairs, and call it "peace"?

It is, of course, but that is just the point. Given all the conceivable reasons for having had a major war in the past four decades—reasons that in any other age would have provided ample justification for such a war—it seems worthy of comment that there has not in fact been one; that despite the unjust and wholly artificial character of the post-World War II settlement, it has now persisted for the better part of half a century. That may not be grounds for celebration, but it is at least grounds for investigation: for trying to comprehend how this great power peace has managed to survive for so long in the face of so much provocation, and for thinking about what might be done to perpetuate that situation. For, after all, we could do worse.

Systems Theory and International Stability

Anyone attempting to understand why there has been no third world war confronts a problem not unlike that of Sherlock Holmes and the dog that did not bark in the night: how does one account for something that did not happen? How does one explain why the great conflict between the United States and the Soviet Union, which by all past standards of historical experience should have developed by now, has not in fact done so? The question involves certain methodological difficulties, to be sure: it is always easier to account for what did happen than what did not. But there is also a curious bias among students of international relations that reinforces this tendency: "For every thousand pages published on the causes of wars," Geoffrey Blainey has commented, "there is less than one page directly on the causes of peace."[1] Even the discipline of "peace studies" suffers from this disproportion: it has given far more attention to the question of what we must do to avoid the apocalypse than it has to the equally interesting question of why, given all the opportunities, it has not happened so far.

It might be easier to deal with this question if the work that has been done on the causes of war had produced something approximating a consensus on why wars develop: we could then apply that analysis to the post-1945 period and see what it is that has been different about it. But, in fact, these studies are not much help. Historians, political scientists, economists, sociologists, statisticians, even meteorologists, have wrestled for years with the question of what causes wars, and yet the most recent review of that literature concludes that "our understanding of war remains at an elementary level. No widely accepted theory of the causes of war exists and little agreement has emerged on the methodology through which these causes might be discovered."[2]

Nor has the comparative work that has been done on international systems shed much more light on the matter. The difficulty here is that our actual experience is limited to the operations of a single system—the balance of power system—operating either within the "multipolar" configuration that characterized international politics until World War II, or the "bipolar" con-

---

1. Geoffrey Blainey, *The Causes of War* (London: Macmillan, 1973), p. 3.
2. Jack S. Levy, *War in the Modern Great Power System, 1495–1975* (Lexington: University Press of Kentucky, 1983), p. 1. Other standard works on this subject, in addition to Blainey, cited above, include: Lewis F. Richardson, *Arms and Insecurity: A Mathematical Study of the Causes and Origins of War* (Pittsburgh: Quadrangle, 1960); Quincy Wright, *A Study of War*, 2nd ed. (Chicago: University of Chicago Press, 1965); Kenneth N. Waltz, *Man, the State and War: A Theoretical Analysis* (New York: Columbia University Press, 1959); Kenneth Boulding, *Conflict and Defense: A General Theory* (New York: Harper and Row, 1962); Raymond Aron, *Peace and War: A Theory of International Relations*, trans. Richard Howard and Annette Baker Fox (New York: Doubleday, 1966); Robert Gilpin, *War and Change in World Politics* (New York: Cambridge University Press, 1981); Melvin Small and J. David Singer, *Resort to Arms: International and Civil Wars, 1816–1980* (Beverly Hills, Calif.: Sage Publications, 1982); and Michael Howard, *The Causes of Wars*, 2nd ed. (Cambridge, Mass.: Harvard University Press, 1984). A valuable overview of conflicting explanations is Keith L. Nelson and Spencer C. Olin, Jr., *Why War? Ideology, Theory, and History* (Berkeley: University of California Press, 1979).

figuration that has characterized them since. Alternative systems remain abstract conceptualizations in the minds of theorists, and are of little use in advancing our knowledge of how wars in the real world do or do not occur.[3]

But "systems theory" itself is something else again: here one can find a useful point of departure for thinking about the nature of international relations since 1945. An "international system" exists, political scientists tell us, when two conditions are met: first, interconnections exist between units within the system, so that changes in some parts of it produce changes in other parts as well; and, second, the collective behavior of the system as a whole differs from the expectations and priorities of the individual units that make it up.[4] Certainly demonstrating the "interconnectedness" of post-World War II international relations is not difficult: one of its most prominent characteristics has been the tendency of major powers to assume that little if anything can happen in the world without in some way enhancing or detracting from their own immediate interests.[5] Nor has the collective behavior of nations corresponded to their individual expectations: the very fact

---

3. The classic example of such abstract conceptualization is Morton A. Kaplan, *System and Process in International Politics* (New York: John Wiley, 1957). For the argument that 1945 marks the transition from a "multipolar" to a "bipolar" international system, see Glenn H. Snyder and Paul Diesing, *Conflict Among Nations: Bargaining, Decision Making, and System Structure in International Crises* (Princeton, N.J.: Princeton University Press, 1977), pp. 419–420; and Kenneth Waltz, *Theory of International Politics* (Reading, Mass.: Addison–Wesley, 1979), pp. 161–163. One can, of course, question whether the postwar international system constitutes true "bipolarity." Peter H. Beckman, for example, provides an elaborate set of indices demonstrating the asymmetrical nature of American and Soviet power after 1945 in his *World Politics in the Twentieth Century* (Englewood Cliffs, N.J.: Prentice Hall, 1984), pp. 207–209, 235–237, 282–285. But such retrospective judgments neglect the perceptions of policymakers *at the time*, who clearly saw their world as bipolar and frequently commented on the phenomenon. See, for example, David S. McLellan, *Dean Acheson: The State Department Years* (New York: Dodd, Mead, 1976), p. 116; and, for Soviet "two camp" theory, William Taubman, *Stalin's America Policy: From Entente to Detente to Cold War* (New York: Norton, 1982), pp. 176–178.
4. I have followed here the definition of Robert Jervis, "Systems Theories and Diplomatic History," in Paul Gordon Lauren, ed., *Diplomacy: New Approaches in History, Theory, and Policy* (New York: Free Press, 1979), p. 212. For a more rigorous discussion of the requirements of systems theory, and a critique of some of its major practitioners, see Waltz, *Theory of International Politics*, pp. 38–78. Akira Iriye is one of the few historians who have sought to apply systems theory to the study of international relations. See his *After Imperialism: The Search for a New Order in the Far East, 1921–1931* (Cambridge: Harvard University Press, 1965); and *The Cold War in Asia: A Historical Introduction* (Englewood Cliffs, N.J.: Prentice Hall, 1974).
5. See, on this point, Robert Jervis, *Perception and Misperception in International Politics* (Princeton, N.J.: Princeton University Press, 1976), pp. 58–62. Jervis points out that "almost by definition, a great power is more tightly connected to larger numbers of other states than is a small power. . . . Growing conflict or growing cooperation between Argentina and Chile would not affect Pakistan, but it would affect America and American policy toward those states. . . ." Jervis, "Systems Theories and Diplomatic History," p. 215.

that the interim arrangements of 1945 have remained largely intact for four decades would have astonished—and quite possibly appalled—the statesmen who cobbled them together in the hectic months that followed the surrender of Germany and Japan.[6]

A particularly valuable feature of systems theory is that it provides criteria for differentiating between stable and unstable political configurations: these can help to account for the fact that some international systems outlast others. Karl Deutsch and J. David Singer have defined "stability" as "the probability that the system retains all of its essential characteristics: that no single nation becomes dominant; that most of its members continue to survive; and that large-scale war does not occur." It is characteristic of such a system, Deutsch and Singer add, that it has the capacity for self-regulation: the ability to counteract stimuli that would otherwise threaten its survival, much as the automatic pilot on an airplane or the governor on a steam engine would do. "Self-regulating" systems are very different from what they call "self-aggravating" systems, situations that get out of control, like forest fires, drug addiction, runaway inflation, nuclear fission, and of course, although they themselves do not cite the example, all-out war.[7] Self-regulating mechanisms are most likely to function, in turn, when there exists some fundamental agreement among major states within the system on the objectives they are seeking to uphold by participating in it, when the structure of the system reflects the way in which power is distributed among its respective members,

---

6. "A future war with the Soviet Union," retiring career diplomat Joseph C. Grew commented in May 1945, "is as certain as anything in this world." Memorandum of May 19, 1945, quoted in Joseph C. Grew, *Turbulent Era: A Diplomatic Record of Forty Years, 1904–1945* (Boston: Houghton Mifflin, 1952), Vol. 2, p. 1446. For other early expressions of pessimism about the stability of the postwar international system, see Walter Lippmann, *The Cold War: A Study in U.S. Foreign Policy* (New York: Harper Brothers, 1947), pp. 26–28, 37–39, 60–62. "There is, after all, something to be explained—about perceptions as well as events—when so much that has been written has dismissed the new state system as no system at all but an unstable transition to something else." A.W. DePorte, *Europe Between the Super-Powers: The Enduring Balance* (New Haven: Yale University Press, 1979), p. 167.
7. Karl W. Deutsch and J. David Singer, "Multipolar Power Systems and International Stability," in James N. Rosenau, ed., *International Politics and Foreign Policy: A Reader in Research and Theory*, rev. ed. (New York: Free Press, 1969), pp. 315–317. Deutsch and Singer equate "self-regulation" with "negative feedback": "By negative—as distinguished from positive or amplifying—feedback, we refer to the phenomenon of self-correction: as stimuli in one particular direction increase, the system exhibits a decreasing response to those stimuli, and increasingly exhibits the tendencies that counteract them." See also Jervis, "Systems Theories and Diplomatic History," p. 220. For Kaplan's more abstract definition of stability, see his *System and Process in International Politics*, p. 8. The concept of "stability" in international systems owes a good deal to "functionalist" theory; see, on this point, Charles Reynolds, *Theory and Explanation in International Politics* (London: Martin Robertson, 1973), p. 30.

and when agreed-upon procedures exist for resolving differences among them.[8]

Does the post-World War II international system fit these criteria for "stability"? Certainly its most basic characteristic—bipolarity—remains intact, in that the gap between the world's two greatest military powers and their nearest rivals is not substantially different from what it was forty years ago.[9] At the same time, neither the Soviet Union nor the United States nor anyone else has been able wholly to dominate that system; the nations most active within it in 1945 are for the most part still active today. And of course the most convincing argument for "stability" is that, so far at least, World War III has not occurred. On the surface, then, the concept of a "stable" international system makes sense as a way of understanding the experience through which we have lived these past forty years.

But what have been the self-regulating mechanisms? How has an environment been created in which they are able to function? In what way do those mechanisms—and the environment in which they function—resemble or differ from the configuration of other international systems, both stable and unstable, in modern history? What circumstances exist that might impair their operation, transforming self-regulation into self-aggravation? These are questions that have not received the attention they deserve from students of the history and politics of the postwar era. What follows is a series of speculations—they can hardly be more than that, given present knowledge—upon these issues, the importance of which hardly needs to be stressed.

I should like to emphasize, though, that this essay's concentration on the way the world is and has been is not intended to excuse or to justify our current predicament. Nor is it meant to preclude the possibility of moving ultimately toward something better. We can all conceive of international systems that combine stability with greater justice and less risk than the present one does, and we ought to continue to think about these things. But short of war, which no one wants, change in international relations tends to be gradual and evolutionary. It does not happen overnight. That means that alternative systems, if they ever develop, probably will not be total rejections

---

8. I have followed here, in slightly modified form, criteria provided in Gordon A. Craig and Alexander L. George, *Force and Statecraft: Diplomatic Problems of Our Time* (New York: Oxford University Press, 1983), p. x, a book that provides an excellent discussion of how international systems have evolved since the beginning of the 18th century. But see also Gilpin, *War and Change in World Politics*, pp. 50–105.

9. See, on this point, Waltz, *Theory of International Politics*, pp. 180–181; also DePorte, *Europe Between the Super-Powers*, p. 167.

of the existing system, but rather variations proceeding from it. All the more reason, then, to try to understand the system we have, to try to distinguish its stabilizing from its destabilizing characteristics, and to try to reinforce the former as a basis from which we might, in time and with luck, do better.

The Structural Elements of Stability

BIPOLARITY

Any such investigation should begin by distinguishing the structure of the international system in question from the behavior of the nations that make it up.[10] The reason for this is simple: behavior alone will not ensure stability if the structural prerequisites for it are absent, but structure can under certain circumstances impose stability even when its behavioral prerequisites are unpromising.[11] One need only compare the settlement of 1945 with its predecessor of 1919 to see the point.

If the intentions of statesmen alone had governed, the Paris Peace Conference of 1919 would have ushered in an era of stability in world politics comparable to the one brought about in Europe by the Congress of Vienna almost a century earlier. Certainly the diplomats at Paris had that earlier precedent very much in mind;[12] conscious of what victory had cost, they approached their task wondering whether war had not altogether lost its usefulness as a means of resolving disputes among nations.[13] Few if any peace negotiators have been able to draw upon such an impressive array of technical expertise as was available in 1919.[14] Moreover, the most influential of them, Woodrow Wilson, had determined to go beyond the practices and procedures of the "old diplomacy" to construct a settlement that would

---

10. Waltz, *Theory of International Politics*, pp. 73–78; Gilpin, *War and Change in World Politics*, pp. 85–88.

11. " . . . [S]tructure designates a set of constraining conditions. . . . [It] acts as a selector, but it cannot be seen, examined, and observed at work. . . . Because structures select by rewarding some behaviors and punishing others, outcomes cannot be inferred from intentions and behaviors." Waltz, *Theory of International Politics*, pp. 73–74.

12. Harold Nicolson, *Peacemaking 1919* (New York: Grosset and Dunlap, 1965), pp. 30–31.

13. Bernadotte E. Schmitt and Harold C. Vedeler, *The World in the Crucible: 1914–1919* (New York: Harper and Row, 1984), p. 470. "Mr Evelyn Waugh's view, that what began as a crusade turned into a tug of war between indistinguishable teams of sweaty louts, is idiosyncratic. Most of us [in World War II] did not feel like that. But it is evident that by the end of the First World War a large number of intelligent people did; and ten years later their doubts had become general." Michael Howard, *Studies in War and Peace* (New York: Viking, 1970), p. 99.

14. Nicolson, *Peacemaking 1919*, pp. 26–29. See also Lawrence E. Gelfand, *The Inquiry: American Preparations for Peace, 1917–1919* (New Haven: Yale University Press, 1963).

integrate power with morality. "Tell me what's right and I'll fight for it," Wilson is said to have demanded of his advisers,[15] and at least as far as the idea of self-determination was concerned, the Versailles Treaty did come about as close as any in modern history to incorporating within itself the principles of justice.[16]

Unfortunately, in so doing, it neglected the realities of power. It broke up the old Austro–Hungarian Empire, a move that reflected accurately enough the aspirations of the nationalities involved, but that failed to provide the successor states of Poland, Czechoslovakia, Austria, and Hungary with the military or economic means necessary to sustain their new-found sovereignty.[17] Even more shortsightedly, the treaty made no effort to accommodate the interests of two nations whose population and industrial strength were certain to guarantee them a major influence over postwar European developments—Germany and Soviet Russia. It should have been no surprise, therefore, that when the Versailles system finally broke down in 1939, it did so largely as the result of a deal cut at the expense of the East Europeans by these two countries whose power had been ignored, twenty years earlier, in the interests of justice.[18]

Nobody, in contrast, would picture the post-World War II settlement as a triumph of justice. That settlement arbitrarily divided sovereign nations like Germany, Austria, and Korea, not because anyone thought it was right to do so, but because neither the United States nor the Soviet Union could agree on whose occupation forces would withdraw first.[19] It did nothing to

---

15. Quoted in John Morton Blum, *Woodrow Wilson and the Politics of Morality* (Boston: Little, Brown, 1956), p. 161. The most convenient overview of Wilson's ideas regarding the peace settlement can be found in N. Gordon Levin, Jr., *Woodrow Wilson and World Politics: America's Response to War and Revolution* (New York: Oxford University Press, 1968), especially pp. 123–251; and Arthur S. Link, *Woodrow Wilson: Revolution, War, and Peace* (Arlington Heights, Ill.: AHM Publishing Corporation, 1979), pp. 72–103.

16. See, on this point, Gelfand, *The Inquiry*, pp. 323–326; Schmitt and Vedeler, *The World in the Crucible*, pp. 474–475; and Klaus Schwabe, *Woodrow Wilson, Revolutionary Germany, and Peacemaking, 1918–1919: Missionary Diplomacy and the Realities of Power* (Chapel Hill, N.C.: University of North Carolina Press, 1985), pp. 395–402.

17. Winston Churchill's is the classic indictment of this decision. See his *The Gathering Storm* (New York: Bantam, 1961), pp. 9–10.

18. Craig and George, *Force and Statecraft*, pp. 87–100; see also Howard, *The Causes of Wars*, pp. 163–164. ". . . [T]he victors at Versailles . . . failed . . . because, as if lulled by their own rhetoric, they continued to assert morality while they neglected armaments." Blainey, *The Causes of War*, p. 163.

19. See, on Germany, Tony Sharp, *The Wartime Alliance and the Zonal Division of Germany* (Oxford: Oxford University Press, 1975), and John H. Backer, *The Decision to Divide Germany: American*

prevent the incorporation of several of the countries whose independence the 1919 settlement had recognized—and, in the case of Poland, whose independence Great Britain had gone to war in 1939 to protect—into a Soviet sphere of influence, where they remain to this day.[20] It witnessed, in response to this, the creation of an American sphere of influence in Western Europe, the Mediterranean, and the Pacific, which although different from its Soviet counterpart in the important fact that the nations lying within it for the most part voluntarily associated themselves with the United States,[21] nonetheless required, however willingly, some sacrifice of national independence as well.

What resulted was the first true polarization of power in modern history. The world had had limited experience with bipolar systems in ancient times, it is true: certainly Thucydides' account of the rivalry between Athens and Sparta carries an eerie resonance for us today; nor could statesmen of the Cold War era forget what they had once learned, as schoolboys, of the antagonism between Rome and Carthage.[22] But these had been regional, not global conflicts: not until 1945 could one plausibly speak of a *world* divided into two competing spheres of influence, or of the *superpowers* that controlled them. The international situation had been reduced, Hans Morgenthau wrote in 1948, "to the primitive spectacle of two giants eyeing each other with watchful suspicion. . . . Thus contain or be contained, conquer or be con-

Foreign Policy in Transition (Durham, N.C.: Duke University Press, 1978); on Austria, William Bader, *Austria Between East and West, 1945–1955* (Stanford: Stanford University Press, 1966), and Sven Allard, *Russia and the Austrian State Treaty: A Case Study of Soviet Policy in Europe* (University Park, Pa.: Pennsylvania State University Press, 1970); on Korea, Charles M. Dobbs, *The Unwanted Symbol: American Foreign Policy, the Cold War, and Korea, 1945–1950* (Kent, Ohio: Kent State University Press, 1981), and Bruce Cumings, *The Origins of the Korean War: Liberation and the Emergence of Separate Regimes, 1945–1947* (Princeton, N.J.: Princeton University Press, 1981). For useful comparative perspectives on the issue of partition, see Thomas E. Hachey, ed., *The Problem of Partition: Peril to World Peace* (Chicago: University of Chicago Press, 1972).

20. Lynn Etheridge Davis, *The Cold War Begins: Soviet–American Conflict Over Eastern Europe* (Princeton, N.J.: Princeton University Press, 1974); Eduard Mark, "American Policy toward Eastern Europe and the Origins of the Cold War, 1941–1946: An Alternative Interpretation," *Journal of American History*, Vol. 68 (September 1981), pp. 313–336; and, for first-person accounts from American diplomats, Thomas T. Hammond, ed., *Witnesses to the Origins of the Cold War* (Seattle: University of Washington Press, 1982).

21. See, on this point, John Lewis Gaddis, "The Emerging Post-Revisionist Synthesis on the Origins of the Cold War," *Diplomatic History*, Vol. 8 (Summer 1983), pp. 181–183. For a perceptive discussion of post-World War II American "imperial" expansion, see Tony Smith, *The Pattern of Imperialism: The United States, Great Britain, and the Late-Industrializing World since 1815* (Cambridge: Cambridge University Press, 1981), pp. 182–202.

22. Robert H. Ferrell, ed., *The Autobiography of Harry S. Truman* (Boulder, Colo.: Colorado Associated University Press, 1980), p. 120; McLellan, *Dean Acheson*, p. 116.

quered, destroy or be destroyed, become the watchwords of the new diplomacy."[23]

Now, bipolarity may seem to many today—as it did forty years ago—an awkward and dangerous way to organize world politics.[24] Simple geometric logic would suggest that a system resting upon three or more points of support would be more stable than one resting upon two. But politics is not geometry: the passage of time and the accumulation of experience has made clear certain structural elements of stability in the bipolar system of international relations that were not present in the multipolar systems that preceded it:

(1) The postwar bipolar system realistically reflected the facts of where military power resided at the end of World War II[25]—and where it still does today, for that matter. In this sense, it differed markedly from the settlement of 1919, which made so little effort to accommodate the interests of Germany and Soviet Russia. It is true that in other categories of power—notably the economic—states have since arisen capable of challenging or even surpassing the Soviet Union and the United States in the production of certain specific commodities. But as the *political* position of nations like West Germany, Brazil, Japan, South Korea, Taiwan, and Hong Kong suggests, the ability to make video recorders, motorcycles, even automobiles and steel efficiently has yet to translate into anything approaching the capacity of Washington or Moscow to shape events in the world as a whole.

(2) The post-1945 bipolar structure was a simple one that did not require sophisticated leadership to maintain it. The great multipolar systems of the 19th century collapsed in large part because of their intricacy: they required a Metternich or a Bismarck to hold them together, and when statesmen of

---

23. Hans J. Morgenthau, *Politics Among Nations: The Struggle for Power and Peace* (New York: Alfred A. Knopf, 1949), p. 285. For the transition from bipolarity to multipolarity, see the 1973 edition of *Politics Among Nations*, pp. 338–342; also Waltz, *Theory of International Politics*, p. 162. For an eloquent history of the Cold War that views it as the product of the polarization of world politics, see Louis J. Halle, *The Cold War as History* (New York: Harper and Row, 1967).

24. Among those who have emphasized the instability of bipolar systems are Morgenthau, *Politics Among Nations*, pp. 350–354; and Wright, *A Study of War*, pp. 763–764. See also Blainey, *The Causes of War*, pp. 110–111.

25. ". . . [W]hat *was* dominant in their consciousness," Michael Howard has written of the immediate post-World War II generation of statesmen, "was the impotence, almost one might say the irrelevance, of ethical aspirations in international politics in the absence of that factor to which so little attention had been devoted by their more eminent predecessors, to which indeed so many of them had been instinctively hostile—military power." Howard, *The Causes of War*, p. 55.

that calibre were no longer available, they tended to come apart.[26] Neither the Soviet nor the American political systems have been geared to identifying statesmen of comparable prowess and entrusting them with responsibility; demonstrated skill in the conduct of foreign policy has hardly been a major prerequisite for leadership in either country. And yet, a bipolar structure of international relations—because of the inescapably high stakes involved for its two major actors—tends, regardless of the personalities involved, to induce in them a sense of caution and restraint, and to discourage irresponsibility. "It is not," Kenneth Waltz notes, "that one entertains the utopian hope that all future American and Russian rulers will combine in their persons . . . nearly perfect virtues, but rather that the pressures of a bipolar world strongly encourage them to act internationally in ways better than their characters may lead one to expect."[27]

(3) Because of its relatively simple structure, alliances in this bipolar system have tended to be more stable than they had been in the 19th century and in the 1919–1939 period. It is striking to consider that the North Atlantic Treaty Organization has now equaled in longevity the most durable of the pre-World War I alliances, that between Germany and Austria–Hungary; it has lasted almost twice as long as the Franco–Russian alliance, and certainly much longer than any of the tenuous alignments of the interwar period. Its principal rival, the Warsaw Treaty Organization, has been in existence for almost as long. The reason for this is simple: alliances, in the end, are the product of insecurity;[28] so long as the Soviet Union and the United States each remain for the other and for their respective clients the major source of insecurity in the world, neither superpower encounters very much difficulty in maintaining its alliances. In a multipolar system, sources of insecurity can vary in much more complicated ways; hence it is not surprising to find alliances shifting to accommodate these variations.[29]

---

26. Henry Kissinger has written two classic accounts dealing with the importance of individual leadership in sustaining international systems. See his *A World Restored* (New York: Grosset and Dunlap, 1957), on Metternich; and, on Bismarck, "The White Revolutionary: Reflections on Bismarck," *Daedalus*, Vol. 97 (Summer 1968), pp. 888–924. For a somewhat different perspective on Bismarck's role, see George F. Kennan, *The Decline of Bismarck's European Order: Franco-Russian Relations, 1875–1890* (Princeton, N.J.: Princeton University Press, 1979), especially pp. 421–422.
27. Waltz, *Theory of International Politics*, p. 176. On the tendency of unstable systemic structures to induce irresponsible leadership, see Ludwig Dehio, *The Precarious Balance: Four Centuries of the European Power Struggle*, trans. Charles Fullman (New York: Alfred A. Knopf, 1962), pp. 257–258.
28. See, on this point, Roger V. Dingman, "Theories of, and Approaches to, Alliance Politics," in Lauren, ed., *Diplomacy*, pp. 247–247.
29. My argument here follows that of Snyder and Diesing, *Conflict Among Nations*, pp. 429–445.

(4) At the same time, though, and probably because of the overall stability of the basic alliance systems, defections from both the American and Soviet coalitions—China, Cuba, Vietnam, Iran, and Nicaragua, in the case of the Americans; Yugoslavia, Albania, Egypt, Somalia, and China again in the case of the Russians—have been tolerated without the major disruptions that might have attended such changes in a more delicately balanced multipolar system. The fact that a state the size of China was able to reverse its alignment twice during the Cold War without any more dramatic effect upon the position of the superpowers says something about the stability bipolarity brings; compare this record with the impact, prior to 1914, of such apparently minor episodes as Austria's annexation of Bosnia and Herzegovina, or the question of who was to control Morocco. It is a curious consequence of bipolarity that although alliances are more durable than in a multipolar system, defections are at the same time more tolerable.[30]

In short, without anyone's having designed it, and without any attempt whatever to consider the requirements of justice, the nations of the postwar era lucked into a system of international relations that, because it has been based upon realities of power, has served the cause of order—if not justice—better than one might have expected.

INDEPENDENCE, NOT INTERDEPENDENCE

But if the structure of bipolarity in itself encouraged stability, so too did certain inherent characteristics of the bilateral Soviet–American relationship. It used to be fashionable to point out, in the days before the Cold War began, that despite periodic outbreaks of tension between them Russians and Americans had never actually gone to war with one another; the same claim could not be made for the history of either country's relations with Great Britain, Germany, Italy, Austria–Hungary, Japan, or (if the Americans' undeclared naval war of 1798–1800 is counted) France. This record was thought to be all the more remarkable in view of the fact that, in ideological terms, Russian and American systems of government could hardly have been more different. Soviet–American friendship would not evolve easily, historian Foster Rhea Dulles noted in the wake of the first meeting between Roosevelt and Stalin in 1943, but the fact that "its roots were so deep in the past, and that it had developed through the years out of common interests transcending all other points of difference, marked the effort toward a new rapprochement as

---

30. Waltz, *Theory of International Politics*, pp. 167–169.

conforming not only to the immediate but also to the long-term interests of the two nations."[31]

The onset of the Cold War made this argument seem less than convincing. To assert that American relations with Russia had once been good, students of the subject now suggested, was to confuse harmony with inactivity: given the infrequency of contacts between Russia and the United States in the 19th century, their tradition of "friendship" had been decidedly unremarkable. Once contacts became more frequent, as they had by the beginning of the 20th century, conflicts quickly followed, even before Western statesmen had begun to worry about the impact of Bolshevism, or the imminence of the international proletarian revolution.[32] But even after this breakdown in cordiality—and regardless of whether that cordiality had been real or imagined—Dulles's point remained valid: there still had been no Russian–American war, despite the fact that Russians and Americans had at one time or another fought virtually every other major power. This raises the question of whether there are not structural elements in the Russian–American relationship itself that contribute to stability, quite apart from the policies actually followed by Russian and American governments.

It has long been an assumption of classical liberalism that the more extensive the contacts that take place between nations, the greater are the chances for peace. Economic interdependence, it has been argued, makes war unlikely because nations who have come to rely upon one another for vital commodities cannot afford it. Cultural exchange, it has been suggested, causes peoples to become more sensitive to each others' concerns, and hence reduces the likelihood of misunderstandings. "People to people" contacts, it has been assumed, make it possible for nations to "know" one another better; the danger of war between them is, as a result, correspondingly reduced.[33]

---

31. Foster Rhea Dulles, *The Road to Teheran: The Story of Russia and America, 1781–1943* (Princeton, N.J.: Princeton University Press, 1944), p. 8.

32. See, for example, Thomas A. Bailey, *America Faces Russia: Russian–American Relations from Early Times to Our Day* (Ithaca: Cornell University Press, 1950), pp. 347–349. A more recent discussion of these developments is in John Lewis Gaddis, *Russia, the Soviet Union, and the United States: An .nterpretive History* (New York: Wiley, 1978), pp. 27–56.

33. The argument is succinctly summarized in Nelson and Olin, *Why War?*, pp. 35–43. Geoffrey Blainey labels the idea "Manchesterism" and satirizes it wickedly: "If those gifted early prophets of the Manchester creed could have seen Chamberlain—during the Czech crisis of September 1938—board the aircraft that was to fly him to Bavaria to meet Hitler at short notice they would have hailed aviation as the latest messenger of peace. If they had known that he met Hitler without even his own German interpreter they would perhaps have wondered whether the conversation was in Esperanto or Volapuk. It seemed that every postage stamp, bilingual

These are pleasant things to believe, but there is remarkably little historical evidence to validate them. As Kenneth Waltz has pointed out, "the fiercest civil wars and the bloodiest international ones are fought within arenas populated by highly similar people whose affairs are closely knit."[34] Consider, as examples, the costliest military conflicts of the past century and a half, using the statistics conveniently available now through the University of Michigan "Correlates of War" project: of the ten bloodiest interstate wars, every one of them grew out of conflicts between countries that either directly adjoined one another, or were involved actively in trade with one another.[35] Certainly economic interdependence did little to prevent Germany, France, Britain, Russia, and Austria–Hungary from going to war in 1914; nor did the fact that the United States was Japan's largest trading partner deter that country from attacking Pearl Harbor in 1941. Since 1945, there have been more civil wars than interstate wars;[36] that fact alone should be sufficient to call into question the proposition that interdependence necessarily breeds peace.

The Russian–American relationship, to a remarkable degree for two nations so extensively involved with the rest of the world, has been one of mutual *in*dependence. The simple fact that the two countries occupy opposite sides of the earth has had something to do with this: geographical remoteness from one another has provided little opportunity for the emergence of irredentist grievances comparable in importance to historic disputes over, say, Alsace–Lorraine, or the Polish Corridor, or the West Bank, the Gaza Strip, and Jerusalem. In the few areas where Soviet and American forces—or their proxies—have come into direct contact, they have erected artificial barriers like the Korean demilitarized zone, or the Berlin Wall, perhaps in unconscious

---

dictionary, railway timetable and trade fair, every peace congress, Olympic race, tourist brochure and international telegram that had ever existed, was gloriously justified when Mr Chamberlain said from the window of number 10 Downing Street on 30 September 1938: 'I believe it is peace for our time.' In retrospect the outbreak of war a year later seems to mark the failure and the end of the policy of appeasement, but the policy survived. The first British air raids over Germany dropped leaflets." *The Causes of War*, p. 28.

34. Waltz, *Theory of International Politics*, p. 138. For Waltz's general argument against interdependence as a necessary cause of peace, see pp. 138–160.

35. Small and Singer, *Resort to Arms*, p. 102. The one questionable case is the Crimean War, which pitted Britain and France against Russia, but that conflict began as a dispute between Russia and Turkey.

36. Small and Singer identify 44 civil wars as having been fought between 1945 and 1980; this compares with 30 interstate and 12 "extra-systemic" wars during the same period. Ibid., pp. 92–95, 98–99, 229–232.

recognition of an American poet's rather chilly precept that "good fences make good neighbors."

Nor have the two nations been economically dependent upon one another in any critical way. Certainly the United States requires nothing in the form of imports from the Soviet Union that it cannot obtain elsewhere. The situation is different for the Russians, to be sure, but even though the Soviet Union imports large quantities of food from the United States—and would like to import advanced technology as well—it is far from being wholly dependent upon these items, as the failure of recent attempts to change Soviet behavior by denying them has shown. The relative invulnerability of Russians and Americans to one another in the economic sphere may be frustrating to their respective policymakers, but it is probably fortunate, from the standpoint of international stability, that the two most powerful nations in the world are also its two most self-sufficient.[37]

But what about the argument that expanded international communication promotes peace? Is not the failure of Russians and Americans to understand one another better a potential source of instability in their relationship? Obviously it can be if misunderstandings occur at the level of national leadership: the most serious Soviet–American confrontation of the postwar era, the Cuban missile crisis, is generally regarded as having arisen from what appear in retrospect to have been quite remarkable misperceptions of each side's intentions by the other.[38] But "people to people" contacts are another matter. The history of international relations is replete with examples of familiarity breeding contempt as well as friendship: there are too many nations whose people have known each other all too well and have, as a result, taken an intense dislike to one another—French and Germans, Russians and Poles, Japanese and Chinese, Greeks and Turks, Arabs and Israelis—to lend very much credence to the invariably pacifying effects of "people to people" contacts.[39] Moreover, foreign policy in the United States depends

---

37. Soviet exports and imports as a percentage of gross national product ranged between 4 and 7 percent between 1955 and 1975; for the United States the comparable figures were 7–14 percent. This compares with figures of 33–52 percent for Great Britain, France, Germany, and Italy in the four years immediately preceding World War I, and figures of 19–41 percent for the same nations plus Japan for the period 1949–1976. Waltz, *Theory of International Politics*, pp. 141, 212.
38. See, on this point, Herbert S. Dinerstein, *The Making of a Missile Crisis, October 1962* (Baltimore: Johns Hopkins University Press, 1976), especially pp. 230–238.
39. See footnote 35, above. It is worth noting, in this connection, the striking tendency of American diplomats who have spent time inside the Soviet Union to become Russophobes. Comparable tendencies seem strikingly absent among China specialists in the Foreign Service. Compare, for the contrast, Hugh DeSantis, *The Diplomacy of Silence: The American Foreign Service,*

only to a limited extent upon mass perceptions; in the Soviet Union, it depends upon them not at all.[40] There is little reason to think that opportunities for travel, academic and cultural exchanges, and even "sister city" contacts have any consistently destabilizing effect on relations between the United States and the Soviet Union; but there is little evidence of their consistently stabilizing effect either.

It may well be, then, that the extent to which the Soviet Union and the United States have been independent of one another rather than interdependent—the fact that there have been so few points of economic leverage available to each, the fact that two such dissimilar people have had so few opportunities for interaction—has in itself constituted a structural support for stability in relations between the two countries, whatever their respective governments have actually done.

DOMESTIC INFLUENCES

Structure can affect diplomacy from another angle, though: that has to do with the domestic roots of foreign policy. It was Karl Marx who first called attention to the effect of social and economic forces upon political behavior; John A. Hobson and V.I. Lenin subsequently derived from this the proposition that capitalism causes both imperialism and war. Meanwhile, Joseph Schumpeter was working out an alternative theory that placed the origins of international conflict in the "atavistic" insecurities of aristocracies, bureaucracies, and individual leaders.[41] Historians of both Marxist and non-Marxist persuasions have stressed the importance of domestic structural influences in bringing about World War I;[42] and there has been increasing scholarly

---

the Soviet Union, and the Cold War, 1933–1947 (Chicago: University of Chicago Press, 1980); and E.J. Kahn, Jr., The China Hands: America's Foreign Service Officers and What Befell Them (New York: Viking, 1975). Whether Soviet diplomats who serve in the United States develop "Americophobic" tendencies is difficult to say, given currently available information.

40. Zbigniew Brzezinski and Samuel P. Huntington, Political Power: USA/USSR (New York: Viking, 1964), pp. 90–104. For a more recent assessment of the extent of public participation in the Soviet political system, see Jerry F. Hough and Merle Fainsod, How the Soviet Union Is Governed (Cambridge: Harvard University Press, 1979), pp. 314–319.

41. For a useful brief review of this literature, see Nelson and Olin, Why War?, pp. 58–84; also Richard J. Barnet, Roots of War (New York: Atheneum, 1972), pp. 208–214.

42. See, most recently, Arno J. Mayer, The Persistence of the Old Regime: Europe to the Great War (New York: Pantheon Books, 1981), especially pp. 304–323; and Paul M. Kennedy, The Rise of the Anglo–German Antagonism, 1860–1914 (Boston: Allen and Unwin, 1980), especially pp. 465–466.

interest as well in the role of such factors in interwar diplomacy.[43] But to what extent can one argue that domestic structures have shaped the behavior of the Soviet Union and the United States toward each other since 1945? What has been the effect of such influences upon the stability of the post-World War II international system?

The literature on the relationship between domestic structures and diplomacy in the United States is both vast and diffuse: certainly there is no clear consensus on how internal influences determine behavior toward the world at large.[44] There has been, though, a persistent effort to link the structure of the American economy to foreign policy, most conspicuously through the assertion that capitalism requires an aggressive search for raw materials, markets, and investment opportunities overseas in order to survive. The theory itself pre-dates the Cold War, having been suggested by Charles A. Beard during the 1920s and 1930s, but it was left to William Appleman Williams to work out the most influential characterization of what he called "open door" expansionism in his classic work, *The Tragedy of American Diplomacy*, first published in 1959.[45] More recently—and in a much more sophis-

---

43. Examples include Charles S. Maier, *Recasting Bourgeois Europe: Stabilization in France, Germany, and Italy in the Decade After World War I* (Princeton, N.J.: Princeton University Press, 1975); Stephen A. Schuker, *The End of French Predominance in Europe: The Financial Crisis of 1924 and the Adoption of the Dawes Plan* (Chapel Hill: University of North Carolina Press, 1976); Michael J. Hogan, *Informal Entente: The Private Structure of Cooperation in Anglo–American Economic Diplomacy, 1918–1928* (Columbia: University of Missouri Press, 1977); Melvyn P. Leffler, *The Elusive Quest: America's Pursuit of European Stability and French Security, 1919–1933* (Chapel Hill: University of North Carolina Press, 1979); Frank Costigliola, *Awkward Dominion: American Political, Economic, and Cultural Relations with Europe, 1919–1933* (Ithaca: Cornell University Press, 1984).
44. For some recent—and sometimes contradictory—attempts to come to grips with this question, see: John Lewis Gaddis, *Strategies of Containment: A Critical Appraisal of Postwar American National Security Policy* (New York: Oxford University Press, 1982), pp. 352–357; Ralph B. Levering, *The Public and American Foreign Policy, 1918–1978* (New York: Foreign Policy Association/Morrow, 1978); William Appleman Williams, *Empire as a Way of Life* (New York: Oxford University Press, 1980); Cecil V. Crabb, Jr., *The Doctrines of American Foreign Policy: Their Meaning, Role, and Future* (Baton Rouge: Louisiana State University Press, 1982), especially pp. 371–386; Robert Dallek, *The American Style of Foreign Policy: Cultural Politics and Foreign Affairs* (New York: Alfred A. Knopf, 1983), especially pp. xi–xx; Lloyd C. Gardner, *A Covenant with Power: America and World Order from Wilson to Reagan* (New York: Oxford University Press, 1984).
45. William Appleman Williams, *The Tragedy of American Diplomacy*, rev. ed. (New York: Dell, 1962). See also Charles A. Beard, *The Idea of National Interest: An Analytical Study in American Foreign Policy* (New York: Macmillan, 1934), and *The Open Door at Home: A Trial Philosophy of National Interest* (New York: Macmillan, 1934). Other important expressions of the Beard/Williams thesis include Gabriel Kolko, *The Roots of American Foreign Policy: An Analysis of Power and Purpose* (Boston: Beacon Press, 1969); and Harry Magdoff, *The Age of Imperialism: The Economics of U.S. Foreign Policy* (New York: Monthly Review Press, 1969).

ticated way—the linkage between domestic economic structure and foreign policy has taken the form of studies demonstrating the effects of "corporatism": the *cooperation* of business, labor, and government to shape a congenial external environment.[46]

Both the "open door" and "corporatist" models have been criticized, with some justification, for their tendency toward reductionism: the explanation of complex phenomena in terms of single causes.[47] But for the purposes of this analysis, these criticisms are beside the point. What is important here is that these most frequently advanced arguments linking the structure of American capitalism with American foreign policy do not assume, from that linkage, the inevitability of war. One of the great advantages of the "open door," Williams has pointed out, was precisely the fact that it *avoided* military confrontations: it was a way to "extend the American system throughout the world without the embarrassment and inefficiency of traditional colonialism"; *"it was conceived and designed to win the victories without the wars."*[48] Similarly, "corporatist" historiography stresses the stabilizing rather than the de-stabilizing effects of American intervention in Europe after World Wars I and II; here, if anything, attempts to replicate domestic structure overseas are seen as reinforcing rather than undermining existing international systems.[49] Neither the "open door" nor the "corporatist" paradigms, therefore, offer evidence sufficient to confirm the old Leninist assertion that a society com-

46. Charles S. Maier, "The Two Postwar Eras and the Conditions for Stability in Twentieth-Century Western Europe," *American Historical Review*, Vol. 86 (April 1981), pp. 327–352; Robert Griffith, "Dwight D. Eisenhower and the Corporate Commonwealth," *American Historical Review*, Vol. 87 (February 1982), pp. 87–122; Michael J. Hogan, "American Marshall Planners and the Search for a European Neocapitalism," *American Historical Review*, Vol. 90 (February 1985), pp. 44–72.
47. The best critiques of the "open door" model are Robert W. Tucker, *The Radical Left and American Foreign Policy* (Baltimore: Johns Hopkins University Press, 1971); Charles S. Maier, "Revisionism and the Interpretation of Cold War Origins," *Perspectives in American History*, Vol. 4 (1970), pp. 313–347; Richard A. Melanson, "Revisionism Subdued? Robert James Maddox and the Origins of the Cold War," *Political Science Reviewer*, Vol. 7 (1977), pp. 229–271, and "The Social and Political Thought of William Appleman Williams," *Western Political Quarterly*, Vol. 31 (1978), pp. 392–409. Kenneth Waltz provides an effective theoretical critique of "reductionism" in his *Theory of International Politics*, pp. 60–67. There is as yet no substantial published critique of "corporatism," although the present author has attempted an insubstantial one soon to be published in *Diplomatic History*.
48. Williams, *The Tragedy of American Diplomacy*, pp. 43, 49 [emphases in original]. See also N. Gordon Levin's elaboration of this key point in *Woodrow Wilson and World Politics*, pp. 2–5.
49. Maier, "The Two Postwar Eras and the Conditions for Stability in Twentieth-Century Western Europe"; Hogan, "American Marshall Planners and the Search for a European Neocapitalism."

mitted to capitalism is necessarily precluded from participation in a stable world order.

There have been, of course, Schumpeterian as well as Leninist explanations of how domestic influences affect American foreign policy. C. Wright Mills some three decades ago stressed the interlocking relationship of business-men, politicians, and military officers whose "power elite" had imposed a form of "naked and arbitrary power" upon the world;[50] subsequent analysts, no doubt encouraged by Dwight D. Eisenhower's perhaps inadvertent en-dorsement of the term,[51] transformed Mills's argument into a full-blown theory of a "military-industrial complex" whose interests necessarily pre-cluded any significant relaxation of world tensions.[52] There were, to be sure, certain difficulties with this model: it did not plausibly explain the Truman administration's low military budgets of the 1945–50 period, nor did it deal easily with the dramatic shift from defense to welfare expenditures presided over by Richard Nixon during the early 1970s.[53] It neglected evidence that a "military-industrial complex" existed inside the Soviet Union as well.[54] But even if one overlooked these problems, it was not clear how the existence of such a "military-industrial complex" necessarily made war any more likely, given the opportunities deterrence offered to develop and deploy a profusion of military hardware without the risks war would pose to one's ability to continue doing precisely this.

More recently, attention has been given to the problems created by the structure of American domestic politics in attempting to formulate coherent policies for dealing with the Soviet Union. There is, of course, nothing new

---

50. C. Wright Mills, *The Power Elite* (New York: Oxford University Press, 1956), p. 360.
51. Eisenhower "farewell address," January 17, 1961, *Public Papers of the Presidents of the United States: Dwight D. Eisenhower, 1960–61* [hereinafter *Eisenhower Public Papers*] (Washington: U.S. Government Printing Office, 1961), p. 1038.
52. Fred J. Cook, *The Warfare State* (New York: Macmillan, 1962); Carroll W. Pursell, Jr., ed., *The Military–Industrial Complex* (New York: Harper and Row, 1972); Bruce M. Russett and Alfred Stepan, *Military Force and American Society* (New York: Harper and Row, 1973); Seymour Melman, *The Permanent War Economy: American Capitalism in Decline* (New York: Simon and Schuster, 1974).
53. See, on the immediate postwar period, Warner R. Schilling, "The Politics of National Defense: Fiscal 1950," in Warner R. Schilling, Paul Y. Hammond, and Glenn H. Snyder, *Strategy, Politics, and Defense Budgets* (New York: Columbia University Press, 1962), pp. 1–266; on the 1970s, Lawrence J. Korb, *The Fall and Rise of the Pentagon: American Defense Policies in the 1970's* (Westport, Conn.: Greenwood Press, 1979).
54. Vernon V. Aspaturian, "The Soviet Military–Industrial Complex—Does It Exist?," *Journal of International Affairs*, Vol. 26 (1972), pp. 1–28; William T. Lee, "The 'Politico–Military–Industrial Complex' of the U.S.S.R.," ibid., pp. 73–86; and Andrew Cockburn, *The Threat: Inside the Soviet Military Machine* (New York: Random House, 1983), pp. 120–149.

about this: the constitutionally mandated division of authority over foreign affairs has always made policy formulation in the United States a less than orderly process. But there is reason to think the problem is getting worse, partly because of the increasing number of government departments, Congressional committees, and interest groups who have a stake in foreign policy decisions, partly because of an increasingly protracted presidential selection process that has eroded an already imperfect tradition of keeping electoral politics apart from world politics.[55] Even here, though, the effect of such disarray on the long-term Soviet–American relationship has not been as great as might have been expected: what is impressive, when one considers all of the domestically motivated mutations American foreign policy has gone through during the past four decades, is how consistent its fundamental objectives in dealing with the Soviet Union have nonetheless remained.[56]

But what about domestic structural constraints inside the Soviet Union? Here, of course, there is much less hard information with which to work; generalizations, as a result, are not as firmly grounded or as richly developed as they are with regard to the United States. One point seems clear enough, though: in attempting to understand the effect of internal influences on Soviet foreign policy, American analysts have found Schumpeter a more reliable guide than Lenin; they have stressed the extent to which the structural requirements of legitimizing internal political authority have affected behavior toward the outside world. It was George F. Kennan who most convincingly suggested this approach with his portrayal, in the famous "long telegram" of February 1946, of a Soviet leadership at once so insecure and so unimaginative that it felt obliged to cultivate external enemies in order to maintain itself in power. Without at least the image of outside adversaries, he argued, "there would be no justification for that tremendous crushing bureaucracy of party, police and army which now lives off the labor and idealism of [the] Russian people."[57] Whatever the validity of this theory—

---

55. Joseph S. Nye, Jr., ed., *The Making of America's Soviet Policy* (New Haven: Yale University Press, 1984); I.M. Destler, Leslie H. Gelb, and Anthony Lake, *Our Own Worst Enemy: The Unmaking of American Foreign Policy* (New York: Simon and Schuster, 1984).
56. See, on this point, Seyom Brown, *The Faces of Power: Constancy and Change in United States Foreign Policy from Truman to Reagan* (New York: Columbia University Press, 1983), pp. 7–14.
57. Kennan to State Department, March 20, 1946, U.S. Department of State, *Foreign Relations of the United States: 1946* [hereinafter FRUS], Vol. 6, p. 721. See also Kennan's famous "long telegram" of February 22, 1946, in ibid., pp. 696–709; and his influential "Mr. X" article, "The Sources of Soviet Conduct," *Foreign Affairs*, Vol. 25 (July 1947), pp. 566–582. The circumstances surrounding the drafting of these documents are discussed in George F. Kennan, *Memoirs: 1925–1950* (Boston: Atlantic/Little, Brown, 1967), pp. 292–295, 354–357.

and however limited Kennan himself considered its application to be[58]—this characterization of a Kremlin leadership condemned by its own nervous ineptitude to perpetual distrust nonetheless remains the most influential explanation in the West of how domestic structure influences Soviet foreign policy.[59]

But this theory, too, did not assume the inevitability of war. Institutionalized suspicion in the U.S.S.R. resulted from weakness, not strength, Kennan argued; as a consequence, the Kremlin was most unlikely actually to initiate military action.[60] With rare exceptions,[61] American officials ever since have accepted this distinction between the likelihood of hostility and the probability of war: indeed, the whole theory of deterrence has been based upon the assumption that paranoia and prudence can co-exist.[62] By this logic, then, the domestic structures of the Soviet state, however geared they may have been to picturing the rest of the world in the worst possible light, have not been seen as likely in and of themselves to produce a war.

One should not make too much of these attempts to attribute to domestic constraints the foreign policy of either the United States or the Soviet Union. International relations, like life itself, is a good deal more complicated than these various models would tend to suggest. But it is significant that these efforts to link internal structure to external behavior reveal no obvious proclivity on either side to risk war; that despite their striking differences, Soviet and American domestic structures appear to have posed no greater impedi-

---

58. Kennan has emphasized that the recommendations advanced in the "long telegram" and the "X" article applied only to the Stalin regime. See his *Memoirs: 1925–1950*, pp. 364–367. But he does still see the role of institutionalized suspicion in Soviet society as making relations with the outside world unnecessarily difficult. See, for example, George F. Kennan, "Letter to a Russian," *New Yorker*, September 24, 1984, pp. 55–73.

59. See, for example, Taubman, *Stalin's American Policy*, pp. 243–255; Vernon V. Aspaturian, "Internal Politics and Foreign Policy in the Soviet System," in Aspaturian, ed., *Process and Power in Soviet Foreign Policy* (Boston: Little, Brown, 1971), pp. 491–551; Seweryn Bialer, "The Political System," in Robert F. Byrnes, ed., *After Brezhnev: Sources of Soviet Conduct in the 1980s* (Bloomington: Indiana University Press, 1983), pp. 10–11, 35–36, 51, 55; Adam Ulam, "The World Outside," in ibid., pp. 345–348.

60. On this point, see Gaddis, *Strategies of Containment*, pp. 34–35, 62, 74, 83–84.

61. The most conspicuous exception would appear to be the authors of NSC-68, the comprehensive reassessment of national security policy drafted early in 1950, who argued that when Soviet *capabilities* reached the point of being able to win a war, Soviet *intentions* would automatically be to provoke one. See NSC-68, "United States Objectives and Programs for National Security," April 14, 1950, *FRUS: 1950*, Vol. 1, especially pp. 251–252, 266–267.

62. See, on this point, Alexander L. George and Richard Smoke, *Deterrence in American Foreign Policy: Theory and Practice* (New York: Columbia University Press, 1974), pp. 527–530; also Patrick M. Morgan, *Deterrence: A Conceptual Analysis* (Beverly Hills: Sage, 1977), pp. 205–207.

ment to the maintenance of a stable international system than has bipolarity itself or the bilateral characteristics of the Soviet–American relationship.

The Behavioral Elements of Stability

NUCLEAR WEAPONS

Stability in international systems is only partly a function of structure, though; it depends as well upon the conscious behavior of the nations that make them up. Even if the World War II settlement had corresponded to the distribution of power in the world, even if the Russian–American relationship had been one of minimal interdependence, even if domestic constraints had not created difficulties, stability in the postwar era still might not have resulted if there had been, among either of the dominant powers in the system, the same willingness to risk war that has existed at other times in the past.

Students of the causes of war have pointed out that war is rarely something that develops from the workings of impersonal social or economic forces, or from the direct effects of arms races, or even by accident. It requires deliberate decisions on the part of national leaders; more than that, it requires calculations that the gains to be derived from war will outweigh the possible costs. "Recurring optimism," Geoffrey Blainey has written, "is a vital prelude to war. Anything which increases that optimism is a cause of war. Anything which dampens that optimism is a cause of peace."[63] Admittedly, those calculations are often in error: as Kennan, in his capacity as a historian, has pointed out, whatever conceivable gains the statesmen of 1914 might have had in mind in risking war, they could not have come anywhere close to approximating the costs the ensuing four-year struggle would actually entail.[64] But it seems hard to deny that it is from such calculations, whether accurately carried out, as Bismarck seemed able to do in his wars against Denmark, Austria, and France in the mid-19th century, or inaccurately carried out, as was the case in 1914, that wars tend to develop. They are not

---

63. Blainey, *The Causes of War*, p. 53. See also Howard, *The Causes of Wars*, pp. 14–15; Paul M. Kennedy, *Strategy and Diplomacy: 1870–1945* (London: Allen and Unwin, 1983), pp. 163–177; and Richard Smoke's perceptive discussion of the role of expectations in escalation in *War: Controlling Escalation* (Cambridge: Harvard University Press, 1977), pp. 268–277.
64. Kennan, *The Decline of Bismarck's European Order*, pp. 3–4.

something that just happens, like earthquakes, locust plagues, or (some might argue) the selection of presidential candidates in the United States.

For whatever reason, it has to be acknowledged that the statesmen of the post-1945 superpowers have, compared to their predecessors, been exceedingly cautious in risking war with one another.[65] In order to see this point, one need only run down the list of crises in Soviet–American relations since the end of World War II: Iran, 1946; Greece, 1947; Berlin and Czechoslovakia, 1948; Korea, 1950; the East Berlin riots, 1953; the Hungarian uprising, 1956; Berlin again, 1958–59; the U-2 incident, 1960; Berlin again, 1961; the Cuban missile crisis, 1962; Czechoslovakia again, 1968; the Yom Kippur war, 1973; Afghanistan, 1979; Poland, 1981; the Korean airliner incident, 1983—one need only run down this list to see how many occasions there have been in relations between Washington and Moscow that in almost any other age, and among almost any other antagonists, would sooner or later have produced war.

That they have not cannot be chalked up to the invariably pacific temperament of the nations involved: the United States participated in eight international wars involving a thousand or more battlefield deaths between 1815 and 1980; Russia participated in nineteen.[66] Nor can this restraint be attributed to any unusual qualities of leadership on either side: the vision and competency of postwar Soviet and American statesmen does not appear to have differed greatly from that of their predecessors. Nor does weariness growing out of participation in two world wars fully explain this unwillingness to resort to arms in their dealings with one another: during the postwar era both nations have employed force against third parties—in the case of the United States in Korea and Vietnam; in the case of the Soviet Union in Afghanistan—for protracted periods of time, and at great cost.

It seems inescapable that what has really made the difference in inducing this unaccustomed caution has been the workings of the nuclear deterrent.[67]

---

65. See Michael Howard's observations on the absence of a "bellicist" mentality among the great powers in the postwar era, in his *The Causes of War*, pp. 271–273.
66. Small and Singer, *Resort to Arms*, pp. 167, 169.
67. For a persuasive elaboration of this argument, with an intriguing comparison of the post-1945 "nuclear" system to the post-1815 "Vienna" system, see Michael Mandelbaum, *The Nuclear Revolution: International Politics Before and After Hiroshima* (New York: Cambridge University Press, 1981), pp. 58–77; also Morgan, *Deterrence*, p. 208; Craig and George, *Force and Statecraft*, pp. 117–120; Howard, *The Causes of War*, pp. 22, 278–279. It is interesting to speculate as to whether Soviet–American bipolarity would have developed if nuclear weapons had never been invented. My own view—obviously unverifiable—is that it would have, because bipolarity resulted from the way in which World War II had been fought; the condition was already evident at the time

Consider, for a moment, what the effect of this mechanism would be on a statesman from either superpower who might be contemplating war. In the past, the horrors and the costs of wars could be forgotten with the passage of time. Generations like the one of 1914 had little sense of what the Napoleonic Wars—or even the American Civil War—had revealed about the brutality, expense, and duration of military conflict. But the existence of nuclear weapons—and, more to the point, the fact that we have direct evidence of what they can do when used against human beings[68]—has given this generation a painfully vivid awareness of the realities of war that no previous generation has had. It is difficult, given this awareness, to produce the optimism that historical experience tells us prepares the way for war; pessimism, it appears, is a permanent accompaniment to our thinking about war, and that, as Blainey reminds us, is a cause of peace.

That same pessimism has provided the superpowers with powerful inducements to control crises resulting from the risk-taking of third parties. It is worth recalling that World War I grew out of the unsuccessful management of a situation neither created nor desired by any of the major actors in the international system. There were simply no mechanisms to put a lid on escalation: to force each nation to balance the short-term temptation to exploit opportunities against the long-term danger that things might get out of hand.[69] The nuclear deterrent provides that mechanism today, and as a result the United States and the Soviet Union have successfully managed a whole series of crises—most notably in the Middle East—that grew out of the actions of neither but that could have involved them both.

None of this is to say, of course, that war cannot occur: if the study of history reveals anything at all it is that one ought to expect, sooner or later,

---

of Hiroshima and Nagasaki. Whether bipolarity would have lasted as long as it has in the absence of nuclear weapons is another matter entirely, though: it seems at least plausible that these weapons have perpetuated bipolarity beyond what one might have expected its normal lifetime to be by minimizing superpower risk-taking while at the same time maintaining an apparently insurmountable power gradient between the superpowers and any potential military rivals.

68. See, on this point, Mandelbaum, *The Nuclear Revolution*, p. 109; also the discussion of the "crystal ball effect" in Albert Carnesale et al., *Living With Nuclear Weapons* (New York: Bantam, 1983), p. 44.

69. For a brief review of the literature on crisis management, together with an illustrative comparison of the July 1914 crisis with the Cuban missile crisis, see Ole R. Holsti, "Theories of Crisis Decision Making," in Lauren, ed., *Diplomacy*, pp. 99–136; also Craig and George, *Force and Statecraft*, pp. 205–219.

the unexpected. Nor is it to say that the nuclear deterrent could not function equally well with half, or a fourth, or even an eighth of the nuclear weapons now in the arsenals of the superpowers. Nor is it intended to deprecate the importance of refraining from steps that might destabilize the existing stalemate, whether through the search for technological breakthroughs that might provide a decisive edge over the other side, or through so mechanical a duplication of what the other side has that one fails to take into account one's own probably quite different security requirements, or through strategies that rely upon the first use of nuclear weapons in the interest of achieving economy, forgetting the far more fundamental systemic interest in maintaining the tradition, dating back four decades now, of never actually employing these weapons for military purposes.

I am suggesting, though, that the development of nuclear weapons has had, on balance, a stabilizing effect on the postwar international system. They have served to discourage the process of escalation that has, in other eras, too casually led to war. They have had a sobering effect upon a whole range of statesmen of varying degrees of responsibility and capability. They have forced national leaders, every day, to confront the reality of what war is really like, indeed to confront the prospect of their own mortality, and that, for those who seek ways to avoid war, is no bad thing.

THE RECONNAISSANCE REVOLUTION

But although nuclear deterrence is the most important behavioral mechanism that has sustained the post-World War II international system, it is by no means the only one. Indeed, the very technology that has made it possible to deliver nuclear weapons anywhere on the face of the earth has functioned also to lower greatly the danger of surprise attack, thereby supplementing the self-regulating features of deterrence with the assurance that comes from knowing a great deal more than in the past about adversary capabilities. I refer here to what might be called the "reconnaissance revolution," a development that may well rival in importance the "nuclear revolution" that preceded it, but one that rarely gets the attention it deserves.

The point was made earlier that nations tend to start wars on the basis of calculated assessments that they have the power to prevail. But it was suggested as well that they have often been wrong about this: they either have failed to anticipate the nature and the costs of war itself, or they have misjudged the intentions and the capabilities of the adversary they have chosen to confront.[70] Certainly the latter is what happened to Napoleon III in choosing to risk war with Prussia in 1870, to the Russians in provoking the Japanese in 1904, to the Germans in World War I when they brought about American entry by resuming unrestricted submarine warfare, to the Japanese in World War II by attacking Pearl Harbor and to Adolf Hitler in that same conflict when he managed within six months to declare war on *both* the Soviet Union and the United States, and most recently, to General Galtieri and the Argentine junta in deciding to take on Mrs. Thatcher.

Now, it would be foolish to argue that Americans and Russians have become any more skillful than they ever were at discerning the other's *intentions:* clearly the United States invasion of Grenada surprised Moscow as much as the Soviet invasion of Afghanistan surprised Washington. The capacity of each nation to behave in ways that seem perfectly logical to it but quite unfathomable to the other remains about what it has been throughout the entire Cold War. But both sides are able—and indeed have been able for at least two decades—to evaluate each other's *capabilities* to a degree that is totally unprecedented in the history of relations between great powers.

What has made this possible, of course, has been the development of the reconnaissance satellite, a device that if rumors are correct allows the reading of automobile license plates or newspaper headlines from a hundred or more miles out in space, together with the equally important custom that has evolved between the superpowers of allowing these objects to pass unhindered over their territories.[71] The effect has been to give each side a far more accurate view of the other's military capabilities—and, to some degree, economic capabilities as well—than could have been provided by an entire phalanx of the best spies in the long history of espionage. The resulting intelligence does not rule out altogether the possibility of surprise attack, but it does render it far less likely, at least as far as the superpowers are concerned. And that is no small matter, if one considers the number of wars in

70. Gilpin, *War and Change in World Politics*, pp. 202–203. Geoffrey Blainey, citing an idea first proposed by the sociologist Georg Simmel, has suggested that, in the past, war was the only means by which nations could gain an exact knowledge of each others' capabilities. Blainey, *The Causes of War*, p. 118.

71. A useful up-to-date assessment of the technology is David Hafemeister, Joseph J. Romm, and Kosta Tsipis, "The Verification of Compliance with Arms-Control Agreements," *Scientific American*, March 1985, pp. 38–45. For the historical evolution of reconnaissance satellites, see Gerald M. Steinberg, *Satellite Reconnaissance: The Role of Informal Bargaining* (New York: Praeger, 1983), pp. 19–70; Paul B. Stares, *The Militarization of Space: U.S. Policy, 1945–1984* (Ithaca, N.Y.: Cornell University Press, 1985), pp. 30–33, 47–57, 62–71; also Walter A. McDougall, *The Heavens and the Earth: A Political History of the Space Age* (New York: Basic Books, 1985), pp. 177–226.

history—from the Trojan War down through Pearl Harbor—in the origins of which deception played a major role.[72]

The "reconnaissance revolution" also corrects, at least to an extent, the asymmetry imposed upon Soviet–American relations by the two countries' sharply different forms of political and social organization. Throughout most of the early Cold War years the Soviet Union enjoyed all the advantages of a closed society in concealing its capabilities from the West; the United States and its allies, in turn, found it difficult to keep anything secret for very long.[73] That problem still exists, but the ability now to see both visually and electronically into almost every part of the Soviet Union helps to compensate for it. And, of course, virtually none of the limited progress the two countries have made in the field of arms control would have been possible had Americans and Russians not tacitly agreed to the use of reconnaissance satellites and other surveillance techniques to monitor compliance;[74] clearly any future progress in that field will depend heavily upon these devices as well.

There is no little irony in the fact that these instruments, which have contributed so significantly toward stabilizing the postwar international system, grew directly out of research on the intercontinental ballistic missile and the U-2 spy plane.[75] Technological innovation is not always a destabilizing force in the Soviet–American relationship. There have been—as in this case—and there could be again instances in which the advance of technology, far from increasing the danger of war, could actually lessen it. It all depends upon the uses to which the technology is put, and that, admittedly, is not an easy thing to foresee.

IDEOLOGICAL MODERATION

If technology has had the potential either to stabilize or destabilize the international system, the same cannot as easily be said of ideology. One

---

72. The most recent assessment, but one whose analysis does not take into account examples prior to 1940, is Richard K. Betts, *Surprise Attack: Lessons for Defense Planning* (Washington, D.C.: Brookings, 1982). See also, on the problem of assessing adversary intentions, Ernest R. May, ed., *Knowing One's Enemies: Intelligence Assessment Before the Two World Wars* (Princeton, N.J.: Princeton University Press, 1984).

73. For a summary of what the open literature reveals about the difficulties faced by American intelligence in the first decade after World War II, see Thomas Powers, *The Man Who Kept the Secrets: Richard Helms and the CIA* (New York: Alfred A. Knopf, 1979), pp. 43–58; and John Prados, *The Soviet Estimate: U.S. Intelligence and Russian Military Strength* (New York: Dial Press, 1982), pp. 24–30.

74. On this point, see Michael Krepon, *Arms Control: Verification and Compliance* (New York: Foreign Policy Association, 1984), especially pp. 8–13.

75. Prados, *The Soviet Estimate*, pp. 30–35, 96–110.

cannot help but be impressed, when one looks at the long history of national liberation movements, or revolutions against established social orders, or racial and religious conflict, by the continuing capacity of ideas to move nations, or groups within nations, to fight one another.[76] It is only by reference to a violent and ultimately self-destructive ideological impulse that one can account for the remarkable career of Adolf Hitler, with all of its chaotic consequences for the post-World War I international system.[77] Since 1945, the ideology of self-determination has not only induced colonies to embroil colonial masters in protracted and costly warfare; it has even led factions within newly independent states forcibly to seek their own separate political existence.[78] Ideologically motivated social revolution, too, has been a prominent feature of the postwar international scene, what with major upheavals in nations as diverse as China, Cuba, Vietnam, Cambodia, and Nicaragua. But the most surprising evidence of the continuing influence of ideology has come in the area of religion, where conflicts between Hindus and Moslems, Arabs and Israelis, Iranians and Iraqis, and even Catholics and Protestants in Northern Ireland provide little reason to think that ideas—even ideas once considered to have little relevance other than for historians—will not continue to have a major disruptive potential for international order.[79]

The relationship between the Soviet Union and the United States has not been free from ideological rivalries: it could be argued, in fact, that these are among the most ideological nations on the face of the earth.[80] Certainly their respective ideologies could hardly have been more antithetical, given the self-proclaimed intention of one to overthrow the other.[81] And yet, since their emergence as superpowers, both nations have demonstrated an impressive

76. See, on this point, Wright, *A Study of War*, pp. 1290–1291; Aron, *Peace and War*, pp. 64–69; Reynolds, *Theory and Explanation in International Politics*, p. 176; also Murray Edelman, *Politics as Symbolic Action: Mass Arousal and Quiescence* (Chicago: Markham, 1971), pp. 53–64.
77. Norman Rich, *Hitler's War Aims: Ideology, the Nazi State, and the Course of Expansion* (New York: Norton, 1973), pp. xxxvi–xxxvii, xlii–xliii, 3–10.
78. One thinks, in this connection, of the successful struggles of the Vietnamese and the Algerians against the French and of Portugal's African colonies against that country, of equally successful separatist movements within India and later Pakistan, and of the unsuccessful Biafran rebellion against Nigeria.
79. On the recent resurgence of religion as an influence on world politics, see Paul Johnson, *Modern Times: The World From the Twenties to the Eighties* (New York: Harper and Row, 1983), pp. 698–710.
80. See, on this point, Halle, *The Cold War as History*, pp. 157–160.
81. Adam B. Ulam, *Expansion and Coexistence: The History of Soviet Foreign Policy, 1917–73*, 2nd ed. (New York: Praeger, 1974), pp. 130–131.

capacity to subordinate antagonistic ideological interests to a common goal of preserving international order. The reasons for this are worth examining.

If there were ever a moment at which the priorities of order overcame those of ideology, it would appear to be the point at which Soviet leaders decided that war would no longer advance the cause of revolution. That clearly had not been Lenin's position: international conflict, for him, was good or evil according to whether it accelerated or retarded the demise of capitalism.[82] Stalin's attitude on this issue was more ambivalent: he encouraged talk of an "inevitable conflict" between the "two camps" of communism and capitalism in the years immediately following World War II, but he also appears shortly before his death to have anticipated the concept of "peaceful coexistence."[83] It was left to Georgii Malenkov to admit publicly, shortly after Stalin's death, that a nuclear war would mean "the destruction of world civilization"; Nikita Khrushchev subsequently refined this idea (which he had initially condemned) into the proposition that the interests of world revolution, as well as those of the Soviet state, would be better served by working within the existing international order than by trying to overthrow it.[84]

The reasons for this shift of position are not difficult to surmise. First, bipolarity—the defining characteristic of the postwar international system—implied unquestioned recognition of the Soviet Union as a great power. It was "no small thing," Khrushchev later acknowledged in his memoirs, "that

---

82. See, on this point, E.H. Carr, *The Bolshevik Revolution, 1917–1923* (New York: Macmillan, 1951–1953), Vol. 3, pp. 549–566; and Marshall D. Shulman, *Stalin's Foreign Policy Reappraised* (New York: Atheneum, 1969), p. 82. It is fashionable now, among Soviet scholars, to minimize the ideological component of Moscow's foreign policy; indeed Lenin himself is now seen as the original architect of "peaceful coexistence," a leader for whom the idea of exporting revolution can hardly have been more alien. See, for example, G.A. Trofimenko, "Uroki mirnogo sosushestvovaniia," *Voprosy istorii*, Number 11 (November 1983), pp. 6–7. It seems not out of place to wonder how the great revolutionary would have received such perfunctory dismissals of the Comintern and all that it implied; certainly most Western students have treated more seriously than this the revolutionary implications of the Bolshevik Revolution.

83. For Stalin's mixed record on this issue, see Shulman, *Stalin's Foreign Policy Reappraised*, *passim*; also Taubman, *Stalin's American Policy*, pp. 128–227; and Adam B. Ulam, *Stalin: The Man and His Era* (New York: Viking, 1973), especially pp. 641–643, 654. It is possible, of course, that Stalin followed both policies intentionally as a means both of intimidating and inducing complacency in the West.

84. Herbert Dinerstein, *War and the Soviet Union: Nuclear Weapons and the Revolution in Soviet Military and Political Thinking* (New York: Praeger, 1959), pp. 65–90; William Zimmerman, *Soviet Perspectives on International Relations, 1956–1967* (Princeton: Princeton University Press, 1969), pp. 251–252.

we have lived to see the day when the Soviet Union is considered, in terms of its economic and military might, one of the two most powerful countries in the world."[85] Second, the international situation in the 1950s and early 1960s seemed favorable, especially because of the decline of colonialism and the rise of newly independent nations likely to be suspicious of the West, to the expansion of Soviet influence in the world.[86] But third, and most important, the proliferation of nuclear capabilities on both sides had confirmed Malenkov's conclusion that in any future war between the great powers, there would be no victors at all, whether capitalist or communist. "[T]he atomic bomb," Soviet leaders reminded their more militant Chinese comrades in 1963, "does not observe the class principle."[87]

The effect was to transform a state which, if ideology alone had governed, should have sought a complete restructuring of the existing international system, into one for whom that system now seemed to have definite benefits, within which it now sought to function, and for whom the goal of overthrowing capitalism had been postponed to some vague and indefinite point in the future.[88] Without this moderation of ideological objectives, it is difficult to see how the stability that has characterized great power relations since the end of World War II could have been possible.

Ideological considerations have traditionally played a less prominent role in shaping American foreign policy, but they have had their influence nonetheless. Certainly the Wilsonian commitment to self-determination, revived and ardently embraced during World War II, did a great deal to alienate Americans from their Soviet allies at the end of that conflict. Nor had their military exertions moderated Americans' long-standing aversion to collectivism—of which the Soviet variety of communism appeared to be the most

---

85. Nikita S. Khrushchev, *Khrushchev Remembers: The Last Testament*, trans. and ed. by Strobe Talbott (Boston: Little, Brown, 1974), p. 529.
86. Zimmerman, *Soviet Perspectives on International Relations*, pp. 252–255.
87. Ibid., pp. 5, 255–259. See also *Khrushchev Remembers*, p. 530.
88. ". . . [P]layers' goals may undergo very little change, but postponing their attainment to the indefinite future fundamentally transforms the meaning of . . . myth by revising its implications for social action. Exactly because myths are dramatic stories, changing their time-frame affects their character profoundly. Those who see only the permanence of professed goals, but who neglect structural changes—the incorporation of common experiences into the myths of both sides, shifts in the image of the opponent ('there are reasonable people also in the other camp'), and modifications in the myths' periodization—overlook the great effects that may result from such contextual changes." Friedrich V. Kratochwil, *International Order and Foreign Policy: A Theoretical Sketch of Post-War International Politics* (Boulder: Westview Press, 1978), p. 117.

extreme example.[89] But there had also developed, during the war, an emphatic hostility toward "totalitarianism" in general: governments that relied upon force to sustain themselves in power, it was thought, could hardly be counted on to refrain from the use of force in the world at large. Demands for the "unconditional surrender" of Germany and Japan reflected this ideological position: there could be no compromise with regimes for whom arbitrary rule was a way of life.[90]

What is interesting is that although the "totalitarian" model came as easily to be applied to the Soviet Union as it had been to Germany and Japan,[91] the absolutist call for "unconditional surrender" was not. To be sure, the United States and the U.S.S.R. were not at war. But levels of tension were about as high as they can get short of war during the late 1940s, and we now know that planning for the *contingency* of war was well under way in Washington—as it presumably was in Moscow as well.[92] Nevertheless, the first of these plans to be approved by President Truman, late in 1948, bluntly stated that, if war came, there would be no "predetermined requirement for unconditional surrender."[93] NSC-68, a comprehensive review of national

---

89. John Lewis Gaddis, *The United States and the Origins of the Cold War, 1941–1947* (New York: Columbia University Press, 1972), pp. 56–62, 133–175.

90. See, on this point, Michael S. Sherry, *Preparing for the Next War: American Plans for Postwar Defense, 1941–45* (New Haven: Yale University Press, 1977), pp. 52–53; Eduard Maximilian Mark, "The Interpretation of Soviet Foreign Policy in the United States, 1928–1947," Ph.D. dissertation, University of Connecticut, 1978, pp. 95–96, 326–329; and, for the Wilsonian background of this idea, Levin, *Woodrow Wilson and World Politics*, pp. 37–45. For the ideological roots of "unconditional surrender," see Anne Armstrong, *Unconditional Surrender: The Impact of the Casablanca Policy Upon World War II* (New Brunswick: Rutgers University Press, 1961), pp. 250–253.

91. See, for example, Hannah Arendt, *The Origins of Totalitarianism* (New York: Harcourt, 1951), and Carl Friedrich and Zbigniew Brzezinski, *Totalitarian Dictatorship and Autocracy* (Cambridge: Harvard University Press, 1956); also Les K. Adler and Thomas G. Paterson, "Red Fascism: The Merger of Nazi Germany and Soviet Russia in the American Image of Totalitarianism, 1930's–1950's," *American Historical Review*, Vol. 75 (April 1970), pp. 1046–1064.

92. The best brief review of early American war plans is in Gregg Herken, *The Winning Weapon: The Atomic Bomb in the Cold War, 1945–1950* (New York: Alfred A. Knopf, 1981), pp. 195–303. A selection from these plans has been published in Thomas H. Etzold and John Lewis Gaddis, eds., *Containment: Documents on American Policy and Strategy, 1945–1950* (New York: Columbia University Press, 1978), pp. 277–381. The Soviet Union has yet to make any comparable selection of its postwar documents available.

93. NSC 20/4, "U.S. Objectives with Respect to the USSR to Counter Soviet Threats to U.S. Security," November 23, 1948, *FRUS: 1948*, Vol. 1, pp. 668–669. In an earlier version of this document, George F. Kennan had explained that "we could not hope to achieve any total assertion of our will on Russian territory, as we have endeavored to do in Germany and Japan. We must recognize that whatever settlement we finally achieve must be a *political* settlement, *politically* negotiated." NSC 20/1, "U.S. Objectives With Respect to Russia," August 18, 1948, in

security policy undertaken two years later, elaborated on the point: "our over-all objectives . . . do not include unconditional surrender, the subjugation of the Russian peoples or a Russia shorn of its economic potential." The ultimate goal, rather, was to convince the Soviet government of the impossibility of achieving its self-proclaimed ideological objectives; the immediate goal was to "induce the Soviet Union to accommodate itself, with or without the conscious abandonment of its [ideological] design, to coexistence on tolerable terms with the non-Soviet world."[94]

It is no easy matter to explain why Americans did not commit themselves to the eradication of Soviet "totalitarianism" with the same single-minded determination they had earlier applied to German and Japanese "totalitarianism." One reason, of course, would have been the daunting prospect of attempting to occupy a country the size of the Soviet Union, when compared to the more manageable adversaries of World War II.[95] Another was the fact that, despite the hostility that had developed since 1945, American officials did not regard their Russian counterparts as irredeemable: the very purpose of "containment" had been to change the *psychology* of the Soviet leadership, but not, as had been the case with Germany and Japan, the leadership itself.[96]

But Washington's aversion to an "unconditional surrender" doctrine for the Soviet Union stemmed from yet another less obvious consideration: it had quickly become clear to American policymakers, after World War II, that insistence on the total defeat of Germany and Japan had profoundly destabilized the postwar balance of power. Only by assuming responsibility for the rehabilitation of these former enemies as well as the countries they had ravaged had the United States been able to restore equilibrium, and even then it was clear that the American role in this regard would have to be a continuing one. It was no accident that the doctrine of "unconditional sur-

---

Thomas H. Etzold and John Lewis Gaddis, eds., *Containment: Documents on American Policy and Strategy, 1945–1950* (New York: 1978), p. 193. George H. Quester has made the point that "containment" itself reflected, by its nature, a repudiation of "unconditional surrender". "Containment, the Soviet Nuclear Buildup, and the Strategic Balance," paper presented at the National Defense University symposium on "Containment and the Future," November 7–8, 1985.

94. NSC 68, "United States Objectives and Programs for National Security," *FRUS: 1950*, Vol. 1, p. 242.

95. Kennan made the point explicitly in NSC 20/1 (Etzold and Gaddis, eds., *Containment*, p. 191); also in his *The Realities of American Foreign Policy* (Princeton: Princeton University Press, 1954), p. 80.

96. On changing Soviet psychology as the ultimate goal of containment, see Gaddis, *Strategies of Containment*, pp. 48–51, 71–83, 98–99, 102–106.

render" came under severe criticism, after 1945, from a new school of "realist" geopoliticians given to viewing international stability in terms of the wary toleration of adversaries rather than, as a point of principle, their annihilation.[97]

Largely as a result of such reasoning, American officials at no point during the history of the Cold War seriously contemplated, as a deliberate political objective, the elimination of the Soviet Union as a major force in world affairs. By the mid-1950s, it is true, war plans had been devised that, if executed, would have quite indiscriminately annihilated not only the Soviet Union but several of its communist and non-communist neighbors as well.[98] What is significant about those plans, though, is that they reflected the organizational convenience of the military services charged with implementing them, not any conscious policy decisions at the top. Both Eisenhower and Kennedy were appalled on learning of them; both considered them ecologically as well as strategically impossible; and during the Kennedy administration steps were initiated to devise strategies that would leave open the possibility of a surviving political entity in Russia even in the extremity of nuclear war.[99]

All of this would appear to confirm, then, the proposition that systemic interests tend to take precedence over ideological interests.[100] Both the Soviet ideological aversion to capitalism and the American ideological aversion to totalitarianism could have produced policies—and indeed had produced policies in the past—aimed at the complete overthrow of their respective adversaries. That such ideological impulses could be muted to the extent they have been during the past four decades testifies to the stake both Washington

97. See, for example, Hans J. Morgenthau, *In Defense of the National Interest: A Critical Examination of American Foreign Policy* (New York: Alfred A. Knopf, 1951), pp. 31–33, 142–146. The critique of "unconditional surrender" can best be followed in Armstrong, *Unconditional Surrender*, pp. 248–262; and in Hanson W. Baldwin, *Great Mistakes of the War* (New York: Harper, 1950), pp. 14–25.

98. David Alan Rosenberg, "'A Smoking, Radiating Ruin at the End of Two Hours': Documents on American Plans for Nuclear War with the Soviet Union, 1954–55," *International Security*, Vol. 6, No. 3 (Winter 1981/82), pp. 3–38, and "The Origins of Overkill: Nuclear Weapons and American Strategy, 1945–1960," *International Security*, Vol. 7, No. 3 (Spring 1983), pp. 3–71. For more general accounts, see Fred Kaplan, *The Wizards of Armageddon* (New York: Simon and Schuster, 1983), especially pp. 263–270; and Gregg Herken, *Counsels of War* (New York: Alfred A. Knopf, 1985), pp. 137–140.

99. Rosenberg, "The Origins of Overkill," pp. 8, 69–71; Kaplan, *Wizards of Armageddon*, pp. 268–285; Herken, *Counsels of War*, pp. 140–165; and Stephen E. Ambrose, *Eisenhower: The President* (New York: Simon and Schuster, 1984), pp. 494, 523, 564.

100. See, on this point, John Spanier, *Games Nations Play: Analyzing International Politics*, 5th ed. (New York: Holt, Rinehart and Winston, 1984), p. 91.

and Moscow have developed in preserving the existing international system: the moderation of ideologies must be considered, then, along with nuclear deterrence and reconnaissance, as a major self-regulating mechanism of postwar politics.

"RULES" OF THE SUPERPOWER "GAME"

The question still arises, though: how can order emerge from a system that functions without any superior authority? Even self-regulating mechanisms like automatic pilots or engine governors cannot operate without someone to set them in motion; the prevention of anarchy, it has generally been assumed, requires hierarchy, both at the level of interpersonal and international relations. Certainly the statesmen of World War II expected that some supra-national structure would be necessary to sustain a future peace, whether in the form of a new collective security organization to replace the ineffectual League of Nations, or through perpetuation of the great-power consensus that Churchill, Roosevelt, and Stalin sought to forge.[101] All of them would have been surprised by the extent to which order has been maintained since 1945 in the absence of any effective supra-national authority of any kind.[102]

This experience has forced students of international politics to recognize that their subject bears less resemblance to local, state, or national politics, where order does in fact depend upon legally constituted authority, than it does to the conduct of games, where order evolves from mutual agreement on a set of "rules" defining the range of behavior each side anticipates from the other. The assumption is that the particular "game" being played promises sufficient advantages to each of its "players" to outweigh whatever might be obtained by trying to upset it; in this way, rivalries can be pursued within an orderly framework, even in the absence of a referee. Game theory therefore helps to account for the paradox of order in the absence of hierarchy that characterizes the postwar superpower relationship: through it one can get a sense of how "rules" establish limits of acceptable behavior on the part of nations who acknowledge only themselves as the arbiters of behavior.[103]

---

101. Gaddis, *The United States and the Origins of the Cold War*, pp. 23–31.
102. The United Nations, regretfully, cannot be considered an effective supra-national authority.
103. My definition here is based on Paul Keal, *Unspoken Rules and Superpower Dominance* (New York: St. Martin's, 1983), pp. 2–3. Other more generalized studies dealing with theories of games and bargaining include Kratochwil, *International Order and Foreign Policy*, passim; Snyder and Diesing, *Conflict Among Nations*, especially pp. 33–182; Anatol Rapaport, *Fights, Games, and*

These "rules" are, of course, implicit rather than explicit: they grow out of a mixture of custom, precedent, and mutual interest that takes shape quite apart from the realm of public rhetoric, diplomacy, or international law. They require the passage of time to become effective; they depend, for that effectiveness, upon the extent to which successive generations of national leadership on each side find them useful. They certainly do not reflect any agreed-upon standard of international morality: indeed they often violate principles of "justice" adhered to by one side or the other. But these "rules" have played an important role in maintaining the international system that has been in place these past four decades: without them the correlation one would normally anticipate between hostility and instability would have become more exact than it has in fact been since 1945.

No two observers of superpower behavior would express these "rules" in precisely the same way; indeed it may well be that their very vagueness has made them more acceptable than they otherwise might have been to the nations that have followed them. What follows is nothing more than my own list, derived from an attempt to identify *regularities* in the postwar Soviet–American relationship whose pattern neither side could now easily disrupt.

(1) RESPECT SPHERES OF INFLUENCE. Neither Russians nor Americans officially admit to having such "spheres," but in fact much of the history of the Cold War can be written in terms of the efforts both have made to consolidate and extend them. One should not, in acknowledging this, fall into so mechanical a comparison of the two spheres as to ignore their obvious differences: the American sphere has been wider in geographical scope than its Soviet counterpart, but it has also been a much looser alignment, participation in which has more often than not been a matter of choice rather than coercion.[104] But what is important from the standpoint of superpower "rules" is the fact that, although neither side has ever publicly endorsed the other's right to a sphere of influence, neither has ever directly challenged it either.[105]

Debates (Ann Arbor: University of Michigan Press, 1960); and Charles Lockhart, *Bargaining in International Conflicts* (New York: Columbia University Press, 1979).
104. On this point, see Geir Lundestad, *America, Scandinavia, and the Cold War, 1945–1949* (New York: Columbia University Press, 1980), especially pp. 327–338. For the formation of spheres of influence, see Keal, *Unspoken Rules and Superpower Dominance*, pp. 66–71, 80–84, 90–98; also John Lewis Gaddis, "The United States and the Question of a Sphere of Influence in Europe, 1945–1949," in Olav Riste, ed., *Western Security: The Formative Years: Europe and Atlantic Defence, 1947–1953* (Oslo: Universitetsforlaget, 1985), pp. 60–91.
105. "In general terms, acquiescence in spheres of influence has taken the form of A disclaiming

Thus, despite publicly condemning it, the United States never attempted seriously to undo Soviet control in Eastern Europe; Moscow reciprocated by tolerating, though never openly approving of, Washington's influence in Western Europe, the Mediterranean, the Near East, and Latin America. A similar pattern held up in East Asia, where the Soviet Union took no more action to oppose United States control over occupied Japan than the Truman administration did to repudiate the Yalta agreement, which left the Soviet Union dominant, at least for the moment, on the Northeast Asian mainland.[106]

Where the relation of particular areas to spheres of influence had been left unclear—as had been the case with the Western-occupied zones of Berlin prior to 1948, or with South Korea prior to 1950—or where the resolve of one side to maintain its sphere appeared to have weakened—as in the case of Cuba following the failure of the Bay of Pigs invasion in 1961—attempts by the other to exploit the situation could not be ruled out: the Berlin blockade, the invasion of South Korea, and the decision to place Soviet missiles in Cuba can all be understood in this way.[107] But it appears also to have been understood, in each case, that the resulting probes would be conducted cautiously, and that they would not be pursued to the point of risking war if resistance was encountered.[108]

Defections from one sphere would be exploited by the other only when it was clear that the first either could not or would not reassert control. Hence, the United States took advantage of departures from the Soviet bloc of Yugoslavia and—ultimately—the Peoples' Republic of China; it did not seek to do so in the case of Hungary in 1956, Czechoslovakia in 1968, or (in what was admittedly a more ambiguous situation) Poland in 1981. Similarly, the Soviet Union exploited the defection of Cuba after 1959, but made no attempt to contest the reassertion of American influence in Iran in 1953, Guatemala in 1954, the Dominican Republic in 1965, or Grenada in 1983.[109]

---

what B does and in fact disapproving of what B does, but at the same time acquiescing by virtue of effectively doing nothing to oppose B." Keal, *Unspoken Rules and Superpower Dominance*, p. 115.
106. For a good overview of this process of consolidation, see ibid., pp. 87–115.
107. George and Smoke, *Deterrence in American Foreign Policy*, pp. 523–526, 557–560.
108. Ibid., pp. 536–543.
109. For a discussion of the Hungarian, Czech, Cuban, and Dominican Republic episodes, see Keal, *Unspoken Rules and Superpower Dominance*, pp. 116–158. There is no adequate comparative analysis of how the United States responded to the defections of Yugoslavia and China.

(2) AVOID DIRECT MILITARY CONFRONTATION. It is remarkable, in retrospect, that at no point during the long history of the Cold War have Soviet and American military forces engaged each other directly in sustained hostilities. The superpowers have fought three major limited wars since 1945, but in no case with each other: the possibility of direct Soviet–American military involvement was greatest—although it never happened—during the Korean War; it was much more remote in Vietnam and has remained so in Afghanistan as well. In those few situations where Soviet and American military units have confronted one another directly—the 1948 Berlin blockade, the construction of the Berlin Wall in 1961, and the Cuban missile crisis the following year—great care was taken on both sides to avoid incidents that might have triggered hostilities.[110]

Where the superpowers have sought to expand or to retain areas of control, they have tended to resort to the use of proxies or other indirect means to accomplish this: examples would include the Soviet Union's decision to sanction a North Korean invasion of South Korea,[111] and its more recent reliance on Cuban troops to promote its interests in sub-Saharan Africa; on the American side covert intervention has been a convenient (if not invariably successful) means of defending spheres of influence.[112] In a curious way, clients and proxies have come to serve as buffers, allowing Russians and Americans to pursue their competition behind a facade of "deniability" that minimizes the risks of open—and presumably less manageable—confrontation.

The two superpowers have also been careful not to allow the disputes of third parties to embroil them directly: this pattern has been most evident in the Middle East, which has witnessed no fewer than five wars between Israel

---

110. Coral Bell, *The Conventions of Crisis: A Study in Diplomatic Management* (New York: Oxford University Press, 1971); Phil Williams, *Crisis Management: Confrontation and Diplomacy in the Nuclear Age* (New York: Wiley, 1976). They have also managed successfully to control incidents at sea: see Sean M. Lynn-Jones, "A Quiet Success for Arms Control: Preventing Incidents at Sea," *International Security*, Vol. 9, No. 3 (Spring 1985), pp. 154–184.
111. This analysis assumes, as do most scholarly examinations of the subject, that the North Korean attack could not have taken place without some form of Soviet authorization. The most thorough assessment of this admittedly unclear episode is Robert R. Simmons, *The Strained Alliance: Peking, Pyongyang, Moscow and the Politics of the Korean Civil War* (New York: Free Press, 1975).
112. Which is not to say that the Soviet Union does not engage in covert operations as well; it is, however, somewhat more successful at concealing them. The best recent overview is John Barron, *KGB Today: The Hidden Hand* (New York: Reader's Digest Press, 1983).

and its Arab neighbors since 1948; but it holds as well for the India–Pakistan conflicts of 1965 and 1971, and for the more recent—and much more protracted—struggle between Iran and Iraq. The contrast between this long tradition of restraint and the casualness with which great powers in the past have allowed the quarrels of others to become their own could hardly be move obvious.[113]

(3) USE NUCLEAR WEAPONS ONLY AS AN ULTIMATE RESORT. One of the most significant—though least often commented upon—of the superpower "rules" has been the tradition that has evolved, since 1945, of maintaining a sharp distinction between conventional and nuclear weapons, and of reserving the military use of the latter only for the extremity of total war. In retrospect, there was nothing at all inevitable about this: the Eisenhower administration announced quite publicly its willingness to use nuclear weapons in limited war situations;[114] Henry Kissinger's *Nuclear Weapons and Foreign Policy* strongly endorsed such use in 1957 as a way to keep alliance commitments credible;[115] and Soviet strategists have traditionally insisted as well that in war both nuclear and conventional means would be employed.[116] It is remarkable, given this history, that the world has not seen a single nuclear weapon used in anger since the destruction of Nagasaki forty-one years ago. Rarely has *practice* of nations so conspicuously departed from proclaimed *doctrine*; rarely, as well, has so great a disparity attracted so little public notice.

This pattern of caution in the use of nuclear weapons did not develop solely, as one might have expected, from the prospect of retaliation. As early as 1950, at a time when the Soviet Union had only just tested an atomic bomb and had only the most problematic methods of delivering it, the United

---

113. The classic case, of course, is the amply documented July 1914 crisis, the implications of which have most recently been reassessed in a special edition of *International Security*, Vol. 9, No. 1 (Summer 1984). But see also Richard Smoke's essays on how the Seven Years War and the Crimean War grew out of a comparable failure of the major powers to limit the escalation of quarrels they did not initiate. Smoke, *War: Controlling Escalation*, pp. 147–236.

114. See Gaddis, *Strategies of Containment*, pp. 145–152; also Glenn H. Snyder, "The 'New Look' of 1953," in Schilling, Hammond, and Snyder, *Strategy, Politics, and Defense Budgets*, pp. 379–524.

115. Henry A. Kissinger, *Nuclear Weapons and Foreign Policy* (New York: Harper, 1957). It should be added, in fairness, that Kissinger by 1961 had repudiated his earlier position on this point. See his *The Necessity for Choice: Prospects of American Foreign Policy* (New York: Harper and Row, 1961).

116. For a summary of Soviet thinking on the subject, see Harriet Fast Scott and William F. Scott, *The Armed Forces of the USSR* (Boulder: Westview Press, 1979), especially pp. 55–56, 61–62.

States nonetheless effectively ruled out the use of its own atomic weapons in Korea because of the opposition of its allies and the fear of an adverse reaction in the world at large. As one State Department official put it: "[W]e must consider that, regardless of the fact that the military results achieved by atomic bombardment may be identical to those attained by conventional weapons, the effect on world opinion will be vastly different."[117] Despite his public position that there was "no reason why [nuclear weapons] shouldn't be used just exactly as you would use a bullet or anything else," President Eisenhower repeatedly rejected recommendations for their use in limited war situations: "You boys must be crazy," he told his advisers at the time of the collapse of Dien Bien Phu in 1954. "We can't use those awful things against Asians for the second time in less than ten years. My God."[118]

It was precisely this sense that nuclear weapons were qualitatively different from other weapons[119] that most effectively deterred their employment by the United States during the first decade of the Cold War, a period in which the tradition of "non-use" had not yet taken hold, within which ample opportunities for their use existed, and during which the possibility of Soviet retaliation could not have been great. The idea of a discrete "threshold" between nuclear and conventional weapons, therefore, may owe more to the moral—and public relations—sensibilities of Washington officials than to any actual fear of escalation. By the time a credible Soviet retaliatory capability was in place, at the end of the 1950s, the "threshold" concept was equally firmly fixed: one simply did not cross it short of all-out war.[120] Subsequent

---

117. John K. Emmerson to Dean Rusk, November 8, 1950, *FRUS: 1950*, Vol. 7, pp. 1098–1099. See also a memorandum by Paul Nitze, November 4, 1950, ibid., pp. 1041–1042; and Philip C. Jessup's notes of a meeting between Truman and Attlee at the White House, December 7, 1950, ibid., pp. 1462–1465. For a comprehensive policy statement on the use of atomic weapons in war, see the Department of State–Joint Strategic Survey Committee paper, "United States Position on Considerations Under Which the United States Will Accept War and on Atomic Warfare," August 3, 1951, *FRUS: 1951*, pp. 866–874.

118. Ambrose, *Eisenhower: The President*, p. 184. For examples of Eisenhower's refusal to authorize the use of nuclear weapons, see ibid., pp. 179, 206, 213, 229–230, 243, 274, 483–484. Eisenhower's "bullet" statement is from his March 16, 1955 press conference, *Eisenhower Public Papers, 1955* (Washington: U.S. Government Printing Office, 1959), p. 332.

119. With the exception of chemical weapons, for which there appears to be an even deeper aversion than to the use of nuclear weapons. See, on this point, Mandelbaum, *The Nuclear Revolution*, especially pp. 29–40. For the distinction between nuclear and conventional weapons, see Thomas C. Schelling, *Arms and Influence* (New Haven: Yale University Press, 1966), pp. 132–134.

120. It is interesting to note that John F. Kennedy began his administration with what appeared to be a pledge never to initiate the use of nuclear weapons against the Soviet Union; after protests from NATO allies, though, this was modified into a promise not to initiate hostilities

limited war situations—notably Vietnam for the Americans, and more recently Afghanistan for the Russians—have confirmed the continued effectiveness of this unstated but important "rule" of superpower behavior, as have the quiet but persistent efforts both Washington and Moscow have made to keep nuclear weapons from falling into the hands of others who might not abide by it.[121]

(4) PREFER PREDICTABLE ANOMALY OVER UNPREDICTABLE RATIONALITY. One of the most curious features of the Cold War has been the extent to which the superpowers—and their respective clients, who have had little choice in the matter—have tolerated a whole series of awkward, artificial, and, on the surface at least, unstable regional arrangements: the division of Germany is, of course, the most obvious example; others would include the Berlin Wall, the position of West Berlin itself within East Germany, the arbitrary and ritualized partition of the Korean peninsula, the existence of an avowed Soviet satellite some ninety miles off the coast of Florida, and, not least, the continued functioning of an important American naval base within it. There is to all of these arrangements an appearance of wildly illogical improvisation: none of them could conceivably have resulted, it seems, from any rational and premeditated design.

And yet, at another level, they have had a kind of logic after all: the fact that these jerry-built but rigidly maintained arrangements have lasted for so long suggests an unwillingness on the part of the superpowers to trade familiarity for unpredictability. To try to rationalize the German, Korean, or Cuban anomalies would, it has long been acknowledged, create the unnerving possibility of an uncertain result; far better, Soviet and American leaders have consistently agreed, to perpetuate the anomalies than to risk the possibilities for destabilization inherent in trying to resolve them. For however unnatural and unjust these situations may be for the people whose lives they directly affect, it seems nonetheless incontestable that the superpowers' preference for predictability over rationality has, on the whole, enhanced more than it has reduced prospects for a stable relationship.

(5) DO NOT SEEK TO UNDERMINE THE OTHER SIDE'S LEADERSHIP. The death of Stalin, in March 1953, set off a flurry of proposals within the United States

---

only. See Michael Mandelbaum, *The Nuclear Question: The United States and Nuclear Weapons, 1946–1976* (Cambridge: Cambridge University Press, 1979), p. 75.
121. For a recent review of non-proliferation efforts, see the National Academy of Sciences study, *Nuclear Arms Control: Background and Issues* (Washington: National Academy Press, 1985), pp. 224–273.

government for exploiting the vulnerability that was thought certain to result: it was a major American objective, Secretary of State Dulles informed embassies overseas, "to sow doubt, confusion, uncertainty about the new regime."[122] And yet, by the following month President Eisenhower was encouraging precisely that successor regime to join in a major new effort to control the arms race and reduce the danger of war.[123] The dilemma here was one that was to recur throughout the Cold War: if what one wanted was stability at the international level, did it make sense to try to destabilize the other side's leadership at the national level?

The answer, it appears, has been no. There have been repeated leadership crises in both the United States and the Soviet Union since Stalin's death: one thinks especially of the decline and ultimate deposition of Khrushchev following the Cuban missile crisis, of the Johnson administration's all-consuming fixation with Vietnam, of the collapse of Nixon's authority as a result of Watergate, and of the recent paralysis in the Kremlin brought about by the illness and death of three Soviet leaders within less than three years. And yet, in none of these instances can one discern a concerted effort by the unaffected side to exploit the other's vulnerability; indeed there appears to have existed in several of these situations a sense of frustration, even regret, over the difficulties its rival was undergoing.[124] From the standpoint of game theory, a "rule" that acknowledges legitimacy of leadership on both sides is hardly surprising: there have to be players in order for the game to proceed. But when compared to other historical—and indeed other current—situations in which that reciprocal tolerance has not existed,[125] its importance as a stabilizing mechanism becomes clear.

Stability, in great power relationships, is not the same thing as politeness. It is worth noting that despite levels of hostile rhetoric unmatched on both

---

122. Dulles to certain diplomatic posts, March 6, 1953, *FRUS: 1952–54*, Vol. 2, pp. 1684–1685. Contingency planning for such an effort had been under way for years, although Eisenhower complained that these had provided no clear conclusions. Ambrose, *Eisenhower: The President*, pp. 67–68.
123. Eisenhower speech to the American Society of Newspaper Editors, April 16, 1953, *Eisenhower Public Papers: 1953* (Washington: U.S. Government Printing Office, 1960), pp. 179–188. For the origins of this speech, see Emmet John Hughes, *The Ordeal of Power: A Political Memoir of the Eisenhower Years* (New York: Atheneum, 1963), pp. 100–112.
124. See, for example, Lyndon B. Johnson, *The Vantage Point: Perspectives of the Presidency, 1963–1969* (New York: Holt, Rinehart and Winston, 1971), pp. 468–469; also Henry Kissinger, *Years of Upheaval* (Boston: Little, Brown, 1982), pp. 287–288.
125. I have in mind here the long history of dynastic struggles in Europe up through the wars of the French Revolution; also, and much more recently, the way in which a refusal to acknowledge leadership legitimacy has perpetuated the Iran–Iraq war.

sides since the earliest days of the Cold War, the Soviet Union and the United States have managed to get through the early 1980s without a single significant military confrontation of any kind. Contrast this with the record of Soviet–American relations in the 1970s: an era of far greater politeness in terms of what the two nations *said* about one another, but one marred by potentially dangerous crises over Soviet submarine bases and combat brigades in Cuba, American bombing and mining activities in Vietnam, and a pattern of Soviet interventionism in Angola, Somalia, Ethiopia, South Yemen, and Afghanistan. There was even a major American nuclear alert during the Yom Kippur War in 1973—the only one since the Cuban missile crisis— ironically enough, this occurred at the height of what is now wistfully remembered as the era of "detente."[126]

What stability does require is a sense of caution, maturity, and responsibility on both sides. It requires the ability to distinguish posturing—something in which all political leaders indulge—from provocation, which is something else again. It requires recognition of the fact that competition is a normal rather than an abnormal state of affairs in relations between nations, much as it is in relations between major corporations, but that this need not preclude the identification of certain common—or corporate, or universal— interests as well. It requires, above all, a sense of the relative rather than the absolute nature of security: that one's own security depends not only upon the measures one takes in one's own defense, but also upon the extent to which these create a sense of insecurity in the mind of one's adversary.

It would be foolish to suggest that the Soviet–American relationship today meets all of these prerequisites: the last one especially deserves a good deal more attention than it has heretofore received, on both sides. But to the extent that the relationship has taken on a new maturity—and to see that it has one need only compare the current mood of wary optimism with the almost total lack of communication that existed at the time of the Korean War, or the extreme swings between alarm and amiability that characterized relations in the late 1950s and early 1960s, or the inflated expectations and resulting disillusionments of the 1970s—that maturity would appear to reflect an increasing commitment on the part of both great nations involved to a "game" played "by the rules."

---

126. I am indebted to Ambassador Jack Matlock for suggesting this point.

Stability and the Future

History, as anyone who has spent any time at all studying it would surely know, has a habit of making bad prophets out of both those who make and those who chronicle it. It tends to take expectations and turn them upside down; it is not at all tolerant of those who would seek too self-confidently to anticipate its future course. One should be exceedingly wary, therefore, of predicting how long the current era of Soviet–American stability will last. Certainly it is easy to conceive of things that might in one way or another undermine it: domestic developments in either country could affect foreign policy in unpredictable ways; the actions of third parties could embroil the superpowers in conflict with each other against their will; opportunities for miscalculation and accident are always present; incompetent leadership is always a risk. All that one can—or should—say is that the relationship has survived these kinds of disruptions in the past: if history made bad prophets out of the warmakers of 1914 and 1939–41, or the peacemakers of 1919, all of whom approached their tasks with a degree of optimism that seems to us foolish in retrospect, then so too has it made bad prophets out of the peacemakers of 1945, who had so little optimism about the future.

Whether the Soviet–American relationship could survive something more serious is another matter entirely. We know the answer when it comes to nuclear war; recent scientific findings have only confirmed visions of catastrophe we have lived with for decades.[127] But what about a substantial decline in the overall influence of either great power that did not immediately result in war? Here, it seems to me, is a more probable—if less often discussed—danger. For if history demonstrates anything at all, it is that the condition of being a great power is a transitory one: sooner or later, the effects of exhaustion, overextension, and lack of imagination take their toll among nations, just as surely as does old age itself among individuals. Nor is it often that history arranges for great powers to decline simultaneously and symmetrically. Past experience also suggests that the point at which a great power perceives its decline to be beginning is a perilous one: behavior can become erratic, even desperate, well before physical strength itself has dissipated.[128]

---

127. See Carl Sagan, "Nuclear War and Climatic Catastrophe: Some Policy Implications," *Foreign Affairs*, Vol. 62 (Winter 1983/84), pp. 257–292.
128. Paul Kennedy has pointed to the significance of the perception among Germans, after

The Soviet–American relationship has yet to face this test, although there is no reason to think it will escape it indefinitely. When that time comes, the preservation of stability may require something new in international relations: the realization that great nations can have a stake, not just in the survival, but also the success and prosperity of their rivals. International systems, like tangoes, require at least two reasonably active and healthy participants; it is always wise, before allowing the dance to end, to consider with what, or with whom, one will replace it.

The Cold War, with all of its rivalries, anxieties, and unquestionable dangers, has produced the longest period of stability in relations among the great powers that the world has known in this century; it now compares favorably as well with some of the longest periods of great power stability in all of modern history. We may argue among ourselves as to whether or not we can legitimately call this "peace": it is not, I daresay, what most of us have in mind when we use that term. But I am not at all certain that the contemporaries of Metternich or Bismarck would have regarded their eras as "peaceful" either, even though historians looking back on those eras today clearly do.

Who is to say, therefore, how the historians of the year 2086—if there are any left by then—will look back on us? Is it not at least plausible that they will see our era, not as "the Cold War" at all, but rather, like those ages of Metternich and Bismarck, as a rare and fondly remembered "Long Peace"? Wishful thinking? Speculation through a rose-tinted word processor? Perhaps. But would it not behoove us to give at least as much attention to the question of how this might happen—to the elements in the contemporary international system that might make it happen—as we do to the fear that it may not?

1900, that British influence in the world was increasing, while their own was not. *The Rise of Anglo–German Antagonism*, p. 313.

The Essential Irrelevance of Nuclear Weapons

John Mueller

Stability in the Postwar World

It is widely assumed that, for better or worse, the existence of nuclear weapons has profoundly shaped our lives and destinies. Some find the weapons supremely beneficial. Defense analyst Edward Luttwak says, "we have lived since 1945 without another world war precisely because rational minds . . . extracted a durable peace from the very terror of nuclear weapons."[1] And Robert Art and Kenneth Waltz conclude, "the probability of war between America and Russia or between NATO and the Warsaw Pact is practically nil precisely because the military planning and deployments of each, together with the fear of escalation to general nuclear war, keep it that way."[2] Others argue that, while we may have been lucky so far, the continued existence of the weapons promises eventual calamity: The doomsday clock on the cover of the *Bulletin of the Atomic Scientists* has been pointedly hovering near midnight for over 40 years now, and in his influential bestseller, *The Fate of the Earth*, Jonathan Schell dramatically concludes that if we do not "rise up and cleanse the earth of nuclear weapons," we will "sink into the final coma and end it all."[3]

This article takes issue with both of these points of view and concludes that nuclear weapons neither crucially define a fundamental stability nor threaten severely to disturb it.

For helpful comments I would like to thank Richard Rosecrance, Karl Mueller, Robert Jervis, MacGregor Knox, Richard Betts, and the anonymous reviewers for *International Security*. This project was supported in part by the University of Rochester and by a Guggenheim Fellowship.

John Mueller is Professor of Political Science at the University of Rochester. He is the author of Retreat from Doomsday: The Obsolescence of Major War, *to be published by Basic Books in 1989.*

1. Edward N. Luttwak, "Of Bombs and Men," *Commentary*, August 1983, p. 82.
2. Robert J. Art and Kenneth N. Waltz, "Technology, Strategy, and the Uses of Force," in Robert J. Art and Kenneth N. Waltz, eds., *The Use of Force* (Lanham, Md.: University Press of America, 1983), p. 28. See also Klaus Knorr, "Controlling Nuclear War," *International Security*, Vol. 9, No. 4 (Spring 1985), p. 79; John J. Mearsheimer, "Nuclear Weapons and Deterrence in Europe," *International Security*, Vol. 9, No. 3 (Winter 1984/85), pp. 25–26; Robert Gilpin, *War and Change in World Politics* (Cambridge: Cambridge University Press, 1981), pp. 213–219.
3. Jonathan Schell, *The Fate of the Earth* (New York: Knopf, 1982), p. 231.

International Security, Fall 1988 (Vol. 13, No. 2)
© 1988 by the President and Fellows of Harvard College and of the Massachusetts Institute of Technology.

The paper is in two parts. In the first it is argued that, while nuclear weapons may have substantially influenced political rhetoric, public discourse, and defense budgets and planning, it is not at all clear that they have had a significant impact on the history of world affairs since World War II. They do not seem to have been necessary to deter World War III, to determine alliance patterns, or to cause the United States and the Soviet Union to behave cautiously.

In the second part, these notions are broadened to a discussion of stability in the postwar world. It is concluded that there may be a long-term trend away from war among developed countries and that the long peace since World War II is less a peculiarity of the nuclear age than the logical conclusion of a substantial historical process. Seen broadly, deterrence seems to be remarkably firm; major war—a war among developed countries, like World War II or worse—is so improbable as to be obsolescent; imbalances in weapons systems are unlikely to have much impact on anything except budgets; and the nuclear arms competition may eventually come under control not so much out of conscious design as out of atrophy born of boredom.

The Impact of Nuclear Weapons

The postwar world might well have turned out much the same even in the absence of nuclear weapons. Without them, world war would have been discouraged by the memory of World War II, by superpower contentment with the postwar status quo, by the nature of Soviet ideology, and by the fear of escalation. Nor do the weapons seem to have been the crucial determinants of Cold War developments, of alliance patterns, or of the way the major powers have behaved in crises.

DETERRENCE OF WORLD WAR

It is true that there has been no world war since 1945 and it is also true that nuclear weapons have been developed and deployed in part to deter such a conflict. It does not follow, however, that it is the weapons that have prevented the war—that peace has been, in Winston Churchill's memorable construction, "the sturdy child of [nuclear] terror." To assert that the ominous presence of nuclear weapons has prevented a war between the two power blocs, one must assume that there would have been a war had these weapons not existed. This assumption ignores several other important war-discouraging factors in the postwar world.

THE MEMORY OF WORLD WAR II. A nuclear war would certainly be vastly destructive, but for the most part nuclear weapons simply compound and dramatize a military reality that by 1945 had already become appalling. Few with the experience of World War II behind them would contemplate its repetition with anything other than horror. Even before the bomb had been perfected, world war had become spectacularly costly and destructive, killing some 50 million worldwide. As former Secretary of State Alexander Haig put it in 1982: "The catastrophic consequences of another world war—with or without nuclear weapons—make deterrence our highest objective and our only rational military strategy."[4]

POSTWAR CONTENTMENT. For many of the combatants, World War I was as destructive as World War II, but its memory did not prevent another world war. Of course, as will be discussed more fully in the second half of this article, most nations *did* conclude from the horrors of World War I that such an event must never be repeated. If the only nations capable of starting World War II had been Britain, France, the Soviet Union, and the United States, the war would probably never have occurred. Unfortunately other major nations sought direct territorial expansion, and conflicts over these desires finally led to war.

Unlike the situation after World War I, however, the only powers capable of creating another world war since 1945 have been the big victors, the United States and the Soviet Union, each of which has emerged comfortably dominant in its respective sphere. As Waltz has observed, "the United States, and the Soviet Union as well, have more reason to be satisfied with the status quo than most earlier great powers had."[5] (Indeed, except for the dismemberment of Germany, even Hitler might have been content with the empire his arch-enemy Stalin controlled at the end of the war.) While there have been many disputes since the war, neither power has had a grievance so

---

4. *New York Times*, April 7, 1982. See also Michael Mandelbaum's comment in a book which in this respect has a curious title, *The Nuclear Revolution* (Cambridge: Cambridge University Press, 1981), p. 21: "The tanks and artillery of the Second World War, and especially the aircraft that reduced Dresden and Tokyo to rubble might have been terrifying enough by themselves to keep the peace between the United States and the Soviet Union." Also see Bruce Russett, "Away from Nuclear Mythology," in Dagobert L. Brito, Michael D. Intriligator, and Adele E. Wick, eds., *Strategies for Managing Nuclear Proliferation* (Lexington, Mass.: Lexington, 1983), pp. 148–150. And of course, given weapons advances, a full-scale *conventional* World War III could be expected to be even more destructive than World War II.
5. Kenneth N. Waltz, *Theory of International Politics* (Reading, Mass.: Addison-Wesley, 1979), p. 190. See also Joseph S. Nye, Jr., "Nuclear Learning and U.S.-Soviet Security Security Regimes," *International Organization*, Vol. 41, No. 3 (Summer 1987), p. 377.

essential as to make a world war—whether nuclear or not—an attractive means for removing the grievance.

SOVIET IDEOLOGY. Although the Soviet Union and international communism have visions of changing the world in a direction they prefer, their ideology stresses revolutionary procedures over major war. The Soviet Union may have hegemonic desires as many have argued but, with a few exceptions (especially the Korean War) to be discussed below, its tactics, inspired by the cautiously pragmatic Lenin, have stressed subversion, revolution, diplomatic and economic pressure, seduction, guerrilla warfare, local uprising, and civil war—levels at which nuclear weapons have little relevance. The communist powers have never—before or after the invention of nuclear weapons— subscribed to a Hitler-style theory of direct, Armageddon-risking conquest, and they have been extremely wary of provoking Western powers into large-scale war.[6] Moreover, if the memory of World War II deters anyone, it

---

6. Arkady N. Shevchenko, while stressing that "the Kremlin is committed to the ultimate vision of a world under its control," gives an "unequivocal no" to the question of whether "the Soviet Union would initiate a nuclear war against the United States"; instead, the Soviets "are patient and take the long view," believing "that eventually [they] will be supreme—not necessarily in this century but certainly in the next." Shevchenko, *Breaking with Moscow* (New York: Knopf, 1985), pp. 285–286. Similarly, Michael Voslensky asserts that Soviet leaders desire "external expansion," but their "aim is to win the struggle between the two systems without fighting"; he notes that Soviet military ventures before and after World War II have consistently been directed only against "weak countries" and only after the Soviets have been careful to cover themselves in advance—often withdrawing when "firm resistance" has been met. Voslensky, *Nomenklatura: The New Soviet Ruling Class* (Garden City, N.Y.: Doubleday, 1984), pp. 320–330. Richard Pipes concludes that "Soviet interests . . . are to avoid general war with the 'imperialist camp' while inciting and exacerbating every possible conflict within it." Pipes, *Survival Is Not Enough* (New York: Simon and Schuster, 1984), p. 65. William Taubman says that Stalin sought "to avert war by playing off one set of capitalist powers against another and to use the same tactic to expand Soviet power and influence without war." Taubman, *Stalin's American Policy* (New York: Norton, 1982), p. 12. MacGregor Knox argues that, for Hitler and Mussolini, "foreign conquest was the decisive prerequisite for a revolution at home," and in this respect those regimes differ importantly from those of Lenin, Stalin, and Mao. Knox, "Conquest, Foreign and Domestic, in Fascist Italy and Nazi Germany," *Journal of Modern History*, Vol. 56, No. 1 (March 1984), p. 57. In his memoirs, Nikita Khrushchev is quite straightforward about the issue: "We've always considered war to be against our own interests." He says he "never once heard Stalin say anything about preparing to commit aggression against another [presumably major] country"; and "we Communists must hasten [the] struggle" against capitalism "by any means at our disposal, *excluding war.*" Khrushchev, *Khrushchev Remembers: The Last Testament*, trans. and ed., Strobe Talbott (Boston: Little, Brown, 1974), pp. 511, 533, 531, emphasis in the original. The Soviets have always been concerned about wars launched *against them* by a decaying capitalist world, but at least since 1935 they have held such wars to be potentially avoidable because of Soviet military strength and of international working class solidarity. Frederic S. Burnin, "The Communist Doctrine of the Inevitability of War," *American Political Science Review*, Vol. 57, No. 2 (June 1963), p. 339. See also Robert Jervis, *The Illogic of American Nuclear Strategy* (Ithaca: Cornell University Press, 1984), p. 156; and Michael MccGwire, "Deterrence: Problem, Not

probably does so to an extreme degree for the Soviets. Officially and unofficially they seem obsessed by the memory of the destruction they suffered. In 1953 Ambassador Averell Harriman, certainly no admirer of Stalin, observed that the Soviet dictator "was determined, if he could avoid it, never again to go through the horrors of another protracted world war."[7]

THE BELIEF IN ESCALATION. Those who started World Wars I and II did so not because they felt that costly wars of attrition were desirable, but because they felt that escalation to wars of attrition could be avoided. In World War I the offensive was believed to be dominant, and it was widely assumed that conflict would be short and decisive.[8] In World War II, both Germany and Japan experienced repeated success with bluster, short wars in peripheral areas, and blitzkrieg, aided by the counterproductive effects of their opponents' appeasement and inaction.[9]

World war in the post-1945 era has been prevented not so much by visions of nuclear horror as by the generally-accepted belief that conflict can easily escalate to a level, nuclear or not, that the essentially satisfied major powers would find intolerably costly.

To deal with the crucial issue of escalation, it is useful to assess two important phenomena of the early post-war years: the Soviet preponderance in conventional arms and the Korean War.

First, it has been argued that the Soviets would have been tempted to take advantage of their conventional strength after World War II to snap up a

---

Solution," *SAIS Review*, Vol. 5, No. 2 (Summer-Fall 1985), p. 122. For a study stressing the Soviet Union's "cautious opportunism" in the Third World, see Stephen T. Hosmer and Thomas W. Wolfe, *Soviet Policy and Practice toward Third World Countries* (Lexington, Mass.: Lexington Books, 1983).

7. *Newsweek*, March 16, 1953, p. 31. The Soviets presumably picked up a few things from World War I as well; as Taubman notes, they learned the "crucial lesson . . . that world war . . . can destroy the Russian regime." Taubman, *Stalin's American Policy*, p. 11.

8. Jack Snyder, *The Ideology of the Offensive* (Ithaca: Cornell University Press, 1984); Stephen Van Evera, "Why Cooperation Failed in 1914," *World Politics*, Vol. 38, No. 1 (October 1985), pp. 80–117. See also the essays on "The Great War and the Nuclear Age" in *International Security*, Vol. 9, No. 1 (Summer 1984), pp. 7–186.

9. Hitler, however, may have anticipated (or at any rate, was planning for) a total war once he had established his expanded empire—a part of his grand scheme he carefully kept from military and industrial leaders who, he knew, would find it unthinkable: see R.J. Overy, "Hitler's War and the German Economy," *Economic History Review*, Vol. 35, No. 2 (May 1982), pp. 272–291. The Japanese did not want a major war, but they were willing to risk it when their anticipated short war in China became a lengthy, enervating one, and they were forced to choose between wider war and the abandonment of the empire to which they were ideologically committed. See Robert J.C. Butow, *Tojo and the Coming of the War* (Stanford, Calif.: Stanford University Press, 1961), ch. 11.

prize like Western Europe if its chief defender, the United States, had not possessed nuclear weapons. As Winston Churchill put it in 1950, "nothing preserves Europe from an overwhelming military attack except the devastating resources of the United States in this awful weapon."[10]

This argument requires at least three questionable assumptions: (1) that the Soviets really think of Western Europe as a prize worth taking risks for;[11] (2) that, even without the atomic bomb to rely on, the United States would have disarmed after 1945 as substantially as it did; and (3) that the Soviets have actually ever had the strength to be quickly and overwhelmingly successful in a conventional attack in Western Europe.[12]

However, even if one accepts these assumptions, the Soviet Union would in all probability still have been deterred from attacking Western Europe by the enormous potential of the American war machine. Even if the USSR had the ability to blitz Western Europe, it could not have stopped the United States from repeating what it did after 1941: mobilizing with deliberate speed, putting its economy onto a wartime footing, and wearing the enemy down in a protracted conventional major war of attrition massively supplied from its unapproachable rear base.

The economic achievement of the United States during the war was astounding. While holding off one major enemy, it concentrated with its allies on defeating another, then turned back to the first. Meanwhile, it supplied everybody. With 8 million of its ablest men out of the labor market, it

---

10. Matthew A. Evangelista, "Stalin's Postwar Army Reappraised," *International Security*, Vol. 7, No. 3 (Winter 1982/83), pp. 110.

11. This assumption was certainly not obvious to Bernard Brodie: "It is difficult to discover what meaningful incentives the Russians might have for attempting to conquer Western Europe." Bernard Brodie, *Escalation and the Nuclear Option* (Princeton: Princeton University Press, 1966), pp. 71–72. Nor to George Kennan: "I have never believed that they have seen it as in their interests to overrun Western Europe militarily, or that they would have launched an attack on that region generally even if the so-called nuclear deterrent had not existed." George Kennan, "Containment Then and Now," *Foreign Affairs*, Vol. 65, No. 4 (Spring 1987), pp. 888–889. Hugh Thomas characterizes Stalin's postwar policy as "conflict which should not be carried into real war, . . . Thus, though expansion should be everywhere attempted, it should not come too close to fighting in zones where the United States, and probably Britain, would resort to arms." Hugh Thomas, *Armed Truce: The Beginnings of the Cold War, 1945–46* (New York: Atheneum, 1986), p. 102.

12. This assumption is strongly questioned in Evangelista, "Stalin's Postwar Army Reappraised," pp. 110–138. See also Adam B. Ulam, *Expansion and Coexistence* (New York: Praeger, 1968), p. 414; John J. Mearsheimer, *Conventional Deterrence* (Ithaca: Cornell University Press, 1983), ch. 6; and Barry R. Posen, "Measuring the European Conventional Balance," *International Security*, Vol. 9, No. 3 (Winter 1984/85). Among Stalin's problems at the time was a major famine in the Ukraine in 1946 and 1947. Khrushchev, *Khrushchev Remembers*, trans. and ed., Strobe Talbott (Boston: Little, Brown, 1970), ch. 7.

increased industrial production 15 percent per year and agricultural production 30 percent overall. Before the end of 1943 it was producing so much that some munitions plants were closed down, and even so it ended the war with a substantial surplus of wheat and over $90 billion in surplus war goods. (National governmental expenditures in the first peacetime year, 1946, were only about $60 billion.) As Denis Brogan observed at the time, "to the Americans war is a business, not an art."[13]

If anyone was in a position to appreciate this, it was the Soviets. By various circuitous routes the United States supplied the Soviet Union with, among other things, 409,526 trucks; 12,161 combat vehicles (more than the Germans had in 1939); 32,200 motorcycles; 1,966 locomotives; 16,000,000 pairs of boots (in two sizes); and over one-half pound of food for every Soviet soldier for every day of the war (much of it Spam).[14] It is the kind of feat that concentrates the mind, and it is extremely difficult to imagine the Soviets willingly taking on this somewhat lethargic, but ultimately hugely effective juggernaut. That Stalin was fully aware of the American achievement—and deeply impressed by it—is clear. Adam Ulam has observed that Stalin had "great respect for the United States' vast economic and hence military potential, quite apart from the bomb," and that his "whole career as dictator had been a testimony to his belief that production figures were a direct indicator of a given country's power."[15] As a member of the Joint Chiefs of Staff put it in

---

13. Despite shortages, rationing, and tax surcharges, American consumer spending increased by 12 percent between 1939 and 1944. Richard R. Lingeman, *Don't You Know There's a War On?* (New York: Putnam, 1970), pp. 133, 357, and ch. 4; Alan S. Milward, *War, Economy and Society 1939–1945* (Berkeley and Los Angeles: University of California Press, 1977), pp. 63–74, 271–275; Mercedes Rosebery, *This Day's Madness* (New York: Macmillan, 1944), p. xii.

14. John R. Deane, *The Strange Alliance* (New York: Viking, 1947), pp. 92–95; Robert Huhn Jones, *The Roads to Russia* (Norman: University of Oklahoma Press, 1969), Appendix A. Additional information from Harvey DeWeerd.

15. Adam Ulam, *The Rivals: America and Russia Since World War II* (New York: Penguin, 1971), pp. 95 and 5. In essence, Stalin seems to have understood that in Great Power wars, as Paul Kennedy put it, "victory has always gone to the side with the greatest material resources." Paul Kennedy, *The Rise and Fall of the Great Powers* (New York: Random House, 1987), p. 439. Nor is it likely that this attitude has changed much: "The men in the Kremlin are absorbed by questions of America's political, military, and economic power, and awed by its technological capacity." Shevchenko, *Breaking with Moscow*, p. 278. Edward Luttwak, while concerned that the Soviets might actually be tempted to start a war, notes the existence of "the great deterrent": the Soviet fear that "more aggressive expansion will precipitate an Alliance-wide mobilization response which could quickly erode the Kremlin's power position down to a 'natural' level—a level, that is, where the power of the Soviet Union begins to approximate its economic capacity." Edward N. Luttwak, *The Grand Strategy of the Soviet Union* (New York: St. Martin's, 1983), p. 116. Or Khrushchev: "those 'rotten' capitalists keep coming up with things which make our jaws drop in surprise." Khrushchev, *The Last Testament*, p. 532.

1949, "if there is any single factor today which would deter a nation seeking world domination, it would be the great industrial capacity of this country rather than its armed strength."[16] Or, as Hugh Thomas has concluded, "if the atomic bomb had not existed, Stalin would still have feared the success of the U.S. wartime economy."[17]

After a successful attack on Western Europe the Soviets would have been in a position similar to that of Japan after Pearl Harbor: they might have gains aplenty, but they would have no way to stop the United States (and its major unapproachable allies, Canada and Japan) from eventually gearing up for, and then launching, a war of attrition.[18] All they could hope for, like the Japanese in 1941, would be that their victories would cause the Americans to lose their fighting spirit. But if Japan's Asian and Pacific gains in 1941 propelled the United States into war, it is to be expected that the United States would find a Soviet military takeover of an area of far greater importance to it—Western Europe—to be alarming in the extreme. Not only would the U.S. be outraged at the American casualties in such an attack and at the loss of an important geographic area, but it would very likely conclude (as many Americans did conclude in the late 1940s even without a Soviet attack) that an eventual attack on the United States itself was inevitable. Any Hitler-style protests by the Soviets that they had no desire for further territorial gains would not be very credible. Thus, even assuming that the Soviets had the conventional capability easily to take over Western Europe, the credible American threat of a huge, continent-hopping war of attrition from south, west, and east could be a highly effective deterrent—all this even in the absence of nuclear weapons.[19]

---

16. Samuel P. Huntington, *The Common Defense* (New York: Columbia University Press, 1961), p. 46. See also Walter Millis, ed., *The Forrestal Diaries* (New York: Viking, 1951), pp. 350–351.
17. Thomas, *Armed Truce*, p. 548.
18. Interestingly, one of Hitler's "terrible anxieties" before Pearl Harbor was that the Americans and Japanese might work out a rapprochement, uniting against Germany. Norman Rich, *Hitler's War Aims: Ideology, the Nazi State, and the Course of Expansion* (New York: Norton, 1973), pp. 228, 231, 246.
19. In fact, in some respects the memory of World War II was more horrible than the prospect of atomic war in the immediate postwar period. Western proponents of an atomic preventive war against the USSR were countered by General Omar Bradley and others who argued that this policy would be "folly" because the Soviets would still be able to respond with an offensive against Western Europe which would lead to something *really* bad: an "extended, bloody and horrible" struggle like World War II. Richard Ned Lebow, "Windows of Opportunity: Do States Jump Through Them?" *International Security,"* Vol. 9, No. 1 (Summer 1984), p. 170. See also Hanson W. Baldwin, "War of Prevention," *New York Times,* September 1, 1950, p. 4. The conventional threat might be more credible than atomic retaliation even in an era of U.S. nuclear

Second, there is the important issue of the Korean War. Despite the vast American superiority in atomic weapons in 1950, Stalin was willing to order, approve, or at least acquiesce in an outright attack by a communist state on a non-communist one, and it must be assumed that he would have done so at least as readily had nuclear weapons not existed. The American response was essentially the result of the lessons learned from the experiences of the 1930s: comparing this to similar incursions in Manchuria, Ethiopia, and Czechoslovakia (and partly also to previous Soviet incursions into neighboring states in East Europe and the Baltic area), Western leaders resolved that such provocations must be nipped in the bud. If they were allowed to succeed, they would only encourage more aggression in more important locales later. Consequently it seems likely that the Korean War would have occurred in much the same way had nuclear weapons not existed.

For the Soviets the lessons of the Korean War must have enhanced those of World War II: once again the United States was caught surprised and under-armed, once again it rushed hastily into action, once again it soon applied itself in a forceful way to combat—in this case for an area that it had previously declared to be of only peripheral concern. If the Korean War was a limited probe of Western resolve, it seems the Soviets drew the lessons the Truman administration intended. Unlike Germany, Japan, and Italy in the 1930s, they were tempted to try no more such probes: there have been no Koreas since Korea. It seems likely that this valuable result would have come about regardless of the existence of nuclear weapons, and it suggests that the Korean War helped to delimit vividly the methods the Soviet Union would be allowed to use to pursue its policy.[20]

---

monopoly because an American retaliatory threat to level Moscow with nuclear weapons could be countered with a threat to make a newly-captured Western city like Paris into a latter-day Lidice. And of course once both sides had nuclear capabilities, the weapons could be mutually deterring, as has often been noted in debates about deterrence in Europe. Moreover, the Soviets could use nuclear weapons to destroy a landing force, as American officials noted in 1950; see Robert Jervis, "The Impact of the Korean War on the Cold War," *Journal of Conflict Resolution*, Vol. 24, No. 4 (December 1980), p. 578.

20. Soviet military intervention in Afghanistan in 1979 was an effort to prop up a faltering pro-Soviet regime. As such it was not like Korea, but more like American escalation in Vietnam in 1965 or like the Soviet interventions in Hungary in 1956 or Czechoslovakia in 1968. For discussions of the importance of the Korean War in shaping Western perspectives on the Cold War, see John Lewis Gaddis, "Was the Truman Doctrine a Real Turning Point?" *Foreign Affairs*, Vol. 52, No. 2 (January 1974), pp. 386–401; Jervis, "The Impact of the Korean War"; and Ernest R. May, "The Cold War" in Joseph S. Nye, Jr., ed., *The Making of America's Soviet Policy* (New Haven: Yale University Press, 1984), pp. 209–230.

It is conceivable that the USSR, in carrying out its ideological commitment to revolution, might have been tempted to try step-by-step, Hitler-style military probes if it felt these would be reasonably cheap and free of risk. The policy of containment, of course, carrying with it the threat of escalation, was designed precisely to counter such probes. If the USSR ever had any thoughts about launching such military probes, the credible Western threat that these probes could escalate (demonstrated most clearly in Korea, but also during such episodes as the Berlin crisis of 1948–49) would be significantly deterring—whether or not nuclear weapons waited at the end of the escalator ride.

The Korean experience may have posed a somewhat similar lesson for the United States. In 1950, amid talk of "rolling back" Communism and sometimes even of liberating China, American-led forces invaded North Korea. This venture led to a costly and demoralizing, if limited, war with China, and resulted in a considerable reduction in American enthusiasm for such maneuvers. Had the United States been successful in taking over North Korea, there might well have been noisy calls for similar ventures elsewhere—though, of course, these calls might well have gone unheeded by the leadership.

It is not at all clear that the United States and the Soviet Union needed the Korean War to become viscerally convinced that escalation was dangerously easy. But the war probably reinforced that belief for both of them and, to the degree that it did, Korea was an important stabilizing event.

COLD WAR AND CRISIS

If nuclear weapons have been unnecessary to prevent world war, they also do not seem to have crucially affected other important developments, including development of the Cold War and patterns of alliance, as well as behavior of the superpowers in crisis.

THE COLD WAR AND ALLIANCE PATTERNS. The Cold War was an outgrowth of various disagreements between the U.S. and the USSR over ideology and over the destinies of Eastern, Central and Southern Europe. The American reaction to the perceived Soviet threat in this period mainly reflects pre-nuclear thinking, especially the lessons of Munich.

For example, the formation of the North Atlantic Treaty Organization and the division of the world into alliances centered on Washington and Moscow suggests that the participants were chiefly influenced by the experience of World War II. If the major determinant of these alliance patterns had been nuclear strategy, one might expect the United States and, to a lesser extent, the Soviet Union, to be only lukewarm members, for in general the alliances include nations that contribute little to nuclear defense but possess the capability unilaterally of getting the core powers into trouble.[21] And one would expect the small countries in each alliance to tie themselves as tightly as possible to the core nuclear power in order to have maximum protection from its nuclear weapons. However, the weakening of the alliances which has taken place over the last three decades has not come from the major partners.

The structure of the alliances therefore better reflects political and ideological bipolarity than sound nuclear strategy. As military economist (and later Defense Secretary) James Schlesinger has noted, the Western alliance "was based on some rather obsolescent notions regarding the strength and importance of the European nations and the direct contribution that they could make to the security of the United States. There was a striking failure to recognize the revolutionary impact that nuclear forces would make with respect to the earlier beliefs regarding European defense."[22] Or, as Warner Schilling has observed, American policies in Europe were "essentially pre-nuclear in their rationale. The advent of nuclear weapons had not influenced the American determination to restore the European balance of power. It was, in fact, an objective which the United States would have had an even greater incentive to undertake if the fission bomb had not been developed."[23]

CRISIS BEHAVIOR. Because of the harrowing image of nuclear war, it is sometimes argued, the United States and the Soviet Union have been notably more restrained than they might otherwise have been, and thus crises that might have escalated to dangerous levels have been resolved safely at low levels.[24]

---

21. As Michael May observes, "the existence of nuclear weapons, especially of nuclear weapons that can survive attack, help[s] make empires and client states questionable sources of security." "The U.S.-Soviet Approach to Nuclear Weapons," *International Security*, Vol. 9, No. 4 (Spring 1985), p. 150.
22. James Schlesinger, *On Relating Non-technical Elements to Systems Studies*, P-3545 (Santa Monica, Cal.: RAND, February 1967), p. 6.
23. Warner R. Schilling, "The H-Bomb Decision," *Political Science Quarterly*, Vol. 76, No. 1 (March 1961), p. 26. See also Waltz: "Nuclear weapons did not cause the condition of bipolarity. . . . Had the atom never been split, [the U.S. and the USSR] would far surpass others in military strength, and each would remain the greatest threat and source of potential damage to the other." Waltz, *Theory of International Politics*, pp. 180–181.
24. John Lewis Gaddis, *The Long Peace* (New York: Oxford University Press, 1987), pp. 229–232; Gilpin, *War and Change in World Politics*, p. 218; Coit D. Blacker, *Reluctant Warriors* (New York: Freeman, 1987), p. 46.

There is, of course, no definitive way to refute this notion since we are unable to run the events of the last forty years over, this time without nuclear weapons. And it is certainly the case that decision-makers are well aware of the horrors of nuclear war and cannot be expected to ignore the possibility that a crisis could lead to such devastation.

However, this idea—that it is the fear of nuclear war that has kept behavior restrained—looks far less convincing when its underlying assumption is directly confronted: that the major powers would have allowed their various crises to escalate if all they had to fear at the end of the escalatory ladder was something like a repetition of World War II. Whatever the rhetoric in these crises, it is difficult to see why the unaugmented horror of repeating World War II, combined with considerable comfort with the status quo, wouldn't have been enough to inspire restraint.

 Once again, escalation is the key: what deters is the belief that escalation to something intolerable will occur, not so much what the details of the ultimate unbearable punishment are believed to be. Where the belief that the conflict will escalate is absent, nuclear countries *have* been militarily challenged with war—as in Korea, Vietnam, Afghanistan, Algeria, and the Falklands.[25]

To be clear: None of this is meant to deny that the sheer horror of nuclear war is impressive and mind-concentratingly dramatic, particularly in the speed with which it could bring about massive destruction. Nor is it meant to deny that decision-makers, both in times of crisis and otherwise, are fully conscious of how horribly destructive a nuclear war could be. It is simply to stress that the sheer horror of repeating World War II is not all that much *less* impressive or dramatic, and that powers essentially satisfied with the status quo will strive to avoid anything that they feel could lead to *either* calamity. World War II did not cause total destruction in the world, but it did utterly annihilate the three national regimes that brought it about. It is probably quite a bit more terrifying to think about a jump from the 50th floor

---

25. On this point, see also Evan Luard: "There is little evidence in history that the existence of supremely destructive weapons alone is capable of deterring war. If the development of bacteriological weapons, poison gas, nerve gases and other chemical armaments did not deter war before 1939, it is not easy to see why nuclear weapons should do so now." Evan Luard, *War in International Society* (New Haven: Yale University Press, 1987), p. 396. For further discussion of this issue and of the belief in many quarters after 1918 that the next war might well destroy the human race, see John Mueller, *Retreat from Doomsday: The Obsolescence of Major War* (New York: Basic Books, forthcoming in 1989).

than about a jump from the 5th floor, but anyone who finds life even minimally satisfying is extremely unlikely to do either.

Did the existence of nuclear weapons keep the Korean conflict restrained? As noted, the communist venture there seems to have been a limited probe— though somewhat more adventurous than usual and one that got out of hand with the massive American and Chinese involvement. As such, there was no particular reason—or meaningful military opportunity—for the Soviets to escalate the war further. In justifying *their* restraint, the Americans contin- ually stressed the danger of escalating to a war with the Soviet Union— something of major concern whether or not the Soviets possessed nuclear weapons.

Nor is it clear that the existence of nuclear weapons has vitally influenced other events. For example, President Harry Truman was of the opinion that his nuclear threat drove the Soviets out of Iran in 1946, and President Dwight Eisenhower, that his nuclear threat drove the Chinese into productive dis- cussions at the end of the Korean War in 1953. McGeorge Bundy's reassess- ment of these events suggests that neither threat was very well communi- cated and that, in any event, other occurrences—the maneuverings of the Iranian government in the one case and the death of Stalin in the other— were more important in determining the outcome.[26] But even if we assume the threats *were* important, it is not clear why the threat had to be peculiarly *nuclear*—a threat to commit destruction on the order of World War II would also have been notably unpleasant and dramatic.

Much the same could be said about other instances in which there was a real or implied threat that nuclear weapons might be brought into play: the Taiwan Straits crises of 1954–55 and 1958, the Berlin blockade of 1948–49, the Soviet-Chinese confrontation of 1969, the Six-day War in 1967, the Yom Kippur War of 1973, Cold War disagreements over Lebanon in 1958, Berlin in 1958 and 1961, offensive weapons in Cuba in 1962. All were resolved, or allowed to dissipate, at rather low rungs on the escalatory ladder. While the horror of a possible nuclear war was doubtless clear to the participants, it is certainly not apparent that they would have been much more casual about

---

26. McGeorge Bundy, "The Unimpressive Record of Atomic Diplomacy," in Gwyn Prins, ed., *The Nuclear Crisis Reader* (New York: Vintage, 1984), p. 44–47. For the argument that Truman never made a threat, see James A. Thorpe, "Truman's Ultimatum to Stalin in the Azerbaijan Crisis: The Making of a Myth," *Journal of Politics*, Vol. 40, No. 1 (February 1978), pp. 188–195. See also Gaddis, *Long Peace*, pp. 124–129; and Richard K. Betts, *Nuclear Blackmail and Nuclear Balance* (Washington, D.C.: Brookings, 1987), pp. 42–47.

escalation if the worst they had to visualize was a repetition of World War II.[27]

Of course nuclear weapons add new elements to international politics: new pieces for the players to move around the board (missiles in and out of Cuba, for example), new terrors to contemplate. But in counter to the remark attributed to Albert Einstein that nuclear weapons have changed everything except our way of thinking, it might be suggested that nuclear weapons have changed little except our way of talking, gesturing, and spending money.

Stability

The argument thus far leads to the conclusion that stability is overdetermined—that the postwar situation contains redundant sources of stability. The United States and the Soviet Union have been essentially satisfied with their lot and, fearing escalation to another costly war, have been quite willing to keep their conflicts limited. Nuclear weapons may well have enhanced this stability—they are certainly dramatic reminders of how horrible a big war could be. But it seems highly unlikely that, in their absence, the leaders of the major powers would be so unimaginative as to need such reminding. Wars are not begun out of casual caprice or idle fancy, but because one country or another decides that it can profit from (not simply win) the war—

---

27. Interestingly, even in the great "nuclear" crisis over Cuba in 1962, Khrushchev seems to have been affected as much by his memories of World War I and II as by the prospect of thermonuclear destruction. See Graham T. Allison, *Essence of Decision* (Boston: Little, Brown, 1971), p. 221. Morton Halperin argues that "the primary military factors in resolving the crisis" in the Taiwan Straits in 1954–55 were "American air and naval superiority in the area," not nuclear threats. Morton H. Halperin, *Nuclear Fallacy* (Cambridge, Mass.: Ballinger, 1987), p. 30. Alexander George and Richard Smoke note that blockade crises in Berlin in 1948–49 and in the Taiwan Straits in 1958 were broken by the ability of the Americans to find a technological solution to them. Alexander L. George and Richard Smoke, *Deterrence in American Foreign Policy* (New York: Columbia University Press, 1974), p. 383. Betts suggests that even if the American alert in 1973 was influential with the Soviets (which is quite questionable), it is "hard to argue against the proposition that the conventional force elements in it were sufficient, the nuclear component superfluous." Betts, *Nuclear Blackmail*, p. 129. As for the Soviet-Chinese confrontation, Roy Medvedev notes Soviet fears of "war with a poorly armed but extremely populous and fanatical China." Roy Medvedev, *China and the Superpowers* (New York: Basil Blackwood, 1986), p. 50; see also Shevchenko, *Breaking with Moscow*, pp. 165–166. On these issues, see also A.F.K. Organski and Jacek Kugler, *The War Ledger* (Chicago: University of Chicago Press, 1980), pp. 147–180.

the combination of risk, gain, and cost appears preferable to peace.[28] Even allowing considerably for stupidity, ineptness, miscalculation, and self-deception in these considerations, it does not appear that a large war, nuclear or otherwise, has been remotely in the interest of the essentially-contented, risk-averse, escalation-anticipating powers that have dominated world affairs since 1945.

It is *conceivable* of course that the leadership of a major power could be seized by a lucky, clever, risk-acceptant, aggressive fanatic like Hitler; or that an unprecedentedly monumental crisis could break out in an area, like Central Europe, that is of vital importance to both sides; or that a major power could be compelled toward war because it is consumed by desperate fears that it is on the verge of catastrophically losing the arms race. It is not obvious that any of these circumstances would necessarily escalate to a major war, but the existence of nuclear weapons probably does make such an escalation less likely; thus there are imaginable circumstances under which it might be useful to have nuclear weapons around. In the world we've actually lived in, however, those extreme conditions haven't come about, and they haven't ever really even been in the cards. This enhancement of stability is, therefore, purely theoretical—extra insurance against unlikely calamity.

CRISIS STABILITY, GENERAL STABILITY, AND DETERRENCE
In further assessing these issues, it seems useful to distinguish crisis stability from a more general form of stability. Much of the literature on defense policy has concentrated on crisis stability, the notion that it is desirable for both sides in a crisis to be so secure that each is able to wait out a surprise attack fully confident that it would be able to respond with a punishing counterattack. In an ideal world, because of its fear of punishing retaliation, neither side would have an incentive to start a war no matter how large or

---

28. Thus the notion that there is a special danger if one side or the other has a "war-winning" capability seems misguided; there would be danger only if a war-*profiting* capability exists. As will be discussed below, the second does not necessarily follow from the first. As Lebow argues: "History indicates that wars rarely start because one side believes it has a military advantage. Rather, they occur when leaders become convinced that force is necessary to achieve important goals." Lebow, "Windows of Opportunity," p. 149. Michael Howard says: "Wars begin with conscious and reasoned decisions based on the calculation, made by *both* parties, that they can achieve more by going to war than by remaining at peace." Michael Howard, "The Causes of Wars," *Wilson Quarterly*, Vol. 8, No. 3 (Summer 1984), p. 103. See also Luard, *War in International Society*, chs. 5, 6; Jervis, *The Illogic of American Nuclear Strategy*, ch. 6; Bruce Bueno de Mesquita, *The War Trap* (New Haven: Yale University Press, 1981), ch. 2; Gaddis, *Long Peace*, p. 232; Geoffrey Blainey, *The Causes of War* (New York: Free Press, 1973), chs. 9, 11.

desperate the disagreement, no matter how intense the crisis. Many have argued that crisis stability is "delicate": easily upset by technological or economic shifts.[29]

There is a more general form of stability, on the other hand, that is concerned with balance derived from broader needs, desires, and concerns. It prevails when two powers, taking all potential benefits, costs, and risks into account, greatly prefer peace to war—in the extreme, even to a victorious war—whether crisis stability exists or not. For example, it can be said that general stability prevails in the relationship between the United States and Canada. The United States enjoys a massive military advantage over its northern neighbor since it could attack at any time with little concern about punishing military retaliation or about the possibility of losing the war (that is, it has a full "first strike capability"), yet the danger that the United States will attack Canada is nil. General stability prevails.

Although the deterrence literature is preoccupied with military considerations, the deterrence concept may be more useful if it is broadened to include non-military incentives and disincentives. For example, it seems meaningful to suggest that the United States is "deterred" from attacking Canada, but not, obviously, by the Canadians' military might. If anyone in Washington currently were even to contemplate a war against Canada (a country, it might be noted, with which the United States has been at war in the past and where, not too long ago, many Americans felt their "manifest destiny" lay), the planner would doubtless be dissuaded by non-military factors. For example, the war would disrupt a beneficial economic relationship; the United States would have the task of occupying a vast new area with sullen and uncooperative inhabitants; the venture would produce political turmoil in the United States. Similar cases can be found in the Soviet sphere. Despite an overwhelming military superiority, the USSR has been far from anxious to attack such troublesome neighboring states as Poland and Romania. It seems likely that the vast majority of wars that never take place are caused by factors which have little to do with military considerations.[30]

---

29. The classic statement of this position is, of course, Albert Wohlstetter, "The Delicate Balance of Terror," *Foreign Affairs*, Vol. 27, No. 2 (January 1959), pp. 211–234. See also Glenn H. Snyder, *Deterrence and Defense* (Princeton: Princeton University Press, 1961), pp. 97–109.

30. Under this approach, if two nations are not at war, then it can be said that they are currently being deterred from attacking each other. That is, deterrence prevails when the expected utility for peace outweighs the expected utility for war. In this sense a deterrence relationship exists not only between the U.S. and the USSR, but also between the U.S. and Canada, and between Bolivia and Pakistan. The usefulness of this approach is that it is not limited exclusively to

Now, it would obviously be too much to suggest that general stability prevails in the relationship between the U.S. and the USSR to the same degree that it does in the relationship between the U.S. and Canada. Yet, as suggested, it is remarkably difficult to imagine how the prevailing stability between the two big powers could be upset to the point that a war could come about: both have a strong interest in peace, and none whatever in major war. Thus many of the concerns about the stability of the military balance, while valid in their own terms, miss a broader point. In the current debate over the Strategic Defense Initiative, for example, it may be the case that the proposed system will make things less stable or more stable, but this change may not alter the picture very much. It is like the millionaire who loses or gains $1000; it is true that he is now poorer or richer than before, but the important point is that his overall status has not changed very much.

If a kind of overwhelming general stability really prevails, it may well be that the concerns about arms and the arms race are substantially overdone. That is, the often-exquisite numerology of the nuclear arms race has probably had little to do with the important dynamics of the Cold War era, most of which have taken place at militarily subtle levels such as subversion, guerrilla war, local uprising, civil war, and diplomatic posturing. As Benjamin Lambeth has observed, "it is perhaps one of the notable ironies of the nuclear age that while both Washington and Moscow have often lauded superiority as a military force-posture goal, neither has ever behaved as though it really believed superiority significantly mattered in the resolution of international conflicts."[31] In their extensive study of the use of threat and force since World War II, Blechman and Kaplan conclude that, "especially noteworthy is the

---

military considerations, and that it comfortably incorporates such important deterring phenomena as satisfaction with the status quo, as well as the restraining effects of economics, morality, good will, inertia, international opinion, national self-image, etc. Thus it can deal with that multitude of cases in which a militarily superior power lives peacefully alongside an inferior one. The approach can also deal with those cases where a nation has become so distressed by the status quo that it starts a war even when it has little hope of military success. For a more formal presentation, see John Mueller, *Approaches to Measurement in International Relations: A Non-Evangelical Survey* (New York: Appleton-Century-Crofts, 1969), pp. 284–286; and Mueller, *Retreat from Doomsday*. See also note 28 above; and Richard Rosecrance, *Strategic Deterrence Reconsidered*, Adelphi Paper No. 116 (London: International Institute for Strategic Studies, Spring 1975), pp. 33–37; Lebow, "Windows of Opportunity," pp. 181–186; and Richard Ned Lebow, "Deterrence Reconsidered," *Survival*, Vol. 27, No. 1 (January/February 1985), pp. 20–28.

31. Benjamin S. Lambeth, "Deterrence in the MIRV Era," *World Politics*, Vol. 24, No. 2 (January 1972), p. 234 n.

Satisfaction w/Status Quo

fact that our data do not support a hypothesis that the strategic weapons balance between the United States and the USSR influences outcomes."[32]

A special danger of weapons imbalance is often cited: a dominant country might be emboldened to use its superiority for purposes of pressure and intimidation. But unless its satisfaction with the status quo falls enormously and unless its opponent's ability to respond becomes very low as well, the superior power is unlikely to push its advantage very far, and certainly not anywhere near the point of major war. Even if the war could be kept non-nuclear and even if that power had a high probability of winning, the gains are likely to be far too low, the costs far too high.[33]

STABILITY: TRENDS

Curiously, in the last twenty-five years crisis stability between the U.S. and the USSR has probably gotten worse while general stability has probably improved.

With the development of highly accurate multiple warhead missiles, there is a danger that one side might be able to obtain a first-strike counterforce capability, at least against the other side's land-based missiles and bombers, or that it might become able to cripple the other side's command and control operations. At the same time, however, it almost seems—to put it very baldly—that the two major powers have forgotten how to get into a war. Although on occasion they still remember how to say nasty things about each other, there hasn't been a true, bone-crunching confrontational crisis

---

32. Barry M. Blechman and Stephen S. Kaplan, *Force Without War* (Washington, D.C.: Brookings, 1978), p. 132. See also Jacek Kugler, "Terror Without Deterrence: Reassessing the Role of Nuclear Weapons," *Journal of Conflict Resolution*, Vol. 28, No. 3 (September 1984), pp. 470–506.

33. Betts finds "scant reason to assume . . . that the nuclear balance would be a prime consideration in a decision about whether to resort to nuclear coercion." Betts, *Nuclear Blackmail*, pp. 218–219. Hannes Adomeit sees "no congruence between increased Soviet military capabilities and enhanced Soviet propensities to take risks." Adomeit, "Soviet Crisis Prevention and Management," *Orbis*, Vol. 30, No. 1 (Spring 1986), pp. 42–43. For an able refutation of the popular notion that it was American nuclear superiority that determined the Soviet backdown in the Cuban missile crisis, see Lambeth, "Deterrence in the MIRV Era," pp. 230–231. Marc Trachtenberg has presented an interesting, if "somewhat speculative" case that Soviet behavior was influenced by Soviet strategic inferiority. His argument is largely based on the observation that the Soviets never went on an official alert, and he suggests this arose from fear of provoking an American preemptive strike. But the essential hopelessness of the tactical situation and the general fear of escalation to what Lambeth (quoting Thomas Schelling) calls "just plain war" would also seem to explain this behavior. Marc Trachtenberg, "Nuclear Weapons and the Cuban Missile Crisis," *International Security*, Vol. 10, No. 1 (Summer 1985), pp. 156–163.

for over a quarter-century. Furthermore, as Bernard Brodie notes, even the last crisis, over missiles in Cuba, was "remarkably different . . . from any previous one in history" in its "unprecedented candor, direct personal contact, and at the same time mutual respect between the chief actors."[34] Events since then that seem to have had some warlike potential, such as the military alert that attended the Yom Kippur War of 1973, fizzled while still at extremely low levels.[35] In fact, as McGeorge Bundy has noted, since 1962 "there has been no open nuclear threat by any government."[36]

It seems reasonable, though perhaps risky, to extrapolate from this trend and to suggest that, whatever happens with crisis stability in the future, general stability is here to stay for quite some time. That is, major war—war among developed countries—seems so unlikely that it may well be appropriate to consider it obsolescent. Perhaps World War II was indeed the war to end war—at least war of that scale and type.

THE HOLLANDIZATION PHENOMENON. There are, of course, other possibilities. Contentment with the status quo could diminish in time and, whatever the traumas of World War II, its lessons could eventually wear off, especially as postwar generations come to power. Somehow the fear of escalation could diminish, and small, cheap wars among major countries could again seem

---

34. Bernard Brodie, *War and Politics* (New York: Macmillan, 1973), p. 426. See also Nye, "Nuclear Learning." Betts concludes that no other Cold War crisis ever "really brought the superpowers close to war." Betts, *Nuclear Blackmail*, p. 132. At the time war did seem close, but Khrushchev's memoirs seem to support Shevchenko's conclusion that from the start the Soviets "were preoccupied almost exclusively with how to extricate themselves from the situation with minimum loss of face and prestige." Shevchenko, *Breaking with Moscow*, p. 118. New evidence demonstrates that President Kennedy was ready to end the crisis even on terms that were substantially embarrassing to the U.S., and thus it appears that, as David Welch and James Blight have concluded, "the odds that the *Americans* would have gone to war were next to zero." David A. Welch and James G. Blight, "The Eleventh Hour of the Cuban Missile Crisis," *International Security*, Vol. 12, No. 3 (Winter 1987/88), p. 27.
35. See Scott D. Sagan, "Nuclear Alerts and Crisis Management," *International Society*, Vol. 9, No. 4 (Spring 1985), pp. 127–129; and Bundy, "The Unimpressive Record of Atomic Diplomacy," pp. 50–51.
36. Bundy, "The Unimpressive Record of Atomic Diplomacy," p. 50. On the improved atmosphere after 1962, see also Brodie, *War and Politics*, p. 431. On the declining use of nuclear threats, see also Blechman and Kaplan, *Force Without War*, pp. 47–49. Public opinion data also reflect relaxed tensions: see John Mueller, "Changes in American Public Attitudes Toward International Involvement," in Ellen Stern, ed., *The Limits of Military Intervention* (Beverly Hills, Cal.: Sage, 1977), pp. 325–328; and Rob Paarlberg, "Forgetting About The Unthinkable," *Foreign Policy*, No. 10 (Spring 1973), pp. 132–140. On the flurry of concern about war in the early 1980s in response to the debate over missiles in Western Europe and to some of Ronald Reagan's rhetoric, see Josef Joffe, "Peace and Populism: Why the European Anti-Nuclear Movement Failed," *International Security*, Vol. 11, No. 4 (Spring 1987), pp. 3–40.

viable and attractive. We could get so used to living with the bomb that its use becomes almost casual. Some sort of conventional war could reemerge as a viable possibility under nuclear stalemate.[37] But, as noted, the trends seem to be substantially in the opposite direction: discontent does not seem to be on the rise, and visceral hostility seems to be on the decline.

Moreover, it might be instructive to look at some broad historical patterns. For centuries now, various countries, once warlike and militaristic, have been quietly dropping out of the war system to pursue neutrality and, insofar as they are allowed to do so, perpetual peace. Their existence tends to go unremarked because chroniclers have preferred to concentrate on the antics of the "Great Powers." "The story of international politics," observes Waltz, "is written in terms of the great powers of an era."[38] But it may be instructive for the story to include Holland, a country which chose in 1713, centuries before the invention of nuclear weapons, to abandon the fabled "struggle for power," or Sweden, which followed Holland's lead in 1721.[39] Spain and Denmark dropped out too, as did Switzerland, a country which fought its last battle in 1798 and has shown a "curious indifference" to "political or territorial aggrandizement," as one historian has put it.[40]

While Holland's bandwagon was quietly gathering riders, an organized movement in opposition to war was arising. The first significant peace organizations in Western history emerged in the wake of the Napoleonic Wars in 1815, and during the next century they sought to promote the idea that war was immoral, repugnant, inefficient, uncivilized, and futile. They also proposed remedies like disarmament, arbitration, and international law and organization, and began to give out prizes for prominent peaceable behavior.

---

37. See Edward N. Luttwak, "An Emerging Postnuclear Era?" *Washington Quarterly*, Vol. 11, No. 1 (Winter 1988), pp. 5–15.

38. Waltz, *Theory of International Politics*, p. 72.

39. They did not drop out of the great power war system merely because they were outclassed economically. With substantial effort Holland and Sweden could have struggled to stay on for a while in the ranks of the great powers, at least enough to rival the less great among them, had they so desired. In 1710 when they were dropping out, each had armies bigger than those of Britain or the Hapsburg Empire and far larger than those of Prussia. See Kennedy, *The Rise and Fall of the Great Powers*, p. 99. The sacrifices would probably have been proportionately no more than those the Soviet Union has borne in its costly effort to keep up militarily with the United States, or those Israel has borne in seeking to pursue its destiny in the Middle East, or those North Vietnam bore to expand its control into South Vietnam, or those Japan paid to enter the great power club early in this century.

40. Lynn Montross, quoted in Jack S. Levy, *War in the Modern Great Power System* (Lexington: University Press of Kentucky), p. 45. On this issue, see also Brodie, *War and Politics*, p. 314.

They had become a noticeable force by 1914 but, as one of their number, Norman Angell, has recalled, they tended to be dismissed as "cranks and faddists . . . who go about in sandals and long beards, live on nuts."[41] Their problem was that most people living within the great power system were inclined to disagree with their central premise: that war was bad. As Michael Howard has observed, "before 1914 war was almost universally considered an acceptable, perhaps an inevitable and for many people a desirable way of settling international differences."[42] One could easily find many prominent thinkers declaring that war was progressive, beneficial, and necessary; or that war was a thrilling test of manhood and a means of moral purification and spiritual enlargement, a promoter of such virtues as orderliness, cleanliness, and personal valor.[43]

It should be remembered that a most powerful effect of World War I on the countries that fought it was to replace that sort of thinking with a revulsion against wars and with an overwhelming, and so far permanent, if not wholly successful, desire to prevent similar wars from taking place. Suddenly after World War I, peace advocates were a decided majority. As A.A. Milne put it in 1935, "in 1913, with a few exceptions we all thought war was a natural and fine thing to happen, so long as we were well prepared for it and had no doubt about coming out the victor. Now, with a few exceptions, we have lost our illusions; we are agreed that war is neither natural nor fine, and that the victor suffers from it equally with the vanquished."[44]

For the few who didn't get the point, the lesson was substantially reinforced by World War II. In fact, it almost seems that after World War I the only person left in Europe who was willing to risk another total war was Adolf Hitler. He had a vision of expansion and carried it out with ruthless

41. Norman Angell, *After All* (New York: Farrar, Straus, and Young, 1951), p. 147. See also A.C.F. Beales, *The History of Peace* (New York: Dial, 1931); Roger Chickering, *Imperial Germany and a World Without War* (Princeton: Princeton University Press, 1975).

42. Howard, "The Causes of Wars," p. 92.

43. See the discussion in Richard Rosecrance, *Action and Reaction in World Politics* (Boston: Little, Brown, 1963), p. 163; Luard, *War in International Society*, pp. 354–365; Van Evera, "Why Cooperation Failed in 1914," pp. 89–92; Roland N. Stromberg, *Redemption by War* (Lawrence: Regents Press of Kansas, 1982); Mueller, *Retreat from Doomsday*. For a sustained and impassioned argument against such thinking, see Norman Angell, *The Great Illusion* (London: Heinemann, 1909).

44. A.A. Milne, *Peace With Honour* (New York: Dutton, 1935), pp. 9–10. See also Paul Fussell, *The Great War and Modern Memory* (New York: Oxford University Press, 1975); I.F. Clarke, *Voices Prophesying War 1763–1984* (London: Oxford University Press, 1966), ch. 5.

and single-minded determination. Many Germans found his vision appealing, but unlike the situation in 1914 where enthusiasm for war was common, Hitler found enormous reluctance at all levels within Germany to use war to quest after the vision. As Gerhard Weinberg has concluded, "whether any other German leader would indeed have taken the plunge is surely doubtful, and the very warnings Hitler received from some of his generals can only have reinforced his belief in his personal role as the one man able, willing, and even eager to lead Germany and drag the world into war."[45] Hitler himself told his generals in 1939 "in all modesty" that he alone possessed the nerve required to lead Germany to fulfill what he took to be its mission.[46] In Italy, Benito Mussolini also sought war, but only a small one, and he had to deceive his own generals to get that.[47] Only in Japan, barely touched by World War I, was the willingness to risk major war fairly widespread.[48]

Since 1945 the major nuclear powers have stayed out of war with each other, but equally interesting is the fact that warfare of *all* sorts seems to have lost its appeal within the developed world. With only minor and fleeting exceptions (the Falklands War of 1982, the Soviet invasions of Hungary and Czechoslovakia), there have been no wars among the 48 wealthiest countries in all that time.[49] Never before have so many well-armed countries spent so much time not using their arms against each other. This phenomenon surely

---

45. Gerhard Weinberg, *The Foreign Policy of Hitler's Germany* (Chicago: University of Chicago Press, 1982), p. 664.

46. Knox, "Conquest, Foreign and Domestic," p. 54.

47. MacGregor Knox, *Mussolini Unleashed 1939–1941* (Cambridge: Cambridge University Press, 1982), ch. 3.

48. On these issues, see note 9 above; Mueller, *Retreat from Doomsday*; Brodie, *War and Politics*, ch. 6; George H. Quester, *Offense and Defense in the International System* (New York: Wiley, 1977), p. 137; Luard, *War in International Society*, p. 365; the arguments by Michael Doyle about the widespread growth of liberal anti-war ideology over the last two centuries in Doyle, "Kant, Liberal Legacies, and Foreign Affairs," *Philosophy and Public Affairs*, Vol. 12, Nos. 3 and 4 (Summer and Fall, 1983); and Doyle, "Liberalism and World Politics," *American Political Science Review*, Vol. 80, No. 4 (December 1986), pp. 1151–1169. See also R.J. Rummel, "Libertarian Propositions on Violence Within and Between Nations," *Journal of Conflict Resolution*, Vol. 29, No. 3 (September 1985), pp. 419–455.

49. For a similar observation, see Luard, *War in International Society*, pp. 395–396. Wealth is per capita, calculated using 1975 data when Iraq and Iran were at their financial peak (ranking 49th and 50th). If 1985 data are used instead, more countries would be on the warless list. Countries like Monaco that have no independent foreign policy are not included in the count. The British-Argentine war over the Falklands cost less than 1000 battle deaths and thus doesn't count as a war by some standards—nor does the bloodless Soviet-Czechoslovak "war" of 1968. The Soviet invasion of Hungary was in some sense requested by the ruling politicians in Hungary and for that reason is also sometimes not classified as an international war. On these issues, see Melvin Small and J. David Singer, *Resort to Arms* (Beverly Hills, Cal.: Sage, 1982), pp. 55, 305.

goes well beyond the issue of nuclear weapons; they have probably been no more crucial to the non-war between, say, Spain and Italy than they have been to the near-war between Greece and Turkey or to the small war between Britain and Argentina.

Consider the remarkable cases of France and Germany, important countries which spent decades and centuries either fighting each other or planning to do so. For this age-old antagonism, World War II was indeed the war to end war. Like Greece and Turkey, they certainly retained the creativity to discover a motivation for war if they had really wanted to, even under an over-arching superpower balance; yet they have now lived side-by-side for nearly half a century, perhaps with some bitterness and recrimination, but without even a glimmer of war fever. They have become Hollandized with respect to one another. The case of Japan is also instructive: another formerly aggressive major power seems now to have embraced fully the virtues and profits of peace.[50]

The existence of nuclear weapons also does not help very much to explain the complete absence since 1945 of civil war in the developed world (with the possible exception of the 1944–49 Greek civil war, which could be viewed instead as an unsettled carryover of World War II). The sporadic violence in Northern Ireland or the Basque region of Spain has not really been sustained enough to be considered civil war, nor have the spurts of terrorism carried out by tiny bands of self-styled revolutionaries elsewhere in Western Europe. Except for the case of Hungary in 1956, Europeans under Soviet domination have not (so far) resorted to major violence, no matter how desperate their disaffection.[51] By one count, 43 civil wars (in addition to scores of anti-colonial wars, bloody coups, communal conflicts, and wars between regions of a country) were begun between 1945 and 1980; none of these civil wars occurred in the developed world.[52]

---

50. See also Richard Rosecrance, *The Rise of the Trading State* (New York: Basic Books, 1986).
51. Even as dedicated a foe of the Soviet regime as Alexandr Solzhenitsyn has said, "I have never advocated physical general revolution. That would entail such destruction of our people's life as would not merit the victory obtained." Quoted in Stephen F. Cohen, *Rethinking the Soviet Experience* (New York: Oxford, 1985), p. 214.
52. Small and Singer, *Resort to Arms*, chs. 12, 13. So traumatic was the Spanish Civil War of the 1930s that it inspired great restraint in the population when that country moved from dictatorship to democracy two generations later. See Edward Schumacher, "Spain Insists U.S. Cut Troops There," *New York Times*, November 20, 1985. The American Civil War seems to have had a similar effect on the United States; although General W.T. Sherman's postwar hope that there would be no war in America for "fifty years to come" proved pessimistic. Lloyd Lewis, *Sherman* (New York: Harcourt, Brace, 1958), p. 585. For the suggestion that internal stability has contrib-

As a form of activity, war in the developed world may be following once-fashionable dueling into obsolescence: the perceived wisdom, value, and efficacy of war may have moved gradually toward terminal disrepute. Where war was often casually seen as beneficial, virtuous, progressive, and glorious, or at least as necessary or inevitable, the conviction has now become widespread that war in the developed world would be intolerably costly, unwise, futile, and debased.

World war could be catastrophic, of course, and so it is sensible to be concerned about it even if its probability is microscopic. Yet general stability seems so firm and the trends so comforting that the concerns of Schell and others about our eventual "final coma" seem substantially overwrought. By themselves, weapons do not start wars, and if nuclear weapons haven't had much difference, reducing their numbers probably won't either.[53] They may be menacing, but a major war seems so spectacularly unlikely that for those who seek to save lives it may make sense to spend less time worrying about something so improbable as major war and more time dealing with limited conventional wars outside the developed world, where war still can seem cheap and tempting, where romantic notions about holy war and purifying revolution still persist and sometimes prevail, and where developed countries sometimes still fight carefully delimited surrogate wars. Wars of that sort are still far from obsolete and have killed millions since 1945.

Over a quarter century ago, strategist Herman Kahn declared that "it is most unlikely that the world can live with an uncontrolled arms race lasting for several decades." He expressed his "firm belief" that "we are not going to reach the year 2000—and maybe not even the year 1965—without a cataclysm" unless we have "much better mechanisms than we have had for forward thinking."[54] Reflecting again on the cases of the United States and Canada, of Sweden and Denmark, of Holland, of Spain and Switzerland, of France and Germany, and of Japan, it might be suggested that there is a long-term solution to the arms competition between the United States and the Soviet Union, and that it doesn't have much to do with "mechanisms."

---

uted to international stability in the developed world, see Luard, *War in International Society*, pp. 398–399.
53. See also the discussion in Jervis, *The Illogic of American Nuclear Strategy*, pp. 158, 195 n. 17.
54. Herman Kahn, *On Thermonuclear War* (Princeton: Princeton University Press, 1961), pp. 574, x, 576.

Should political tensions decline, as to a considerable degree they have since the classic Cold War era of 1945–63, it may be that the arms race will gradually dissipate.[55] And it seems possible that this condition might be brought about not principally by ingenious agreements over arms control, but by atrophy stemming from a dawning realization that, since preparations for major war are essentially irrelevant, they are profoundly foolish.

---

55. In 1817 there was an arms control agreement between the United States and British Canada about warships on the Great Lakes, but conflict, hostility, and an arms competition continued between the two neighbors for 45 years after that. By the 1870s, however, the claims and controversies had resolved themselves or been settled, and mutual disarmament gradually took place without further formal agreement. Peace happened mainly because both sides became accustomed to, and generally pleased with, the status quo. In later decades there was substantial rearmament on the Great Lakes, by agreement, because both sides found them convenient areas for naval training. See C.P. Stacey, *The Undefended Border: The Myth and the Reality* (Ottawa: Canadian Historical Association, 1955).

The Political Effects of Nuclear Weapons

Robert Jervis

A Comment

Perhaps the most striking characteristic of the postwar world is just that—it can be called "postwar" because the major powers have not fought each other since 1945. Such a lengthy period of peace among the most powerful states is unprecedented.[1] Almost as unusual is the caution with which each superpower has treated the other. Although we often model superpower relations as a game of chicken, in fact the U.S. and USSR have not behaved like reckless teenagers. Indeed, superpower crises are becoming at least as rare as wars were in the past. Unless one strains and counts 1973, we have gone over a quarter of a century without a severe crisis. Furthermore, in those that have occurred, each side has been willing to make concessions to avoid venturing too near the brink of war. Thus the more we see of the Cuban missile crisis, the more it appears as a compromise rather than an American victory. Kennedy was not willing to withhold all inducements and push the Russians as hard as he could if this required using force or even continuing the volatile confrontation.[2]

It has been common to attribute these effects to the existence of nuclear weapons. Because neither side could successfully protect itself in an all-out war, no one could win—or, to use John Mueller's phrase, profit from it.[3] Of

The author would like to thank John Mueller for comments.

Robert Jervis is a Professor in the Department of Political Science and the Institute of War and Peace Studies, Columbia University. He is the author of the forthcoming Implications of the Nuclear Revolution.

1. Paul Schroeder, "Does Murphy's Law Apply to History?" *Wilson Quarterly*, Vol. 9, No. 1 (New Year's 1985), p. 88; Joseph S. Nye, Jr., "The Long-Term Future of Nuclear Deterrence," in Roman Kolkowicz, *The Logic of Nuclear Terror* (Boston: Allen & Unwin, 1987), p. 234.
2. See the recent information in McGeorge Bundy, transcriber, and James G. Blight, ed., "October 27, 1962: Transcripts of the Meetings of the ExComm," *International Security*, Vol. 12, No. 3 (Winter 1987/88), pp. 30–92; and James G. Blight, Joseph S. Nye, Jr., and David A. Welch, "The Cuban Missile Crisis Revisited," *Foreign Affairs*, Vol. 66 (Fall 1987), pp. 178–179. Long before this evidence became available, Alexander George stressed Kennedy's moderation; see Alexander L. George, David K. Hall, and William E. Simons, *The Limits of Coercive Diplomacy: Laos, Cuba, Vietnam* (Boston: Little Brown, 1971), pp. 86–143.
3. "The Essential Irrelevance of Nuclear Weapons: Stability in the Postwar World," *International Security*, Vol. 13, No. 2 (Fall 1988) pp. 55–79. But as we will discuss below, it can be rational for states to fight even when profit is not expected.

International Security, Fall 1988 (Vol. 13, No. 2)

course this does not mean that wars will not occur. It is rational to start a war one does not expect to win (to be more technical, whose expected utility is negative), if it is believed that the likely consequences of not fighting are even worse.[4] War could also come through inadvertence, loss of contol, or irrationality. But if decision-makers are "sensible,"[5] peace is the most likely outcome. Furthermore, nuclear weapons can explain superpower caution: when the cost of seeking excessive gains is an increased probability of total destruction, moderation makes sense.

Some analysts have argued that these effects either have not occurred or are not likely to be sustained in the future. Thus Fred Iklé is not alone in asking whether nuclear deterrence can last out the century.[6] It is often claimed that the threat of all-out retaliation is credible only as a response to the other side's all-out attack: thus Robert McNamara agrees with more conservative analysts whose views he usually does not share that the "sole purpose" of strategic nuclear force "is to deter the other side's first use of its strategic forces."[7] At best, then, nuclear weapons will keep the nuclear peace; they will not prevent—and, indeed, may even facilitate—the use of lower levels of violence.[8] It is then not surprising that some observers attribute Soviet adventurism, particularly in Africa, to the Russians' ability to use the nuclear stalemate as a shield behind which they can deploy pressure, military aid, surrogate troops, and even their own forces in areas they had not previously controlled. The moderation mentioned earlier seems, to some, to be only one-sided. Indeed, American defense policy in the past decade has been driven by the felt need to create limited nuclear options to deter Soviet incursions that, while deeply menacing to our values, fall short of threatening immediate destruction of the U.S.

---

4. Alternatively, to be even more technical, a decision-maker could expect to lose a war and at the same time could see its expected utility as positive if the slight chance of victory was justified by the size of the gains that victory would bring. But the analysis here requires only the simpler formulation.
5. See the discussion in Patrick M. Morgan, *Deterrence: A Conceptual Analysis* (Beverly Hills, Cal.: Sage, 1977), pp. 101–124.
6. Fred Iklé, "Can Nuclear Deterrence Last Out the Century?" *Foreign Affairs*, Vol. 51, No. 2 (January 1973), pp. 267–285.
7. Robert McNamara, "The Military Role of Nuclear Weapons," *Foreign Affairs*, Vol. 62, No. 4 (Fall 1983), p. 68. For his comments on how he came to this view, see his interview in Michael Charlton, *From Deterrence to Defense* (Cambridge: Harvard University Press, 1987), p. 18.
8. See Glenn Snyder's discussion of the "stability-instability paradox," in "The Balance of Power and the Balance of Terror," in Paul Seabury, ed., *The Balance of Power* (San Francisco: Chandler, 1965), pp. 184–201.

Furthermore, while nuclear weapons may have helped keep the peace between the U.S. and USSR, ominous possibilities for the future are hinted at by other states' experiences. Allies of nuclear-armed states have been attacked: Vietnam conquered Cambodia and China attacked Vietnam. Two nuclear powers have fought each other, albeit on a very small scale: Russia and China skirmished on their common border. A nonnuclear power has even threatened the heartland of a nuclear power: Syria nearly pushed Israel off the Golan Heights in 1973 and there was no reason for Israel to be confident that Syria was not trying to move into Israel proper. Some of those who do not expect the U.S. to face such a menace have predicted that continued reliance on the threat of mutual destruction "would lead eventually to the demoralization of the West. It is not possible indefinitely to tell democratic republics that their security depends on the mass extermination of civilians . . . without sooner or later producing pacifism and unilateral disarmament."[9]

John Mueller has posed a different kind of challenge to claims for a "nuclear revolution." He disputes, not the existence of a pattern of peace and stability, but the attributed cause. Nuclear weapons are "essentially irrelevant" to this effect; modernity and highly destructive nonnuclear weapons would have brought us pretty much to the same situation had it not been possible to split the atom.[10] Such intelligent revisionism makes us think about questions whose answers had seemed self-evident. But I think that, on closer inspection, the conventional wisdom turns out to be correct. Nevertheless, there is much force in Mueller's arguments, particularly in the importance of what he calls "general stability" and the reminder that the fact that nuclear war would be so disastrous does not mean that conventional wars would be cheap.

Mueller is certainly right that the atom does not have magical properties. There is nothing crucial about the fact that people, weapons, industry, and agriculture may be destroyed as a result of a particular kind of explosion,

---

9. Henry Kissinger, "After Reykjavik. Current East-West Negotiations," *The San Francisco Meeting of the Tri-Lateral Commission, March 1987.* (New York: The Trilateral Commission, 1987), p. 4; see also ibid., p. 7, and his interview in Charlton, *From Deterrence to Defense,* p. 34.
10. Mueller, "The Essential Irrelevance." Waltz offers yet a third explanation for peace and stability—the bipolar nature of the international system, which, he argues, is not merely a product of nuclear weapons. See Kenneth Waltz, *Theory of International Politics* (Reading, Mass.: Addison-Wesley, 1979). But in a later publication he places more weight on the stabilizing effect of nuclear weapons: *The Spread of Nuclear Weapons: More May Be Better,* Adelphi Paper No. 171 (London: International Institute for Strategic Studies, 1981).

although fission and fusion do produce special by-products like fallout and electromagnetic pulse. What is important are the political effects that nuclear weapons produce, not the physics and chemistry of the explosion. We need to determine what these effects are, how they are produced, and whether modern conventional weapons would replicate them.

Political Effects of Nuclear Weapons

The existence of large nuclear stockpiles influences superpower politics from three directions. Two perspectives are familiar: First, the devastation of an all-out war would be unimaginably enormous. Second, neither side—nor, indeed, third parties—would be spared this devastation. As Bernard Brodie, Thomas Schelling, and many others have noted, what is significant about nuclear weapons is not "overkill" but "mutual kill."[11] That is, no country could win an all-out nuclear war, not only in the sense of coming out of the war better than it went in, but in the sense of being better off fighting than making the concessions needed to avoid the conflict. It should be noted that although many past wars, such as World War II for all the allies except the U.S. (and, perhaps, the USSR), would not pass the first test, they would pass the second. For example: although Britain and France did not improve their positions by fighting, they were better off than they would have been had the Nazis succeeded. Thus it made sense for them to fight even though, as they feared at the outset, they would not profit from the conflict. Furthermore, had the allies lost the war, the Germans—or at least the Nazis— would have won in a very meaningful sense, even if the cost had been extremely high. But "a nuclear war," as Reagan and Gorbachev affirmed in their joint statement after the November 1985 summit, "cannot be won and must never be fought."[12]

A third effect of nuclear weapons on superpower politics springs from the fact that the devastation could occur extremely quickly, within a matter of days or even hours. This is not to argue that a severe crisis or the limited use of force—even nuclear force—would inevitably trigger total destruction, but only that this is a possibility that cannot be dismissed. At any point, even in calm times, one side or the other could decide to launch an unpro-

---

11. Bernard Brodie, ed., *The Absolute Weapon: Atomic Power and World Order* (New York: Harcourt Brace, 1946); Thomas Schelling, *Arms and Influence* (New Haven: Yale University Press, 1966).
12. *New York Times*, November 22, 1985, p. A12.

voked all-out strike. More likely, a crisis could lead to limited uses of force which in turn, through a variety of mechanisms, could produce an all-out war. Even if neither side initially wanted this result, there is a significant, although impossible to quantify, possibility of quick and deadly escalation.

Mueller overstates the extent to which conventional explosives could substitute for nuclear ones in these characteristics of destructiveness, evenhandedness, and speed. One does not have to underestimate the horrors of previous wars to stress that the level of destruction we are now contemplating is much greater. Here, as in other areas, there comes a point at which a quantitative difference becomes a qualitative one. Charles De Gaulle put it eloquently: after a nuclear war, the "two sides would have neither powers, nor laws, nor cities, nor cultures, nor cradles, nor tombs."[13] While a total "nuclear winter" and the extermination of human life would not follow a nuclear war, the world-wide effects would be an order of magnitude greater than those of any previous war.[14] Mueller understates the differences in the scale of potential destruction: "World War II did not cause total destruction in the world, but it did utterly annihilate the three national regimes that brought it about. It is probably quite a bit more terrifying to think about a jump from the 50th floor than about a jump from the 5th floor, but anyone who finds life even minimally satisfying is extremely unlikely to do either."[15] The war did indeed destroy these national regimes, but it did not utterly destroy the country itself or even all the values the previous regimes supported. Most people in the Axis countries survived World War II; many went on to prosper. Their children, by and large, have done well. There is an enormous gulf between this outcome—even for the states that lost the war— and a nuclear holocaust. It is far from clear whether societies could ever be reconstituted after a nuclear war or whether economies would ever recover.[16] Furthermore, we should not neglect the impact of the prospect of destruction of culture, art, and national heritage: even a decision-maker who was willing

---

13. Speech of May 31, 1960, in Charles De Gaulle, *Discours Et Messages*, Vol. 3 (Paris: Plon, 1970), p. 218. I am grateful to McGeorge Bundy for the reference and translation.
14. Starley Thompson and Stephen Schneider, "Nuclear Winter Reappraised," *Foreign Affairs*, Vol. 64, No. 5 (Summer 1986), pp. 981–1005.
15. "The Essential Irrelevance," pp. 66–67.
16. For a discussion of economic recovery models, see Michael Kennedy and Kevin Lewis, "On Keeping Them Down: Or, Why Do Recovery Models Recover So Fast?" in Desmond Ball and Jeffrey Richelson, *Strategic Nuclear Targeting* (Ithaca: Cornell University Press, 1986), pp. 194–208.

to risk the lives of half his population might hesitate at the thought of destroying what has been treasured throughout history.

Mueller's argument just quoted is misleading on a second count as well: the countries that started World War II were destroyed, but the Allies were not. It was more than an accident but less than predetermined that the countries that were destroyed were those that sought to overturn the status quo; what is crucial in this context is that with conventional weapons at least one side can hope, if not expect, to profit from the war. Mueller is quite correct to argue that near-absolute levels of punishment are rarely required for deterrence, even when the conflict of interest between the two sides is great—i.e., when states believe that the gross gains (as contrasted with the net gains) from war would be quite high. The United States, after all, could have defeated North Vietnam. Similarly, as Mueller notes, the United States was deterred from trying to liberate East Europe even in the era of American nuclear monopoly.

But, again, one should not lose sight of the change in scale that nuclear explosives produce. In a nuclear war the "winner" might end up distinguishably less worse off than the "loser," but we should not make too much of this difference. Some have. As Harold Brown put it when he was Secretary of the Air Force, "if the Soviets thought they may be able to recover in some period of time while the U.S. would take three or four times as long, or would never recover, then the Soviets might not be deterred."[17] Similarly, one of the criteria that Secretary of Defense Melvin Laird held necessary for the essential equivalence of Soviet and American forces was: "preventing the Soviet Union from gaining the ability to cause considerably greater urban/ industrial destruction than the United States would in a nuclear war."[18] A secret White House memorandum in 1972 used a similar formulation when it defined "strategic sufficiency" as the forces necessary "to ensure that the United States would emerge from a nuclear war in discernably better shape than the Soviet Union."[19]

---

17. U.S. Senate, Preparedness Investigating Subcommittee of the Committee on Armed Services, *Hearings on Status of U.S. Strategic Power*, 90th Cong., 2d sess., April 30, 1968 (Washington, D.C.: U.S. Government Printing Office, 1968), p. 186.
18. U.S. House of Representatives, Subcommittee on Department of Defense, *Appropriations for the FY 1973 Defense Budget and FY 1973–1977 Program*, 92nd Cong., 2d sess., February 22, 1972, p. 65.
19. Quoted in Gregg Herken, *Counsels of War* (New York: Knopf, 1985), p. 266. This conception leads to measuring the peacetime strategic balance and the projected balance during a hypothetical war by looking at which side has more capability (e.g., amount of megatonnage, number

But this view is a remarkably apolitical one. It does not relate the costs of the war to the objectives and ask whether the destruction would be so great that the "winner," as well as the loser, would regret having fought it. Mueller avoids this trap, but does not sufficiently consider the possibility that, absent nuclear explosives, the kinds of analyses quoted above would in fact be appropriate. Even very high levels of destruction can rationally be compatible with a focus on who will come out ahead in an armed conflict. A state strongly motivated to change the status quo could believe that the advantages of domination were sufficiently great to justify enormous blood-letting. For example, the Russians may feel that World War II was worth the cost not only when compared with being conquered by Hitler, but also when compared with the enormous increase in Soviet prestige, influence, and relative power.

Furthermore, without nuclear weapons, states almost surely would devote great energies to seeking ways of reducing the costs of victory. The two world wars were enormously destructive because they lasted so long. Modern technology, especially when combined with nationalism and with alliances that can bring others to the rescue of a defeated state, makes it likely that wars will last long: defense is generally more efficacious than offense. But this is not automatically true; conventional wars are not necessarily wars of attrition, as the successes of Germany in 1939–40 and Israel in 1967 remind us. Blitzkrieg can work under special circumstances, and when these are believed to apply, conventional deterrence will no longer be strong.[20] Over an extended period of time, one side or the other could on occasion come to believe that a quick victory was possible. Indeed, for many years most American officials have believed not only that the Soviets could win a conventional war in Europe or the Persian Gulf, but that they could do so at low cost. Were the United States to be pushed off the continent, the considerations Mueller gives might well lead it to make peace rather than pay the

---

of warheads, numbers of warheads capable of destroying hardened targets). I have discussed the problems with this approach in "Cognition and Political Behavior," in Richard Lau and David Sears, eds., *Political Cognition* (Hillsdale, N.J.: Earlbaum, 1986), pp. 330–333; and "The Drunkard's Search" (unpublished ms.).

20. John J. Mearsheimer, *Conventional Deterrence* (Ithaca: Cornell University Press, 1983). It should be noted, however, that even a quick and militarily decisive war might not bring the fruits of victory. Modern societies may be even harder to conquer than are modern governments. A high degree of civilian cooperation is required if the victor is to reach many goals. We should not assume it will be forthcoming. See Gene Sharp, *Making Europe Unconquerable* (Cambridge, Mass.: Ballinger, 1985).

price of re-fighting World War II. Thus, extended deterrence could be more difficult without nuclear weapons. Of course, in their absence, NATO might build up a larger army and better defenses, but each side would continually explore new weapons and tactics that might permit a successful attack. At worst, such efforts would succeed. At best, they would heighten arms competition, national anxiety, and international tension. If both sides were certain that any new conventional war would last for years, the chances of war would be slight. But we should not be too quick to assume that conventional war with modern societies and weapons is synonymous with wars of attrition.

The length of the war is important in a related way as well. The fact that a war of attrition is slow makes a difference. It is true, as George Quester notes, that for some purposes all that matters is the amount of costs and pain the state has to bear, not the length of time over which it is spread.[21] But a conventional war would have to last a long time to do an enormous amount of damage; and it would not *necessarily* last a long time. Either side can open negotiations or make concessions during the war if the expected costs of continued fighting seem intolerable. Obviously, a timely termination is not guaranteed—the fitful attempts at negotiation during World War II and the stronger attempts during World War I were not fruitful. But the possibility of ending the war before the costs become excessive is never foreclosed. Of course, states can believe that a nuclear war would be prolonged, with relatively little damage being done each day, thus permitting intra-war bargaining. But no one can overlook the possibility that at any point the war could escalate to all-out destruction. Unlike the past, neither side could be certain that there would be a prolonged period for negotiation and intimidation. This blocks another path which statesmen in nonnuclear eras could see as a route to meaningful victory.

Furthermore, the possibility that escalation could occur even though neither side desires this outcome—what Schelling calls "the threat that leaves something to chance"[22]—induces caution in crises as well. The fact that sharp

21. George Quester, "Crisis and the Unexpected," *Journal of Interdisciplinary History*, Vol. 18, No. 3 (Spring 1988), pp. 701–703.
22. Thomas Schelling, *The Strategy of Conflict* (Cambridge: Harvard University Press, 1960), pp. 187–203; Schelling, *Arms and Influence*, pp. 92–125. Also see Jervis, *The Illogic of American Nuclear Strategy* (Ithaca: Cornell University Press, 1984), ch. 5; Jervis, "'MAD is a Fact, not a Policy': Getting the Arguments Straight," in Jervis, *Implications of the Nuclear Revolution* (Ithaca: Cornell University Press, forthcoming); and Robert Powell, "The Theoretical Foundations of Strategic Nuclear Deterrence," *Political Science Quarterly*, Vol. 100, No. 1 (Spring 1985), pp. 75–96.

confrontations can get out of control, leading to the eventual destruction of both sides, means that states will trigger them only when the incentives to do so are extremely high. Of course, crises in the conventional era also could escalate, but the possibility of quick and total destruction means that the risk, while struggling near the brink, of falling into the abyss is greater and harder to control than it was in the past. Fears of this type dominated the bargaining during the Cuban missile crisis: Kennedy's worry was "based on fear, not of Khrushchev's intention, but of human error, of something going terribly wrong down the line." Thus when Kennedy was told that a U-2 had made a navigational error and was flying over Russia, he commented: "There is always some so-and-so who doesn't get the word."[23] The knowledge of these dangers—which does not seem lacking on the Soviet side as well[24]—is a powerful force for caution.

Empirical findings on deterrence failure in the nuclear era confirm this argument. George and Smoke show that: "The initiator's belief that the risks of his action are calculable and that the unacceptable risks of it can be controlled and avoided is, with very few exceptions, a necessary (though not sufficient) condition for a decision to challenge deterrence."[25] The possibility of rapid escalation obviously does not make such beliefs impossible, but it does discourage them. The chance of escalation means that local military advantage cannot be confidently and safely employed to drive the defender out of areas in which its interests are deeply involved. Were status quo states able to threaten only a war of attrition, extended deterrence would be more difficult.

General Stability

But is very much deterrence needed? Is either superpower strongly driven to try to change the status quo? On these points I agree with much of Mueller's argument—the likely gains from war are now relatively low, thus

---

23. Arthur M. Schlesinger, Jr., *Robert Kennedy and His Times* (Boston: Houghton Mifflin, 1978), p. 529; quoted in Roger Hilsman, *To Move A Nation* (Garden City, N.Y.: Doubleday, 1964), p. 221.
24. See Benjamin Lambeth, "Uncertainties for the Soviet War Planner," *International Security*, Vol. 7, No. 3 (Winter 1982/83), pp. 139–66.
25. Alexander L. George and Richard Smoke, *Deterrence in American Foreign Policy* (New York: Columbia University Press, 1974), p. 529.

producing what he calls general stability.[26] The set of transformations that go under the heading of "modernization" have not only increased the costs of war, but have created alternative paths to established goals, and, more profoundly, have altered values in ways that make peace more likely. Our focus on deterrence and, even more narrowly, on matters military has led to a distorted view of international behavior. In a parallel manner, it has adversely affected policy prescriptions. We have not paid sufficient attention to the incentives states feel to change the status quo, or to the need to use inducements and reassurance, as well as threats and deterrence.[27]

States that are strongly motivated to challenge the status quo may try to do so even if the military prospects are bleak and the chances of destruction considerable. Not only can rational calculation lead such states to challenge the status quo, but people who believe that a situation is intolerable feel strong psychological pressures to conclude that it can be changed.[28] Thus nuclear weapons by themselves—and even mutual second-strike capability— might not be sufficient to produce peace. Contrary to Waltz's argument, proliferation among strongly dissatisfied countries would not necessarily recapitulate the Soviet-American pattern of stability.[29]

The crucial questions in this context are the strength of the Soviet motivation to change the status quo and the effect of American policy on Soviet drives and calculations. Indeed, differences of opinion on these matters explain much of the debate over the application of deterrence strategies toward the USSR.[30] Most of this dispute is beyond our scope here. Two points, however, are not. I think Mueller is correct to stress that not only Nazi Germany, but Hitler himself, was exceptional in the willingness to chance an enormously destructive war in order to try to dominate the world.

---

26. Mueller, "Essential Irrelevance," pp. 69–70; also see Waltz, *Theory of International Politics*, p. 190.
27. For discussions of this topic, see George, Hall, and Simons, *Limits of Coercive Diplomacy*; George and Smoke, *Deterrence in American Foreign Policy*; Richard Ned Lebow, *Between Peace and War* (Baltimore: Johns Hopkins University Press, 1981); Robert Jervis, "Deterrence Theory Revisited," *World Politics*, Vol. 31, No. 2 (January 1979), pp. 289–324; Jervis, Lebow, and Janice Gross Stein, *Psychology and Deterrence* (Baltimore: Johns Hopkins University Press, 1985); David Baldwin, "The Power of Positive Sanctions," *World Politics*, Vol. 24, No. 1 (October 1971), pp. 19–38; and Janice Gross Stein, "Deterrence and Reassurance," in Philip E. Tetlock, et al., eds., *Behavior, Society, and Nuclear War*, Vol. 2 (New York: Oxford University Press, forthcoming, 1989).
28. George and Smoke, *Deterrence in American Foreign Policy*; Lebow, *Between Peace and War*; Jervis, Lebow, and Stein, *Psychology and Deterrence*.
29. Waltz, *Spread of Nuclear Weapons*.
30. See Robert Jervis, *Perception and Misperception in International Politics* (Princeton: Princeton University Press, 1976), ch. 3.

While of course such a leader could recur, we should not let either our theories or our policies be dominated by this possibility.

A second point is one of disagreement: even if Mueller is correct to believe that the Soviet Union is basically a satisfied power—and I share his conclusion—war is still possible. Wars have broken out in the past between countries whose primary goal was to preserve the status quo. States' conceptions of what is necessary for their security often clash with one another. Because one state may be able to increase its security only by making others less secure, the premise that both sides are basically satisfied with the status quo does not lead to the conclusion that the relations between them will be peaceful and stable. But here too nuclear weapons may help. As long as all-out war means mutual devastation, it cannot be seen as a path to security. The general question of how nuclear weapons make mutual security more feasible than it often was in the past is too large a topic to engage here.[31] But I can at least suggest that they permit the superpowers to adopt military doctrines and bargaining tactics that make it possible for them to take advantage of their shared interest in preserving the status quo. Winston Churchill was right: "Safety [may] be the sturdy child of terror."

---

31. I have discussed it in the concluding chapter of *Implications of the Nuclear Revolution*.

Is War Obsolete? | *Carl Kaysen*

A Review Essay

John Mueller, *Retreat from Doomsday: The Obsolescence of Major War*. New York: Basic Books, 1989.

The forty-five years that have now passed since the end of World War II without interstate war in Europe is the longest such period in its post-medieval history.[1] Many scholars and commentators have attributed the present "long peace" among the major powers to the deterrent effect of nuclear weapons. When President Ronald Reagan and General Secretary Mikhail Gorbachev agreed that a nuclear war cannot be won and must not be fought, they were only reiterating what has become an almost universally accepted piety in current public and scholarly discussion of international relations.[2]

John Mueller's *Retreat from Doomsday*[3] advances a much stronger thesis: major war was already becoming obsolete by the time of the First World War;

The author thanks Francis Bator, McGeorge Bundy and Marc Trachtenberg for many helpful comments on an earlier draft of this essay. They encouraged him in writing down his speculations without necessarily endorsing them, and read the result with critical eyes.

Carl Kaysen is David W. Skinner Professor of Political Economy in the Program in Science, Technology and Society at the Massachusetts Institute of Technology, and a member of MIT's program in Defense and Arms Control Studies.

1. See J.S. Levy, *War in the Modern Great Power System, 1495–1975* (Lexington: University Press of Kentucky, 1983); and Evan Luard, *War in International Society* (London: I.B. Taurus, 1986). Luard's analysis covers 1400–1984, and includes civil wars, colonial wars and revolts, and some other wars outside the European system. Both Levy and Luard find the nineteenth century— 1816–99 in Levy, 1815–1914 in Luard—the most peaceful of the long periods they studied. Luard records the periods of 1815–54 and 1871–1914, forty and forty-three years, as free of major power wars. The longest such period in the eighteenth century was 1720–27, and in earlier centuries war raged even more frequently.
2. See Department of State *Bulletin*, Vol. 86, No. 2106 (January 1988), p. 8, for the joint communiqué at the end of the Reagan-Gorbachev meeting in Geneva, November 19–21, 1985. Agreement is not universal. See for example ch. 4 in Paul Seabury and Angelo Codevilla, *War: Ends and Means* (New York: Basic Books, 1989). See also Richard Pipes, "Why the Soviets Think They Could Fight and Win a Nuclear War," *Commentary*, Vol. 64 (July 1977), pp. 21–34.
3. John Mueller, *Retreat from Doomsday: The Obsolescence of Major War* (New York: Basic Books, 1989); most subsequent references to this book appear parenthetically in the text. See also Mueller, "The Essential Irrelevance of Nuclear Weapons: Stability in the Postwar World," *International Security*, Vol. 13, No. 2 (Fall 1988), pp. 55–79.

International Security, Spring 1990 (Vol. 14, No. 4)
© 1990 by the President and Fellows of Harvard College and of the Massachusetts Institute of Technology.

World War II repeated and reinforced that lesson. The development of nuclear weapons was accordingly irrelevant to the process; it was, so to speak, the flourish under the *finis* at the end of the story.

Mueller's central argument is that war—among "western," modernized nations—has become "subrationally unthinkable."

> An idea becomes impossible not when it becomes reprehensible or has been renounced, but when it fails to percolate into one's consciousness as a conceivable option. Thus, two somewhat paradoxical conclusions about the avoidance of war can be drawn. On the one hand, peace is likely to be firm when war's repulsiveness and futility are fully evident—as when its horrors are dramatically and inevitably catastrophic. On the other hand, peace is most secure when it gravitates away from conscious rationality to become a subrational, unexamined mental habit. At first, war becomes rationally unthinkable—rejected because it's calculated to be ineffective and/or undesirable. Then it becomes subrationally unthinkable—rejected not because it's a bad idea but because it remains subconscious and never comes off as a coherent possibility. Peace in other words, can prove to be habit forming, addictive. (p. 240.)

The obsolescence of war, argues Mueller, is thus the result of a change in mental habits through socio-cultural evolution, not a change in the terms of a calculation: "unthinkable," not "unprofitable."

When the whole postwar European security system is rapidly changing, Mueller's claims merit careful consideration. The burden of this essay is that Mueller is right in his result, but that his argument fails to sustain his conclusion. Mueller hardly explains the cultural change that has made wars unthinkable, and fails to explore the interconnections among cultural, political, and economic changes in the evaluation of interstate war. It is because wars of the kind under consideration have become unprofitable, both economically and politically, that they have become unthinkable. Finally, he is too cavalier in his dismissal of the significance of nuclear weapons.

Mueller's Analysis

Mueller sets the stage for his examination of the change in attitudes toward war by probing two other social institutions that have disappeared through a similar cultural change: duelling and slavery. Duelling, for centuries a natural and appropriate response to offense and insult between gentlemen, became ridiculous and therefore unthinkable in the course of the last century (pp. 9–11). Slavery has had a similar fate:

From the dawn of pre-history until about 1788 it had occurred to almost no one that there was anything the least bit peculiar about the institution of slavery. Like war, it could be found just about everywhere, in one form or another, and it flourished in every age . . . . The abolitionist movement that broke out at the end of the century in Britain and the United States was something new, not the culmination of a substantial historical process.

As it happened, it was a new idea whose time had come. . . . Within a century, slavery, and most similar institutions like serfdom, had been all but eradicated from the face of the globe. Slavery had become controversial, then peculiar, then obsolete. (pp. 11–12.)

Mueller refers to the parallels of duelling and slavery several times in later chapters, but more as emblems than explanations.

More directly in point is Mueller's brief account of those nations that have "opted out" of the war system: Holland and Sweden. Both were at one time great powers; both had been militarily strong and active. But, notes Mueller,

After 1713, [Holland] dropped out of the great power system and concentrated on commercial and colonial ventures. . . . For over two-and-one-half centuries, Holland has generally . . . sought to avoid all international war in Europe, a pattern that can be called Hollandization.

Sweden, a Great Power—and a very warlike one—in the seventeenth century lost that status by 1721. . . . Swedish kings tried warfare again a few times between 1741 and 1814 [unsuccessfully]. Thereafter, [they] lost whatever residual enthusiasm for war they could still muster, and . . . have now been at peace for over a century and a half. (p. 20.)

He cites Switzerland, Spain, Denmark and Portugal as other "Hollandized" nations, which at earlier times had been, or, in terms of resources, could have been, Great Powers, but simply opted out.

After a brief discussion of the century-long peace between the United States and Canada, and an even briefer reference to the rise of the liberal state and the absence of war among liberal democracies, Mueller directly addresses his main theme, the changing social evaluation of war.[4] Before World War I, he argues, only a small minority spoke against war. Quakers opposed war as immoral, as they did slavery, religious intolerance, and many other then-

---

4. Mueller fails to cite Michael Doyle's brilliant discussion of why liberal states have never fought with each other. See Doyle, "Kant, Liberal Legacies, and Foreign Affairs", parts 1 and 2 in *Philosophy and Public Affairs*, Vol. 12, No. 3, No. 4 (Summer, Fall 1983), pp. 205–235 and 325–353. I am indebted to Marc Trachtenberg for calling Doyle's work to my attention after reading an earlier draft of this paper. Doyle's argument overlaps my own with respect to changes in the political rewards of war, but is not identical to it.

widespread and socially-approved practices embodying man's inhumanity to man. Non-religious humanists shared these views. So did those who saw war as inimical to commerce and economically ruinous, from Montesquieu, Kant, Buckle, and Adam Smith in the seventeenth and eighteenth centuries to Norman Angell in the twentieth. The majority view, however (or at least the majority of those who recorded their views), approved of war. War was an admirable stage for the display of heroism and virility for the individual and glory for the nation at one end of the spectrum of ideas, and a psychologically inevitable product of aggressiveness rooted in human nature and a necessary element of human progress in social Darwinian terms at the other.

The First World War changed these ideas. The magnitude of the slaughter, the costs to both victors and vanquished, the horribly inhuman and degrading circumstances of combat itself led to a "bone-deep revulsion," a "colossal confirmation [of] the repulsiveness, immorality and futility of war."[5]

According to Mueller, there were three possible lessons to be drawn from the experience of World War I: collective security had somehow to be substituted for individual self-help; military preparations, including newer and more formidable weapons, had to be maintained at a level that would deter war; conflicts had to be negotiated out rather than fought out. Most of the world drew the third lesson.

Unfortunately, Mussolini, Hitler, and the leaders of Japan were socially and culturally outsiders who had not shared the lessons of the First World War. They continued to believe in both the nobility and necessity of war. Mussolini was a foolish romantic pushing an unwilling Italian people into military adventures. The Japanese leadership was an ideological remnant of pre–World War I times, with a romantic view of war and a belief in the positive political and social role of the military in their own great task of modernization. Hitler, with his racist ideology, resentment against Versailles and quest for *Lebensraum,* was an entrepreneurial genius of both politics and war. None of them wanted genuinely to negotiate conflicts: the attempts of the other European states to do so, and the United States to avoid them—in

---

5. Mueller, *Retreat from Doomsday,* p. 55. It is striking that Mueller neither quotes nor cites the novels and memoirs of the twenties that expressed these feelings profoundly and gave them wide circulation: Erich Maria Remarque, *All Quiet on the Western Front;* Robert Graves, *Goodbye to All That;* Henri Barbusse, *Fire;* e.e. cummings, *The Enormous Room;* or Paul Fussell's overview of this literature in *The Great War and Modern Memory* (New York: Oxford University Press, 1975). Nor does Mueller explain why the American Civil War, the first modern war, which was equally costly and bloody relative to its extent, did not have the same effect in changing attitudes.

short, "appeasement"—led to the Second World War. For Mueller, Hitler's leadership in Germany was a necessary condition for the outbreak of war; he is silent on whether it was also sufficient.

The Second World War repeated and reinforced the lessons of the first and this time they were better learned. Among the developed nations there were now no dropouts who had failed to attend class. The atomic bomb played no significant part in these lessons. The war taught that U.S. productive power was itself a great deterrent; Detroit was as important as the atom bomb (pp. 82–84). Further, the actual use of the bomb against Japan was significant only because half of its leadership was already prepared to surrender (pp. 87–88). Finally, the absence of civil war against the occupying Nazis and their puppet governments (beyond the relatively small scale guerrilla resistance in occupied Europe) showed that the population had lost its stomach for war (pp. 91–92).

Roughly half of Mueller's book, chapters 5–9, depicts the major events of the period of the long peace since World War II. Mueller sees the success of containment as reflecting the satisfaction of the victors with and acceptance by the losers of the postwar situation; nuclear weapons are essentially irrelevant. The Korean War was a stabilizing event; it demonstrated the inutility of limited war. Khrushchev's policy of bluster and crisis-creation similarly failed, as did his efforts at seduction of the non-communist world by the examples of Soviet success in competitive economic growth—"we will bury you"—and the space race. The failure of U.S. intervention in Vietnam's civil war was followed by China's abandonment of the Cold War, and in turn by Soviet recognition of its "overreach" in the Third World and the demise of the cold war.

WEAKNESSES AND LIMITATIONS OF MUELLER'S ANALYSIS
Mueller's analysis reveals inadequacies at three different levels. The inadequacies detract least from the author's central argument at the first level, which characterizes the chapters summarized immediately above. These chapters present a curious and inconsistent mixture of Mueller's central thesis with a more conventional, neo-realist analysis of events. The fears of the advocates of containment and the consequent military responses in Korea and Vietnam were, Mueller argues, not all unreasonable at the time (p. 213); thus U.S. intervention in Vietnam may well have prevented a third world war, by stimulating a premature Chinese attempt at a coup in Indonesia. If delayed, the coup attempt might well have succeeded, emboldening Khru-

shchev and Mao to further use of force and accordingly creating a panic reaction in the United States leading to major war. Mueller recognizes this as speculation, but says it should not be dismissed (pp. 181–187). But Mueller's discussion of the Vietnam War gives almost no attention to the internal situation within South Vietnam. Mueller is unsympathetic to U.S. and West European cold warriors, yet sneers at Congressional constraints on executive action in Vietnam and Africa. He is contemptuous of Soviet performance, yet omits any discussion of why communism might have been attractive in the Third World.

These, however, are superficial flaws that do not detract from the force of Mueller's larger thesis, even if they weaken readers' confidence in the care with which he marshals evidence and advances argument.

At a second and deeper level, Mueller fails to confront the traditional realist and neo-realist argument that war is an inescapable feature of the anarchic international system in which independent states seek power and security. After all, this is one of the dominant models of international relations, if not the dominant one, and Mueller simply does not engage with it.

Kenneth Waltz offers a clear statement of the realist view: conflict is the inevitable result of the structure of the international system.[6] Independent states seeking security in an anarchic system in which war is the *ultima ratio* of statecraft will inevitably be in conflict, and conflict will regularly issue in war, as it has throughout history. However, a bipolar system has better prospects than a multipolar one for stability and the avoidance of war. With formidable nuclear, arsenals on both sides, the prospects for avoiding war become better still; indeed, "the probability of major war among states having nuclear weapons approaches zero."[7] Waltz thus supports Mueller's conclu-

---

6. Kenneth Waltz, "The Origins of War in Neo-Realist Theory," *Journal of Interdisciplinary History*, Vol. 17, No. 3 (Spring 1988), pp. 615–628; Waltz, *Man, the State, and War* (New York: Columbia University Press, 1959); and Waltz, *Theory of International Politics* (Reading, Mass.: Addison Wesley, 1979). The whole of that issue of the *Journal of Interdisciplinary History*, devoted to the "origins and prevention of major wars," has been published as Robert I. Rotberg and Theodore K. Rabb, eds., *The Origin and Prevention of Major Wars* (Cambridge: Cambridge University Press, 1989). A much cruder exposition of a much less subtle realist view is presented by Seabury and Codevilla in *War: Ends and Means*. Combining a primer with a present-oriented polemic, it depicts war as the inevitable consequence of the often ideologically-driven aggressive plans of some states. This situation has persisted through history and will continue in the future, they argue; wars must be expected, prepared for, if possible deterred, and if necessary fought. Neither preparation for war at all levels nor willingness to fight it using all available and imaginable weapons can be avoided, except by submitting to the will of the aggressor.
7. Waltz, "The Origins of War in Neo-Realist Theory," p. 627.

sion, at least for so long as the world of international politics remains bipolar, but for entirely different reasons. And as bipolarity disintegrates, it is not clear where Waltz's argument leads: will the stability effect of "absolute" weapons outweigh the instability of shifting alliances that multipolarity breeds?[8]

Though Mueller essentially dismisses the neo-realist case by ignoring it, he does not hesitate to make use of neo-realist arguments himself. He explains the stability of the post–World War II settlement in essentially neo-realist terms: the war resulted in a stable structure of power (pp. 95–97).

At the third and deepest level, Mueller fails to account for the socio-cultural change that he relies on to explain the "retreat from doomsday." The retreat appears to take place in a vacuum, or at best in a highly rarefied atmosphere in which the forces of technological change, economic change, and change in the internal structures and workings of the polities that fight or avoid wars are barely detectable. In his analysis, social ideas and attitudes seem to change of themselves, or at best to reflect changes in the ideas and attitudes of individuals, aggregated in an unstructured way. But this is not the way the world works. It is to this that the rest of this essay is addressed.

Toward a More Comprehensive Explanation: The Historical Background

Understanding why war has become obsolescent requires an examination of the political and economic calculus of war. A necessary and sufficient, or almost sufficient, condition for the disappearance of war is that all parties concerned calculate a negative cost benefit ratio *ex ante*.[9] No nation will start

---

8. See also Waltz's essay "Toward Nuclear Peace," pp. 684–712, in Robert Art and Kenneth Waltz, eds., *The Use of Force: Military Power and International Politics*, 3rd ed. (Lanham, Md.: University Press of America, 1988). Focusing on nuclear proliferation rather than directly on multipolarity, Waltz sees it as contributing to an increase in stability rather than the reverse. For the opposite conclusion see Lewis Dunn, "What Difference Will It Make?" in Art and Waltz, *The Use of Force*, pp. 713–725.

9. This condition is almost sufficient in that it appears to omit the possibility of inadvertent war. But inadvertent wars, if they occur at all, occur only in situations of conflict in which at least some of the actors have mobilized military forces and are threatening or contemplating their use. In such a situation, one or more actors must expect that making the threat of war, even allowing for the possibility that it may in fact occur, will produce a positive outcome. See Bruce Bueno de Mesquita, *The War Trap* (New Haven: Yale University Press, 1981), and Bueno de Mesquita, "The Contribution of Expected Utility Theory to the Study of International Conflict," in *Journal of Interdisciplinary History*, Vol. 43, No. 4 (Spring 1988), pp. 629–652 (also in Rotberg and Rabb, *The Origin and Prevention of Major Wars*). Luard, *War in International Society*, devotes chapter 5 to examining the decision processes that led to wars and concludes by asking:

a war unless it expects to gain in some way by doing so. Of course the prospective gain may be a virtual rather than an absolute one: the avoidance of an even greater loss where the alternative course of action requires submission in one way or another to the will of the adversary.

In the starkest and simplest terms, the key proposition of the more comprehensive explanation is that for most of human history, societies were so organized that war could be profitable for the victors, in both economic and political terms. But profound changes in economics and politics in the last century and a half, following the Industrial Revolution, have changed the terms of the calculation.

For millennia, societies were organized around landholding as the chief basis of both economic and political power. Agriculture was the overwhelmingly dominant economic activity; land and relatively unskilled labor were its major inputs, and typically—though not invariably—land was relatively the more scarce. Political power was based on the control of land, the mobilization of agricultural surpluses, and their conversion into military power and symbolic display in the shape of political and religious buildings and ceremonies. For these millennia, most labor was more or less tied to the landholder and land, either institutionally through slavery and serfdom, or less formally through simple immobility.

In such societies, successful war yielded a clear gain: control over territory—additional land and the associated labor force—that added directly to both economic and political power. Compared to the potential returns, costs, at least for the winner, were small. The instruments of war were simple and its scale typically small. The land itself suffered from war at most for one harvest season beyond the war's duration. While there were some losses of labor force in terms of civilian casualties and more in spread of famine and disease, these losses too were usually transient, and in general added little to the ambient levels of famine and disease.

In the political structure characteristic of these societies, the power holders were themselves the warriors, and the connection between those who fought

---

"Can war nonetheless occur accidentally?" His answer: "The evidence of history provides no indication that this is likely. Throughout the whole of the period we have been surveying it is impossible to identify a single case in which it can be said that a war started accidentally: in which it was not, at the time when war broke out, the deliberate intentions of at least one party that war should take place. . . . Whether a decision to make war results from active desire or passive willingness, therefore, it remains the case that the decision, when it occurs, is deliberate and intentional" (p. 232).

wars and those who, in victory, gained from them was direct and immediate. Conversely, the large mass of the population was separated entirely from political power and almost entirely from war. Shifts in political control and rule over the land on which they lived and worked had little effect on ordinary people's lives, except as one of the variations of fortune visited upon them by fate or the gods, like flood, drought, or plague.

In such societies, the romanticization of war and the high value given to the warrior hero were clearly functional. Even without a discussion of causation, it is clear that the social valuation of war corresponded well with its role as an instrument for gaining and enlarging political and economic power for those who both decided on war and waged it.[10] To be sure, this direct connection meant that the warriors and kings who decided on war risked their own lives, and could and did lose them in victory as well as defeat. They confronted this risk sustained not only by ideas of honor and glory, but by familial and dynastic as well as personal bases of reckoning gains and losses.

This is, of course, a highly schematic account, but as a set of stylized facts, it serves well to characterize most of Europe from the ninth to the fifteenth centuries. By the end of the fifteenth century, the scheme needs enlargement. Cities and trade, including overseas trade, became important; the machinery of government became more elaborate, and leaders other than warriors played an important role in it. Professional armies and gunpowder, used in both small arms and artillery, began to play an increasing role in warfare; the mounted knight disappeared; and the scale of war grew.[11] These changes continued, and increased in importance in the next three centuries. Still, the political, economic, and technical parameters remained such that war could still be seen as an enterprise in which possible gains outweighed costs.

Through the eighteenth century, political structures still concentrated power in the hands of a small elite who decided on peace and war; kings

---

10. See Homer's *Iliad*, passim.

11. For changes in the scale of war in the early part of the period, see Luard, *War in International Society*, chap. 2. He divides the time from 1400 into five periods: 1400–1559, the age of dynasties; 1559–1648, the age of religions; 1648–1789, the age of sovereignty; 1789–1917, the age of nationalism; and 1917 to the present, the age of ideology. His first period would correspond to the simple pre-industrial model of society; a more elaborate industrial model covers his next two, and at least part of the fourth. During the first of Luard's periods, wars involved armies ranging from 10–15,000 men on a side at first, rising to 30–40,000 by its end. By the end of the next period they had grown as much as tenfold. In the age of sovereignty wars tended to be smaller, and nothing matched the scale of the Thirty Years War, either in terms of forces mobilized or of relative casualties.

remained centrally important. The great majority of the population was still so distant from the ruling elites as to be almost totally disconnected from them. Land and immobile labor remained important though not as overwhelmingly dominant. The new spheres of economic activity in cities and trade also provided assets capturable by war. The cities themselves contained appropriable wealth in the form of stocks of food, materials, and (handicraft) manufactures. Trade was typically conducted in a mercantilist framework, often by licensed monopolies, so that political rulers retained both a substantial interest in it and control via access to ports and shipping. The scale of war was growing, but the scale of destruction was still small. Cities of course were more vulnerable to destruction than agricultural land, but they often had the option to surrender rather than endure siege and bombardment. Their inhabitants, too, while not tied to the land, were not particularly mobile. This was especially true of the economically most valuable ones, the skilled craftsmen and commercially active traders, who in much of Europe were more closely tied, politically, socially, and culturally, to their cities than to the sovereign king or emperor who nominally ruled them.[12] Thus they sometimes were available as intact or nearly intact spoils of war.

In the late sixteenth and early seventeenth centuries, religion assumed a salience in European wars that it has not had before or since.[13] But religious issues were still intermingled with issues of power, and Catholic sovereigns were often allied with Protestant ones in the wars of the period.

Though the societies of the eighteenth century differed greatly from those of the previous millennia in which the ideas of heroic valor and the romance of war developed, the ideas remained lively among elites, and thus still functional, since these remained the war-deciding, if no longer the chief warmaking, classes.

THE GREAT CHANGE

In the nineteenth century, economy, polity, society, and culture were all transformed in ways that fundamentally changed the calculus of war. The

---

12. For the situation in Germany, see Mack Walker, *German Small Towns: Community, State and General Estate, 1648–1871* (Ithaca: Cornell University Press, 1971).

13. Luard found 26 civil wars over religious conflict and the same number of international wars concerned partly with religion in Europe between 1559 and 1648. These were more than half of the civil wars and about half of the international wars in the period. See *War in International Society,* Tables 3 and 4, pp. 36, 37, and also p. 93. Of course the wars of Islamic expansion and the European responses thereto in the Middle East and Spain were also wars of religion.

industrial revolution replaced animal by mechanical and then electric power, natural and traditional materials by steel and manufactured chemicals, and small-scale handicraft by large-scale factory production; transportation and communication sped up by orders of magnitude. By the end of the century, urban outweighed rural populations in half of Europe and, by the middle of the next, in most of the rest of Europe and North America, too. War, too, was industrialized: more powerful weapons, larger and more complexly organized armies, and great improvements in supply, transport, and communication changed its scale and intensity. After the American and French Revolutions, the fundamental basis of political legitimacy changed. The polity became both more inclusive and more integrated. More and more of the population were included in the politically significant classes. The spread of literacy as well as the growth of urban middle classes meant that there was no longer as profound a gulf of thought and feeling separating a small governing elite from a huge mass that belonged almost to a different species. The development of the polity was part of the larger process by which states become nations. The separate, isolated localities and regions of the peasant world were fused into a truly national state. Schooling played a significant role in this process, as did military service, but other less-organized forces, for example, the growth of railroad and road systems, were also important.[14]

The nation-states that were being created at the end of the last century and the first part of the twentieth formed a new kind of polity, culturally as well as politically. They became the chief focus of popular loyalty. The individual citizen identified directly with the nation on the basis of the cultural style he shared with his fellows. This was a literate culture, based on a nationally organized system of education that reached all the nation's inhabitants. The individual's membership in the culture was direct, rather than mediated through membership in smaller sub-groups. Sub-groups existed, of course, but were flexible rather than rigid, and typically did not evoke the same strong identification as the nation. The population was anonymous, fluid, mobile. Homogeneity, literacy, anonymity are the key words for describing the members of the new nation-state.[15]

---

14. See Eugen Weber, *Peasants into Frenchmen, 1870–1914* (Stanford: Stanford University Press, 1976), for detailed examination of this transformation in France.
15. This characterization is drawn from Ernest Gellner, *Nations and Nationalism* (Ithaca: Cornell University Press, 1983). The passage above is adapted from p. 138. Gellner's short book is an incisive, penetrating, and persuasive discussion of how the nation-states of the modern industrial world differ from earlier states, which were typically segmented, often multinational, and

DOES WAR STILL PAY? THE ECONOMIC CALCULUS

All of these nineteenth-century changes affected both the potential gains and the potential costs of war. In the economic sphere, land greatly diminished in importance as a resource. Capital in the tangible forms of machinery, buildings, and the infrastructure of transportation, communication, and urban life, and especially intangible human capital, in the form of the accumulated knowledge and skills of the work force at all levels, became relatively much more important. The integration of all or nearly all of the population into the unified society of the nation-state meant that the mere acquisition of territory did not by itself convey effective control of the resources sited on it, especially the all-important human resources (but of this more below).

The economic balance changed on the cost side as well. Industrialization multiplied both the scale and cost of war; industrial wars involved the whole nation, not the typically small fraction of population and output drawn into earlier wars. World Wars I and II far outweighed anything that had gone before in destructiveness.[16]

Destruction of a significant part of the stock of tangible capital in the battlefield countries was one element, and not even the most important, in the economic costs of the great wars. Loss of life, especially in the cohorts of young men in military service, was significant. Finally, there was the loss of four or five years of economic growth by the diversion to war-making of those resources that would otherwise have created new capital, tangible and human.[17]

---

not at all marked by a common literate culture. Gellner uses this analysis to explain the force of nationalism in the modern world. A more extended summary of Gellner's argument is provided on the last four pages of his book (pp. 139–143). See also his essays collected in Gellner, *Culture, Identity, and Politics* (Cambridge: Cambridge University Press, 1987). Much of the noneconomic part of the argument of this essay rests on Gellner's insights.

16. See Levy, *War in the Modern Great Power System*, Table 41, pp. 88–91. The two world wars (102 and 113 in his list) exceeded all others in measures of severity, intensity, and concentration, measured respectively in total battle deaths, battle deaths/population, and battle deaths/nation-year. The nearest competitors in these measures—the Napoleonic Wars, the War of the Spanish Succession, and the Thirty Years War—were far behind.

17. The case of the United States in World War II is exceptional. U.S. involvement came at a time when the economy was operating far below capacity, and started slowly with a buildup to provide equipment and supplies to France and the United Kingdom. Thus the United States was able to increase both war production, including substantial investments in new capacity for making weapons, and civilian consumption. There probably was a gain in total growth in both civilian consumption and investment usable for further growth over what would have been achieved in the absence of war. In contrast, the demographic losses of Britain and France in the First World War have often been seen as a contributing factor to their sluggish economic performance in the 1920s and 1930s.

On the other side of the ledger, the extent to which the conquest of new territory added to the economic strength of the conqueror is questionable. The one-time opportunity for looting—seizure and removal of stocks of materials and finished goods, and movable capital equipment such as vehicles, ships, aircraft, machinery—remained. Compared to pre-industrial times, the available loot was much greater, since industrial societies have a much higher ratio of physical capital stock (other than land) to output than do agricultural-commercial ones. However, assuming that the conqueror aims to retain his conquests for a long period and wring from them a continuing economic surplus, the comparative balance is not so clear. The question is whether the economy of a different society, all or part of another industrial nation, can be effectively incorporated by conquest against the will of its inhabitants. The continuing political hostility of the conquered, and its effects on the level of energy and efficiency with which their economy operates, may lead to poorer results than those the conqueror could have achieved by avoiding the cost of the war and of continuing suppression of the conquered, and instead investing the equivalent in production for home consumption or trade with the rest of the world.

How long does political hostility endure? How high are its economic costs directly in terms of political repression, and indirectly in terms of political strikes, sabotage, low productivity? There has been no systematic study that could provide answers to these questions. Available evidence is fragmentary and non-quantitative.

Perhaps the first example of the conquest of a part of one industrial society by another is the German annexation of Alsace-Lorraine after the Franco-Prussian war. But, despite its forty-year duration, the episode provides no clear lesson. The area certainly functioned as part of the German economy, and was integrated into it to a substantial degree.[18] But on the other side, the primary purpose of the annexation was military. German military investment in garrison troops was high, and German policy did little to promote maximum integration and economic performance. Throughout the pe-

---

18. Alsatian potash was an important input to German agriculture, as were the phosphate by-products of the Thomas steelmaking process, which utilized the minette ores of Lorraine. The use of these ores by the Ruhr steelmakers helped the German steel industry reach first place in world production just before the First World War. Yet the ores came from *French* Lorraine; the boundary had been drawn two decades before the Thomas process came into wide use. Had the process been available in 1871, the Germans might well have sought to draw the boundary differently. I am indebted to Marc Trachtenberg for pointing this out.

riod, conflict continued between German military and civilian authorities, and between the local "particularists" who wished to improve the region's relations to the Reich, and an alliance of Catholic clergy and liberals who were hostile to Protestant, authoritarian Prussia. A clumsy and clumsily managed political structure did nothing to diminish these conflicts. Though three-quarters of the population lived in primarily German-speaking communities, and only one-eighth in primarily French-speaking ones, popular hostility to German rule remained strong. Almost a quarter of the original population migrated to France during this period, but some of this loss was replaced by immigration from Germany. The attempt to apply the German military call-up to the young men of the territories was a failure, with evasion rates running 25 percent or more in the early years after annexation.

The textile industry in Alsace, which earlier had been a European leader, grew much more slowly than it did in other parts of the Reich during the same period. The interests of firms and localities in the other parts of the Reich in restricting competition from the newly-annexed territories were effective in preventing investments in canals and ports, and in slowing the development of railroad connections with France, all of which could have increased productivity in the newly conquered "Reichsland."[19]

It is difficult to strike a balance on the basis of the information available, and even more difficult to speculate definitively what Germany could have achieved with an effective policy directed to promoting the economic and political integration of the territories.

Another example to test the proposition is that of German-occupied Europe between 1940 and 1944. Alan Milward, studying the economics of the Second World War, finds that the conquest and occupation of France was a profitable operation for Germany.[20] On one set of calculations, the levies that the Germans imposed on France rose from some 9–10 percent of French output in 1940 to about a third in 1943, then declined to a quarter in 1944. These flows represented some 3 to 8 or 9 percent of the German GNP in the corresponding years, falling to about 6 percent in 1944. On the basis of a crude estimate of the costs of conquest and occupation, Milward further

---

19. This account is drawn primarily from Dan P. Silverman, *Reluctant Union: Alsace-Lorraine and Imperial Germany, 1871–1918* (University Park: Pennsylvania State University Press, 1972), which appears to be the only recent study. See also Hajo Holborn, *A History of Modern Germany*, Vol. 3, *1840–1945*, (New York: Knopf, 1965).
20. Alan Milward, *War, Economy, and Society, 1939–1945* (Berkeley: University of California Press, 1979), ch. 5, "The Economics of Occupation."

concludes that the returns substantially outweighed the cost.[21] Although showing no similarly comprehensive calculations, Milward concludes that Belgium and the Netherlands also yielded a surplus to the Germans, but Norway did not, because of its smaller economy, dependence on imported raw materials, and the cost of the relatively large number of active German forces stationed there.

The significance of these calculations is unclear. The period is a short one. In France, and to a lesser extent in Belgium, governments and substantial segments of the population were sympathetic to the Nazis, but there was also active resistance in all three countries. The strongest conclusions that these and the other examples sustain is that the question of the economic costs and benefits of conquest is open.

Milward discusses at some length the part played in Germany's calculus of war by German concepts of *Grossraumwirtschaft*, the idea that Germany needed to expand the area it controlled in order to sustain its role as a great military power. More agricultural land was particularly needed, but so was access to raw materials, especially iron ore, bauxite, and oil. There is no easy way to assess how much weight this economic motive had in driving Germany's policy, compared to the mix of desire for revenge for the wrongs of Versailles, racist ideology, Nazi dreams of a New Order, hatred and fear of Bolshevism, and Hitler's simple lust for power. The economic goals were certainly present; that does not say that they were correctly assessed.

Aside from the particular goals of Germany in 1939, access to and control of critical raw materials—oil and metal ores in particular—have often been advanced as economic bases for war. Japanese actions in the thirties provide another example of this type. However, the proposition does not stand up to analysis. Raw material inputs have long been declining in overall economic importance; the ratios of primary production in general, and minerals specifically, to GNP have been steadily declining in industrial countries at least since the First World War. Further, any single material usually has substitutes and, at higher prices, alternative sources of supply. Even crude oil, often cited as indispensable to modern society and modern military power, can be substituted by coal-based synthetics, as Germany did successfully during the Second World War, although at much higher costs. But if the calculation were made of the economic balance between securing these materials by

---

21. Ibid., pp. 137–147, esp. tables 21 and 22, p. 140, and discussion on pp. 144–145.

conquest, and securing them in the ordinary ways by trade or by the search for substitutes and alternate sources of supply, it would be a peculiar situation indeed that gave the advantage to war. The typical discussion of critical materials takes for granted the necessity of wartime access or alternately the threat of hostile denial, thus begging the question of whether they are worth fighting for. But the question should rather be seen as a long-run one: is it cheaper for a nation to secure the supply of raw materials not found within its borders by trade, or by conquest?[22]

DOES WAR STILL PAY? THE POLITICAL CALCULUS

So far, the discussion of how the coming of industrialization has changed the calculus of war has focused on its economic elements. But the political calculus is at least as important, if not more so. It is presidents, prime ministers, and party secretaries who play central roles in making decisions about war and peace, not finance ministers, budget directors, and central bankers. Here, too, the last century-and-a-half has brought a profound trans-formation. Governments have become popular and populist even when not democratic; the welfare of the general population, conceived in a broad sense, is their chief business, and it is to achieving this that they bend their efforts. Of course, this is true *a fortiori* in democratic societies, in which the question, "are you better off now than you were however many years ago?" is always a useful electoral cry for one or another of the political competitors.[23] But even authoritarian and repressive governments in modern societies need the consent, however tacit and grudging, of the mass of the governed. Economic well-being and social peace are the chief elements on which this consent rests.

Making war can rarely contribute positively to these goals. In the short run, the mass of the public bears heavy costs. The public, not a small army of professionals, pays the price in blood, whether as soldiers or as city dwellers subject to attack from the air. They suffer the immediate hardships consequent on wartime economic mobilization. If the arguments above are correct, it is most unlikely that there is compensation in the long run sufficient to outweigh the costs, even to families that have not suffered death or injury.

---

22. These issues are discussed further in E.N. Castle and K.A. Price, eds., *U.S. Interests and Global Natural Resources* (Baltimore: Johns Hopkins University Press, 1983). See especially the essays of McGeorge Bundy and Carl Kaysen.
23. Michael Doyle's two-part article "Kant, Liberal Legacies and Foreign Policy," examines this question at length.

Welfare-oriented societies typically produce leaders who are attuned to and reflect their societies' goals. They compete for their positions by appealing to the public as improvers of public welfare, whether by positive action, or by promising to unleash the natural forces of progress. Peace, not war, is seen as the natural state of affairs by leaders as well as the public. Further, the dominance of the nation-state as a focus of popular sentiment has delegitimated wars of conquest; they are not only unlikely to be profitable, they are viewed as wrong. Gellner quotes Lord Acton: "Thus began a time when the text simply was, that nations would not be governed by foreigners. Power legitimately attained, and exercised with moderation, was declared invalid."[24] Germany's annexation of Alsace-Lorraine exemplified just such an illegitimate change of rule. Current examples are even clearer. The Israeli military occupation of the West Bank and the Soviet-installed regimes in Eastern Europe have all been characterized by an extremely high level of persisting political hostility between their populations and the dominant power.

Economy, Polity, and the Social Evaluation of War

The changes in society, economy, and polity sketched in the preceding pages provide both the context for and a substantial part of the explanation of the cultural change that Mueller invokes as the chief reason for the obsolescence of major war in the industrialized world. New relations of individuals to a new kind of society, new leaders with new conceptions of their task, and new ways of making war explain new ideas about war. An additional question Mueller simply does not address is, what governed the pace of change in the social evaluation of war? Why did the lessons of the First World War require the experience of the Second before they were widely absorbed? Part of the answer is that the two wars themselves were the agents of consummation for the social changes described. The First World War greatly accelerated the disappearance of regimes ruled by hereditary elites that were still imbued with old ideas of war. The experiences of the inter-war years and the Second World War solidified the recognition and acceptance of the guarantee of popular welfare as a major duty of the state.

Viewed another way, the time scale for these changes was surprisingly short. In general, social ideas—cultures—change much more slowly than

---

24. Gellner, *Nations and Nationalism*, p. 159.

social institutions.[25] Although the transformations consequent on industrialization were well underway in the major states of Europe by 1914, the culture of politics was still nearer to that of 1815 than that of 1945. In 1914, when the Germans took the steps that set themselves and the other combatants on the path to war, they hoped for a short war not much different from the other wars they had experienced since 1815. They put their faith in a war plan that called for the rapid defeat of France, and their hope in the neutrality of Britain. The final steps to the Second World War were more compressed in time than those that led to the first: just six years from Hitler's assumption of power to the German invasion of Poland. The responses to his moves by other European nations were reluctant, not eager; there were not two sides pushing for war. If anything, some of the lessons of the first war had been overlearned in France, Britain, and the United States. The cap to all this was the improbable conjuncture of situation and personal talents that brought Hitler to his key role in the process.

To be sure, the cultural transformation is far from complete. Wars still mobilize national sentiments, and create a heightened emotional state with an intensified sense of community and sharing. Even the threat of war or the display of force brings out such feelings. The nationalization and integration of modern societies sketched above reinforces and amplifies these sentiments, and their instant dissemination and multiple reflection in the media does so even more.[26]

A short, small war, ending in victory at little cost in blood or treasure, by mobilizing just these sentiments, can still produce political gains for the leaders who initiate it. The recent Falklands/Malvinas War produced a substantial gain for Prime Minister Thatcher, and the United States' intervention in Grenada—hardly a war—a similar one for President Reagan. But such wars may be hard to choose successfully. As Yehoshafat Harkabi has pointed out, nations that have initiated wars in this century have generally come out the loser.[27]

---

25. See Clifford Geertz, *The Interpretation of Cultures* (New York: Basic Books, 1973), passim.

26. See John Mueller, *War, Presidents, and Public Opinion* (Lanham, Md.: University Press of America, 1985). This is a reprint of the original published in 1973. Mueller traces the public response, as shown in polls, to the actions of Presidents Truman in Korea and Johnson in Vietnam. Initially strongly positive, public opinion declined and turned negative as the wars dragged on and casualties grew.

27. Yehoshafat Harkabi, "Directions of Change in the World Strategic Order," a comment on a paper of the same title given by Karl Kaiser at the 30th Anniversary Conference of the International Institute for Strategic Studies (IISS), in Brighton, and reprinted in *The Changing Strategic*

Broad Arguments and the Evidence, Such As It Is

The foregoing comments on the recentness of change in the social accept-
ability of war are consistent with such quantitative evidence as there is on
the frequency and intensity of war. Melvin Small and David Singer, in their
1982 study *Resort to Arms*, find no trends at all in the frequency or intensity
of wars between 1816 and 1980.[28]

J.S. Levy's longer study of wars in the great power system does identify
some trends. His regression analysis shows that the frequency of wars involving the great powers, measured in terms of 25-year periods, declined
modestly over the 1495–1975 period of his study. So did the duration of wars
and their magnitude, in terms of nation-years of wars. However, their severity in terms of casualties increased.[29]

Organizing his material somewhat differently, Levy compares the five long
periods, "modified centuries," covered by his data: 1500–1599, 1600–1713,
1714–1789, 1816–1899, 1900–1975 (a periodization that excludes the wars of
the French Revolution and Napoleon). The seventeenth century appears as
the most warlike, followed by the sixteenth, the eighteenth, and the twentieth; with the nineteenth most peaceable.[30]

Luard, with a somewhat different periodization and less attempt at refined
measurement, paints a broadly similar picture. His age of nationalism (1789–
1917) is of course more warlike than Levy's nineteenth century, since it
includes the great wars of 1789–1815 and 1914–1917. He too comments on
the peaceable century of 1815–1914 in Europe: Prussia, which led in the
number of its wars, was involved in international war for only five years,
Russia for eight, France for five, Austria for four, and Britain for three.[31] But
relative peaceableness extended only to international wars in Europe. The
same period that saw only twenty-eight international wars in Europe saw
244 wars worldwide, including 107 of colonial conquest or colonial revolt and
47 civil wars in Europe.[32]

Landscape: IISS Conference Papers, 1988, Part II, Adelphi Paper No. 237 (London: IISS, 1989), pp.
21–23. Harkabi makes, in highly compressed form, some of the broader arguments made here.
28. Melvin Small and J. David Singer, *Resort to Arms: International and Civil Wars, 1816–1980*
(Beverly Hills: Sage, 1982).
29. Levy, *War in the Modern Great Power System,* Table 6.3, p. 134.
30. Ibid., Table 6.5, p. 143.
31. See Luard, *War in International Society,* ch. 2 and appendices 1–5.
32. Luard reminds us that the long peace since World War II was a long peace in Europe, not
in the rest of the world, ibid., pp. 72–79.

Does the Nuclear Revolution Matter?

The argument so far has made no mention of the nuclear revolution, and so far is in accord with Mueller's contention that major war between modern nations was on its way to obsolescence before the development of nuclear weapons. However, this is not to accept that the profound revolution in the technology of war brought by nuclear and thermonuclear weapons and long-range ballistic missiles does not matter; quite the contrary. These new technologies of war have amplified the message of this century's war experiences by many decibels, and set it firmly in the minds of the wide public as well as those of political and military leaders. Contemplating what a dozen thermonuclear warheads can do to a modern society, much less a thousand dozen, leads all concerned to a much more subtle, careful, and discriminating calculation of what the national interest is, in any conflict situation, and how it can best be pursued. And all *are* concerned. The downside risks of wrong decisions have become so immense and immediate that it is almost inconceivable that haste and wishfulness will again play the roles in initiating wars that they have in the past. It is equally difficult to think what interest other than sheer survival can be placed on the other pan of the balance, and there is simply no rational way to believe that, in a world of long-range missiles carrying thermonuclear warheads, the initiation of nuclear war is a way to ensure survival.[33] Nor have nuclear weapons made the world safe for non-nuclear war, if it involves the interests of nuclear-armed nations on both sides of a conflict, since the risks of escalation must be counted into a balance already unfavorable to war.

Another way to make clear that the nuclear-missile revolution in military technology has had a profound effect is to imagine, *per impossibile*, that the revolution had taken place in the world of the eighteenth century. Even the most calculating of absolute monarchs, completely focused on their dynastic interests, and totally unconcerned with the welfare of their powerless peasant populations, would nevertheless have had to take a different view of war than they had previously held. The prospect that they themselves, their families, their capitals, and their hunting lodges as well as their palaces would all vaporize in the thermonuclear fire would certainly change their

---

33. See McGeorge Bundy, *Danger and Survival: Choices about the Bomb in the First Fifty Years* (New York: Random House, 1988), for a penetrating and meticulous examination of the cautious behavior of the leaders of the superpowers in periods of tension and moments of crisis.

assessment of the relative virtues of war and peace. The question for this imagined world is whether the elites would have had the time to contemplate the lesson of Hiroshima and Nagasaki, or whether their survivors would have had to learn it by bitter experience.

Concluding Observations

If wars among modern nations truly serve no possible rational purpose, why is there not wide, even universal, recognition of this proposition, especially by the political leadership of these nations? What leads them to persist in supporting large military forces, and building their relations to other nations around military alliances and the threat, if not actual use, of force? These questions can be answered at both a general and a quite specific level.

The general answer is that cultures change much more slowly than technologies and institutions. As Keynes said, most living politicians are slaves of some dead scribbler. Despite Mueller's assertion, war has not yet become "subrationally unthinkable," even though conscious attitudes toward war have indeed changed.

For most governmental and political elites in modern states, the old ideas of military power and "defense" as the core of national sovereignty still carry great weight. Accordingly, providing the capability for war, and being in some sense prepared to use it, still command a large share of the resources and energies of governments. This has been true over a wide range of the political spectrum, wide enough to cover most of the actual and potentially eligible ruling groups. Disarmers and pacifists in opposition have changed their views when they led or joined governments. Those who have maintained these views have remained outsiders and critics, because most of the publics share their governors' views of these questions.

On a more concrete level, the powerful grip of ideology on governments and publics on both sides of the great postwar East-West divide has diverted attention from the changes sketched in the preceding pages. The West has combined abhorrence of communism as a mode of social organization with belief in its inherent expansionism and its goal of conquest. These beliefs, and a reading of the lessons of the 1930s that focused on the failure of will in France, Great Britain, and the United States, have justified the place of military power and the threat of war in the center of our international picture. On the other side of the divide, ideological commitment to the idea that capitalists must and will resist the inevitable triumph of communism, and the fear of capitalist encirclement, together with a reading of history since 1917 that justifies that fear, have produced a complementary world picture.

It is just the revolutionary change in military technology, especially in the last twenty-five years, that has loosened the grip of ideology on both sides of the divide. The self-confessed failure of communist ideology as a blueprint for successful social organization is helping to complete the process, and opening the way to new thinking in the West as well as the East.

Assuming that the foregoing analysis is correct, and assuming further that it can be made widely persuasive (which may be two independent assumptions), does not imply that the world is on the threshold of universal and perpetual peace. Fully modern industrial nations are still in the minority in the world in both number and population. Civil wars, and forms of violent international conflict falling short of war, are widespread and will continue to be so in the foreseeable future.

Nonetheless, this analysis reinforces Mueller's to offer a real basis for hope. The international system that relies on the national use of military force as the ultimate guarantor of security, and the threat of its use as the basis of order, is not the only possible one. To seek a different system with a more secure and a more humane basis for order is no longer the pursuit of an illusion, but a necessary effort toward a necessary goal. The industrialized nations, which are also the most heavily and dangerously armed, must lead the way to this transformation by their own example of changed behavior. That may not be enough to persuade the others, but it is certainly the indispensable first step.

Postscript

The first draft of this essay, ending just above, was finished in the middle of October 1989. At that time, nothing foreshadowed the accelerating pace of revolutionary political change in Eastern Europe shown in each morning's headlines and each evening's broadcasts, not quite two months later. To be sure, the internal politics of the Soviet Union had been undergoing far-reaching changes since Gorbachev's ascension to leadership in 1985, and these changes were having their reflection in Soviet relations with the rest of the world. By last spring, Poland's government had taken the first steps away from the Communists' monopoly of political power by relegitimizing Solidarity and engaging in negotiations about the composition of the government with its leadership. But even in October 1989, no one expected the dizzying changes of November and December.[34]

So far, the focus of change is the internal political order in Poland, Hungary, Czechoslovakia, the German Democratic Republic, Rumania, and Bulgaria. But the first signs of their equally profound international consequences are appearing. The same crowds in the streets of Leipzig and East Berlin that have demanded and achieved the dismissal of their country's Communist leadership are displaying banners reading, *"Ein Volk, Ein Land"* (One People, One Country). The sentiment for German reunification is echoed in more guarded language in Bonn and Washington, and bluntly rejected in Moscow.[35] As seen from Moscow, the simultaneous reunification of Germany and the strengthening of its ties with the West, specifically with NATO, pose a threat to the entire postwar settlement that was finally ratified in Helsinki after twenty-five years of Western denial, and threaten to undo the results of the Second World War. As seen from Washington, a reunification of Germany that required the withdrawal of American and other NATO troops from West Germany as well as Soviet troops from East Germany would mean the destruction of the whole Western security structure that has been arduously built up since the North Atlantic Treaty of 1949.

Both views will have to change. Have not the heads of both governments been saying that the will of the people should prevail? It is clear that a profound transformation of the international structure of power in Europe— and the whole world—is underway. In the past, such changes have regularly been consummated by war. The argument presented in this essay supports the prediction that this time the changes can take place without war (although not necessarily without domestic violence within the states concerned). So far—mid-January—so good. The author and his readers will be eagerly and anxiously testing the prediction each day.

---

34. See, for example, Seweryn Bialer and Michael Mandelbaum, *The Global Rivals* (New York: Vintage Books, 1989). Here two leading students of the Soviet Union and East-West relations write: "Whatever happens in Europe itself, the two military blocs will not dissolve. . . . The Soviet Union will not release its grip on its East European satellites, nor will the West be powerful enough to break that grip by force" (p. 193).

35. See Timothy Garton Ash, "The German Revolution," *New York Review of Books*, December 21, 1989, pp. 14–19. (The article was dated November 21, 1989.)

Averting Anarchy in the New Europe

Jack Snyder

For the past four decades, the division of Europe and the repression of political pluralism in its eastern half have coincided with an unprecedented period of peace among the great powers.[1] Now, however, social change in the Soviet bloc and "new thinking" in Soviet foreign policy are undermining the stable Cold War stalemate in Europe. Simultaneously, mass political participation is expanding in Communist Europe, the legitimacy of the old institutions of the Communist era is collapsing, and international alignments are becoming more fluid.[2]

This article presents three views of the demise of the bipolar division Europe. First, some Western observers have seen these developments as all to the good: Liberal "end of history" optimism envisions that, as illegitimate Communist rule is rolled back and replaced by liberal, market-oriented regimes, the sources of conflict in Europe will be eliminated and peace will break out. But the difficulties facing *perestroika* in the Soviet Union and the potential for nationalist conflicts throughout the erstwhile Soviet bloc raise the possibility of a much grimmer outcome.

Hobbesian pessimism anticipates a reversion to pre-1945 patterns of multipolar instability and nationalism. While agreeing with some of the diagnosis

Jeff Frieden, Gregory Gause, Joseph Grieco, Ted Hopf, Samuel Huntington, Robert Jervis, Robert Keohane, John Mearsheimer, Helen Milner, Alexander Motyl, David Spiro, Stephen Walt, Stephen Van Evera, an anonymous reviewer, and several participants at seminars at Columbia and Harvard Universities provided helpful comments on this article or discussed the ideas leading to it. Gary Sick urged me to write them down.

Jack Snyder is Associate Professor in the Political Science department at Columbia University.

This is a revised version of an article in *International Security*, Spring 1990 (Vol. 14, No. 4)
© 1990 by the President and Fellows of Harvard College and of the Massachusetts Institute of Technology.

1. The best treatment is John Lewis Gaddis, "The Long Peace: Elements of Stability in the Postwar International System," *International Security*, Vol. 10, No. 4 (Spring 1986), pp. 99–142, reprinted in this volume, pp. 1–44.
2. For background on East European developments in 1989, see William E. Griffith, ed., *Central and Eastern Europe: The Opening Curtain?* (Boulder, Colo.: Westview, 1989). See also Mark Kramer, "Beyond the Brezhnev Doctrine: A New Era in Soviet-East European Relations?" *International Security*, Vol. 14, No. 3 (Winter 1989–90), pp. 25–67.

International Security, Winter 1990/91 (Vol. 15, No. 3)
© 1990 by the President and Fellows of Harvard College and of the Massachusetts Institute of Technology.

of Hobbesian pessimisim, I question its policy prescriptions of shoring up the Cold War *status quo ante* and, if that fails, keeping at arm's length from the impending East European maelstrom.

As an alternative to these solutions, I explore a third view that is conditionally optimistic: neo-liberal institutionalism prescribes the implantation of cooperative international institutions as an antidote to the consequences of Hobbesian anarchy.[3]

The Soviet Union and Eastern Europe are facing the classic problem that Samuel Huntington described in *Political Order in Changing Societies*: a gap between booming political participation and ineffectual political institutions. In Huntington's analysis, this gap is typically filled by the pernicious pattern of "praetorian" politics. "In a praetorian system," says Huntington:

social forces confront each other nakedly; no political institutions, no corps of professional political leaders are recognized or accepted as the legitimate intermediaries to moderate group conflict. Equally important, no agreement exists among the groups as to the legitimate and authoritative methods for resolving conflicts. . . . Each group employs means which reflect its peculiar nature and capabilities. The wealthy bribe; students riot; workers strike; mobs demonstrate; and the military coup.[4]

Other studies of praetorian societies add that nationalist demagogy becomes a common political instrument to advance group interests and to help unstable governments rule.[5]

Praetorian societies such as Germany and Japan have accounted for most of this century's international security problems among the great powers.[6]

---

3. These three viewpoints do not precisely reflect the views of any particular author. Rather, in sketching each view, I have taken the arguments of several theorists and commentators on current events, to present a logically coherent view of their underlying principles.

4. Samuel P. Huntington, *Political Order in Changing Societies* (New Haven: Yale University Press, 1968), p. 196. Philip Roeder, "Modernization and Participation in the Leninist Developmental Strategy," *American Political Science Review*, Vol. 83, No. 3 (September 1989), pp. 859–884, also invokes Huntington in analyzing current Soviet developments.

5. Myron Weiner, "The Macedonian Syndrome: An Historical Model of International Relations and Political Development," *World Politics*, Vol. 23, No. 4 (July 1971), pp. 665–683, examines praetorian-type states from this aspect. Huntington, *Political Order*, pp. 304–305, writes about nationalism as a response to foreign domination.

6. The Nazi period was not praetorian in my use of the term, since central state authority dominated parochial interests, but the foreign policy ideology that spurred Hitler's expansionism was an outgrowth of earlier praetorian periods. It developed from ideas that flourished in the political competition among imperialist, militarist, and protectionist groups in the Wilhelmine era. See Woodruff Smith, *The Ideological Origins of Nazi Imperialism* (New York: Oxford University Press, 1986). More generally, arguments about the international aggressiveness of praetorian regimes dominated by imperialist elite coalitions are developed in Jack Snyder, *Myths of Empire: Domestic Politics and Strategic Ideology* (Ithaca: Cornell University Press, forthcoming).

In both cases, weak democratic institutions were unable to channel the exploding energies of increasing mass political participation in constructive directions. Instead, elite groups interested in militarism, protectionism, and imperialism used nationalist appeals to recruit mass backing for their parochial ends. Consequently, the Western democracies have a powerful incentive to head off the emergence of more states of this type, especially in the Soviet Union but also in Eastern Europe.

One possible solution to the contemporary dangers signaled by Huntington's model would be to recruit reformist Eastern regimes into the West's already well-developed supra-national political order, especially the European Community.[7] As in the cases of Spain and Greece, this would create incentives for the emergence of liberal rather than praetorian political patterns, as well as a ready-made institutional framework for acting on those incentives.[8]

In this article, I evaluate the competing policy prescriptions of these three views of change in the European order: "end of history" optimism, Hobbesian realism, and neo-liberal institutionalism.

Focusing on the latter, I argue that the changing European political order requires that the field of international security studies enrich its rather limited repertoire of Hobbesian realist theories with borrowings from the fields of comparative politics and international political economy. I lay out a theoretical scheme that will help focus the questions that policy advocates ought to address. I conclude that a strategy of international institution-building might be able to avert "the war of all against all" that the Hobbesian pessimists see looming on the horizon in Central and Eastern Europe.

Liberal End-of-History Optimism

Liberal optimism anticipates that the erosion of the bipolar division of Europe will make the European political order more peaceful. The Cold War division

---

7. Arguing for this policy, although not linking it to Huntington's analysis, is Robert D. Hormats, "Redefining Europe and the Atlantic Link," *Foreign Affairs*, Vol. 68, No. 4 (Fall 1989), pp. 71–91. Anne-Marie Burley, "The Once and Future German Question," *Foreign Affairs*, Vol. 68, No. 5 (Winter 1989–90), pp. 65–83, esp. 66, 70–73, notes that this sort of conception was the conventional wisdom in mainstream West German political circles for most of the 1980s.
8. On the lure of EC membership as a factor promoting the democratic political outcome in Spain, see Edward Malefakis, "Spain and Its Francoist Heritage," in John H. Herz, ed., *From Dictatorship to Democracy* (Westport, Conn.: Greenwood, 1982), pp. 217–219; and Mary Barker Cascallar, "International Influences in the Transition to Democracy in Spain" (unpub. ms., Columbia University, Spring 1988).

of the continent has been, in this view, an inherently tense, war-prone situation. The imposition of illegitimate regimes in Europe's Eastern half has been a cause of political frustration and potential violent conflict. If these illegitimate Communist regimes in Eastern Europe and the Soviet Union are replaced by liberal, market-oriented, democratic regimes, neither internal nor international bloodshed is likely. As the historical record shows, liberal democratic regimes do not fight wars against each other.[9] Insofar as the boom in mass political participation and free speech in the Soviet bloc is a harbinger of democracy, it will also bring a more peaceful international order along with it.

Some might think that this outcome is already all-but-achieved, due to the intellectual discrediting of Marxism-Leninism and the impending victory of liberal ideology throughout the developed world.[10] Others might think that the West should help along this "ending of history" by a strategy of fomenting liberal change in the Communist bloc. To promote such developments, the West should, in this view, use whatever leverage it has, short of military intervention, to roll back Soviet influence and to strengthen liberal, democratic, capitalist forces in the East European countries. No attempt should be made, in this view, to mitigate Gorbachev's fear of "exporting capitalism."[11] Economic aid should be targeted on strengthening the private sector. Trade and financial concessions should be conditional on movement toward a multi-party, market model.[12] Arms control should aim at removing Soviet troops from Eastern Europe. Liberal ideological rhetoric should be used to undermine the social support for what is left of Communist authority in Eastern Europe and even in the Soviet Baltic republics. Some elements of current American policy embody this thinking, such as targeting economic

---

9. On this point, see Michael Doyle, "Liberalism and World Politics," *American Political Science Review*, Vol. 80, No. 4 (December 1986), pp. 1151–1169; Doyle, "Kant, Liberal Legacies, and Foreign Affairs," *Philosophy and Public Affairs*, Vol. 12, No. 3 (Summer 1983), pp. 205–235, and Part II of that article in No. 4 (Fall 1983), pp. 323–353. Also relevant is John Mueller, *Retreat from Doomsday? The Obsolescence of Major War* (New York: Basic Books, 1989), and Jack S. Levy, "Domestic Politics and War," *Journal of Interdisciplinary History*, Vol. 43, No. 4 (Spring 1988), pp. 653–673.

10. Francis Fukuyama, "The End of History?" *The National Interest*, No. 16 (Summer 1989), pp. 3–18. It should be pointed out that Fukuyama is neither an unvarnished liberal nor an optimist, since he expresses some regret over the universal victory of liberal ideology (p. 18).

11. Gorbachev, quoted in the *New York Times*, November 15, 1989, p. 1. For this kind of liberal roll-back argument, see "Z" [pseud.], "To the Stalin Mausoleum," *Daedalus*, Vol. 119, No. 1 (Winter 1990), pp. 295–344.

12. See Mark Palmer, "U.S. and Western Policy—New Opportunities for Action," in Griffith, ed., *Central and Eastern Europe*, pp. 388–400.

aid to the private sector in Poland and Hungary and jawboning in favor of market-oriented pluralism.

In short, the plausibility of liberal end-of-history optimism rests on two assumptions: first, that when states are well-ordered internally, they make for a good international order;[13] and second, that states naturally become well-ordered when unnatural, illegitimate oppressors are banished. Such sanguine assumptions are challenged, in different ways, by Hobbesian pessimism and by the premises of a strategy of neo-liberal institution-building.

Hobbesian Pessimism

The currently prevailing Realist theory of international politics holds that the bipolar stalemate between the two superpowers is the most stable possible power configuration, given the realities of an anarchic international system.[14] This brand of Realism anticipates that the waning of Soviet power and the erosion of the bipolar division of Europe are likely to lead to the breakup of NATO, the reunification of Germany, and the consequent emergence of an unstable, multipolar balance-of-power system. As a result, major war may come again for the same reasons it came in 1914 and 1939, through the uncertain workings of the multipolar balancing process.[15] Likewise, the balance-of-power policies of small East European states, released from the grip of Soviet hegemony, may help catalyze war among the great powers, as it did before the First World War.[16]

---

13. For the seminal critique of this kind of "second image" theory of war and peace, see Kenneth Waltz, *Man, the State, and War* (New York: Columbia University Press, 1959).
14. Kenneth Waltz, *Theory of International Politics* (Reading, Mass.: Addison-Wesley, 1979). In the following discussion, I use the word "anarchy" when I mean the lack of a central authority to adjudicate disputes between competitors; I use "disorder" or "chaos" to describe the results of anarchic political conflict. On conceptual confusion in the use of the term "anarchy", see Helen Milner, "Anarchy and Interdependence," in Robert Art and Robert Jervis, eds. *International Politics*, (New York: Harper Collins, forthcoming).
15. Thomas Christensen and Jack Snyder, "Chain Gangs and Passed Bucks: Predicting Alliance Patterns in Multipolarity," *International Organization*, Vol. 44, No. 2 (Spring 1990), pp. 137–168, present a discussion of the pathologies of multipolar balancing in these cases that builds on, but revises Waltz's basic insights.
16. Most of the points in this paragraph were discussed by John Mearsheimer in presentations to meetings in Chicago and Princeton in the spring and summer, 1989, and in "The Future of Europe," a paper prepared for the Flagstaff Conference at Ditchley Park, England, in February 1990; published in revised form as "Back to the Future: Instability in Europe After the Cold War," *International Security*, Vol. 15, No. 1 (Summer 1990), pp. 5–56, and reprinted in this volume. See also Stephen M. Walt, "The Case for Finite Containment: Analyzing U.S. Grand Strategy,"

Not only recent scholarship, but some high Bush administration officials seem to hold to this theory. Deputy Secretary of State Lawrence Eagleburger has noted that "we are moving into, or I should say back into—for such has been the nature of international affairs since time immemorial—a world in which power and influence is diffused among a multiplicity of states." This multipolar world, he continues, is not "necessarily going to be a safer place than the Cold War era from which we are emerging. . . . For all its risks and uncertainties, the Cold War was characterized by a remarkably stable and predictable set of relations among the great powers. A brief look at the history books will tell us that we cannot say as much about the period leading from the birth of the European nation states up through the outbreak of the Second World War."[17]

However, if the anarchic international setting were the only problem, Hobbesian thinking might not necessarily lead to such pessimistic conclusions. Modern Realist thinking includes the idea that the perverse consequences of international anarchy can be mitigated by arms control measures that make states more secure by limiting offensive military capabilities. Though this is harder to contrive in multipolar settings, solutions could be found if international insecurity were really the major, sufficient cause of war.[18]

International Security, Vol. 14, No. 1 (Summer 1989), pp. 5–49, esp. 39–40. Walt and Mearsheimer have been very helpful in discussing with me the implications of Realist theory for the changing situation in Europe. Their ideas served as background, helping me to write this section. However, for the direction in which I have developed these ideas, they bear no responsibility. The label "Hobbesian pessimist" is mine, not theirs. Waltz says that his ideas on anarchy were inspired by Rousseau, not Hobbes. To my knowledge, Waltz has not taken a position on the current European changes.

17. Eagleburger speech at Georgetown University, September 13, 1989, reported in the *New York Times*, September 16, 1989, pp. 1, 6. Subsequent statements by President Bush and Secretary of State Baker appear to have rejected this view, however, and Eagleburger has aligned his own subsequent statements with theirs. Andrew Rosenthal, "U.S. Finds Relief in Stand by Gorbachev on the East," *New York Times*, November 16, 1989, p. 21. See also Samuel Huntington, "No Exit: The Errors of Endism," *The National Interest*, No. 17 (Fall 1989), pp. 3–11, for a critique of end-of-history optimism.

18. One difficulty with solving the security dilemma through arms control in multipolarity is that allies arrayed in the typical multipolar checkerboard pattern need offensive capabilities to honor their alliance commitments. One solution would be a truly radical adjustment of force postures in a defensive direction, such that every state could be secure against any combination of contiguous states without the assistance of non-contiguous allies. For a discussion of the general problem, see Stephen Van Evera, "Offense, Defense, and Strategy: When Is Offense Best?" paper presented to the annual meeting of the American Political Science Association, Chicago, 1987. The seminal theoretical work on the security dilemma is Robert Jervis, "Cooperation under the Security Dilemma," *World Politics* Vol. 30, No. 2 (January 1978), pp. 167–214.

However, Hobbesian pessimism stems not only from the consequences of international anarchy, but from the effects of international military competition on the domestic political order and from the anarchic nature of domestic political competition itself. Unlike liberal optimism, Hobbesian pessimism sees domestic order not as arising from a harmonious society but as imposed by a coercive state organization—a "Leviathan," in Hobbes's term. The state simultaneously struggles to defend itself against other states, to maintain its monopoly of violence against would-be domestic opponents, and to extract resources from its society for both purposes.

In order to facilitate the achievement of these tasks, the state relies above all on powerful military bureaucracies and nationalist mythmaking.[19] These twin pillars of the modern state form a domestic order that is prone to nationalistic international aggression. It is not only, as Charles Tilly put it, that "war made the state and the state made war."[20] Beyond this, the state, to carry out its triple tasks of external defense, monopolizing domestic violence, and extracting social resources for these state purposes, must have nationalistic myths, which make war more likely.[21] Eagleburger recognized the danger that multipolar international anarchy will promote nationalism, remarking that "the process of reform in the Soviet bloc and the relaxation of Soviet control over Eastern Europe are bringing long-suppressed ethnic antagonisms and national rivalries to the surface, and putting the German question back on the international agenda."[22]

Some Realists acknowledge that liberal states sometimes find ways to mitigate the inherently nationalistic tendencies of the modern state, for example, by allowing detailed public scrutiny of the state's conduct of foreign affairs and creating a free marketplace of ideas to evaluate policy.[23] Still, this is the exception rather than the rule. The nature of states in their anarchical setting works against it, in the Hobbesian view. The bipolar post-1945 stale-

---

19. Exploring these issues is Stephen Van Evera, "Causes of War" (Ph.D. dissertation, University of California, Berkeley 1984).
20. Charles Tilly, "Reflections on the History of European State-making," in Tilly, ed., *The Formation of National States in Western Europe* (Princeton: Princeton University Press, 1975), p. 42.
21. For a discussion of the nexus among war, the state, and nationalist myths, see Van Evera, "Causes of War." See also Stephen Walt, "The Foreign Policy of Revolutionary States," paper presented to the annual meeting of the American Political Science Association, Chicago, 1987, who quotes Tilly in this connection.
22. *New York Times*, September 16, 1989, p. 6. See also Kramer, "Beyond the Brezhnev Doctrine," pp. 51–54.
23. Van Evera, "Causes of War," notes that societies with open policy debates are more able to contain nationalist mythmaking by state organizations.

mate has created unusual international circumstances, which have mitigated the exigencies of international anarchy for West European societies, allowing the luxury of the welfare state and widespread anti-war ideology. But to the extent that these benign domestic conditions may in part be consequences of the bipolar stalemate, a shift in international structure may undermine them.[24]

Likewise, Hobbesians view as spurious the connection between economic interdependence among the capitalist powers and the post-war peace. The former does not cause the latter; rather, both are caused by the bipolar stalemate, according to the Realist view.[25] Once the power structure changes, the vulnerabilities inherent in economic interdependence are likely to be a cause of conflict, not of harmony. Extending economic interdependence throughout a new "European Common Home" would, from this point of view, only exacerbate international tensions.[26] Interwar Japan, for example, might have lived much more harmoniously with its neighbors if its fate had not been shaped by its economic dependence on them.

In short, Hobbesian pessimism sees political order as deriving not from a harmony of interests but from a hegemony that quashes the disorder inherent in political anarchy. Tight co-hegemonic leadership in a bipolar division of Europe is the best that can be hoped for in a Hobbesian world.

Based on these theoretical underpinnings, Hobbesian pessimism can only expect the worst as a result of the erosion of the bipolar order. The structural deformities of multipolarity will mean that small disturbances will reverberate into major clashes, and such disturbances are almost certain to result from the militarism and nationalism fostered by multipolar insecurity.

Nationalist tendencies may have been tamed in welfare-state Western Europe, but they are nevertheless more likely to emerge in the East. In the anarchic conditions prevailing in the reforming states of Eastern Europe, social groups are likely to use nationalist appeals to establish their right to seize control of an existing state or to create a new state. Once they achieve

---

24. John Mearsheimer, "The Future of Europe," makes this point.
25. Waltz, *Theory of International Politics*, p. 71. For an argument that there is a connection between interdependence and peaceful foreign policy, see Edward L. Morse, "The Transformation of Foreign Policies: Modernization, Interdependence, and Externalization," *World Politics*, Vol. 22, No. 3 (April 1970), pp. 371–392.
26. Stephen Walt discusses the points in this paragraph in "Preserving Peace in Europe: The Case for the Status Quo," a paper presented to a conference on U.S.-Soviet relations sponsored by the International Research and Exchanges Board (IREX) in Princeton, New Jersey, August 1989.

power, they will find nationalism useful in strengthening state control over society.

Such Hobbesian worries are not without foundation. Conflict-causing nationalism is already proving an indispensable tool for seizing and maintaining power in the increasingly pluralistic former Soviet bloc.[27] In Soviet Azerbaijan, local intellectuals recently used their comparative advantage in propaganda to exacerbate ethnic feeling against Armenia, and succeeded in placing themselves at the head of a popular nationalist movement. Exploiting the power this confers on them, these intellectuals have successfully bargained with Moscow so that they have virtually supplanted the Communist Party as the governing institution of Azerbaijan. Though Moscow has rejected their plea to be allowed to set up a separate Azerbaijani army, the mass movement they head seems to be creating one *de facto*.[28]

Several policy prescriptions follow from Hobbesian assumptions: If at all possible, the West should try to maintain the bipolar order intact, avoid policies that weaken the Soviet Union's resource base, and refrain from undercutting what remains of the Soviet position in Eastern Europe and the Baltic.

But if this is not possible, the West should try to isolate the relatively healthy Western half of the European order, where the effects of anarchy have been partially mitigated, and nationalism and militarism controlled, from Europe's increasingly volatile Eastern half. The West should not tinker with NATO and the European Community in pursuit of the will-o'-the-wisp of the European Common Home; this would only embroil the West in the insoluble troubles of the East. The prospects for liberal change in the East—and the West's stake in such changes—should not be oversold to Western publics. The West must continue to look to nuclear deterrence to maintain the peace, as a last resort.

But such a quarantine strategy is likely to be difficult to sustain, given the risks and temptations inherent in the emerging multipolar configuration of power. Under Hobbesian assumptions, at any rate, Germany would be ex-

---

27. On the problem of nationalism under conditions of Moscow's declining power, see Zbigniew Brzezinski, "Post-Communist Nationalism," *Foreign Affairs*, Vol. 68, No. 5 (Winter 1989–90), pp. 1–25; and Seweryn Bialer, ed., *Politics, Society, and Nationality inside Gorbachev's Russia* (Boulder: Westview, 1989).

28. Bill Keller, "Nationalists in Azerbaijan Win Big Concessions from Party Chief," *New York Times*, October 13, 1989, pp. 1, 6. For background, see Mirza Michaeli and William Reese, "The Popular Front in Azerbaijan and Its Program," Radio Liberty, *Report on the USSR*, August 25, 1989, pp. 29–32.

pected to watch political developments in the East with a wary eye, to be sensitive to threats that might emerge from the unsettled conditions there, and to intervene diplomatically, if not militarily, to forestall such threats. Germany might in fact choose to play a less interventionist role in Eastern troubles, but if so, Hobbesian assumptions could not explain it.

A more innovative Hobbesian strategy might be to give up the bipolar stalemate as lost, and switch to a Bismarckian strategy of defensive multipolar alliances.[29] For example, France, Britain, and the United States might guarantee the security of a reunited Germany against attack by Russia, while also insuring Russia against aggression by Germany. Likewise, small East European states would be guaranteed security assistance only if they were the party attacked, not if they were the attacker. The Locarno Treaty's two-way guarantee of Germany's Western border might also provide a model for such a strategy.

Such a scheme might be stabilizing, but history and theory point to many pitfalls along that path. Neither Bismarck's defensive alliances nor Locarno lasted very long. In the multipolarity of the interwar period, some states were tempted to ride free, relying on the balancing efforts of others, so defensive alliances lost credibility. Conversely, before 1914 alliance commitments that were originally defensive came to be unconditional, because the power of each major ally was considered essential to maintaining the balance. In such circumstances, as with the German blank check to Austria in 1914, allies had to be supported even if they were the aggressors.[30] Moreover, in checkerboard multipolar alliance patterns, it may be difficult to honor alliance commitments, even defensive ones, without the development of offensive military capabilities and strategies to attack an aggressor in the rear.[31] But such capabilities would exacerbate security fears and undermine the pacific aims of a system of defensive alliances. There is little reason to believe that a strategy of defensive alliances would by itself produce stability. Still, this does not exclude the possibility that in a system moderated by other factors,

---

29. Stephen Van Evera mentions this approach in "The Future of Europe," unpublished ms., November 1989. On the distinction between Bismarck's defensive alliances and the offensive ones that supplanted them, see Stephen Van Evera, "The Cult of the Offensive and the Origins of the First World War," *International Security*, Vol. 9, No. 1 (Summer 1984), pp. 96–103.
30. Waltz, *Theory of International Politics*, pp. 166–169; Christensen and Snyder, "Chain Gangs and Passed Bucks."
31. Van Evera, "When Is Offense Best?"; and Scott Sagan, "1914 Revisited: Allies, Offense, and Instability," *International Security*, Vol. 11, No. 2 (Fall 1986), pp. 151–176.

such as benign patterns of domestic politics, defensive alliances might make a beneficial contribution.

Finally, reliance on a multipolar nuclear stand-off to insure stability also seems problematic. First, the Soviet Union's nuclear arsenal will not protect it from the real challenges to its integrity as a state: economic colonization of its periphery by more advanced powers, and ethnic separatism. Second, most of the newly emerging power centers, including Germany, will not have nuclear weapons. In light of the nuclear allergy which currently dominates European thinking, decisions to acquire nuclear weapons might well take place only *after* a severe worsening of international tension made them seem necessary. In that context, the uneven proliferation of nascent, vulnerable nuclear forces could be a provocation to war, not a deterrent against it.

The enormity of Hobbesian predictions and the weakness of Hobbesian prescriptions virtually demand asking whether other kinds of measures can be devised to head off such dire developments. If the pressure of international and domestic anarchy is indeed likely to foster a miscarriage of the balance of power and the spread of militaristic nationalism, then it is natural to ask whether steps can be taken to mitigate this anarchic pressure. Neoliberal institution-building takes up this issue.

Neo-liberal Institutionalism

Neo-liberal institution-building offers a more constructive perspective on the creation of a stable political order in Europe. This approach assumes that the Hobbesian condition can be mitigated by an institutional structure that provides legitimate and effective channels for reconciling conflicting interests. Whereas liberal optimism sees political order as arising spontaneously from a harmony of interests, and Hobbesian pessimism sees it as imposed by hegemonic power, neo-liberal institutionalism sees it as arising from organized procedures for articulating interests and settling conflicts among them.[32]

When institutions are strong, there is order; the effects of anarchy are mitigated. When institutions are weak, there is disorder; politics are marked

---

32. Differentiating betweeen neo-liberal institutionalism and classical liberalism is Robert Keohane, *International Institutions and State Power* (Boulder, Colo.: Westview, 1989), pp. 10–11.

by the perverse effects of anarchy.[33] Thus, from this perspective, the problem of creating a new European security order to supplant that of the bipolar stalemate is above all a problem of building institutions. Institutionalist theories borrowed form the fields of comparative politics and international political economy may help illuminate the task ahead.

The classic statement of the institutionalist understanding of political order is Samuel Huntington's *Political Order in Changing Societies*. Huntington is concerned with the consequences for political order when intense political demands are advanced by a mobilized society, but governing institutions are too weak to reconcile those competing claims effectively. In particular, he examines the disorder that emerges in a modernizing society when industrialization, urbanization, and expanding literacy lead to an expansion of political demands, which the traditional political institutions of the *ancien regime* cannot process efficiently and authoritatively.[34]

In such circumstances, politics becomes disordered. Groups and individuals cannot defend their interests by appealing to legitimate governing institutions and orderly procedures for resolving conflicts, because such channels are unavailable. As a result, narrow groups form to defend their parochial interests through self-help, including direct violent action, as in any anarchical environment. Social groups like students and organized labor may take to the streets or use other means of direct, coercive action, like political strikes, to advance their selfish parochial interests. Government institutions, unable to create order and pursue the state's interests on the basis of legitimate authority, also act as self-interested, coercive groups. The military, because the dominant means of violent coercion lie in its hands, tends to play a central role in this pattern of "praetorian" politics. As Huntington quotes Hobbes, "when nothing else is turned up, clubs are trumps."[35]

In praetorian societies the problem is not in a lack of organization, but in the character of the institutions that are well organized. Various parochial interests—e.g., the military and the trade unions—may be well-organized. But institutions for aggregating competing interests—e.g., elected

---

33. Two influential studies embodying this type of analysis are Stephen Krasner, ed., *International Regimes* (Ithaca: Cornell University Press, 1983), first appearing as a special issue of *International Organization*, Vol. 36, No. 2 (Spring 1982), and Robert Keohane, *After Hegemony* (Princeton: Princeton University Press, 1984).
34. Huntington, *Political Order*, chapter 1.
35. Quoted in Ibid., *Political Order*, p. 196; chapter 4 discusses praetorian systems.

representative institutions and mass political parties—are weak and ineffective.[36]

Is this theory relevant to political change in the former Soviet bloc? At first glance, it might appear not. Huntington applied his theory to some historical European states, but primarily to modernizing states in the Third World. Moreover, he thought that Leninist party-states were antidotes to praetorianism, not causes of it.

Huntington wrote in 1968 that the appeal of the Leninist party-state model to newly-modernizing countries was that it would help close the gap between high levels of political participation and low levels of political institutionalization.[37] From the vantage point of two subsequent decades, however, it seems clear that Leninist organization was merely an expedient papering over of that gap, not a permanent, stable solution. The Leninist variety of "participation" was too perfunctory and manipulated to serve the real function of channeling and integrating social demands. Likewise, Leninist party-state institutions tended to ossify, thus violating Huntington's dictum that successful institutions must be not just strong, but flexible. Even in the Soviet bloc itself, let alone the Third World, such party-states have failed to meet the challenge of creating a legitimate order.[38]

But will the collapse of Leninist orders produce a praetorian pattern of politics, just as the collapse of institutionally weak traditional political orders often did? Obviously, the situations are not identical. The problem of replacing discredited Leninist institutions is not necessarily the same as the problem of creating strong, diversified, modern governing institutions from scratch in the institutional poverty of a traditional society.

On the other hand, many of the elements of Huntington's praetorian pattern seem present in former Soviet bloc states today. In a political environment where governmental legitimacy is weak, the military, organized labor, and intellectuals—indeed almost all the same actors that Huntington found in his examples of praetorian societies—could be among the players taking direct action in defense of their threatened interests.[39]

---

36. Huntington, *Political Order*, chapter 4, can be read this way.
37. Huntington, Ibid., pp. 334–343, esp. 340.
38. On the failure of Leninist regimes to institutionalize participation successfully, see Roeder, "Modernization and Participation," pp. 859–872. For additional background, see Seweryn Bialer, "Gorbachev's Program of Change," and other essays in Seweryn Bialer and Michael Mandelbaum, eds., *Gorbachev's Russia and American Foreign Policy* (Boulder, Colo.: Westview, 1987).
39. Offering country-by-country analyses of such social forces are Griffith, *Central and Eastern*

The main potential difference between collapsing Leninist states and rising traditional ones is that enough of the institutional structure from the Communist period might remain to allow a quicker reestablishment of political order than a traditional society could manage. But this could be part of the problem, rather than the solution, if the bureaucratic institutions left over from Communist rule act as self-regarding interest groups. In that case, the praetorian pattern would only be reinforced.

Huntington sees the praetorian society as only one model of domestic politics. The Hobbesian condition is not universal in domestic politics. Advanced democracies, says Huntington, have developed strong, flexible institutions that allow groups and individuals to articulate and defend their interests through orderly, universally accepted channels. This pattern he calls the civic polity.[40] By implication, if the states of the former Soviet bloc succeed in creating democratic institutions of this type, the praetorian pattern can be avoided. In this sense, Huntington's theory of the civic polity might be said to agree with the liberal optimists, though it would be more skeptical about the ease of achieving this favorable outcome.

THREE INSTITUTIONALIST SETTINGS FOR PLURALIST POLITICS

Within the neo-liberal institutional approach, three patterns of pluralistic politics—civic democracy, pretorianism, and corporatism—can be used to analyze the future of the former Soviet bloc. Each offers a description of how interests are aggregated in pluralistic politics; their differences are based in part on differing assumptions about the institutional context of political action.

CIVIC DEMOCRACY. In a civic democracy, well-institutionalized electoral competition drives politicians to compete for the favor of the average voter. In this context, most politicians tend to promise similar, middle-of-the-road policies that appeal to moderate segments of public opinion, rather than to

---

Europe, chapters 6, 8–13; J. F. Brown, *Eastern Europe and Communist Rule* (Durham, N.C.: Duke University Press, 1988); and the special issue of *International Organization,* Vol. 40, No. 2 (Spring 1986), on "Power, Purpose, and Collective Choice: Economic Strategy in Socialist States," edited by Ellen Comisso and Laura Tyson. The issue of *International Organization* addresses in particular the effect of changes in the international economic environment on the economic policies and domestic politics of East European states.

40. For Huntington's discussion of the civic polity and the the contrast with praetorianism, see Huntington, *Political Order,* pp. 78–92.

ideological extremes. Pandering to narrow interest groups is politically un-
advisable if it entails large costs to the broad electorate.[41]

As a result, costly, reckless foreign policies usually lose out in electoral
competition in a well-institutionalized democracy, at least in the long run.
Mature democracies have been reasonably good at retrenching from strategic
overextension and other self-defeating aggressive behavior, because such
policies threaten the interests of prudent average voters.[42] Moreover, well-
developed democratic institutions normally foster a relatively open marketplace of ideas, so that average voters have access to the information and
analysis that they need to calculate their interests at least roughly.[43] This
does not always work smoothly, but in comparative terms mature democracies have been much better than the German and Japanese praetorian states
at avoiding strategic disasters.

PRAETORIANISM. In the praetorian pattern, competing groups face each
other nakedly, their struggle unmediated by any effective institutional framework. Compact groups with intense preferences—e.g., the military or industrialists—are more likely to organize politically than are large groups
with diffuse interests, like average voters. As a result national policy—
both foreign and domestic—can be captured by narrow interest groups, who
use their disproportionate influence to extract benefits from and pass
costs on to unorganized sectors of society, like consumers and taxpayers.
The organized sectors may collude in a "logroll" that exploits the unorganized
sectors, or they may try to exploit both the unorganized sectors and each
other.[44]

---

41. See Anthony Downs, *An Economic Theory of Democracy* (New York: Harper, 1959). Benjamin
I. Page, *Choices and Echoes in Presidential Elections* (Chicago: University of Chicago Press, 1978),
presents tests of and modifications to Downs's basic argument.
42. Downs himself does not make this deduction from his theory. For theoretical and empirical
support for it, see Jack Snyder, *Myths of Empire.* I do not mean to argue that democracies are
always pacific or that systems with competitive elections invariably produce moderate, optimal
policies. Rather, I argue merely that Downs's reasoning helps to explain why democracies have
been good strategic learners who have avoided the extreme forms of self-defeating expansionism
characteristic of the praetorian great powers. Paul Kennedy's essays on "The Tradition of
Appeasement in British Foreign Policy, 1865–1939," and "Why Did the British Empire Last So
Long?", in Kennedy, *Strategy and Diplomacy, 1870–1945* (London: Allen & Unwin, 1983), Chaps.
1 and 8, might be read with this in view.
43. I thank Stephen Van Evera for discussion of this point.
44. See Mancur Olson, *The Rise and Decline of Nations* (New Haven: Yale University Press, 1982),
on political systems dominated by selfish interest groups; and Olson, *The Logic of Collective Action*
(Cambridge: Harvard University Press, 1965) for the underlying theory. Olson applies his theory
primarily to advanced democracies, not to the undemocratic pluralistic societies that Huntington
labels praetorian, but Olson's hypotheses should hold even more strongly in such cases, where

When praetorian patterns hold, foreign policy can be dominated by the interests of narrow military, ideological, economic, or colonial lobbies, who may benefit from reckless policies while they pass their costs on to the taxpayers. In a praetorian system, mass interests that suffer from such policies will lack adequate means of redress at the polls.[45]

DEMOCRATIC CORPORATISM. In the third pattern, democratic corporatism, an overarching coalition may encompass the bulk of the organized interests in the whole society. Because the deals brokered within this encompassing umbrella must aggregate a broad spectrum of society's interests, the power of narrower interest groups is held in check.[46] Such corporatist arrangements are especially common in small European states, who use corporatist brokerage to negotiate the domestic terms of adjusting to the rigors of the international market.[47] Democratic corporatist regimes have typically shunned excessive nationalism and pursued benign foreign policies.

Emerging Patterns of Pluralism in the Former Soviet Bloc

Any of these three patterns may emerge in the states of the former Soviet bloc. Civic or corporatist democracy is more likely in the northern tier of Eastern Europe (Poland, Hungary, and Czechoslovakia) than in the Soviet Union.

On the one hand, these societies seem rife with self-seeking interest groups, many of them the detritus of the period of Leninist rule. Workers and managers in uncompetitive heavy industry, the military, and Communist Party apparatchiks are compact groups, each with a strong incentive for political action in defense of its threatened corporate interests. Nationalist groups and ethnic minorities are also likely candidates for narrowly self-interested behavior, like the Baltic reformers who press their parochial agenda at the expense of the collective interest in *perestroika's* success throughout the Soviet Union. Indeed varied groups are rapidly organizing to push their

---

diffuse interests lack electoral power to check self-interested compact groups. On bargaining among organized interest groups, see Olson, *Rise and Decline*, p. 37.

45. Olson does not discuss these implications of his argument for foreign policy. I make those deductions and support them with historical evidence in *Myths of Empire*.

46. Olson, *Rise and Decline*, pp. 47–53.

47. Peter Katzenstein, *Small States in World Markets* (Ithaca: Cornell University Press, 1985), p. 24 and *passim*.

special interests: wildcat strike committees in Soviet heavy industry, trade unions in the Soviet military,[48] the Great Russian *Rossiya* bloc in the Supreme Soviet, and various ethnic "national fronts."[49]

On the other hand, reforming Soviet bloc states are also creating competitive electoral institutions which should help take power away from compact interest groups and give it to the average voter. A well-developed electoral system with well-developed political parties should prevent the emergence of praetorian politics, according to Huntington's logic.

The problem is that the electoral systems emerging in reformist Soviet bloc countries have a truncated quality that is closer to the Wilhelmine German system than to the modern civic polity. The Wilhelmine precedent offers a sobering example of the consequences of a popularly elected legislature which is not directly responsible for policymaking.[50] The Reichstag, elected on the basis of universal manhood suffrage, had authority to raise taxes, approve budgets, and approve the conscription of soldiers, but it had no power to topple government ministers, who were selected by the Kaiser. Forming governments in the Wilhelmine Reich meant logrolling among the members of the uneasy coalition of "iron and rye," including aristocratic Junker landowners, Ruhr heavy industrialists, Prussian bureaucrats, the army, and the navy. But getting government policies funded meant also coopting swing votes in the Reichstag. For example, to win votes for the expansion of the fleet, the Chancellor paid off the Center Party with concessions to the narrow concerns of the Catholics who were that party's sole constituency. In short, the Wilhelmine pattern of elite-managed, truncated democracy is more likely to yield a praetorian politics of interest-group logrolling than a civic politics dominated by the diffuse, moderate interests of the average voter.[51]

A similar pattern may be unfolding in some of the truncated democracies in the former Soviet bloc. Despite universal suffrage, contested elections,

---

48. "Soviet Army Officers Plan to Create Trade Union," Radio Free Europe / Radio Liberty *Daily Report*, October 18, 1989; Bill Keller, "Soviet Military Officers Pressing for Changes and a Trade Union," *New York Times*, October 22, 1989, pp. 1, 16.

49. On the *Rossiya* bloc, Esther B. Fein, "Soviet Legislature Votes to Abolish Official Seats," *New York Times*, October 25, 1989, p. 13. On the national fronts, see Radio Liberty, *Report on the Soviet Union*, August 25, September 15, and October 6, 1989.

50. David Blackbourn, *Populists and Patricians* (London: Allen and Unwin, 1987), pp. 102, 161–162, 190, and esp. 211.

51. See Eckart Kehr, *Economic Interest, Militarism, and Foreign Policy* (Berkeley: University of California, 1977), esp. 272–276; and the chapter on Germany in Jack Snyder, *Myths of Empire*.

and diverse representation in a national parliament, the average voter exercises only an oblique influence on state policy in systems like that of Poland, let alone the Soviet Union's, for two reasons.

First, in the Soviet case, safe seats for party apparatchiks and members of conservative nationalist organizations like the Great Russian writers' union function like "rotten boroughs," skewing the outcome away from average voter preferences for the benefit of privileged organized groups. Although the Soviets intend to eliminate the safe seats, Party manipulation of the local nominating and campaigning process may still produce a group of delegates to the Congress of People's Deputies that disproportionately favors conservative coalitions; so will Party manipulation of the Congress itself, which acts as a further filter in selecting Supreme Soviet legislators.[52]

But the second and more important flaw is that the resulting elected body has limited authority over policy and over the composition of the governing cabinet. In Poland, the defense bureaucracy and the unelected president are now being brought under electoral control. In the Soviet Union the main holders of executive power in all issue areas are only loosely accountable to the Supreme Soviet, although that body has rejected some proposed ministers and is establishing a veneer of legislative oversight even in the military field.[53]

It could be argued that Poland is nearing the threshold of responsible party government, with the holders of real power directly accountable to fully enfranchised voters. In this view, Poland already passed through a praetorian period in the early 1980s, during which a military dictator aligned himself with conservative industrial and governing elites against a trade union aligned with militant intellectuals. Indeed, this is a common pattern in Huntington's praetorian systems.[54] But now the emergence of real electoral institutions may give Solidarity a strong incentive to act like a Western political party, appealing to the average voters' interest in expanding the economic pie, rather than like a parochial trade union, appealing to the narrow instincts

---

52. Fein, "Soviet Legislature," p. 13.

53. Jack Snyder and Andrei Kortunov, "French Syndrome on Soviet Soil?" *New Times* (Moscow), No. 44 (October 27, 1989), pp. 18–20, offer a critical discussion of current Soviet attempts to institutionalize civilian control of the military. David Holloway, "State, Society, and the Military under Gorbachev," *International Security*, Vol. 14, No. 3 (Winter 1989–90), pp. 5–24, stresses the progress that has been made in asserting democratic control over Soviet military policy.

54. Huntington, *Political Order*, p. 214, citing the Chilean case, and chapter 4, *passim*.

of organized labor.[55] At present, Solidarity is adopting market-oriented policies, which should further undercut the power of Poland's protected heavy industries, while reducing subsidies, which would retain the hothouse environment of the planned economy. Only if the new system works will the military's interest in political intervention to prevent disorder wane. If so, the praetorian pattern may be averted.

In Hungary, elements of all three patterns—democratic, praetorian, and corporatist—can be discerned in recent events. Since the spring of 1989, all major constitutional and economic questions have been the subject of detailed bargaining; representatives of the government, the main political parties, and organized labor have sat down together for "roundtable" discussions.[56] If this pattern holds, Hungary may quickly take the route of the small corporatist states, like its neighbor Austria.[57]

However, benign corporatist arrangements serving the broad social interest are not the only deals being struck in pluralist Hungary's smoke-filled back rooms. The plan for the early election of a president, concocted through collusion between Communists and conservative nationalists and narrowly defeated in November 1989, smacked of a logroll between parochial interest groups. The Communists (now called Socialists) had hoped that a monopoly on name recognition would insure the victory of their candidate for president, Imre Pozsgay, if the election were held in January 1990 on the basis of direct popular vote. Pozsgay allegedly expected to use the several months before a new legislature would be elected in the spring of 1990 to assert strong presidential control over the state bureaucracy. The Socialists were supported in this plan by the Democratic Forum, a non-socialist party whose members include many conservative nationalists and anti-semites. It is widely believed that the Forum, some of whose members have longstanding ties to the Communist bureaucracy, was offered the premiership as a quid pro quo.[58]

If successful, this scheme would have shifted Hungarian politics toward a praetorian pattern of truncated democracy, not managed by a benign cor-

55. For background, see Roman Stefanowski, "Trade Unions and Politics in Poland," Radio Free Europe Reports, *Situation Report*, Poland, No. 15, October 12, 1989.
56. Radio Free Europe, *Situation Report*, Hungary, No. 10, June 23, 1989.
57. Peter Katzenstein, *Corporatism and Change: Austria, Switzerland, and the Politics of Industry* (Ithaca: Cornell University Press, 1984).
58. David K. Shipler, "Letter from Budapest," *New Yorker*, Nov. 20, 1989, pp. 74–101, esp. 90–91, 97; Henry Kamm, "Hungary Opposition Splits," *New York Times*, November 25, 1989, p. 8; Kamm, "Hungarians Hold First Free Vote in 42 Years," *New York Times*, Nov. 27, 1989, pp. 1, 11. On the Democratic Forum, see also Radio Free Europe, *Situation Report*, Hungary, No. 3, February 24, 1989, pp. 35–6, and No. 5, March 31, 1989, pp. 19–24.

poratism, but manipulated through a narrow marriage of Communist bureaucrats and Hungarian nationalists. The would-be praetorian logroll was defeated, however, through the power of the average voter at the ballot box. The Alliance of Free Democrats, a truly democratic Western-oriented party, demanded a referendum on the plan for a hasty presidential election. Overcoming a Socialist-Forum boycott, the democratic opposition parties generated the necessary minimum turnout needed to delay a presidential vote until the new constitution and legislature are in place.[59] Since then, the power of the average voter has helped move the Democratic Forum to the center of the political spectrum, away from nationalist extremes.

Whether the reforming East European states are over the crucial democratic threshold remains to be seen. The Soviet Union is of course much farther from having a system of real democratic accountability. Praetorian Wilhelmine Germany's truncated democracy may be the model that describes the Soviet future. But civic polity or democratic corporatism may have a better chance to prevail in the smaller states of the Northern tier of Eastern Europe.

International Consequences of Praetorian Politics

The emergence of praetorian societies in Eastern Europe would have grave implications for international politics. Two such societies, Japan and Germany, have been the most egregious disturbers of the peace in this century. In Eastern Europe in the first half of this century, even small powers with praetorian political systems provoked international conflicts, which embroiled the great powers.

Wilhelmine Germany again illustrates why this occurred.[60] Wilhelmine aggressiveness stemmed from two sources. The first source was the terms of the intra-elite logroll. Many of the elite groups had vested interests in policies that embroiled Germany with other powers—e.g., the interests of heavy industry and the navy in fleet construction, the Army's offensive Schlieffen Plan, the Junkers' need for farm tariffs that hurt Russian interests.

---

59. Henry Kamm, "Hungarians Hold First Free Vote."
60. The following discussion of German politics is based on Hans-Ulrich Wehler, *The German Empire, 1871–1918* (Leamington Spa/Dover, N.H.: Berg, 1985); Geoff Eley, *Reshaping the German Right* (New Haven: Yale Univeersity Press, 1980); and ideas developed in the chapter on Germany in Snyder, *Myths of Empire.*

In the praetorian Wilhelmine society, there was neither a strong central authority nor strong accountability to the median voter to constrain these parochial interests and establish strategic priorities. As a result, Germany made too many enemies, and once encircled, tried to break out of that encirclement through aggression.

The second element feeding Wilhelmine aggressiveness was the relationship between the elites and the mass groups suddenly mobilized into German political life in the 1880s and 1890s. This sudden burst of political participation was due in part to the processes of industrialization and urbanization, and in part also to the strategies of elite groups who sought to recruit mass allies against competing elites. Thus, Junker landowners recruited small-holding agrarian populists, while industrial and naval circles used the middle class Navy League to create popular pressure for their pet project. Many of these agricultural and middle class groups had been whipsawed by market forces which had disrupted their traditional economic activities in the late 19th century. Because liberal *laissez faire* had been discredited by its disruption of traditional, regulated markets, these mass groups were not hard to recruit for the elites' illiberal protectionist and imperialist schemes. Added to this volatile mixture was nationalistic propaganda, which the elites used as part of their "social imperialist" strategy for managing the explosion of popular participation in politics.

A similar pattern can also be observed in the history of Eastern Europe's small powers during the first half of the twentieth century. Myron Weiner has noted what he calls the "Macedonian syndrome," in which the weak, modernizing states of Central and Eastern Europe were often captured by ethnic groups, the military, and intellectuals touting nationalist themes as tools for their parochial purposes.[61] Their irredentist nationalism embroiled these states in conflicts with their neighbors, contributing further to the hyper-patriotic cultural atmosphere and the praetorian character of domestic politics. Squabbles among the praetorian East European states gave rise to the familiar multipolar "checkerboard" balance-of-power pattern and triggered interventions by outside great powers. In short, nationalistic, praeto-

---

61. Myron Weiner, "The Macedonian Syndrome: An Historical Model of International Relations and Political Development," *World Politics*, Vol. 23, No. 4 (July 1971), pp. 665–683. Weiner's cases include almost every East European and Balkan state, before either World War I or II.

rian domestic politics both fed and was fed by sharp competition in the anarchical international setting.[62]

Despite Weiner's findings, the broader historical record does not show that praetorian societies necessarily become nationalistic and expansionist. Huntington's instances of praetorianism include many societies that turned their violence strictly inward. Perhaps the East Europeans internationalized their praetorian violence because of the prevalence of ethnic irredenta in their region, an historical pattern which largely persists today.[63] Another difference between Weiner's cases and Huntington's might be the distinctive historical role played by praetorian Germany as a model of belligerence for its smaller East European praetorian neighbors. If so, a well-behaved united Germany might exert a more benign influence on Central and Eastern Europe in the present era.

How likely is it that the Soviet Union will recapitulate the Wilhelmine pattern of domestic and foreign policy, or that Eastern Europe will relive the Macedonian syndrome? Some obvious parallels can be mentioned. The Soviet Union is a state undergoing a huge leap in mass political participation in the context of an authoritarian tradition and a demonstrable de-legitimation of its previous governing institutions. "Traditional" elite groups, in this case the conservative sectors of the Party and the military, have corporate interests that in the past have inclined them toward a conflictual approach to international politics.[64] Labor, ethnic groups, the military, and intellectuals are forming organized groups. Existing institutions, including the Communist government and truncated democratic bodies, are hard pressed to reconcile competing demands of these groups in ways that serve collective rather than parochial interests. The mass populace, moreover, is being mobilized into political life at the same time as it is being threatened with unparalleled economic disruptions due to the introduction of market reforms. Potential or actual ethnic conflicts in the Soviet periphery and between some East

---

62. The best extended treatment of these problems is Joseph Rothschild, *East Central Europe between the Two World Wars* (Seattle: University of Washington Press, 1974).
63. Brzezinski, "Post-Communist Nationalism," p. 3.
64. Jack Snyder, "The Gorbachev Revolution: A Waning of Soviet Expansionism?" *International Security*, Vol. 12, No. 3 (Winter 1987/88), pp. 93–131. Celeste Wallander, "Third-World Conflict in Soviet Military Thought: Does the 'New Thinking' Grow Prematurely Grey?" *World Politics*, Vol. 42, No. 1 (October 1989), pp. 31–63, presents evidence that the Soviet military has manifested such tendencies even after the emergence of "new thinking" among Soviet civilians.

European states may contribute to an international environment where intense nationalism seems the norm and where peace and security cannot be taken for granted.[65]

Gorbachev himself worries that the pluralism unleashed by *perestroika* has the potential to degenerate into a praetorian chaos. Explaining the need to maintain the leading role of the Communist Party, he asserts that "in the efforts to renew socialism, the party may not concede the initiative to either populist demagoguery, nationalist or chauvinistic currents or to the spontaneity of group interests."[66]

On the more positive side, Gorbachev may be in a stronger position and is more liberal than analogous reform leaders in Germany or Japan, like Gustav Stresemann and Shidehara Kijuro in the 1920s.[67] The Soviet military, though an active lobbyist for offensive military programs under Brezhnev, does not have anything like the deep-rooted traditions of domestic interventionism and international belligerency that its German and Japanese counterparts had. Soviet intellectuals, notwithstanding ethnic chauvinist elements among the Great Russians and other national groups, are playing a much more positive role than did the infamous "fleet professors" of the Wilhelmine era and the white-washers of German war guilt in Weimar Germany.[68]

More generally, the passing of Social Darwinism from pan-European culture, due in part to the passing of praetorian regimes, has made nationalist appeals harder to sell, as have the lessons of two world wars.[69] Inside the erstwhile Soviet bloc, nationalism seems virulent especially among stateless ethnic groups—Armenians, Azerbaijanis, Balts. Three reforming nationalities who already form the core of nation-states—Russians, Poles, and Hungarians—have not so far tried to exploit excessive nationalism as a solution to the problems of governing increasingly pluralistic societies. The

---

65. For a theoretically informed analysis of Soviet nationality problems, see Alexander Motyl, *Will the Non-Russians Rebel? State, Ethnicity, and Stability in the USSR* (Ithaca: Cornell University Press, 1987).

66. Mikhail Gorbachev, "The Socialist Idea and Revolutionary Perestroika," *Pravda*, November 26, 1989, as translated in the *New York Times*, November 27, 1989, p. 12.

67. For a comparison of "tentatively liberalizing regimes" in their international contexts, see Jack Snyder, "International Leverage on Soviet Domestic Change," *World Politics*, Vol. 42, No. 1 (October 1989), pp. 1–30.

68. Holger Herwig, "Clio Deceived: Patriotic Self-Censorship in Germany after the Great War," *International Security*, Vol. 12, No. 2 (Fall 1987), pp. 5–44.

69. Mueller, *Retreat from Doomsday*; and Mueller, "The Essential Irrelevance of Nuclear Weapons," *International Security*, Vol. 13, No. 2 (Fall 1988), pp. 55–79, esp. 75–78.

nationalism and anti-semitism of elements within the Democratic Forum is not yet playing a dominant role in Hungarian politics. However, one such core nationality, Yugoslavia's Serbs, has been asserting its parochial claims at the expense of the Albanians in Kosovo province. In Bulgaria, reformers' efforts to recognize the rights of the Turkish minority have led to a backlash among ethnic Bulgarians. In Romania, the overthrow of the Ceausescu government has halted plans to bulldoze ethnic Hungarian villages, but the long-run fate of ethnic relations in a pluralistic political setting remains in doubt.[70]

The states of the former Soviet bloc, including the Soviet Union, may degenerate into praetorian politics in response to the problems associated with expanding political participation and the retrenchment of Soviet power, or they may not. And if they do slip into that pattern, they may recapitulate the Wilhelmine and "Macedonian" patterns of foreign policy, or they may not. Precisely because the outcome remains in doubt, it seems plausible that the nature of the broader international environment, including the policies of the West, will affect the result. Nationalism may be kept under wraps in Hungary, for example, because the public calculates that a show of overt chauvinistic irredentism toward Romania over the Hungarian minority in Transylvania would kill Hungary's incipient opening to the West.[71] It is therefore to the effects of the international setting that I now turn.

International Causes of Praetorian Politics

Whether a society takes the praetorian path is determined largely by its domestic pattern of development. The prime candidates are late, rapid developers with elites who have a strong interest in resisting the diffusion of political power.[72] But the international environment may also play a role, either for good or ill.

---

70. For background on these nationalisms, see Griffith, ed., *Central and Eastern Europe: The Opening Curtain?*, chapters 8–14, especially chapters 11–12 on the Balkans. For recent developments in the Balkans, see "Rights of the Turks Protested," *New York Times*, January 3, 1990, p. 12; and Mary Ellen Fischer, "Rumania up for Grabs," *New York Times*, December 28, 1989, p. 21.

71. On the Transylvania issue and the Democratic Forum's relatively guarded attempts to exploit it politically, see Radio Free Europe, *Situation Report*, Hungary, No. 3, February 24, 1989, pp. 35–38; No. 5, March 31, 1989, p. 21; No. 12, July 28, 1989, pp. 37–40.

72. Barrington Moore, *Social Origins of Dictatorship and Democracy* (Boston: Beacon, 1966); and Alexander Gerschenkron, *Bread and Democracy in Germany* (Ithaca: Cornell University Press, 1989; orig. ed. 1943).

Among small states, one would expect the international environment to play a major role in shaping domestic institutions and their expression in foreign policy. Small, vulnerable states must adapt to their international position, since they cannot buffer themselves from its influence. As I suggested above, the especially malign international setting may explain why Weiner's aggressive "Macedonian syndrome" prevailed in Eastern Europe in the first half of this century, whereas it was less prevalent in praetorian states elsewhere.[73] Likewise, Peter Katzenstein finds that an "authoritarian version" of corporatism was prevalent in small European states in the 1930s, whereas later a "democratic form of corporatism" was "nourished by the strong effect of a liberal United States on the postwar global economy."[74]

The effect of the international setting on large, would-be praetorian states is just as dramatic. In the 1920s, for example, Weimar Germany and Taisho Japan were societies on the cusp of emerging from praetorian patterns. Liberal, democratic, free-trading, non-militarist institutions were potentially emerging in these two states in the 1920s, facilitated in part by a fairly benign international environment. The Washington Naval Treaty of 1922 and the Locarno Pact of 1925 institutionalized a security environment that made aggressive behavior seem unnecessary for achieving security. Financial flows from America, in the form of Dawes Plan loans to Germany and Japanese profits from the textile trade, bankrolled liberal, free-trading coalitions, which counted on an expanded electoral franchise to maintain their position against military, protectionist, and conservative elites. When this relatively liberal international order collapsed with the Depression at the end of the 1920s, however, the liberal regimes in Germany and Japan collapsed along with it.[75]

The lessons of this case may cut both ways. One lesson is cautionary: unless links between a tentatively liberalizing state and a liberal international order are strong and permanent, they may be counterproductive. Forging

---

73. For a related argument and evidence about the 1930s, see Deborah Welch Larson, "Bandwagon Images in American Foreign Policy: Myth or Reality?" In Robert Jervis and Jack Snyder, eds., *Dominoes and Bandwagons: Strategic Beliefs and Superpower Competition in the Eurasian Rimland* (New York: Oxford University Press, forthcoming).
74. Katzenstein, *Small States*, p. 38. The corporatisms of the 1930s included both democratic and authoritarian variants, but the latter was more prevalent in the 1930s than it was in the liberal international order after 1945.
75. Snyder, "International Leverage," pp. 6–8; Peter Gourevitch, *Politics in Hard Times* (Ithaca: Cornell University Press, 1986). Of course, Weimar's comparatively restrained foreign policy was also due in part to its military weakness.

such ties and then having them broken is probably more disruptive to domestic political order than never forging them at all.

A more optimistic lesson, however, is that even a relatively weak liberal international order can exert positive effects even on hard-case praetorian societies like Germany and Japan, by creating incentives for the formation of liberal coalitions. By implication, a much stronger liberal regime, like the one that the advanced capitalist countries have forged today, should be able to exert an even stronger positive effect on easier cases, like most of today's East bloc states.

The next section uses the neo-liberal institutionalist theory of international regimes to examine the current policy implications of this proposition.

How International Institutions May Create Political Order

How might international institution-building contribute to the creation of a stable, democratic order in the former Soviet bloc? In addressing this question, it will be worthwhile to consider theories of international regimes and to look back to the origins of the post-war order.

Neo-liberal regime theory, as articulated by such students of international political economy as Stephen Krasner and Robert Keohane, accepts the proposition that cooperation rarely emerges spontaneously in anarchic conditions.[76] To overcome problems of organizing collective action, successful cooperation requires a push from some powerful provider of incentives to cooperate and the creation of institutions that coordinate the participants' expectations and actions. But once in place, a cooperative regime and its institutions tend to create habits and constituencies that make them self-perpetuating.

One version of the institutionalist view places particular stress on the role of the structures of institutions in channeling interests toward certain outcomes. This is the part of the institutionalist argument that I draw on most heavily. Kenneth Arrow's famous "impossibility theorem" showed that it is impossible to predict a unique outcome of pluralistic policy-making from the

---

76. Krasner, *International Regimes*; Keohane, *After Hegemony*. See also Joseph Grieco, "Anarchy and Cooperation: A Realist Critique of the Newest Liberal Institutionalism," *International Organization*, Vol. 42, No. 3 (Summer 1988), pp. 485–508.

preferences of the participants. A variety of different coalitions and policy outcomes are all possible; there is no stable equilibrium. Subsequent theorists have shown, however, that the prevailing institutional setting increases the probability of certain outcomes and favors the emergence of some potential coalitions over others.[77]

The canonical example of a successful attempt to use international institution-building to load the dice in favor of liberal outcomes is the post-1945 international economic regime. Initially underwritten by American power and leadership, this regime is now firmly rooted in its participants' domestic and international institutions in ways that go beyond simple power relations among states. In light of the frequent calls for a "new Marshall Plan" for Eastern Europe, it is especially appropriate to remember precisely how the original Marshall Plan worked to forge the liberal post-war order.[78]

The Marshall Plan's effectiveness lay in its political and institutional strategy, not just in its dollar amount. American money was only a small fraction of the total investment in Western Europe in the late 1940s. America did not just buy a liberal international order. Rather, the Marshall Plan worked primarily because it linked its financial aid to the beneficiary countries' acceptance of institutions of transnational economic cooperation. These included multilateral institutions like the General Agreement on Tariffs and Trade (GATT), and also regional European cooperative efforts like the European Coal and Steel Community (ECSC) and the European Payments Union (EPU). This had a multiplier effect on economic efficiency, while politically it strengthened internationally-oriented sectors and coalitions against their insular, protectionist competitors. In short, the Marshall Plan worked by creating international institutions to channel domestic interests in a direction favorable to international cooperation and stability.[79]

Proponents of a new Marshall Plan for Eastern Europe should think in similar terms. More than just economic investment, the former Soviet bloc needs to develop a workable set of economic and political institutions that

---

77. A good review of this literature is Kenneth Shepsle, "Studying Institutions: Some Lessons from the Rational Choice Approach," *Journal of Theoretical Politics*, Vol. 1, No. 2 (April 1989), pp. 131–147. The seminal work is Kenneth Arrow, *Social Choice and Individual Values*, 2d ed. (New Haven: Yale University Press, 1963).

78. On the call for a new Marshall Plan, see Flora Lewis, "Watershed for Europe," *New York Times*, November 22, 1989, p. 25.

79. Robert Pollard, *Economic Security and the Origins of the Cold War, 1945–1950* (New York: Columbia, 1985), pp. 158–167, 248–249.

will allow that investment to be put to stable, productive use. Western loans and investment in Eastern Europe in the 1970s failed to spark meaningful economic growth and political change because they were not tied to institutional reform. Moreover, just as Marshall aid backed regional European organizations like ECSC and EPU, so too today's efforts might work best through regional European institutions like the European Community.

SPECIFIC PROPOSALS FOR BUILDING PAN-EUROPEAN INSTITUTIONS

Like the original Marshall Plan, the "new Marshall Plan" needs a strategy for using international institutions to fill the gap between booming political participation and a weak domestic order threatened by the competing demands of illiberal organized interests. Below I evaluate some ideas of this type that have already been advanced by prominent figures in the West, and add some specific ideas of my own to this framework.[80]

The most effective scheme would gradually integrate reforming Soviet bloc states into the European Community. The EC is a strong, well-developed supranational institution with a proven record of successfully assimilating less-developed European states into its economic system, with favorable effects on their political development. Germany, the nation that Soviet bloc states are most eager to trade with, is a member of the EC. With backing from Washington and a benign attitude from Moscow, the EC would surely have sufficient resources to play the leadership role that is helpful in setting up a strong international regime. There are economic incentives for the EC to play a more active role in the East, as well as ideological and security incentives.[81]

This is *not* a scheme that relies simply on the erroneous notion that economic interdependence breeds peace. The favorable political effect comes

---

80. In addition to Hormats, "Redefining Europe"; Brzezinski, "Post-Communist Nationalism"; and Burley, "The Once and Future German Question," see various statements by European leaders on the need to manage German reunification and East-West rapprochement within a context of broader European institutions, all as reported in the *New York Times*: German Chancellor Helmut Kohl, November 29, 1989, pp. 1, 17; German Foreign Minister Hans-Dietrich Genscher, November 6, 1989, p. 10; former French President Valery Giscard d'Estaing, November, 11, 1989, p. 8; and post-Malta statements by President George Bush and West European leaders, December 5, 1989, p. 17.

81. On possible security motives for the EC's 1992 plans, see Wayne Sandholtz and John Zysman, "1992: Recasting the European Bargain," *World Politics*, Vol. 42, No. 1 (October 1989), pp. 95–128, esp. 95–96.

not just from interdependence, but from the institutional structures and changes in domestic interests that may or may not accompany high levels of interdependence. In previous eras of extensive foreign trade and loans, multilateral economic institutions were weaker, as were the effects of interdependence on domestic economic structure. Though trade may have been at high levels, the production process of individual firms was rarely internationalized, as it is now. Consequently, the political effects of a liberal order were not deeply rooted in international institutions and domestic interests.[82] Thus, merely pointing out that high levels of trade preceded World War I is not an argument against a strategy of neo-liberal institution-building in the former Soviet bloc.

How would such a strategy work? According to the most commonly discussed ideas, different East European states would be granted different levels of association with the EC and integrated into its institutions at varying paces. Progress toward market reforms and full-fledged electoral democracy would be the price of admission to greater participation. Access to capital and markets would be the carrot. The institutionalized, legal character of the relationship would make for predictability, irreversibility, and deeply penetrating effects on the domestic order of the state.

The regime should also have a security component. Alliances that the Soviet Union would find threatening (e.g., between NATO and Poland) should be forsworn. Arms control should be designed to stabilize not only the East-West balance but also East-East balances.[83]

Two principles should be considered in designing military postures. First, states that have potential irredentist ethnic claims should not be militarily stronger than their neighbors. Thus, Hungary is—and should be—militarily weaker than Romania, which deters irredentism over Transylvania. Romania, in turn, is weaker than the Soviet Union, which deters irredentism over the status of Romanian-speaking Soviet Moldavia. Since Poland is weaker than Germany and worries about German irredentist claims, Germany should unilaterally curtail its ability to attack Poland and other Eastern states by adopting non-threatening military doctrines and postures.[84]

---

82. On the internationalization of firms' operations and interests, see Helen Milner, *Resisting Protectionism* (Princeton: Princeton University Press, 1988). On the institutional aspect, see Robert Keohane and Joseph Nye, *Power and Interdependence* (Boston: Little, Brown, 1977).
83. Henry Kissinger, "Untangling Alliances," *Los Angeles Times*, April 16, 1989, part V, pp. 1, 6, discusses conventional arms control in the context of the broader European political order.
84. For figures on these states' current and potential military power, see International Institute for Strategic Studies (IISS), *The Military Balance, 1989–1990* (London: IISS, 1989).

Second, individual states and the two alliances should have force postures that are optimized for defense. Tank-heavy mobile strike forces and deep-strike ground-attack aircraft should be sharply limited, whereas fixed defenses should be encouraged.[85] Whenever possible, states should prepare to defend their allies by moving forces into defensive positions on the allies' own territory, not by preparing to attack the aggressor on the aggressor's home territory.[86] For non-contiguous allies, this might involve airlifting troops into previously prepared defensive positions.

A cooperative, pan-European security regime should also lay out the rights and responsibilities of ethnic and religious minorities. The purpose would be to head off nationalistic conflicts before they get started. Adherence to such a regime would be a precondition for the extension of a state's participation in East-West economic ties. Social science has developed a number of ideas about how to prevent ethnic tension from creating political instability. Applied social scientists should think about how to use these ideas in the construction of a European minorities regime.[87]

One new institution that could advance a stabilizing minorities regime would be an International Academy for Nationalities Studies. Its aim would be to get local intellectuals out of their self-created hothouses of nationalistic mythology and into the broader Euro-Atlantic intellectual community. Throughout the history of nationalism, intellectuals and publicists have played a major role by creating a wave of nationalist myth and then riding it to positions of prestige and influence.[88] The international community should try to create alternative incentives for restless intellectuals and on-the-make journalists. Conferences, fellowships, and mid-career retraining at the Academy should expose them to objective accounts of the history

85. For details, see Jack Snyder, "Limiting Offensive Conventional Forces: Soviet Proposals and Western Options," *International Security*, Vol. 12, No. 4 (Spring 1988), pp. 48–77.
86. Van Evera, "When Is Offense Best?" discusses the reasons for this and also the difficulties involved in implementing such a strategy.
87. See Arend Lijphart, *The Politics of Accommodation: Pluralism and Democracy in the Netherlands* (Berkeley: University of California Press, 1968), and other works discussed and cited in Katzenstein, *Small States*, pp. 35, 88, 185, 213–215. Note also the proposals for voluntary ethnic confederations in Brzezinski, "Post-Communist Nationalism."
88. Stephen Van Evera, "Causes of War," has been the pioneer in reopening the question of the origins and consequences of nationalist mythmaking. See also Paul Kennedy, "The Decline of Nationalistic History in the West, 1900–1970," *Journal of Contemporary History*, Vol. 8, No. 1 (January 1973), pp. 77–100; and Saburo Ienaga, *The Pacific War, 1931–1945* (New York: Pantheon, 1978), chapter 2. On the return of nationalistic history, see Richard J. Evans, *In Hitler's Shadow: West German Historians and the Attempt to Escape from the Nazi Past* (New York: Pantheon, 1989).

of their region and its relations with others, and to modern theories of conflict management in multi-ethnic societies. To participate, intellectuals and their local institutes would have to be accredited by some international body (much as the international psychiatric organization now imposes professional preconditions that have affected Soviet participation). Conditions might include international standards of archival openness, availability of books by international authors, accurate labeling of fact and opinion in journalistic writings, and academic promotions based on international scholarly standards.

MANAGING THE GERMAN QUESTION IN AN EC CONTEXT Perhaps the most important benefit of giving the EC a high profile role in Eastern Europe is that it would ease the problem of the unification of Germany. The emergence of a strong, unified German power will be less destabilizing insofar as it takes place within the framework of the EC and other international legal and institutional arrangements. For example, international agreements and institutions are regulating German military power and multinationalizing German economic activities in the East.

It might be objected that managing the German problem within the EC will simply provide a fig leaf for the eastward expansion of German influence. For example, the 1989 economic summit of Western leaders decided that the EC should take the lead in coordinating economic aid to reforming East Bloc states, but in fact the most significant measures were taken by Germany unilaterally. Thus, German capital operating under the EC aegis might dominate the economies of the states of Eastern Europe, with the rest of Western Europe playing merely a token role. German economic penetration of Eastern Europe in the 1930s, and the political influence that went along with it, might be recreated.[89] Far from solving the problem of an emerging German superpower, the EC strategy might help to legitimate it.

However, German economic domination of East Central Europe is a possibility whether or not German unification is managed through the EC. Purely bilateral deals, as in the 1930s, could produce the same result. Moreover, if the EC is involved, Germany would be more constrained to secure the assent of its EC partners. Likewise, there would be an institutionalized framework for East European protests if Germany tries to link investment to narrowly

---

89. The classic study is Albert Hirschman, *National Power and the Structure of Foreign Trade* (Berkeley: University of California Press, 1945).

German political goals, such as political autonomy for Germans in Polish Silesia.

A ROLE FOR THE UNITED STATES AND THE USSR

Germany's EC partners should not be left alone to bear the institutional burden of channeling German strength and ambitions. The United States and the Soviet Union must also play a role in the European Common Home. For example, the EC solution to the German problem should not be seen as obviating the function of NATO, which still has an irreplaceable role to play in providing Germany with a secure nuclear unbrella. Without a NATO nuclear guarantee, Germany might feel insecure if tensions developed in Soviet-East European relations, provoking anxious calls for a German nuclear deterrent, which would further complicate any crisis.

Economic arrangements must also include the two superpowers. The strategy of extending Western economic institutions eastward must include the Russian core of the Soviet Union. Otherwise, the enterprise would seem to Moscow like capitalist imperialism and might therefore provoke a backlash. At all costs, the expansion of the EC must not look like a lure to encourage Baltic separatism, while leaving Muscovy to sink into its economic bog.[90] Though the Soviet Union might be included in the European Common Home more loosely than some other East European states, arrangements must be designed to offer Moscow a net benefit in security and economic terms. A moderate dose of easy credits for consumer purchases, joint ventures, reassuring arms control, and the symbolism of an opening to the West might suffice to achieve this effect. President Bush's proposals on GATT and Most Favored Nation status for the Soviet Union at the December 1989 Malta summit are steps in the right direction.

The United States would also have to be included in the Euro-Atlantic system. An Open Door to an American economic presence in Eastern Europe would help prevent the EC move eastward from becoming a thin veil covering an all-German show. American treaty commitments to NATO and the Four Power Berlin regime should be maintained.

---

90. For a discussion of constructive steps that the West can take with regard to the Baltic states, see Alexander Motyl, "Identity Crisis in the Soviet West," *Bulletin of the Atomic Scientists*, March 1989, pp. 21–4.

How International Institutions Could Prevent Praetorianism

A system of international institutions would work to prevent the emergence of praetorian regimes in the former Soviet bloc, first, because increased openness to trading on the world market would help break the power of the self-interested cartels that are characteristic of praetorian politics. As conventional wisdom has phrased it, "the tariff is the mother of trusts."[91] The Bismarckian marriage of iron and rye, for example, was consummated expressly to establish tariff protection for both sectors, which would have been severely weakened without it. In contrast, free trading would make it impossible to return to the domestic political alliances, comprising obsolete industry, the military, and the orthodox Communist Party, that characterized Brezhnev's Russia and Gierek's Poland.

Second, a negotiated security environment would undercut the plausibility of nationalist appeals and threat exaggeration by the military. Since civilian control over the military would be thereby easier, one of the ingredients of praetorian politics—military intervention in domestic politics—would be missing. At the same time, by co-opting intellectuals into pan-European networks, another potential source of virulent nationalism would be lured toward more benign pursuits.

Third, a democratic institutional requirement for EC membership would directly strengthen the moderating voice of the average citizen in Eastern Europe. Recent developments in Hungary already show this process at work. The Hungarians admit that one motive for their democratic constitutional reforms is to make them acceptable economic partners for EC countries. Democratic voting, in turn, has helped to stymie a would-be Communist-nationalist ruling cartel in that country.

Finally, successful economic integration into the EC would expand the economic pie in Eastern countries, and thus lubricate the process of political transformation, just as the mid-Victorian economic boom, fueled by expanding international trade, facilitated Britain's transition to a full-fledged, two-party, universal-suffrage democracy.

In short, given the importance of heading off the emergence of praetorian states in the former Sovet bloc, the West has an incentive to extend its successful international regimes eastward in order to help fill the gap between

---

91. Ronald Rogowski, *Commerce and Coalitions: How Trade Affects Political Alignments* (Princeton: Princeton University Press, 1989); Olson, *Rise and Decline*, chapter 5.

rising political participation and weak governing institutions. One promising scheme would center on an expanded EC as its core, with the United States and the Soviet Union as more loosely associated members of a Euro-Atlantic Common Home.

Evaluating the Competing Perspectives

The burden of this paper is to clarify the reasoning behind three competing perspectives on security in the changing European order, and in particular to explore the logic behind the neo-liberal institutionalist view. A definitive evaluation of the three views is a task for the cumulative work of many scholars and public commentators.

Nonetheless, a few judgments are in order. First, liberal optimism seems more like ideological self-indulgence or politicians' rhetoric than a serious analytical position. Any worthwhile analysis must recognize that the dismantling of a stable political order entails grave dangers.

Hobbesian pessimism, in contrast, enjoys a firmer theoretical foundation and offers some insightful diagnoses, but suffers from a few significant flaws. It exaggerates the inevitability that international conflict and nationalistic excesses will follow from the erosion of the bipolar division of Europe. Its assumption that profound changes in the domestic character of states since the interwar period will be readily reversed as a consequence of changes in the structure of the international system is untenable. The past pathologies of German politics, for example, were caused not primarily by Germany's vulnerable position in the multipolar system, but by the social tensions associated with Germany's pattern of late development.[92] Since this particular phase of development was outgrown long ago, the coming period of multipolarity will take place in a more benign domestic context. If this favorable pattern is reinforced by liberal international institutions, there is no reason to expect a revival of the Hobbesian war of all against all in Europe.

Nor does the Hobbesian viewpoint generate any plausible solutions to the problem of European order. The solution that *is* consistent with its theoretical assumptions—maintaining the bipolar Cold War division of Europe—is no longer available. Russia is too weak and irresolute, and East European publics

---

92. See Moore, *Social Origins;* Gerschenkron, *Bread and Democracy;* and Wehler, *German Empire.*

are too restive for the *status quo ante* to be restored. More plausible would be a unilateral decision by the NATO alliance to insulate itself from the coming crisis in the East, but this fits poorly with the theoretical assumptions of Hobbesian theory, which posits as unlikely that a state would impose on itself a geopolitical sphere of abstention, and that an alliance would be maintained after the opposing alliance breaks up.

The third Hobbesian solution, Bismarckian defensive alliances, had a weak track record when it was tried before. If it is to do better this time, it will have to be embedded in a political order of more favorable domestic and international institutions. Insuring that all states in the multipolar checkerboard are simultaneously secure will require elaborate arms control arrangements negotiated on the principles of non-offensive defense in a well-institutionalized setting. Otherwise, the logic of the strategic situation will increase pressures to develop offensive military capabilities to come to the aid of non-contiguous allies.

Neo-liberal institutionalism also entails several serious problems. It envisages a cooperative security regime involving all of the world's great powers, which would be a historical event almost unprecedented, apart from the short-lived post-Napoleonic Concert of Europe.[93] Moreover, it fails to reckon with the problem of compensating the many powerful social groups who would be losers in any scheme integrating Eastern societies into the Western political order—e.g., internationally uncompetitive economic sectors, those who control locally scarce resources,[94] and the institutional remnants of the Soviet period. Integrating these societies into Western market economies is bound to be disruptive, if not outright explosive.

Inclusion of the Soviet Union in the Western order is the *sine qua non* of the whole scheme, yet it is by far the most difficult to accomplish. Its economy is too big for the EC to digest as it could a Spain, a Greece, or a Hungary. Moreover, the Soviet economy and polity seem more inherently resistant to successful reform than does Hungary's, for example. The nuclear-armed Soviet Union must be included because a praetorian outcome there would

---

93. On the Concert of Europe security regime, see Robert Jervis, "Security Regimes," *International Organization*, Vol. 36, No. 2 (Spring 1982), pp. 357–378, esp. 362–368.
94. Rogowski, *Commerce and Coalitions*, pp. 106–107, 121–122, 175–177, discusses Eastern Europe and the USSR in light of the hypothesis that increasing exposure to trade harms holders of locally scarce factors of production (land, labor, or capital), but benefits holders the locally abundant factors.

do the most damage, but it is the country for which that outcome may be hardest to prevent.[95]

Finally, neo-liberal institution-building will do great damage if it is attempted, but doesn't work. It will damage the West by embroiling it deeply in the possibly insoluble problems of the East. A new Marshall Plan may convince Americans that to spread liberalism in Eastern Europe is their "manifest destiny," and they may get so absorbed in the task that they refuse to give it up if it turns sour. As the example of the 1920s suggested, international institution-building might also damage the East by engaging it in disruptive, but unsustainable economic ties with the West. Shaking up the social order in order to forge such links, and then breaking them if they fail to work, could generate more profound social disorder than would failing to forge them in the first place.

On balance, a middle road between the Hobbesian instinct for insulation and the neo-liberal instinct for institutionalized activism is probably best. Hungary and Czechoslovakia should probably eventually be admitted into the Western institutional framework. Poland's role in western institutions should be tailored to fit Soviet sensibilities, which would probably tolerate a high degree of Polish economic integration with the West, but not close military ties.

The Soviet Union should be offered generous security guarantees, a full seat in Europe's diplomatic councils, and beneficial economic relationships with the West. Given the apparent unripeness of the Soviet economy for reform, however, it is highly risky to encourage a leap into the dark in the form of total integration of the Soviet economy into Western markets. Judging from current evidence, this would disrupt Soviet society more than it would

---

95. According to some critics, EC expansion into Central Europe might strengthen a German-dominated European Community, creating what amounts to a tripolar configuration of power: the United States, the Soviet Union, and the EC. If, as Waltz argues in *Theory of International Politics*, p. 163, tripolar configurations are unstable, this outcome could be dangerous. But the United States and the Soviet Union should be included as major participants in the European regime, which thus would not exist as a separate pole. Moreover, if the institutional scheme worked, the consequences of tripolar anarchy would be muted. In any event, Waltz's deductions about the instability of tripolar configurations are speculative and not logically compelling. By the broader logic of Waltz's own theory, an attack by one pole should lead to an alliance of the other two, to prevent the achievement of system-wide hegemony by the attacker. The attacker, anticipating this, should be dissuaded from aggression. Finally, adding Japan and/or China would make the global configuration multipolar, not tripolar.

spur increased productivity, and consequently might provoke praetorian tendencies rather than dampen them.

Analyzing European security can no longer be reduced to positing the vectors of billiard-ball states and counting their tanks. The European order is being remade by social and economic change, no less than by shifts in the international configuration of power. Strategies to maintain international security must, in this new world, comprehend all of these varied facets of social life.

Back to the Future | *John J. Mearsheimer*

Instability in Europe After the Cold War

The profound changes now underway in Europe have been widely viewed as harbingers of a new age of peace. With the Cold War over, it is said, the threat of war that has hung over Europe for more than four decades is lifting. Swords can now be beaten into ploughshares; harmony can reign among the states and peoples of Europe. Central Europe, which long groaned under the massive forces of the two military blocs, can convert its military bases into industrial parks, playgrounds, and condominiums. Scholars of security affairs can stop their dreary quarrels over military doctrine and balance assessments, and turn their attention to finding ways to prevent global warming and preserve the ozone layer. European leaders can contemplate how to spend peace dividends. So goes the common view.

This article assesses this optimistic view by exploring in detail the consequences for Europe of an end to the Cold War. Specifically, I examine the effects of a scenario under which the Cold War comes to a complete end. The Soviet Union withdraws all of its forces from Eastern Europe, leaving the states in that region fully independent. Voices are thereupon raised in the United States, Britain, and Germany, arguing that American and British military forces in Germany have lost their principal *raison d'être*, and these forces are withdrawn from the Continent. NATO and the Warsaw Pact then dissolve; they may persist on paper, but each ceases to function as an alliance.[1] As a result, the bipolar structure that has characterized Europe since

This article emerged from a paper written for a February 1990 conference at Ditchley Park, England, on the future of Europe, organized by James Callaghan, Gerald Ford, Valéry Giscard d'Estaing, and Helmut Schmidt. An abridged version of this article appears in the *Atlantic*, August 1990. I am grateful to Robert Art, Stacy Bergstrom, Richard Betts, Anne-Marie Burley, Dale Copeland, Michael Desch, Markus Fischer, Henk Goemans, Joseph Grieco, Ted Hopf, Craig Koerner, Andrew Kydd, Alicia Levine, James Nolt, Roger Petersen, Barry Posen, Denny Roy, Jack Snyder, Ashley Tellis, Marc Trachtenberg, Stephen Van Evera, Andrew Wallace, and Stephen Walt for their most helpful comments.

John Mearsheimer is Professor and Chair of the Department of Political Science, University of Chicago.

1. There is considerable support within NATO's higher circles, including the Bush administration, for maintaining NATO beyond the Cold War. NATO leaders have not clearly articulated the concrete goals that NATO would serve in a post–Cold War Europe, but they appear to conceive the future NATO as a means for ensuring German security, thereby removing possible German motives for aggressive policies; and as a means to protect other NATO states against

International Security, Summer 1990 (Vol. 15, No. 1)
© 1990 by the President and Fellows of Harvard College and of the Massachusetts Institute of Technology.

the end of World War II is replaced by a multipolar structure. In essence, the Cold War we have known for almost half a century is over, and the postwar order in Europe is ended.[2]

How would such a fundamental change affect the prospects for peace in Europe?[3] Would it raise or lower the risk of war?

I argue that the prospects for major crises and war in Europe are likely to increase markedly if the Cold War ends and this scenario unfolds. The next decades in a Europe without the superpowers would probably not be as violent as the first 45 years of this century, but would probably be substantially more prone to violence than the past 45 years.

This pessimistic conclusion rests on the argument that the distribution and character of military power are the root causes of war and peace. Specifically, the absence of war in Europe since 1945 has been a consequence of three factors: the bipolar distribution of military power on the Continent; the rough military equality between the two states comprising the two poles in Europe,

---

German aggression. However, the Germans, who now provide the largest portion of the Alliance's standing forces, are likely to resist such a role for NATO. A security structure of this sort assumes that Germany cannot be trusted and that NATO must be maintained to keep it in line. A united Germany is not likely to accept for very long a structure that rests on this premise. Germans accepted NATO throughout the Cold War because it secured Germany against the Soviet threat that developed in the wake of World War II. Without that specific threat, which now appears to be diminishing rapidly, Germany is likely to reject the continued maintenance of NATO as we know it.

2. I am not arguing that a complete end to the Cold War is inevitable; also quite likely is an intermediate outcome, under which the status quo is substantially modified, but the main outlines of the current order remain in place. Specifically, the Soviet Union may withdraw much of its force from Eastern Europe, but leave significant forces behind. If so, NATO force levels would probably shrink markedly, but NATO may continue to maintain significant forces in Germany. Britain and the United States would withdraw some but not all of their troops from the Continent. If this outcome develops, the basic bipolar military competition that has defined the map of Europe throughout the Cold War will continue. I leave this scenario unexamined, and instead explore what follows from a complete end to the Cold War in Europe because this latter scenario is the less examined of the two, and because the consequences, and therefore the desirability, of completely ending the Cold War would still remain an issue if the intermediate outcome occurred.

3. The impact of such a change on human rights in Eastern Europe will not be considered directly in this article. Eastern Europeans have suffered great hardship as a result of the Soviet occupation. The Soviets have imposed oppressive political regimes on the region, denying Eastern Europeans basic freedoms. Soviet withdrawal from Eastern Europe will probably change that situation for the better, although the change is likely to be more of a mixed blessing than most realize. First, it is not clear that communism will be promptly replaced in all Eastern European countries with political systems that place a high premium on protecting minority rights and civil liberties. Second, the longstanding blood feuds among the nationalities in Eastern Europe are likely to re-emerge in a multipolar Europe, regardless of the existing political order. If wars break out in Eastern Europe, human rights are sure to suffer.

the United States and the Soviet Union; and the fact that each superpower was armed with a large nuclear arsenal.[4] Domestic factors also affect the likelihood of war, and have helped cause the postwar peace. Most importantly, hyper-nationalism helped cause the two world wars, and the decline of nationalism in Europe since 1945 has contributed to the peacefulness of the postwar world. However, factors of military power have been most important in shaping past events, and will remain central in the future.

The departure of the superpowers from Central Europe would transform Europe from a bipolar to a multipolar system.[5] Germany, France, Britain, and perhaps Italy would assume major power status; the Soviet Union would decline from superpower status but would remain a major European power, giving rise to a system of five major powers and a number of lesser powers. The resulting system would suffer the problems common to multipolar systems, and would therefore be more prone to instability.[6] Power inequities could also appear; if so, stability would be undermined further.

The departure of the superpowers would also remove the large nuclear arsenals they now maintain in Central Europe. This would remove the pacifying effect that these weapons have had on European politics. Four principal scenarios are possible. Under the first scenario, Europe would become nuclear-free, thus eliminating a central pillar of order in the Cold War era. Under the second scenario, the European states do not expand their arsenals to compensate for the departure of the superpowers' weapons. In a third scenario, nuclear proliferation takes place, but is mismanaged; no steps are

---

4. It is commonplace to characterize the polarity—bipolar or multipolar—of the international system at large, not a specific region. The focus in this article, however, is not on the global distribution of power, but on the distribution of power in Europe. Polarity arguments can be used to assess the prospects for stability in a particular region, provided the global and regional balances are distinguished from one another and the analysis is focused on the structure of power in the relevant region.

5. To qualify as a pole in a global or regional system, a state must have a reasonable prospect of defending itself against the leading state in the system by its own efforts. The United States and the Soviet Union have enjoyed clear military superiority over other European states, and all non-European states, throughout the Cold War; hence they have formed the two poles of both the global and European systems. What is happening to change this is that both the Soviet Union and the United States are moving forces out of Central Europe, which makes it more difficult for them to project power on the Continent and thus weakens their influence there; and reducing the size of those forces, leaving them less military power to project. Because of its proximity to Europe, the Soviet Union will remain a pole in the European system as long as it retains substantial military forces on its own territory. The United States can remain a pole in Europe only if it retains the capacity to project significant military power into Central Europe.

6. Stability is simply defined as the absence of wars and major crises.

taken to dampen the many dangers inherent in the proliferation process. All three of these scenarios would raise serious risks of war.

In the fourth and least dangerous scenario, nuclear weapons proliferate in Europe, but the process is well-managed by the current nuclear powers. They take steps to deter preventive strikes on emerging nuclear powers, to set boundaries on the proliferation process by extending security umbrellas over the neighbors of emerging nuclear powers, to help emerging nuclear powers build secure deterrent forces, and to discourage them from deploying counterforce systems that threaten their neighbors' deterrents. This outcome probably provides the best hope for maintaining peace in Europe. However, it would still be more dangerous than the world of 1945–90. Moreover, it is not likely that proliferation would be well-managed.

Three counter-arguments might be advanced against this pessimistic set of predictions of Europe's future. The first argument holds that the peace will be preserved by the effects of the liberal international economic order that has evolved since World War II. The second rests on the observation that liberal democracies very seldom fight wars against each other, and holds that the past spread of democracy in Europe has bolstered peace, and that the ongoing democratization of Eastern Europe makes war still less likely. The third argument maintains that Europeans have learned from their disastrous experiences in this century that war, whether conventional or nuclear, is so costly that it is no longer a sensible option for states.

But the theories behind these arguments are flawed, as I explain; hence their prediction of peace in a multipolar Europe is flawed as well.

Three principal policy prescriptions follow from this analysis. First, the United States should encourage a process of limited nuclear proliferation in Europe. Specifically, Europe will be more stable if Germany acquires a secure nuclear deterrent, but proliferation does not go beyond that point. Second, the United States should not withdraw fully from Europe, even if the Soviet Union pulls its forces out of Eastern Europe. Third, the United States should take steps to forestall the re-emergence of hyper-nationalism in Europe.

METHODOLOGY: HOW SHOULD WE THINK ABOUT EUROPE'S FUTURE?
Predictions on the future risk of war and prescriptions about how best to maintain peace should rest on general theories about the causes of war and peace. This point is true for both academics and policymakers. The latter are seldom self-conscious in their uses of theory. Nevertheless, policymakers'

views on the future of Europe are shaped by their implicit preference for one theory of international relations over another. Our task, then, is to decide which theories best explain the past, and will most directly apply to the future; and then to employ these theories to explore the consequences of probable scenarios.

Specifically, we should first survey the inventory of international relations theories that bear on the problem. What theories best explain the period of violence before the Cold War? What theories best explain the peace of the past 45 years? Are there other theories that explain little about pre–Cold War Europe, or Cold War Europe, but are well-suited for explaining what is likely to occur in a Europe without a Soviet and American military presence?

Next, we should ask what these theories predict about the nature of international politics in a post–Cold War multipolar Europe. Will the causes of the postwar peace persist, will the causes of the two world wars return, or will other causes arise?

We can then assess whether we should expect the next decades to be more peaceful, or at least as peaceful, as the past 45 years, or whether the future is more likely to resemble the first 45 years of the century. We can also ask what policy prescriptions these theories suggest.

The study of international relations, like the other social sciences, does not yet resemble the hard sciences. Our stock of theories is spotty and often poorly tested. The conditions required for the operation of established theories are often poorly understood. Moreover, political phenomena are highly complex; hence precise political predictions are impossible without very powerful theoretical tools, superior to those we now possess. As a result, all political forecasting is bound to include some error. Those who venture to predict, as I do here, should therefore proceed with humility, take care not to claim unwarranted confidence, and admit that later hindsight will undoubtedly reveal surprises and mistakes.

Nevertheless, social science *should* offer predictions on the occurrence of momentous and fluid events like those now unfolding in Europe. Predictions can inform policy discourse. They help even those who disagree to frame their ideas, by clarifying points of disagreement. Moreover, predictions of events soon to unfold provide the best tests of social science theories, by making clear what it was that given theories have predicted about those events. In short, the world can be used as a laboratory to decide which theories best explain international politics. In this article I employ the body of theories that I find most persuasive to peer into the future. Time will reveal whether these theories in fact have much power to explain international politics.

The next section offers an explanation for the peacefulness of the post–World War II order. The section that follows argues that the end of the Cold War is likely to lead to a less stable Europe. Next comes an examination of the theories underlying claims that a multipolar Europe is likely to be as peaceful, if not more peaceful, than Cold War Europe. The concluding section suggests policy implications that follow from my analysis.

Explaining the "Long Peace"

The past 45 years represent the longest period of peace in European history.[7] During these years Europe saw no major war, and only two minor conflicts (the 1956 Soviet intervention in Hungary and the 1974 Greco-Turkish war in Cyprus). Neither conflict threatened to widen to other countries. The early years of the Cold War (1945–63) were marked by a handful of major crises, although none brought Europe to the brink of war. Since 1963, however, there have been no East-West crises in Europe. It has been difficult—if not impossible—for the last two decades to find serious national security analysts who have seen a real chance that the Soviet Union would attack Western Europe.

The Cold War peace contrasts sharply with European politics during the first 45 years of this century, which saw two world wars, a handful of minor wars, and a number of crises that almost resulted in war. Some 50 million Europeans were killed in the two world wars; in contrast, probably no more than 15,000 died in the two post-1945 European conflicts.[8] Cold War Europe is far more peaceful than early twentieth-century Europe.

Both Europeans and Americans increasingly assume that peace and calm are the natural order of things in Europe and that the first 45 years of this century, not the most recent, were the aberration. This is understandable,

---

7. The term "long peace" was coined by John Lewis Gaddis, "The Long Peace: Elements of Stability in the Postwar International System," *International Security,* Vol. 10, No. 4 (Spring 1986), pp. 99–142.
8. There were approximately 10,000 battle deaths in the Russo-Hungarian War of October–November 1956, and some 1500–5000 battle deaths in the July–August 1974 war in Cyprus. See Ruth Leger Sivard, *World Military and Social Expenditures 1989* (Washington, D.C.: World Priorities, 1989), p. 22; and Melvin Small and J. David Singer, *Resort to Arms: International and Civil Wars, 1816–1980* (Beverly Hills, Calif.: Sage, 1982), pp. 93–94.

since Europe has been free of war for so long that an ever-growing proportion of the Western public, born after World War II, has no direct experience with great-power war. However, this optimistic view is incorrect.

The European state system has been plagued with war since its inception. During much of the seventeenth and eighteenth centuries war was underway somewhere on the European Continent.[9] The nineteenth century held longer periods of peace, but also several major wars and crises. The first half of that century witnessed the protracted and bloody Napoleonic Wars; later came the Crimean War, and the Italian and German wars of unification.[10] The wars of 1914–45 continued this long historical pattern. They represented a break from the events of previous centuries only in the enormous increase in their scale of destruction.

This era of warfare came to an abrupt end with the conclusion of World War II. A wholly new and remarkably peaceful order then developed on the Continent.

THE CAUSES OF THE LONG PEACE: MILITARY POWER AND STABILITY

What caused the era of violence before 1945? Why has the postwar era been so much more peaceful? The wars before 1945 each had their particular and unique causes, but the distribution of power in Europe—its multipolarity and the imbalances of power that often occurred among the major states in that multipolar system—was the crucial permissive condition that allowed these particular causes to operate. The peacefulness of the postwar era arose for three principal reasons: the bipolarity of the distribution of power on the Continent, the rough equality in military power between those two polar states, and the appearance of nuclear weapons, which vastly expanded the violence of war, making deterrence far more robust.[11]

---

9. For inventories of past wars, see Jack S. Levy, *War In the Modern Great Power System, 1495–1975* (Lexington: University Press of Kentucky, 1983); and Small and Singer, *Resort to Arms.*

10. Europe saw no major war from 1815–1853 and from 1871–1914, two periods almost as long as the 45 years of the Cold War. There is a crucial distinction, however, between the Cold War and these earlier periods. Relations among the great powers deteriorated markedly in the closing years of the two earlier periods, leading in each case to a major war. On the other hand, the Cold War order has become increasingly stable with the passage of time and there is now no serious threat of war between NATO and the Warsaw Pact. Europe would surely remain at peace for the foreseeable future if the Cold War were to continue, a point that highlights the exceptional stability of the present European order.

11. The relative importance of these three factors cannot be stated precisely, but all three had substantial importance.

These factors are aspects of the European state system—of the character of military power and its distribution among states—and not of the states themselves. Thus the keys to war and peace lie more in the structure of the international system than in the nature of the individual states. Domestic factors—most notably hyper-nationalism—also helped cause the wars of the pre-1945 era, and the domestic structures of post-1945 European states have been more conducive to peace, but these domestic factors were less important than the character and distribution of military power between states. Moreover, hyper-nationalism was caused in large part by security competition among the European states, which compelled European elites to mobilize publics to support national defense efforts; hence even this important domestic factor was a more remote consequence of the international system.

Conflict is common among states because the international system creates powerful incentives for aggression.[12] The root cause of the problem is the anarchic nature of the international system. In anarchy there is no higher body or sovereign that protects states from one another. Hence each state living under anarchy faces the ever-present possibility that another state will use force to harm or conquer it. Offensive military action is always a threat to all states in the system.

Anarchy has two principal consequences. First, there is little room for trust among states because a state may be unable to recover if its trust is betrayed. Second, each state must guarantee its own survival since no other actor will provide its security. All other states are potential threats, and no international institution is capable of enforcing order or punishing powerful aggressors.

States seek to survive under anarchy by maximizing their power relative to other states, in order to maintain the means for self-defense. Relative power, not absolute levels of power, matters most to states. Thus, states seek opportunities to weaken potential adversaries and improve their relative power position. They sometimes see aggression as the best way to accumulate more power at the expense of rivals.

This competitive world is peaceful when it is obvious that the costs and risks of going to war are high, and the benefits of going to war are low. Two aspects of military power are at the heart of this incentive structure: the distribution of power between states, and the nature of the military power

---

12. The two classic works on this subject are Hans J. Morgenthau, *Politics Among Nations: The Struggle for Power and Peace*, 5th ed. (New York: Knopf, 1973); and Kenneth N. Waltz, *Theory of International Politics* (Reading, Mass.: Addison-Wesley, 1979).

available to them. The distribution of power between states tells us how well-positioned states are to commit aggression, and whether other states are able to check their aggression. This distribution is a function of the number of poles in the system, and their relative power. The nature of military power directly affects the costs, risks, and benefits of going to war. If the military weaponry available guarantees that warfare will be very destructive, states are more likely to be deterred by the cost of war.[13] If available weaponry favors the defense over the offense, aggressors are more likely to be deterred by the futility of aggression, and all states feel less need to commit aggression, since they enjoy greater security to begin with, and therefore feel less need to enhance their security by expansion.[14] If available weaponry tends to equalize the relative power of states, aggressors are discouraged from going to war. If military weaponry makes it easier to estimate the relative power of states, unwarranted optimism is discouraged and wars of miscalculation are less likely.

One can establish that peace in Europe during the Cold War has resulted from bipolarity, the approximate military balance between the superpowers, and the presence of large numbers of nuclear weapons on both sides in three ways: first, by showing that the general theories on which it rests are valid; second, by demonstrating that these theories can explain the conflicts of the pre-1945 era and the peace of the post-1945 era; and third, by showing that competing theories cannot account for the postwar peace.

THE VIRTUES OF BIPOLARITY OVER MULTIPOLARITY. The two principal arrangements of power possible among states are bipolarity and multipolarity.[15]

---

13. The prospects for deterrence can also be affected by crisis stability calculations. See John J. Mearsheimer, "A Strategic Misstep: The Maritime Strategy and Deterrence in Europe," *International Security*, Vol. 11, No. 2 (Fall 1986), pp. 6–8.

14. See Robert Jervis, "Cooperation Under the Security Dilemma," *World Politics*, Vol. 30, No. 2 (January 1978), pp. 167–214; and Stephen Van Evera, "Causes of War" (unpub. PhD dissertation, University of California at Berkeley, 1984), chap. 3. As noted below, I believe that the distinction between offensive and defensive weapons and, more generally, the concept of an offense-defense balance, is relevant at the nuclear level. However, I do not believe those ideas are relevant at the conventional level. See John J. Mearsheimer, *Conventional Deterrence* (Ithaca: Cornell University Press, 1983), pp. 25–27.

15. Hegemony represents a third possible distribution. Under a hegemony there is only one major power in the system. The rest are minor powers that cannot challenge the major power, but must act in accordance with the dictates of the major power. Every state would like to gain hegemony, because hegemony confers abundant security: no challenger poses a serious threat. Hegemony is rarely achieved, however, because power tends to be somewhat evenly distributed among states, because threatened states have strong incentives to join together to thwart an aspiring hegemon, and because the costs of expansion usually outrun the benefits before domination is achieved, causing extension to become overextension. Hegemony has never

A bipolar system is more peaceful for three main reasons. First, the number of conflict dyads is fewer, leaving fewer possibilities for war. Second, deterrence is easier, because imbalances of power are fewer and more easily averted. Third, the prospects for deterrence are greater because miscalculations of relative power and of opponents' resolve are fewer and less likely.[16]

In a bipolar system two major powers dominate. The minor powers find it difficult to remain unattached to one of the major powers, because the major powers generally demand allegiance from lesser states. (This is especially true in core geographical areas, less so in peripheral areas.) Furthermore, lesser states have little opportunity to play the major powers off against each other, because when great powers are fewer in number, the system is more rigid. As a result, lesser states are hard-pressed to preserve their autonomy.

In a multipolar system, by contrast, three or more major powers dominate. Minor powers in such a system have considerable flexibility regarding alliance partners and can opt to be free floaters. The exact form of a multipolar system can vary markedly, depending on the number of major and minor powers in the system, and their geographical arrangement.

A bipolar system has only one dyad across which war might break out: only two major powers contend with one another, and the minor powers are not likely to be in a position to attack each other. A multipolar system has many potential conflict situations. Major power dyads are more numerous, each posing the potential for conflict. Conflict could also erupt across dyads involving major and minor powers. Dyads between minor powers could also lead to war. Therefore, *ceteris paribus*, war is more likely in a multipolar system than a bipolar one.

Wars in a multipolar world involving just minor powers or only one major power are not likely to be as devastating as a conflict between two major

---

characterized the European state system at any point since it arose in the seventeenth century, and there is no prospect for hegemony in the foreseeable future; hence hegemony is not relevant to assessing the prospects for peace in Europe

16. The key works on bipolarity and multipolarity include Thomas J. Christensen and Jack Snyder, "Chain Gangs and Passed Bucks: Predicting Alliance Patterns in Multipolarity," *International Organization*, Vol. 44, No. 2 (Spring 1990), pp. 137–168; Karl W. Deutsch and J. David Singer, "Multipolar Power Systems and International Stability," *World Politics*, Vol. 16, No. 3 (April 1964), pp. 390–406; Richard N. Rosecrance, "Bipolarity, Multipolarity, and the Future," *Journal of Conflict Resolution*, Vol. 10, No. 3 (September 1966), pp. 314–327; Kenneth N. Waltz, "The Stability of a Bipolar World," *Daedalus*, Vol. 93, No. 3 (Summer 1964), pp. 881–909; and Waltz, *Theory of International Politics*, chap. 8. My conclusions about bipolarity are similar to Waltz's, although there are important differences in our explanations, as will be seen below.

powers. However, local wars tend to widen and escalate. Hence there is always a chance that a small war will trigger a general conflict.

Deterrence is more difficult in a multipolar world because power imbalances are commonplace, and when power is unbalanced, the strong become hard to deter.[17] Power imbalances can lead to conflict in two ways. First, two states can gang up to attack a third state. Second, a major power might simply bully a weaker power in a one-on-one encounter, using its superior strength to coerce or defeat the minor state.[18]

Balance of power dynamics can counter such power imbalances, but only if they operate efficiently.[19] No state can dominate another, either by ganging up or by bullying, if the others coalesce firmly against it, but problems of geography or coordination often hinder the formation of such coalitions.[20] These hindrances may disappear in wartime, but are prevalent in peacetime, and can cause deterrence failure, even where an efficient coalition will eventually form to defeat the aggressor on the battlefield.

First, geography sometimes prevents balancing states from putting meaningful pressure on a potential aggressor. For example, a major power may not be able to put effective military pressure on a state threatening to cause trouble, because buffer states lie in between.

In addition, balancing in a multipolar world must also surmount difficult coordination problems. Four phenomena make coordination difficult. First, alliances provide collective goods, hence allies face the formidable dilemmas of collective action. Specifically, each state may try to shift alliance burdens onto the shoulders of its putative allies. Such "buck-passing" is a common feature of alliance politics.[21] It is most common when the number of states

---

17. Although a balance of power is more likely to produce deterrence than an imbalance of power, a balance of power between states does not guarantee that deterrence will obtain. States sometimes find innovative military strategies that allow them to win on the battlefield, even without marked advantage in the balance of raw military capabilities. Furthermore, the broader political forces that move a state towards war sometimes force leaders to pursue very risky military strategies, impelling states to challenge opponents of equal or even superior strength. See Mearsheimer, *Conventional Deterrence*, especially chap. 2.
18. This discussion of polarity assumes that the military strength of the major powers is roughly equal. The consequences of power asymmetries among great powers is discussed below.
19. See Stephen M. Walt, *The Origins of Alliances* (Ithaca: Cornell University Press, 1987); and Waltz, *Theory of International Politics*, pp. 123–128.
20. One exception bears mention: ganging up is still possible under multipolarity in the restricted case where there are only three powers in the system, and thus no allies available for the victim state.
21. See Mancur Olson and Richard Zeckhauser, "An Economic Theory of Alliances," *Review of Economics and Statistics*, Vol. 48, No. 3 (August 1966), pp. 266–279; and Barry R. Posen, *The*

required to form an effective blocking coalition is large. Second, a state faced with two potential adversaries might conclude that a protracted war between those adversaries would weaken both, even if one side triumphed; hence it may stay on the sidelines, hoping thereby to improve its power position relative to each of the combatants. (This strategy can fail, however, if one of the warring states quickly conquers the other and ends up more powerful, not less powerful, than before the war.) Third, some states may opt out of the balancing process because they believe that they will not be targeted by the aggressor, failing to recognize that they face danger until after the aggressor has won some initial victories. Fourth, diplomacy is an uncertain process, and thus it can take time to build a defensive coalition. A potential aggressor may conclude that it can succeed at aggression before the coalition is completed, and further may be prompted to exploit the window of opportunity that this situation presents before it closes.[22]

If these problems of geography and coordination are severe, states can lose faith in the balancing process. If so, they become more likely to bandwagon with the aggressor, since solitary resistance is futile.[23] Thus factors that weaken the balancing process can generate snowball effects that weaken the process still further.

The third major problem with multipolarity lies in its tendency to foster miscalculation of the resolve of opposing individual states, and of the strength of opposing coalitions.

War is more likely when a state underestimates the willingness of an opposing state to stand firm on issues of difference. It then may push the other state too far, expecting the other to concede, when in fact the opponent will choose to fight. Such miscalculation is more likely under multipolarity because the shape of the international order tends to remain fluid, due to the tendency of coalitions to shift. As a result, the international "rules of the road"—norms of state behavior, and agreed divisions of territorial rights and other privileges—tend to change constantly. No sooner are the rules of a given adversarial relationship worked out, than that relationship may become a friendship, a new adversarial relationship may emerge with a previous

---

Sources of Military Doctrine: France, Britain, and Germany between the World Wars (Ithaca: Cornell University Press, 1984).

22. Domestic political considerations can also sometimes impede balancing behavior. For example, Britain and France were reluctant to ally with the Soviet Union in the 1930s because of their deep-seated antipathy to communism.

23. See Walt, *Origins of Alliances*, pp. 28–32, 173–178.

friend or neutral, and new rules must be established. Under these circumstances, one state may unwittingly push another too far, because ambiguities as to national rights and obligations leave a wider range of issues on which a state may miscalculate another's resolve. Norms of state behavior can come to be broadly understood and accepted by all states, even in multipolarity, just as basic norms of diplomatic conduct became generally accepted by the European powers during the eighteenth century. Nevertheless, a well-defined division of rights is generally more difficult when the number of states is large, and relations among them are in flux, as is the case with multipolarity.

War is also more likely when states underestimate the relative power of an opposing coalition, either because they underestimate the number of states who will oppose them, or because they exaggerate the number of allies who will fight on their own side.[24] Such errors are more likely in a system of many states, since states then must accurately predict the behavior of many states, not just one, in order to calculate the balance of power between coalitions.

A bipolar system is superior to a multipolar system on all of these dimensions. Bullying and ganging up are unknown, since only two actors compete. Hence the power asymmetries produced by bullying and ganging up are also unknown. When balancing is required, it is achieved efficiently. States can balance by either internal means—military buildup—or external means—diplomacy and alliances. Under multipolarity states tend to balance by external means; under bipolarity they are compelled to use internal means. Internal means are more fully under state control, hence are more efficient, and are more certain to produce real balance.[25] The problems that attend efforts to balance by diplomatic methods—geographic complications and coordination difficulties—are bypassed. Finally, miscalculation is less likely than in a multipolar world. States are less likely to miscalculate others' resolve, because the rules of the road with the main opponent become settled over time, leading both parties to recognize the limits beyond which they cannot push the other. States also cannot miscalculate the membership of the opposing coalition, since each side faces only one main enemy. Simplicity breeds certainty; certainty bolsters peace.

---

24. This point is the central theme of Waltz, "The Stability of a Bipolar World." Also see Geoffrey Blainey, *The Causes of War* (New York: Free Press, 1973), chap. 3.
25. Noting the greater efficiency of internal over external balancing is Waltz, *Theory of International Politics*, pp. 163, 168.

There are no empirical studies that provide conclusive evidence of the effects of bipolarity and multipolarity on the likelihood of war. This undoubtedly reflects the difficulty of the task: from its beginning until 1945, the European state system was multipolar, leaving this history barren of comparisons that would reveal the differing effects of multipolarity and bipolarity. Earlier history does afford some apparent examples of bipolar systems, including some that were warlike—Athens and Sparta, Rome and Carthage—but this history is inconclusive, because it is sketchy and incomplete and therefore does not offer enough detail to validate the comparisons. Lacking a comprehensive survey of history, we cannot progress beyond offering examples pro and con, without knowing which set of examples best represents the universe of cases. As a result the case made here stops short of empirical demonstration, and rests chiefly on deduction. However, I believe that this deductive case provides a sound basis for accepting the argument that bipolarity is more peaceful than multipolarity; the deductive logic seems compelling, and there is no obvious historical evidence that cuts against it. I show below that the ideas developed here apply to events in twentieth century Europe, both before and after 1945.

THE VIRTUES OF EQUALITY OF POWER OVER INEQUALITY. Power can be more or less equally distributed among the major powers of both bipolar and multipolar systems. Both systems are more peaceful when equality is greatest among the poles. Power inequalities invite war by increasing the potential for successful aggression; hence war is minimized when inequalities are least.[26]

How should the degree of equality in the distribution of power in a system be assessed? Under bipolarity, the overall equality of the system is simply a function of the balance of power between the two poles—an equal balance creates an equal system, a skewed balance produces an unequal system. Under multipolarity the focus is on the power balance between the two leading states in the system, but the power ratios across other potential conflict dyads also matter. The net system equality is an aggregate of the degree of equality among all of the poles. However, most general wars under multipolarity have arisen from wars of hegemony that have pitted the leading state—an aspiring hegemon—against the other major powers in the system. Such wars are most probable when a leading state emerges, and can hope

---

26. This discussion does not encompass the situation where power asymmetries are so great that one state emerges as a hegemon. See note 15.

to defeat each of the others if it can isolate them. This pattern characterized the wars that grew from the attempts at hegemony by Charles V, Philip II, Louis XIV, Revolutionary and Napoleonic France, Wilhelmine Germany, and Nazi Germany.[27] Hence the ratio between the leader and its nearest competitor—in bipolarity or multipolarity—has more effect on the stability of the system than do other ratios, and is therefore the key ratio that describes the equality of the system. Close equality in this ratio lowers the risk of war.

The polarity of an international system and the degree of power equality of the system are related: bipolar systems tend more toward equality, because, as noted above, states are then compelled to balance by internal methods, and internal balancing is more efficient than external balancing. Specifically, the number-two state in a bipolar system can only hope to balance against the leader by mobilizing its own resources to reduce the gap between the two, since it has no potential major alliance partners. On the other hand, the second-strongest state in a multipolar system can seek security through alliances with others, and may be tempted to pass the buck to them, instead of building up its own strength. External balancing of this sort is especially attractive because it is cheap and fast. However, such behavior leaves intact the power gap between the two leading states, and thus leaves in place the dangers that such a power gap creates. Hence another source of stability under bipolarity lies in the greater tendency for its poles to be equal.

THE VIRTUES OF NUCLEAR DETERRENCE. Deterrence is most likely to hold when the costs and risks of going to war are obviously great. The more horrible the prospect of war, the less likely it is to occur. Deterrence is also most robust when conquest is most difficult. Aggressors then are more likely to be deterred by the futility of expansion, and all states feel less compelled to expand to increase their security, making them easier to deter because they are less compelled to commit aggression.

---

27. This point is the central theme of Ludwig Dehio, *The Precarious Balance: Four Centuries of the European Power Struggle*, trans. Charles Fullman (New York: Knopf, 1962). Also see Randolph M. Siverson and Michael R. Tennefoss, "Power, Alliance, and the Escalation of International Conflict, 1815–1965," *American Political Science Review*, Vol. 78, No. 4 (December 1984), pp. 1057–1069. The two lengthy periods of peace in the nineteenth century (see note 10 above) were mainly caused by the equal distribution of power among the major European states. Specifically, there was no aspiring hegemon in Europe for most of these two periods. France, the most powerful state in Europe at the beginning of the nineteenth century, soon declined to a position of rough equality with its chief competitors, while Germany only emerged as a potential hegemon in the early twentieth century.

Nuclear weapons favor peace on both counts. They are weapons of mass destruction, and would produce horrendous devastation if used in any numbers. Moreover, if both sides' nuclear arsenals are secure from attack, creating a mutually assured retaliation capability (mutual assured destruction or MAD), nuclear weapons make conquest more difficult; international conflicts revert from tests of capability and will to purer tests of will, won by the side willing to run greater risks and pay greater costs. This gives defenders the advantage, because defenders usually value their freedom more than aggressors value new conquests. Thus nuclear weapons are a superb deterrent: they guarantee high costs, and are more useful for self-defense than for aggression.[28]

In addition, nuclear weapons affect the degree of equality in the system. Specifically, the situation created by MAD bolsters peace by moving power relations among states toward equality. States that possess nuclear deterrents can stand up to one another, even if their nuclear arsenals vary greatly in size, as long as both sides' nuclear arsenals are secure from attack. This situation of closer equality has the stabilizing effects noted above.

Finally, MAD also bolsters peace by clarifying the relative power of states and coalitions.[29] States can still miscalculate each other's will, but miscalculations of relative capability are less likely, since nuclear capabilities are not elastic to the specific size and characteristics of forces; once an assured destruction capability is achieved, further increments of nuclear power have little strategic importance. Hence errors in assessing these specific characteristics have little effect. Errors in predicting membership in war coalitions also have less effect, since unforeseen additions or subtractions from such coalitions will not influence war outcomes unless they produce a huge change in the nuclear balance—enough to give one side meaningful nuclear superiority.

THE DANGERS OF HYPER-NATIONALISM. Nationalism is best defined as a set of political beliefs which holds that a nation—a body of individuals with characteristics that purportedly distinguish them from other individuals—

---

28. Works developing the argument that nuclear weapons are essentially defensive in nature are Shai Feldman, *Israeli Nuclear Deterrence: A Strategy for the 1980s* (New York: Columbia University Press, 1982), pp. 45–49; Stephen Van Evera, "Why Europe Matters, Why the Third World Doesn't: American Grand Strategy after the Cold War," *Journal of Strategic Studies*, Vol. 13, No. 2 (June 1990, forthcoming); and Van Evera, "Causes of War," chap. 13.
29. See Feldman, *Israeli Nuclear Deterrence*, pp. 50–52; and Van Evera, "Causes of War," pp. 697–699.

should have its own state.[30] Although nationalists often believe that their nation is unique or special, this conclusion does not necessarily mean that they think they are superior to other peoples, merely that they take pride in their own nation.

However, this benevolent nationalism frequently turns into ugly hyper-nationalism—the belief that other nations or nation-states are both inferior and threatening and must therefore be dealt with harshly. In the past, hyper-nationalism among European states has arisen largely because most European states are nation-states—states comprised of one principal nation—and these nation-states exist in an anarchic world, under constant threat from other states. In such a situation people who love their own nation and state can develop an attitude of contempt and loathing toward the nations who inhabit opposing states. The problem is exacerbated by the fact that political elites often feel compelled to portray adversary nations in the most negative way so as to mobilize public support for national security policies.

Malevolent nationalism is most likely to develop under military systems that require reliance on mass armies; the state may exploit nationalist appeals to mobilize its citizenry for the sacrifices required to sustain large standing armies. On the other hand, hyper-nationalism is least likely when states can rely on small professional armies, or on complex high-technology military organizations that do not require vast manpower. For this reason nuclear weapons work to dampen nationalism, since they shift the basis of military power away from pure reliance on mass armies, and toward greater reliance on smaller high-technology organizations.

In sum, hyper-nationalism is the most important domestic cause of war, although it is still a second-order force in world politics. Furthermore, its causes lie largely in the international system.

THE CAUSES OF THE LONG PEACE: EVIDENCE

The historical record shows a perfect correlation between bipolarity, equality of military power, and nuclear weapons, on the one hand, and the long peace, on the other hand. When an equal bipolarity arose and nuclear weapons appeared, peace broke out. This correlation suggests that the bipolarity

---

30. This definition is drawn from Ernest Gellner, *Nations and Nationalism* (Ithaca: Cornell University Press, 1983), which is an excellent study of the origins of nationalism. Nevertheless, Gellner pays little attention to how nationalism turns into a malevolent force that contributes to instability in the international system.

theory, the equality theory, and the nuclear theory of the long peace are all valid. However, correlation alone does not prove causation. Other factors still may account for the long peace. One way to rule out this possibility is to enumerate what the three theories predict about both the pre-war and postwar eras, and then to ask if these predictions came true in detail during those different periods.

BEFORE THE COLD WAR. The dangers of multipolarity are highlighted by events before both world wars. The existence of many dyads of potential conflict provided many possible ways to light the fuse to war in Europe. Diplomacy before World War I involved intense interactions among five major powers (Britain, France, Russia, Austria-Hungary, and Germany), and two minor powers (Serbia, and Belgium). At least six significant adversarial relationships emerged: Germany versus Britain, France, Russia, and Belgium; and Austria-Hungary versus Serbia and Russia. Before World War II five major powers (Britain, France, the Soviet Union, Germany, and Italy) and seven minor powers (Belgium, Poland, Czechoslovakia, Austria, Hungary, Romania, and Finland) interacted. These relations produced some thirteen important conflicts: Germany versus Britain, France, the Soviet Union, Czechoslovakia, Poland, and Austria; Italy versus Britain and France; the Soviet Union versus Finland and Poland; Czechoslovakia versus Poland and Hungary; and Romania versus Hungary. This multiplicity of conflicts made the outbreak of war inherently more likely. Moreover, many of the state interests at issue in each of these conflicts were interconnected, raising the risk that any single conflict that turned violent would trigger a general war, as happened in both 1914 and 1939.

Before World War II Germany was able to gang up with others against some minor states, and to bully others into joining with it. In 1939 Germany bolstered its power by ganging up with Poland and Hungary to partition Czechoslovakia, and then ganged up with the Soviet Union against Poland. In 1938 Germany bullied the Czechs into surrendering the Sudetenland, and also bullied the Austrians into complete surrender.[31] By these successes Germany expanded its power, leaving it far stronger than its immediate neighbors, and thereby making deterrence much harder.

German power could have been countered before both world wars had the other European powers balanced efficiently against Germany. If so, Ger-

---

31. Austria is not a pure case of bullying; there was also considerable pro-German support in Austria during the late 1930s.

many might have been deterred, and war prevented on both occasions. However, the other powers twice failed to do so. Before 1914 the scope of this failure was less pronounced; France and Russia balanced forcefully against Germany, while only Britain failed to commit firmly against Germany before war began.[32]

Before 1939, failure to balance was far more widespread.[33] The Soviet Union failed to aid Czechoslovakia against Germany in 1938, partly for geographic reasons: they shared no common border, leaving the Soviets with no direct access to Czech territory. France failed to give effective aid to the Czechs and Poles, partly because French military doctrine was defensively oriented, but also because France had no direct access to Czech or Polish territory, and therefore could not easily deploy forces to bolster Czech and Polish defenses.

Britain and France each passed the buck by transferring the cost of deterring Germany onto the other, thereby weakening their combined effort. The Soviet Union, with the Molotov-Ribbentrop Pact, sought to turn the German armies westward, hoping that they would become bogged down in a war of attrition similar to World War I on the Western Front. Some of the minor European powers, including Belgium, the Netherlands, Denmark, and the Scandinavian states, passed the buck to the major powers by standing on the sidelines during the crises of 1938 and 1939.

Britain and the United States failed to recognize that they were threatened by Germany until late in the game—1939 for Britain, 1940 for the United States—and they therefore failed to take an early stand. When they finally recognized the danger posed by Germany and resolved to respond, they lacked appropriate military forces. Britain could not pose a significant military threat to Germany until after it built up its own military forces and coordinated its plans and doctrine with its French and Polish allies. In the meantime

---

32. Britain's failure to commit itself explicitly to a Continental war before the July Crisis was probably a mistake of great proportions. There is evidence that the German chancellor, Bethmann-Hollweg, tried to stop the slide towards war once it became apparent that Britain would fight with France and Russia against Germany, turning a Continental war into a world war. See Imanuel Geiss, ed., *July 1914: The Outbreak of the First World War* (New York: Norton, 1967), chap. 7. Had the Germans clearly understood British intentions before the crisis, they might have displayed much greater caution in the early stages of the crisis, when it was still possible to avoid war.

33. See Williamson Murray, *The Change in the European Balance of Power, 1938–1939: The Path to Ruin* (Princeton: Princeton University Press, 1984); Posen, *Sources of Military Doctrine;* and Arnold Wolfers, *Britain and France between Two Wars: Conflicting Strategies of Peace from Versailles to World War II* (New York: Norton, 1968); and Barry R. Posen, "Competing Images of the Soviet Union," *World Politics,* Vol. 39, No. 4 (July 1987), pp. 579–597.

deterrence failed. The United States did not launch a significant military buildup until after the war broke out.

Multipolarity also created conditions that permitted serious miscalculation before both world wars, which encouraged German aggression on both occasions. Before 1914, Germany was not certain of British opposition if it reached for continental hegemony, and Germany completely failed to foresee that the United States would eventually move to contain it. In 1939, Germany hoped that France and Britain would stand aside as it conquered Poland, and again failed to foresee eventual American entry into the war. As a result Germany exaggerated its prospects for success. This undermined deterrence by encouraging German adventurism.

In sum, the events leading up to the world wars amply illustrate the risks that arise in a multipolar world. Deterrence was undermined in both cases by phenomena that are more common under a multipolar rather than a bipolar distribution of power.[34]

Deterrence was also difficult before both wars because power was distributed asymmetrically among the major European powers. Specifically, Germany was markedly stronger than any of its immediate neighbors. In 1914 Germany clearly held military superiority over all of its European rivals; only together were they able to defeat it, and then only with American help. 1939 is a more ambiguous case. The results of the war reveal that the Soviet Union had the capacity to stand up to Germany, but this was not apparent at the beginning of the war. Hitler was confident that Germany would defeat the Soviet Union, and this confidence was key to his decision to attack in 1941.

Finally, the events leading up to both world wars also illustrate the risks that arise in a world of pure conventional deterrence in which weapons of mass destruction are absent. World War I broke out partly because all of the important states believed that the costs of war would be small, and that successful offense was feasible.[35] Before World War II these beliefs were less widespread, but had the same effect.[36] The lesser powers thought war would

---

34. The problems associated with multipolarity were also common in Europe before 1900. Consider, for example, that inefficient balancing resulted in the collapse of the first four coalitions arrayed against Napoleonic France. See Steven T. Ross, *European Diplomatic History, 1789–1815: France Against Europe* (Garden City, N.Y.: Doubleday, 1969).

35. Stephen Van Evera, "The Cult of the Offensive and the Origins of the First World War," *International Security*, Vol. 9, No. 1 (Summer 1984), pp. 58–107. Also see Jack Snyder, *The Ideology of the Offensive: Military Decision-Making and the Disasters of 1914* (Ithaca: Cornell University Press, 1984).

36. Mearsheimer, *Conventional Deterrence*, chaps. 3–4.

be costly and conquest difficult, but the leaders of the strongest state—Germany—saw the prospect of cheap victory, and this belief was enough to destroy deterrence and produce war. Had nuclear weapons existed, these beliefs would have been undercut, removing a key condition that permitted both wars.

What was the role of internal German politics in causing the world wars? So far I have focused on aspects of the international system surrounding Germany. This focus reflects my view that systemic factors were more important. But German domestic political and social developments also played a significant role, contributing to the aggressive character of German foreign policy. Specifically, German society was infected with a virulent nationalism between 1870 and 1945 that laid the basis for expansionist foreign policies.[37]

However, two points should be borne in mind. First, German hyper-nationalism was in part fueled by Germany's pronounced sense of insecurity, which reflected Germany's vulnerable location at the center of Europe, with relatively open borders on both sides. These geographic facts made German security problems especially acute; this situation gave German elites a uniquely strong motive to mobilize their public for war, which they did largely by fanning nationalism. Thus even German hyper-nationalism can be ascribed in part to the nature of the pre-1945 international system.

Second, the horror of Germany's murderous conduct during World War II should be distinguished from the scope of the aggressiveness of German foreign policy.[38] Germany was indeed aggressive, but not unprecedentedly so. Other states have aspired to hegemony in Europe, and sparked wars by their efforts; Germany was merely the latest to attempt to convert dominant into hegemonic power. What was unique about Germany's conduct was its policy of mass murder toward many of the peoples of Europe. The causes of this murderous policy should not be conflated with the causes of the two

---

37. See Ludwig Dehio, *Germany and World Politics in the Twentieth Century*, trans. Dieter Pevsner (New York: Norton, 1967); Fritz Fischer, *War of Illusions: German Policies from 1911 to 1914*, trans. Marian Jackson (New York: Norton, 1975); Paul M. Kennedy, *The Rise of the Anglo-German Antagonism, 1860–1914* (London: Allen and Unwin, 1980), chap. 18; Hans Kohn, *The Mind of Germany: The Education of a Nation* (New York: Harper Torchbook, 1965), chaps. 7–12; and Louis L. Snyder, *German Nationalism: The Tragedy of a People* (Harrisburg, Pa.: Telegraph Press, 1952).
38. There is a voluminous literature on the German killing machine in World War II. Among the best overviews of the subject are Ian Kershaw, *The Nazi Dictatorship: Problems and Perspectives of Interpretation*, 2nd ed. (London: Arnold, 1989), chaps. 5, 8, 9; Henry L. Mason, "Imponderables of the Holocaust," *World Politics*, Vol. 34, No. 1 (October 1981), pp. 90–113; and Mason, "Implementing the Final Solution: The Ordinary Regulating of the Extraordinary," *World Politics*, Vol. 40, No. 4 (July 1988), pp. 542–569.

world wars. The policy of murder arose chiefly from domestic sources; the wars arose mainly from aspects of the distribution and character of power in Europe.

THE COLD WAR RECORD. The European state system abruptly shifted from multipolar to bipolar after 1945. Three factors were responsible: the near-complete destruction of German power, the growth of Soviet power, and the permanent American commitment to the European Continent. The weakening of the German Reich was accomplished by allied occupation and dismemberment. Silesia, Pomerania, East Prussia, and parts of West Prussia and Brandenburg were given to other countries, the Sudetenland was returned to Czechoslovakia, and Austria was restored to independence. The rest of the German Reich was divided into two countries, East and West Germany, which became enemies. This reduction of German power, coupled with the physical presence of American and Soviet military might in the heart of Europe, eliminated the threat of German aggression.[39]

Meanwhile the Soviet Union extended its power westward, becoming the dominant power on the Continent and one of the two strongest powers in the world. There is no reason to think that the Soviets would not have reached for continental hegemony, as the Spanish, French, and Germans did earlier, had they believed they could win a hegemonic war. But the Soviets, unlike their predecessors, made no attempt to gain hegemony by force, leaving Europe in peace.

Bipolarity supplies part of the reason. Bipolarity made Europe a simpler place in which only one point of friction—the East-West conflict—had to be managed to avoid war. The two blocs encompassed most of Europe, leaving few unprotected weak states for the Soviets to conquer. As a result the Soviets have had few targets to bully. They have also been unable to gang up on the few states that are unprotected, because their West-bloc adversary has been their only potential ganging-up partner.

Bipolarity also left less room for miscalculation of both resolve and capability. During the first fifteen years of the Cold War, the rules of the road for the conflict were not yet established, giving rise to several serious crises. However, over time each side gained a clear sense of how far it could push the other, and what the other would not tolerate. A set of rules came to be agreed upon: an understanding on the division of rights in Austria, Berlin,

---

39. See Anton W. DePorte, *Europe between the Superpowers: The Enduring Balance*, 2nd ed. (New Haven: Yale University Press, 1986).

and elsewhere in Europe; a proscription on secret unilateral re-deployment of large nuclear forces to areas contiguous to the opponent; mutual toleration of reconnaissance satellites; agreement on rules of peacetime engagement between naval forces; and so forth. The absence of serious crises during 1963–90 was due in part to the growth of such agreements on the rights of both sides, and the rules of conduct. These could develop in large part because the system was bipolar in character. Bipolarity meant that the same two states remained adversaries for a long period, giving them time to learn how to manage their conflict without war. By contrast, a multipolar world of shifting coalitions would repeatedly have forced adversaries to re-learn how their opponents defined interests, reach new accords on the division of rights, and establish new rules of competitive conduct.

Bipolarity also left less room to miscalculate the relative strength of the opposing coalitions. The composition of possible war coalitions has been clear because only two blocs have existed, each led by an overwhelmingly dominant power that could discipline its members. Either side could have miscalculated its relative military strength, but bipolarity removed ambiguity about relative strength of adversarial coalitions arising from diplomatic uncertainties.

The East-West military balance in Europe has been roughly equal throughout the Cold War, which has further bolstered stability. This approximate parity strengthened deterrence by ensuring that no state was tempted to use force to exploit a power advantage. Parity resulted partly from bipolarity: because the two blocs already encompassed all the states of Europe, both sides have balanced mainly by internal rather than external means. These more efficient means have produced a more nearly equal balance.

Nuclear weapons also played a key role in preventing war in post–World War II Europe.

Western elites on both sides of the Atlantic quickly recognized that nuclear weapons were vastly destructive and that their widespread use in Europe would cause unprecedented devastation. The famous *Carte Blanche* exercises conducted in Germany in 1955 made it manifestly clear that a nuclear war in Europe would involve far greater costs than another World War II.[40] Accordingly, Western policymakers rarely suggested that nuclear war could be "won," and instead emphasized the horrors that would attend nuclear war.

---

40. See Hans Speier, *German Rearmament and Atomic War: The Views of German Military and Political Leaders* (Evanston, Ill.: Row, Peterson, 1957), chap. 10.

Moreover, they have understood that conventional war could well escalate to the nuclear level, and have in fact based NATO strategy on that reality.

Soviet leaders also recognized the horrendous results that a nuclear war would produce.[41] Some Soviet military officers have asserted that victory is possible in nuclear war, but even they have acknowledged that such a victory would be Pyrrhic. Soviet civilians have generally argued that victory is impossible. Furthermore, the Soviets long maintained that it was not possible to fight a purely conventional war in Europe, and that conventional victory would only prompt the loser to engage in nuclear escalation.[42] The Soviets later granted more possibility that a conventional war might be controlled, but still recognized that escalation is likely.[43] Under Gorbachev, Soviet military thinking has placed even greater emphasis on the need to avoid nuclear war and devoted more attention to the dangers of inadvertent nuclear war.[44]

Official rhetoric aside, policymakers on both sides have also behaved very cautiously in the presence of nuclear weapons. There is not a single case of a leader brandishing nuclear weapons during a crisis, or behaving as if nuclear war might be a viable option for solving important political problems. On the contrary, policymakers have never gone beyond nuclear threats of a very subtle sort, and have shown great caution when the possibility of nuclear confrontation has emerged.[45] This cautious conduct has lowered the risk of war.

Nuclear weapons also imposed an equality and clarity on the power relations between the superpowers. This equality and clarity represented a

---

41. See Robert L. Arnett, "Soviet Attitudes Towards Nuclear War: Do They Really Think They Can Win?" *Journal of Strategic Studies*, Vol. 2, No. 2 (September 1979), pp. 172–191; and David Holloway, *The Soviet Union and the Arms Race* (New Haven: Yale University Press, 1983).
42. Thus Nikita Khrushchev explained, "Now that the big countries have thermonuclear weapons at their disposal, they are sure to resort to those weapons if they begin to lose a war fought with conventional means. If it ever comes down to a question of whether or not to face defeat, there is sure to be someone who will be in favor of pushing the button, and the missiles will begin to fly." Nikita Khrushchev, *Khrushchev Remembers: The Last Testament*, trans. and ed. by Strobe Talbott (New York: Bantam, 1976), pp. 603–604.
43. See James M. McConnell, "Shifts in Soviet Views on the Proper Focus of Military Development," *World Politics*, Vol. 37, No. 3 (April 1985), pp. 317–343.
44. See Stephen M. Meyer, "The Sources and Prospects of Gorbachev's New Political Thinking on Security," *International Security*, Vol. 13, No. 2 (Fall 1988), pp. 134–138.
45. See Hannes Adomeit, *Soviet Risk-taking and Crisis Behavior: A Theoretical and Empirical Analysis* (London: Allen and Unwin, 1982); Richard K. Betts, *Nuclear Blackmail and Nuclear Balance* (Washington, D.C.: Brookings, 1987); and McGeorge Bundy, *Danger and Survival: Choices about the Bomb in the First Fifty Years* (New York: Random House, 1988). Also see Joseph S. Nye, Jr., "Nuclear Learning and U.S.-Soviet Security Regimes," *International Organization*, Vol. 41, No. 3 (Summer 1987), pp. 371–402.

marked change from the earlier non-nuclear world, in which sharp power inequalities and miscalculations of relative power were common.[46]

During the Cold War, the United States and the Soviet Union have exhibited markedly less hyper-nationalism than did the European powers before 1945. After World War II, nationalism declined sharply within Europe, partly because the occupation forces took active steps to dampen it,[47] and also because the European states, no longer providing their own security, now lacked the incentive to purvey hyper-nationalism in order to bolster public support for national defense. More importantly, however, the locus of European politics shifted to the United States and the Soviet Union—two states that, each for its own reasons, had not exhibited nationalism of the virulent type found earlier in Europe. Nor has nationalism become virulent in either superpower during the Cold War. In part this reflects the greater stability of the postwar order, arising from bipolarity, military equality, and nuclear weapons; with less expectation of war, neither superpower has faced the need to mobilize its population for war. It also reflects a second effect of nuclear weapons: they have reduced the importance of mass armies for preserving sovereignty, thus diminishing the importance of maintaining a hyper-nationalized pool of manpower.

THE CAUSES OF THE LONG PEACE: COMPETING EXPLANATIONS

The claim that bipolarity, equality, and nuclear weapons have been largely responsible for the stability of the past 45 years is further strengthened by the absence of persuasive competing explanations. Two of the most popular theories of peace—*economic liberalism* and *peace-loving democracies*—are not relevant to the issue at hand.

Economic liberalism, which posits that a liberal economic order bolsters peace (discussed in more detail below), cannot explain the stability of postwar Europe, because there has been little economic exchange between the Soviet Union and the West over the past 45 years. Although economic flows be-

---

46. Some experts acknowledge that nuclear weapons had deterrent value in the early decades of the Cold War, but maintain that they had lost their deterrent value by the mid-1960s when the Soviets finally acquired the capability to retaliate massively against the American homeland. I reject this argument and have outlined my views in John J. Mearsheimer, "Nuclear Weapons and Deterrence in Europe," *International Security*, Vol. 9, No. 3 (Winter 1984/85), pp. 19–46.

47. See Paul M. Kennedy, "The Decline of Nationalistic History in the West, 1900–1970," *Journal of Contemporary History*, Vol. 8, No. 1 (January 1973), pp. 77–100; and E.H. Dance, *History the Betrayer* (London: Hutchinson, 1960).

tween Eastern and Western Europe have been somewhat greater, in no sense has all of Europe been encompassed by a liberal economic order.

The peace-loving democracies theory (also discussed below) holds that democracies do not go to war against other democracies, but concedes that democracies are not especially pacific when facing authoritarian states. This theory cannot account for post–World War II stability because the Soviet Union and its allies in Eastern Europe have not been democratic over the past 45 years.

A third theory of peace, *obsolescence of war*, proposes that modern conventional war had become so deadly by the twentieth century that it was no longer possible to think of war as a sensible means to achieve national goals.[48] It took the two world wars to drive this point home, but by 1945 it was clear that large-scale conventional war had become irrational and morally unacceptable, like institutions such as slavery and dueling. Thus, even without nuclear weapons, statesmen in the Cold War would not seriously have countenanced war, which had become an anachronism. This theory, it should be emphasized, does not ascribe the absence of war to nuclear weapons, but instead points to the horrors of modern conventional war.

This argument probably provides the most persuasive alternative explanation for the stability of the Cold War, but it is not convincing on close inspection. The fact that World War II occurred casts serious doubt on this theory; if any war could have convinced Europeans to forswear conventional war, it should have been World War I, with its vast casualties. There is no doubt that conventional war among modern states could devastate the participants. Nevertheless, this explanation misses one crucial difference between nuclear and conventional war, a difference that explains why war is still a viable option for states. Proponents of this theory assume that all conventional wars are protracted and bloody wars of attrition, like World War I on the Western front. However, it is possible to score a quick and decisive victory in a conventional war and avoid the devastation that usually attends a protracted conventional war.[49] Conventional war can be won; nuclear war cannot be, since neither side can escape devastation by the other, regardless of the outcome on the battlefield. Thus, the incentives to avoid

---

48. This theory is most clearly articulated by John E. Mueller, *Retreat from Doomsday: The Obsolescence of Major War* (New York: Basic Books, 1989). See also Carl Kaysen, "Is War Obsolete? A Review Essay," *International Security*, Vol. 14, No. 4 (Spring 1990), pp. 42–64.
49. See Mearsheimer, *Conventional Deterrence*, chaps. 1–2.

war are far greater in a nuclear than a conventional world, making nuclear deterrence much more robust than conventional deterrence.[50]

Predicting the Future: The Balkanization of Europe?

What new order will emerge in Europe if the Soviets and Americans withdraw to their homelands and the Cold War order dissolves? What characteristics will it have? How dangerous will it be?

It is certain that bipolarity will disappear, and multipolarity will emerge in the new European order. The other two dimensions of the new order—the distribution of power among the major states, and the distribution of nuclear weapons among them—are not pre-determined, and several possible arrangements could develop. The probable stability of these arrangements would vary markedly. This section examines the scope of the dangers that each arrangement would present, and the likelihood that each will emerge.

The distribution and deployment patterns of nuclear weapons in the new Europe is the least certain, and probably the most important, element of the new order. Accordingly, this section proceeds by exploring the character of the four principal nuclear worlds that might develop: a denuclearized Europe, continuation of the current patterns of nuclear ownership, and nuclear proliferation either well- or ill-managed.

The best new order would incorporate the limited, managed proliferation of nuclear weapons. This would be more dangerous than the current order, but considerably safer than 1900–45. The worst order would be a non-nuclear Europe in which power inequities emerge between the principal poles of power. This order would be more dangerous than the current world, perhaps almost as dangerous as the world before 1945. Continuation of the current

---

50. German decision-making in the early years of World War II underscores this point. See Mearsheimer, *Conventional Deterrence*, chap. 4. The Germans were well aware from their experience in World War I that conventional war among major powers could have devastating consequences. Nevertheless, they decided three times to launch major land offensives: Poland (1939); France (1940); and the Soviet Union (1941). In each case, the Germans believed that they could win a quick and decisive victory and avoid a costly protracted war like World War I. Their calculations proved correct against Poland and France. They were wrong about the Soviets, who thwarted their blitzkrieg and eventually played the central role in bringing down the Third Reich. The Germans surely would have been deterred from attacking the Soviet Union if they had foreseen the consequences. However, the key point is that they saw some possibility of winning an easy and relatively cheap victory against the Red Army. That option is not available in a nuclear war.

pattern, or mismanaged proliferation, would be worse than the world of today, but safer than the pre-1945 world.

EUROPE WITHOUT NUCLEAR WEAPONS

Some Europeans and Americans seek to eliminate nuclear weapons from Europe, and would replace the Cold War order with a wholly non-nuclear order. Constructing this nuclear-free Europe would require Britain, France and the Soviet Union to rid themselves of nuclear weapons. Proponents believe that a Europe without nuclear weapons would be the most peaceful possible arrangement; in fact, however, a nuclear-free Europe would be the most dangerous among possible post–Cold War orders. The pacifying effects of nuclear weapons—the security they provide, the caution they generate, the rough equality they impose, and the clarity of relative power they create— would be lost. Peace would then depend on the other dimensions of the new order—the number of poles, and the distribution of power among them. However, the new order will certainly be multipolar, and may be unequal; hence the system may be very prone to violence. The structure of power in Europe would look much like it did between the world wars, and it could well produce similar results.

The two most powerful states in post–Cold War Europe would probably be Germany and the Soviet Union. They would be physically separated by a band of small, independent states in Eastern Europe. Not much would change in Western Europe, although the states in that area would have to be concerned about a possible German threat on their eastern flank.

The potential for conflict in this system would be considerable. There would be many possible dyads across which war might break out. Power imbalances would be commonplace as a result of the opportunities this system would present for bullying and ganging up. There would be considerable opportunity for miscalculation. The problem of containing German power would emerge once again, but the configuration of power in Europe would make it difficult to form an effective counterbalancing coalition, for much the same reason that an effective counterbalancing coalition failed to form in the 1930s. Eventually the problem of containing the Soviet Union could also re-emerge. Finally, conflicts may erupt in Eastern Europe, providing the vortex that could pull others into a wider confrontation.

A reunified Germany would be surrounded by weaker states that would find it difficult to balance against German aggression. Without forces stationed in states adjacent to Germany, neither the Soviets nor the Americans would be in a good position to help them contain German power. Furthermore, those small states lying between Germany and the Soviet Union might fear the Soviets as much as the Germans, and hence may not be disposed to cooperate with the Soviets to deter German aggression. This problem in fact arose in the 1930s, and 45 years of Soviet occupation in the interim have done nothing to ease East European fears of a Soviet military presence. Thus, scenarios in which Germany uses military force against Poland, Czechoslovakia, or even Austria become possible.

The Soviet Union also might eventually threaten the new status quo. Soviet withdrawal from Eastern Europe does not mean that the Soviets will never feel compelled to return to Eastern Europe. The historical record provides abundant instances of Russian or Soviet involvement in Eastern Europe. Indeed, the Russian presence in Eastern Europe has surged and ebbed repeatedly over the past few centuries.[51] Thus, Soviet withdrawal now hardly guarantees a permanent exit.

Conflict between Eastern European states is also likely to produce instability in a multipolar Europe. There has been no war among the states in that region during the Cold War because the Soviets have tightly controlled them. This point is illustrated by the serious tensions that now exist between Hungary and Romania over Romanian treatment of the Hungarian minority in Transylvania, a region that previously belonged to Hungary and still has roughly 2 million Hungarians living within its borders. Were it not for the Soviet presence in Eastern Europe, this conflict could have brought Romania and Hungary to war by now, and it may bring them to war in the future.[52] This will not be the only danger spot within Eastern Europe if the Soviet empire crumbles.[53]

Warfare in Eastern Europe would cause great suffering to Eastern Europeans. It also might widen to include the major powers, because they would

---

51. See, inter alia: Ivo J. Lederer, ed., *Russian Foreign Policy: Essays in Historical Perspective* (New Haven: Yale University Press, 1962); Andrei Lobanov-Rostovsky, *Russia and Europe, 1825–1878* (Ann Arbor, Mich.: George Wahr Publishing, 1954); and Marc Raeff, *Imperial Russia, 1682–1825: The Coming of Age of Modern Russia* (New York: Knopf, 1971), chap. 2.

52. To get a sense of the antipathy between Hungary and Romania over this issue, see *Witnesses to Cultural Genocide: First-Hand Reports on Romania's Minority Policies Today* (New York: American Transylvanian Federation and the Committee for Human Rights in Romania, 1979). The March 1990 clashes between ethnic Hungarians and Romanians in Tîrgu Mures (Romanian Transylvania) indicate the potential for savage violence that is inherent in these ethnic conflicts.

53. See Zbigniew Brzezinski, "Post-Communist Nationalism," *Foreign Affairs*, Vol. 68, No. 5 (Winter 1989/1990), pp. 1–13; and Mark Kramer, "Beyond the Brezhnev Doctrine: A New Era in Soviet-East European Relations?" *International Security*, Vol. 14, No. 3 (Winter 1989/90), pp. 51–54.

be drawn to compete for influence in that region, especially if disorder created fluid politics that offered opportunities for wider influence, or threatened defeat for friendly states. During the Cold War, both superpowers were drawn into Third World conflicts across the globe, often in distant areas of little strategic importance. Eastern Europe is directly adjacent to both the Soviet Union and Germany, and has considerable economic and strategic importance; thus trouble in Eastern Europe could offer even greater temptations to these powers than past conflicts in the Third World offered the superpowers. Furthermore, because the results of local conflicts will be largely determined by the relative success of each party in finding external allies, Eastern European states will have strong incentives to drag the major powers into their local conflicts.[54] Thus both push and pull considerations would operate to enmesh outside powers in local Eastern European wars.

Miscalculation is also likely to be a problem in a multipolar Europe. For example, the new order might well witness shifting patterns of conflict, leaving insufficient time for adversaries to develop agreed divisions of rights and agreed rules of interaction, or constantly forcing them to re-establish new agreements and rules as old antagonisms fade and new ones arise. It is not likely that circumstances would allow the development of a robust set of agreements of the sort that have stabilized the Cold War since 1963. Instead, Europe would resemble the pattern of the early Cold War, in which the absence of rules led to repeated crises. In addition, the multipolar character of the system is likely to give rise to miscalculation regarding the strength of the opposing coalitions.

It is difficult to predict the precise balance of conventional military power that would emerge between the two largest powers in post–Cold War Europe, especially since the future of Soviet power is now hard to forecast. The Soviet Union might recover its strength soon after withdrawing from Central Europe; if so, Soviet power would overmatch German power. Or centrifugal national forces may pull the Soviet Union apart, leaving no remnant state that is the equal of a united Germany.[55] What seems most likely is that

---

54. The new prime minister of Hungary, Jozsef Antall, has already spoken of the need for a "European solution" to the problem of Romania's treatment of Hungarians in Transylvania. Celestine Bohlen, "Victor in Hungary Sees '45 as the Best of Times," *New York Times*, April 10, 1990, p. A8.

55. This article focuses on how changes in the strength of Soviet power and retraction of the Soviet empire would affect the prospects for stability in Europe. However, the dissolution of the Soviet Union, a scenario not explored here in any detail, would raise dangers that would be different from and in addition to those discussed here.

Germany and the Soviet Union might emerge as powers of roughly equal strength. The first two scenarios, with their marked inequality between the two leading powers, would be especially worrisome, although there is cause for concern even if Soviet and German power are balanced.

Resurgent hyper-nationalism will probably pose less danger than the problems described above, but some nationalism is likely to resurface in the absence of the Cold War and may provide additional incentives for war. A non-nuclear Europe is likely to be especially troubled by nationalism, since security in such an order will largely be provided by mass armies, which often cannot be maintained without infusing societies with hyper-nationalism. The problem is likely to be most acute in Eastern Europe, but there is also potential for trouble in Germany. The Germans have generally done an admirable job combatting nationalism over the past 45 years, and in remembering the dark side of their past. Nevertheless, worrisome portents are now visible; of greatest concern, some prominent Germans have lately advised a return to greater nationalism in historical education.[56] Moreover, nationalism will be exacerbated by the unresolved border disputes that will be uncovered by the retreat of American and Soviet power. Especially prominent is that of the border between Germany and Poland, which some Germans would change in Germany's favor.

However, it seems very unlikely that Europe will actually be denuclearized, despite the present strength of anti-nuclear feeling in Europe. For example, it is unlikely that the French, in the absence of America's protective cover and faced with a newly unified Germany, would get rid of their nuclear weapons. Also, the Soviets surely would remain concerned about balancing the American nuclear deterrent, and will therefore retain a deterrent of their own.

THE CURRENT OWNERSHIP PATTERN CONTINUES

A more plausible order for post–Cold War Europe is one in which Britain, France and the Soviet Union keep their nuclear weapons, but no new nuclear powers emerge in Europe. This scenario sees a nuclear-free zone in Central Europe, but leaves nuclear weapons on the European flanks.

---

56. Aspects of this story are recounted in Richard J. Evans, *In Hitler's Shadow: West German Historians and the Attempt to Escape from the Nazi Past* (New York: Pantheon, 1989). A study of past German efforts to mischaracterize history is Holger H. Herwig, "Clio Deceived: Patriotic Self-Censorship in Germany After the Great War," *International Security*, Vol. 12, No. 2 (Fall 1987), pp. 5–44.

This scenario, too, also seems unlikely, since the non-nuclear states will have substantial incentives to acquire their own nuclear weapons. Germany would probably not need nuclear weapons to deter a conventional attack by its neighbors, since neither the French nor any of the Eastern European states would be capable of defeating a reunified Germany in a conventional war. The Soviet Union would be Germany's only legitimate conventional threat, but as long as the states of Eastern Europe remained independent, Soviet ground forces would be blocked from a direct attack. The Germans, however, might not be willing to rely on the Poles or the Czechs to provide a barrier and might instead see nuclear weapons as the best way to deter a Soviet conventional attack into Central Europe. The Germans might choose to go nuclear to protect themselves from blackmail by other nuclear powers. Finally, given that Germany would have greater economic strength than Britain or France, it might therefore seek nuclear weapons to raise its military status to a level commensurate with its economic status.

The minor powers of Eastern Europe would have strong incentives to acquire nuclear weapons. Without nuclear weapons, these Eastern European states would be open to nuclear blackmail from the Soviet Union and, if it acquired nuclear weapons, from Germany. No Eastern European state could match the conventional strength of Germany or the Soviet Union, which gives these minor powers a powerful incentive to acquire a nuclear deterrent, even if the major powers had none. In short, a continuation of the current pattern of ownership without proliferation seems unlikely.

How stable would this order be? The continued presence of nuclear weapons in Europe would have some pacifying effects. Nuclear weapons would induce greater caution in their owners, give the nuclear powers greater security, tend to equalize the relative power of states that possess them, and reduce the risk of miscalculation. However, these benefits would be limited if nuclear weapons did not proliferate beyond their current owners, for four main reasons.

First, the caution and the security that nuclear weapons impose would be missing from the vast center of Europe. The entire region between France and the Soviet Union, extending from the Arctic in the north to the Mediterranean in the south, and comprising some eighteen significant states, would become a large zone thereby made "safe" for conventional war. Second, asymmetrical power relations would be bound to develop, between nuclear and non-nuclear states and among non-nuclear states, raising the dangers that attend such asymmetries. Third, the risk of miscalculation would rise, reflecting the multipolar character of this system and the absence of nuclear weapons from a large portion of it. A durable agreed political order would be hard to build because political coalitions would tend to shift over time, causing miscalculations of resolve between adversaries. The relative strength of potential war coalitions would be hard to calculate because coalition strength would depend heavily on the vagaries of diplomacy. Such uncertainties about relative capabilities would be mitigated in conflicts that arose among nuclear powers: nuclear weapons tend to equalize power even among states or coalitions of widely disparate resources, and thus to diminish the importance of additions or defections from each coalition. However, uncertainty would still be acute among the many states that would remain non-nuclear. Fourth, the conventionally-armed states of Central Europe would depend for their security on mass armies, giving them an incentive to infuse their societies with dangerous nationalism in order to maintain public support for national defense efforts.

NUCLEAR PROLIFERATION, WELL-MANAGED OR OTHERWISE

The most likely scenario in the wake of the Cold War is further nuclear proliferation in Europe. This outcome is laden with dangers, but also might provide the best hope for maintaining stability on the Continent. Its effects depend greatly on how it is managed. Mismanaged proliferation could produce disaster, while well-managed proliferation could produce an order nearly as stable as the current order. Unfortunately, however, any proliferation is likely to be mismanaged.

Four principal dangers could arise if proliferation is not properly managed. First, the proliferation process itself could give the existing nuclear powers strong incentives to use force to prevent their non-nuclear neighbors from gaining nuclear weapons, much as Israel used force to preempt Iraq from acquiring a nuclear capability.

Second, even after proliferation was completed, a stable nuclear competition might not emerge between the new nuclear states. The lesser European powers might lack the resources needed to make their nuclear forces survivable; if the emerging nuclear forces were vulnerable, this could create first-strike incentives and attendant crisis instability. Because their economies are far smaller, they would not be able to develop arsenals as large as those of the major powers; arsenals of small absolute size might thus be vulnerable. Furthermore, their lack of territorial expanse deprives them of possible basing modes, such as mobile missile basing, that would secure their deterrents.

Several are landlocked, so they could not base nuclear weapons at sea, the most secure basing mode used by the superpowers. Moreover, their close proximity to one another deprives them of warning time, and thus of basing schemes that exploit warning to achieve invulnerability, such as by the quick launch of alert bombers. Finally, the emerging nuclear powers might also lack the resources required to develop secure command and control and adequate safety procedures for weapons management, thus raising the risk of accidental launch, or of terrorist seizure and use of nuclear weapons.

Third, the elites and publics of the emerging nuclear European states might not quickly develop doctrines and attitudes that reflect a grasp of the devastating consequences and basic unwinnability of nuclear war. There will probably be voices in post–Cold War Europe arguing that limited nuclear war is feasible, and that nuclear wars can be fought and won. These claims might be taken seriously in states that have not had much direct experience with the nuclear revolution.

Fourth, widespread proliferation would increase the number of fingers on the nuclear trigger, which in turn would increase the likelihood that nuclear weapons could be fired due to accident, unauthorized use, terrorist seizure, or irrational decision-making.

If these problems are not resolved, proliferation would present grave dangers. However, the existing nuclear powers can take steps to reduce these dangers. They can help deter preventive attack on emerging nuclear states by extending security guarantees. They can provide technical assistance to help newly nuclear-armed powers to secure their deterrents. And they can help socialize emerging nuclear societies to understand the nature of the forces they are acquiring. Proliferation managed in this manner can help bolster peace.

How broadly should nuclear weapons be permitted to spread? It would be best if proliferation were extended to Germany but not beyond.[57] Germany has a large economic base, and can therefore sustain a secure nuclear force. Moreover, Germany will feel insecure without nuclear weapons; and Germany's great conventional strength gives it significant capacity to disturb Europe if it feels insecure. Other states—especially in Eastern Europe—may also want nuclear weapons, but it would be best to prevent further proliferation. The reasons are, as noted above, that these states may be unable to

---

57. See David Garnham, "Extending Deterrence with German Nuclear Weapons," *International Security*, Vol. 10, No. 1 (Summer 1985), pp. 96–110.

secure their nuclear deterrents, and the unlimited spread of nuclear weapons raises the risk of terrorist seizure or possession by states led by irrational elites. However, if the broader spread of nuclear weapons proves impossible to prevent without taking extreme steps, the existing nuclear powers should let the process happen, while doing their best to channel it in safe directions.

However, even if proliferation were well-managed, significant dangers would remain. If all the major powers in Europe possessed nuclear weapons, history suggests that they would still compete for influence among the lesser powers and be drawn into lesser-power conflicts. The superpowers, despite the security that their huge nuclear arsenals provide, have competed intensely for influence in remote, strategically unimportant areas such as South Asia, Southeast Asia, and Central America. The European powers are likely to exhibit the same competitive conduct, especially in Eastern Europe, even if they possess secure nuclear deterrents.

The possibility of ganging up would remain: several nuclear states could join against a solitary nuclear state, perhaps aggregating enough strength to overwhelm its deterrent. Nuclear states also might bully their non-nuclear neighbors. This problem is mitigated if unbounded proliferation takes place, leaving few non-nuclear states subject to bullying by the nuclear states, but such widespread proliferation raises risks of its own, as noted above.

Well-managed proliferation would reduce the danger that states might miscalculate the relative strength of coalitions, since nuclear weapons clarify the relative power of all states, and diminish the importance of unforeseen additions and defections from alliances. However, the risk remains that resolve will be miscalculated, because patterns of conflict are likely to be somewhat fluid in a multipolar Europe, thus precluding the establishment of well-defined spheres of rights and rules of conduct.

Unbounded proliferation, even if it is well-managed, will raise the risks that appear when there are many fingers on the nuclear trigger—accident, unauthorized or irrational use, or terrorist seizure.

In any case, it is not likely that proliferation will be well-managed. The nuclear powers cannot easily work to manage proliferation while at the same time resisting it; there is a natural tension between the two goals. But they have several motives to resist. The established nuclear powers will be reluctant to give the new nuclear powers technical help in building secure deterrents, because it runs against the grain of state behavior to transfer military power to others, and because of the fear that sensitive military technology could be turned against the donor state if that technology were further transferred to its adversaries. The nuclear powers will also be reluctant to undermine the legitimacy of the 1968 Nuclear Non-Proliferation Treaty by allowing any signatories to acquire nuclear weapons, since this could open the floodgates to the wider proliferation that they seek to avoid, even if they would otherwise favor very limited proliferation. For these reasons the nuclear powers are more likely to spend their energy trying to thwart the process of proliferation, rather than managing it.

Proliferation can be more easily managed if it occurs during a period of relative international calm. Proliferation that occurred during a time of crisis would be especially dangerous, since states in conflict with the emerging nuclear powers would then have a strong incentive to interrupt the process by force. However, proliferation is likely not to begin until the outbreak of crisis, because there will be significant domestic opposition to proliferation within the potential nuclear powers, as well as significant external resistance from the established nuclear powers. Hence it may require a crisis to motivate the potential nuclear powers to pay the domestic and international costs of moving to build a nuclear force. Thus, proliferation is more likely to happen under disadvantageous international conditions than in a period of calm.

Finally, there are limits to the ability of the established nuclear powers to assist small emerging nuclear powers to build secure deterrents. For example, small landlocked powers cannot be given access to sea-based deterrents or land-mobile missile systems requiring vast expanses of land; these are geographic problems that technology cannot erase. Therefore even if the existing nuclear powers move to manage the proliferation process early and wisely, that process still may raise dangers that they cannot control.

Alternative Theories that Predict Peace

Many students of European politics will reject my pessimistic analysis of post–Cold War Europe and instead argue that a multipolar Europe is likely to be at least as peaceful as the present order. Three specific scenarios for a peaceful future have been advanced. Each rests on a well known theory of international relations. However, each of these theories is flawed and thus cannot serve as the basis for reliable predictions of a peaceful order in a multipolar Europe; hence the hopeful scenarios they support lack plausibility.

Under the first optimistic scenario, even a non-nuclear Europe would remain peaceful because Europeans recognize that even a conventional war would be horrific. Sobered by history, national leaders will take great care to avoid war. This scenario rests on the "obsolescence of war" theory.

Although modern conventional war can certainly be very costly, there are several flaws in this argument. There is no systematic evidence demonstrating that Europeans believe war is obsolete. However, even if it were widely believed in Europe that war is no longer thinkable, attitudes could change. Public opinion on national security issues is notoriously fickle and responsive to elite manipulation and world events. Moreover, only one country need decide war is thinkable to make war possible again. Finally, it is possible that a conventional war could be fought and won without suffering grave losses, and elites who saw this possibility could believe war is a viable option.

Under the second optimistic scenario, the existing European Community (EC) grows stronger with time, a development heralded by the Single European Act, designed to create a unified Western European market by 1992. A strong EC then ensures that this economic order remains open and prosperous, and the open and prosperous character of the European economy keeps the states of Western Europe cooperating with each other. In this view, the present EC structure grows stronger, but not larger. Therefore, while conflict might emerge in Eastern Europe, the threat of an aggressive Germany would be removed by enmeshing the newly unified German state deeply in the EC. The theory underpinning this scenario is "economic liberalism."

A variant of this second scenario posits that the EC will spread to include Eastern Europe and possibly the Soviet Union, bringing prosperity and peace to these regions as well.[58] Some also maintain that the EC is likely to be so successful in the decade ahead that it will develop into a state apparatus: a unified Western European super-state would emerge and Germany would be subsumed in it. At some future point, the remainder of Europe would be incorporated into that super-state. Either way, suggest the proponents of this second scenario and its variants, peace will be bolstered.

Under the third scenario, war is avoided because many European states have become democratic since the early twentieth century, and liberal democracies simply do not fight against each other. At a minimum, the presence of liberal democracies in Western Europe renders that half of Europe free from armed conflict. At a maximum, as democracy spreads to Eastern Europe and the Soviet Union, it bolsters peace among these states, and between

---

58. Jack Snyder, "Averting Anarchy in the New Europe," *International Security*, Vol. 14, No. 4 (Spring 1990), pp. 5–41.

these states and Western Europe. This scenario is based on the theory that can be called "peace-loving democracies."

ECONOMIC LIBERALISM

THE LOGIC OF THE THEORY. Economic liberalism rejects the notion that the prospects for peace are tightly linked to calculations about military power, and posits instead that stability is mainly a function of international economic considerations. It assumes that modern states are primarily motivated by the desire to achieve prosperity, and that national leaders place the material welfare of their publics above all other considerations, including security. This is especially true of liberal democracies, where policymakers are under special pressure to ensure the economic well-being of their populations.[59] Thus, the key to achieving peace is establishment of an international economic system that fosters prosperity for all states.

The taproot of stability, according to this theory, is the creation and maintenance of a liberal economic order that allows free economic exchange between states. Such an order works to dampen conflict and enhance political cooperation in three ways.[60]

First, it makes states more prosperous; this bolsters peace because prosperous states are more economically satisfied, and satisfied states are more

---

59. This point about liberal democracies highlights the fact that economic liberalism and the theory of peace-loving democracies are often linked in the writings of international relations scholars. The basis of the linkage is what each theory has to say about peoples' motives. The claim that individuals mainly desire material prosperity, central to economic liberalism, meshes nicely with the belief that the citizenry are a powerful force against war, which, as discussed below, is central to the theory of peace-loving democracies.

60. The three explanations discussed here rest on three of the most prominent theories advanced in the international political economy (IPE) literature. These three are usually treated as distinct theories and are given various labels. However, they share important common elements. Hence, for purposes of parsimony, I treat them as three strands of one general theory: economic liberalism. A caveat is in order. The IPE literature often fails to state its theories in a clear fashion, making them difficult to evaluate. Thus, I have construed these theories from sometimes opaque writings that might be open to contrary interpretations. My description of economic liberalism is drawn from the following works, which are among the best of the IPE genre: Richard N. Cooper, "Economic Interdependence and Foreign Policies in the Seventies," *World Politics*, Vol. 24, No. 2 (January 1972), pp. 158–181; Ernst B. Haas, "Technology, Pluralism, and the New Europe," in Joseph S. Nye, Jr., ed., *International Regionalism* (Boston: Little, Brown, 1968), pp. 149–176; Robert O. Keohane and Joseph S. Nye, Jr., *Power and Interdependence: World Politics in Transition* (Boston: Little, Brown, 1977); Robert O. Keohane, *After Hegemony: Cooperation and Discord in the World Political Economy* (Princeton: Princeton University Press, 1984); David Mitrany, *A Working Peace System* (Chicago: Quadrangle Press, 1966); Edward L. Morse, "The Transformation of Foreign Policies: Modernization, Interdependence, and Externalization," *World Politics*, Vol. 22, No. 3 (April 1970), pp. 371–392; and Richard N. Rosecrance, *The Rise of the Trading State: Commerce and Conquest in the Modern World* (New York: Basic Books, 1986).

peaceful. Many wars are waged to gain or preserve wealth, but states have less motive for such wars if they are already wealthy. Wealthy societies also stand to lose more if their societies are laid waste by war. For both reasons they avoid war.

Moreover, the prosperity spawned by economic liberalism feeds itself, by promoting international institutions that foster greater liberalism, which in turn promotes still greater prosperity. To function smoothly, a liberal economic order requires international regimes or institutions, such as the EC, the General Agreement on Tariffs and Trade (GATT), and the International Monetary Fund (IMF). These institutions perform two limited but important functions. First, they help states to verify that partners keep their cooperative commitments. Second, they provide resources to governments experiencing short-term problems arising from their exposure to international markets, and by doing so they allow states to eschew beggar-thy-neighbor policies that might otherwise undermine the existing economic order. Once in place, these institutions and regimes bolster economic cooperation, hence bolster prosperity. They also bolster themselves: once in existence they cause the expansion of their own size and influence, by proving their worth and selling themselves to states and publics. And as their power grows they become better able to promote cooperation, which promotes greater prosperity, which further bolsters their prestige and influence. In essence, a benevolent spiral-like relationship sets in between cooperation-promoting regimes and prosperity, in which each feeds the other.

Second, a liberal economic order fosters economic interdependence among states. Interdependence is defined as a situation in which two states are mutually vulnerable; each is a hostage of the other in the economic realm.[61] When interdependence is high, this theory holds, there is less temptation to cheat or behave aggressively towards other states because all states could retaliate. Interdependence allows states to compel each other to cooperate on economic matters, much as mutual assured destruction allows nuclear powers to compel each other to respect their security. All states are forced by the others to act as partners in the provision of material comfort for their home publics.

Third, some theorists argue that with ever-increasing political cooperation, international regimes will become so powerful that they will assume an

---

61. See Kenneth N. Waltz, "The Myth of National Interdependence," in Charles P. Kindelberger, ed., *The International Corporation* (Cambridge: MIT Press, 1970), pp. 205–223.

independent life of their own, eventually growing into a super-state. This is a minority view; most economic liberals do not argue that regimes can become so powerful that they can coerce states to act against their own narrow interests. Instead most maintain that regimes essentially reflect the interests of the states that created and maintain them, and remain subordinate to other interests of these states. However, the "growth to super-statehood" view does represent an important strand of thought among economic liberals.

The main flaw in this theory is that the principal assumption underpinning it—that states are primarily motivated by the desire to achieve prosperity—is wrong. States are surely concerned about prosperity, and thus economic calculations are hardly trivial for them. However, states operate in both an international political environment and an international economic environment, and the former dominates the latter in cases where the two systems come into conflict. The reason is straightforward: the international political system is anarchic, which means that each state must always be concerned to ensure its own survival. Since a state can have no higher goal than survival, when push comes to shove, international political considerations will be paramount in the minds of decision-makers.

Proponents of economic liberalism largely ignore the effects of anarchy on state behavior and concentrate instead on economic considerations. When this omission is corrected, however, their arguments collapse, for two reasons.

First, competition for security makes it very difficult for states to cooperate. When security is scarce, states become more concerned about relative gains than absolute gains.[62] They ask of an exchange not, "will both of us gain?" but instead, "who will gain more?"[63] When security is scarce, they reject even cooperation that would yield an absolute economic gain, if the other state would gain more of the yield, from fear that the other might convert its gain to military strength, and then use this strength to win by coercion in later rounds.[64] Cooperation is much easier to achieve if states worry only about absolute gains, as they are more likely to do when security is not so

---

62. See Joseph M. Grieco, "Anarchy and the Limits of Cooperation: A Realist Critique of the Newest Liberal Institutionalism," *International Organization*, Vol. 42, No. 3 (Summer 1988), pp. 485–507; and Grieco, *Cooperation among Nations: Europe, America and Non-Tariff Barriers to Trade* (Ithaca: Cornell University Press, 1990).
63. Waltz, *Theory of International Politics*, p. 105.
64. It is important to emphasize that because military power is in good part a function of economic might, the consequences of economic dealings among states sometimes have important security implications.

scarce. The goal then is simply to insure that the overall economic pie is expanding and each state is getting at least some part of the resulting benefits. However, anarchy guarantees that security will often be scarce; this heightens states' concerns about relative gains, which makes cooperation difficult unless gains can be finely sliced to reflect, and thus not disturb, the current balance of power.

In contrast to this view, economic liberals generally assume that states worry little about relative gains when designing cooperative agreements, but instead are concerned mainly about absolute gains. This assumption underlies their optimism over the prospects for international cooperation. However, it is not well-based: anarchy forces states to reject agreements that result in asymmetrical payoffs that shift the balance of power against them.

Second, interdependence is as likely to lead to conflict as cooperation, because states will struggle to escape the vulnerability that interdependence creates, in order to bolster their national security. States that depend on others for critical economic supplies will fear cutoff or blackmail in time of crisis or war; they may try to extend political control to the source of supply, giving rise to conflict with the source or with its other customers. Interdependence, in other words, might very well lead to greater competition, not to cooperation.[65]

Several other considerations, independent of the consequences of anarchy, also raise doubts about the claims of economic liberals.

First, economic interactions between states often cause serious frictions, even if the overall consequences are positive. There will invariably be winners and losers within each state, and losers rarely accept defeat gracefully. In modern states, where leaders have to pay careful attention to their constit-

---

65. There are numerous examples in the historical record of vulnerable states pursuing aggressive military policies for the purpose of achieving autarky. For example, this pattern of behavior was reflected in both Japan's and Germany's actions during the interwar period. On Japan, see Michael A. Barnhart, *Japan Prepares for Total War: The Search for Economic Security, 1919–1941* (Ithaca: Cornell University Press, 1987); and James B. Crowley, *Japan's Quest for Autonomy* (Princeton: Princeton University Press, 1966). On Germany, see William Carr, *Arms, Autarky and Aggression: A Study in German Foreign Policy, 1933–39* (New York: Norton, 1973). It is also worth noting that during the Arab oil embargo of the early 1970s, when it became apparent that the United States was vulnerable to OPEC pressure, there was much talk in America about using military force to seize Arab oil fields. See, for example, Robert W. Tucker, "Oil: The Issue of American Intervention," *Commentary*, January 1975, pp. 21–31; Miles Ignotus [said to be a pseudonym for Edward Luttwak], "Seizing Arab Oil," *Harpers*, March 1975, pp. 45–62; and U.S. Congress, House Committee on International Relations, *Report on Oil Fields as Military Objectives: A Feasibility Study*, prepared by John M. Collins and Clyde R. Mark, 94th Cong., 1st sess. (Washington, D.C.: U.S. Government Printing Office [U.S. GPO], August 21, 1975).

uents, losers can cause considerable trouble. Even in cases where only winners are involved, there are sometimes squabbles over how the spoils are divided. In a sense, then, expanding the network of contacts among states increases the scope for international disagreements among them. They now have more to squabble about.

Second, there will be opportunities for blackmail and for brinkmanship in a highly dynamic economic system where states are dependent on each other. For example, although mutual vulnerabilities may arise among states, it is likely that the actual levels of dependence will not be equal. The less vulnerable states would probably have greater bargaining power over the more dependent states and might attempt to coerce them into making extravagant concessions. Furthermore, different political systems, not to mention individual leaders, have different capacities for engaging in tough bargaining situations.

THE HISTORICAL RECORD. During two periods in the twentieth century, Europe witnessed a liberal economic order with high levels of interdependence. Stability should have obtained during those periods, according to economic liberalism.

The first case clearly contradicts the theory. The years between 1890 and 1914 were probably the time of greatest economic interdependence in Europe's history. Yet World War I broke out following this period.[66]

The second case covers the Cold War years. During this period there has been much interdependence among the EC states, while relations among these states have been very peaceful. This case, not surprisingly, is the centerpiece of the economic liberals' argument.

The correlation in this second case does not mean, however, that interdependence has *caused* cooperation among the Western democracies. It is more likely that the prime cause was the Cold War, and that this was the main reason that intra-EC relations have flourished.[67] The Cold War caused these results in two different but mutually reinforcing ways.

First, old-fashioned balance of power logic mandated cooperation among the Western democracies. A powerful and potentially dangerous Soviet

---

66. See Richard N. Rosecrance, et al., "Whither Interdependence?" *International Organization,* Vol. 31, No. 3 (Summer 1977), pp. 432–434.
67. This theme is reflected in Barry Buzan, "Economic Structure and International Security: The Limits of the Liberal Case," *International Organization,* Vol. 38, No. 4 (Autumn 1984), pp. 597–624; Robert Gilpin, *U.S. Power and the Multinational Corporation: The Political Economy of Foreign Direct Investment* (New York: Basic Books, 1975); and Robert A. Pollard, *Economic Security and the Origins of the Cold War, 1945–1950* (New York: Columbia University Press, 1985).

Union forced the Western democracies to band together to meet the common threat. Britain, Germany, and France no longer worried about each other, because all faced a greater menace from the Soviets. This Soviet threat muted concerns about relative gains arising from economic cooperation among the EC states by giving each Western democracy a vested interest in seeing its alliance partners grow powerful, since each additional increment of power helped deter the Soviets. The Soviet threat also muted relative-gains fears among Western European states by giving them all a powerful incentive to avoid conflict with each other while the Soviet Union loomed to the east, ready to harvest the gains of Western quarrels. This gave each Western state greater confidence that its Western partners would not turn their gains against it, as long as these partners behaved rationally.

Second, America's hegemonic position in NATO, the military counterpart to the EC, mitigated the effects of anarchy on the Western democracies and facilitated cooperation among them.[68] As emphasized, states do not trust each other in anarchy and they have incentives to commit aggression against each other. America, however, not only provided protection against the Soviet threat, but also guaranteed that no EC state would aggress against another. For example, France did not have to fear Germany as it rearmed, because the American presence in Germany meant that the Germans were not free to attack anyone. With the United States serving as night watchman, relative-gains concerns among the Western European states were mitigated and, moreover, those states were willing to allow their economies to become tightly interdependent.

In effect, relations among EC states were spared the effects of anarchy—fears about relative gains and an obsession with autonomy—because the United States served as the ultimate arbiter within the Alliance.

If the present Soviet threat to Western Europe is removed, and American forces depart for home, relations among the EC states will be fundamentally altered. Without a common Soviet threat and without the American night watchman, Western European states will begin viewing each other with greater fear and suspicion, as they did for centuries before the onset of the Cold War. Consequently, they will worry about the imbalances in gains as well as the loss of autonomy that results from cooperation.[69] Cooperation in

---

68. See Josef Joffe, "Europe's American Pacifier," *Foreign Policy*, No. 54 (Spring 1984), pp. 64–82.
69. Consider, for example, a situation where the European Community is successfully extended

this new order will be more difficult than it has been in the Cold War. Conflict will be more likely.

In sum, there are good reasons for looking with skepticism upon the claim that peace can be maintained in a multipolar Europe on the basis of a more powerful EC.

PEACE-LOVING DEMOCRACIES

The peace-loving democracies theory holds that domestic political factors, not calculations about military power or the international economic system, are the principal determinant of peace. Specifically, the argument is that the presence of liberal democracies in the international system will help to produce a stable order.[70] The claim is not that democracies go to war less often than authoritarian states. In fact, the historical record shows clearly that such is not the case.[71] Instead, the argument is that democracies do not go to war against other democracies. Thus, democracy must spread to Eastern Europe and the Soviet Union to insure peace in post–Cold War Europe.

It is not certain that democracy will take root among the states of Eastern Europe or in the Soviet Union. They lack a strong tradition of democracy; institutions that can accommodate the growth of democracy will have to be built from scratch. That task will probably prove to be difficult, especially in an unstable Europe. But whether democracy takes root in the East matters

---

to include Eastern Europe and the Soviet Union, and that over time all states achieve greater prosperity. The Germans, however, do significantly better than all other states. Hence their relative power position, which is already quite strong, begins to improve markedly. It is likely that the French and the Soviets, just to name two states, would be deeply concerned by this situation.

70. This theory has been recently articulated by Michael Doyle in three articles: "Liberalism and World Politics," *American Political Science Review*, Vol. 80, No. 4 (December 1986), pp. 1151–1169; "Kant, Liberal Legacies, and Foreign Affairs," *Philosophy and Public Affairs*, Vol. 12, No. 3 (Summer 1983), pp. 205–235; and "Kant, Liberal Legacies, and Foreign Affairs, Part 2," *Philosophy and Public Affairs*, Vol. 12, No. 4 (Fall 1983), pp. 323–353. Doyle draws heavily on Immanuel Kant's classic writings on the subject. This theory also provides the central argument in Francis Fukuyama's widely publicized essay on "The End of History?" in *The National Interest*, No. 16 (Summer 1989), pp. 3–18. For an excellent critique of the theory, see Samuel P. Huntington, "No Exit: The Errors of Endism," *The National Interest*, No. 17 (Fall 1989), pp. 3–11.
71. There is a good empirical literature on the relationship between democracy and war. See, for example, Steve Chan, "Mirror, Mirror on the Wall . . . Are the Freer Countries More Pacific?" *Journal of Conflict Resolution*, Vol. 28, No. 4 (December 1984), pp. 617–648; Erich Weede, "Democracy and War Involvement," in ibid., pp. 649–664; Bruce M. Russett and R. Joseph Monsen, "Bureaucracy and Polyarchy As Predictors of Performance," *Comparative Political Studies*, Vol. 8, No. 1 (April 1975), pp. 5–31; and Melvin Small and J. David Singer, "The War-Proneness of Democratic Regimes, 1816–1965," *The Jerusalem Journal of International Relations*, Vol. 1, No. 4 (Summer 1976), pp. 50–69.

little for stability in Europe, since the theory of peace-loving democracies is unsound.

THE LOGIC OF THE THEORY. Two explanations are offered in support of the claim that democracies do not go to war against one another.

First, some claim that authoritarian leaders are more prone to go to war than leaders of democracies, because authoritarian leaders are not accountable to their publics, which carry the main burdens of war. In a democracy, by contrast, the citizenry that pays the price of war has greater say in the decision-making process. The people, so the argument goes, are more hesitant to start trouble because it is they who pay the blood price; hence the greater their power, the fewer wars.

The second argument rests on the claim that the citizens of liberal democracies respect popular democratic rights—those of their fellow countrymen, and those of individuals in other states. As a result they are reluctant to wage war against other democracies, because they view democratic governments as more legitimate than others, and are loath to impose a foreign regime on a democratic state by force. This would violate their own democratic principles and values. Thus an inhibition on war is introduced when two democracies face each other that is missing in other international relationships.

The first of these arguments is flawed because it is not possible to sustain the claim that the people in a democracy are especially sensitive to the costs of war and therefore less willing than authoritarian leaders to fight wars. In fact, the historical record shows that democracies are every bit as likely to fight wars as are authoritarian states.

Furthermore, mass publics, whether democratic or not, can become deeply imbued with nationalistic or religious fervor, making them prone to support aggression, regardless of costs. The widespread public support in post-revolutionary France for Napoleon's wars of aggression is just one example of this phenomenon. On the other hand, authoritarian leaders are just as likely as democratic publics to fear going to war, because war tends to unleash democratic forces that can undermine the regime.[72] War can impose high costs on authoritarian leaders as well as on their citizenries.

The second argument, which emphasizes the transnational respect for democratic rights among democracies, rests on a weaker factor that is usually

---

72. See, for example, Stanislav Andreski, "On the Peaceful Disposition of Military Dictatorships," *Journal of Strategic Studies*, Vol. 3, No. 3 (December 1980), pp. 3–10.

overridden by other factors such as nationalism and religious fundamental-ism. There is also another problem with the argument. The possibility always exists that a democracy will revert to an authoritarian state. This threat of backsliding means that one democratic state can never be sure that another democratic state will not change its stripes and turn on it sometime in the future. Liberal democracies must therefore worry about relative power among themselves, which is tantamount to saying that each has an incentive to consider aggression against the other to forestall future trouble. Lamentably, it is not possible for even liberal democracies to transcend anarchy.

THE HISTORICAL RECORD. Problems with the deductive logic aside, the his-torical record seems to offer strong support for the theory of peace-loving democracies. There appears to have been no case where liberal democracies fought against each other. Although this evidence looks impressive at first glance, closer examination shows it to be indecisive. In fact, history provides no clear test of the theory. Four evidentiary problems leave the issue in doubt.

First, democracies have been few in number over the past two centuries, and thus there have not been many cases where two democracies were in a position to fight with each other. Only three prominent cases are usually cited: Britain and the United States (1832–present); Britain and France (1832–49, 1871–1940); and the Western democracies since 1945.

Second, there are other persuasive explanations for why war did not occur in those three cases, and these competing explanations must be ruled out before the peace-loving democracies theory can be accepted. While relations between the British and the Americans during the nineteenth century were hardly free of conflict,[73] their relations in the twentieth century were quite harmonious, and thus fit closely with how the theory would expect two democracies to behave towards each other. That harmony, however, can easily be explained by the presence of a common threat that forced Britain and the United States to work closely together.[74] Both faced a serious German threat in the first part of the century, and a Soviet threat later. The same basic argument applies to France and Britain. While Franco-British relations

---

73. For a discussion of the hostile relations that existed between the United States and Britain during the nineteenth century, see H.C. Allen, *Great Britain and the United States: A History of Anglo-American Relations, 1783–1952* (London: Odhams, 1954).
74. For a discussion of this rapprochement, see Stephen R. Rock, *Why Peace Breaks Out: Great Power Rapprochement in Historical Perspective* (Chapel Hill: University of North Carolina Press, 1989), chap. 2.

were not the best throughout most of the nineteenth century,[75] they improved significantly around the turn of the century with the rise of a common threat: Germany.[76] Finally, as noted above, the Soviet threat can explain the absence of war among the Western democracies since 1945.

Third, it bears mention that several democracies have come close to fighting one another, which suggests that the absence of war may be due simply to chance. France and Britain approached war during the Fashoda crisis of 1898. France and Weimar Germany might have come to blows over the Rhineland during the 1920s, had Germany possessed the military strength to challenge France. The United States has clashed with a number of elected governments in the Third World during the Cold War, including the Allende regime in Chile and the Arbenz regime in Guatemala.

Lastly, some would classify Wilhelmine Germany as a democracy, or at least a quasi-democracy; if so, World War I becomes a war among democracies.[77]

Conclusion

This article argues that bipolarity, an equal military balance, and nuclear weapons have fostered peace in Europe over the past 45 years. The Cold War confrontation produced these phenomena; thus the Cold War was principally responsible for transforming a historically violent region into a very peaceful place.

There is no doubt that the costs of the Cold War have been substantial. It inflicted oppressive political regimes on the peoples of Eastern Europe, who were denied basic human rights by their forced membership in the Soviet

---

75. For a good discussion of Franco-British relations during the nineteenth century, see P.J.V. Rolo, *Entente Cordiale: The Origins and Negotiation of the Anglo-French Agreements of 8 April 1904* (New York: St. Martins, 1969), pp. 16–109.

76. Stephen Rock, who has examined the rapprochement between Britain and France, argues that the principal motivating force behind their improved relations derived from geopolitical considerations, not shared political beliefs. See Rock, *Why Peace Breaks Out*, chap. 4.

77. Doyle recognizes this problem and thus has a lengthy footnote that attempts to deal with it. See "Kant, Liberal Legacies, and Foreign Affairs [Part One]," pp. 216–217, n. 8. He argues that "Germany was a liberal state under republican law for domestic issues," but that the "emperor's active role in foreign affairs . . . made imperial Germany a state divorced from the control of its citizenry in foreign affairs." However, an examination of the decision-making process leading to World War I reveals that the emperor (Wilhelm II) was not a prime mover in foreign affairs and that he was no more bellicose than other members of the German elite, including the leading civilian official, Chancellor Bethmann-Hollweg.

empire. It consumed national wealth, by giving rise to large and costly defense establishments in both East and West. It spawned bloody conflicts in the Third World; these produced modest casualties for the superpowers, but large casualties for the Third World nations. Nevertheless, the net human and economic cost of the Cold War order has been far less than the cost of the European order of 1900–45, with its vast violence and suffering.

A Cold War order without confrontation would have been preferable to the order that actually developed; then the peace that the Cold War order produced could have been enjoyed without its attendant costs. However, it was East-West enmity that gave rise to the Cold War order; there would have been no bipolarity, no equality, and no large Soviet and American nuclear forces in Europe without it. The costs of the Cold War arose from the same cause—East-West confrontation—as did its benefits. The good could not be had without the bad.

This article further argues that the demise of the Cold War order is likely to increase the chances that war and major crises will occur in Europe. Many observers now suggest that a new age of peace is dawning; in fact the opposite is true.

The implications of my analysis are straightforward, if paradoxical. The West has an interest in maintaining peace in Europe. It therefore has an interest in maintaining the Cold War order, and hence has an interest in the continuation of the Cold War confrontation; developments that threaten to end it are dangerous. The Cold War antagonism could be continued at lower levels of East-West tension than have prevailed in the past; hence the West is not injured by relaxing East-West tension, but a complete end to the Cold War would create more problems than it would solve.

The fate of the Cold War, however, is mainly in the hands of the Soviet Union. The Soviet Union is the only superpower that can seriously threaten to overrun Europe; it is the Soviet threat that provides the glue that holds NATO together. Take away that offensive threat and the United States is likely to abandon the Continent, whereupon the defensive alliance it has headed for forty years may disintegrate. This would bring to an end the bipolar order that has characterized Europe for the past 45 years.

The foregoing analysis suggests that the West paradoxically has an interest in the continued existence of a powerful Soviet Union with substantial military forces in Eastern Europe. Western interests are wholly reversed from those that Western leaders saw in the late 1940s: instead of seeking the retraction of Soviet power, as the West did then, the West now should hope that the Soviet Union retains at least some military forces in the Eastern European region.

There is little the Americans or the Western Europeans can or are likely to do to perpetuate the Cold War, for three reasons.

First, domestic political considerations preclude such an approach. Western leaders obviously cannot base national security policy on the need to maintain forces in Central Europe for the purpose simply of keeping the Soviets there. The idea of deploying large forces in order to bait the Soviets into an order-keeping competition would be dismissed as bizarre, and contrary to the general belief that ending the Cold War and removing the Soviet yoke from Eastern Europe would make the world safer and better.[78]

Second, the idea of propping up a declining rival runs counter to the basic behavior of states. States are principally concerned about their relative power position in the system; hence, they look for opportunities to take advantage of each other. If anything, they prefer to see adversaries decline, and thus will do whatever they can to speed up the process and maximize the distance of the fall. In other words, states do not ask which distribution of power best facilitates stability and then do everything possible to build or maintain such an order. Instead, they each tend to pursue the more narrow aim of maximizing their power advantage over potential adversaries. The particular international order that results is simply a byproduct of that competition, as illustrated by the origins of the Cold War order in Europe. No state intended to create it. In fact, both the United States and the Soviet Union worked hard in the early years of the Cold War to undermine each other's position in Europe, which would have ended the bipolar order on the Continent. The remarkably stable system that emerged in Europe in the late 1940s was the unintended consequence of an intense competition between the superpowers.

Third, even if the Americans and the Western Europeans wanted to help the Soviets maintain their status as a superpower, it is not apparent that they could do so. The Soviet Union is leaving Eastern Europe and cutting its

---

78. This point is illustrated by the 1976 controversy over the so-called "Sonnenfeldt Doctrine." Helmut Sonnenfeldt, an adviser to Secretary of State Henry Kissinger, was reported to have said in late 1975 that the United States should support Soviet domination of Eastern Europe. It was clear from the ensuing debate that whether or not Sonnenfeldt in fact made such a claim, no administration could publicly adopt that position. See U.S. Congress, House Committee on International Relations, *Hearings on United States National Security Policy Vis-à-Vis Eastern Europe (The "Sonnenfeldt Doctrine")*, 94th Cong., 2nd sess. (Washington, D.C.: U.S. GPO, April 12, 1976).

military forces largely because its economy is foundering. It is not clear that the Soviets themselves know how to fix their economy, and there is little that Western governments can do to help them solve their economic problems. The West can and should avoid doing malicious mischief to the Soviet economy, but at this juncture it is difficult to see how the West can have significant positive influence.[79]

The fact that the West cannot sustain the Cold War does not mean that the United States should abandon all attempts to preserve the current order. The United States should do what it can to direct events toward averting a complete mutual superpower withdrawal from Europe. For instance, the American negotiating position at the conventional arms control talks should aim toward large mutual force reductions, but should not contemplate complete mutual withdrawal. The Soviets may opt to withdraw all their forces unilaterally anyway; there is little the United States could do to prevent this.

POLICY RECOMMENDATIONS

If complete Soviet withdrawal from Eastern Europe proves unavoidable, the West faces the question of how to maintain peace in a multipolar Europe. Three policy prescriptions are in order.

First, the United States should encourage the limited and carefully managed proliferation of nuclear weapons in Europe. The best hope for avoiding war in post–Cold War Europe is nuclear deterrence; hence some nuclear proliferation is necessary to compensate for the withdrawal of the Soviet and American nuclear arsenals from Central Europe. Ideally, as I have argued, nuclear weapons would spread to Germany, but to no other state.

Second, Britain and the United States, as well as the Continental states, will have to balance actively and efficiently against any emerging aggressor to offset the ganging up and bullying problems that are sure to arise in post–Cold War Europe. Balancing in a multipolar system, however, is usually a problem-ridden enterprise, either because of geography or because of significant coordination problems. Nevertheless, two steps can be taken to maximize the prospects of efficient balancing.

The initial measure concerns Britain and the United States, the two prospective balancing states that, physically separated from the Continent, may

---

79. For an optimistic assessment of how the West can enhance Gorbachev's prospects of succeeding, see Jack Snyder, "International Leverage on Soviet Domestic Change," *World Politics*, Vol. 42, No. 1 (October 1989), pp. 1–30.

thus conclude that they have little interest in what happens there. They would then be abandoning their responsibilities and, more importantly, their interests as off-shore balancers. Both states' failure to balance against Germany before the two world wars made war more likely in each case. It is essential for peace in Europe that they not repeat their past mistakes, but instead remain actively involved in maintaining the balance of power in Europe.

Specifically, both states must maintain military forces that can be deployed to the Continent to balance against states that threaten to start a war. To do this they must also socialize their publics to support a policy of continued Continental commitment. Support for such a commitment will be more difficult to mobilize than in the past, because its principal purpose would be to preserve peace, rather than to prevent an imminent hegemony, and the latter is a simpler goal to explain publicly. Moreover, it is the basic nature of states to focus on maximizing relative power, not on bolstering stability, so this prescription asks them to take on an unaccustomed task. Nevertheless, the British and American stake in peace is real, especially since there is a sure risk that a European war might involve large-scale use of nuclear weapons. It should therefore be possible for both countries to lead their publics to recognize this interest and support policies that protect it.[80]

The other measure concerns American attitudes and actions toward the Soviet Union. The Soviets may eventually return to their past expansionism and threaten to upset the status quo. If so, we are back to the Cold War; the West should respond as quickly and efficiently as it did the first time. However, if the Soviets adhere to status quo policies, Soviet power could play a key role in balancing against Germany and in maintaining order in Eastern Europe. It is important that, in those cases where the Soviets are acting in a balancing capacity, the United States recognize this, cooperate with its former adversary, and not let residual distrust from the Cold War interfere with the balancing process.

Third, a concerted effort should be made to keep hyper-nationalism at bay, especially in Eastern Europe. This powerful force has deep roots in Europe and has contributed to the outbreak of past European conflicts. Nationalism has been contained during the Cold War, but it is likely to reemerge once

---

80. Advancing this argument is Van Evera, "Why Europe Matters, Why the Third World Doesn't."

Soviet and American forces leave the heart of Europe.[81] It will be a force for trouble unless it is curbed. The teaching of honest national history is especially important, since the teaching of false chauvinist history is the main vehicle for spreading virulent nationalism. States that teach a dishonestly self-exculpating or self-glorifying history should be publicly criticized and sanctioned.[82]

On this count it is especially important that relations between Germany and its neighbors be handled carefully. Many Germans rightly feel that Germany has behaved very responsibly for 45 years, and has made an honest effort to remember and make amends for an ugly period of its past. Therefore, Germans quickly tire of lectures from foreigners demanding that they apologize once again for crimes committed before most of the current German population was born. On the other hand, peoples who have suffered at the hands of the Germans cannot forget their enormous suffering, and inevitably ask for repeated assurance that the past will not be repeated. This dialogue has the potential to spiral into mutual recriminations that could spark a renewed sense of persecution among Germans, and with it, a rebirth of German-nationalism. It is therefore incumbent on all parties in this discourse to proceed with understanding and respect for one another's feelings and experience. Specifically, others should not ask today's Germans to apologize for crimes they did not commit, but Germans must understand that others' ceaseless demands for reassurance have a legitimate basis in history, and should view these demands with patience and understanding.

None of these tasks will be easy to accomplish. In fact, I expect that the bulk of my prescriptions will not be followed; most run contrary to powerful strains of domestic American and European opinion, and to the basic nature of state behavior. Moreover, even if they are followed, this will not guarantee the peace in Europe. If the Cold War is truly behind us, the stability of the past 45 years is not likely to be seen again in the coming decades.

---

81. On the evolution of nationalistic history-teaching in Europe see Kennedy, "The Decline of Nationalistic History," and Dance, *History the Betrayer*
82. My thinking on this matter has been influenced by conversations with Stephen Van Evera.

Primed for Peace | *Stephen Van Evera*

Europe After the Cold War

$\mathbf{O}$ne year has passed since the Berlin Wall and the communist regimes of Eastern Europe came crashing down in the revolutions of 1989. The euphoria first evoked by these events has been replaced by a more sober contemplation of the realities and challenges of the new Europe. For all its flaws, the postwar order that divided Europe into two rival blocs kept the peace for 45 years, a new European record. Now this order is rapidly crumbling. Soviet forces will be gone from Germany by 1994, and Soviet leaders have declared their readiness to withdraw all Soviet troops from Eastern Europe by 1995.[1] U.S. forces, too, will certainly be reduced in Central Europe. Germany has been reunified, the Warsaw Pact has effectively dissolved, and the Soviet Union shows signs of political fragmentation. These dramatic changes have sparked worried debate on the opportunities and dangers facing the new Europe, and on the best way to preserve peace.

This article explores two questions raised by these events. First, how will the end of the Cold War affect the probability of war in Europe? In particular, what risks will arise from the Soviet withdrawal from Eastern Europe, and from the possible further transformation or splintering of the Soviet Union? Second, what U.S. and Western policies would best contribute to preserving Europe's long peace?

Some observers warn that Europe may return to its historic warlike ways once the superpowers are gone. One such view holds that bipolar state systems are inherently more peaceful than multipolar systems; that the Cold War peace was caused partly by the bipolar character of the Cold War

I wish to thank Beverly Crawford, Charles Glaser, Robert Jervis, Chaim Kaufmann, John Mearsheimer, Jack Snyder, Marc Trachtenberg, Stephen Walt, and David Yanowski for their thoughtful comments on drafts of this article. Research for this article was supported by the Ford Foundation through the Consensus Project of the Olin Institute at Harvard University.

Stephen Van Evera is Assistant Professor in the political science department at the Massachusetts Institute of Technology. He was managing editor of International Security *from 1984 to 1987.*

1. Thomas L. Friedman, "Pact on European Armies May Skip Troop Limits to Speed Accord," *New York Times*, September 12, 1990, p. A14; Michael Parks, "USSR talks of full European pullout," *Boston Globe*, February 12, 1990, p. 20.

International Security, Winter 1990/91 (Vol. 15, No. 3)
© 1990 by the President and Fellows of Harvard College and of the Massachusetts Institute of Technology.

international order; and that the withdrawal of U.S. and Soviet forces will now produce a less stable multipolar system like those that spawned Europe's centuries of war, including the two great wars of this century.[2]

A second pessimistic perspective suggests that Germany may return to the aggressive course that caused both World Wars, once it is united and free from the police presence of the superpowers. Proponents of this view believe that past German aggression was driven largely by flaws in German national character; that Germany has behaved well since 1945 largely because it was not free to behave badly; and that a united and more autonomous Germany may return to its old ways.[3] This fear is often thought, sometimes whispered, but rarely stated baldly.[4] It nonetheless is implicit in fears that Germany will be the focus of instability in post–Cold War Europe.

Third, some worry that the promise of democracy in Eastern Europe, so great in the heady days of late 1989 and early 1990, will go unfulfilled. Instead of developing Western-style democracy, the post-communist regimes of the region may evolve into "praetorian states"—flawed democracies that lack the

---

2. See John J. Mearsheimer, "Back to the Future: Instability in Europe After the Cold War," *International Security*, Vol. 15, No. 1 (Summer 1990), pp. 5–56. Mearsheimer is a qualified pessimist: he does not forecast a complete return to the levels of danger of 1914 or 1939, and he sees some possibility of dampening the dangers he outlines. He also recognizes the importance of factors other than the polarity of the international system in causing war, although he believes these factors are less important than the structure of the international system. However, he does warn that the new European order will be substantially more dangerous than the Cold War order, largely because the system will be multipolar.

3. A variant of this view suggests that Germany was aggressive in the past because it found itself surrounded by strong neighbors, with borders that offered few physical barriers to invasion; hence it expanded to bolster its security. In this view, these unchanging geographic facts may stir renewed German aggression once Germany is reunified and unoccupied.

4. A crude example is Leopold Bellak, "Why I Fear the Germans" (op-ed), *New York Times*, April 25, 1990, p. A29. Bellak argues that German children are abused more often than children in other societies, and grow up to become aggressive adults "whom I don't trust to be peaceful, democratic people." For replies, see letters to the editor by Werner M. Graf, Mark Tobak, and Joseph Dolgin, *New York Times*, May 10, 1990, p. A30. See also Dominic Lawson, "Saying the Unsayable About the Germans" (an interview with British then–Secretary of State for Industry Nicholas Ridley), *The Spectator* (London), July 14, 1990, pp. 8–10, in which Ridley expressed fears of Germany. Prime Minister Margaret Thatcher reportedly shares Ridley's views: see Anthony Bevins, "Bitter memories shape views on Germany," *The Independent* (London), July 13, 1990, p. 3. Likewise, former NATO Secretary General Joseph Luns warned that a united Germany someday might seek to expand beyond its current borders, adding: "Ridley said out loud what many Europeans think. We all know about the German character, don't we? Germans naturally become a little arrogant when they are powerful." Robert Melcher and Roman Rollnick, "Axis urged to counter Bonn," *The European*, July 27–29, 1990. *The Economist* reported that "Mr. Ridley's words . . . reflect the visceral feelings of millions of fellow-Britons, thousands of Tory party workers and scores, if not hundreds, of Tory MPs." "Nick and his mouth," July 14, 1990, p. 33.

institutions required to channel growing popular participation. In such states, governments are often captured by narrow interest groups. If this occurs, these groups may pursue aggressive policies that benefit themselves, even if these policies harm the larger society.[5]

A fourth school of thought suggests that Europe's virulent ethnic hatreds and latent border conflicts will re-emerge, like plagues from Pandora's box, if the superpowers lift the lid by withdrawing. These conflicts are most likely between and within the post-communist countries of Eastern Europe, and among the nationalities inside the Soviet Union.[6]

I argue that all but the last of these pessimistic views rest on false fears, and that the risk of a return to the warlike Europe of old is low. The European wars of this century grew mainly from military factors and domestic conditions that are largely gone, and will not return in force. The nuclear revolution has dampened security motives for expansion, and the domestic orders of most European states have changed in ways that make renewed aggression unlikely. The most significant domestic changes include the waning of militarism and hyper-nationalism. Secondary changes include the spread of democracy, the leveling of highly stratified European societies, the resulting evaporation of "social imperial" motives for war, and the disappearance of states governed by revolutionary elites.

Europe's past multipolar systems would have been far more peaceful without these conditions and factors. A return to multipolarity poses no special risks in their absence. Germany has undergone a social transformation that removed the roots of its past aggressiveness, and unified Germany can be expected to remain a responsible member of the European community. The risks of imperfect or stunted democratization are real, but these problems are confined to a small number of Eastern European states. Even in that

---

5. See Jack Snyder, "Averting Anarchy in the New Europe," *International Security*, Vol. 14, No. 4 (Spring 1990), pp. 5–41; and for historical background on the problem of praetorianism, Jack Snyder, *Myths of Empire* (Ithaca: Cornell University Press, forthcoming). Snyder is the main exponent of the praetorian scenario, but others also fear the emergence of flawed democracies in the East. See, for example, Timothy Garton Ash, "Eastern Europe: Après Le Déluge, Nous," *New York Review of Books*, August 16, 1990, pp. 51–57; and Valerie Bunce, "Rising Above the Past: The Struggle for Liberal Democracy in Eastern Europe," *World Policy Journal*, Vol. 7, No. 3 (Summer 1990), pp. 395–430.

6. See Zbigniew Brzezinski, "Post-Communist Nationalism," *Foreign Affairs*, Vol. 68, No. 5 (Winter 1989/90), pp. 1–25; F. Stephen Larrabee, "Long Memories and Short Fuses: Change and Instability in the Balkans," *International Security*, Vol. 15, No. 3 (Winter 1990/91), pp. 58–91; Paul Kennedy, "The 'Powder Keg' Revisited," *Los Angeles Times*, November 1, 1989, p. B7; and Samuel R. Williamson, "1914's Shadow on the Europe of Today," *Newsday*, July 27, 1989, p. 61.

region, communism has removed much of the social and economic stratification that gives rise to hyper-nationalism, militarism, and aggressive praetorianism.

The risks of renewed ethnic conflict in Eastern Europe are more serious, however, and constitute the most important reason for concern in the new Europe. The immediate dangers raised by the break-up of the Soviet Union and by resurgent border and inter-ethnic conflicts in the Balkans would be confined to that region, but a conflict arising there could spread westward, giving the Western states a major stake in preserving peace in the East.

Overall, the risk of war in the new Europe may be greater than under the Cold War order, but only slightly so. Western Europe seems very secure from war, and any dangers that might arise in that region could be dampened by appropriate American policies. The main dangers lie in the East, where potential causes of war are more potent, and the West has less capacity to promote peace.

To bolster Europe's peace, the West should seek a general Cold War peace settlement with the Soviet Union, and should revamp NATO into a collective security system. The United States should retain its membership in this new NATO, and should maintain a significant military force on the European continent to symbolize the continuing U.S. commitment to Europe. The United States should also take active steps to dampen hyper-nationalism and militarism in Western Europe, and the West should use economic leverage to encourage Eastern European states to adopt democracy, protect the rights of national minorities, accept current borders, and eschew the propagation of hyper-nationalism.

The following discussion is necessarily speculative. Our knowledge of the causes of war is incomplete; our stock of hypotheses is small, and many plausible hypotheses have not been tested empirically. I believe the propositions that underpin my analysis are deductively sound, but many are still untested. The ongoing transformation of Europe will not wait for further empirical studies to accumulate, however, and social science owes the world what it knows about this transformation, however incomplete that knowledge may be.

The next section reviews the many causes of past European conflicts that have disappeared over the past few decades, or are now disappearing, and offers reasons why these causes are unlikely to recur. In the section that follows, I assess the specific dangers of multipolarity, German aggression, and praetorianism, and indicates why they pose little danger. Causes of war that may persist or reappear are noted in the subsequent section. The last section offers prescriptions for American and Western policy.

Why Europe is Primed for Peace: Vanished and Vanishing Causes of War

The case for optimism about Europe's future rests chiefly on the diminution or disappearance of many of the principal causes of wars of the past century. Specifically, eight significant causes of past wars have markedly diminished, or are now diminishing. Of these eight, the waning of the first three—offense-dominance, militarism, and hyper-nationalism—is most significant. The following list also progresses from largely systemic causes (the first) to unit-level domestic factors (the last seven).

OFFENSE-DOMINANCE

War is far more likely when offense appears easy and conquest seems feasible, for five main reasons.[7] First and most important, arguments for territorial expansion are more persuasive: states want more territory because their current borders appear less defensible, and the seizure of others' territory seems more feasible. Second, the incentive to launch preemptive attack increases, because a successful surprise attack provides larger rewards, and averts greater dangers. When the offense is strong, smaller shifts in ratios of forces between states create greater shifts in their relative capacity to conquer and defend territory. As a result, a state has greater incentive to strike first—in order to gain the advantage of striking the first blow, or to deny that advantage to its opponent—if a first strike will shift the force ratio in its favor. This increases the danger of pre-emptive war and makes crises more explosive.

Third, arguments for preventive war are more powerful. Since smaller shifts in force ratios have larger effects on relative capacity to conquer or defend territory, smaller prospective shifts in force ratios cause greater hope and alarm, bolstering arguments for shutting "windows of vulnerability" by force. Fourth, states are quicker to use diplomatic tactics that risk war in order to gain diplomatic victories. Since security is scarcer, more competitive behavior seems justified when assets that provide security are disputed

---

7. These and other dangers are detailed in Robert Jervis, "Cooperation Under the Security Dilemma," *World Politics*, Vol. 30, No. 2 (January 1978), pp. 167–214; and Stephen Van Evera, "Causes of War" (Ph.D. dissertation, University of California at Berkeley, 1984), pp. 77–123.

between states. As a result, states use competitive tactics, like brinkmanship and presenting opponents with *faits accomplis*, which raise the risk of war.

Fifth, states enforce tighter political and military secrecy, since national security is threatened more directly if enemies win the contest for information. Hence states try harder to gain the advantage and avoid the disadvantage of disclosure, leading them to carefully conceal military plans and forces. This can lead opponents to underestimate one another's capabilities and blunder into a war of optimistic miscalculation.[8] It also may ease surprise attack, by concealing preparations from the opponent, and may prevent arms control agreements, by making compliance more difficult to verify.

These dangers have been ubiquitous causes of past European wars, and faith in the relative ease of conquest played a major role in the outbreak of both World Wars, especially the First.[9] However, three changes since 1945—the nuclear revolution, the evolution of industrial economies toward knowledge-based forms of production, and the transformation of American foreign policy interests and thinking—have powerfully strengthened the defense, and largely erased the rationale for security competition among the European powers.

THE NUCLEAR REVOLUTION. As many observers note, nuclear weapons have bolstered peace by vastly raising the cost of war; states therefore behave far more cautiously.[10] If this were the sole effect of the nuclear revolution, however, it would represent little net gain for peace, and would provide little basis for optimism about Europe's future. Wars would be far fewer, but far more destructive. Over the long run the number of war-deaths might be as

---

8. On wars of optimistic miscalculation, see Geoffrey Blainey, *The Causes of War* (New York: Free Press, 1973), pp. 35–56.

9. On World War I, see Stephen Van Evera, "The Cult of the Offensive and the Origins of the First World War," in Steven E. Miller, ed., *Military Strategy and the Origins of the First World War* (Princeton: Princeton University Press, 1984), pp. 58–107; and Jack Snyder, *The Ideology of the Offensive: Military Decision Making and the Disasters of 1914* (Ithaca: Cornell University Press, 1984). The effect of offense-defense calculations on the outbreak of World War II is more complicated; a "cult of the defensive" among the states opposing Hitler also played a role in setting the stage for that war. See Barry R. Posen, *The Sources of Military Doctrine: France, Britain, and Germany Between the World Wars* (Ithaca: Cornell University Press, 1984), p. 232; and Thomas Christensen and Jack Snyder, "Chain Gangs and Passed Bucks: Predicting Alliance Patterns in Multipolarity," *International Organization*, Vol. 44, No. 2 (Spring 1990), pp. 137–168, at 166. However, this defensive cult was not shared by Hitler, who believed that offensive military action was feasible, if not easy, and who exaggerated the ease of conquest overall by underestimating the political forces that would gather against an aggressor.

10. See, for example, John Lewis Gaddis, "The Long Peace: Elements of Stability in the Postwar International System," *International Security*, Vol. 10, No. 4 (Spring 1986), pp. 99–142, at 120–123.

large as always; the difference is merely that the dead would die in a smaller number of more violent conflicts.

A second effect of nuclear weapons is far more important: they strengthen defending states against aggressors. States with developed nuclear arsenals can annihilate each other even after absorbing an all-out attack, giving rise to a world of mutual assured destruction (MAD). In a MAD world, conquest is far harder than before, because international conflicts shift from tests of will and capability to purer tests of will—to be won by the side willing to run greater risks and pay greater costs. This strengthens defenders, because they nearly always value their freedom more than aggressors value new conquests; hence they will have more resolve than aggressors, hence their threats are more credible, hence they are bound to prevail in a confrontation.

For these reasons the nuclear revolution makes conquest among great powers virtually impossible. A victor now must destroy almost all of an opponent's nuclear arsenal—an enormous task requiring massive technical and material superiority. As a result, even lesser powers can now stand alone against states with far greater resources, as they never could before.

Britain, France and Soviet Union are Europe's only nuclear powers today, but a number of others could develop powerful deterrents if they ever faced serious threats to their security. This potential greatly diminishes the risk of war. Before 1945, states sought to redress insecurity by territorial expansion and preventive war. The nuclear revolution has given states the option of achieving security without resort to war, by peacefully acquiring superior defensive weapons. As a result of this increased security, competition for security will be muted in the new Europe; arguments for preemptive and preventive war will be less common; diplomacy will be conducted with less reckless search for unilateral advantage; and foreign and security policies will be relatively open.[11]

---

11. The Cold War "reconnaissance revolution"—embodied in the deployment of reconnaissance satellites by both superpowers—reflects this last effect. As John Gaddis notes, this revolution helped stabilize the Cold War, by preventing optimistic miscalculation, inhibiting surprise attack, and facilitating arms control. Gaddis, "Long Peace," pp. 123–125. See also John Lewis Gaddis, *The Long Peace: Inquiries into the History of the Cold War* (New York: Oxford University Press, 1987), pp. 195–214. The reconnaissance revolution, in turn, was largely a product of the nuclear revolution. It required the development of ballistic missiles that could loft satellites into space, but it also required tacit acceptance by both superpowers, who otherwise could have developed and used anti-satellite weapons to prevent satellite overflights. Nuclear weapons made the superpowers better able to agree tacitly to allow mutual surveillance, even if one side gained more information than the other from such surveillance. Such unilateral gains made little difference in a world of redundant, secure nuclear arsenals, since even a large advantage to one

The possibility of nuclear proliferation should thus be seen as a net benefit to peace in Europe. Proliferation would entail obvious dangers. For example, new nuclear states might develop frail deterrents that are not secure from terrorism, accident, or surprise attack, raising the risk of terrorist use, and of accidental or preemptive war; and surrounding states might be tempted to launch preventive wars against emerging nuclear powers. However, these dangers can be managed by the existing nuclear powers. These powers can limit proliferation to states capable of maintaining secure deterrents, by guaranteeing the security of other non-nuclear states, thereby reducing their need for nuclear weapons. They also can manage any proliferation that does occur by deterring preventive attack on emerging nuclear states when proliferation is deemed acceptable, and by giving them the technical help required to build secure arsenals. If proliferation is constrained and managed in this fashion, it can bolster Europe's peace by making conquest infeasible.[12] Things would be safest if all European states that might someday desire nuclear deterrents already possessed them; the dangers of the proliferation process would then be avoided. Overall, however, the possibility of proliferation makes Europe far safer than it would be if that possibility did not exist.

ECONOMIC CHANGE: THE END OF THE AGE OF EXTRACTION. The shift toward knowledge-based forms of production in advanced industrial economies since 1945 has reduced the ability of conquerors to extract resources from conquered territories. This change, too, diminishes the risk of war in Europe by making conquest more difficult and less rewarding.

Today's high-technology post-industrial economies depend increasingly on free access to technical and social information. This access requires a free domestic press, and access to foreign publications, foreign travel, personal computers, and photocopiers. But the police measures needed to subdue a conquered society require that these technologies and practices be forbidden, because they also carry subversive ideas. Thus critical elements of the eco-

---

side would not give it a strategic first-strike capability. Hence both sides felt that the danger of allowing the other side to gain a unilateral information advantage was outweighed by the mutual gain provided by an open information regime.

12. Some pessimists expect that if nuclear proliferation occurs, it is likely to be mismanaged, and argue that the possibility of proliferation therefore poses a net danger. See, for example, Mearsheimer, "Back to the Future," pp. 37–40. However, if the United States remains in Europe, it seems implausible that the Americans will stand idly by while a botched proliferation process unfolds. Hence proliferation poses a danger only if the United States withdraws fully from Europe—which seems unlikely, as I note below. Moreover, even if the United States does withdraw, the European nuclear powers also have the wherewithal to manage any proliferation that might occur, and have every interest in doing so.

nomic fabric now must be ripped out to maintain control over conquered polities.

As a result of these changes, states can afford to compete less aggressively for control of industrial areas, since control adds little to national power, and control by others would give them little power-gain. Hence it poses little threat. This change undercuts the geopolitical motives that produced past European balance-of-power wars. It is now far harder to conquer Europe piecemeal, using each conquest to gain strength for the next, since incremental conquests would provide little gain in power, and might even produce a net loss. Hence would-be aggressors have less motive to expand, and defenders less reason to compete fiercely to prevent others' gain.[13]

This is a marked change from the smokestack-economy era, when societies could be conquered and policed with far less collateral economic harm. The Nazis sustained fairly high levels of production in France and Czechoslovakia, even while they subjugated the conquered populations. Likewise, the Soviet regime was able until recently to squeeze high production from a society that was also subject to tight police controls, including severe limits on information technology, foreign publications, and travel. The slowdown of Soviet economic growth after 1970, and the stall in Soviet economic growth during the 1980s, reflect the new economic reality. The Soviet economy hit the wall partly because Soviet means of political control now collide with the imperatives of post-industrial economic productivity. The Soviet Union had to institute *glasnost* and other democratic reforms if it hoped to re-start its economy, because the police measures required to sustain the Bolshevik dictatorship would also stifle Soviet efforts to escape the smokestack age.

Any expansionist European state would confront the same dilemma. It would have to adopt harsh police measures to control its newly-acquired empire, but these measures would wreck productivity. Industrial economies could once be domesticated and milked; now they would wither in captivity. Hence any future European state that pursued successful military expansion would then face only two options: liberalize and lose control politically, or maintain tight political control and impoverish the empire. This change

---

13. Carl Kaysen notes further reasons why conquest now pays smaller strategic and economic rewards than in the past. See Carl Kaysen, "Is War Obsolete? A Review Essay," *International Security*, Vol. 14, No. 4 (Spring 1990), pp. 42–64, at 48–58. However, most of the factors he identifies have evolved over several centuries, and thus provide little reason to hope that the world is significantly safer now than it was in 1914 or 1939.

dampens the balance-of-power concerns, and the attendant competition for control of industrial regions, that helped cause both world wars.[14]

AMERICA AS BALANCER: THE TRANSFORMATION OF AMERICAN FOREIGN POLICY INTERESTS AND IDEAS. When diplomatic coalitions fail to form against aggressors, aggression becomes easier, making war more likely. Such failure represents a diplomatic variety of offense-dominance, and has the same effects as the military variety. Thus the two world wars were caused partly by American and British failure to balance firmly against German aggression in both 1914 and 1939, and Soviet failure to balance in 1939. This left Germany's neighbors less secure, and allowed Germany to hope that hegemony was possible. Peace has been preserved since 1945 partly because the United States and Britain reversed course after 1945, playing an active role in counterbalancing Soviet power on the European Continent.

American foreign policy interests and thinking have changed dramatically since the 1930s. The United States is therefore likely to continue playing an active balancing role, at least in Western Europe, even after the Soviet withdrawal from Eastern Europe.[15] As a result, the danger of inadequate diplomatic balancing is unlikely to recur in the new Europe.

The nuclear revolution reduces the threat posed by a hegemonic European state to American sovereignty, since a nuclear-armed America could defend itself against such a hegemon far more easily than it could in the pre-nuclear era. This lowers America's geopolitical interest in balancing actively against a potential European hegemon. However, the nuclear revolution also heightens America's interest in avoiding war in Europe, since such a war would now inflict far more harm on America if it spread to engulf the United States. America could well be drawn into such a war, because it has deep cultural and ethnic ties to Europe, and would find it difficult to stand aside while

---

14. This change does have a downside: by slackening the impulse to balance against aggression, it could weaken the resistance that aggressors face, weakening deterrence. However, the new economics would cause net damage to peace through this effect only if aggressors' motives to commit aggression are not reduced by the new economics, while defenders' will to defend is weakened. This asymmetry might develop, but there is no clear reason why it should be expected.

15. A continued American military commitment to Europe will not diminish the risk of war in Eastern Europe unless the United States guarantees the security of the Eastern European states against attack by one another—a policy I do not expect or recommend—but it will inhibit aggression in Western Europe, and dampen the spread of war from Eastern to Western Europe. Moreover, the United States can use measures short of military commitment, such as economic incentives, to punish aggressors and reward good conduct in Eastern Europe, as I note below. This would constitute a balancing policy implemented by non-military means.

the homelands of American ethnic groups were conquered or destroyed. A future European war could also harm American commercial or other interests, drawing in the United States by a process parallel to that which pulled it into the French Revolutionary Wars and the First World War. Thus while one argument for balancing has diminished, another has become more persuasive. As a result, the United States is unlikely to return to its pre–World War II policy of isolation.[16]

The experience of the two world wars has also changed American foreign policy thinking in ways that will probably not be reversed. Before both wars, the United States remained aloof from Europe in the belief that it could stand aside from Europe's wars, but this proved impossible both times. National historical learning is often ephemeral, but this experience forms a large part of American historical consciousness, and its main lesson—that the United States could be drawn into any future European conflagration—is relatively unambiguous. As a result, it is difficult to imagine a return to the simple isolationism of the 1930s. The disastrous results of that policy are too difficult to explain away. Moreover, during the Cold War the United States developed a large military establishment whose main reason for existence lies in the American commitment to Europe. This establishment has an institutional interest in reminding Americans of the history of 1914–45, if they begin to forget it.

The post–Cold War world has yet to emerge, but early signs indicate that those who forecast a complete American withdrawal from Europe will be proven wrong.[17] During the 1980s some Americans called for such a withdrawal,[18] but these voices have now largely faded away. The current American administration seems committed to staying in Europe even after the Soviet withdrawal from Eastern Europe,[19] and there is little dissent from this policy in the United States.

---

16. For further discussion of America's post–Cold War interest in Europe, see Stephen Van Evera, "Why Europe Matters, Why the Third World Doesn't: American Grand Strategy After the Cold War," *Journal of Strategic Studies*, Vol. 13, No. 2 (June 1990), pp. 1–51, at 2–12.

17. Mearsheimer suggests that the dissolution of NATO and the complete withdrawal of American and British forces from the European continent are likely if the Soviet Union withdraws fully from Eastern Europe. "Back to the Future," pp. 5–6.

18. For examples, see Van Evera, "Why Europe Matters, Why the Third World Doesn't," pp. 1, 34–35n.

19. President Bush has declared that American forces are needed to provide a "stabilizing presence" in Europe even if the Soviet Union withdraws fully from Eastern Europe, and in early 1990 he successfully pressed Moscow to agree that American forces in Western Europe would be reduced more slowly than Soviet forces in the East. See Michael Gordon, "American Troops

MILITARISM

World War I and the Pacific War of 1941–45 were caused in part by the domination of civilian discourse by military propaganda that primed the world for war. This domination has now disappeared in Europe.

As a general matter, professional military officers are nearly as cautious as civilians in recommending decisions for war.[20] However, militaries do sometimes cause war as a side-effect of their efforts to protect their organizational interests. They infuse the surrounding society with organizationally self-serving myths; these myths then have the unintended effect of persuading the rest of society that war is necessary or desirable. Militaries purvey these myths to convince society to grant them the size, wealth, autonomy, and prestige that all bureaucracies seek—not to provoke war. Yet these myths also support arguments for war; hence societies infused with military propaganda will be warlike, even if their militaries want peace.[21] Wilhelmine Germany and Imperial Japan are prime examples of societies that were infused with such myths, and waged war because of them.[22] Other European powers also fell under the sway of militarist mythology before 1914, although to a lesser extent than Germany.[23]

Needed in Europe, President Asserts," *New York Times,* February 13, 1990, p. 1; and Thomas Friedman, "Soviets, Ending Objections, Agree to U.S. Edge on Soldiers in Europe," *New York Times,* February 14, 1990, p. 1.

20. The only empirical study on this question is Richard K. Betts, *Soldiers, Statesmen and Cold War Crises* (Cambridge: Harvard University Press, 1977). Betts found that America's Cold War military leaders were as cautious as American civilian leaders in recommending war, although military leaders were notably more hawkish than civilians when the escalation of warfare was considered.

21. I develop this argument in Van Evera, "Causes of War," pp. 206–398.

22. Thus Hans-Ulrich Wehler notes "the spread of military values throughout German society" before 1914, and argues that "this 'social militarism' not only placed the military highest on the scale of social prestige, but permeated the whole of society with its ways of thinking, patterns of behavior, and its values and notions of honor." Wehler, *The German Empire 1871–1918,* trans. Kim Traynor (Leamington Spa/Dover, N.H.: Berg Publishers, 1985), p. 156. German Admiral George von Müller later explained German pre-war bellicosity by noting that "a great part of the German people . . . had been whipped into a high-grade chauvinism by Navalists and Pan-Germans"; quoted in Fritz Stern, *The Failure of Liberalism* (London: George Allen and Unwin, 1972), p. 94. For more on the role of the military in Wilhelmine Germany see Gordon Craig, *The Politics of the Prussian Army, 1640–1945* (New York: Oxford University Press, 1955); and Martin Kitchen, *The German Officer Corps, 1890–1914* (Oxford: Clarendon Press, 1968). On Japan see Saburo Ienaga, *The Pacific War, 1931–1945* (New York: Pantheon, 1978), pp. 13–54. A survey on the problem of militarism is Volker R. Berghahn, *Militarism: The History of an International Debate, 1861–1979* (New York: St. Martin's, 1982).

23. I summarize the beliefs purveyed by European militaries before 1914 in Stephen Van Evera, "Why Cooperation Failed in 1914," *World Politics,* Vol. 37, No. 1 (October 1985), pp. 80–117, at 83–99.

Five principal myths have been prominent in past military arguments and propaganda. First, militaries exaggerate the power of the offense relative to the defense, and the ease of conquest among states. Before World War I the German army's chief propagandist, General Friedrich von Bernhardi, expressed the common military prejudice when he wrongly asserted that "the offensive mode of action is by far superior to the defensive mode," and that new technology favored the attacker.[24] Such illusions bolster arguments that larger forces are needed to defend against aggression, and support arguments for the offensive military doctrines that militaries strongly prefer.[25] However, they also cause war, by conjuring up the many dangers (noted above) that arise when national leaders believe that security is scarce and conquest is easy.[26]

Second, military propaganda exaggerates the hostility of other states, painting neighbors as malevolent and aggressive. This bolsters the military's case for large budgets by exaggerating the likelihood of war, but also causes war by bolstering arguments that enemies should be forestalled by launching preemptive or preventive war.[27]

---

24. Friedrich von Bernhardi, *How Germany Makes War* (New York: Doran, 1914), p. 155. Before 1914, British generals likewise declared that "the defensive is never an acceptable role to the Briton, and he makes little or no study of it," and that the offensive "will win as sure as there is a sun in the heavens." Generals W.G. Knox and R.C.B. Haking, quoted in T.H.E. Travers, "Technology, Tactics, and Morale: Jean de Bloch, the Boer War, and British Military Theory, 1900–1914," *Journal of Modern History*, Vol. 51 (June 1979), pp. 264–286, at 275. For more details on British thought and practice see Tim Travers, *The Killing Ground: The British Army, the Western Front and the Emergence of Modern Warfare, 1900–1918* (Boston: Allen and Unwin, 1987). On offensive thinking in Germany, France, and Russia before 1914, see Snyder, *Ideology of the Offensive*, pp. 41–198; on France, see also Basil Liddell Hart, "French Military Ideas before the First World War," in Martin Gilbert, ed., *A Century of Conflict, 1850–1950* (London: Hamish Hamilton, 1966), pp. 135–148; and for further examples see Van Evera, "Causes of War," pp. 280–324, 571–607.
25. The reasons for this preference are detailed in Posen, *Sources of Military Doctrine*, pp. 47–51, 58, 67–74; and Snyder, *Ideology of the Offensive*, pp. 24–25.
26. See pp. 11–12, above.
27. Thus German officers in the Wilhelmine era depicted a Germany encircled by envious neighbors about to attack, and naval officers in imperial Japan warned of an aggressive encirclement of Japan by America, Britain, China, and the Netherlands in the 1930s. Such warnings created a general belief that war was inevitable, which strengthened the arguments of German and Japanese advocates of preventive war. For an example from Germany see Imanuel Geiss, *German Foreign Policy, 1871–1914* (Boston: Routledge and Kegan Paul, 1976), pp. 121–122, quoting General Alfred von Schlieffen; for other pre-1914 examples from Germany, Britain, and Russia, see Van Evera, "Why Cooperation Failed," p. 85. On Japan see Asada Sadao, "The Japanese Navy and the United States," in Dorothy Borg and Shumpei Okamoto with Dale K.A. Finlayson, eds., *Pearl Harbor as History: Japanese-American Relations 1931–1941* (New York: Columbia University Press, 1973), pp. 225–260, at 243–244, 251.

Third, militaries exaggerate the tendency of other states to give in to threats—to "bandwagon" with the threat instead of "balancing" against it.[28] Such myths bolster the military's arguments for larger forces by reinforcing claims that a bigger force can be used to make diplomatic gains, but also cause war by feeding confidence that belligerent behavior will bring political rewards.[29]

Fourth, militaries commonly overstate the strategic and economic value of empire.[30] These exaggerations strengthen arguments for forces required to gain or defend imperial conquests, but also feed arguments for waging imperial wars.

Finally, militaries often understate the costs of warfare, sometimes even portraying it as healthy or beneficial.[31] This raises the prestige of the military by increasing the apparent utility of the instrument it wields, but it causes war by encouraging states to behave recklessly. The bizarre pre-1914 popular belief that a European war would "cleanse" and "rejuvenate" society largely sprang from such military propaganda, and helped set the stage for war.

The scourge of militarism kept the world in turmoil until 1945, but has now almost vanished in Europe. European militarism diminished sharply

---

28. On bandwagoning and balancing, and the prevalence of the latter over the former, see Stephen M. Walt, *The Origins of Alliances* (Ithaca: Cornell University Press, 1987), pp. 17–33, 147–180, 263–266, 274–280.

29. Thus the Wilhelmine German Navy justified its big fleet with its famous "risk theory," which proposed that a large German fleet could be used to cow Britain into neutrality while Germany moved aggressively. See Theodore Ropp, *War in the Modern World*, rev. ed. (New York: Collier, 1962), pp. 212–213; Paul Kennedy, *Strategy and Diplomacy, 1870–1945* (London: Fontana, 1984), pp. 127–162, and specifically on the intimidation of Britain, pp. 133, 135, 139. Germany's General Schlieffen similarly contended that even if Britain fought to contain Germany, it would abandon the war in discouragement once the German army had defeated France. Gerhard Ritter, *The Schlieffen Plan: Critique of a Myth*, trans. Andrew and Eva Wilson (London: Oswald Wolff, 1958; reprint ed., Westport, Conn.: Greenwood, 1972), p. 163. These notions strengthened the arguments of German war-hawks in 1914.

30. For example, before 1914 the German Admiral George von Müller saw Germany locked in a "great battle for economic survival"; without new territories "the artificial [German] economic edifice would start to crumble and existence therein would become very unpleasant indeed." Müller memorandum to the Kaiser's brother, quoted in J.C.G. Röhl, ed., *From Bismarck to Hitler: The Problem of Continuity in German History* (London: Longman, 1970), pp. 56–57, 59. General Bernhardi likewise declared that "flourishing nations . . . require a continual expansion of their frontiers; they require new territory for the accommodation of their surplus population." Friedrich von Bernhardi, *Germany and the Next War*, trans. Allen H. Powles (New York: Longmans, Green, 1914), p. 21, and see also pp. 82–83. In France Marshall Ferdinand Foch spoke in similar terms; see Foch, *The Principles of War*, trans. de Morinni (New York: Fly, 1918), pp. 36–37. For more examples see Van Evera, "Causes of War," pp. 339–347.

31. For examples see Van Evera, "Causes of War," pp. 348–360; and Van Evera, "Why Cooperation Failed," pp. 90–92.

after World War I, when Europe's militaries were widely blamed both for causing the war and for waging it foolishly. This reduced the military's ability to shape public opinion by lowering its prestige.

Since World War II the potential for militarism has diminished further, with the end of the deep social barriers between the military establishment and civilian society. Before 1914 European militaries stood apart from society in two ways. First, military officers were socially segregated and isolated. This allowed them to develop a separate culture, including an arrogant sense of a right to command civilian ideas on foreign and military policy. Second, the military officer corps were preserves of the upper class, especially in Germany and France, and were seen by that class as pillars of its social dominance.[32] Hence militaries had a double motive to sow propaganda that enhanced their prestige: to advance the interests of military institutions, at the expense of wider societies with which they felt little identification; and to advance the interests of the upper class as a whole.[33] Three changes, which began after World War I and gathered momentum after World War II, have now diminished these motives: European officers are more integrated into civilian society; the officer corps are no longer an upper-class preserve, instead representing a wider cross-section of society; and European societies have undergone a process of social leveling, which has sharply reduced class conflict.

In addition, new barriers have been built against a militarist revival. These barriers are embodied in the spread of democracy in Europe, the development in the West of governmental institutions for the civilian evaluation and control of defense policy, the growth in Western Europe of university-based civilian expertise in military affairs—which is weaker than in the United States but is nevertheless significant—and the awareness of European military officers that their institutions did great harm in the past. The growth of official and unofficial civilian defense analysis, combined with democracy and norms of free speech, guarantees that military propaganda would face greater public criticism than before 1914. The greater historical awareness of European military officers—a product of their greater social integration,

---

32. On Germany see Wehler, *The German Empire*, pp. 125–127, 145–146, 155–170; on France see Snyder, *Ideology of the Offensive*, chap. 3.
33. In France the military also believed that its social purity could best be preserved by an offensive doctrine that would require a fully professional army, untainted by masses of middle-class reserves, and for this reason as well it purveyed offensive ideas. See Snyder, *Ideology of the Offensive*, chap. 3.

which brings them into greater contact with common historical discourse—causes militaries to use more self-restraint than before in defending their institutional interests.

The permanent disappearance of European militarism is not guaranteed, however, and logic suggests that militarism could make a modest comeback in the future. This danger lies in the same dynamic that makes great powers more vulnerable to militarism than medium powers. Great powers must provide for their own security, which causes them to maintain larger militaries, which then have larger effects on the discourse of surrounding society. More importantly, great power militaries stand to gain more from the propagation of militarist myths than do medium-power militaries, because great powers address the foreign threats that these myths depict by counter-buildup, while medium powers more often respond by seeking support from allies. Hence great power militaries gain a greater budgetary payoff from propagating such myths, giving them greater incentive to do so.

This dynamic helps explain the marked confinement of past militarism to great powers, or to isolated medium powers that lacked allies to provide security. It also suggests that Europe will become more prone to militarism as the superpowers reduce their European presence. European states will then be forced to provide more of their own security; hence their security policies will come to more closely resemble those of great powers, restoring one condition for militarism.

The risk of militarism will also increase in the Soviet Union, due to *glasnost* (in the short run) and the end of the Bolshevik dictatorship (in the longer run). Some argue that these changes will reduce the influence of the military, by allowing greater public criticism of military policies.[34] However, *glasnost* also gives the military new freedom to purvey propaganda, and the end of the Bolshevik monopoly on power will lift the longstanding Communist Party monopoly on political ideas, giving the military an even greater opportunity. There is still no sign that the Soviet military has begun to exploit these opportunities, but it may not remain quiescent forever. Moreover, unlike the West, the Soviet Union lacks established academic or governmental civilian institutions with military expertise, so civilians are poorly prepared to use their new freedom.[35] Hence it seems possible that the Soviet military will

---

34. David Holloway, "State, Society, and the Military under Gorbachev," *International Security*, Vol. 14, No. 3 (Winter 1989/90), pp. 5–24.
35. See Stephen M. Meyer, "Civilian and Military Influence in Managing the Arms Race in the

gain more power than it loses from Soviet liberalization, at least until strong civilian analytic institutions are developed.

However, a resurgence of European militarism to the levels seen during 1900–14 seems unlikely, because pre-1914 militarism arose partly from social conditions unique to those times, and because European societies are at least partly immunized against a repetition by the memory of its results.

HYPER-NATIONALISM AND ITS MYTHS AND MISPERCEPTIONS

During the period 1871–1939, a great wave of hyper-nationalism swept over Europe. Each state taught itself a mythical history of its own and others' national past, and glorified its own national character while denigrating that of others.[36] The schools, the universities, the press, and the politicians all joined in this orgy of mythmaking and self-glorification. Boyd Shafer summarized the common tenor of European education:

Text and teacher alike, with a few notable exceptions, taught the student that his own country was high-minded, great, and glorious. If his nation went to war, it was for defense, while the foe was the aggressor. If his nation won its wars, that was because his countrymen were braver and God was on their side. If his nation was defeated, that was due only to the enemy's overwhelmingly superior forces and treachery. If his country lost territory, as the French lost Alsace-Lorraine in 1870, that was a crime; whatever it gained was for the good of humanity and but its rightful due. The enemy was "harsh," "cruel," "backward." His own people "kind," "civilized," "progressive."[37]

This chauvinist mythmaking poisoned international relations by convincing each state of the legitimacy of its own claims, the rightness of its own

---

U.S.S.R.," in Robert J. Art, Vincent Davis, and Samuel P. Huntington, eds., *Reorganizing America's Defense: Leadership in War and Peace* (Washington, D.C.: Pergamon-Brassey's, 1985), pp. 37–61. The danger presented by enlarged military influence is seen in the sharp difference between Soviet military and civilian views on foreign and military policy; this difference is described in Celeste A. Wallander, "Third World Conflict in Soviet Military Thought: Does the 'New Thinking' Grow Prematurely Grey?" *World Politics*, Vol. 42, No. 1 (October 1989), pp. 31–63; and R. Hyland Phillips and Jeffrey I. Sands, "Reasonable Sufficiency and Soviet Conventional Defense: A Research Note," *International Security*, Vol. 13, No. 2 (Fall 1988), pp. 164–178.

36. For examples from before 1914 see Van Evera, "Why Cooperation Failed," pp. 93–95. On the doctoring of history in Germany during the interwar years and its consequences, see Holger H. Herwig, "Clio Deceived: Patriotic Self-Censorship in Germany After the Great War," *International Security*, Vol. 12, No. 2 (Fall 1987), pp. 5–44. A general survey on nationalism is Boyd C. Shafer, *Faces of Nationalism: New Realities and Old Myths* (New York: Harcourt Brace Jovanovich, 1972).

37. Boyd Shafer, *Nationalism: Myth and Reality* (New York: Harcourt, Brace, 1955), p. 185.

cause, and the wrongfulness and maliciousness of the grievances of others. Oblivious that its own past conduct had often provoked others' hostility, each country ascribed hostility to others' innate and boundless aggressiveness. This led each to assume that others could not be appeased, and should be dealt with harshly.[38] Countries also approached war with a reckless confidence engendered by a sense of innate superiority. Such ideas fed the climate that fostered both world wars.[39]

The stability of postwar Europe has been partly due to the remarkable decline of nationalist propaganda, especially in European schools.[40] As I note below, this decline resulted in part from the social and economic leveling of European societies after the 1930s, and the less competitive relations that developed among Western European states after 1945. It also grew from the Allied occupation of Germany, which destroyed the Nazi textbooks and imposed a more honest history curriculum in German schools;[41] and from the concerted efforts of international agencies and educational institutions, most notably the U.N. Educational, Scientific, and Cultural Organization (UNESCO), and the Brunswick International Schoolbook Institute in Germany.[42] These institutions oversaw textbook exchanges whose purpose was to force the educators of each country to answer foreign complaints about their curricula, with the aim of causing Europe to converge on a single shared version of European history. Their efforts were a dramatic success, largely ridding Western Europe of hyper-nationalism. Nothing suggests that this achievement will soon be undone. Moreover, the social leveling of Eastern

---

38. I suspect that such nationalist mythmaking is the main cause of the "spiral model" pattern of conflict described by Robert Jervis, *Perception and Misperception in International Politics* (Princeton, N.J.: Princeton University Press, 1976), pp. 58–113. Jervis emphasizes psychological causes; empirical research comparing these explanations would be useful.

39. During World War I an American historian reflected on the responsibility of chauvinist historical writing for causing the European war: "Woe unto us! professional historians, professional historical students, professional teachers of history, if we cannot see written in blood, in the dying civilization of Europe, the dreadful result of exaggerated nationalism as set forth in the patriotic histories of some of the most eloquent historians of the nineteenth century." H. Morse Stephens, "Nationality and History," *American Historical Review*, Vol. 21 (January 1916), pp. 225–236, at 236.

40. See Paul M. Kennedy, "The Decline of Nationalistic History in the West, 1900–1970," *Journal of Contemporary History*, Vol. 8, No. 1 (January 1973), pp. 77–100.

41. A survey of this often-mismanaged but ultimately successful endeavor is Nicholas Pronay and Keith Wilson, eds., *The Political Re-education of German and Her Allies After World War II* (Totowa, N.J.: Barnes and Noble Books, 1985).

42. An account is E.H. Dance, *History the Betrayer* (London: Hutchinson, 1960), pp. 126–150. The Brunswick Institute has since been renamed the Georg Eckert Institute for International Schoolbook Research, after its founder, Dr. Georg Eckert.

Europe makes the emergence of hyper-nationalism unlikely in that region as well, as I note below.

SOCIAL IMPERIALISM

During the late nineteenth and early twentieth centuries European elites sometimes sought to bolster their domestic position by distracting publics with foreign confrontations, or by seeking successful foreign wars.[43] Russian bellicosity toward Japan before the Russo-Japanese war of 1904–05 has been ascribed partly to such motives.[44] Hans-Ulrich Wehler argues that the Prussian government launched the wars of 1864, 1866, and 1870 partly "to legitimize the prevailing political system against the striving for social and political emancipation of the middle classes."[45] Before 1914 some Germans feared the domestic effects of war,[46] but others favored bellicose policies because they thought a victorious war would strengthen the monarchy.[47]

This cause of war has been removed from Europe by the democratization of European politics, and the leveling of European societies. The coming of democracy has legitimized Europe's regimes, and social leveling has reduced popular discontent with the existing social order. Both changes have reduced the elites' need to use foreign policy to bolster their legitimacy. Today's

---

43. On social imperialism in Germany see Wehler, *The German Empire*, pp. 24–28, 103–104, 171–179, 200; Volker Berghahn, *Germany and the Approach of War in 1914* (London: Macmillan, 1973), pp. 81–82, 93–94, 97, 185; Fritz Fischer, *War of Illusions: German Policies from 1911 to 1914*, trans. Marian Jackson (New York: W.W. Norton, 1975), pp. 253–254; and Arno Mayer, "Domestic Causes of the First World War," in Leonard Krieger and Fritz Stern, eds., *The Responsibility of Power* (New York: Macmillan, 1968), pp. 286–300. Some have ascribed Soviet Cold War expansionism to similar causes; a discussion is Gaddis, "Long Peace," pp. 118–119. A criticism of the social imperial explanation for German conduct is Marc Trachtenberg, "The Social Interpretation of Foreign Policy," *Review of Politics*, Vol. 40, No. 3 (July 1978), pp. 328–350, at 341–344. A more general discussion of social imperialism and other scapegoat theories of war is Jack S. Levy, "The Diversionary Theory of War: A Critique," in Manus I. Midlarsky, ed., *Handbook of War Studies* (Boston: Unwin Hyman, 1989), pp. 259–288; a criticism of these theories is Blainey, *Causes of War*, pp. 72–86.

44. The Russian minister of the interior, Viascheslav Plehve, stated at the time: "What this country needs is a short victorious war to stem the tide of revolution." Quoted in Levy, "Diversionary Theory of War," p. 264.

45. Wehler, *German Empire*, p. 26.

46. For examples see Berghahn, *Germany and the Approach of War*, pp. 82, 97, 185; and Wehler, *German Empire*, p. 200.

47. Thus shortly before the war, former Chancellor Bernhard von Bulow wrote that an expansionist policy was the "true antidote against social democracy," and Chancellor Bethmann Hollweg noted in June 1914 that belligerent German agrarian interests "expected a war to turn domestic politics in a conservative direction." Quoted in Wehler, *German Empire*, pp. 177–178; and Berghahn, *Germany and the Approach of War*, p. 185.

European elites face less pressure from below, and hence have less motive to divert that pressure by foreign adventurism.

UNDEMOCRATIC POLITIES

European societies are more democratic than before 1914 or 1939, and democracy is spreading rapidly in Eastern Europe. This trend is bound to continue, because key pre-conditions for democracy—high levels of literacy and industrial development, and a relatively equal distribution of land, wealth, and income—are now far more widespread in Europe than they were 80 years ago.[48] This change bolsters peace.

Empirical evidence suggests that democracies are not generally more peaceful than other states, but that relations among democracies are more peaceful than relations among non-democratic states, or between democracies and non-democracies.[49] Logic suggests two related reasons why relations among democracies should be peaceful.[50] First, the ideologies of democracies do not incorporate a claim to rule other democracies, so they have no ideological motives for expansion against one another. The democratic presumption of the right of peoples to choose their own political path precludes the idea that world democracy should be run from a single center, or that any democracy has a claim to rule another. The communist world has long been rent with conflict over who would be the leader, most clearly manifest in the Sino-Soviet and Yugoslav-Soviet conflicts.[51] The Arab states have likewise clashed over leadership of the Arab world.[52] The democratic world has suffered no parallel conflict, because democratic ideology preempts the question "who should lead?" with the answer that "no one should lead."[53] This dampens expansionism among democratic states, and eases their fears of one another.

---

48. The prerequisites for democracy are discussed in Robert A. Dahl, *Polyarchy: Participation and Opposition* (New Haven: Yale University Press, 1971), pp. 48–188; and Seymour Martin Lipset, *Political Man: The Social Bases of Politics,* expanded ed. (Baltimore: Johns Hopkins University Press, 1981), pp. 27–63.

49. For empirical studies see Steve Chan, "Mirror, Mirror on the Wall . . . Are the Freer Countries More Pacific?" *Journal of Conflict Resolution,* Vol. 28, No. 4 (December 1984), pp. 617–648; and Erich Weede, "Democracy and War Involvement," in ibid., pp. 649–664.

50. Developing these arguments is Michael Doyle: "Kant, Liberal Legacies, and Foreign Affairs," Parts 1 and 2, *Philosophy and Public Affairs,* Vol. 12, No. 3, No. 4 (Summer, Fall 1983), pp. 205–235, and 325–353; and Michael Doyle, "Liberalism and World Politics," *American Political Science Review,* Vol. 80, No. 4 (December, 1986), pp. 1151–1169.

51. A general account through the early 1960s is Richard Lowenthal, *World Communism: The Disintegration of a Secular Faith* (New York: Oxford University Press, 1964).

52. See Walt, *Origins of Alliances,* pp. 206–212.

53. Making this point is Walt, *Origins of Alliances,* pp. 35–37, 211–214.

Second, democratic elites would have more difficulty legitimating a war against another democracy. They could not claim that they fought to free the people of the opposing state, since these people would already be free. The elite would also face arguments that warring to overthrow another democratic regime is anti-democratic, since such a war would seek to undo the popular will of the other society. Thus democracies have less motive to attack each other, and would face greater domestic opposition if they chose to do so.

Deduction suggests two additional reasons why democracies should be more peaceful. First, war-causing national misperceptions—militarist myths, hyper-nationalist myths, or elite arguments for "social imperial" wars, for example—should be dampened by norms of free speech, which permit the development of evaluative institutions that can challenge errant ideas. Even in democracies the evaluation of public policy is seldom very good, and fatuous ideas can often influence state action; but this danger is smallest in societies that permit free debate, as all democracies must to some degree. Second, democracy tends to limit social stratification. This limits the elite's motive to purvey nationalist myths or to pursue war for social-imperial reasons, and removes a past cause of militarism.[54]

These last two deductions suggest that democracies should have more peaceful relations with both democracies and non-democracies; hence they are contradicted by empirical studies showing that democracies have in fact not been more pacific in their relations with non-democratic states.[55] However, these studies have not controlled for perturbing variables that may explain the discrepancy, hence they do not definitively disprove these deductions.[56] Moreover, this question need not be resolved to establish the effect of the spread of democracy in Europe. It has created a homogeneously democratic Western Europe, and most Eastern states are likely to become democracies also. If so, nearly all international relations in Europe will be

---

54. Thus democracy and social leveling are reciprocally related; each bolsters the other.
55. See Chan, "Mirror, Mirror"; and Weede, "Democracy and War Involvement."
56. For example, these studies did not control for the strength of states. This omission may make democracies appear more warlike, because democracy tends to develop in industrialized states; industrial states tend to be strong states; and strong states tend to be involved in more wars. See Quincy Wright, *A Study of War*, 2nd ed. (Chicago: University of Chicago Press, 1965) pp. 220–222, who notes that European great powers have averaged twice as many wars as lesser states since 1700. Moreover, case studies of the origins of wars indicate that hyper-nationalism, unchallenged official propaganda, and social imperialism have sometimes played a role in their outbreak; this supports the argument that democracies are more peaceful overall, since democracy should dampen these diseases. Thus the total body of empirical evidence points both ways.

intra-democratic, and most scholars agree that intra-democratic relations are more peaceful.

SOCIAL AND ECONOMIC STRATIFICATION

European societies are now far less socially and economically stratified than they were before 1914 or 1939.[57] In Western Europe, stratification was ended by democracy and the political mobilization of the working class. In Eastern Europe it was ended by communism. This transformation has operated as a remote cause of peace by contributing to the four changes just discussed— the growth of democracy, and the decline of militarism, hyper-nationalism, and social imperialism.

These four effects of social leveling vary in importance. The demilitarization and democratization of Europe have removed important causes of war, but social leveling was not the sole cause, nor perhaps even the main cause, of these changes. It played a large role in eliminating social-imperial motives for war, but this cause of war, while significant, probably mattered less than others. The most significant effect of leveling has been the reduction of hyper-nationalism; leveling removed the taproot of the great wave of hyper-nationalism that swept Europe during 1870–1939.

This wave of hyper-nationalism was a largely artificial phenomenon, engineered by elites who resorted to nationalism to persuade publics to tolerate the steep stratification of late nineteenth century and early twentieth century European societies. As the nineteenth century progressed, Europe's elites faced increasing challenge because industrialization weakened previous

---

57. For data on the evolution of income inequality in Europe, see Peter Flora, Franz Kraus, and Winfried Pfenning, *State, Economy, and Society in Western Europe, 1815–1975: A Data Handbook in Two Volumes*, Vol. 1: *The Growth of Industrial Societies and Capitalist Economies* (Chicago: St. James, 1987), pp. 611–674. They report inequality diminishing over the past several decades in eight of nine countries covered. For example, the share of national income received by the top 10 percent of the British population fell from 38.8 percent to 25.8 percent between 1938 and 1976 (p. 672); in Germany the share received by the top 10 percent fell from 40.5 to 31.7 percent between 1913 and 1974 (p. 652). Inequality in the distribution of wealth in Europe has diminished even more markedly. For example, in England and Wales the share of total wealth controlled by the richest 1 percent of the population fell from 61 percent to 32 percent between 1923 and 1972; in Sweden the share of total taxed net worth controlled by the richest 1 percent fell from 50 percent to 17 percent from 1920 to 1975. See A.B. Atkinson and A.J. Harrison, "Trends in the Distribution of Wealth in Britain," in A.B. Atkinson, ed., *Wealth, Income and Inequality*, 2nd ed. (Oxford: Oxford University Press, 1980), pp. 214–229, at 218; and Roland Spånt, "Wealth Distribution in Sweden, 1920–1983," in Edward N. Wolf, ed., *International Comparisons of the Distribution of Household Wealth* (Oxford: Clarendon Press, 1987), pp. 51–71. On the United States see H.P. Miller, "Income Distribution in the United States," in A.B. Atkinson, ed., *Wealth, Income and Inequality* (Harmondsworth: Penguin, 1973), pp. 111–135, at 113, 125–126.

methods of social control. The spread of mass literacy and the rural migration to the cities broke the elites' monopoly of information and caused the spread of egalitarian ideas. The development of mass armies, caused partly by the invention of mass production methods to make small arms, forced each state to arm its citizenry to avoid defeat by mass foreign armies; this broke the elites' monopoly of force. These changes impelled elites to seek new instruments of social control—so they switched from coercion to persuasion. Hyper-nationalism, purveyed chiefly through public education, was their prime weapon. This hyper-nationalism was crafted to persuade publics to continue to serve and obey the state loyally.[58]

The profound leveling of European societies, however, now allows European elites to command public loyalty without resort to hyper-nationalism. Hence this motive for the propagation of nationalism has largely disappeared, which suggests that hyper-nationalism will not return in force.

Social stratification was not the sole cause of European hypernationalism: a secondary cause lay in the felt need to mobilize publics to support the costly defense efforts required by the competitive international politics of the era.[59] This cause may reappear as the European states begin providing more of their own security, and their elites may be motivated to propagate somewhat more nationalism in order to persuade publics to back enlarged defense programs. The elites of seceding Soviet republics will also fan nationalism to mobilize popular support if they face long liberation struggles. However, the United States can dampen security motives for the propagation of nationalism in Western Europe by continuing its military presence in Europe. And any nationalism fanned by liberation struggles in the Soviet republics will be weakened by the absence of the social inequities that nourished hyper-nationalism in the past.

---

58. Overall, as Hans-Ulrich Wehler notes, the German "teaching of history was used as an anti-revolutionary mind-drug for the inculcation of a patriotic mentality." *German Empire*, p. 121. However, see also Geoff Eley, *Reshaping the German Right: Radical Nationalism and Political Change After Bismarck* (New Haven: Yale University Press, 1980). Eley argues that nationalist propaganda had its main effect on the German middle class, while leaving the working class relatively unaffected. And for a different view on the causes of nationalism, see Ernest Gellner, *Nations and Nationalism* (Ithaca: Cornell University Press, 1983). Gellner explains nationalism without reference to social stratification.

59. Thus the Kaiser's government instructed German teachers to produce "self-denying subjects . . . who will be glad to pay the supreme sacrifice for king and country," by teaching "the power and greatness of our people in the past and in the present." Quoted in Walter Consuelo Langsam, "Nationalism and History in the Prussian Elementary Schools Under William II," in Edward Mead Earle, ed., *Nationalism and Internationalism* (New York: Columbia University Press, 1950), pp. 243–245.

AGGRESSIVE REVOLUTIONARY STATES

War spawned by revolution is another danger absent from the new Europe. States led by movements that seized power through mass revolution are more war-prone for a number of reasons. Once in power, revolutionary elites fear counter-revolution, leading them to defensive wars of expansion to remove threatening counter-revolutionaries from their borders. They infuse themselves with self-glorifying myths to motivate supporters during the revolution; these myths live on after the revolution, fueling chauvinism toward other countries. They frequently adopt universalist aims and rhetoric to inspire supporters to sacrifice for the revolution, but these universalist aims often become dogma that outlives the revolutionary struggle, fueling messianic expansion later on. They demand a monopoly of ideas and suppress dissent during the revolution itself; this habit later leads to the suppression of free speech and public debate, allowing misperceptions and illusions to govern state conduct. Neighboring regimes with different social systems may fear the contagious impact of a revolutionary example on their own publics—especially if these regimes lack domestic legitimacy—and may foment the counter-revolution that the revolution fears, or even attack it directly. Neighbors may also be influenced to attack by emigrés who flee the revolution and then work to persuade neighboring states to restore them to power. Thus revolutionary states are more prone to attack others, and more likely to be attacked.[60] Revolutionary France, the Soviet Union, Khomeini's Iran, and Castro's Cuba all suffered these syndromes and sparked these reactions, leading them into international confrontation.[61]

This cause of war will not arise in the new Europe, because Europe is devoid of revolutionary states, and of illegitimate regimes that might be threatened by them. The revolutionary cycle has burned itself out in the Soviet Union. The new regimes of Eastern Europe gained power in popular upheavals, but these were not mass revolutions; they involved no long insurgencies of the sort that nurture battle-hardened, myth-ridden revolutionary organizations. Revolutionary regimes might arise in republics seced-

60. Advancing these hypotheses is Stephen Walt, "The Foreign Policy of Revolutionary States: Hypotheses and Illustrations," paper prepared for the annual meeting of the American Political Science Association, Chicago, 1987; and Stephen Walt, "Revolution and War," paper prepared for the annual meeting of the American Political Science Association, San Francisco, 1990.
61. See T.C.W. Blanning, *The Origins of the French Revolutionary Wars* (New York: Longman, 1986); Marvin Zonis and Daniel Brumberg, *Khomeini, the Islamic Republic of Iran, and the Arab World* (Cambridge: Harvard Center for Middle East Studies, 1987); Jorge I. Dominguez, *To Make a Word Safe for Revolution: Cuba's Foreign Policy* (Cambridge: Harvard University Press, 1989).

ing from the Soviet Union if they are forced to gain freedom by lengthy wars, but this scenario, while plausible, now seems unlikely. Moreover, the older regimes of Europe would feel less threatened by revolution, and would respond more temperately if a revolutionary regime did appear, because they are now democratic, socially leveled, and legitimate.

AGGRESSIVE CAPITALIST STATES

Some scholars, mostly Marxist, have blamed distempers of capitalism for past troubles in Europe. Such arguments have been overblown, but they also contain a grain of truth. During the 1890s many Europeans and Americans came to believe that the conquest of colonies could avert or cure economic depression by providing a market for unsold goods. Such ideas played a major role in American imperial expansion during 1898–1902.[62] They soon lost fashion, with the worldwide recovery from the great depression of the 1890s, and with the failure of markets to appear in conquered colonies. However, after-echoes of these ideas continued in Germany, where arguments that Germany should seize territory to create markets for unsold goods played a minor part in the expansionist propaganda that fueled German chauvinism and set the stage for war in 1914.[63] After-echoes also continued in the United States; after World War II American policymakers feared a new depression, and America's early Cold War belligerence was given an extra push by arguments that the United States should acquire or protect overseas markets to avert it.[64]

---

62. See David Healy, *U.S. Expansionism: The Imperialist Urge in the 1890s* (Madison: University of Wisconsin Press, 1970), pp. 42–46, 159–177.

63. Thus German journalist Arthur Dix explained in 1901 that a world power requires "extensive territory . . . as a market for [its] manufactures," and General Bernhardi in 1911 saw a Germany "compelled to obtain space for our increasing population and markets for our growing industries." Wallace Notestein and Elmer E. Stoll, *Conquest and Kultur: Aims of the Germans in Their Own Words* (Washington, D.C.: U.S. Government Printing Office, 1917), p. 51; *Germany and the Next War*, p. 103. See also ibid., pp. 82–83. France's Marshall Foch explained that modern states needed "commercial outlets to an industrial system which produces more than it can sell, and therefore is constantly smothered by competition," and argued that "new markets are opened by force of arms." Foch, *Principles of War*, p. 37.

64. For examples see Walter LaFeber, *America, Russia, and the Cold War 1945–1980*, 4th ed. (New York: Wiley, 1980), pp. 10–11, 18, 27, 45, 52, 55, 59–61, 110–111, 179–180, 235. It may not follow that these ideas helped cause the Cold War, however: perhaps they fueled American belligerence, but this belligerence may have deterred the Soviets from further aggression, thus dampening the Cold War, as much or more than it provoked them. Making this argument is Vojtech Mastny, *Russia's Road to the Cold War: Diplomacy, Warfare, and the Politics of Communism, 1941–1945* (New York: Columbia University Press, 1979). A good survey of the debate on Cold War origins is John Lewis Gaddis, "The Emerging Post-Revisionist Synthesis on the Origins of the Cold War," *Diplomatic History*, Vol. 7, No. 3 (Summer 1983), pp. 171–204.

This problem, never large, has now disappeared completely. Fears of economic depression have abated throughout the West, with the development of fiscal and monetary tools for managing the business cycle. The European and American colonial experience has delegitimated the concept of colonialism in general, and with it the concept of regulating the business cycle by imperial expansion. Reflection has brought the realization that any attempt to relieve depression by one-way colonial trade could last only until the colony's currency reserves were exhausted, which would happen quickly. These changes remove the main causes of any past capitalist belligerence.

SUMMARY: ABSENT AGGRESSOR STATES

If all states accept the status quo and none wish to change it, wars are far fewer. Indeed, if no aggressor state is on the scene, war can only occur by accident or misunderstanding.[65] The causes of war discussed above all operate primarily by fueling expansionism, thereby creating aggressor states that reject the status quo. Aggressor states will be rare in the new Europe, because both domestic and systemic factors will provide little stimulus to aggression, and powerful dissuasion. This is a vast change from 1914, 1939, and 1945.

This auspicious condition is likely to persist. Today's Western European states are far less bellicose in their general approach to foreign relations than the European states of 1914 and 1939. In part this reflects their status as smaller powers, which are generally less bellicose than great powers, reflecting their smaller, tamer militaries. This could fade as they assume their own security burdens, if both superpowers withdraw from Europe completely. But it also reflects the nuclear revolution, the knowledge revolution in economics, and the transformation of European domestic societies, which are far more healthy than those of the European states of 1914 or 1939. The emerging societies of Eastern Europe are likely to develop eventually along similar lines.[66]

---

65. I use the term "aggressor state" to refer to states that seek to expand for any reason. Others often use the term to refer only to states that seek to expand for reasons other than security, while classifying expansionist states that are driven mainly by security concerns as status quo powers. See, for example, Charles Glaser, "International Political Consequences of Military Doctrine" (manuscript, July 1990), p. 4.

66. Some observers have suggested that two additional changes since 1945 may prevent renewed conflict in Europe. John Mueller has argued that the great horrors of past conventional wars have delegitimated even conventional war, and that warfare is therefore now largely obsolete. See John Mueller, *Retreat From Doomsday: The Obsolescence of Major War* (New York: Basic Books,

False Fears: Illusory New Causes of European War

Pessimists about the future peace of Europe have said little about these propitious changes, focusing instead on four dangers: the multipolar character of the emerging Europe, the possibility of renewed German aggression, the risk of praetorian states emerging in the East, and the problem of national and border conflicts in Eastern Europe and the Soviet Union. However, the first three dangers (discussed next) are largely illusory; only the fourth poses large risks, as I explain in the subsequent section.

A MULTIPOLAR EUROPE

Prominent scholars have argued that bipolar systems are more peaceful than multipolar systems. John Mearsheimer recently used this theory to predict that the emergence of multipolarity in Europe will raise the risk of war.[67]

1989). Others point to the spread of free economic exchange in Europe since 1945, the greater prosperity and economic interdependence that this change produces, and the development of international institutions, including the European Economic Community (EC) and the General Agreement on Tariffs and Trade (GATT), to foster and protect these changes. They argue that prosperity and interdependence promote peace, by dampening economic motives for war, and by raising the economic cost of war. Some also argue that international economic institutions could grow stronger, developing into a kind of super-state that could bolster peace by playing a police role. I find both views largely unpersuasive. Even the horrors of World War I failed to delegitimate war, and if World War I cannot do the job, nothing can. (Germany developed a large war-celebrating literature only a decade after World War I ended: see Wolfram Wette, "From Kellogg to Hitler [1928–1933]: German Public Opinion Concerning the Rejection or Glorification of War," in Wilhelm Deist, ed., *The German Military in the Age of Total War* [Dover, N.H.: Berg, 1985], pp. 71–99. For a general criticism of Mueller's argument see Kaysen, "Is War Obsolete?")

The prosperity promoted by economic liberalism probably promotes peace indirectly, by bolstering democracy, and by pushing economies further toward knowledge-based forms of production. However, there is little reason to believe that prosperity reduces economic motives for war. Economic interdependence is more likely to cause war than peace, by inducing states toward aggressive policies to relieve dependence on other states they feel they cannot trust. Such motives drove Germany and Japan to seek economic autarky through expansion in World War II, and arguments that America depends on Third World raw materials have often been advanced by American advocates of U.S. Third World intervention. Finally, the European liberal economic order is likely to dissolve if other causes of war appear to produce conflict in the new Europe; instead of dampening these causes, the European economic order will succumb to them. Mearsheimer convincingly criticizes both theories on these and other grounds: see "Back to the Future," pp. 29–31, 40–48; and Mearsheimer, "Correspondence: Back to the Future, Part II: International Relations Theory and Post-Cold War Europe," *International Security*, Vol. 15, No. 2 (Fall 1990), pp. 194–199. On interdependence see also Gaddis, "Long Peace," pp. 110–114; and, for examples of arguments for American intervention premised on American raw-materials dependence, Van Evera, "Why Europe Matters, Why the Third World Doesn't," pp. 19, 43n.

67. Kenneth N. Waltz, "The Stability of a Bipolar World," *Daedalus*, Vol. 93, No. 3 (Summer

The European system is indeed losing its bipolar Cold War character with the decline of Soviet power and the Soviet withdrawal from Eastern Europe. It will become fully multipolar if the United States also withdraws from the West. However, those who fear this development rest their case on weak theory. Some aspects of bipolarity favor peace, but others favor war. Still other aspects of bipolarity have indeterminate effects. Overall, the two types of systems seem about equally prone to war.[68]

FACTORS FAVORING BIPOLARITY. Four aspects of bipolarity favor peace. First, the two poles of a bipolar system comprise larger states whose size makes them more difficult to conquer; hence states are more secure, and aggression is better deterred.[69] This argument assumes that the size of states is not held constant in our analysis, and that we instead compare the effects of bipolar or multipolar arrangements in a given region; if so, the poles of a multipolar system must be smaller than those in a bipolar system, since multipolarity subdivides the same territory into more poles. This assumption seems appropriate in an analysis of the future of Europe, however, since the evolution of Europe toward multipolarity entails the subdivision of two vast blocs led by very large states into a system of smaller states that can be more easily overrun.[70]

Second, bipolarity facilitates cooperation on arms control and other matters, and makes it easier to establish and maintain "rules of the game" and agreed spheres of influence.[71] Cooperation is easiest among the few;[72] a

---

1964), pp. 881–909; Kenneth N. Waltz, *Theory of International Politics* (Reading, Mass.: Addison-Wesley, 1979), pp. 161–176; Gaddis, "Long Peace," pp. 105–110; Mearsheimer, "Back to the Future," pp. 13–19, 21–29.

68. My thinking on the effects of multipolarity has profited greatly from conversations with Chaim Kaufmann.

69. Chaim Kaufmann suggests this argument. I find it the strongest element of the case for bipolarity; yet it has not been advanced by bipolarity advocates, although Waltz comes close. Waltz clearly assumes that bipolar poles are larger than multipolar poles; see Waltz, *Theory of International Politics*, pp. 146–160. However, Waltz does not suggest that this size differential makes conquest harder under bipolarity.

70. As Kaufmann notes, however, a case could be made for holding size constant even when analyzing the effects of multipolarity in Europe, because the nuclear revolution largely eliminates the effects of small size. If the size of states is held constant, the case for bipolarity is substantially weakened.

71. See Waltz, *Theory of International Politics*, pp. 174; Mearsheimer, "Back to the Future," pp. 16–17. Waltz stresses the greater ease of cooperation under bipolarity; Mearsheimer stresses the greater ease of establishing and maintaining rules of the game and spheres of influence.

72. On the effects of the number of players on the feasibility of cooperation see Kenneth A. Oye, "Explaining Cooperation Under Anarchy: Hypotheses and Strategies," in Kenneth A. Oye, ed., *Cooperation Under Anarchy* (Princeton, N.J.: Princeton University Press, 1986), pp. 1–24, at 18–20.

bipolar order has the fewest players. An agreed order is most easily created and maintained in an unchanging world; a bipolar world changes least. Under multipolarity, by contrast, cooperation faces the difficulties of complex diplomacy among many states, and an agreed international order is harder to maintain because the whirl of shifting coalitions sweeps away the facts on which the old order was premised. Consequently, arms control and other forms of cooperation are more difficult, rules of the game are harder to establish, and agreed .pheres of influence are harder to maintain.

Third, misunderstandings and miscalculations are less likely under bipolarity, because great powers face a simpler world. States face only one opponent, and have many years to study that opponent. Hence they are less likely to misconstrue its interests, or to underestimate its strength or resolve. This lowers the risk of wars arising from misunderstanding or optimistic miscalculation. A multipolar world is more complex, creating greater room for error.[73] It forces states to diffuse their focus of attention toward a number of states, causing them to know less about each. As a result, states can more easily stumble into conflict by misconstruing another state's interests. States also must do more complex calculations to predict the results of war—they must estimate the strength and resolve of their opponent's potential allies, in addition to those of their opponent. This uncertainty magnifies the likelihood of war-causing optimistic miscalculation.[74]

Fourth, the greater complexity of multipolarity increases the possibility that defending states will underestimate how much effort is necessary to balance against aggressors, and will therefore do too little or act too late. This can happen if defending states exaggerate the willingness of other defenders to balance, and fail to make military preparations of their own adequate to compensate for this unwillingness. If so, balancing will be too weak, and opportunities for aggression will appear. With bipolarity, in contrast, defenders know that they can secure themselves only by their own efforts. They are therefore less likely to place fruitless reliance on others.[75]

---

73. See Waltz, *Theory of International Politics*, pp. 168, 170, 172–173.

74. The greater uncertainty produced by multipolarity may also prevent some wars, by fostering pessimistic miscalculation that leads states to avoid wars that they would otherwise fight. However, it seems likely that overall, wars would be fewer if all states always accurately foresaw their outcome. Losers would then fight only if they thought a losing contest was still worthwhile to preserve their honor and credibility.

75. This possibility is partly offset by its converse: defending states in a multipolar system may underestimate others' willingness to balance, and may therefore make extra efforts to balance internally, producing a stronger defending coalition than would otherwise develop. However,

FACTORS FAVORING MULTIPOLARITY. These factors are counter-balanced by two others that operate to make multipolarity more peaceful. First, the coalition politics of a multipolar world usually produce defensive coalitions that overmatch aggressors by a greater margin than is possible under bipolarity. This effect makes conquest more difficult, and offsets the offense-strengthening effect produced by the smaller size of states under multipolarity, and by the possibility that defenders will not balance adequately because they exaggerate others' willingness to balance.

In a bipolar system, the ratio of defending to aggressing states never falls below 1:1, but also never exceeds 1:1. Under multipolarity, an aggressor can gain advantages of more than 1:1 against a defender if other states bandwagon with the aggressor. If others coalesce against the aggressor, however, it can face overwhelming superiority. Since balancing behavior is the prevalent tendency of states, the latter pattern prevails over the former—large defensive coalitions usually form against aggressors, confronting them with stronger opposition than they would face under bipolarity. If so, a successful defense is more certain, and the penalty for aggression is higher. The aggressor will certainly be thwarted, and may also be smashed—a penalty that is unlikely under bipolarity. Hence aggressors are better deterred, and all states are more secure.

Balancing can break down if appropriate conditions are absent.[76] Thus effective defending coalitions failed to form against ancient Rome, against Chi'n in ancient China, and against American expansion in North America during the nineteenth century. However, history indicates that such cases are the exception, not the rule.[77] This has been true in Europe, where over the past 500 years every hegemonic aggressor eventually faced a coalition that outgunned it. Moreover, even if balancing fails, multipolarity is no worse than bipolarity on this count. International conflict then reduces to duels that

---

this often bolsters a balance that is already adequate, and thus merely makes less likely wars that are already unlikely, hence it does not fully offset the risks raised by the possibility of failures to balance due to exaggerated expectations of balancing by others.

76. Specifically, balancing is inhibited if geography prevents states from coming to the aid of the victim, for example, if states are arranged in a geographically linear fashion, leaving some remote from others; if geography allows the aggressor to sever communications between the victim and others; if diplomacy is hobbled by poor communication among states (as occurred in ancient times); or if the system is composed of small states whose size makes them less prone to balance.

77. A survey concluding that balancing has prevailed over bandwagoning in both the Middle East and worldwide during the Cold War is Walt, *Origins of Alliances*, pp. 147–180, 263–266, 274–280.

assume a bipolar character, in which conquest is no easier than it would be under bipolarity. Alliance dynamics make conquest easier under multipolarity than bipolarity only in the rare event that states bandwagon—or if, as noted above, states fail to balance adequately because they exaggerate others' willingness to do so.[78]

Under bipolarity, as Kenneth Waltz notes, competition extends widely and hard as the two poles quickly move to contest each other everywhere, because if each does not check the other, no one else will. This ensures that aggressors will not get a free ride, which is good; but it also reflects the greater insecurity produced by the absence of potential allies under bipolarity, and highlights the dangers that this insecurity creates. States compete widely and hard precisely because they know they have no one to fall back on if the balance of power turns against them. This knowledge persuades them to balance, but it may also lead them to adopt exceedingly competitive or aggressive policies that may trigger crises and war. By contrast, desperate states in multipolarity can call on allies for help. Such recourse to allies is often a safer solution than early and belligerent confrontation.[79]

Second, militarism is a greater danger under bipolarity than multipolarity. With bipolarity, the military captures the full benefit of the myths it sows, while under multipolarity this benefit is dissipated as the government re-

---

78. Bipolarity advocates claim that the balancing mechanism is more efficient under bipolarity; each side will be quick to resist the other's aggressive moves, and will counter-balance the other's military effort with its own. Balancing by such internal methods (direct action to thwart aggression, or arms buildup) is more certain and effective than the external methods (seeking allies) that are possible with multipolarity. Thus under bipolarity, they argue, a fairly defense-dominant world results, in which each side cannot easily commit aggression because the other prevents it. In contrast, states often "pass the buck" under multipolarity, leaving the burden of balancing to their allies; but if all states buck-pass, they will fail to counter-balance the aggressor. See Waltz, *Theory of International Politics*, pp. 164–165, 168; and Mearsheimer, "Back to the Future," pp. 15–16. (Waltz wrote before discussion of the effects of the offense-defense balance became common currency, and I embellish his concepts by using offense-defense terminology, but this terminology is consistent with his meaning.) The logic of this argument for the greater peacefulness of bipolarity is flawed, however. If states balance at all under multipolarity, aggressors will face greater opposition than under bipolarity, even if states buck-pass quite a lot. Even if states buck-pass all the time, multipolarity is no worse than bipolarity. States then must fully provide for their own security; hence they should exhibit the same rapid and forceful internal balancing behavior that Waltz predicts for bipolarity.

79. Waltz's argument that bipolarity forces states to behave prudently implicitly concedes the same point. See Waltz, *Theory of International Politics*, p. 176. As I note below, he suggests that states must be prudent because there is no one to save them from disaster. However, prudence that is forced by insecurity, while beneficial in itself, arises from a cause that has other, dangerous effects.

sponds by forging alliances rather than building forces.[80] Bipolarity therefore gives the military greater incentive to propagate militarist myths, raising the risk of militarism.

At first glance history seems to disprove this hypothesis: militarism flourished in the multipolar Europe of 1890–1914, but was far less evident in the United States and the Soviet Union during the bipolar Cold War. However, this merely demonstrates that militarism has a number of causes, and other causes that matter were abundant before World War I, but absent during the Cold War. Most important, the domestic political systems and culture of both superpowers were notably unconducive to militarism: the Soviet Union's Communist Party insisted on a strict civilian monopoly of all political ideas, and America's democratic free-speech culture demanded civil control of the military, and guaranteed some public challenge to military propaganda. Even so, a case could be made that the United States, and perhaps both superpowers, were mildly infected by the militarism virus.

Finally, another test provides opposite results. History shows that militarism is a disease confined to great powers or isolated states,[81] and is never found in medium powers allied to others. If we extrapolate from this pattern, a system whose powers reach the top limit of power and isolation—bipolarity—should see militarism most often. In any case, scattered instances do not provide a persuasive test of a theory, so at this stage the verdict on the hypothesis that multipolarity lessens militarism should rest chiefly on its deductive soundness.

INDETERMINATE FACTORS. Bipolarity advocates argue that two additional aspects of bipolarity favor peace, but deduction suggests that these factors are in fact indeterminate.

---

80. Bipolarity also may foster militarism by causing states to maintain larger military establishments. This occurs because states cannot "free-ride" on allies, and must instead rely wholly on their own efforts for security. See Mancur Olson, Jr., and Richard Zeckhauser, "An Economic Theory of Alliances," *The Review of Economics and Statistics*, Vol. 48, No. 3 (August 1966), pp. 266–279. Some increase in militarism may result, as larger size gives militaries greater domestic influence. However, this effect is at least partly offset by the greater security afforded by the greater size of states under bipolarity, which should reduce their military requirements.

81. Wilhelmine Germany and imperial Japan are prime cases of militarized great powers. Both also saw themselves as largely isolated, and thus also illustrate the militarizing effects of isolation. Lesser states largely isolated from great-power allies that have suffered at least some militarization include South Africa, Brazil, Argentina, and Chile. On the latter three, see Jack Child, *Geopolitics and Conflict in South America: Quarrels Among Neighbors* (New York: Praeger, 1985), pp. 19–85, 98–105. On South Africa see Kenneth W. Grundy, *The Militarization of South African Politics* (Bloomington: Indiana University Press, 1986), pp. 58–67.

First, some assert that bipolarity bolsters peace by removing the possibility that benign great powers will be dragged into wars begun by more reckless powers. Multipolarity raises the risk of the "chain gang" phenomenon—a circumstance in which the whole system is led to war by its most bellicose states, who drag in their allies. Bipolarity eliminates this risk; the system only goes to war if one of the two poles are themselves bellicose.[82]

However, this argument cuts both ways. The alliances that form under multipolarity can pull states back from war as well as pulling them in. The "chain gang" phenomenon is a danger, especially when elites believe they live in an offense-dominant world (as in 1914), because states then must join wars that their allies provoke, since they cannot afford to see the ally defeated.[83] However, the opposite can also happen, especially when the defense is believed to be dominant. An alliance then functions like a "drunk tank," containing and calming its most aggressive members.[84] The aggressive state must explain its policies to its allies, and listen to their counter-arguments. These allies can afford to stay out of the aggressor's reckless adventures, and can further threaten to cancel their ties of alliance if it moves aggressively, leaving it without protection against aggression by others. Knowing this, it may not move at all. Thus American membership in NATO helped restrain the United States in the 1950s: the cases for preventive war against the Soviet Union, for escalating the Korean War, for intervening in Indochina in 1954, and for using nuclear weapons against China during the 1954–55 Taiwan Straits crisis were all dampened by arguments that European NATO states would not help, or would actively disapprove.[85]

---

82. See Waltz, *Theory of International Politics*, p. 167; and on the chain gang metaphor, Christensen and Snyder, "Chain Gangs and Passed Bucks." Mearsheimer makes a similar argument using different logic; see "Back to the Future," pp. 14–15. He notes that multipolarity creates more dyadic relationships than bipolarity, creating more relationships that could flare into war. He further notes that war has a general propensity to spread, hence each dyadic war could bear the seed of a system-wide war, creating more possibilities for general war under multipolarity than bipolarity. Thus Waltz focuses on the chain gang phenomenon, Mearsheimer on the general tendency of war to spread, as the mechanism by which one bellicose state can trigger system-wide war.

83. See Christensen and Snyder, "Chain Gangs and Passed Bucks."

84. Suggesting that alliances often served to restrain alliance members in Europe during 1815–1945 is Paul W. Schroeder, "Alliances, 1815–1945: Weapons of Power and Tools of Management," in Klaus Knorr, ed., *Historical Dimensions of National Security Problems* (Lawrence: University Press of Kansas, 1976), pp. 227–262.

85. On American consideration of preventive war in the 1950s see Marc Trachtenberg, "A 'Wasting Asset': American Strategy and the Shifting Nuclear Balance, 1949–1954," *International Security*, Vol. 13, No. 3 (Winter 1988/89), pp. 5–49; and Russell D. Buhite and William Christopher Hamel, "War for Peace: The Question of an American Preventive War against the Soviet Union,"

The allies of a bellicose state can also go further by moving to balance actively against it if it moves aggressively.[86] If so, multipolarity operates to prevent or shorten local wars by facing the aggressor with overwhelming opposition. Thus, overall, a multipolar system creates the possibility that other states in the system can be drawn into local wars, but it can also operate to dampen or prevent such wars—by threatening adventurous states with the loss of its allies, or by facing them with an overwhelming coalition.

Second, some suggest that bipolarity creates greater incentives to behave cautiously, and to choose wise national leadership. Under multipolarity states can hope to rely on each other, but with bipolarity they must rely on themselves, and hence on their leaders. This leads societies to behave carefully, and to choose prudent leaders.[87]

However, this argument clashes with other elements of the case for bipolarity. Some favor bipolarity because states in bipolarity compete widely and hard, hence aggressors face strong opposition; however this competitive conduct can cross the line to become reckless conduct. Bipolarity advocates also argue that multipolarity is more complex and confusing, raising greater risks of war—but if so, states in multipolarity should try harder to find wise leaders who can cope with these complexities. Overall, it is not clear which system best fosters cautious conduct and wise leadership.

The total case for each system is hard to assess, since we have no way to measure the power of the factors favoring each system. Overall, the case for each seems equally persuasive. Moreover, even if bipolarity is somewhat safer, the difference between the two systems is not dramatic, and forms a frail basis upon which to argue that the risk of war will rise sharply in the new Europe.

Diplomatic History, Vol. 14, No. 3 (Summer 1990), pp. 367–384. Trachtenberg mentions (but does not elaborate) Dulles's view that the likelihood that American allies would refuse to support such a policy was an important consideration against it (pp. 42–43). On Korea, see Rosemary Foot, *The Wrong War: American Policy and the Dimensions of the Korean Conflict, 1950–1953* (Ithaca: Cornell University Press, 1985), pp. 127, 145–146, 200–201, 217–219; and Robert Divine, *Eisenhower and the Cold War* (New York: Oxford University Press, 1981), pp. 28–29. On Indochina see George C. Herring, *America's Longest War: The United States and Vietnam 1950–1975* (New York: Wiley, 1979), pp. 31–36. On the Taiwan Straits crisis see Buhite and Hamel, "War for Peace," p. 382. These examples are especially noteworthy because they show lesser powers restraining a superpower in a bipolar system; in a multi-polar system, allies should be better able to restrain each other, since power is distributed more equally among them.

86. The Soviet decision to balance against expansion by its Iraqi ally during the 1990 Persian Gulf crisis provides a recent example.

87. See Waltz, *Theory of International Politics*, p. 176.

GERMAN AGGRESSION?

The argument that a free and united Germany will return to its past aggressiveness is refuted by the dramatic transformation of German society since 1945. Five changes have erased the roots of past German aggressiveness. First, German society, like the rest of Europe, has undergone a dramatic social leveling process.[88] The Junkers and big industrial barons are history. Their departure removed the arrogant elite whose stubborn defense of its class privilege helped provoke World War I and, less directly, World War II.

Second, Germany is an established democracy. German society contains all the preconditions for democracy in abundance, so we can be confident that this democracy is robust and durable.

Third, flowing in part from the first and second changes, German hypernationalism has dissipated, and a powerful barrier against its return has been erected by a strong movement in Germany for the honest discussion of German history. German secondary schools and the German media generally provide accurate coverage of Germany's past crimes.[89] German academic historians have largely abandoned the nationalist habits of their Wilhelmine predecessors, often taking a more critical view of German conduct than foreign historians do. For example, Fritz Fischer and his students have assigned more of the blame for the First World War to Germany than many British and American historians do.[90] A few German historians have tried to justify Germany's conduct in the Second World War, but many others have beaten them down.[91]

---

88. See World Bank, *World Development Report 1990* (New York: Oxford University Press, 1990), p. 237. The distribution of income in Germany is more equal than in most other major industrialized states, including the United States, Canada, Britain, France, Italy, Switzerland, Finland, Denmark, Australia, and New Zealand; it is less equal than in Sweden, Japan, the Netherlands, and Belgium; and is roughly comparable to the distribution in Norway and Spain.

89. See Anne P. Young, "Germans, History, and the Nazi Past," *Social Education*, Vol. 4, No. 2 (February 1981), pp. 86–98; and Hildegund M. Calvert, "Germany's Nazi Past: A Critical Analysis of the Period in West German High School History Textbooks" (Ph.D. dissertation, Ball State University, 1987). Calvert notes some objectionable omissions, but concludes that German textbooks "satisfactorily covered the majority of the topics examined" (p. ii).

90. The Fischer school's views are summarized in Geiss, *German Foreign Policy;* and Fischer, *War of Illusions*. A good survey of the controversy stirred by the Fischer school is John A. Moses, *The Politics of Illusion: The Fischer Controversy in German Historiography* (London: George Prior, 1975). As Moses notes, most German historians now accept Fischer's argument that Germany deliberately unleashed the First World War in June–July 1914, disputing only Fisher's contention that the war was planned long in advance (p. 73). An example of a non-German interpretation far more sympathetic to Germany than the Fischer school is L.C.F. Turner, *Origins of the First World War* (London: Edward Arnold, 1970).

91. On this dramatic debate see Richard J. Evans, *In Hitler's Shadow: West German Historians and*

If historical mythmaking did make a comeback in Germany, an acute danger would arise. Germany was badly mutilated by the two world wars, losing 34 percent of its pre-1914 territory,[92] and suffering the expulsion of 13.8 million Germans from the lost territories.[93] Germans who forget that German conduct was the main cause of this mutilation would begin blaming others, and could develop an extreme sense of grievance. The potential danger is even larger than in 1914 and 1939, since Germany was whole in 1914, and had less "lost" territory in 1939 than it has now. Hence German behavior is highly dependent upon German historical memory, and benign German behavior depends on sound memory. However, the commitment to honest history now seems stronger in Germany than anywhere else in Europe, and the main causes of past historical mythmaking have disappeared with the leveling of German society and the growth of German democracy.

Fourth, German civil-military relations have been transformed since the 1930s. The German military is no longer an upper-class preserve, and is integrated into German society. As a result, German officers understand the civilian viewpoint, and largely accept the civilian right to determine foreign and defense policy. German military officers learn the history of the German military's past misdeeds, which creates a barrier against their repetition.[94] German mass media contain no echoes of past military propaganda.

Fifth, the nuclear revolution has made available weapons of absolute security, should Germany ever need them. If Germany again faces a serious threat from without, it will not need to reach for more defensible borders or

---

the Attempt to Escape from the Nazi Past (New York: Pantheon, 1989); and Peter Baldwin, "The Historikerstreit in Context," in Peter Baldwin, ed., *Reworking the Past: Hitler, the Holocaust and the Historian's Debate* (Boston: Beacon, 1990), pp. 3–37. Noting the defeat of the German apologists in this debate are Baldwin, ibid., p. 29; and Hans-Ulrich Wehler, "Unburdening the German Past? A Preliminary Assessment," in Baldwin, *Reworking the Past*, pp. 214–223, at 214–215. Noting the absence of chauvinism in Germany today is Hans Mommsen, who concludes that "Germany today is ahead of its neighbors in its wariness of patriotic appeals and violent solutions to domestic conflicts." Hans Mommsen, "Reappraisal and Repression: The Third Reich in West German Historical Consciousness," in ibid, pp. 173–184, at 183.

92. *World Almanac and Book of Facts 1990* (New York; World Almanac, 1989), pp. 712–713.

93. At the end of World War II a total of 13,841,000 Germans were expelled from formerly German territories annexed by Poland and the Soviet Union, and from other East European countries; of these, 2,111,000 died during the expulsion, leaving 11,730,000 expellees alive during 1945–50. Most settled in West Germany, some in East Germany, and small fraction in Austria and other western countries. Alfred M. de Zayas, *Nemesis at Potsdam: The Expulsion of the Germans From the East*, 3rd rev. ed. (Lincoln: University of Nebraska Press, 1988), p. xxv.

94. I am indebted to Dr. Roland E. Foerster, Director of the Department of Education, Information, and Special Studies at the Military Historical Research Institute at Freiburg, and to Professor David Large of Montana State University, for sharing information on this question.

for wider territories to provide economic autarky, as it once did; now it can secure itself by building a nuclear deterrent. Germany's transition to nuclear power would not be without danger, in the form of possible preventive attack by outsiders. However, outside powers, most notably the United States, have the power to deter such an attack. Moreover, they would have every reason to do so, since a secure Germany is a more benign Germany, and is thus in the common interest.

In short, the new Germany is very unlikely to launch a new campaign of aggression. Its benign behavior since 1945 was due less to its divided and occupied condition than to the postwar transformation of German society, which removed the causes of its past belligerence. It is time for the rest of the world to stop viewing Germany with suspicion, and begin treating it with the respect that its responsible conduct deserves. The world should ask that Germans remember their past, if they ever need reminding. It should also ask that Germans accept a continuing obligation to reassure Germany's victims that Germany's past crimes will not be repeated. But the world should not ask for penance from a German generation that was not yet born in 1945, and should not make them pariahs for crimes committed by Germans who are long gone.

PRAETORIAN STATES IN THE EAST?

Jack Snyder has suggested that the tide of democracy in Eastern Europe and the Soviet Union may produce flawed praetorian polities, reminiscent of Wilhelmine Germany, rather than the civic-democratic or corporate-democratic states now found in the West.[95] Fledgling democratic institutions may be inadequate to channel growing popular political participation. This could leave control in the hands of narrow elites. These elites might then pursue aggressive foreign policies that would profit these elites, even if they produced net harm for the whole society.

However, this danger has been sharply reduced by the social leveling imposed by Soviet communist rule. Praetorianism is largely a disease of stratified societies; in praetorian states political institutions are inadequate to channel rising participation chiefly because elites want to exclude the public from politics, not because democratic channels for participation would be hard to establish if elites wished to create them. Communism has done great

---

95. Snyder, "Averting Anarchy in the New Europe," pp. 18–38.

harm throughout the East, but its egalitarian policies have ended steep class stratification, and thereby reduced the elites' motive to constrict democracy and create praetorianism.

The possibility of praetorianism is not gone altogether, because some social stratification persists in the East. The upper-class elites are gone, but the communist party bureaucracies and military establishments form elites of a different sort. Their power has not been broken in the Soviet Union, Romania, and Bulgaria, where this old guard still clings to its privileges, and seeks to choke off democratic reforms. In the Soviet Union it also recommends belligerent foreign policies, and criticizes President Gorbachev's withdrawal from Eastern Europe.[96] Nevertheless, praetorianism will probably be muted, because the net stratification of Eastern European societies seems substantially smaller than in past states where praetorianism flourished.

The states in the East might also suffer from other maladies of new democracies. Most notably, they lack developed non-governmental institutions for the evaluation and criticism of public policy—free universities, a skilled free press, and free research institutions. This raises the risk of the debasement of public discourse, political demagoguery, and the domination of dishonest propaganda purveyed by the government or private special interests. As a result, these states are likely to elect more than a few crackpot politicians of the Theodore Bilbo–Joe McCarthy–Jesse Helms–Gus Savage variety, and find their public debates polluted by European Al Sharptons. However, this is a short-term problem: these societies have the resources to develop evaluative institutions, and should be able to build them fairly quickly.

Why Peace Isn't Assured: Persisting and Emerging Causes of War

Two major dangers will emerge in the new Europe: the breakdown of established international and domestic order in Eastern Europe, and the reappearance of nationality conflicts and border disputes in the East. These two

---

96. Yegor Ligachev, a spokesman for the Communists Party old guard, has warned of the dangers of German reunification, and criticized acquiescence to this reunion as a "new Munich." "Excerpts From Speech By Ligachev to Party," *New York Times*, February 7, 1990, p. A12. Army General Albert Makashov has complained that "because of the so-called victories of our diplomacy the Soviet army is being driven without combat out of the countries which our fathers liberated from fascism." "Loyal to Lenin, Soviet general blasts Gorbachev," *Boston Globe*, June 20, 1990, p. 17. See also Helen Womack, "Kremlin under fire from generals," *The Independent*, July 6, 1990, p. 9.

dangers feed and magnify one another: the breakdown of order allows latent border and national conflicts to resurface, while these conflicts magnify the dangers created by the breakdown of order.

THE BREAKDOWN OF INTERNATIONAL AND DOMESTIC ORDER
Peace among states is most durable when spheres of influence, the "rules of the game," and the rights and responsibilities of all parties are clear. Dangers rise when these are ambiguous; each state then tends to define its own rights broadly and others' narrowly, and to dispute the others' definitions. Crises erupt as states issue threats and stage *faits accomplis* to force others to accept their own definition of their rights. The breakdown of established order could take two forms, both of which are now appearing in Europe.

INTERNATIONAL BREAKDOWN. Agreements on spheres of influence and regimes governing international behavior can dissolve if new events make them obsolete, or new issues arise. Thus the Cold War erupted partly because World War II demolished the old European order, leaving the Soviet Union and United States facing each other in Central Europe with only the sketchy rules of the wartime agreements to define their rights. Both then jockeyed hard to stake their claims, and collided on questions where rights and rules were ambiguous—most notably, over Western access rights to Berlin, and the Soviet Union's right to deploy nuclear weapons in Cuba. The later Cold War saw fewer crises largely because the rules of the game and the boundaries of the two superpowers' spheres of influence were more clearly worked out after 1962.[97]

The Soviet withdrawal from Eastern Europe creates a situation that resembles the early Cold War. The Soviets have blundered by withdrawing without first demanding an accord on the new status of Eastern Europe. Now a huge zone of Europe has re-entered the international system, but no agreement defines the rights of outside powers in Eastern Europe, or the responsibilities

---

97. The outbreak of the Seven Years War illustrates the same dynamics. The origins of that war lay partly in the lack of clarity over ownership of the Ohio Valley, which allowed Britain and France each to convince itself that it owned the valley and the other was encroaching. See, e.g., Patrice L.R. Higonnet, "The Origins of the Seven Years War," *Journal of Modern History*, Vol. 40 (1968), pp. 57–90; and Richard Smoke, *War: Controlling Escalation* (Cambridge: Harvard University Press, 1977), pp. 195–236. Likewise, each of the many European "wars of succession" in the eighteenth century grew from the breakdown of agreed international spheres of influence upon the death of a monarch; states then struggled to establish successions that would favor their own states or dynasties, or to avert such gains by others.

of the East European states to one another.[98] This ambiguity raises the risk of misunderstandings and collisions, as states inside and outside the region struggle to establish their rights.

DOMESTIC BREAKDOWN. Order can also unravel with the domestic collapse of imperial states, and the secession of outlying provinces. As imperial control wanes, outer territories spin off from the center; but absent prior agreements, there will be no rules to delineate others' rights in these territories, or to define their inhabitants' responsibilities to one another. This can spark an unregulated competition for control among outsiders, and fighting among the newly-free peoples. These dangers are magnified if the borders of the newly-emerging states are poorly defined, as they often are. Imperial collapse can also cause collisions between outside powers and the imperial metropole, as that metropole struggles to retain or regain control of areas that it still defines as its own, but others have come to define as free states.[99]

Collisions of the last sort are made more intense by the insecurity felt by the declining metropole, and its resulting willingness to take extreme measures to sustain itself. The domestic weakness of the metropole creates a domestic-political version of offense-dominance: the metropole is insecure not because military or diplomatic factors favor the offense, but because its own domestic weakness enables an "offensive" against it in the form of outside subversion or support for secessionist movements. Thus the domestic weakness of Austria-Hungary before 1914 caused it to fear Serbian subversion in Bosnia-Herzegovina. This spurred Austria to counter-attack against Serbia, sparking World War I.

The Soviet Union is Europe's last colonial empire. It is now riddled with secessionist movements among the many non-Russian peoples that Russia

---

98. For example, there is no explicit East-West understanding on whether the East European states can join NATO, whether NATO states can base forces in Eastern Europe, or whether Soviet forces can return to Eastern Europe, either to police civil or inter-state wars or for some other reason.

99. The crises surrounding the slow collapse of the Ottoman empire after the Napoleonic Wars illustrate these dangers. This collapse spawned three great crises, in 1832–33, 1839–40, and 1875–78, and two great wars—the Crimean War and World War I—plus the Balkan wars of 1912–13. The territories escaping Turkish control were of relatively little strategic value, but the undefined nature of other states' rights in these territories caused outsiders to collide over their possession. Thus Britain and France clashed over Egypt and Syria in the crisis of 1839–40, and Austria and Russia collided over the Balkans in 1914. The collapse of Ottoman authority also produced violent conflicts among the newly independent Balkan states. A general account is M.S. Anderson, *The Eastern Question 1774–1923* (New York: Macmillan, 1966). A summary is Rene Albrecht-Carrie, *A Diplomatic History of Europe Since the Congress of Vienna* (New York: Harper and Row, 1958), pp. 40–55, 84–92, 167–177, 280–286, 321–334.

conquered under the Tsars. It seems inevitable that this empire will eventually go the way of the British, French, Dutch, and Belgian empires. Its demise will raise greater dangers than the dismantling of the other colonial empires, however, for three main reasons. First, its seceding provinces lie closer to its imperial core, making that core more nervous about their possible alignment with hostile powers.[100] Second, the boundaries between metropole and colony are relatively unclear; for example, are the Ukraine and Byelorussia colonial provinces, or in some sense part "Russian"? And third (as I discuss below), the populations of the Soviet Union have intermingled, leaving millions of Russians living outside the metropole, and millions of other nationalities living outside their home republics. This situation creates immense potential for conflict over each group's rights and status, and gives the metropole a potent reason to refuse them independence. Some voices in the United States have already begun to call for treating the seceding nationalities as independent states, and for lending them support; this could cause a Soviet-Western confrontation if the Soviet leadership decides not to permit their unilateral secession.[101]

BORDER DISPUTES AND INTERMINGLED OR DIVIDED NATIONALITIES
The Soviet withdrawal from Eastern Europe uncovers border disputes and revanchist claims that were previously suppressed by the Soviet imperium, and similar conflicts will doubtless emerge among the Soviet republics as they gain independence from the Soviet Union. These conflicts arise partly from border shifts produced by past wars that have not been accepted by the loser. They also arise from the intermingling of nationalities in Eastern Europe and the Soviet Union, which sparks claims for territories inhabited by nationals living outside the home territory. Finally, the intermingling of nationalities also raises the risk of confrontations even across settled borders, as one state is aroused against the oppression of its nationals in another.[102]

---

100. On the other hand, the nuclear revolution should dampen fears in the Russian metropole that the secession of nearby republics will leave it insecure. However, this logic does not always prevail, as shown by the great nervousness that the United States has displayed in the past over the appearance of Soviet-aligned states and movements in the Caribbean and Central America.
101. For example, see Richard L. Berke, "Nine GOP Senators Attack Bush on Lithuania," *New York Times*, April 28, 1990, p. 4; and Richard L. Berke, "On Right, Signs of Discontent With Bush," *New York Times*, May 1, 1990, p. A18.
102. Such nationality conflicts should be distinguished from those arising from the hyper-nationalism discussed above (pp. 23–25, 28–29.) Hyper-nationalism is artificially generated or magnified by chauvinist myths. Conflicts arising from hyper-nationalism thus derive from the

These conflicts heighten the dangers posed by the absence of an agreed international order for Eastern Europe and the breakup of the Soviet internal empire, by providing concrete cause for the unregulated competition that these conditions permit.

These dangers have diminished since World War II. Eastern Europe's borders are more widely accepted now than fifty years ago, and Eastern Europe's nationalities are less intermingled because in the cataclysm of World War II millions of Germans were expelled from Eastern Europe, and the Nazis mass-murdered East European Jews and Gypsies. Nevertheless, a tour of the map of Eastern Europe reveals at least nine potential border disputes, and at least thirteen significant ethnic pockets that may either seek independence or be claimed by other countries.[103] If Yugoslavia breaks up, as now seems possible, additional border disputes would arise among its successor states, and ethnic pockets would exist within them.

In the Soviet Union, nationalities are even more intermingled than in Eastern Europe. The Soviet population totals some 262 million people, comprising 104 nationalities living in 15 Soviet republics. Of these, a total of 64 million (24 percent) either live outside their home republic, or are among the 89 small nationalities with no republic of their own, and thus would be minorities in the successor states to a dismantled Soviet Union (assuming that all 14 non-Russian republics secede but are not further sub-divided).[104] Of these 64 million, some 39 million (15 percent of total Soviet population) are members of nationalities that have their own republic, but live outside it; these include 24 million Russians (17 percent of all Russians) and 15 million

---

beliefs of nations. The national conflicts discussed here arise from the *circumstances* of nations— from their intermingling or their division by international borders. Such conflicts can be magnified by nationalist myths, but do not require them. Even nations that are not imbued with false self-glorifying history will tend to fall into conflict if they are intermingled or divided.

103. Frontiers that may be disputed include the Romanian-Soviet, Romanian-Hungarian, Polish-Soviet, Polish-German, Polish-Czechoslovakian, Hungarian-Czechoslovakian, Yugoslav-Albanian, Greek-Albanian, Greek-Turkish, and Greek-Yugoslav-Bulgarian. Ethnic pockets include Romanians in Soviet Bessarabia; Hungarians in Romania, Czechoslovakia, and the Soviet Union; Poles in the Soviet Union and Czechoslovakia; Germans in Poland, Czechoslovakia and Romania; Macedonians in Bulgaria and Greece; Turks in Bulgaria; Greeks in Albania, and Albanians in Yugoslavia. Summaries include Larrabee, "Long Memories and Short Fuses"; Istvan Deak, "Uncovering Eastern Europe's Dark History," *Orbis*, Vol. 34, No. 1 (Winter 1989), pp. 51–65; and Barry James, "Central Europe Tinderboxes: Old Border Disputes," *International Herald Tribune*, January 1, 1990, p. 5.

104. All demographic figures are for 1979, the most recent Soviet census, and are calculated from John L. Scherer, ed., *USSR Facts and Figures Annual*, Vol. 5 (Gulf Breeze, Fla.: Academic International Press, 1981), pp. 49–51.

members of other nationalities (15 percent of all such nationalities). Another 25 million people (9 percent of the total Soviet population) are members of smaller nationalities without home republics, who would be minorities wherever they live.[105]

A dismantled Soviet Union would thus be riddled with national conflicts.[106] These could arise from a nationality's demand to annex territory in another republic inhabited by its own members; from complaints against the oppression of national brethren who live across accepted borders;[107] and from demands by the small, stateless nationalities for autonomy or secession from the republics where they reside. Border disputes could also arise because some nationalities may claim larger borders dating from the days of their independent pre-colonial greatness. Armenian nationalists have already laid claim to Nagorno-Karabakh in Azerbaijan, and radical Georgian nationalists claim parts of Azerbaijan, Armenia, Turkey, and Russia. Other claims will doubtless be lodged by nationalists in other republics.

These ethnic conflicts and territorial disputes will pose significant dangers in the years ahead to both Eastern and Western Europe. Western Europe itself is largely free of such problems; its borders are well-settled,[108] and its populations are not significantly intermingled. However, war anywhere in Europe could spread to engulf others; hence the whole continent has an interest in dampening conflict in the East. The risk that an Eastern conflict could spread westward is smaller than in the past, because the nuclear revolution has made conquest harder, and the high-technology revolution has reduced the strategic value of empire; these changes reduce the security implications of affairs in the East for other European states, which lowers their impulse to intervene in Eastern wars. Nevertheless, some risk of spread

---

105. This excludes the Kazakh residents of Kazakhstan, but a literal accounting would include them, because the Russians outnumber them in Kazakhstan, 41 percent to 36 percent. In all other Russian republics the nationality after whom the republic is named are the majority or (in Kirgizia) a plurality.

106. A survey of relations among Soviet nationalities is Rasma Karklins, *Ethnic Relations in the U.S.S.R.* (Boston: Allen and Unwin, 1986).

107. The Soviet Union already has over 600,000 internal refugees who have fled from such oppression, and hundreds have died in communal violence. Francis X. Clines, "40 Reported Dead in Soviet Clashes," *New York Times,* June 9, 1990, p. 1.

108. The Polish-German boundary is the only Western frontier that might be disputed. Before unification the East and West German governments both agreed to guarantee the current German-Polish border; if the united German government adheres to this agreement, this border dispute is settled. See Serge Schmemann, "Two Germanys Adopt Unity Treaty and Guarantee Poland's Borders," *New York Times,* June 22, 1990, p. 1; and Thomas L. Friedman, "Two Germanys Vow to Accept Border With The Poles," *New York Times,* July 18, 1990, P. 1.

remains; hence the Western countries should take active measures to dampen conflicts in the East, and be prepared to prevent the spread of any wars they might ignite.

Policy Prescriptions

The United States has a large interest in preserving peace in Europe. Accordingly, the United States should be active to keep the risk of war as low as possible. Four specific policies are recommended.

PURSUE A GENERAL EUROPEAN SETTLEMENT
The world sails dangerously if it allows momentous changes without moving early to agree on the rights and responsibilities of all in the new world. Eastern Europe and the Soviet Union will be a magnet for outside interference, and a possible wellspring of general conflict, unless the main NATO powers and the Soviet Union promptly agree on the rights of all powers in the Eastern region. This need is made more urgent by the Eastern conflicts over borders and among nationalities. Without prior understandings, outside powers might be drawn into these conflicts, perhaps in response to pleas from states in the region, who can be expected to exert themselves to find outside allies.

These dangers could be reduced by a comprehensive Cold War peace settlement. Such a settlement should attempt to balance the security interests of all states against human rights concerns. Two questions are foremost: the status of Eastern Europe, and the status of seceding Soviet republics.[109] Eastern Europe's status should be settled by "Finlandizing" the region: the West would promise not to incorporate East European states into Western military alliances or to base forces on their territory, while the Soviet Union would guarantee their complete domestic freedom. Such a settlement would seem to strike the best balance between Soviet security interests and Western human rights concerns

The West should also seek an accord with the Soviet Union on the rights of all peoples in the Soviet republics. The Soviet nationalities conflicts, and the international effects of a breakdown of the Soviet empire, are best dampened by reaching an understanding before these crises are manifest.

---

109. A third major issue, the status of Germany, has recently been settled by agreement that a united Germany will be incorporated into NATO.

Specifically, the West should agree not to support or encourage the unilateral secession of Soviet republics. In exchange, the West should ask that the Soviet Union establish a fair and expeditious procedure for legal secession, if its current procedure is deemed too unwieldy. Western agreement to refrain from support for unilateral secessions makes sense for three reasons.

First, an unregulated breakup of the Soviet Union could produce a human rights disaster, by risking communal violence against the 64 million Soviet citizens who are now minorities in the republics where they live. In a worst case, a chain of non-negotiated secessions could trigger violence like the slaughter in India after the British withdrawal that killed 800,000 people and created millions of refugees during 1946–48, and killed many more in later years.[110] Bloody post-independence communal conflicts in Uganda, Rwanda, Burundi, Nigeria, Sudan, Zaire, Angola, Mozambique, Iraq, and Lebanon further illustrate this danger. It can best be averted if the republics negotiate their departure from the Soviet Union, and are not allowed to leave until they provide robust guarantees of the political and economic rights of their minorities. The West should favor their continued membership in the Soviet Union until they accept these obligations.

Second, non-negotiated secessions from the Soviet Union would also raise the risk of inter-state warfare among republics after they gain independence. Peace will be most robust if seceding republics first settle their borders and their post-independence economic and political relations with Russia and the other republics by negotiation. Otherwise these issues will later brew conflicts. Third, American support for unilateral secessions could spark a Soviet-American collision. States facing breakup seldom accept it gracefully, and outside interference in such situations can spark war, just as Serbian support for secessionists in Bosnia-Herzegovina sparked the Austrian counter-attack that triggered World War I. Western support for separatist groups in the Soviet Union might have similar results.

As a general matter, the West should seek a moderate settlement with the Soviet Union, and should not seek to exploit current Soviet weakness to press home every advantage. Perhaps the West could now impose a harsh peace, but this would fuel Soviet revisionism once the Soviet Union recovers from its current malaise. Just as Germany overthrew the Versailles peace once it recovered its strength, a later Soviet or Russian regime would some-

---

110. Casualty data are from Ruth Leger Sivard, *World Military and Social Expenditures 1989* (Washington, D.C.: World Priorities, 1989), p. 22.

day move to overthrow today's harsh settlement, and might disturb the peace of Europe in the process. Instead, the West should seek a settlement that will stand the test of time. A settlement that does not last is worse than none at all, since it provides no benefits and its breakdown will sow bitterness and suspicion, just as the breakdown of the wartime accords added bitterness to East-West relations early in the Cold War.

DAMPEN HYPER-NATIONALISM, MILITARISM, AND CONFLICT AMONG NATIONALITIES; PROMOTE DEMOCRACY

The experience of both world wars warns that hyper-nationalism and militarism can be potent causes of conflict. Accordingly, the United States should take active measures to combat these syndromes in the new Europe. Both are at low ebb in Europe today, and are unlikely to return to their former levels, for reasons noted above. However, their permanent disappearance is not guaranteed; hence the United States should act to prevent their resurgence. Otherwise we waste lessons that the world paid dearly to learn.

To dampen nationalism, the United States should monitor historical education in Europe, and should object when it finds omissions or distortions.[111] American relations with NATO states should be conditioned on their willingness to teach honest history in the schools, and the West's economic relations with the East should be likewise conditioned on the East's willingness to teach truthful history. The United States should also be willing to examine its own treatment of history, and to meet the same standard it sets for others.[112]

Some argue that the United States lacks the means to influence education in other countries. However, education is largely controlled by the state; and since historical education affects foreign policy conduct, and thereby affects the interests of other states, it is a legitimate subject of international negotiation. The United States has negotiated details of strategic nuclear force

---

111. This prescription has even more relevance in Japan, where the government has been slowly moving to re-patriotize education. See Tracy Dahlby, "Japan's Texts Revise WWII: 'Invasion' Becomes 'Advance'; Asians Become Irate," *Washington Post*, July 28, 1982, p. A1; Urban C. Lehner, "More Japanese Deny Nation Was Aggressor During World War II," *Wall Street Journal*, September 8, 1988, p. 1; Colin Nickerson, "In Japan, war and forgetfulness," *Boston Globe*, August 15, 1988, p. 1; and Patrick L. Smith, "A Textbook Warrior in Japan," *International Herald Tribune*, November 1, 1989, p. 18. Ominously, these moves have met little domestic resistance in Japan, and no objection from the United States government.

112. American historical education is not above criticism; see, for example, Frances Fitzgerald, *America Revised: History Schoolbooks in the Twentieth Century* (Boston: Little, Brown, 1979); and William L. Griffin and John Marciano, *Teaching the Vietnam War* (Montclair, N.J.: Allenheld, Osmun, 1979).

posture with the Soviet Union, and intimate aspects of domestic economic policy with Japan;[113] historical education policy surely can be negotiated as well. The content of historical education is public, hence compliance with understandings on education would be easy to verify. Arms control diplomacy has overcome more difficult verification problems.[114]

The problem of militarism seems even more distant in today's Europe, with its level-headed professional militaries and pacific publics, but this situation could deteriorate. This possibility can best be averted by promoting public understanding of security affairs, especially by fostering the scholarly study of security affairs in European universities; and by ensuring that the education of military officers includes discussion of the past disasters that militarism produced in Germany, Japan, and elsewhere. Again, such education could be monitored and negotiated among states.

The United States and other governments will hesitate to move against hyper-nationalism and militarism, because these problems are now largely invisible. However, these governments should recognize that both nationalism and militarism are best contained by early action, and may be uncontrollable if the world waits until they are manifest. After a society develops full-blown symptoms it is very difficult to bring it back to sanity, because its regime closes it off to outside influence. The best medicine is prevention.

Finally, the West should also act to dampen nationality conflicts and promote democracy in the East. Specifically, the Western countries should ask that the East European countries protect the rights of their national minorities, accept current boundaries, and adopt democratic reforms. Western economic relations with the East should be conditional on Eastern compliance

---

113. In 1990 the United States and Japan reached a trade accord that undertook to change fundamental characteristics of both economies that inhibit commerce between them. For example, Japan undertook to increase public works spending, reduce its protection of small retail shops, and enforce laws against bid-rigging and price-fixing. The United States undertook to cut its budget deficit, provide greater education for the American workforce, and increase spending on scientific and commercial research. See David E. Sanger, "U.S. and Japan Set Accord to Rectify Trade Imbalances," *New York Times*, June 29, 1990, p. 1. International accord on the content of national historical education seems far less difficult to reach and verify than these accords.

114. Such negotiation would be complicated by the fact that education is controlled by local governments in many countries (as in the United States and West Germany), and that in a few (such as Britain), standard textbooks are seldom used in history teaching. See Volker R. Berghahn and Hanna Schissler, "Introduction: History Textbooks and Perceptions of the Past," in Volker R. Berghahn and Hanna Schissler, eds., *Perceptions of History: An Analysis of School Textbooks* (New York: Berg Publishers, 1982) pp. 1–16, at 5–7, 13. However, even states whose school curricula are locally controlled could agree to provide incentives to local school districts to eliminate mythical and distorted history, and such incentives could be negotiated between countries.

with these requests. Full membership in the Western economy, and in Western economic institutions, should be offered as carrots; trade and investment embargoes should be held in reserve as sticks.[115] These incentives should be effective tools, since the states of the East will be eager to draw on Western resources to rebuild their economies.

BOUND AND MANAGE NUCLEAR PROLIFERATION

The proliferation of nuclear weapons in Europe would be a traumatic event, and is best deferred as long as Europe's non-nuclear states are content with their existing security arrangements. However, one or more European powers may eventually decide that its national security requires a nuclear deterrent. If so, the United States should not seek to prevent any proliferation. Rather, it should seek to bound and manage the process. If Germany decides to become a nuclear power, the United States should not resist: Germany has proven its responsibility, and it has the resources needed to develop an invulnerable deterrent secure from accident or terrorism. However, Europe is more dangerous with 20 or 25 fingers on the nuclear trigger than with a handful, because the additional states might be unable to secure any nuclear forces that they build.[116] Hence the United States should seek to confine proliferation sharply—ideally, to Germany alone.[117] It should also actively manage any proliferation that might occur, by deterring preventive attack on emerging nuclear powers, and by giving new nuclear states technical help to secure their deterrents.

CONTINUE AMERICA'S MILITARY PRESENCE IN EUROPE

The Soviet withdrawal from Eastern Europe will allow large American troop withdrawals from Western Europe, but the United States should leave a sizable residual force in Europe. Such a presence will allow the United States to deter aggression and play the balancing role that it failed to play in 1914 and 1939. It will also strengthen America's hand if America hopes to build

---

115. A full discussion of this idea is Snyder, "Averting Anarchy in the New Europe," pp. 31–36.

116. Explaining this danger is Mearsheimer, "Back to the Future," pp. 37–40.

117. America's ability to dampen proliferation in Eastern Europe will be hampered if the United States follows my recommendation that Eastern Europe be "Finlandized," since the United States would thereby forswear the right to extend the alliance protection to East European states that might be required to persuade them not to acquire nuclear weapons. However, the main stimulus to proliferation in the East would probably lie in German acquisition of nuclear weapons; the United States can unilaterally guarantee the East European states against German aggression without forming broader alliances with those states or putting forces in Eastern Europe.

barriers against hyper-nationalism and militarism, to exert leverage over East European states, and to bound and manage proliferation. The American force should be small enough to forestall taxpayer demands for further cuts, but large enough to provide some military capability, to serve as a visible token of America's commitment to Europe, and to remind Americans and Europeans of that commitment. A force of roughly 50,000–100,000 troops, backed by large additional forces in the United States, would seem to fit this requirement.

Such a deployment requires an institutional framework to define its purpose, and to bolster its legitimacy in the eyes of the American and European publics. The current NATO framework seems unsatisfactory. A continued American deployment would have the purpose of deterring aggression from any quarter, while NATO exists only to address the now-fading Soviet military threat; hence NATO's aim and the aim of the American deployment no longer match.

One solution would be to revamp NATO into an explicit collective security system, whose members guarantee each other against attack by any state, including other member states.[118] Collective security systems have a dismal history; the hapless League of Nations is the main exemplar. However, a NATO collective security system need not work like a Swiss watch. Its main purpose would simply be to provide a public rationale for a continued American presence in Europe, and to legitimate American action if action is ever needed. This task is far less demanding than the tasks faced by the League. Moreover, the League of Nations failed because it lacked strong leaders, but if the United States decides to continue playing a peacekeeping role in Europe, NATO already has the strong leader it needs.

Some instead propose constructing a single Europe-wide collective security system, perhaps based on the 35-country Conference on Security and Cooperation in Europe (CSCE).[119] Such a system would have the merit of

---

118. This would require a new NATO Charter. The current Charter obliges NATO members to defend one another from attack from any quarter, but it uses language implying that it does not contemplate attack by NATO members on one another. See "The North Atlantic Treaty, April 4, 1949," in Ernest R. May, ed., *Anxiety and Affluence: 1945–1965* (New York: McGraw-Hill, 1966), pp. 85–89, at 87. Nor does it define a process for triggering and operating the alliance against aggression by its own members, and the alliance has refused pleas from member states for guarantees against other NATO members. See, for example, Athanassios Platias, "High Politics in Small Countries: An Inquiry into the Security Policies of Greece, Israel, and Sweden" (Ph.D. dissertation, Cornell University, 1986), pp. 165–166, recounting Greek requests for NATO guarantees against Turkey, and NATO refusal on grounds that NATO's purpose does not include the defense of NATO members against each other.

119. Discussing this possibility are Jane M.O. Sharp and Gerhard Wachter, *Looking Beyond the*

providing security for all the states of Europe; no one is left out. However, a smaller system based on NATO would have two advantages over a single pan-European system. First, it would operate more smoothly, for several reasons: the internal politics of a smaller system would be less unwieldy; it would build on a developed alliance (NATO) which already has a shared sense of culture and interest, whereas a single system would build on a thinner institutional base, and would encompass a more diverse membership; and the residue of the Soviet threat would tend to hold it together. Second, a large system is incompatible with a "Finlandization" agreement for Eastern Europe. Under Finlandization, the West agrees to keep its forces out of the East, but a comprehensive Europe-wide collective security system would draw Western forces into the East for peacekeeping if war broke out there. Thus the Western-Soviet disengagement achieved by Finlandization is undone by a CSCE security order.

The main disadvantage of a small NATO system lies in its inability to address conflict in the East. This is a serious shortcoming, since war in the East is the main danger facing Europe. However, the Western countries could still use economic incentives to induce peaceful conduct—to include truth-telling in historical education, the protection of national minorities, the adoption of democratic reforms, and the acceptance of national boundaries—from Eastern countries.

Finally, however, Americans should not blithely assume that American power in Europe will automatically be wisely applied for peaceful purposes. If the United States pursues fickle or short-sighted policies, the American presence in Europe could cause more problems than it solves.

A peaceful American policy therefore requires conscious effort to maintain national self-control. In the past the United States has often allowed its policies to be shaped by foreign governments or ethnic special interests. A recurrence would shake the steady hand that the United States must apply if it is to act as peacekeeper in Europe. This danger is a special threat to America's European policy, because many Americans have ethnic ties to Europe. Hence American policy should be actively protected against manip-

Blocs: European Security in 2020, Paper No. 16, Peace Paper/Common Security Series (Cambridge, Mass.: Institute for Peace and International Security, December 1989), pp. 71–81; and Malcolm Chalmers, "Beyond the Alliance System: The Case for a European Security Organization," *World Policy Journal*, Vol. 7, No. 2 (Spring 1990), pp. 215–250.

ulation by foreign governments, or capture by domestic special interests. This can be achieved by reminding the American public and foreign policy-makers of the damage that such manipulation and capture have done in the past.[120] Domestic interests and foreign governments should make their case, but all Americans must understand that America's European policy affects the general welfare, and should insist that it reflect the general will.

---

120. Scholarship on both subjects is thin, and more is needed. Existing studies include Ross Y. Koen, *The China Lobby in American Politics* (New York: Harper and Row, 1974); and Horace Cornelius Peterson, *Propaganda for War: The Campaign Against American Neutrality, 1914–1917* (Norman: University of Oklahoma Press, 1939).

The Unipolar Illusion

Christopher Layne

Why New Great Powers Will Rise

The Soviet Union's collapse transformed the international system from bipolarity to unipolarity. To be sure, the United States has not imposed a "universal monarchy" on the international system. There are other states that are formidable militarily (Russia) or economically (Japan and Germany).[1] However, because only the United States possesses imposing strength in all categories of great power capability, it enjoys a preeminent role in international politics.[2] Following the Gulf War and the Soviet Union's collapse, many commentators suggested that America should adopt a new grand strategy that would aim at perpetuating unipolarity.[3] Belief that unipolarity favors the United States, and hence should be maintained, resonated in official Washington as well. This became apparent in March 1992, when the initial draft of the Pentagon's Defense

Christopher Layne teaches international politics at UCLA.

I am grateful to the following for their perceptive and helpful comments on the drafts of this article: John Arquilla, Ted Galen Carpenter, Kerry Andrew Chase, John Mearsheimer, Ben Schwarz, Alan Tonelson, Kenneth Waltz, and an anonymous reviewer. I am also indebted to Harry Kreisler (Institute of International Studies, UC Berkeley) and Jed Snyder (Washington Strategy Seminar) for providing stimulating intellectual forums that helped refine my thinking about unipolarity and prompted me to write this article.

1. Germany, Japan and Russia certainly have the potential to be great powers. Germany and Japan cannot today be considered great powers, however, because they lack the requisite military capabilities, especially strategic nuclear arsenals that would give them deterrence self-sufficiency. Notwithstanding Russia's still formidable nuclear and conventional military capabilities, economic difficulties and domestic political uncertainties have undercut its great power status. China will be a strong contender for great power status if it can maintain its internal cohesion. Buoyed by its vibrant economy, China has embarked on a major modernization and expansion of its air, naval, and ground forces, including its power-projection capabilities. Nicholas D. Kristof, "China Builds Its Military Muscle, Making Some Neighbors Nervous," *New York Times*, January 11, 1993, p. A1.
2. I define a unipolar system as one in which a single power is geopolitically preponderant because its capabilities are formidable enough to preclude the formation of an overwhelming balancing coalition against it.
3. Analysts of such diverse views as the liberal internationalist Joseph S. Nye, Jr., and neoconservatives Charles Krauthammer and Joshua Muravchick agree that a unipolar world is highly conducive to American interests. See Joseph S. Nye, Jr., *Bound to Lead: The Changing Nature of American Power* (New York: Basic Books, 1990); Charles Krauthammer, "The Unipolar Moment," *Foreign Affairs: America and the World*, Vol. 70, No. 1 (1990/91) and "What's Wrong With The 'Pentagon Paper'?" *Washington Post*, March 13, 1992; Joshua Muravchick, "At Last, Pax Americana," *New York Times*, January 24, 1991, p. A19.

International Security, Vol. 17, No. 4 (Spring 1993)
© 1993 by the President and Fellows of Harvard College and the Massachusetts Institute of Technology.

Planning Guidance (DPG) for Fiscal Years 1994–99 was leaked to the *New York Times*.[4] Specifically, the document stated that, "We must account sufficiently for the interests of the large industrial nations to discourage them from challenging our leadership or seeking to overturn the established political or economic order" and that "we must maintain the mechanisms for *deterring potential competitors from even aspiring to a larger regional or global role.*"[5]

The initial draft of the DPG was controversial, and a subsequent draft deleted the language referring to the goal of preserving unipolarity.[6] Nevertheless, the available evidence suggests that the DPG accurately reflected official views about unipolarity. For example, the 1991 Summer Study organized by the Pentagon's Director of Net Assessment defined a "manageable" world as one in which there is no threat to America's superpower role.[7] The main risk to American security, the study argued, is that of "Germany and/or Japan disconnecting from multilateral security and economic arrangements and pursuing an independent course."[8] During late 1992 and early 1993, the Pentagon's Joint Staff was preparing a "new NSC 68" intended to establish an intellectual framework for America's post–Cold War grand strategy. One of this document's key themes is that a multipolar world is, by definition, dangerously unstable. There is as yet no evidence that the Clinton administration's view of unipolarity will differ from the Bush administration's.[9]

Although there are shadings of difference among the various proposals for perpetuating unipolarity, it is fair to speak of a single strategy of predomi-

---

4. Patrick E. Tyler, "U.S. Strategy Plan Calls for Insuring No Rivals Develop," *New York Times*, March 8, 1992, p. A1.
5. "Excerpts From Pentagon's Plan: 'Prevent the Re-emergence of a New Rival'," *New York Times*, March 8, 1992, p. A14 (emphasis added).
6. See Leslie H. Gelb, "They're Kidding," *New York Times*, March 9, 1992, p. A15; William Pfaff, "Does America Want to Lead Through Intimidation?" *Los Angeles Times*, March 11, 1992, p. B7; and the comments of Senator Joseph Biden (D-Del.) and the Brookings Institution's John D. Steinbruner quoted in Melissa Healy, "Pentagon Cool to Sharing Its Power," *Los Angeles Times*, March 9, 1992, p. A8; Patrick E. Tyler, "Pentagon Drops Goal of Blocking New Superpowers," *New York Times*, May 24, 1992, p. A1; Melissa Healy, "Pentagon Maps Post–Cold War Defense Plans," *Los Angeles Times*, May 24, 1992, p. A1; Barton Gellman, "On Second Thought, We Don't Want to Rule the World," *Washington Post National Weekly Edition*, June 1–7, 1992, p. 31.
7. Undersecretary of Defense (Policy), *1991 Summer Study*, Organized by the Director, Net Assessment, held at Newport, R.I., August 5–13, 1991, p. 17.
8. Ibid., p. 73.
9. Post-election analyses stressed the likelihood of substantial continuity between the Clinton and Bush foreign policies. At his first post-election news conference, President-elect Clinton referred to the responsibilities imposed on the United States by virtue of its position as the "sole superpower." "Excerpts from President-Elect's News Conference in Arkansas," *New York Times*, November 13, 1992, p. A8.

nance. This strategy is not overtly aggressive; the use of preventive measures to suppress the emergence of new great powers is not contemplated. It is not, in other words, a strategy of heavy-handed American dominance. Rather the strategy of preponderance seeks to preserve unipolarity by persuading Japan and Germany that they are better off remaining within the orbit of an American-led security and economic system than they would be if they became great powers. The strategy of preponderance assumes that rather than balancing against the United States, other states will bandwagon with it. Important benefits are thought to flow from the perpetuation of unipolarity. In a unipolar system, it is argued, the United States could avoid the unpredictable geopolitical consequences that would attend the emergence of new great powers. Unipolarity would, it is said, minimize the risks of both strategic uncertainty and instability. In effect, the strategy of preponderance aims at preserving the Cold War status quo, even though the Cold War is over.

In this article, I use neorealist theory to analyze the implications of unipolarity. I argue that the "unipolar moment" is just that, a geopolitical interlude that will give way to multipolarity between 2000–2010. I start with a very simple premise: states balance against hegemons, even those like the United States that seek to maintain their preeminence by employing strategies based more on benevolence than coercion. As Kenneth N. Waltz says, "In international politics, overwhelming power repels and leads other states to balance against it."[10] In a unipolar world, systemic constraints—balancing, uneven growth rates, and the sameness effect—impel eligible states (i.e., those with the capability to do so) to become great powers. I use neorealist theory to explain the process of great power emergence.

My theoretical argument is supported by an extensive historical discussion. A unipolar world is not *terra incognita*. There have been two other comparable unipolar moments in modern international history. The evidence from those two eras confirms the expectations derived from structural realism: (1) unipolar systems contain the seeds of their own demise because the hegemon's unbalanced power creates an environment conducive to the emergence of new great powers; and (2) the entry of new great powers into the international system erodes the hegemon's relative power and, ultimately, its preeminence. In the final section of this article, I consider the policy implications,

---

10. Kenneth N. Waltz, "America as a Model for the World? A Foreign Policy Perspective," *PS*, December 1991, p. 669.

and I argue that the strategy of preponderance is unlikely to be successful.[11] It will be difficult for the United States to maintain the Cold War status quo because structural change has destroyed the bipolar foundation of the post-1945 international system. I conclude by outlining a new grand strategy that could accomplish the two main geopolitical tasks facing the United States in the years ahead: (1) managing the potentially difficult transition from unipolarity to multipolarity; and (2) advancing American interests in the multipolar world that inevitably will emerge.

Why Great Powers Rise—The Role of Systemic Constraints

Whether the United States can maintain its standing as the sole great power depends largely on whether new great powers will rise. To answer that question, we need to understand why states become great powers.[12] This is

---

11. In a sense, this article extends Mearsheimer's examination of post–Cold War Europe's geopolitical future to the global level. See John Mearsheimer, "Back to the Future: Instability in Europe After the Cold War," *International Security*, Vol. 15, No. 1 (Summer 1990), pp. 5–56. It should be noted that Mearsheimer and I come to very different policy conclusions regarding the American military commitment to Europe (and no doubt we would not agree on some of the other policy recommendations made in this article), notwithstanding the similarity of our analyses.

12. As Kenneth Waltz writes, great powers are defined by capabilities: "States, because they are in a self-help system, have to use their combined capabilities in order to serve their interests. The economic, military, and other capabilities of nations cannot be sectored and separately weighed. States are not placed in the top rank because they excel in one way or another. Their rank depends on how they score on all of the following items: size of population and territory; resource endowment; military strength; political stability; and competence." Kenneth N. Waltz, *Theory of International Politics* (Reading, Mass.: Addison-Wesley, 1979), p. 131. Because of their capabilities, great powers tend to behave differently than other states. Jack Levy writes that great powers are distinguished from others by: 1) a high level of military capability that makes them relatively self-sufficient strategically and capable of projecting power beyond their borders; 2) a broad concept of security that embraces a concern with regional and/or global power balances; and 3) a greater assertiveness than lesser powers in defining and defending their interests. Jack Levy, *War and the Modern Great Power System, 1495–1975* (Lexington: University Press of Kentucky, 1983), pp. 11–19.

Recently there have been several questionable attempts to redefine great power status. For example, Joseph S. Nye, Jr., and Samuel P. Huntington argue that only the United States has the "soft" power resources (socio-cultural and ideological attractiveness to other states) that Nye and Huntington claim are a prerequisite of great power status. Nye, *Bound to Lead*; Huntington, "The U.S.—Decline or Renewal?" *Foreign Affairs*, Vol. 67, No. 2 (Winter 1988/89), pp. 90–93. This argument has three weaknesses. First, it is far from clear that others view U.S. culture and ideology in the same positive light that Nye and Huntington do. America's racial, economic, educational, and social problems have eroded others' admiration for the United States. Second, it is not unusual for great powers to see themselves as cultural or ideological role models; examples include nineteenth-century Britain and France, pre-1914 Germany and, of course, the Soviet Union. Finally, when it comes to setting great powers apart from others, soft power may

a critical issue because the emergence (or disappearance) of great powers can have a decisive effect on international politics; a consequential shift in the number of great powers changes the international system's structure. Waltz defines a "consequential" shift as "variations in number that lead to different expectations about the effect of structure on units."[13] Examples are shifts from: bipolarity to either unipolarity or multipolarity; unipolarity to bipolarity or multipolarity; multipolarity to bipolarity or unipolarity; from a multipolar system with three great powers to one of four or more (or vice versa).[14]

Throughout modern international history, there has been an observable pattern of great power emergence. Although neorealism does not, and cannot, purport to predict the foreign policies of specific states, it can account for outcomes and patterns of behavior that happen recurrently in international politics. Great power emergence is a structually driven phenomenon. Specifically, it results from the interaction of two factors: (1) differential growth rates and (2) anarchy.

Although great power emergence is shaped by structural factors, and can cause structural effects, it results from unit-level actions. In other words, a feedback loop of sorts is at work: (1) structural constraints press eligible states to become great powers; (2) such states make unit-level decisions whether to pursue great power status in response to these structural constraints; (3) if a unit-level decision to seek great power status produces a consequential shift in polarity, it has a structural impact. Rising states have choices about whether to become great powers. However, a state's freedom to choose whether to seek great power status is in reality tightly constrained by structural factors. Eligible states that fail to attain great power status are predictably punished. If policymakers of eligible states are socialized to the inter-

---

be a helpful supplement to the other instruments of statecraft, but states with the requisite hard power capabilities (per Waltz's definition) are great powers regardless of whether they "stand for an idea with appeal beyond [their] borders."

Another popular intellectual fashion holds that Japan and Germany will carve out niches in international politics as the first "global civilian powers." Hanns Maull, "Germany and Japan: The New Civilian Powers," *Foreign Affairs*, Vol. 69, No. 5 (Winter 1990/91), pp. 91–106. As civilian powers, it is argued, they will eschew military strength in favor of economic power, work through international institutions to promote global cooperation, and "furnish international public goods, such as refugee resettlement, national disaster relief, development of economic infrastructure, and human resources improvements." Yoichi Funabashi, "Japan and America: Global Partners," *Foreign Policy*, No. 86 (Spring 1992), p. 37. In the real world, however, one does not find traditional great powers and "civilian" great powers. One finds only states that are great powers and those that are not.

13. Waltz, *Theory of International Politics*, p. 162.
14. Ibid., pp. 163–170.

national system's constraints, they understand that attaining great power status is a prerequisite if their states are to be secure and autonomous.[15] The fate that befell nineteenth-century China illustrates what can happen to an eligible state when its leaders ignore structural imperatives. But nineteenth-century China is a rather singular exception to the pattern of great power emergence. Far more typical is post-1860 Italy, a state that tried hard to attain great power status notwithstanding that it "had more in common with . . . a small Balkan state or a colony than a Great Power" in that it was economically backward, financially weak, and resource-poor.[16]

DIFFERENTIAL GROWTH RATES

The process of great power emergence is underpinned by the fact that the economic (and technological and military) power of states grows at differential, not parallel rates. That is, in relative terms, some states are gaining power while others are losing it. As Robert Gilpin notes, over time, "the differential growth in the power of various states in the system causes a fundamental redistribution of power in the system."[17] The result, as Paul Kennedy has shown, is that time and again relative "economic shifts heralded the rise of new Great Powers which one day would have a decisive impact on the military/territorial order."[18] The link between differential growth rates

---

15. Kenneth N. Waltz, "A Reply to My Critics" in Robert O. Keohane, ed., *Neorealism and Its Critics* (New York: Columbia University Press, 1986), p. 343.

16. R.J.B. Bosworth, *Italy, the Least of the Great Powers: Italian Foreign Policy before the First World War* (Cambridge: Cambridge University Press, 1979), p. 2. In mid to late nineteenth-century China, some attempts were made at "self-strengthening"—adoption of Western industrial, technological, and military innovations. However, the initiative for such efforts came more from regional strongmen like Li Hongzang than from the central government in Peking. Economic problems resulting from unfavorable demographics, and social and cultural factors, especially Peking's inability to mobilize the elite for a centrally-directed reform program, undercut the modernization effort. "Late imperial China experienced a profound structural breakdown brought on by traditional forces that propelled dynastic cycles. At this unfortunate juncture between dynastic breakdown and foreign intrusion, the leadership simply lacked the internal resources to protect China from other expansive nations in search of wealth and glory." June Grasso, Jay Corrin, and Michael Kort, *Modernization and Revolution in China* (Armonk, N.Y.: M.E. Sharpe, 1991), p. 69.

17. Robert Gilpin, *War and Change in World Politics* (Cambridge: Cambridge University Press, 1981), p. 13. The role of uneven growth rates in the rise of great powers is closely connected to long cycle explanations. See Joshua S. Goldstein, *Long Cycles: Prosperity and War in the Modern Age* (New Haven: Yale University Press, 1988); George Modelski, *Long Cycles in World Politics* (Seattle: University of Washington Press, 1987); and William R. Thompson, "Dehio, Long Cycles, and the Geohistorical Context of Structural Transition," *World Politics*, Vol. 45, No. 1 (October 1992), pp. 127–152.

18. Paul Kennedy, *The Rise and Fall of Great Powers: Economic Change and Military Conflict From 1500 to 2000* (New York: Random House, 1987), p. xxii.

and great power emergence has important implications for unipolarity. Unipolarity is likely to be short-lived because new great powers will emerge as the uneven growth process narrows the gap between the hegemon and the eligible states that are positioned to emerge as its competitors.

There are at least three other respects in which great power emergence is affected by differential growth rates. First, as eligible states gain relative power, they are more likely to attempt to advance their standing in the international system. As Gilpin points out, "The critical significance of the differential growth of power among states is that it alters the cost of changing the international system and therefore the incentives for changing the international system."[19] Second, Gilpin observes, rising power leads to increasing ambition. Rising powers seek to enhance their security by increasing their capabilities and their control over the external environment.[20] Third, as Kennedy explains, rising power leads also to increased international interests and commitments. Oftentimes for great powers, geopolitical and military capabilities are the consequence of a process that begins with economic expansion. Economic expansion leads to new overseas obligations (access to markets and raw materials, alliances, bases), which then must be defended.[21]

THE CONSEQUENCES OF ANARCHY: BALANCING AND SAMENESS

Because it is anarchic, the international political system is a self-help system in which states' foremost concern must be with survival.[22] In an anarchic system, states must provide for their own security and they face many real or apparent threats.[23] International politics thus is a competitive realm, a fact that in itself constrains eligible states to attain great power status. Specifically, there are two manifestations of this competitiveness that shape great power emergence: balancing and the "sameness effect."[24]

BALANCING. The competitiveness of international politics is manifested in the tendency of states to balance.[25] Balancing has especially strong explana-

---

19. Gilpin, *War and Change*, p. 95.
20. Ibid., pp. 94–95. As Gilpin notes, rising power can tempt a state to seek change in the international system, which can trigger "hegemonic war." This problem is discussed in more detail in the conclusion.
21. Kennedy, *Rise and Fall of Great Powers*, p. xxiii.
22. Waltz, *Theory of International Politics*, pp. 107, 127.
23. Kenneth N. Waltz, "The Origins of War in Neorealist Theory," in Robert I. Rotberg and Theodore K. Rabb, eds., *The Origin and Prevention of Major Wars* (Cambridge: Cambridge University Press, 1989), p. 43.
24. The phrase "sameness effect" is from Waltz, *Theory of International Politics*, p. 128.
25. For discussion of the differences between bandwagoning and balancing behavior, see Waltz,

tory power in accounting for the facts that unipolarity tends to be short-lived and that would-be hegemons invariably fail to achieve lasting dominance. Structural realism leads to the expectation that hegemony should generate the rise of countervailing power in the form of new great powers.

The reason states balance is to correct a skewed distribution of relative power in the international system. States are highly attentive to changes in their relative power position because relative power shifts have crucial security implications.[26] It is the interaction of differential growth rates—the main cause of changes in the relative distribution of power among states—and anarchy that produces important effects. In an anarchic, self-help system, states must always be concerned that others will use increased relative capabilities against them. By enhancing their own relative capabilities or diminishing those of an adversary, states get a double payoff: greater security and a wider range of strategic options.[27] The reverse is true for states that remain indifferent to relative power relationships. Thus, as Gilpin says, the international system's competitiveness "stimulates, and may compel, a state to increase its power; at the least, it necessitates that the prudent state prevent relative increase in the powers of competitor states."[28] By definition, the distribution of relative power in a unipolar system is extremely unbalanced. Consequently, in a unipolar system, the structural pressures on eligible states to increase their relative capabilities and become great powers should be overwhelming. If they do not acquire great power capabilities, they may be exploited by the hegemon. Of course, an eligible state's quest for security may give rise to the security dilemma because actions intended to bolster its own security may have the unintended consequence of threatening others.[29]

It can be argued on the basis of hegemonic stability theory and balance of threat theory that a "benign" hegemon might be able to prevent new great powers from emerging and balancing against it.[30] These arguments are unpersuasive. Although hegemonic stability theory is usually employed in the

Theory of International Politics, pp. 125–126; Stephen M. Walt, *The Origins of Alliances* (Ithaca: Cornell University Press, 1987), pp. 17–33.

26. Waltz, *Theory of International Politics*, p. 126.

27. Gilpin, *War and Change*, pp. 86–87.

28. Ibid., pp. 87–88.

29. John Herz, "Idealist Internationalism and the Security Dilemma," *World Politics*, Vol. 2, No. 2 (January 1950), pp. 157–180.

30. On balance of threat theory, see Walt, *The Origins of Alliances*, pp. 17–26. For an overview of the benevolent and coercive strands of hegemonic stability theory, see Duncan Snidal, "The Limits of Hegemonic Stability Theory," *International Organization*, Vol. 39, No. 4 (Autumn 1985), pp. 579–614.

context of international political economy, it can be extended to other aspects of international politics. The logic of collective goods underlying the notion of a benign hegemon assumes that all states will cooperate because they derive absolute benefit from the collective goods the hegemon provides. Because they are better off, the argument goes, others should willingly accept a benign hegemon and even help to prop it up if it is declining. However, as Michael C. Webb and Stephen D. Krasner point out, the benign version of hegemonic stability theory assumes that states are indifferent to the distribution of relative gains.[31] This is, as noted, a dubious assumption. As Joseph Grieco points out, because states worry that today's ally could become tomorrow's rival, "they pay close attention to how cooperation might affect relative *capabilities* in the future."[32] Moreover, if stability is equated with the dominant state's continuing preeminence, the stability of hegemonic systems is questionable once the hegemon's power begins to erode noticeably. As Gilpin points out, over time a hegemon declines from its dominant position because: (1) the costs of sustaining its preeminence begin to erode the hegemon's economic strength, thereby diminishing its military and economic capabilities; and (2) the hegemonic paradox results in the diffusion of economic, technological, and organizational skills to other states, thereby causing the hegemon to lose its "comparative advantage" over them.[33] Frequently, these others are eligible states that will rise to great power status and challenge the hegemon's predominance.

This last point suggests that in unipolar systems, states do indeed balance against the hegemon's unchecked power. This reflects the fact that in unipolar systems there is no clear-cut distinction between balancing against threat and balancing against power. This is because the threat inheres in the hegemon's power.[34] In a unipolar world, others must worry about the he-

---

31. Michael C. Webb and Stephen D. Krasner, "Hegemonic Stability Theory: An Empirical Assessment," *Review of International Studies*, Vol. 15, No. 2 (April 1989), pp. 184–185.
32. Joseph M. Grieco, "Anarchy and the Limits of Cooperation: A Realist Critique of the Newest Liberal Institutionalism," *International Organization*, Vol. 42, No. 3 (Summer 1988), p. 500 (emphasis in original).
33. Gilpin, *War and Change*, pp. 156–210.
34. Traditional balance-of-power theory postulates that states align against others that are excessively powerful. Stephen Walt refined balance of power theory by arguing that states actually balance against threats rather than against power *per se*. However, Walt's balance-of-threat analysis is more ambiguous than it might seem at first glance. For example, he admits that every post-1648 bid for European hegemony was repulsed by a balancing coalition. *Origins of Alliances*, pp. 28–29. Why? Because would-be hegemons were powerful or because they were threatening? He does not say directly but one suspects that his answer would be "both." Walt

gemon's capabilities, not its intentions. The preeminent power's intentions may be benign today but may not be tomorrow. Robert Jervis cuts to the heart of the matter when he notes, "Minds can be changed, new leaders can come to power, values can shift, new opportunities and dangers can arise."[35] Unless they are prepared to run the risk of being vulnerable to a change in the hegemon's intentions, other states must be prepared to counter its capabilities. Moreover, even a hegemon animated by benign motives may pursue policies that run counter to others' interests. Thus, as Waltz says, "Balance-of-power theory leads one to expect that states, if they are free to do so, will flock to the weaker side. The stronger, not the weaker side, threatens them if only by pressing its preferred policies on other states."[36]

Invariably, the very fact that others believe a state is excessively powerful redounds to its disadvantage by provoking others to balance against it. It was precisely for this reason that, responding to Sir Eyre Crowe's 1907 "German danger" memorandum, Lord Thomas Sanderson counseled that London should try hard to accommodate rising great powers while simultaneously moderating its own geopolitical demands. Showing commendable empathy for other states' views of Britain's policies and its power, he observed that it would be unwise for Britain to act as if every change in international politics menaced its interests. "It has sometimes seemed to me that to a foreigner . . . the British Empire must appear in the light of some huge giant sprawling over the globe, with gouty fingers and toes stretching in every direction, which cannot be approached without eliciting a scream."[37]

---

does not downplay the importance of power as a factor in inducing balancing behavior; he simply says it is not the *only* factor (p. 21). Indeed, power and threat blend together almost imperceptibly. Note that two of his threat variables, geographic proximity and offensive capabilities, correlate closely with military *power*. When Walt says that states do not necessarily balance against the most powerful actor in the system he essentially is equating power with GNP. When he says that states balance against threat he is saying that they balance against military power (coupled with aggressive intentions). Obviously, power is more than just GNP. What states appear to balance against in reality is actual or latent military capabilities. In a unipolar world, the hegemon's possession of actual or latent military capabilities will result in balancing regardless of its intentions. If, in a unipolar world, capabilities matter more than intentions, the U.S. monopoly on long-range power-projection capabilities—that is, its preponderance of military power—probably will be viewed by others as threatening.

35. Robert Jervis, "Cooperation Under the Security Dilemma," *World Politics*, Vol. 30, No. 2 (January 1978), p. 105.
36. Kenneth N. Waltz, "The Emerging Structure of International Politics," paper presented at the annual meeting of the American Political Science Association, San Francisco, California, August 1990, p. 32.
37. "Memorandum by Lord Sanderson," in G.P. Gooch and Harold Temperley, eds., *British Documents on the Origins of the War, 1898–1914*, Volume III (London: His Majesty's Stationery Office [HMSO], 1928), p. 430.

It is unsurprising that counter-hegemonic balancing has occurred even during periods of *perceived* unipolarity. After the 1962 Cuban missile crisis, for instance, French policy was driven by the belief that the scales of power in the U.S.-Soviet competition were weighted too heavily in America's favor. French President DeGaulle said that the United States had become the greatest power and that it was driven "automatically" to extend its influence and "to exercise a preponderant weight, that is to say, a hegemony over others."[38] DeGaulle's policy was animated by the need to redress this perceived imbalance. As Edward Kolodziej observes, "In the closing years of Gaullist rule, *the possible development of a unipolar system became one of the major concerns of the French government.*"[39] One of the most important questions concerning international politics today is whether this pattern of balancing against the dominant power in a unipolar system (actual or perceived) will recur in the post–Cold War world.

SAMENESS. As Waltz points out, "competition produces a tendency toward sameness of the competitors"; that is, toward imitating their rivals' successful characteristics.[40] Such characteristics include not only military strategies, tactics, weaponry, and technology, but also administrative and organizational techniques. If others do well in developing effective instruments of competition, a state must emulate its rivals or face the consequences of falling behind. Fear drives states to duplicate others' successful policies because policymakers know that, as Arthur Stein observes, "failure in the anarchic international system can mean the disappearance of their states."[41] From this standpoint, it is to be expected that in crucial respects, great powers will look and act very much alike. It is also to be expected that sameness-effect imperatives will impel eligible states to become great powers and to acquire all the capabilities attendant to that status. As Waltz observes, "In a self-help system, the possession of most but not all of the capabilities of a great power leaves a state vulnerable to others who have the instruments that the lesser state lacks."[42]

Additional light is shed on the sameness effect by the "second image reversed" perspective, which posits a linkage between the international sys-

---

38. Quoted in Edward A. Kolodziej, *French International Policy Under DeGaulle and Pompidou: The Politics of Grandeur* (Ithaca: Cornell University Press, 1974), p. 91.
39. Ibid., pp. 90–91 (emphasis added).
40. Waltz, *Theory of International Politics*, p. 127.
41. Arthur Stein, *Why Nations Cooperate: Circumstance and Choice in International Relations* (Ithaca, New York: Cornell University Press, 1990), pp. 115–116.
42. Waltz, "Emerging Structure," p. 21.

tem's structural constraints and a state's domestic structure. Charles Tilly's famous aphorism, "War made the state, and the state made war" neatly captures the concept.[43] Tilly shows how the need to protect against external danger compelled states in early modern Europe to develop administrative and bureaucratic structures to maintain, supply, and finance permanent military establishments. But there is more to it than that. As is discussed below, the evidence from 1660–1713 and 1860–1910 suggests that great power emergence reflects an eligible state's adjustment to the international system's structural constraints. Otto Hinze observed that the way in which states are organized internally reflects "their position relative to each other and their overall position in the world" and that "throughout the ages pressure from without has been a determining influence on internal structure."[44]

Great powers are similar because they are not, and cannot be, functionally differentiated. This is not to say that great powers are identical. They may adopt different strategies and approaches; however, ultimately they all must be able to perform satisfactorily the same security-related tasks necessary to survive and succeed in the competitive realm of international politics. The sameness effect reflects the enormous pressure that the international system places on great powers to imitate the successful policies of others. Hinze's discussion of Prussia-Germany and England is illustrative. Their respective domestic, political and economic systems developed dissimilarly, in large part because each was affected differently by international pressures. (Maritime England was far more secure than continental Germany.) But, as is true for all great powers, in other crucial respects Prussia-Germany and England were very much alike. That is, both were organized for war and trade in order to maximize their security in a competitive international environment.

Response to Unipolarity: 1660–1714

In this and the following section, I use historical evidence to test my hypotheses about great power emergence. Such a test should be especially useful because there have been two prior occasions in history similar to

---

43. Charles Tilly, "Reflections on the History of European State Making," in Charles Tilly, ed., *The Formation of National States in Western Europe* (Princeton: Princeton University Press, 1975), p. 42.
44. Otto Hinze, "Military Organization and the Organization of the State," in Felix Gilbert, ed., *The Historical Essays of Otto Hinze* (Princeton: Princeton University Press, 1975), p. 183.

today's unipolar moment. France in 1660 and Great Britain in 1860 were as dominant in the international system as the United States is today. In neither case, however, did unipolarity last beyond fifty years. France's unipolar moment ended when Britain and Austria emerged as great powers; Britain's when Germany, Japan and the United States ascended to great power status. If the emergence of those great powers correlates strongly with uneven growth rates, the sameness effect, and balancing against hegemonic power, it can be expected that the present unipolar moment will be displaced by multipolarity within a reasonably short time.

FRENCH HEGEMONY IN A UNIPOLAR WORLD

It is generally agreed that in 1660, when Louis XIV ascended the French throne, France was Europe's sole great power, "the strongest and richest state in the world"; it was "a rare situation of preeminence."[45] France's dominant position reflected her own strength and the relative weakness of Europe's other states. In 1660, France was Europe's most populous state, had Europe's most efficient centralized administration, was (by the standards of the age) rich agriculturally, and had the potential to develop a dynamic industrial base.[46] In contrast, France's rivals were declining powers (Spain), or beset by internal troubles (England), or lacked France's capabilities or the means to mobilize them (Habsburg Austria).[47]

France achieved hegemonic standing by developing the means to mobilize its assets and convert them into effective diplomatic, military, and economic power.[48] France under Louis XIV was responsible for what G.R.R. Treasure calls the "*étatisation*" of war: "the mobilization of the total resources of the state, of the economy, as well as of manpower."[49] Under War Minister Michel Le Tellier, and his son and successor Louvois, the army was brought under the administrative control of the central government and a standing professional military force was created. The Military Revolution was completed and the French army was drastically altered and improved in such areas as

---

45. G.R.R. Treasure, *Seventeenth Century France* (London: Rivingtons, 1966), pp. 257–258. Agreeing that France was Europe's only great power in 1660 are Derek McKay and H.M. Scott, *The Rise of the Great Powers, 1648–1815* (London: Longman, 1983); John B. Wolf, *Toward a European Balance of Power, 1620–1715* (Chicago: Rand McNally, 1970), p. 1.
46. McKay and Scott, *Rise of the Great Powers*, pp. 14–15.
47. Treasure, *Seventeenth Century France*, pp. 210–215, surveys the relative weakness of France's European rivals.
48. McKay and Scott, *Rise of the Great Powers*, pp. 14–15.
49. Treasure, *Seventeenth Century France*, pp. 219–220.

selection of officers, recruitment, weapons, tactics, training and logistics. Finance Minister Colbert labored to strengthen France's financial and economic base to provide the wherewithal to support its enhanced military capabilities. These military, economic, and financial initiatives were made possible by the administrative reforms that strengthened the central government's power and made it more efficient.[50]

Although France was Europe's only great power in 1660, by 1713 England and Habsburg Austria, as well as Russia, had emerged as great powers. The rise of England and Habsburg Austria—that is, the international system's transformation from unipolarity to multipolarity—is directly traceable to anarchy and its consequences: the sameness effect and balancing. Because French dominance threatened their security and autonomy, England and Austria responded by: (1) organizing the Grand Alliances that, in the Nine Years' War and War of the Spanish Succession, sought to contain France and counter its power; and (2) reorganizing themselves administratively, military, and economically to acquire great power capabilities comparable to France's. Treasure observes that, "France's example forced change on other states"; Derek McKay and H.M. Scott point out that, to compete with France, France's opponents "had begun to copy the French model."[51] The increasing power of governments was a response to external danger: "International competition and war," says William Doyle, "were the main spur to domestic innovation."[52] The danger to their security posed by French hegemony forced England and Austria to emulate France and to develop the capabilities that would enable them to stand on an equal geopolitical footing with France.

England's rise to great power status was a direct response to France's preeminent position in international politics. The English King William III was concerned with maintaining England's security by establishing a balance of power to preserve "the peace, liberties, and well-being of Europe, which happened in his lifetime to be threatened by overgrown French power."[53] In

---

50. For brief discussions of the administrative, military, and economic bases of French power, see John B. Wolf, *The Emergence of the Great Powers, 1685–1715* (New York: Harper and Brothers, 1951), pp. 97–103, pp. 181–187; Treasure, *Seventeenth Century France*, pp. 231–244, 288–320; and William Doyle, *The Old European Order, 1660–1800* (Oxford: Oxford University Press, 1978), pp. 244–245. Ultimately, of course, fiscal reforms were only partially successful and France was unable to bear the huge financial costs of the Nine Years' War and War of the Spanish Succession.
51. Treasure, *Seventeenth Century France*, p. 241; McKay and Scott, *Rise of the Great Powers*, pp. 41–42.
52. Doyle, *The Old Order*, p. 265.
53. G.C. Gibbs, "The Revolution in Foreign Policy," in Geoffrey Holmes, ed., *Britain After the Glorious Revolution, 1689–1714* (London: Macmillan, 1989), p. 61.

rising to great power status, England was balancing at least as much against France's hegemonic power as against the French threat. Indeed, the distinction between power and threat was blurred.[54] After 1688, England was at war with France almost continuously for twenty-five years and the extent of its military involvement on the continent increased dramatically. England maintained a sizeable standing army and the largest and most powerful navy in the world. The imperatives of war meant that the state had to improve its ability to extract and mobilize the nation's wealth and, as in France, England's administrative capabilities were greatly expanded for this purpose between 1688 and 1713. France's hegemonic challenge was the most powerful stimulus to the growth of power of the English state: England "became, like her main rivals, a fiscal-military state, one dominated by the task of waging war."[55]

Habsburg Austria, too, emerged as a great power in response to France's hegemonic power, and also the Ottoman threat to Austria's eastern interests. The goals of Austria's western policy were "establishment of a recognized great power position and the fight against the supremacy of France."[56] In this context, for Austria, the stakes in the War of the Spanish Succession were survival and emergence as a great power.[57] Like Britain and France, Austria undertook administrative reforms aimed at increasing the state's warmaking capabilities. "The centralizing drive of the Habsburg government, latent in the sixteenth and conscious in the seventeenth centuries, was based upon a desire to consolidate power for the purpose of state security."[58]

---

54. Secretary of State Charles Hedges said, "We are awake and sensible to the too great growth of our dangerous neighbor, and are taking vigorous measures for the preservation of ourselves, and the peace of Europe." And in June 1701, King William III instructed the Duke of Marlborough to commence negotiations for an anti-French coalition "for the Preservation of the Liberties of Europe, the Property and Peace of England, and for reducing the Exorbitant Power of France." Quoted in John B. Hattendorf, "Alliance, Encirclement, and Attrition: British Grand Strategy in the War of the Spanish Succession," in Paul Kennedy, ed., *Grand Strategy in War and Peace* (New Haven: Yale University Press, 1991), p. 16.

55. John Brewer, *The Sinews of Power: War, Money, and the English State, 1688–1783* (London: Unwin Hyman, 1989), p. 27.

56. Robert A. Kann, *A History of the Habsburg Empire* (Berkeley: University of California Press, 1974), pp. 77–78.

57. Ibid., pp. 84–85.

58. Thomas M. Barker, *Double Eagle and Crescent: Vienna's Second Turkish Siege and Its Historical Setting* (Albany: State University of New York Press, 1967), p. 19. In the administrative sphere, efforts were stepped up to subject Hungary (the bulk of which only came under firm Austrian control after the Ottomans were defeated in 1683) to Vienna's control so that Austria could draw upon its resources; a central organ, the *Hofkanzlei*, was established to conduct foreign and domestic affairs; the *Hofkammer* was established to exert central control over the finances of Habsburg Austria's possessions; and the *Hofkriegsrat* was created to administer Austria's army centrally and remodel it as a standing professional army on French lines. See Wolf, *Emergence*

Austria was considerably less successful than France and England in creating administrative mechanisms for the efficient mobilization of national resources. Nevertheless, it remains the case that the need for security in the face of French hegemony forced Austria (like England) both to emulate France and to balance against it in order to attain great power status.[59]

Response to Unipolarity: 1860–1910

In 1860, Britain was in a position of apparently unequaled dominance in an international system that has been characterized as unipolar.[60] Because it was Europe's arbiter and possessor of a worldwide and unchallenged colonial empire, "Britain could not have been met with an overwhelming balancing coalition."[61] Indeed, Britain's dominance was so pronounced that it was able in the early 1860s largely to turn its back on European security affairs and withdraw into a "splendid isolation" that lasted until the turn of the century. Britain's hegemony was a function of its naval power, its colonial empire, and its overwhelming economic and financial strength.[62] The Royal Navy was as strong as those of the next three or four naval powers combined. Britain's level of per capita industrialization was more than twice that of the

---

of the Great Powers, pp. 126–137; R.J.W. Evans, The Making of the Habsburg Monarchy (Oxford: Clarendon Press, 1979), pp. 148–150.

59. Although Russia's rise to great power status paralleled England's and Austria's, I do not discuss it at length because it was unconnected to the wars against French hegemony.

60. The phrase "unequaled dominance" is from Paul Kennedy, Rise and Fall of Great Powers, p. 152. Michael Doyle describes the international system in 1860 as "unipolar-peripheral"; that is, in the extra-European world, Britain's power was unchallenged. Doyle, Empires (Ithaca: Cornell University Press, 1986), p. 236. Building on Doyle, Fareed Zakaria drops the qualifier and describes the mid-nineteenth century international system as unipolar. Zakaria, "Realism and Domestic Politics: A Review Essay," International Security, Vol. 17, No. 1 (Summer 1992), pp. 186–187.

61. Zakaria, "Realism and Domestic Politics," p. 187. There is empirical support for Zakaria's statement. William B. Moul's measurement of the power capability shares of Europe's great powers confirms Britain's hegemonic standing. In 1860, Britain's share was 43.8 percent, while the combined shares of Prussia, France, Austria, Russia and Italy was 56.2 percent. France was the second-ranked power at 19.7 percent. Moul, "Measuring the 'Balances of Power': A Look at Some Numbers," Review of International Studies, Vol. 15, No. 2 (April 1989), p. 120.

62. This discussion, and the figures cited, are based on Kennedy, Rise and Fall of Great Powers, pp. 152–157. In the United States there is a spirited debate about the contemporary implications of Britain's decline. For contrasting views in a policy context, see Nye, Bound to Lead, pp. 49–68, which rejects the British analogy's relevance; and David P. Calleo, Beyond American Hegemony: The Future of the Western Alliance (New York: Basic Books, 1987), pp. 129–149, which sees a strong parallel between the Pax Britannica's demise and the likely demise of the post-1945 Pax Americana.

next ranking power (France), and Britain in 1860 accounted for 53.2 percent of world manufacturing output (a bit more than America's share in 1945).

In the following discussion, I look at the great power emergence of Germany, the United States, and Japan (but not Italy's attempted rise to great power status), and analyze how each was affected by relative power shifts and the consequences of anarchy. Germany's rise to world power status was most obviously a direct response to Britain's hegemony, while in the American and Japanese cases the connection between unipolarity and great power emergence, though less direct, is still discernible.

BRITISH HEGEMONY IN A UNIPOLAR WORLD

Britain's preeminence cast a shadow over the international system. By 1880, it was widely (and correctly) perceived that the European great power system was evolving into a system of three or four "world" powers (what today are called superpowers).[63] International politics was profoundly affected by this trend, which alerted policymakers to the security and economic consequences of the relative distribution of power in the international system. After 1880, there was among statesmen "a prevailing view of the world order which stressed struggle, change, competition, the use of force and the organization of national resources to enhance state power."[64] Britain was the first world power and it was the model that other rising powers sought to imitate as they climbed to great power status. In other words, the sameness effect was very much in evidence. Speaking of Germany, Japan, and Italy, Paul Kennedy says:

In all three societies there were impulses to emulate the established powers. By the 1880s and 1890s each was acquiring overseas territories; each, too, began to build a modern fleet to complement its standing army. Each was a significant element in the diplomatic calculus of the age and, at the least by 1902, had become an alliance partner of an older power.[65]

---

63. See Kennedy, *Rise and Fall of Great Powers*, pp. 194–202. This transformation is illustrated by the great powers' respective shares of total industrial potential and world manufacturing output. In 1880 Germany, France, and Russia were tightly bunched and well behind both Britain and the United States in terms of both total industrial potential and shares of world manufacturing output. However, by 1913 Britain, the United States, and Germany had widely distanced themselves from the rest of the great power pack. In terms of total industrial potential and share of world manufacturing output, third-place Germany held nearly a 2:1 advantage over Russia, the next ranking power.
64. Ibid., p. 196.
65. Ibid., pp. 202–203.

Kennedy does not mention the United States in this passage but he could have. Although the United States did not need a large army and was able to refrain from joining a great power alliance, it followed the same pattern of building a powerful modern navy, acquiring overseas colonies, and becoming a major factor in great power diplomacy.

GERMANY'S RISE TO WORLD POWER

The effect of differential growth rates was an important factor in Germany's rise to great power status. As Paul Kennedy has pointed out, Germany's economic growth after 1860 was "explosive."[66] Between 1860 and 1913, Germany's share of world manufacturing output rose from 4.9 percent to 14.8 percent and its share of world trade from 9.7 percent to 13 percent.[67] In 1913, Germany's share of world exports was 13 percent (compared to Britain's 14 percent).[68] Germany's rising power facilitated Berlin's decision to seek change in the international system. As Kennedy observes, Germany "either already possessed the instruments of power to alter the status quo or had the material resources to create such instruments."[69] As Kurt Reiszler, political confidant of pre–World War I Chancellor Bethmann Hollweg, observed, *Weltpolitik* was tightly linked to the dynamic growth of Germany's export-driven economy.[70] Reiszler also noted how Germany's demands for power and prestige increased in proportion to its rising strength.[71] Predictably, Germany's increasing ambition reflected Berlin's concern with protecting its deepening stakes in the international system. For a rising power such behavior is typical: "In order to increase its own security, it will try to expand its political, economic and territorial control; it will try to change the international system in accordance with its particular interests."[72]

Germany's rise to world power status was a direct response to Britain's preeminence in international politics. "The Germans came to resent British power and even British efforts to maintain their position unimpaired."[73] *Weltpolitik*—Germany's push for a big navy, colonies, and equality with Brit-

---

66. Ibid., p. 210.
67. Ibid., pp. 149, 202; Paul Kennedy, *The Rise of the Anglo-German Antagonism, 1860–1914* (London: George Allen and Unwin, 1980), pp. 44, 292.
68. Kennedy, *Anglo-German Antagonism*, p. 292.
69. Kennedy, *Rise and Fall of Great Powers*, p. 211.
70. Quoted in Imanuel Geiss, *German Foreign Policy, 1871–1914* (London: Routledge and Kegan Paul, 1976), p. 9.
71. Ibid., p. 81.
72. Gilpin, *War and Change*, pp. 94–95.
73. William L. Langer, *The Diplomacy of Imperialism, 1890–1902*, 2d ed. (New York: Alfred A. Knopf, 1965), p. 416.

ain in political influence and prestige—was driven by security concerns and was a clear manifestation of the sameness effect. German leaders were concerned that unless Germany developed countervailing naval power, its independence and interests in international politics would be circumscribed by Britain.[74] Chancellor Chlodwig Hohenlohe-Schillingfurst said in 1896: "Unless we are prepared to yield at all times and to give up the role of world power, then we must be respected. Even the most friendly word makes no impression in international relations if it is not supported by adequate material strength. Therefore, a fleet is necessary in the face of other naval powers." Notwithstanding the consequences, in an anarchic world Germany had little choice but to emulate Britain by building a powerful navy.[75]

Germany's rise to world power status and the resulting Anglo-German antagonism were structurally determined. Unless Germany acquired world power capabilities, it would have been vulnerable to states like Britain that did have them.[76] William L. Langer points out that Germany's increasing international interests and the need to defend them in the face of Britain's

---

74. Grand Admiral Alfred von Tirpitz believed Germany could not remain a great power unless it developed into a first-rank maritime power. Volker R. Berghahn, *Germany and the Approach of War in 1914* (London: MacMillan, 1973), p. 29. "Naval power," Tirpitz said, "is essential if Germany does not want to go under"; Ivor Lambi, *The Navy and German Power Politics, 1862–1914* (Boston: George Allen and Unwin, 1984), p. 139.

75. Quotation from Lambi, *The Navy and German Power Politics*, p. 114. Even Sir Eyre Crowe, the British Foreign Office's leading anti-German hardliner, recognized this in his famous 1907 memorandum. Crowe conceded that it was for Berlin, not London, to determine the size of the navy necessary to defend German interests. Crowe also understood that British opposition to Germany's naval buildup would serve only to accentuate Berlin's security dilemma: "Apart from the question of right and wrong, it may also be urged that nothing would be more likely than an attempt at such dictation, to impel Germany to persevere with her shipbuilding programs." "Memorandum by Mr. [Sir] Eyre Crow," in Gooch and Temperley, *Documents on the Origins of the War*, p. 418.

76. In the late nineteenth and early twentieth century, Germany's international behavior differed little from Britain's or America's. But unlike Britain, Germany's outward thrust did not go into a geopolitical vacuum, and unlike the United States, Germany lacked a secure strategic and economic base of continental dimension. Germany was hemmed in and its rise to great power status was too rapid, and too freighted with implications for others' interests, to be accommodated. David Calleo, *The German Problem Reconsidered: Germany and the World Order, 1870 to the Present* (Cambridge: Cambridge University Press, 1978), pp. 83–84. As W.E. Mosse observes, Germany's rise to great power status "could not but affect the interests and policies of all others. It was bound to frustrate and arouse the opposition of some at least of the older powers." W.E. Mosse, *The European Powers and the German Question, 1848–1871: With Special Reference to England and Russia* (Cambridge: Cambridge University Press, 1958), p. 2. In a real sense, therefore, Germany was born encircled. Merely by existing, it posed a threat to others. There is an important lesson here. A state must decide for itself whether to strive for great power status, but success hinges on how others react. Some states (such as pre-1914 Germany) may face a difficult path to great power status, while for others (e.g., the United States) the going is relatively easy. Environmental factors, such as geographic positioning, have a lot to do with the difficulties that may confront an eligible state as it attempts to rise to great power status.

preeminence meant that Berlin was "virtually driven" into imitating London by pursuing a policy of naval and colonial expansion. Given these circumstances, "it is hard to see how Germany could have avoided colliding with England."[77] The Anglo-German rivalry was a textbook example of the security dilemma. Because Germany's rise to world power status challenged a *status quo* that primarily reflected Britain's predominance and interests, *Weltpolitik* made Britain less secure and prompted London to take counteraction. Thus, the Anglo-German rivalry illustrates that the process of great power emergence can trigger a Hertz/Avis dynamic if a rising great power emerges as the clear challenger to a preeminent state's position.[78]

Such states are fated to engage in intense competition. The effect of Germany's emergence to great power status on Anglo-German relations is suggestive. In 1880, for example, Germany's power position (measured by share of world manufacturing output and total industrial potential) was similar to that of France and Russia.[79] While London and Berlin were on close terms during the 1880s (which at times verged on *de facto* alliance), France and Russia were Britain's main rivals.[80] By 1900, however, the Anglo-German rivalry had heated up and Germany had by a decisive margin established

---

77. Langer, *Diplomacy of Imperialism*, p. 794.
78. The competition between the largest and second-largest U.S. automobile rental companies (Hertz and Avis, respectively) became famous when Avis ran an advertising campaign with the slogan, "We're number two; we try harder." The analogy of the Anglo-German rivalry to commercial competition was apparent to Tirpitz, who wrote, "the older and stronger firm inevitably seeks to strangle the new and rising one before it is too late." Paul Kennedy, "The Kaiser and German *Weltpolitik*: Reflexions on Wilhelm II's Place in the Making of German Foreign Policy," in John C.G. Röhl and Nicolaus Sombart, *Kaiser Wilhelm II: New Interpretations* (Cambridge: Cambridge University Press, 1982), p. 149.
79. In 1880, the total industrial potential of the four powers was: Britain (73.3, where Britain in 1900 is the index benchmark of 100), Germany (27.4), France (25.1), Russia (24.5). The four powers' shares of world manufacturing output were: Britain (22.9 percent), Germany (8.5 percent), France (7.8 percent), Russian (7.6 percent). Kennedy, *Rise and Fall of Great Powers*, pp. 201–202.
80. This does not contradict my argument that Germany's rise to world power status was a balancing response to Britain's hegemony. On the contrary: during the 1880s, Berlin and London were able to mantain a cordial relationship because Germany's relative power had not risen to a point that thrust Germany into the challenger's role. It should also be noted that during the 1880s the Anglo-German relationship was indirect. London was aligned not with Berlin itself but with Germany's allies, Austria-Hungary and Italy. This alignment was part of Bismarck's intricate alliance scheme and was meant to counter Russian ambitions in the Near East and Mediterranean, an objective that overlapped Britain's interests. Bismarck's system also was intended to isolate France while simultaneously keeping Berlin on friendly terms with Europe's other great powers. After 1890, the stunning rise in Germany's relative power became manifest. Inexorably, Germany was pushed down the path to world power status, and to confrontation with Britain.

itself as Europe's second-ranking power. Indeed, Germany was closing in on Britain in terms of share of world manufacturing output and total industrial potential, and by 1913, Germany would pass Britain in these two categories.[81] The dramatic change in the two states' relative power positions fueled the deterioration in Anglo-German relations, and led to a shift in European geopolitical alignments as London sought ententes with its erstwhile rivals, France and Russia, as counterweights to German power.

EMBRYONIC SUPERPOWER: AMERICA'S RISE TO WORLD POWER

It has been argued that the United States did not seek to become a great power but rather had that status thrust upon it.[82] This view does not hold up, however. By the mid-1870s, the United States was contemplating a new role in world affairs, however tentatively.[83] This outward thrust was underpinned by the effect of differential growth rates. In the decades after the War Between the States, the United States acquired enormous economic capabilities including a rapidly expanding manufacturing and industrial base, leadership in advanced technology, a highly productive agricultural sector, abundant raw materials, ample foreign (and later internally generated) capital.[84] In 1880, the United States (at 14.7 percent) ranked second behind Great Britain (at 22.9 percent) in world manufacturing output. By 1913, the United States (at 32 percent) held a commanding advantage in share of world manufacturing production over Germany (14.8 percent) and Britain (13.6 percent).[85] As Kennedy has observed, given the economic, technological, and

---

81. In 1900, the total industrial potential of the four powers was: Britain, 100; Germany, 71.3; Russia, 47.6; France, 36.8. The four powers' shares of world manufacturing output were: Britain, 18.5 percent, Germany, 13.2 percent, Russia, 8.8 percent, France, 6.8 percent. Kennedy, *Rise and Fall of Great Powers*, pp. 201–202.
82. Ernest R. May, *Imperial Democracy: The Emergence of America as a Great Power* (New York: Harcourt, Brace and World, 1961), pp. 269–270.
83. Milton Plesur, *America's Outward Thrust: Approaches to Foreign Affairs, 1865–1890* (DeKalb: Northern Illinois University Press, 1971). "Whether great power status came in the 1890s or earlier, it is certain that the United States did not make the decision for colonialism and world involvement in a sudden movement which caught the national psyche offguard. The new departure had its roots in the quiet years of the Gilded Age." Ibid., pp. 9–10. Edward P. Crapol has recently surveyed the state of the historiography of late nineteenth-century American foreign policy. Many recent works take the view that the United States consciously sought world power status. Crapol, "Coming to Terms with Empire: The Historiography of Late Nineteenth Century American Foreign Relations," *Diplomatic History*, Vol. 16, No. 4 (Fall 1992), pp. 573–597.
84. See Kennedy, *Rise and Fall of Great Powers*, pp. 178–182, 242–249.
85. Ibid., pp. 201–202.

resource advantages the United States enjoyed, there "was a virtual inevitability to the whole process" of its rise to great power status.[86]

In the late nineteenth century, the historian Frederick Jackson Turner noted that because states develop significant international political interests as their international economic interests deepen, the United States was already on the way to becoming a great power.[87] During the Benjamin Harrison administration, the United States began engaging in what Secretary of State James G. Blaine (echoing William Pitt the younger) called "the annexation of trade."[88] Focusing first on Latin America, U.S. overseas economic interests expanded later to encompass Asia and Europe as well. Like Germany, as America's overseas economic stakes grew (or were perceived to grow), its international political interests also increased.[89] Paul Kennedy observes that the "growth of American industrial power and overseas trade was accompanied, perhaps inevitably, by a more assertive diplomacy and by an American-style rhetoric of *Weltpolitik*."[90]

Again like Germany, as America's stakes in the international system deepened, Washington began acquiring the capabilities to defend its interests. As early as the 1870s, proponents of naval expansion argued that, lacking an enlarged and modernized fleet, the United States would be vulnerable and powerless to defend its interests.[91] In the 1880s, Alfred Thayer Mahan argued that attainment of world power status was the key to America's security. His arguments about the "influence of sea power upon history" displayed an intuitive understanding of the sameness effect and he presciently argued that, to become a world power, the United States would have to emulate Britain's naval, colonial, and trade policies.[92] America's naval buildup began during the Harrison administration (1889–93) when Navy Secretary Tracy

---

86. Kennedy, *Rise and Fall of Great Powers*, p. 242.
87. Quoted in Walter LaFeber, *The New Empire: An Interpretation of American Expansion, 1860–1898* (Ithaca: Cornell University Press, 1963), pp. 69–70.
88. Quoted in ibid., p. 106.
89. American policymakers believed that overseas markets were more crucial to the nation's economic health than in fact was true. By 1913, foreign trade accounted for only 8 percent of GNP, compared with 26 percent for Britain. Kennedy, *Rise and Fall of Great Powers*, p. 244.
90. Kennedy, *Rise and Fall of Great Powers*, p. 246.
91. J.A.S. Grenville and George B. Young, *Politics, Strategy, and American Diplomacy: Studies in American Foreign Policy, 1873–1917* (New Haven: Yale University Press, 1966), pp. 5–6.
92. On Mahan's views, see Harold and Margaret Sprout, *The Rise of American Naval Power, 1776–1918* (Princeton: Princeton University Press, 1944), pp. 202–222; LaFeber, *The New Empire*, pp. 80–95.

persuaded Congress to authorize construction of a modern battleship fleet.[93] This building program signalled a break with the navy's traditional strategy of protecting American commerce, in favor of one challenging rivals for command of the sea. Responding to an increasingly competitive international environment, the navy chose "to make itself into a European-style force ready for combat with the navies of the other major powers."[94] America's naval buildup was underpinned by its rising economic power. Naval expenditures as a percentage of federal spending rose from 6.9 percent in 1890 to 19 percent in 1914 and Kennedy recounts the shock of a famous British warship designer when he discovered during a 1904 visit that America's industrial capabilities were such that the United States was simultaneously building 14 battleships and 13 armored cruisers.[95]

The extent to which America's great power emergence was a direct response to unipolarity is unclear. It is apparent, however, that Britain's preeminence was at least an important factor. The impetus for America's naval buildup and growing geopolitical assertiveness was deepening apprehension about the Western hemisphere's vulnerabilty to European encroachment, especially if the European great powers shifted the focus of their colonial rivalries from Asia to the Americas.[96] Policymakers became convinced that "American claims in Latin America would only be as strong as the military force behind them. Consequently, as American stakes in Central and South America increased, so did American military [i.e., naval] strength."[97] Thus, America's rise to great power status was a defensive reaction to the threat posed by others to its expanding overseas interests. Until 1898, the United States regarded Britain as the main danger to its strategic and commercial interests in the Western hemisphere.[98] No doubt, American feelings toward

---

93. For a brief discussion, see Kenneth J. Hagan, *This People's Navy: The Making of American Sea Power* (New York: The Free Press, 1991), pp. 194–197.
94. Ibid., p. 186.
95. Kennedy, *Rise and Fall of Great Powers*, pp. 243, 247.
96. The relationship between security worries and American foreign and strategic policy is explored in Richard D. Challener, *Admirals, Generals and Foreign Policy, 1898–1914* (Princeton: Princeton University Press, 1973); and Grenville and Young, *Politics, Strategy and American Diplomacy*.
97. LaFeber, *New Empire*, p. 229.
98. Kinley J. Brauer has argued that between 1815 and 1860, American leaders were concerned about the implications of Britain's expanding global interests, and various strategies were contemplated to counter the threat posed by Britain's naval and economic power and its formal and informal empire. Although these proposed strategic responses to British power did not

Britian were ambivalent because not only was the United States threatened by Britain's hegemony but simultaneously it was also a major beneficiary of London's preeminence. Nevertheless, Britain's predominance was tolerated only until the United States was strong enough to challenge it. Backed by growing naval power and unlimited industrial potential, in the mid-1890s the United States launched a diplomatic offensive against Britain. In 1895–96, the United States provoked a crisis with Britain over the seemingly obscure boundary dispute between Venezuela and British Guiana.[99] London was compelled to back down and to acknowledge America's hemispheric primacy. By 1903, Britain had given in completely to American demands concerning control over the proposed isthmian canal and the boundary between Alaska and Canada. Shortly thereafter, Britain bowed to the reality of America's overwhelming regional power and withdrew its naval and military forces from North America.

JAPAN: EXTERNAL THREAT, INTERNAL RESPONSE

Japan's great power emergence differed from Germany's and America's. The effect of differential growth rates was not a factor. Between 1860 and 1938, comparative measures of great power capabilities put Japan at or near the bottom of the list. For example, between 1860 and 1938, Japan's share of world manufacturing output rose only from 2.6 percent to 3.8 percent.[100] Japan's great power emergence was, rather, driven by its extreme vulnerability. Indeed, in the 1860s, Japan's very existence as a nation-state was at risk.

Although Japan's security-driven great power emergence was not a direct response to unipolarity, here too Britain's preeminence had its effect. Specifically, it was Britain's defeat of China in the Opium Wars, and China's consequent loss of independence, that provided an object lesson for the

---

come to fruition before the War Between the States, they nevertheless laid the groundwork for America's subsequent rise to world power status. Kinley J. Brauer, "The United States and British Imperial Expansion," *Diplomatic History*, Vol. 12, No. 1 (Winter 1988), pp. 19–38.

99. For brief discussions of the Venezuela crisis, see J.A.S. Grenville, *Lord Salisbury and Foreign Policy at the Close of the Nineteenth Century* (London: Athlone Press, 1964), pp. 54–73; May, *Imperial Democracy*, pp. 35–55; LaFeber, *The New Empire*, pp. 242–283; and "The Background of Cleveland's Venezuelan Policy: A Reconsideration," *American Historical Review*, Vol. 66, No. 4 (July 1961), pp. 947–967.

100. Kennedy, *Rise and Fall of Great Powers*, pp. 198–209.

reformers who led the Meiji Restoration.[101] They were determined that Japan would not suffer China's fate. As Shumpei Okamoto notes, the Meiji reformers shared a common purpose: "Throughout the Meiji period, the aspiration and resolve shared by all those concerned with the fate of the nation were that Japan strive to maintain its independence in a world dominated by the Western powers."[102] The reformers' aim was neatly expressed in the slogan *fukoku kyohei*—"enrich the country, strengthen the army"—which "became the official program of the Meiji government, geared to achieving the strength with which Japan could resist the West."[103]

Driven by security concerns, Japan's great power emergence reflected the sameness effect. To be secure Japan needed to develop the kind of military and economic capabilities that would enable it to compete with the West. In Meiji Japan, therefore, domestic politics was shaped by foreign policy concerns.[104] The era's governmental and administrative reforms, for example, were intended to reorganize Japan's central governmental structure along Western lines; centralized government was seen to be necessary if Japan were to organize itself to defend its interests from foreign encroachment.[105] Similarly, the Imperial Edict abolishing the feudal domains (1871) justified the action by observing that Japan needed a strong central government if it was "to stand on an equal footing with countries abroad."[106]

Recognizing the link between economics and national power, the Meiji era reformers worked hard to expand Japan's industrial and commercial strength. Toshimichi Okubo said in 1874:

A country's strength depends on the prosperity of its people . . . [which] in turn depends upon their productive capacity. And although the amount of production is determined in large measure by the diligence of the people

---

101. The intellectual background of the Meiji Restoration is discussed in W.G. Beasley, *The Meiji Restoration* (Stanford: Stanford University Press, 1972), pp. 74–139.
102. Shumpei Okamoto, *The Japanese Oligarchy and the Russo-Japanese War* (New York: Columbia University Press, 1960), p. 43.
103. Beasley, *The Meiji Restoration*, p. 379.
104. See James B. Crowley, "Japan's Military Foreign Policies," in James W. Morley, ed., *Japan's Foreign Policy, 1868–1941: A Research Guide* (New York: Columbia University Press, 1974). Also see W.G. Beasley, *The Rise of Modern Japan* (London: Weidenfeld and Nicolson, 1990), p. 21, where it is similarly pointed out that the Meiji Restoration, and its consequent reforms, were based on the assumption that a causal relationship existed between modernization at home and success in foreign policy.
105. See Beasley, *Rise of Modern Japan*, pp. 68–69; and *The Meiji Restoration*, pp. 303–304.
106. Quoted in Beasley, *The Meiji Restoration*, p. 347.

engaged in manufacturing industries, a deeper probe for the ultimate determinate reveals no instance when a country's productive power was increased without the patronage and encouragement of the government and its officials.[107]

Okubo, a key figure in the early Restoration governments, had visited Europe, including Bismarckian Germany. His travels underscored for Okubo the competitive nature of international politics and "convinced him that he must establish for Japan the same bases upon which the world powers of the day had founded their wealth and strength."[108] Under his direction, the government supported the expansion of manufacturing, trade, and shipping. At all times, there was a sense of urgency about Japan's internal efforts to enhance its national security by becoming a great power. Field Marshal Aritomo Yamagata, one of the Meiji era's towering political and military figures, said in 1898 that if Japan wanted to avoid lagging behind the West, "we cannot relax for even a day from encouraging education, greater production, communications and trade."[109]

From the beginning, almost every aspect of Meiji policy was directed toward safeguarding Japan's security and to vindicating its claim to equal status with the Western powers. To this end, Field Marshal Yamagata stressed, no effort must be spared to expand Japan's army and navy and to revise the post-1853 unequal treaties that the Western powers had forced upon Tokyo. These goals had largely been accomplished by 1890. A rising Japan then began to project its power outwards. The fear that the European powers would try to deny Japan economic access to China led the Japanese leadership to conclude that Japan must establish its own sphere of influence on the mainland.[110] Japan "found that a concern with defense led easily to arguments for expansion."[111] Japan's policy led to the Sino-Japanese War of 1894–95 and eventually to the Russo-Japanese War of 1904–05. Japan's mili-

---

107. Quoted in Masakazu Iwata, *Okubo Toshimichi: The Bismarck of Modern Japan* (Berkeley: University of California Press, 1964), p. 236.
108. Ibid., p. 175.
109. Quoted in Roger F. Hackett, *Yamagata Aritomo and the Rise of Modern Japan, 1838–1922* (Cambridge: Harvard University Press, 1971), p. 195.
110. Crowley, "Japan's Military Foreign Policies," p. 14.
111. Beasley, *Rise of Modern Japan*, p. 140. Beasley's observation seems entirely correct. Fear begets expansion. And expansion has its own consequences. As John Lewis Gaddis comments, "the principal occupational hazard as a general rule of being a great power is paranoia . . . and the exhaustion it ultimately produces." "Toward the Post–Cold War World," in John Lewis Gaddis, *The United States and the End of the Cold War: Implications, Reconsiderations, Provocations* (New York: Oxford University Press, 1992), p. 215.

tary successes in these conflicts established it as the leading power in Northeast Asia, and Japan's victory over Russia "secured her recognition as a major world power."[112]

HISTORY, UNIPOLARITY AND GREAT POWER EMERGENCE

There is a strong correlation between unipolarity and great power emergence. Late seventeenth-century England and Austria and late nineteenth-century Germany balanced against the dominant pole in the system. Moreover, even when great power emergence was not driven primarily by the need to counterbalance the hegemon's power, the shadow of preeminence was an important factor.[113] This is illustrated by the rise of the United States and Japan to great power status in the late nineteenth century. It is, therefore, apparent that a general tendency exists during unipolar moments: several new great powers simultaneously enter the international system. The events of the late nineteenth century also illustrate how competition from established great powers combined with challenges from rising great powers to diminish Britain's relative power and erode its primacy. During the last years of the nineteenth century, Britain, the most powerful state in the system, was the target of others' balancing policies. "The story of European international relations in the 1890s is the story of the assault of Russia and France upon the territorial position of Britain in Asia and Africa, and the story of the great economic duel between England and her all-too-efficient German rival."[114]

In the late nineteenth century, the growth of American, German, and Japanese naval power compelled Britain to forgo its policy of maintaining global naval supremacy.[115] Indeed, Britain was pressed hard by its rivals on all fronts. By 1900, it was apparent that London could not simultaneously meet the German challenge across the North Sea, defend its imperial and colonial interests from French and Russian pressure, and preserve its position in the Western hemisphere. Britain withdrew from the Western hemisphere

---

112. Ian Nish, *Japanese Foreign Policy, 1869–1942* (London: Routledge and Kegan Paul, 1977), p. 78.
113. The shadow effect is a consequence of anarchy. The unbalanced distribution of power in the hegemon's favor implicitly threatens others' security. This is because states must react to the hegemon's capabilities rather than to its intentions. In a unipolar system, concern with security is a compelling reason for eligible states to acquire great power capabilities, even if they are not immediately menaced by the hegemon.
114. Langer, *The Diplomacy of Imperialism*, p. 415.
115. See Aaron L. Friedberg, *The Weary Titan: Britain and the Experience of Relative Decline, 1895–1905* (Princeton: Princeton University Press, 1988), pp. 135–208.

because London realized it lacked the resources to compete successfully against the United States and that the naval forces deployed in North American waters could better be used elsewhere.[116] The Anglo-Japanese alliance was driven, from London's standpoint, by the need to use Japanese naval power to protect Britain's East Asian interests and thereby allow the Royal Navy units in the Far East to be redeployed to home waters. Like the rapprochment with Washington and the alliance with Tokyo, the ententes with France and Russia also evidenced Britain's declining relative power. By 1907, Britain's geopolitical position "depended upon the kindness of strangers." Over the longer term, the great power emergence of the United States and Japan paved the way for Britain's eclipse, first as hegemon and then as a great power. In the 1930s, Japanese power cost Britain its Far Eastern position, and America's relative power ultimately rose to a point where it could displace Britain as hegemon. Such was the result of Britain's policy of benign hegemony, a policy that did not merely abstain from opposing, but actually had the effect of facilitating the emergence of new great powers.

After the Cold War: America in a Unipolar World?

The historical evidence from 1660–1714 and 1860–1914 strongly supports the hypothesis derived from neorealist theory: unipolar moments cause geopolitical backlashes that lead to multipolarity. Nevertheless, in principle, a declining hegemon does have an alternative to a policy of tolerating the rise of new great powers: it can actively attempt to suppress their emergence. Thus, if Washington were prepared to contemplate preventive measures (including the use of force), it might be able to beat back rising challengers.[117] But, although prevention may seem attractive at first blush, it is a stop-gap measure. It may work once, but over time the effect of differential growth rates ensures that other challengers will subsequently appear. Given its probable costs and risks, prevention is not a strategy that would lend itself to repetition.

---

116. See C.J. Lowe and M.L. Dockrill, *The Mirage of Power*, Vol. I: *British Foreign Policy, 1902–14* (London: Routledge and Kegan Paul, 1972), pp. 96–106.
117. When a hegemon finds its primacy threatened, the best strategy is "to eliminate the source of the problem." Gilpin, *War and Change*, p. 191.

THE STRATEGY OF PREPONDERANCE

In any event, the United States has chosen a somewhat different strategy to maintain its primacy. Essentially the United States is trying to maintain intact the international order it constructed in World War II's aftermath. As Melvyn Leffler points out, after 1945 American strategy aimed at achieving a "preponderance of power" in the international system.[118] Washington sought to incorporate Western Europe, West Germany, and Japan into an American-led alliance; create an open global economy that would permit the unfettered movement of goods, capital and technology; and create an international environment conducive to America's democratic values. While committed to reviving Western Europe, Germany, and Japan economically and politically, Washington also believed that "neither an integrated Europe nor a united Germany nor an independent Japan must be permitted to emerge as a third force or a neutral bloc."[119] To maintain its preeminence in the non-Soviet world, American strategy used both benevolent and coercive incentives.

In attempting to perpetuate unipolarity, the United States is pursuing essentially the same goals, and using the same means to achieve them, that it pursued in its postwar quest for preponderance.[120] The "new NSC 68" argues that American grand strategy should actively attempt to mold the international environment by creating a secure world in which American interests are protected. American alliances with Japan and Germany are viewed as an integral part of a strategy that seeks: (1) to prevent multipolar rivalries; (2) to discourage the rise of global hegemons; and (3) to preserve a cooperative and healthy world economy. The forward deployment of U.S. military forces abroad is now viewed primarily as a means of preserving unipolarity. If the United States continues to extend security guarantees to Japan and Germany, it is reasoned, they will have no incentive to develop great power capabilities. Indeed, fear that Japan and Germany will acquire independent capabilities—that is, that they will become great powers—per-

---

118. Melvyn P. Leffler, *A Preponderance of Power: National Security, the Truman Administration, and the Cold War* (Stanford: Stanford University Press, 1992).

119. Ibid., p. 17. For second-image theorists, America's rejection of a preventive war strategy is unsurprising. It has been argued that in addition to not fighting other democracies, declining democratic powers also do not engage in preventive war against rising challengers. Randall Schweller, "Domestic Structure and Preventive War: Are Democracies More Pacific?" *World Politics*, Vol. 44, No. 2 (January 1992), pp. 235–269.

120. As I discuss below, it was the bipolar structure of the postwar system that allowed Washington to pursue a strategy of preponderance successfully and thereby smother the re-emergence of Japan and Germany as great powers.

vades the thinking of American strategists. For example, a recent RAND study of American strategy in the Pacific says that Washington must manage relations with Tokyo to maintain "the current alliance and reduce Japanese incentives for major rearmament."[121] A RAND study of the future of U.S. forces in Europe suggests that American withdrawal from Europe could result in Germany reemerging as "a heavy handed rogue elephant in Central Europe" because it would drive Germany in the "direction of militarization, nuclearization, and chronically insecure policies."[122]

Inevitably, a strategy of preponderance will fail. A strategy of more or less benign hegemony does not prevent the emergence of new great powers. The fate of nineteenth-century Britain, which followed such a strategy, is illustrative. A strategy of benign hegemony allows others to free-ride militarily and economically. Over time, the effect is to erode the hegemon's preeminence. A hegemon tends to overpay for security, which eventually weakens the internal foundation of its external position. Other states underpay for security, which allows them to shift additional resources into economically productive investments. Moreover, benign hegemony facilitates the diffusion of wealth and technology to potential rivals. As a consequence, differential growth rates trigger shifts in relative economic power that ultimately result in the emergence of new great powers. No doubt, the strategy of preponderance could prolong unipolarity somewhat, as long as eligible states calculate that the benefits of free riding outweigh the constraints imposed on them by American hegemony. Over time, however, such a policy will accelerate the hegemon's relative decline.

There is another reason why a strategy of preponderance will not work. Such a strategy articulates a vision of an American-led international order. George Bush's New World Order and Bill Clinton's apparent commitment to assertive projection of America's democratic and human rights values reflect America's desire to "press its preferred policies" on others.[123] But there is more to it than that. Other states can justifiably infer that Washington's

121. James A. Winnefeld, et al., *A New Strategy and Fewer Forces: The Pacific Dimension*, R-4089/1-USDP (Santa Monica, Calif.: RAND 1992), p. 111.

122. Richard L. Kugler, *The Future U.S. Military Presence in Europe: Forces and Requirements for the Post–Cold War Era*, R-4194-EUCOM/NA (Santa Monica, Calif.: RAND, 1992), pp. 11, 16.

123. As Waltz points out, other states cannot trust an excessively powerful state to behave with moderation. The United States may believe it is acting for the noblest of reasons. But, he notes, America's definition of peace, justice, and world order reflects American interests and may conflict with the interests of other states. "With benign intent, the United States has behaved, and until its power is brought into some semblance of balance, will continue to behave in ways that frighten and annoy others." Waltz, "America as a Model?" p. 669.

unipolar aspirations will result in the deliberate application of American power to compel them to adhere to the United States' policy preferences. For example, in a February 1991 address to the New York Economic Club, Bush said that because the United States had taken the leader's role in the Gulf militarily, America's renewed credibility would cause Germany and Japan to be more forthcoming in their economic relations with Washington.[124] Several weeks later, Harvard professor Joseph S. Nye, Jr. suggested that the deployment of United States forces in Europe and Japan could be used as a bargaining chip in trade negotiations with those countries.[125] Such a "leverage strategy" is no mere abstraction. In February 1992, then–Vice President Dan Quayle linked the continuance of America's security commitment to NATO with West European concessions in the GATT negotiations.[126]

The leverage strategy is the hegemonic stability theory's dark side. It calls for the United States to use its military power to compel other states to give in on issue areas where America has less power. It is a coercive strategy that attempts to take advantage of the asymmetries in great power capabilities that favor the United States. The leverage strategy is not new. Washington employed it from time to time in intra-alliance relations during the Cold War. However, American policies that others found merely irritating in a bipolar world may seem quite threatening in a unipolar world. For example, Japan almost certainly must realize that its lack of power projection capability renders it potentially vulnerable to leverage policies based on America's present ability to control the flow of Persian Gulf oil. Proponents of America's preponderance have missed a fundamental point: other states react to the threat of hegemony, not to the hegemon's identity. American leaders may regard the United States as a benevolent hegemon, but others cannot afford to take such a relaxed view.

REACTION TO UNIPOLARITY: TOWARDS A MULTIPOLAR WORLD

There is ample evidence that widespread concern exists today about America's currently unchallenged dominance in international politics.[127] In Sep-

---

124. Quoted in Norman Kempster, "U.S., Allies Might Help Iraq Rebuild After War, Baker Says," *Los Angeles Times*, February 17, 1991, p. A1.
125. William J. Eaton, "Democrats Groping For Image Building Issues," *Los Angeles Times*, March 9, 1991, p. A14.
126. William Tuohy, "Quayle Remarks Spark European Alarm on Trade vs. Security," *Los Angeles Times*, February 11, 1992, p. A4; Craig R. Whitney, "Quayle, Ending European Trip, Lobbies for New Trade Accord," *New York Times*, February 12, 1992, p. A4.
127. It has been suggested that the Persian Gulf War demonstrates that other states welcome, rather than fear, America's post–Cold War preeminence. However, this simply is not the case.

tember 1991, French Foreign Minister Roland Dumas warned that American "might reigns without balancing weight" and he and European Community Commission President Jacques Delors called for the EC to counterbalance the United States.[128] Some European policy analysts have said that the Soviet Union's collapse means that Europe is now threatened mainly by unchallenged American ascendancy in world politics.[129] This viewpoint was echoed in Japan in the Gulf War's aftermath. A number of commentators worried that the United States—a "fearsome" country—would impose a Pax Americana in which other states would be compelled to accept roles "as America's underlings."[130] China, too, has reacted adversely to America's post–Cold War preeminence. "Chinese analysts reacted with great alarm to President George Bush's 'New World Order' proclamations, and maintained that this was a ruse for extending U.S. hegemony throughout the globe. From China's perspective, unipolarity was a far worse state of affairs than bipolarity."[131] Similar sentiments have been echoed in the Third World. Although the reactions of these smaller states are not as significant as those of potential new great powers, they confirm that unipolarity has engendered general unease throughout the international system. At the September 1992 Nonaligned Movement Meeting, Indonesian President Suharto warned that the New World Order cannot be allowed to become "a new version of the same old

---

First, it was *after* the Persian Gulf crisis began that others began voicing their concerns about unipolarity. Second, to the extent that the Gulf War is an example of states bandwagoning with the United States, it is easily explainable. As Walt points out, weak powers threatened by a powerful neighbor will often turn to an outside great power for defensive support. Walt, *Origins of Alliances*, p. 266. Third, as Jean Edward Smith points out, the United States had to exert considerable pressure on both Egypt and Saudi Arabia to get these nations to accept the Bush administration's decision to confront Iraq militarily after the invasion of Kuwait. Jean Edward Smith, *George Bush's War* (New York: Henry Holt and Company, 1992), pp. 63–95. Finally, it should be remembered that during the war, the Arab coalition partners restrained the United States from overthrowing Saddam Hussein and that, in July and August 1992, Egypt, Turkey and Syria restrained the United States when it appeared that the Bush administration was going to provoke a military showdown over the issue of UN weapons inspectors' access to Iraq's Agricultural Ministry.

128. Quoted in "France to U.S.: Don't Rule," *New York Times*, September 3, 1991, p. A8.
129. Rone Tempest, "French Revive Pastime Fretting About U.S. 'Imperialism'," *Los Angeles Times*, February 15, 1989, p. A9.
130. See the views of Waseda University Professor Sakuji Yoshimura, quoted in Paul Blustein, "In Japan, Seeing The War On A Five-Inch Screen," *Washington Post National Weekly Edition*, February 25–March 3, 1991, and of Tokyo University Professor Yasusuke Murakami and Opposition Diet Member Masao Kunihiro, in Urban C. Lehner, "Japanese See A More 'Fearsome' U.S. Following American Success in the Gulf," *Wall Street Journal*, March 14, 1991.
131. David Shambaugh, "China's Security Policy in the Post–Cold War Era," *Survival*, Vol. 34, No. 2 (Summer 1992), p. 92.

patterns of domination of the strong over the weak and the rich over the poor." At this same meeting, UN Secretary General Boutros-Ghali warned that "the temptation to dominate, whether worldwide or regionally, remains"; Malaysian Prime Minister Mahathir Mohammed pointedly stated that a "unipolar world is every bit as threatening as a bipolar world."[132]

As has been shown, the post–Cold War world's geopolitical constellation is not unique. Twice before in international history there have been "unipolar moments." Both were fleeting. On both occasions, the effect of the entry of new great powers in the international system was to redress the one-sided distribution of power in the international system. There is every reason to expect that the pattern of the late seventeenth and nineteenth centuries will recur. The impact of differential growth rates has increased the relative power of Japan and Germany in a way that clearly marks them as eligible states. As their stakes in the international system deepen, so will their ambitions and interests. Security considerations will cause Japan and Germany to emulate the United States and acquire the full spectrum of great power capabilities, including nuclear weapons.[133] It can be expected that both will seek recognition by others of their great power status. Evidence confirming the expectation of Japan's and Germany's great power emergence already exists.

Germany is beginning to exert its leadership in European security affairs. It has assumed primary responsibility for providing economic assistance to the former Soviet Union and Eastern Europe, and took the lead in securing EC recognition of the breakaway Yugoslav republics of Croatia and Slovenia. In a sure sign that the scope of German geopolitical interests is expanding, Defense Minister Volker Rühe is advocating acquisition of large military transport aircraft.[134] Chancellor Kohl's decision to meet with outgoing Austrian President Kurt Waldheim suggests that Germany is rejecting the external constraints heretofore imposed on its behavior. Germany is also insisting that henceforth its diplomats (who had previously spoken in French or

---

132. Quoted in Charles B. Wallace, "Nonaligned Nations Question New World Order," *Los Angeles Times*, September 2, 1992, p. A4.
133. The nuclear issue is being debated, albeit gingerly, in Japan but not in Germany (or at least not openly). Nevertheless it seems to be widely understood, in the United States and in Germany and Japan, that their accession to the nuclear club is only a matter of time. See Doyle McManus, "Thinking the Once Unthinkable: Japan, Germany With A-Bombs," *Los Angeles Times* (Washington D.C. ed.), June 10, 1992, p. A8. For a discussion of a nuclear Germany's strategic implications, see Mearsheimer, "Back to the Future."
134. Terrence Roth, "New German Defense Chief Is Redefining Agency's Role," *Wall Street Journal*, August 14, 1992, p. A10.

English) will use only German when addressing international conferences.[135] Finally, Germany's open expression of interest in permanent membership on the UN Security Council is another indication that Berlin is moving toward great power status. In making Germany's position known, Foreign Minister Klaus Kinkel pointedly noted that the Security Council should be restructured because as now constituted it reflects, not the present distribution of power, but the international order that existed at the end of World War II.[136]

Notwithstanding legal and historical inhibitions, Japan is beginning to seek strategic autonomy. An important step is the decision to develop the capability to gather and analyze politico-military and economic intelligence independently of the United States.[137] Japan has also begun importing huge amounts of plutonium from Europe. The plutonium is to be used by Japan's fast breeder reactors, thereby enabling Tokyo to free itself of dependence on Persian Gulf oil and American uranium. Plutonium imports plus the acquisition of other materials in recent years mean that Japan has the capability of moving quickly to become a nuclear power.[138] After prolonged debate, Japan has finally authorized unarmed Japanese military personnel to participate in UN peacekeeping operations. This may well be the opening wedge for Japan to develop military capabilities commensurate with great power status. As a special panel of the Liberal Democratic Party argued in February 1992, "Now that we have become one of the very few economic powerhouses, it would fly in the face of the world's common sense if we did not play a military role for the maintenance and restoration of global peace."[139] As Japan becomes more active on the international stage, military power will be needed to support its policies and ensure it is not at a bargaining disadvantage in its dealings with others. Unsurprisingly, Japan has plans to build a full-spectrum

135. Stephen Kinzer, "Thus Sprake Helmut Kohl Auf Deutsch," *New York Times*, February 23, 1992, p. A4.
136. "Germany Seeks a Permanent Council Seat," *Los Angeles Times*, September 24, 1992, p. A9; Paul Lewis, "Germany Seeks Permanent UN Council Seat," *New York Times*, September 24, 1992, p. A1.
137. David E. Sanger, "Tired of Relying on U.S., Japan Seeks to Expand Its Own Intelligence Efforts," *New York Times*, January 1, 1992, p. A6.
138. Jim Mann, "Japan's Energy Future Linked to Risky Cargo," *Los Angeles Times*, February 23, 1992, p. A1. The initial plutonium shipment left for Japan from Cherbourg, France, in early November 1992 and arrived in Japan in early January 1993. There has been speculation that the mere fact that Japan will possess a substantial plutonium stockpile may serve as a deterrent even if Tokyo does not acquire nuclear weapons. See David Sanger, "Japan's Atom Fuel Shipment Is Worrying Asians," *New York Times*, November 9, 1992, p. A3.
139. Quoted in Teresa Watanabe, "Shift Urged on Sending Japan's Troops Abroad," *Los Angeles Times*, February 22, 1992, p. A10.

navy (including aircraft carriers) capable of operating independently of the American Seventh Fleet.[140] In January 1993, Foreign Minister Michio Watanabe openly called for Japan to acquire long-range air and naval power-projection capabilities. Japan is also showing signs of diplomatic assertiveness, and its leading role in the UN effort to rebuild Cambodia is viewed by Tokyo as the beginning of a more forceful and independent foreign policy course now that Japan no longer is constrained to "obey U.S. demands."[141] Japan's policies toward Russia, China, and Iran demonstrate a growing willingness to follow an independent course, even if doing so leads to open friction with Washington. It is suggestive of Japan's view of the evolving international system that its recently appointed ambassador to the United States has spoken of the emergence of a "multipolar world in which the United States could no longer play the kind of dominant role it used to play."[142] That Japan is measuring itself for a great power role is reflected in its expressed desire for permanent membership of the UN Security Council.[143]

Back to the Future: The Political Consequences of Structural Change

Since 1945, the West has enjoyed a Long Peace.[144] During the post–World War II era, American leadership has been maintained, Germany and Japan have been prevented from becoming great powers, a cooperative economic order has been established, and the spread of democratic values has been

---

140. This information provided by John Arquilla based on his discussions with Japanese defense analysts. See also David E. Sanger, "Japanese Discuss an Expanded Peacekeeping Role for the Military," *New York Times*, January 10, 1993, p. A9. The issue of constitutional reform and elimination of the "peace clause" has been raised again recently; Jacob M. Schlesinger, "Japan's Ruling Party Will Seek a Review of 1946 Constitution," *Wall Street Journal*, January 14, 1993, p. A13; David E. Sanger, "Japanese Debate Taboo Topic of Military's Role," *New York Times*, January 17, 1993, p. A7.
141. Quoted in Teresa Watanabe, "Putting Cambodia Together Again," *Los Angeles Times*, March 3, 1992, p. HI.
142. Quoted in Sam Jameson, "Japan's New Envoy to U.S. Sees 'Crucial Period' Ahead," *Los Angeles Times*, February 18, 1992, p. A4.
143. Sam Jameson, "Japan to Seek U.N. Security Council Seat," *Los Angeles Times*, January 29, 1992, p. A1.
144. See John Lewis Gaddis, "The Long Peace: Elements of Stability in the Postwar International System," *International Security*, Vol. 10, No. 4 (Spring 1986), pp. 99–142, where Gaddis probed for an explanation of the absence of great power war during the Cold War rivalry between the Soviet Union and the United States. Gaddis has revisited the issue and asked whether certain factors (nuclear weapons, polarity, hegemonic stability, "triumphant" liberalism, and long cycles) have implications for the possible prolongation of the Long Peace into the post–Cold War era. Gaddis, "Great Illusions, the Long Peace, and the Future of the International System," in *The United States and the End of the Cold War.*

promoted. The strategy of preponderance seeks to maintain the geopolitical status quo that the Long Peace reflects. American strategic planners and scholars alike believe the United States can successfully perpetuate this status quo. This sanguine outlook is predicated on the belief that second-image factors (economic interdependence, common democratic institutions) militate against the reappearance of traditional forms of great power competition while promoting new forms of international cooperation.[145] Neorealists, however, believe that the Long Peace was rooted primarily in the bipolar structure of the international system, although the unit-level factor of nuclear deterrence also played a role.[146] Because they expect structural change to lead to changed international political outcomes, neorealists are not sanguine that the Long Peace can endure in the coming era of systemic change. Neorealist theory leads to the expectation that the world beyond unipolarity will be one of great power rivalry in a multipolar setting.

During the Cold War era, international politics was profoundly shaped by the bipolar competition between the United States and the Soviet Union.[147] The Soviet threat to their common security caused the United States, Western Europe, and Japan to form an anti-Soviet coalition. Because of America's military preeminence in a bipolar system, Western Europe and Japan did not have to internalize their security costs because they benefited from the protective mantle of Washington's containment policy. At the same time, because Western Europe's and Japan's political and economic stability were critical to containment's success, the United States resolved the "hegemon's dilemma"

---

145. For scholarly elaborations of this viewpoint, see John Mueller, *Retreat from Doomsday: The Obsolescence of Major War* (New York: Basic Books, 1989); Richard Rosecrance, *The Rise of the Trading State: Commerce and Conquest in the Modern World* (New York: Basic Books, 1986); Robert Jervis, "The Future of World Politics: Will It Resemble the Past?" *International Security*, Vol. 16, No. 3 (Winter 1991/92), pp. 39–73; Carl Kaysen, "Is War Obsolete?" *International Security*, Vol. 14, No. 4 (Spring 1990), pp. 42–64; Charles Kupchan and Clifford Kupchan, "Concerts, Collective Security and the Future of Europe," *International Security*, Vol. 16, No. 1 (Summer 1991), pp. 114–161; Richard Rosecrance, "A New Concert of Powers," *Foreign Affairs*, Vol. 71, No. 2 (Spring 1992), pp. 64–82; James M. Goldgeier and Michael McFaul, "A Tale of Two Worlds: Core and Periphery in the Post–Cold War Era," *International Organization*, Vol. 46, No. 3 (Spring 1992), pp. 467–491. The Defense Planning Guidance and similar documents also stress that the spread of democracy and economic interdependence are crucial to the success of the strategy of preponderance. The classic discussion of the second and third images of international politics is Kenneth N. Waltz, *Man, the State, and War* (New York: Columbia University Press, 1958).
146. This argument is presented in the European context in Mearsheimer, "Back to the Future."
147. For a different view, see Ted Hopf, "Polarity, the Offense-Defense Balance, and War," *American Political Science Review*, Vol. 81, No. 3 (June 1991), pp. 475–494. Hopf argues that the international system's stability during the Cold War era was attributable to nuclear deterrence and that bipolarity was an irrelevant factor.

by forgoing maximization of its relative gains and pursuing instead a policy of promoting absolute gains for all members of the anti-Soviet coalition.[148] For strategic reasons, the United States encouraged Western Europe's economic integration and Japan's discriminatory trade and foreign investment policies, even though the inevitable consequence of these policies was to enhance Western Europe's and Japan's relative power at America's expense.

Bipolarity was the decisive variable in the West's Long Peace because it removed the security dilemma and the relative gains problem from the agenda of relations among the Western powers. Even non-neorealists implicitly acknowledge the salience of structural factors in securing the postwar "liberal peace." Michael Doyle, for example, admits that American military leadership was crucial because it dampened the need for Western Europe and Japan to become strategically independent (which would rekindle the security dilemma) and reinforced the bonds of economic interdependence (thereby alleviating the relative gains problem). Doyle says the erosion of American preeminence could imperil the liberal peace "if independent and substantial military forces were established" by Western Europe and Japan.[149] In other words, if liberated from the bipolar structural constraints that, with Washington's help, smothered their great power emergence, states like Germany and Japan might respond to new international systemic constraints by becoming—*and acting like*—great powers. Here, Doyle is correct and that is precisely the point: structure affects outcomes.

AMERICA IN A MULTIPOLAR WORLD: IMPLICATIONS AND RECOMMENDATIONS

The Cold War structure has been swept away. American policymakers must now think about international politics from a wholly new analytical framework. This will not be easy. Richard Rosecrance observed in 1976, when it was already apparent that the bipolar system was beginning to erode, that

---

148 Arthur A. Stein, "The Hegemon's Dilemma: Great Britain, the United States, and the International Economic Order," *International Organization*, Vol. 38, No. 2 (Spring 1984), pp. 355–386. Stein delineates the hegemon's dilemma as follows:

A hegemonic power's decision to enrich itself is also a decision to enrich others more than itself. Over time, such policies will come at the expense of the hegemon's relative standing and will bring forth challengers. Yet choosing to sustain its relative standing . . . is a choice to keep others impoverished at the cost of increasing its own wealth. Maintaining its relative position has obvious costs not only to others but to itself. Alternatively, maximizing its absolute wealth has obvious benefits but brings forth even greater ones to others.

Stein, *Why Nations Cooperate*, p. 139.

149. Michael Doyle, "Kant, Liberal Legacies and Foreign Affairs," Part 1, *Philosophy and Public Affairs*, Vol. 12, No. 3 (Summer 1983), p. 233.

Washington has, since 1945, always had difficulty in understanding how Western Europe and Japan could have different interests than the United States.[150] More recently, Stephen Krasner has observed that "U.S. policymakers have paid little attention to the possibility that a loss of power *vis-à-vis* friends could present serious and unforeseen difficulties, either because friends can become enemies or because managing the international system may be more difficult in a world in which power is more evenly distributed."[151] The impending structural shift from unipolarity to multipolarity means that the security dilemma and the relative gains problem will again dominate policymakers' concerns. As Japan and Germany become great powers, the quality of their relations with the United States will be profoundly altered.[152] Relations will become significantly more competitive, great power security rivalries and even war will be likely, and cooperation will correspondingly become more difficult.

The implications of multipolarity will be especially evident in the United States-Japan relationship.[153] Summarizing his incisive analysis of the pre-1914 Anglo-German antagonism, Paul Kennedy states that the "most profound cause, surely, was *economic.*"[154] By this, Kennedy does not mean the commercial competition between British and German firms, but rather that economic shifts had radically transformed the relative power relationship between Britain and Germany. Kennedy asks if the relative power relationship of two great powers has ever changed so remarkably with the span of a single lifetime. The answer may now be "yes."

There is a very good chance that early in the next decade Japan's GNP may equal or surpass America's.[155] Such an economic change would be a fact

---

150. Richard Rosecrance, "Introduction," in Rosecrance, ed., *America as an Ordinary Country* (Ithaca: Cornell University Press, 1976), p. 12.
151. Stephen Krasner, "Trade Conflicts and the Common Defense: The United States and Japan," *Political Science Quarterly*, Vol. 101, No. 5 (1986), pp. 787–806.
152. Others have argued that America's relations with Japan and Germany will become more competitive in the post–Cold War era. A notable example is Jeffrey E. Garten, *A Cold Peace: America, Japan, Germany and the Struggle for Supremacy* (New York: Times Books, 1992). Garten's argument differs from mine in two critical respects. First, Garten pinpoints the locus of rivalry in second-image factors; specifically the different cultural, political, and economic traditions of the three countries. Second, he discounts the possibility of war or of security competitions and argues that the rivalry will be primarily economic.
153. An interesting albeit flawed attempt to consider the geopolitical consequences of the altered relative power relationship of Japan and the United States is George Friedman and Meredith Lebard, *The Coming War With Japan* (New York: St. Martin's Press, 1991).
154. Kennedy, *Anglo-German Antagonism*, p. 464.
155. This is C. Fred Bergsten's projection based on the following assumptions: Japan's annual

of enormous geopolitical significance. Should this relative power shift occur, no doubt Japan would demand that power and prestige in the international system be redistributed to reflect its new status. Besides demands for UN Security Council membership, Tokyo might: (1) insist on the decisive vote in international economic institutions; (2) demand that the yen become the international economy's primary reserve currency; (3) exploit advantageous technological, economic, and fiscal asymmetries to advance its strategic interests; and (4) become a much more assertive actor geopolitically.

Whether the United States could comfortably accommodate a Japan of equal or greater power is an open question. The answer would depend on the moderation, and the moderate tone, of Japan's *desiderata* and on the willingness of the United States to make reasonable concessions gracefully. But even skillful and patient diplomacy on both sides could fail to avert conflict. In that case, the question is not so much who as *what* would be responsible for conflict between the United States and Japan: I argue that it would be the international political system's structure and the constraints it exerts on great power behavior.

Again, history may provide insight. At the turn of the century, Great Britain was able to reach an accommodation with the United States because America's ambitions did not immediately seem to threaten London's most vital security concerns.[156] On the other hand, Germany's rising power did appear to present such a threat. It is worrisome that the changing relative power relationship between the United States and Japan contains the same Hertz/Avis dynamic that fueled the Anglo-German antagonism. Thus once again, the prospect of hegemonic war, thought to have been banished from international politics, must be reckoned with even as we hope to avoid it. Indeed, it must be reckoned with *especially* if we hope to avoid it. The main point of the hegemonic war theory is that:

there is incompatibility between crucial elements of the existing international system and the changing distribution of power among the states within the system. . . . The resolution of the disequilibrium between the superstructure of the system and the underlying distribution of power is

---

growth is about 4 percent, the United States' is 2 to 2½ percent, and the yen appreciates to 100 to 1 against the dollar. Bergsten, "Primacy of Economics," *Foreign Policy*, No. 87 (Summer 1992), p. 6.
156. See Charles S. Campbell, *Anglo-American Understanding, 1898–1903* (Baltimore: The Johns Hopkins University Press, 1957); Dexter Perkins, *The Great Rapprochement: England and the United States, 1895–1914* (New York: Atheneum, 1968).

found in the outbreak and intensification of what becomes a hegemonic war.[157]

Great power war is not a certainty, because some factors could reduce the war-proneness of the coming multipolar system. At the unit level, nuclear deterrence could maintain the peace among the great powers in a multipolar system where each has nuclear weapons.[158] In such a system, great power conflict might be played out in the economic, rather than the military, arena.[159] Still, the shadow of war will loom over a multipolar system. Consequently, the United States will have to rethink the answer it gave in the late 1940s to "the hegemon's dilemma." Put another way, Washington will have to come to grips with the *declining* hegemon's dilemma. Precisely because major shifts in relative economic power presage change in the relative distribution of power geopolitically, the United States must begin to concern itself with maintaining its relative power rather than pursuing absolute gains for itself and those who are its partners today but may become its rivals tomorrow. Although states can cooperate readily to promote absolute gains

---

157. Robert Gilpin, "The Theory of Hegemonic War," in Rotberg and Rabb, *Origin and Prevention of Major Wars*, pp. 25–26.

158. Kenneth N. Waltz, "Nuclear Myths and Political Realities," *American Political Science Review*, Vol. 81, No. 3 (September 1991), pp. 731–746; *The Spread of Nuclear Weapons: More May Be Better*, Adelphi Paper No. 171 (London: International Institute for Strategic Studies, 1981). For a more pessimistic view of the possible consequences of the spread of nuclear weapons, see Barry R. Posen, *Inadvertent Escalation: Conventional War and Nuclear Weapons* (Ithaca: Cornell University Press, 1991).

159. If deterrence holds among the great powers in a multipolar world, the prevailing conventional wisdom is that economic competitions would replace security competitions as the primary means of great power rivalry. Under the shadow of war, trade wars that improve a state's relative position by inflicting more pain on a rival could become a rational strategy. States in a position to do so could also use their financial power or control over access to key technologies to advance their interests relative to rivals. For a suggestive first cut at the possible role of "economic statecraft" in great power relations in the emerging multipolar system, see Aaron L. Friedberg, "The Changing Relationship Between Economics and National Security," *Political Science Quarterly*, Vol. 106, No. 2 (1991), pp. 272–274.

One should be careful about assuming that economics will entirely displace military power. Deterrence rests on military strength. Moreover, it could be expected that arms races and tests of resolve would be employed by the great powers as substitutes for actual fighting. A great power nuclear stalemate could have two other important military effects. Just as the Cold War superpowers did in Korea, Vietnam, Angola and Afghanistan, the great powers in a multipolar system could wage war through proxies. Also, deterrence at the nuclear level could, notwithstanding the risk of escalation, cause the great powers to fight (or attempt to fight) limited conventional wars. Here, it may be useful to revisit the early Cold War literature on limited war. See Henry Kissinger, *Nuclear Weapons and Foreign Policy* (New York: Harper and Row, 1957); Robert E. Osgood, *Limited War* (Chicago: University of Chicago Press, 1957).

for all when the shadow of war is absent from their relations, the barriers to cooperation become formidable when the shadow of war is present.[160]

STRATEGIC INDEPENDENCE IN A MULTIPOLAR WORLD

Because multipolarity is inevitable, it is pointless to debate the comparative merits of unipolar, bipolar, and multipolar systems. Rather than vainly and counterproductively pursuing a strategy of preponderance, the United States needs to design a strategy that will (1) safeguard its interests during the difficult transition from unipolarity to multipolarity; and (2) enable the United States to do as well as possible in a multipolar world. America's optimal strategy is to make its power position similar to Goldilocks' porridge: not too strong, which would frighten others into balancing against the United States; not too weak, which would invite others to exploit American vulnerabilities; but just right—strong enough to defend American interests, without provoking others.

The transition from unipolarity to multipolarity will challenge the United States to devise a policy that will arrest its relative decline while minimizing the chances that other states will be provoked into balancing against the United States. Relative decline has internal and external causes. Relative decline can be addressed by policies that focus on either or both of these causes. It would be counterproductive for the United States to attempt to maintain its relative power position by attempting to suppress the emergence of new great powers. This approach would heighten others' concerns about the malign effects of unchecked American power, which probably would accelerate the rise of new great powers, and increase the probability that balancing behavior would be directed against the United States. American policymakers need to remember that other states balance against hegemons

---

160. Robert Powell, "The Problem of Absolute and Relative Gains in International Relations Theory," *American Political Science Review*, Vol. 81, No. 4 (December 1991), pp. 1303–1320. Joanne Gowa points out that free trade is more likely to prevail in bipolar international systems than in multipolar ones. Because the risk of exit from a bipolar alliance is less than from an alliance in a multipolar system, bipolar alignments are more stable. Consequently, bipolar alliances are better able to internalize the security externalities of free trade (the members do not need to be concerned with relative gains because today's ally is unlikely to be tomorrow's rival). Moreover, in a bipolar alliance, the dominant partner has incentives to act altruistically towards its allies because it benefits when they do. All of these incentives are reversed in multipolar systems where exit risks (i.e., defection of allies) and buck passing/free rider tendencies force states to ponder the relative gains problem and to think hard about the wisdom of acting unselfishly. Free trade thus is problematic in a multipolar system. Gowa, "Bipolarity, Multipolarity and Free Trade," *American Political Science Review*, Vol. 79, No. 4 (December 1989), pp. 1245–1266.

and they should not want the United States to be seen by others as a "sprawling giant with gouty fingers and toes." A policy that concentrates U.S. energies on redressing the internal causes of relative decline would be perceived by others as less threatening than a strategy of preponderance. Although vigorous internal renewal might cause frictions with others over economic policy, it is less likely to have negative geopolitical repercussions than a policy that aims at perpetuating unipolarity.

Washington also needs to remember that while the United States may regard its hegemony as benign, others will have different perceptions. The international order objectives embedded in a strategy of preponderance reinforce others' mistrust of American preeminence. The more the United States attempts to press its preferences and values on others, the more likely it is that they will react against what is, in their view, overweening American power. Moreover, policies that arouse others' fear of America today could carry over into the emerging multipolar system. It makes no sense to alienate needlessly states (such as China) that could be strategically useful to the United States in a multipolar world. To avoid frightening others, the United States should eschew a value-projection policy and moderate both its rhetoric and its ambitions.[161]

The United States must adjust to the inevitable emergence of new great powers. The primary role of forward-deployed American forces now is to dissuade Japan and Germany from becoming great powers. There are three reasons why American forward deployments in Europe and Northeast Asia should be phased out soon. First, a policy of forward deployment could unnecessarily entangle the United States in overseas conflicts where the stakes are more important to others than to itself. Second, because the United States faces severe fiscal and economic constraints, the opportunity costs of such a strategy are high. Third, such a policy cannot work. Indeed, the strategy of preponderance is probably the worst option available to the United States because it is not coercive enough to prevent Japan and Germany from becoming great powers, but it is coercive enough to antagonize them and cause them to balance against the United States. If the analysis presented in this article is correct, a policy of attempting to smother Germany's and Japan's great power emergence would be unavailing because

---

161. For a discussion of value projection as a grand strategic option see Terry L. Deibel, "Strategies Before Containment: Patterns for the Future," *International Security*, Vol. 16, No. 4 (Spring 1992), pp. 79–108.

structural pressures will impel them to become great powers regardless of what the United States does or does not do. Simply stated, the declining hegemon's dilemma is acute: neither benign nor preventive strategies will prevent the emergence of challengers and the consequent end of the hegemon's predominance in the international system.

American grand strategy must be redesigned for a multipolar world. In a multipolar system, the United States should follow a policy of strategic independence by assuming the posture of an offshore balancer.[162] Traditionally, America's overriding strategic objective has been to ensure that a hegemon does not dominate Eurasia.[163] That objective would not change under strategic independence, but the means of attaining it would. Rather than assuming primary responsibility for containing the rise of a potential hegemon, the United States would rely on global and regional power balances to attain that goal. Strategic independence is not an isolationist policy that rules out the use of American power abroad.[164] Strategic independence also differs from the selective-commitment variant of offshore balancing articulated by John Mearsheimer and Stephen Van Evera, whereby the United States would be relatively indifferent to Third World events but would remain militarily engaged in Europe and Northeast Asia in order to preserve "stability."[165] Strategic independence is a hedging strategy that would commit the United States militarily if, but only if, other states failed to balance effectively against a rising Eurasian hegemon. The United States would need to remain alert to

---

162. I first used the term "strategic independence" in 1983 and I elaborated on it in 1989. Christopher Layne, "Ending the Alliance," *Journal of Contemporary Studies*, Vol. 6, No. 3 (Summer 1983), pp. 5–31; and Layne, "Realism Redux: Strategic Independence in a Multipolar World," *SAIS Review*, Vol. 9, No. 2 (Summer–Fall 1989), pp. 19–44. Ted Galen Carpenter, who has also embraced a form of strategic independence, has acknowledged that I was the first to articulate the concept and to so name it. Ted Galen Carpenter, "Introduction," in Carpenter, ed., *Collective Defense of Strategic Independence: Alternative Strategies for the Future* (Washington, D.C.: Cato Institute, 1989), p. xx, n. 7. The most recent explication of his views on strategic independence is Carpenter, *A Search for Enemies: America's Alliances After the Cold War* (Washington, D.C.: Cato Institute, 1992).

163. See John Lewis Gaddis, *Strategies of Containment* (New York: Oxford University Press, 1982), chap. 2; George F. Kennan, *Realities of American Foreign Policy* (Princeton: Princeton University Press, 1954), pp. 63–65; Hans Morgenthau, *In Defense of the National Interest* (Lanham, Md.: University Press of America, 1982, reprint of 1951 edition), pp. 5–7; Nicholas Spykman, *America's Strategy in World Politics: The United States and the Balance of Power* (New York: Harcourt, Brace, 1942), part 1.

164. For the isolationist approach to post–Cold War American grand strategy, see Earl C. Ravenal, "The Case For Adjustment," *Foreign Policy*, No. 81 (Winter 1990/91), pp. 3–19.

165. Mearsheimer, "Back to the Future"; Stephen Van Evera, "Why Europe Matters, Why the Third World Doesn't: American Grand Strategy After the Cold War," *Journal of Strategic Studies*, Vol. 13, No. 2 (June 1990), pp. 1–51.

the events that would require a more engaged policy: (1) the appearance of a "careful" challenger able to cloak its ambitions and ward off external balancing against it; (2) a dramatic narrowing of America's relative power margin over Japan; or (3) the inability of other states to act as effective counterweights due to internal difficulties.[166]

Strategic independence aims to capitalize on America's inherent geopolitical advantages.[167] First, in a relative sense, the United States is probably the most secure great power in history because of the interlocking effects of geography, nuclear weapons, and capabilities which, although diminished relatively, are still formidable in absolute terms. Such "strategic security enables the balancer to stay outside the central balance until the moment when its intervention can be decisive."[168] America's insularity means that it can benefit strategically from geography in another way, as well. Because America is distant from the likely theaters of great power conflict, in a multipolar world others are unlikely to view it as a threat to their security. Indeed distance would enhance America's attractiveness as an ally. (In a unipolar world the United States loses this advantage because hegemons repel others rather than attracting them). Finally, because of its still considerable great power capabilities, in a multipolar world America's intervention would decisively tip the scales against an aspiring hegemon.

---

166. For a discussion of the "careful" challenger, see John Arquilla, "Balances Without Balancing," paper presented at the annual meeting of the American Political Science Association, Chicago, Illinois, September 1992.

167. It is not neorealist heresy to suggest that the United States can play an offshore balancer's role. I do not claim that there is a functionally differentiated role for a balancer in the international system. Rather, like Waltz, I am saying that under "narrowly defined and historically unlikely conditions," certain states can play this role because of their unit-level attributes (especially geography and capabilities). The United States today meets Waltz's criteria: (1) American strength added to a weaker coalition would redress the balance; (2) America has (or ought to have) no positive ends—its goal is the negative one of thwarting an aspiring hegemon; (3) America's power for the foreseeable future will be at least the equal of any other state's. Waltz, *Theory of International Politics,* pp. 163–164. It should also be noted that balancers often are attractive allies precisely because they do not have ambitions that threaten others. As George Liska notes, Britain benefited from its "attractiveness in Europe whenever she was ready to meet an actual or potential hegemonical threat" from Europe. To win allies, "Britain had only to abstain from direct acquisitions on the continent and, when called, limit voluntarily her wartime gains overseas." George Liska, *The Quest for Equilibrium: America and the Balance of Power on Land and Sea* (Baltimore: The John Hopkins University Press, 1977), p. 13. For additional discussion of the criteria that a state should meet to be an effective balancer, see Michael Sheehan, "The Place of the Balancer in Balance of Power Theory," *Review of International Studies,* Vol. 15, No. 2 (April 1989), pp. 123–133.

168. Sheehan, "The Place of the Balancer," p. 128.

An insular great power in a multipolar system enjoys a wider range of strategic options than less fortunately placed states.[169] This would certainly be true for the United States. Because of its relative immunity from external threat, in a multipolar world the United States could stand by and could rationally adopt buck-passing strategies that force others to "go first."[170] The emerging great powers are located in regions where other potentially powerful actors are present (Ukraine, Russia, China, and Korea, which probably will be reunified in the next decade) and where the potential for intense security competitions also exists. The emerging great powers (and these other actors) are likely to be kept in check by their own rivalries. There are three reasons why this situation could be beneficial to the United States. First, the fact that the emerging great powers are involved in regional rivalries will have the effect of enhancing America's relative power.[171] Second, Japan, America's most likely future geopolitical rival, could be contained by others without the United States having to risk direct confrontation. Third, if the emerging great powers are compelled to internalize their security costs, they no longer will be free to concentrate primarily on trading-state strategies that give them an advantage in their economic competition with the United States.

Strategic independence is responsive to the constraints of the impending structural changes in the international system. It is a strategy that would serve America's interests in the emerging multipolar system. It is, admittedly, a competitive strategy. But such a strategy is needed in a world where great power rivalries, with both security and economic dimensions, will be a fact of international life. At the same time, strategic independence is a restrained

---

169. Liska, *Quest for Equilibrium*, p. 12.
170. For a discussion of the "buck-passing" phenomenon see Thomas J. Christensen and Jack Snyder, "Chain Gangs and Passed Bucks: Predicting Alliance Patterns in Multipolarity," *International Organization*, Vol. 44, No. 2 (Spring 1990), pp. 137–168; Waltz, *Theory of International Politics*, p. 165. John Arquilla defines "bystanding" as a state's propensity to avoid conflicts, if it can do so, for self-preservation reasons. Arquilla, "Balances Without Balancing."
171. An offshore balancer can benefit from others' rivalries: by the mid-1890s, America's navy was powerful, though still smaller than Britain's and those of Europe's lending powers. But "such equality was not necessary. The growing instability of the European political equilibrium seriously tied the hands of the Great Powers of that Continent, and rendered progressively improbable any determined aggression from that quarter against the interests of the United States in the northern part of the Western Hemisphere. European instability, in short, enhanced the *relative* power and security of the United States." Harold and Margaret Sprout, *Rise of American Naval Power*, p. 222 (emphasis in original). Similarly, during the nineteenth century, Britain was able to enjoy a relatively high degree of security while spending proportionately less on defense than the European powers, precisely because the European states were preoccupied with security competitions among themselves.

and prudent policy that would (1) avoid provocative actions that would cause others to regard the United States as an overpowerful hegemon; (2) minimize the risks of open confrontation with the emerging great powers; and (3) attempt to enhance America's relative power indirectly through skillful manipulation of the dynamics of multipolarity.

Strategic independence is also a more realistic policy than the strategy of preponderance, which is based on preserving the status quo and on maintaining stability. "Stability" is defined as a world where the United States is unchallenged by rivals and its interests are undisturbed by international political unheaval.[172] The strategy of preponderance aims at attaining a condition that approximates absolute security for the United States. In this respect, it is another form of American exceptionalism. It is a transcendant strategy that seeks nothing less than the end of international politics. However, unwanted and unanticipated events happen all the time in international politics; in this respect, "instability" is normal. War, the security dilemma, the rise and fall of great powers, the formation and dissolution of alliances,

---

172. For a devastating critique of America's stability obsession, see Benjamin C. Schwarz, "Rights and Foreign Policy: Morality is No Mantra," *New York Times*, November 20, 1992, p. A19. The focus on instability means that the strategy of preponderance leads inexorably to the open-ended proliferation of American commitments, all of which are seen as "interdependent." The United States must, under this strategy, worry about both the rise of new great powers and turmoil in strategically peripheral areas. The latter, it is feared, could set off a cascading series of effects that would spill over and affect important American interests. There is particular concern that American economic interests could be harmed by instability. As Bush's Secretary of Defense Dick Cheney said: "We are a trading nation, and our prosperity is linked to peace and stability in the world. . . . Simply stated, the worldwide market that we're part of cannot thrive where regional violence, instability, and aggression put it at peril." Dick Cheney, "The Military We Need in the Future," *Vital Speeches of the Day*, Vol. 59, No. 1 (October 15, 1992), p. 13. For a similar argument see Van Evera, "Why Europe Matters," pp. 10–11.

This line of thinking is an ironic twist on the interdependence/trading state concept, which holds that territorial conquest does not pay because the most effective means of increasing national power is through trade, and that war is too costly to be a viable option for economically powerful states. Rather than being a stimulus for peace, under the strategy of preponderance economic interdependence means that the United States must maintain a forward military presence and be prepared to wage war, in order to ensure that it is not cut off from the markets with which it has become economically interconnected. Here, two flaws of the stability-oriented strategy of preponderance become clear. First, there is a failure to consider whether the benefits of maintaining stability outweigh the costs of attempting to do so. Admittedly, instability abroad conceivably could harm the United States. The issue, however, is whether this harm would exceed the certain costs of maintaining American forward-deployed forces and the possible costs if commitment leads to involvement in a conflict. Second, there is no consideration of alternative strategies. For example, by relying on its large domestic market (which will get bigger if the North American Free Trade Agreement goes into effect) and diversifying its overseas markets, the United States could minimize the economic disruption that could accompany possible geopolitical disturbances in Europe and East Asia.

and great power rivalries are enduring features of international politics. The goal of a unipolar world in which the United States is unthreatened and able to shape the international environment is alluring but it is a chimera. No state can achieve absolute security because no state, not even the United States, can rise above the international political system's structural constraints.

THE COMING TEST

The coming years will be ones of turmoil in international politics. Systemic change occasioned by the rise and fall of great powers has always been traumatic. No doubt neorealism's critics will continue to point to second-image factors as reasons to take an optimistic view of the future. No doubt, too, the debate between neorealists and their critics will continue. But this one is not fated to drag on inconclusively. In coming years, the international system will provide a definitive field test of the contending views of international politics offered by neorealists and their critics. Fifty years from now, and probably much sooner, we will know who was right and who was wrong. Structural realists can be confident that events will vindicate their predictions: (1) Because of structural factors, an American strategy of preponderance or an attempt to perpetuate unipolarity is doomed to failure; (2) unipolarity will stimulate the emergence of eligible states as great powers; (3) unipolarity will cause other states to balance against the United States; (4) in a multipolar system, traditional patterns of great power competition will reemerge notwithstanding the effect of second-image factors; and (5) if differential growth rate effects allow Japan to challenge America's leading position, the United States–Japan relationship will become highly competitive and the possibility of hegemonic war will be present.

International Primacy | *Robert Jervis*

Is the Game Worth the Candle?

$\mathbf{D}$oes international primacy matter? In the past, this question was not worth asking. The great powers—and the term is suggestive—always struggled for position, and the top two or three of them, with the glaring exception of the United States in the 1920s and 1930s, sought to be the leading state.[1] Disagreements about who had succeeded and who was slipping were common and usually of more than academic interest, as was true of the debates in the 1980s about whether the United States was or would remain "number one."[2] Today, however, the important argument is whether the United States needs to strive to maintain its primacy. One could take more than an article to define this concept, but I think that for most purposes a simple definition will do: primacy means being much more powerful than any other state according to the usual and crude measures of power (e.g., gross national product; size of the armed forces; lack of economic, political, and geographic vulnerabilities). This in turn implies that the state has greater ability than any rival to

Robert Jervis is Adlai E. Stevenson Professor of International Relations at Columbia University and a member of its Institute of War and Peace Studies. His most recent book is The Meaning of the Nuclear Revolution *(Cornell University Press, 1989), for which he received the Grawemeyer Award.*

1. See, for example, Robert Gilpin, *War and Change in the International System* (New York: Cambridge University Press, 1981); Paul Kennedy, *The Rise and Fall of the Great Powers: Economic Change and Military Conflict From 1500–2000* (New York: Random House, 1987); Charles Doran, *Systems in Crisis: New Imperatives of High Politics at Century's End* (New York: Cambridge University Press, 1991). I use the term primacy rather than hegemony because the latter has two connotations, neither intended here. It is often used to describe a state like Hitler's Germany or Napoleon's France that seeks to dominate the international system, leaving others only token autonomy. More recently, it has been used to describe a state sufficiently powerful to influence strongly the economic practices prevailing in much of the world. Because I am concerned more with political than with economic arrangements (although of course the two are hard to separate), I wish to avoid the second meaning; because I do not mean to bring to mind either complete domination or malign intentions, I want to avoid the connotations of the first meaning of hegemony.
2. Among the responses to Kennedy are Samuel Huntington, "The U.S.—Decline or Renewal?" *Foreign Affairs*, Vol. 67, No. 2 (Winter 1988–89), pp. 76–96; and Joseph Nye, Jr., *Bound to Lead: The Changing Nature of American Power* (New York: Basic Books, 1990). Kennedy's response to the first wave of criticisms can be found in "Can the U.S. Remain Number One?" *New York Review of Books*, March 16, 1989, pp. 36–42. For the debate within early twentieth-century Great Britain on whether that country was still the strongest in Europe, see Aaron Friedberg, *The Weary Titan: Britain and the Experience of Relative Decline, 1895–1905* (Princeton: Princeton University Press, 1988).

International Security, Vol. 17, No. 4 (Spring 1993)
© 1993 by the President and Fellows of Harvard College and the Massachusetts Institute of Technology.

influence a broad range of issues and a large number of states. Furthermore, a state with primacy can establish, or at least strongly influence, "the rules of the game" by which international politics is played, the intellectual frameworks employed by many states, and the standards by which behavior is judged to be legitimate.[3] In the past, any state in this position could protect and benefit itself. But is the game still worth the candle?

As usual, Bernard Brodie put the key question well and, again as usual, Samuel Huntington cut to the heart of the matter with a clear and important statement, although one I believe to be incorrect. In explaining the continuing relevance of Clausewitz, Brodie uses as the title of the first chapter of his classic *War and Politics*[4] the question posed by Marshal Foch: "*De quoi s'agit-il?*"—what is it all about? Foch, Clausewitz, and Brodie were referring to the use of force in international politics, but it is now appropriate to apply the question more broadly. Most Realists would accept Lenin's answer, "*kto kovo*"—who-whom, meaning which state or class will dominate and which will be dominated. In parallel, when Huntington discusses why Americans are so concerned about growing Japanese economic power, he argues: "The United States is obsessed with Japan for the same reason that it was once obsessed with the Soviet Union. It sees that country as a major threat to its primacy in a crucial arena of power."[5] A related position is expressed in the Pentagon's draft Defense Planning Guidance for the Fiscal Years 1994–99:

Our first objective is to prevent the reemergence of a new rival, either on the territory of the former Soviet Union or elsewhere, that poses a threat on the order posed formerly by the Soviet Union. . . . [Aside from the former USSR,] there are other potential nations or coalitions that could, in the further future, develop strategic aims and a defense posture of region-wide or global

---

3. The notion of "meta-power" captures some of this: see T. Baumgartner and T.R. Burns, "The Structuring of International Economic Relations," *International Studies Quarterly*, Vol. 19, No. 2 (June 1975), pp. 126–159; and Stephen Krasner, *Structural Conflict: The Third World Against Global Liberalism* (Berkeley. University of California Press, 1985). For discussions of socialization, see Kenneth Waltz, *Theory of International Politics* (Reading, Mass.. Addison-Wesley, 1979), pp. 74–77; 127–28; G. John Ikenberry and Charles Kupchan, "Socialization and Hegemonic Power," *International Organization*, Vol. 44, No. 3 (Summer 1990), pp. 283–316.
4. Bernard Brodie, *War and Politics* (New York: Macmillian, 1973).
5. Samuel Huntington, "America's Changing Strategic Interests," *Survival*, Vol. 23, No. 1 (January/February 1991), p. 8. Also see Edward Luttwak, "From Geopolitics to Geo-Economics: Logic of Conflict, Grammar of Commerce," *National Interest*, No. 20 (Summer 1990), pp. 17–23; Edward Olsen, "Target Japan as America's Economic Foe," *Orbis*, Vol. 36, No. 4 (Fall 1992), pp. 491–504. For a reply to Olsen, see Edward Hudgins, "Japan's Prosperity Is Not a Danger," ibid., pp. 505–510.

domination. Our strategy must now refocus on precluding the emergence of any potential future global competitor.[6]

I do not think that Huntington, the Pentagon, or most of us have come to grips with Foch's question, which must provide the foundations for foreign policy. We need to ask what goals the United States seeks and whether they are likely to be menaced by the growing power of other states.[7]

Relative Versus Absolute Gains

Foreign policy debates tend to degenerate into assertion of preferences and unsupported predictions unless they are rooted in theories about how international politics works.[8] Many of the issues involved in whether the United States should seek primacy can be understood in terms of the importance of relative as contrasted with absolute gains. Arguments that the United States must beat back challenges for economic or political dominance are couched in terms of zero-sum competition and positional advantages. The claim is that, now as in the past, the anarchic nature of international politics requires states to be deeply concerned not only with how various policies and outcomes directly affect them, but also with the question of whether they are gaining more (or losing less) than others. Indeed, this is a fundamental postulate of Realism. "When faced with the possibility of cooperating for mutual gain, states that feel insecure must ask how the gain will be divided. They are compelled to ask not 'Will both of us gain?' but 'Who will gain more?'."[9] The reason is not envy or a mindless desire for status, but rather a preoccupation with power, which in most formulations has at least an element of comparison built into it. A state may then reasonably reject an arrangement that increases its territory and resources if others gain even more than it does. To the extent that economic advantage produces military

---

6. "Excerpts from Pentagon's Plan: 'Prevent the Re-Emergence of a New Rival'," *New York Times*, March 8, 1992, p. 14. Because this document was leaked to the press, public pressure led to a revision that apparently took a less controversial position; see Patrick Tyler, "Pentagon Drops Goal of Blocking New Superpowers," *New York Times*, May 24, 1992, pp. 1, 14. But it is not yet clear which document best represents the thrust of American policy.
7. For the purposes of this discussion, I will neglect the Russian nuclear threat to the United States.
8. A good discussion of this point along with useful examples can be found in Stephen Walt, "Alliance, Threats, and U.S. Grand Strategy," *Security Studies*, Vol. 1, No. 3 (Spring 1992), pp. 465–469.
9. Waltz, *Theory of International Politics*, p. 105.

strength or can be used to produce further gains, the same logic applies in this realm as well.[10]

PRIMACY, RELATIVE GAINS AND THE POSSIBILITY OF WAR
The importance of relative gains is obvious when war is a real possibility. In that case, the state must be concerned about how it will fare in an armed contest with its rivals and therefore will want to maximize its advantage over them—or at least be sure that it is not disadvantaged. In the current era, we need to begin by asking whether nuclear weapons, especially the possession of second-strike capability, have rendered this approach obsolete. It is no accident that Bernard Brodie and his colleagues titled their classic book written at the beginning of the atomic age *The Absolute Weapon:*[11] What mattered was that the state had the absolute ability to destroy the other, not the relative size of the two states' stockpiles. Of course the validity of this position is hotly contested in a debate that forms the backbone of arguments about alternative nuclear strategies. These issues matter now only if the United States needs to worry about the possibility of a war with another developed country. This is not out of the question: forms of Realism that stress the conflict-generating nature of the structure of the international system lead to the conclusion that cooperation among the western states was, in significant

---

10. The question of whether, and the conditions under which, states seek absolute or relative gains has received much attention recently: see, for example, Arthur Stein, "The Hegemon's Dilemma," *International Organization*, Vol. 38, No. 2 (Spring 1984), pp. 355–386; Stein, *Why Nations Cooperate: Circumstance and Choice in International Relations* (Ithaca: Cornell University Press, 1990), chapter 5; Joseph Grieco, "Anarchy and the Limits of Cooperation: A Realist Critique of the Newest Liberal Institutionalism," *International Organization*, Vol. 42, No. 3 (Summer 1988), pp. 485–508; Grieco, *Cooperation Among Nations: Europe, America, and Non-Tariff Barriers to Trade* (Ithaca: Cornell University Press, 1990); Robert Jervis, "Realism, Game Theory, and Cooperation," *World Politics*, Vol. 40, No. 3 (April 1988), pp. 334–336; Duncan Snidal, "Relative Gains and International Cooperation," *American Political Science Review*, Vol. 83, No. 3 (September 1991), pp. 701–726; Robert Powell, "Absolute and Relative Gains in International Relations Theory," *American Political Science Review*, Vol. 85, No. 4 (December 1991), pp. 1303–1320; Powell, "Intrinsic Ends and Instrumental Means in International Politics," *American Political Science Review*, forthcoming; Michael Mastanduno, "Do Relative Gains Matter? America's Response to Japanese Industrial Policy," *International Security*, Vol. 16, No. 1 (Summer 1991), pp. 73–113; Jonathan Tucker, "Partners and Rivals: A Model of International Collaboration in Advanced Technology," *International Organization*, Vol. 45, No. 1 (Winter 1991), pp. 83–120. The most recent contributions are Joseph Grieco, "Understanding the Problem of International Cooperation: The Limits of Neoliberal Institutionalism, and the Future of Realist Theory"; and Robert Keohane, "Institutionalist Theory and the Realist Challenge After the Cold War" in David Baldwin, ed., *Neorealism and Neoliberalism: The Contemporary Debate* (New York: Columbia University Press, forthcoming), which also reprints several of the articles cited above.
11. Bernard Brodie, et al., *The Absolute Weapon* (New York: Harcourt Brace, 1946).

measure, caused by the Cold War and may well disappear with the end of that era.[12] By contrast, more eclectic Realism that looks at the costs and benefits that war and its alternatives are likely to bring, as well as at changing national goals and outlooks, indicates that cooperation among the developed countries is likely to continue.[13] Although I have taken the latter position and argued that it is hard to imagine the rise of a conflict sufficiently severe to lead any developed country to believe that a war with one of its peers is an appropriate solution to its problems, Richard Betts issues an appropriate warning:

Major discontinuities in international relations are seldom predicted. Who would not have been derided and dismissed in 1988 for predicting that within a mere three years Eastern Europe would be liberated, the Communist Party of the Soviet Union deposed, and the Union itself on the ash heap of history? Yet it is hard to believe that the probability of equally revolutionary negative developments, of economic crisis and ideological disillusionment with democracy, of scapegoating and instability leading to miscalculation, escalation, and war several years from now is lower than the probability of the current peace seemed several years ago.[14]

Of course American policy can influence the chance of war. Some would argue that the United States can decrease the chance that others will develop dangerous ambitions and destabilizing fears by showing that it will do everything it can to maintain its primacy. This was the rationale for the recommendation in the Pentagon's draft Defense Guidance that the United States should seek to prevent other countries—including its current allies—from seeking to challenge its position. To this end, it is argued, the United States should be prepared not only to deter challengers, but also to protect many of their interests so that they do not need to greatly increase their own military forces.[15] But an American policy that stresses the possibility of great power wars and the concomitant continued importance of relative gains

---

12. John Mearsheimer, "Back to the Future: Instability in Europe After the Cold War," *International Security*, Vol. 15, No. 1 (Summer 1990), pp. 5–56.
13. John Mueller, *Retreat From Doomsday: The Obsolescence of Major War* (New York: Basic Books, 1989); Jervis, "The Future of World Politics: Will It Resemble the Past?" *International Security*, Vol. 16, No. 3 (Winter 1991/92), pp. 39–73.
14. Richard Betts, "Systems for Peace or Causes of War? Collective Security, Arms Control, and the New Europe," *International Security*, Vol. 17, No. 1 (Summer 1992), p. 14.
15. "Excerpts From Pentagon's Plan: 'Prevent the Re-Emergence of a New Rival'." The revised version of this document seems to have dropped the emphasis on deterrence but retained the discussion of protecting others' interests; Tyler, "Pentagon Drops Goal of Blocking New Superpowers."

might turn out to be a self-fulfilling prophecy that will make such wars more likely.[16]

Primacy Without Great Power War

At this point, however, the possibility of war is not the major reason for concern with relative gains. They also are sought if it is believed that they will lead to increased absolute gains in the future: positive feedback can be at work when states use competitive advantages to increase later benefits and when falling behind concomitantly would lead to greater distress later. While states, like individuals who are not influenced by envy, care only about costs and benefits to themselves, these can be influenced by the fates of others. To the extent that the future well-being of the United States is threatened by the success of others, it has to seek to prevent them from doing better (or less worse) than it does. (The other side of this coin is that conflict is generated as others will symmetrically seek relative gains of their own.) Even without fear of war, a state that was ultimately concerned only about the welfare of its citizens would have to be concerned about the growth rates of others if it believed that for others to grow faster than it (or to dominate certain industrial sectors) would lower the state's absolute level of well-being in the future. This result could come about through either the natural operation of the economic system or the other state's coercive policy. Thus some analysts argue that "the growth of Japanese economic power threatens American economic well-being,"[17] but whether this is in fact the case is far from clear. Recently the American economy has grown slowly and investment and productivity have lagged: simultaneously the Japanese economy has done quite well and the result has been the distress of a number of American industries. But whether Japan's success is the *cause* of America's problems has yet to be established. The implication that the United States would do better if Japan did worse is an unsubstantiated hypothesis. Eco-

---

16. This is a version of the familiar argument between proponents of deterrence theory and the spiral model of conflict: see Robert Jervis, *Perception and Misperception in International Politics* (Princeton: Princeton University Press, 1976), chapter 3. For a summary of the recent arguments in several arenas, see Paul Stern, et al., eds., *Perspectives on Deterrence* (New York: Oxford University Press, 1989). I suspect that those who think that war remains a real possibility also believe that an assertive American policy is more likely to prevent it, and that those who think that there is no longer much reason for developed states to fight each other are prone to worry that the American pursuit of primacy is not only wasteful, but might also be dangerous.
17. Huntington, "America's Changing Strategic Interests," p. 10.

nomic competition is not necessarily like military competition: gains on the part of a rival do not automatically make the state worse off.[18]

Strategic trade theory argues that those who start with a small advantage can reap much greater gains in the future if they can thereby move up the learning curve more rapidly than their competitors and therefore are able to keep the latter from challenging them. By protecting home markets and subsidizing exports, the state and industry can gain so great a lead over rivals that the state can later afford to remove the protectionist measures without sacrificing its dominance.[19] But there is only limited evidence on this point, and the models apply only under restricted conditions and may have little prescriptive value.[20]

Even when positive feedback is not at work, competition and a struggle for primacy are required for goods that are inherently positional. Status, prestige, and some kinds of self-images fit in this category.[21] Only one country can win the most medals in the Olympics; Americans may simply feel less good about themselves if the Japanese economy grows faster than the American one. If one country gains prestige, other countries have to lose it if the standard of judgment is comparative. The sense of being better or doing better than other countries may also produce self-confidence that helps convince leaders, elites, and the general public to take on important and difficult international tasks. Would the United States have sent forces to Somalia if its citizens (and, even more, its president) had not felt that it was

---

18. Paul Krugman, "Myths and Realities of U.S. Competitiveness," *Science*, Vol. 254 (November 1991), pp. 811–815.

19. The literature on strategic trade theory is large: see, for example, Paul Krugman, *Strategic Trade Policy and the New International Economics* (Cambridge: MIT Press, 1986); Klaus Stegemann, "Policy Rivalry Among Industrial States: What Can We Learn from Models of Strategic Trade Policy?" *International Organization*, Vol. 43, No. 1 (Winter 1989), pp. 73–100; Helen Milner and David Yoffie, "Between Free Trade and Protectionism: Strategic Trade Policy and the Theory of Corporate Trade Demand," *International Organization*, Vol. 43, No. 2 (Spring 1989), pp. 239–272. A similar argument was made a generation ago in E.J. Hobsbawm, *Industry and Empire: The Making of Modern English Society*, Vol. 2: *1750 to the Present Day* (New York: Pantheon, 1968).

20. Some limitations on the theory are explained by Paul Krugman, "Introduction: New Thinking about Trade Policy," in Krugman, ed., *Strategic Trade Policy and the New International Economics* (Cambridge: MIT Press, 1986), pp. 14–20; for a critique see Gene Grossman, "Strategic Export Promotion: A Critique," in Krugman, ed., *Strategic Trade Policy and the New International Economics*, chapter 3. For a reaffirmation of the value of the theory and its applicability, see J. David Richardson, "'New' Trade Theory and Policy a Decade Old: Assessment in a Pacific Context," in John Ravenhill, ed., *Pacific Economic Relations in the 1990s* (New York: Columbia University Press, forthcoming).

21. For a superb study of positional goods, see Fred Hirsch, *The Social Limits to Growth* (Cambridge: Harvard University Press, 1976).

the prime if not dominant state in world politics? These considerations are elusive, but they may play a role in establishing national moods which influence behavior.[22]

For further discussion, we can usefully separate arguments about the importance of primacy that focus on conflict from those that stress the need for cooperation. That is, the most obvious line of argument is that the United States needs to maintain its dominant position because there are important conflicts of interest between it and other developed countries. But a different chain of reasoning sees the main problem not as others gaining at America's expense, but as the need to provide public or collective goods. In this view, it is still important for the United States to maintain primacy, but doing so is in the interests of other developed countries as well.

COMPETITIVE REASONS FOR SEEKING PRIMACY

If statesmen expect peace among the developed countries, what are the competitive reasons for seeking primacy? What does the United States want that brings it into conflict with others? The wording of the draft Defense Guidance was interesting: "Our first objective is to prevent the re-emergence of a new rival . . . *that poses a threat on the order of that posed formerly by the Soviet Union. This* . . . requires that we endeavor to prevent any *hostile* power from dominating a region whose resources would, under consolidated control, be sufficient to generate global power."[23] Realism that is based on structural considerations and that assumes a constant struggle for power would not need the emphasized phrases because *any* rival would be seen as posing a serious threat. But it is far from clear that this is an accurate view of the world. We can make the question concrete by asking whether it is in the American interest for Europe to unite. If this were to occur, the new entity would be at least as strong as the United States by almost all indicators of power. It is not surprising that the United States encouraged a high degree of European unity during the Cold War in order to strengthen the anti-Soviet coalition, but, contrary to what should be the case if there were strong

---

22. See, for example, Robert Dallek, *The American Style of Foreign Policy: Cultural Politics and Foreign Affairs* (New York: Knopf, 1983). Discussion of national mood is often linked to arguments about cycles: see Frank Klingberg, "The Historical Alternation of Moods in American Foreign Policy," *World Politics*, Vol. 4, No. 2 (January 1952), pp. 239–273; Klingberg, *Cyclical Trends in American Foreign Policy Moods: The Unfolding of America's World Role* (Lanham, Md.: University Press of America, 1983); Arthur Schlesinger, Jr., *The Cycles of American History* (Boston: Houghton Mifflin, 1986), chapters 2–3.
23. "Excerpts From Pentagon's Plan: 'Prevent the Re-Emergence of a New Rival'."

competitive reasons for the United States to maintain primacy, this attitude has continued. Although some have voiced concern that American firms might suffer because tariffs on American goods will remain while those within Europe would disappear, few have seen dire international political consequences in the rise of what would clearly be another superpower. To the contrary, it appears that most Americans believe that a united Europe would both increase world-wide prosperity and constitute an entity that will cooperate effectively with the United States to reach common goals.

One can argue that increased European power will be dangerous because throughout the Cold War the Europeans were less willing than the United States to sacrifice commercial gain for generally shared political objectives—for example, European countries did little to restrain their firms from selling materials that would enable other countries to develop nuclear and chemical weapons and associated delivery systems. But this difference in behavior may have stemmed in part from the fact that the European states were small enough to be "free riders" and take advantage of the American willingness to bear a disproportionate share of the non-proliferation burden. A united Europe would presumably play a larger role in world politics and therefore might be more responsible on these issues. Similarly, Japanese behavior, both diplomatic and economic, may well change as its influence increases. Although not all countries use their power for the same ends, in part because of differences in values and domestic systems (if Hitler had won World War II, it is unlikely that the Nazi hegemony would have produced an open economic system), we should not exaggerate the difference between Japanese and Western trading practices or neglect the extent to which growing trade and investment abroad will change behavior.[24]

Where disagreements stem from differences in values, interests, or beliefs rather than different placements in the structure of the international system, American preferences will suffer as others grow stronger. For example, the Europeans have traditionally been more "even-handed" (or, from a different perspective, more "pro-Arab") in Middle Eastern issues than has the United States. Whether this is due to Europe's greater reliance on Arab oil, its closer ties to the Arab world, lack of a strong pro-Israeli lobby, or different views of the merits of the case (or some combination of these) cannot be readily determined. Although the American position has changed some in recent

---

24. On the latter point, see Richard Rosecrance and Jennifer Taw, "Japan and the Theory of Leadership," *World Politics*, Vol. 42, No. 2 (January 1990), pp. 184–209.

years, the difference in policy has not disappeared and a stronger Europe could therefore more effectively present a policy that conflicted with the American one. Surely other policy differences will arise in the future as well. Thus September 1992 saw German-American disputes over interest rates, rescheduling of the debts of the former Soviet Union, and the possibility of a permanent seat on the Security Council for Germany.[25] Shortly thereafter, the United States and Europe engaged in a game of Chicken over agriculture that nearly led to a trade war. Issues like these are likely to be staples of future international politics among developed countries. But there does not seem to be any reason to expect them to concern central values or to lead either Europe or the United States to regret that the other is a major power or to seek to weaken the other. Although each state will want to have significant bargaining resources and leverage over others in order to protect and further its interests, the stakes and the intensity of the competition will be much lower than was the case when international politics was infused with deep concerns for survival and security.

Perhaps American primacy would bring with it major economic advantages. In part, this raises the question of the fungibility of power, which may have a different answer in a world of decreased security concerns than it did during the Cold War. Under many circumstances political power can contribute to economic goals. Indeed, in the event of major international conflict, a weaker country may not be able to maintain its desired economic and domestic system in the face of pressure, let alone out-right attack, by a stronger rival. No one expects Japan or Europe to present this kind of pressure to the United States, nor is anyone recommending that the United States try to develop sufficient military and political power that it could use threats to extort economic benefit from its allies. But during the Cold War, there seem to have been implicit bargains between the United States and its allies that involved trade-offs between security and economic issues, and related arrangements might still be possible.[26] Perhaps the United States could turn military and diplomatic resources into economic benefits by either coercing others or performing services for them for which it would receive payment. Convincing others to pay for military ventures might be possible,

---

25. Keith Bradsher, "Talks on Rescheduling Moscow's Debt Pits U.S. and Russia Against Germany," *New York Times,* September 21, 1992; Paul Lewis, "Germany Tells U.N. It Wants a Permanent Seat on the Council," *New York Times,* September 23, 1992.
26. The classic article is Robert Gilpin, "The Politics of Transnational Economic Relations," *International Organization,* Vol. 25, No. 3 (Summer 1971), pp. 398–419.

but even in the Gulf War the United States did little more than break even. It seems unlikely that in a world of low security threats and great common interests among the developed countries, the route to economic strength for the United States would lie through gaining significant unilateral military and political advantage over Europe and Japan.

NON-COMPETITIVE REASONS FOR PRIMACY

Even if there are few competitive reasons to seek primacy, there may be cooperative ones. Here, the problem is not that the United States needs to be number one, as much as it is that some state has to fill this role in order to provide general or public goods.[27] It may be true that the other developed countries share with the United States the most important foreign policy goals—e.g., the maintenance of an open economic system, non-proliferation of nuclear weapons, fostering human rights, deterring aggression, protecting the environment—but pursuing these goals involves significant costs and if power is distributed relatively equally among many countries, no one of them will have the incentives to make the effort that is necessary to reach these goals. In principle, a country that not only increased its power relative to that of the United States but surpassed it could provide the leadership that would be in the common interest. But even a fully united Europe could not do this for decades. Thus the result of other states gaining power at the expense of the United States would not be that any of them would become the leading state, but that power would become diffused.

Increased diffusion of power may not mean that the problems of organizing the international system for collective action will be much greater than they have been in the recent past, however. Just as it is important not to exaggerate the decline of American power,[28] so it is also important to remember that even at its height America could only bargain with other developed countries, not dictate to them. Furthermore, even if Japan and Europe grow faster than the United States in economic strength and diplomatic influence, the change from the current situation will be slow and, by most scales, slight. The collective goods problem would indeed be very great if we were moving

27. This is the argument of the cooperative or benign form of hegemonic stability theory, well represented by Charles Kindleberger, *The World in Depression, 1929–1939* (Berkeley: University of California Press, 1973).
28. Bruce Russett, "The Mysterious Case of Vanishing Hegemony; Or, Is Mark Twain Really Dead?" *International Organization*, Vol. 39, No. 2 (Spring 1985), pp. 207–232; Huntington, "The U.S.: Decline or Renewal?"

from a situation in which one country was dominant to one in which power was evenly spread over ten or fifteen states. But this is not the case. There are only a few powerful and highly developed countries. We are not confronting the classic problem in which every actor is so small that it knows that its behavior will not make a noticeable difference in whether collective goods are provided or not. To the contrary, each knows that a refusal to do its share can undermine the system and, in so doing, endanger its own welfare. Cooperation of course is not guaranteed, but at least is possible.[29]

In the economic arena it is often argued that the end of American primacy and the continued diffusion of power will lead to the division of the world into three trading blocs—a group in Asia dominated by Japan, a Europe dominated by Germany, and the Americas under U.S. hegemony.[30] These fears arose even before the collapse of the Soviet Union and the end of the Cold War removed some of the inhibitions restraining states from moving toward the formation of blocs. Without dismissing these concerns, I think two points are warranted. First, no amount of American effort, hard bargaining with its trading partners, or domestic growth will return the United States to the position of economic dominance it held in the 1950s. If a world of trading blocs is to be avoided, it will have to be through negotiations and shared understandings among states of relatively equal resources. Second, the fact that the fears of widespread protectionism are by now longstanding gives us some grounds for optimism since previous predictions of economic closure have not been borne out. Most countries see this path as undesirable and are willing to pay a significant price to block it. There is a good chance they will do so; not only is the number of major states sufficiently small that the pessimistic framework of collective goods does not apply, but those who engage in protectionism may suffer retaliation rather than gaining a free ride, thereby increasing the chances of cooperation.[31]

---

29. The literature on cooperation in situations that approximate a Prisoner's Dilemma is vast: see, for example, Kenneth Oye, ed., *Cooperation Under Anarchy* (Princeton: Princeton University Press, 1985); Robert Jervis, "Realism, Game Theory, and Cooperation," pp. 317–349.

30. For a discussion of this possibility, see Robert Gilpin, *The Political Economy of International Relations* (Princeton: Princeton University Press, 1987), pp. 397–406.

31. John Conybeare, "Public Goods, Prisoners' Dilemma, and the International Political Economy," *International Studies Quarterly*, Vol. 28, No. 1 (March 1984), pp. 5–22; for an argument to the contrary, see Joanne Gowa, "Rational Hegemons, Excludable Goods, and Small Groups: An Epitaph For Hegemonic Stability Theory?" *World Politics*, Vol. 41, No. 3 (April 1989), pp. 307–324. For further arguments that the diffusion of power is compatible with a high degree of international economic cooperation, see David Lake, *Power, Protection, and Free Trade: International Sources of U.S. Commercial Strategy, 1887–1939* (Ithaca: Cornell University Press, 1988); Helen

Problems of reaching common goals of course also arise on political questions. If the United States does not take the lead, nuclear weapons may spread more rapidly because no one will restrain the sales of nuclear materials and because countries throughout the world will have greater fears for their security—and greater hopes for coercing others. If the United States does not lead a coalition to block aggression, the world may become much more insecure and war-prone. Proponents of these arguments point to the fact that aggression was punished and reversed in the Gulf under U.S. leadership, but not in Yugoslavia when the United States, rather than firmly taking the lead, largely left it to the Europeans. Indeed, the strongest international measures to contain Serbia—first the economic embargo and then the prohibition of flights over Bosnia—were taken only on the American initiative. Furthermore, no country other than the United States was willing and able to move into the chaos of Somalia. As President Bush said when explaining why he was sending in 28,000 troops to enable food to be distributed, "I understand the United States alone cannot right the world's wrongs, but. . . . only the United States has the global reach to place a large security force on the ground in such a distant place quickly and efficiently and thus save thousands of innocents from death."[32]

A related argument is that the United States needs to maintain world order to discourage others from believing that the only way they can protect their own interests is by increasing their power. Thus the draft Defense Guidance argues:

The U.S. must show the leadership necessary to establish and protect a new order that holds the promise of convincing potential competitors that they need not aspire to a greater role or pursue a more aggressive posture to protect their legitimate interests. . . . [The U.S.] will retain the pre-eminent responsibility for addressing selectively those wrongs which threaten not only our interests, but those of our allies or friends.[33]

Milner, *Resisting Protectionism: Global Industries and the Politics of International Trade* (Princeton: Princeton University Press, 1988); Richard Rosecrance, "The Prospect of World Economic Conflict: Implications for the Global System and for Europe," in Beverly Crawford, ed., *The Future of European Security* (Berkeley: University of California at Berkeley International and Area Studies Research Series, No. 84, 1992), pp. 122–151. The argument can be traced to the discussion of k-groups in Thomas Schelling, *Micromotives and Microbehavior* (New York: Norton, 1978), chapter 7.

32. "Transcript of President's Address on Somalia," *New York Times*, December 5, 1992, p. 4.

33. "Excerpts From Pentagon's Plan: 'Prevent the Re-Emergence of a New Rival'."

There is a good deal to this argument that American primacy is needed to maintain international cooperation for common goals, but it is not entirely convincing. First, the difference between the Gulf and Yugoslavia is not entirely to be explained by differences in American behavior. Or, to put it slightly differently, differences in American behavior were in part the product of differences in expectations about how others would behave.[34] Second, the exercise of strong leadership may be self-limiting if others resent the American role. Maintaining the Gulf War coalition was a marvelous feat of diplomacy and many other countries presumably feel they benefited by letting the United States set the policy. But they may have been disturbed and resentful as well because they did not have much influence; they might be less willing to be junior partners in future endeavors. Third, even if the United States remains the leading world power, it may not have sufficient resources to provide public goods. The United States will never regain the position it held in the 1950s and 1960s. In the political as in the economic arena, even if the diffusion of power is arrested, it is not likely to be reversed.

But cooperative action is still possible: the number of leading states is small, the conflicts among them are not enormous, and the contribution made by each is large enough to have a significant impact on the outcome. Concerts have provided a significant measure of security in the past, and the conditions for establishing related arrangements are propitious: the developed countries have relatively little to gain by exploiting each other, and much to lose if mutual cooperation breaks down.[35] A decrease in the American ability to reach many common goals through its own efforts would not necessarily mean that such goals would not be reached. Contrary to President Bush's claim, the size of the force required for Somalia in December 1992 was not beyond the reach of the NATO allies, either singly or acting together, especially if the United States provided logistical support. Indeed, the United

---

34. For a discussion of followership, see Andrew Cooper, Richard Higgott, and Kim Nossal, "Bound to Follow? Leadership and Followership in the Gulf Conflict," *Political Science Quarterly,* Vol. 106, No. 3 (Fall 1991), pp. 391–410.

35. For discussions of the Concert, how it functioned historically, the conditions that produced it, and how a concert might function in the future, see Richard Elrod, "The Concert of Europe: A Fresh Look at an International System," *World Politics,* Vol. 28, No. 2 (January 1976), pp. 159–174; Paul Schroeder, "The 19th-Century International System: Changes in Structure," *World Politics,* Vol. 39, No. 1 (October 1986), pp. 1–26; Robert Jervis, "Security Regimes," *International Organization,* Vol. 36, No. 2 (Spring 1982), pp. 362–368; Jervis, "From Balance to Concert: A Study of International Security Cooperation," *World Politics,* Vol. 38, No. 1 (October 1985), pp. 58–79; Charles Kupchan and Clifford Kupchan, "Concerts, Collective Security, and the Future of Europe," *International Security,* Vol. 16, No. 1 (Summer 1991), pp. 114–161.

States may benefit if it cannot do the job on its own. As long as cases in which it would want to intervene on a large scale also deeply involve the interests of other developed states as well,[36] the costs, responsibilities, and decisions also can be shared. If it is only the United States that believes intervention is necessary and if the other developed countries disagree, a distribution of power that precludes American action might not, on average, serve it badly: the American judgment in cases like this may be no better than the judgment of others. Furthermore, if intervention were possible only if it were truly joint, then other developed countries could not avoid the question of what sort of "world order" is worth seeking; they could not rely on pious pronouncements and the expectations of a division of labor whereby the United States takes the bulk of the responsibility, risk, and cost while they share in the benefit.

We should also not forget the admonition of balance of power theory that even the most benign state cannot be trusted with excessive power. Both Edmund Burke and François Fénélon, a French thinker of the late seventeenth century, argue that even with good values and moderate domestic politics, a state will behave with moderation and decency only if it is checked by others.[37] Kenneth Waltz draws the important conclusion about what will follow from the destruction of Soviet power: "Despite good intentions, the United States will often act in accordance with Fénélon's theorem."[38] Binding itself to act multilaterally by forgoing the capability to use large-scale force on its own would then provide a safeguard against the excessive use of American power. This might benefit all concerned: the United States would not be able to act on its own worst impulses; others would share the costs of interventions and would also be less fearful of the United States and so, perhaps, more prone to cooperate with it.

In summary, the pursuit of primacy was what great power politics was all about in the past. But with the development of nuclear weapons, the spread of liberal democracy to all the developed countries, and the diminution of nationalism, war among the most powerful actors is unlikely. The first reason

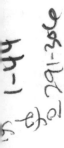

ada and Panama did not involve the interests of allies, but the military forces
ture needed to intervene there were not large.
, "Remarks on the Policy of the Allies With Respect to France," *Works*, Vol.
own, 1899), p. 457; Herbert Butterfield, "The Balance of Power," in Herbert
rtin Wight, eds., *Diplomatic Investigations* (Cambridge: Harvard University

, "America as a Model for the World? A Foreign Policy Perspective," *PS:
Politics*, Vol. 24, No. 4 (December 1991), p. 699.

for striving for international primacy has then disappeared. Other reasons, both competitive and cooperative, seem weak, although the latter are stronger than the former. The United States might be able to recreate some of the unfortunate but necessary patterns from the past by behaving as though nothing has changed. But it is not forced down this path by the international environment.

Why International Primacy Matters

Samuel P. Huntington

$\mathbf{D}$oes international primacy matter? The answer seems so obvious that one first wonders why someone as intelligent, perceptive, and knowledgeable as Robert Jervis raises the question. On further thought, however, one sees that while the answer may be obvious for most people, the reasons why it is obvious may not be all that clear and may have been forgotten or lost in the other concerns of political scientists and economists studying international relations. By posing this question at this time of change in world affairs Jervis has constructively forced us to rethink why primacy is of central importance. This issue involves several subordinate questions.

Primacy in What?

First, what do we mean by primacy? Primacy in what? Politics is concerned with primacy in power. In international politics power is the ability of one actor, usually but not always a government, to influence the behavior of others, who may or may not be governments. International primacy means that a government is able to exercise more influence on the behavior of more actors with respect to more issues than any other government can. Or, as Lasswell and Kaplan put it in their classic formulation, the amount of power an actor possesses is a function of weight (degree of participation in decision-making), scope (the values that are influenced), and domain (the people who are influenced).[1]

To ask whether primacy matters is to ask whether power matters. And the answer can only be: of course, it matters in most human relationships, even in families, and it obviously matters in national and international affairs. It does make a difference whether one party, politician, branch of government, interest group, public official, or national government has more or less power

Samuel P. Huntington is Eaton Professor of the Science of Government at Harvard University, where he is Director of the John M. Olin Institute for Strategic Studies. His most recent book is The Third Wave: Democratization in the Late Twentieth Century (University of Oklahoma Press, 1991), for which he received the Grawemeyer Award.

1. Harold D. Lasswell and Abraham Kaplan, *Power and Society: A Framework for Political Inquiry* (New Haven: Yale University Press, 1950), p. 77.

International Security, Vol. 17, No. 4 (Spring 1993)
© 1993 by the President and Fellows of Harvard College and the Massachusetts Institute of Technology.

than another. It mattered to a hundred million American voters whether George Bush or Bill Clinton or Ross Perot has primacy in shaping decisions affecting the United States. It matters to hundreds of millions of people throughout the world whether the United States, Japan, Germany, Europe, Russia, China, or some other entity has primacy in shaping decisions affecting the world. Political science is, indeed, the study of why, how, and with what consequences people get and exercise power in major collective entities. If power and primacy did not matter, political scientists would have to look for other work.

Those who are skeptical concerning the value of primacy often approach the issue in terms of relative and absolute gains. The argument is that, given a choice, Actor A should prefer to achieve a gain of x even though Actor B is scoring a gain of $x + y$, rather than achieving a gain of $x - y$ while Actor B is scoring a gain of $x - 2y$. The crucial issue, however, in the debate of absolute versus relative gains is: gain in what? Whether absolute or relative gains are to be preferred depends on the values at stake. If it is gains in health, Actor A probably will prefer a gain of x as against a gain of $x - y$, no matter what health gains Actor B may be achieving. With respect to wealth, in some circumstances actors may prefer absolute gains and in others relative gains. In Olympic competitions, probably most athletes would prefer to run the 1,000 meters in time t and win a gold medal than to run it in time $t - y$ if another athlete was making off with the gold by running it in time $t - 2y$. With respect to power, however, absolute gains are meaningless. An actor gains or loses power compared to other people. Since it concerns the ability of people to influence each other, power is only relative. Lord Acton and others may have talked about "absolute power," but they do not mean absolute in the meaning it has in the term absolute gains. Absolute power itself is relative: it means that relative to other actors, Actor A monopolizes decision-making on all issues concerning all people in a given universe. International primacy means a state has more power than other actors and hence primacy is inherently relative.

Even if power is relative, the question remains: Why do people want power? A variety of motives are possible. The contest for power itself may be satisfying and enjoyable. So also may be the exercise of power once it is acquired. To be powerful and to be viewed by others as such surely enhances the self-esteem of individuals and nations. Power enables an actor to shape his environment so as to reflect his interests. In particular it enables a state to protect its security and prevent, deflect, or defeat threats to that security.

It also enables a state to promote its values among other peoples and to shape the international environment so as to reflect its values. States and other actors who are powerful can, and do, do evil. But power is also the prerequisite to doing good and promoting collective goods. Almost nothing beneficial in the world happens except by the exercise of power.

Is History Ending?

It is a fact well-known since Thucydides that it matters which state exercises the most power in the international system. At no time in history has this been more true than in the twentieth century: one has only to consider what the world would have looked like if Nazi Germany had won World War II or the Soviet Union won the Cold War.[2] No reason exists to assume that what has been true for millennia will cease to be true in the next hundred years.

Does it matter to the United States or the world that American primacy be maintained? Obviously that depends on what the alternative distributions of power might be. Logically there are two other possibilities. Some other state could displace the United States as the only superpower in the world, or there could be a condition in which no state was in a position of international primacy and there was a rough equilibrium of power among the major states. Would either of these situations be more desirable for the United States or for the world than the maintenance of U.S. primacy?

It is quite erroneous to think that the principal reason states pursue international primacy is to be able to win wars, and that hence if war is unlikely primacy is unimportant. States pursue primacy in order to be able to insure their security, promote their interests, and shape the international environment in ways that will reflect their interests and values. Primacy is desirable not primarily to achieve victory in war but to achieve the state's goals without recourse to war. Primacy is thus an alternative to war. A state such as the United States that has achieved international primacy has every reason to attempt to maintain that primacy through peaceful means so as to preclude the need of having to fight a war to maintain it.

---

2. For an imaginative and quite persuasive picture (which could not be published in Germany) of what a Nazi victory would have meant, and also for a good read, see Richard Harris, *Fatherland* (New York: Random House, 1992). For a brilliant discussion of this book, see Josef Joffe, "The Mother of All Fatherlands," *The National Interest*, No. 29 (Fall 1992), pp. 85–88.

Some argue that the end of the Cold War means the end of history as we have known it. Unfortunately every day's newspaper contains dramatic and tragic evidence that the end of the Cold War means the return to history as we used to know it. Conflicts among nations and ethnic groups are escalating. Controversies are intensifying between the United States and other major powers. This is to be expected. The end of a significant war or conflict, whether among individuals, groups, or states, creates the basis for the generation of new conflicts. The end of war leads to the breakup of the coalition of powers fighting the war. There is no reason why the end of the Cold War should have any different consequences. The alliances of the United States with Japan and with the Western European countries in NATO rested on three fundamentals: shared political and economic values; common economic interests; and the Soviet security threat. Without the last of these three, the alliances would never have come into existence. Now, however, the Soviet threat is gone, and common economic interests are giving way to competing economic interests. Shared political and economic values remain the principal glue holding together the grand alliances of the Cold War. Those common values are real, and they mean that wars are most unlikely between these countries.[3] They do not mean that these countries will have shared or even congruent interests. Instead the disappearance of the common enemy means that conflicting interests that were subordinated to the common need to unite against the Soviet security threat during the Cold War will now emerge with a vengeance. This is not likely to lead to the physical mayhem that occurred in Bosnia, but it will lead to intense conflicts over political and economic interests. Competition—the struggle for primacy—we all recognize as natural among individuals, corporations, political parties, athletes, and universities; it is no less natural among countries.

Does Economic Primacy Matter?

In the coming years, the principal conflicts of interests involving the United States and the major powers are likely to be over economic issues. U.S. economic primacy is now being challenged by Japan and is likely to be challenged in the future by Europe. Obviously the United States, Japan, and

---

3. Michael N. Doyle, "Liberalism and World Politics,"*American Political Science Review*, Vol. 80, No. 4 (December 1986), pp. 1151–1169; and Doyle, "Kant, Liberal Legacies, and Foreign Affairs," *Philosophy and Public Affairs*, Vol. 12 (Summer/Fall 1983), pp. 205–235, 323, 353.

Europe have common interests in promoting economic development and international trade. They also, however, have deeply conflicting interests over the distribution of the benefits and costs of economic growth and the distribution of the costs of economic stagnation or decline. The idea that economics is primarily a non-zero-sum game is a favorite conceit of tenured academics. It has little connection to reality. In the course of the economic competition that may produce economic growth, companies go bankrupt; bankers forfeit their investments; factories are closed; managers and workers lose their jobs; money, wealth, well-being, and power are shifted from one industry, region, or country to another.

Economists argue that in economic competition what counts are absolute not relative gains; to economists this is a self-evident truth. It is, however, self-evident to almost no one but economists. The American public as a whole, various groups in American society, and the leaders and publics in other societies do not buy it for a moment.[4] Why are the economists out in left field? They are there because they are blind to the fact that economic activity is a source of power as well as well-being. It is, indeed, probably the most important source of power, and in a world in which military conflict between major states is unlikely, economic power will be increasingly important in determining the primacy or subordination of states. Precisely for this reason Americans have every reason to be concerned by the current challenge to American economic primacy posed by Japan and the possible future challenge that could come from Europe.

The threat to American economic primacy from Japan is serious because Japanese policy makes it serious. Since the 1950s Japan has pursued a strategy designed not to promote Japanese economic welfare but to maximize Japanese economic power. For decades Japan has acted in a way totally consistent with the "realist" theory of international relations, which holds that international politics is basically anarchic and that to insure their security states act to maximize their power.[5] Realist theorists have focused overwhelmingly on military power. Japan has accepted all the assumptions of realism but applied them purely in the economic realm. Abjuring military power, it has acted precisely as realist theory would predict in the pursuit of economic

---

4. See, e.g., Michael Mastanduno, "Do Relative Gains Matter? America's Response to Japanese Industrial Policy," *International Security*, Vol. 16, No. 1 (Summer 1991), pp. 73–74.
5. Here and a few other places in this essay, I draw on my "America's Changing Strategic Interests," *Survival*, Vol. 33 (January/February 1991), pp. 3–7; and "The Economic Renewal of America," *The National Interest*, No. 28 (Spring 1992), pp. 14–18.

power. In the realm of military competition, the instruments of power are missiles, planes, warships, bombs, tanks, divisions. In the realm of economic competition, the instruments of power are productive efficiency, market control, trade surplus, strong currency, foreign exchange reserves, ownership of foreign companies, factories, and technology. These are the objectives that Japan has unremittingly pursued.

The Japanese strategy of economic power maximization has had several components:

PRODUCER DOMINANCE

Japanese strategy has given producer interests total priority over consumer interests. Among the industrialized democracies Japan is unique in the extent to which it gives priority to economic power over economic well-being. This outcome is the result of conscious decisions made by Japanese policymakers in the 1950s. In 1954 private consumption accounted for 66.2 percent of the Japanese GNP and 63.5 percent of the U.S. GNP. In 1971 the U.S. percentage was virtually the same, 62.7 percent. Japanese private consumption, in contrast, had been driven down to 53.5 percent of GNP. Japanese investment, on the other hand, rose from 23.5 percent of GNP in 1954 to 35.8 percent in 1971.[6] This reduction in the proportion of GNP devoted to consumption was comparable in scale to that which Stalin imposed on the Soviet Union between the late 1920s and late 1930s during the five-year plans and the massive industrialization drive.

INDUSTRY TARGETING

The Japanese government has consistently pursued a systematic strategy of targeting particular industries for development first for the home market and then for foreign markets. After World War II, as the U.S. Office of Technology Assessment put it, "policymakers felt that Japan should be strong in manufacturing iron and steel, ships, machinery, heavy electrical equipment, and chemicals. Later, the automobile, petrochemical, nuclear power, computer and semiconductor, and aircraft industries were added to the list." As the list suggests, this strategy has involved an increasingly successful "unrelenting emphasis" on "strategic, high-technology, high-value-added industries."

---

6. Thomas K. McCraw, "From Partners to Competitors: An Overview of the Period Since World War II," in McCraw, ed., *America versus Japan* (Boston: Harvard Business School Press, 1986), pp. 2–3.

The purpose of these policies, according to the Ministry of International Trade and Industry, is to enhance Japan's "autonomy and bargaining power."[7]

MARKET SHARES

Japanese corporations rate the expansion of market share higher than profit or other objectives. They overexpand their production capability in order to achieve this goal: "Deliberate investment in losses for the sake of ultimate domination of an industry is one of the characteristics of Japan's headquarters strategy."[8] Japanese strategy, in short, is to pursue *relative* gains in terms of market shares, rather than *absolute* gains in terms of profits. While Japanese firms accept lower profits in order to increase market shares, American firms increase prices in order to increase profits at the expense of market shares.[9] Japanese shareholders as well as Japanese consumers thus pay the costs of the Japanese pursuit of economic power.

IMPORT RESTRICTION

Aggressive support for Japanese firms in targeted industries plus the pursuit of market share by those firms are the key offensive elements in Japanese economic strategy. The central defensive elements of its strategy are the restriction of both imports of goods to Japan and foreign direct investment in Japan. By any measure, Japanese imports, apart from primary products, are extremely small compared to those of the other industrialized democracies. "Japan's pattern of trade on imports," as one careful 1990 study concluded, "has been and remains very peculiar when compared to with those of other countries—a peculiarity that cannot be explained through standard economic factors. Japan does indeed exhibit an aversion to manufactured imports and avoids the two-way trade in many manufactured products that characterizes the international trade of other nations."[10]

---

7. Office of Technology Assessment, *Competing Economies: America, Europe, and the Pacific Rim* (Washington, D.C.: U.S. GPO, October 1991), p. 9; William S. Dietrich, *In the Shadow of the Rising Sun* (University Park: Pennsylvania State University Press, 1991), p. 63; Clyde V. Prestowicz, Jr., *Trading Places* (New York: Basic Books, 1988), pp. 125, 131ff.

8. Leon Hollerman, "The Headquarters Nation," *The National Interest*, No. 25 (Fall 1991), pp. 22–23.

9. *The International Economy*, Vol. 5 (March-April 1991), p. 8; Shin'ichi Yamamoto, "Japan's Trade Lead: Blame Profit-Hungry American Firms," *Brookings Review*, Vol. 8 (Winter 1989–90), p. 18.

10. Edward J. Lincoln, *Japan's Unequal Trade* (Washington, D.C.: Brookings Institution, 1990), pp. 2–3; International Institute for Global Peace, *Containing Global Frictions: Creating a Common Economic Foundation*, Policy Paper 55E (Tokyo: IIGP, June 1991), p. 2; James Fallows, "Playing

SUSTAINED SURPLUS

The goal and the effect of Japan's economic power maximization strategy has been to create sustained trade surpluses, which have defied all efforts by the international economic community to reduce them. The classic economic correction measures which have reduced the U.S. deficit with Europe have not worked with Japan. The maintenance of this surplus both generally and particularly with respect to the United States creates the economic capabilities by which Japan exercises power in relation to other countries. The sustained surplus provides the wherewithal for the purchase of facilities, property, companies, technology, lobbies, research institutes, opinion leaders, and politicians, all of which and of whom could serve Japanese interests. The goal of a power maximization strategy is to counter the effects of economic forces and to maintain both a strong currency *and* a trade surplus. Japan has done just that.

Sophisticated analysts such as Joseph Nye argue that Japanese-American "economic competition can leave both sides better off, albeit not in every case and sometimes with considerable stresses." Hence it is "inappropriate" to speak of an "economic cold war" between the two countries.[11] It takes only one side, however, to produce a cold war. Japanese strategy is a strategy of economic warfare. Japanese leaders regularly assert that economic competition is central to the relations among nations, that Japan must prevail in this competition, and that Japan is, indeed, prevailing in the competition. As usual, Shintaro Ishihara put it most bluntly: "Economic warfare is the basis for existence in the free world . . . . The twenty-first century will be a century of economic warfare . . . . There is no hope for the United States." These views are not limited to populist Japanese politicians. They are widely shared by members of the Japanese elite and public. "We are going to have *a totally new configuration in the balance of power in the world,*" argued Akio Morita. "The time will never again come when America will regain its strength in industry."[12] Japan, its ambassador-to-be to the United States said

---

by Different Rules," *Atlantic Monthly*, Vol. 260 (September 1987), p. 28; and "The Real Japan," *New York Review of Books*, July 20, 1989, p. 27; *The International Economy*, Vol. 4 (June/July 1990), p. 9.
11. Joseph S. Nye, Jr., "Coping with Japan," *Foreign Policy*, No. 89 (Winter 1992–93), pp. 97, 115.
12. Shintaro Ishihara and Akio Morita, quoted by Flora Lewis, "Japan's Looking Glass", *New York Times*, November 8, 1989, p. A31 (emphasis added).

in 1985, is "rapidly overtaking" the United States in economic and technological strength.[13] "The Asian economic zone," Kiichi Miyazawa said, shortly
before becoming prime minister, "will outdo the North American economic
zone and European economic zone at the beginning of the twenty-first century and assume a very crucial role."[14] In 1991 some Japanese thought they
were already the victor. "Americans," a senior Japanese Foreign Ministry
official said, "simply don't want to recognize that Japan has won the economic race against the West."[15] The United States is like the Soviet Union, a
leading editor said, "just another ailing giant." The United States is losing
the economic competition, a Japanese professor agreed, and will become "a
premier agrarian power, a giant version of Denmark."[16]

Japanese strategy, behavior, and declarations all posit the existence of an
economic cold war between Japan and the United States. In the 1930s Chamberlain and Daladier did not take seriously what Hitler said in *Mein Kampf*.
Truman and his successors did take it seriously when Stalin and Khrushchev
said, "We will bury you." Americans would do well to take equally seriously
both Japanese declarations of their goal of achieving economic dominance
and the strategy they are pursuing to achieve that goal.

The Japanese challenge to American economic primacy affects the United
States in a variety of ways. First, American national security, in a narrow
sense, could be affected if the Japanese expand their lead in a variety of
militarily important technologies. In 1988, for instance, the Defense Science
Board identified 22 areas of critical technology and judged the Soviet Union
to be "significantly" ahead of the United States in "some niches of technology" in two areas, but Japan to be ahead in six.[17] A 1990 Commerce Department study found Japan to be ahead of the United States in five of twelve
emerging technologies and rapidly gaining in another five.[18] American na-

---

13. Ryohei Murata, quoted in *Washington Post National Weekly Edition*, December 4–10, 1989,
p. 19.
14. Kiichi Miyazawa, quoted in Kenneth B. Pyle, "How Japan Sees Itself," *American Enterprise*,
Vol. 2 (November–December 1991), p. 33.
15. Kazuo Ogura, director of cultural affairs, Japanese Foreign Ministry, quoted in Steven R.
Weisman, "Japan and U.S. Struggle with Resentment," *New York Times*, December 3, 1991, p.
A16.
16. Takano Hajime, editor of *Insider*, quoted in Colin Nickerson, "U.S., Japan Drift Dangerously
Apart," *Boston Globe*, November 25, 1991, p. 8; Barry H. Hillenbrand and James Walsh, "Fleeing
the Past?" *Time*, December 2, 1991, p. 70.
17. U.S. Department of Defense, *Critical Technologies Plan* (Washington, D.C.: Department of
Defense, March 15, 1990), pp. 10–12.
18. U.S. Department of Commerce, Technology Administration, *Emerging Technologies: A Survey*

tional security obviously is weakened to the extent to which the United States becomes dependent upon Japanese technology for its sophisticated weapons. In the Gulf War, U.S. defense contractors had to obtain from Japan semiconductors, video display equipment, circuits for missile guidance systems, and other key electronic products. As a senior Japanese Foreign Ministry official noted, Japan supplied these products, but the Japanese public has "a strong abhorrence" to exporting arms, and the sale of weapons parts to the United States "meets some psychological resistance."[19] In a future war where the United States was not so clearly fighting in Japan's interests, the willingness to supply those parts could easily evaporate.

Second, the growth of Japanese economic power threatens American economic well-being. The loss of markets means that American factories close and jobs migrate offshore. Profits go down, business go bankrupt, investors suffer. American per capita income increases at a slower rate or even decreases. The economic decline and even collapse manifest in so many industries targeted by the Japanese will appear in still others. The Japanese government, for instance, has targeted aerospace for rapid development with government "subsidies, loans, and political support."[20] If Japan is successful, the future of Seattle can be seen in Detroit.

The Japanese also use their financial resources to acquire and to transfer to their country technologies critical for military or essential civilian purposes and generally to move home the high-value-added operations of the companies they acquire. In contrast to European and Canadian firms, Japanese firms investing in the United States "have been prone to keep top management, high value-added productions, and research and development operations at home, often preferring to build 'screwdriver' assembly plants [abroad] that pay lower wages."[21]

Third, American influence in third countries declines relative to that of Japan. In 1989 Japan supplanted the United States as the largest provider of economic assistance. Japanese influence over Third World developing countries has increased compared to that of the United States[22] By the early 1990s

---

of Technical and Economic Opportunities (Washington, D.C.: Department of Commerce, Spring 1990), pp. 12–14.

19. Washington Post National Weekly Edition, April 1–7, 1991, p. 11.

20. Richard W. Stevenson, "Will Aerospace Be the Next Casualty?" New York Times, March 15, 1992, Sec. 3, pp. 1, 6.

21. Thomas Omestad, "Selling Off America," Foreign Policy, No. 76 (Fall 1989), pp. 134–135.

22. See, e.g., Victor H. Palmieri, "U.S. Takes Back Seat in Third World," New York Times, August 26, 1990, p. F13.

the tremendous expansion of Japanese investment and trade with Southeast Asia, combined with economic and technological assistance, had made Japan the most influential outside power in that region. Japanese influence in southern Asia has also risen, fueled by Japan's concerns for its oil supplies. The Japanese similarly moved to expand their involvements in Mexico, Brazil and other Latin American countries, constructing factories there whose products they plan to export to the United States.

Fourth, the influence that Japan exercises over the United States increases. To the extent that the United States becomes dependent on imports of goods and money from Japan, it also becomes vulnerable to Japanese threats to restrict those outflows. The United States, as Kiichi Miyazawa pointed out just before becoming prime minister, requires Japanese electronic components for its weapons, and cutting the flow of Japanese exports would produce "problems in the U.S. economy." "The real trigger" of the October 19, 1987, stock market crash, according to Treasury Secretary Nicholas Brady, "was that the Japanese came in for their own reasons and sold an enormous amount of government bonds, and drove the 30-year government bond rate up through 10 percent. And when it got through 10 percent, that got a lot of people thinking, Gee, that's four times the return you get on equity. Here we go, inflation again. That, to me, is what really started the 19th—a worry by the Japanese about U.S. currency."[23]

Japan has regularly used its financial power as a threat against the United States. "During the tensest period of the Super-301 [trade] negotiations with the U.S.," one leading Japanese journalist reports, "voices in the leadership argued, for the first time, for retaliation over concessions. They hinted that in financial markets, Japanese institutional investors would begin dumping dollar-denominated securities." In January 1991, the vice minister of finance "indicated Tokyo's awareness of its leverage. He bluntly commented, in public, that Japan would reduce capital investments in America if the United States applied sanctions for not giving U.S. financial institutions opportunities in Japan similar to those Japanese firms have in America." In the fall of 1991, as controversies intensified over Japanese exports of automobiles and other goods, reports repeatedly surfaced of Japan threatening a "'second

---

23. Kiichi Miyazawa, *International Herald Tribune*, October 19–20, 1991, p. 5; Nicholas Brady, quoted in Catherine Collins, "Could Japan Realty Holdings Hurt U.S.?" *Los Angeles Times*, May 7, 1989, Sect. VIII, p. 3.

strike': if Washington cuts off Japanese imports, Tokyo can strangle the American economy by cutting off investments or purchases of Treasury bonds." Japan, two distinguished economists concluded, "has the financial capacity—and begins, in public, to threaten to use that capacity—to influence American exchange rate and monetary conditions."[24]

Economic power increases Japan's ability to shape American public attitudes and decision-making so as to favor Japanese interests. In the 1940s the Soviet Union used its ideology to enlist influential Americans to serve its interests; in the 1990s Japan uses its money to enlist influential Americans to serve its interests. The Japanese government and Japanese corporations have worked closely together to achieve this goal and they have achieved significant success. In 1989 more than 250 Japanese government agencies and Japanese corporations were funding Washington lobbyists; second-place Canada had only 90 groups so engaged. Japanese spending on Washington lobbying was variously estimated from $60 to $100 million, the latter figure being more than that spent by the next six largest spenders combined. With this money Japanese organizations hire well-placed and well-connected former executive branch officials, members of Congress, and congressional staffers.[25]

Japanese investments in the United States expand Japanese political influence and in part appear to be designed to have that effect. In the 1980s, for instance, the Japanese government targeted the U.S. movie industry and began to provide substantial tax incentives for Japanese investments in that industry. By 1990 about 40 percent of the investment in new Hollywood

---

24. Yoichi Funabashi, "Japan as Superpower: Will It Say 'Yes' or 'No'?" *Economic Insights*, Vol. 1 (July–August 1990), p. 20; William J. Barnds, "The United States and Japan: A Time of Troubles," CAPA Report No. 2, June 1991, The Asia Foundation, Center for Asian Pacific Affairs, p. 2; Steven R. Weisman, "Pearl Harbor in the Mind of Japan," *New York Times Magazine*, November 3, 1991, p. 68; Nickerson, "U.S., Japan Drift Dangerously Apart"; Steven R. Weisman, "Japanese-U.S. Relations Undergoing a Redesign," *New York Times*, June 4, 1990, p. A2; *Washington Post National Weekly Edition*, February 19–25, 1990, p. 23; C. Michael Aho and Bruce Stokes, "The Year the World Economy Turned," *Foreign Affairs*, Vol. 70, No. 1 (America and the World 1990–91), p. 166; Michael Borrus and John Zysman, "The Highest Stakes: Industrial Competitiveness and National Strategy," BRIE Working Paper No. 39, April 1991, Berkeley Roundtable on the International Economy, p. 41.
25. Clyde Farnsworth, "Japan's Loud Voice in Washington," *New York Times*, December 10, 1989, p. F1; James Fallows, "Agents of Influence: How Japan's Lobbyists in the United States Manipulate America's Political and Economic System," *New York Review of Books*, November 8, 1990, p. 35; James Fallows, "The Japan-Handlers," *Atlantic Monthly*, Vol. 264 (August 1989), p. 18; Pat Choate, *Agents of Influence* (New York: Alfred A. Knopf, 1990), pp. 109–120.

movies came from Japan. The result was the ability to influence public opinion: the chairman of Matsushita made it clear that MCA would not be allowed to produce movies critical of or offensive to Japan.[26]

The Japanese effort to influence policy outcomes in Washington necessarily leads Japan to attempt to influence who becomes a policymaker in Washington. "Japan should use its economic power," said Keniche Ohmae, a leading Tokyo economic analyst, "to put a stop to one-sided Japan-bashing in the U.S." Akio Morita agreed: "If a congressman or a politician bashes his friend [Japan], then that politician will lose the election." He is right. In 1988 candidates supported by the Auto Dealers and Drivers for Free Trade PAC (AUTOPAC), the political action committee representing Japanese auto dealers and the importers of Japanese cars in the United States, won six of their seven congressional races. AUTOPAC financial support was crucial to the victory of Republican Connie Mack in a very close Florida Senate race over the Democratic candidate Buddy MacKay, who said afterwards, "I was beaten in Tokyo." Two years later AUTOPAC targeted Sen. John Durkin (D-N.H.) for defeat, and late in the campaign bought $357,000 worth of television time in New Hampshire to attack Durkin, effectively securing the election of his Republican opponent, Bob Smith. "We depend heavily on the element of surprise," AUTOPAC's director remarked.[27]

The Japanese also make substantial efforts to cultivate intellectuals and scholars and to influence the output of universities and research centers. Japanese corporations have endowed thirteen professorships at MIT and nine at Harvard. Between 1970 and 1991, Harvard received $30 million from Japanese corporations. "According to Harvard insiders," the Harvard alumni magazine reported, "these donors wanted the funds to provide an antidote to 'Japan-bashing' through the creation at Harvard of a public forum for explaining Japan's position on such sensitive issues as investment and trade with the United States." The head of at least one think tank that received Japanese support resigned "after protesting efforts by Japanese sponsors to influence the organization's research."[28] "The U.S. has been *penetrated*," a

---

26. David E. Sanger, "Politics and Multinational Movies," *New York Times*, November 27, 1990, p. D7; Eamon Fingleton, "YMCA," *New Republic*, December 31, 1990, pp. 13–14.
27. Akio Morita, quoted in William J. Holstein, *The Japanese Power Game* (New York: Charles Scribner's Sons, 1990) pp. 234–235; Choate, *Agents of Influence*, pp. 110–112; David Nyhan, "The GOP-Japanese Connection in N.H.," *Boston Globe*, February 9, 1992, p. 77.
28. Sol Hurwitz, "The Japanese Connection," *Harvard Magazine*, Vol. 94 (January–February 1992), p. 94; Choate, *Agents of Influence*, pp. 39–41; Holstein, *Japanese Power Game*, pp. 230–232; Steven Kelman, "The 'Japanization' of America," *The Public Interest*, No. 98 (Winter 1990), p. 81.

1989 study prepared at the U.S. Foreign Service Institute concluded, "not only by Japanese autos and VCRs, but by Japanese influence peddling at every level. Thousands of American lawyers, lobbyists, former officials, bankers, and scholars are funded by Japanese corporations or the Government of Japan."[29]

"Economics," as Daniel Bell has said, "is the continuation of war by other means."[30] Economic primacy matters because economic power is both the most fundamental and the most fungible form of power. For the United States, the loss of economic primacy to Japan could be highly damaging, as would have been the loss of political-military primacy to the Soviet Union. This loss to Japan would, first, make U.S. influence in world affairs subordinate to that of Japan and, second, reduce long-term U.S. economic welfare, as Japan used its power, as its leaders and policies have said that it would, to accumulate high-technology, high-value-added industries in Japan, and to reduce the United States to the status of a "giant Denmark." The American public, in the phrase that provoked Robert Jervis, very justifiably "is obsessed with Japan for the same reasons that it was once obsessed with the Soviet Union. It sees that country as a major threat to its primacy in a crucial arena of power." Does Professor Jervis really believe that Americans are wrong for not wanting to live in a world where the major decisions affecting them economically are made in Tokyo? Does he really think that those decisions would be the same as decisions made in Washington, New York, Chicago, Atlanta, Houston, and Los Angeles?

To restore its economic primacy *vis-à-vis* Japan requires the United States to take two broad types of measures. First, the United States needs to recognize the Japanese economic power maximization strategy for what it is and to pursue a much more concerted and consistent course to prevent Japan from exploiting the openness of the American economy and to induce Japan to open its own economy further to foreign goods, investment, and participation. Second, the United States needs to take the measures which it should take in any event to renew its economic health: reducing the federal deficit, increasing savings and investment, increasing productivity, promoting research and development, improving its educational system. Good reason

---

29. Kenneth J. Dillon, *Worlds in Collision: The U.S. and Japan Beyond the Year 2000* (U.S. Department of State, Foreign Service Institute, Center for the Study of Foreign Affairs, Center Paper No. 2, April 1989), p. 27 (emphasis added).
30. Daniel Bell, "Germany: The Enduring Fear," *Dissent*, Vol. 37 (Fall 1990), p. 466.

exists to do all of these things even if there were no Japanese challenge. The existence of such a challenge provides additional incentive for these actions in order to insure America's primacy in the world.

What's the World's Interest?

The maintenance of U.S. primacy matters for the world as well as for the United States.

First, no other country can make comparable contributions to international order and stability. The security consequences of a multipolar world have been dramatically evident in the dismal failure of the major European powers to deal with the Yugoslav catastrophe on their doorstep. Leaders and publics throughout the world recognize the need for an American presence and American leadership in maintaining stability in their region. These are, as the prime ministers of Japan and Korea said, "indispensable" to Asian security.[31] Crowds chanting "Americans go home!" are not much in evidence these days. The fear is, instead, that Americans may well turn isolationist again and do exactly that. The ability of the United States to provide international order is obviously limited and, despite the constant demands, the United States cannot settle every dispute in every part of the world. Yet the fact remains that, as General Colin Powell, chairman of the Joint Chiefs of Staff, put it, "One of the fondest expressions around here is that we can't be the world's policeman. But guess who gets called when suddenly someone needs a cop?"[32] As Bosnia, Somalia, and many other places evidence, the answer to that question is obvious. And, given the nature of the world as it is, is there any remotely plausible alternative answer or better answer? If the United States is unable to maintain security in the world's trouble spots, no other single country or combination of countries is likely to provide a substitute.

Second, the collapse of the Soviet Union leaves the United States as the only major power whose national identity is defined by a set of universal political and economic values. For the United States these are liberty, democracy, equality, private property, and markets. In varying degrees other major countries may from time to time support these values. Their identity,

---

31. "Asian Allies Say U.S. Military Presence Is Indispensable," *Christian Science Monitor*, November 10, 1992, p. 3.
32. "The Global Constable," *The Economist*, September 1, 1990, p. 26.

however, is not defined by these values, and hence they have far less commitment to them and less interest in promoting them than does the United States. This is not, obviously, to argue that these values are always at the forefront of American foreign policy; other concerns and needs have to be taken into consideration. It is, rather, to argue that the promotion of democracy, human rights, and markets are far more central to American policy than to the policy of any other country. Following in the footsteps of both Jimmy Carter and Ronald Reagan, Bill Clinton has committed himself to a foreign policy of "democratic realism" in which the central goal of the United States will be the promotion of democracy in the world. The maintenance of American primacy and the strengthening of American influence in the world are indispensable to achieving that goal. To argue that primacy does not matter is to argue that political and economic values do not matter and that democracy does not or should not matter.

A world without U.S. primacy will be a world with more violence and disorder and less democracy and economic growth than a world where the United States continues to have more influence than any other country in shaping global affairs. The sustained international primacy of the United States is central to the welfare and security of Americans and to the future of freedom, democracy, open economies, and international order in the world.

International Relations Theory and the End of the Cold War

John Lewis Gaddis

$\mathbf{P}$rinces have always sought out soothsayers of one kind or another for the purpose of learning what the future holds. These hired visionaries have found portents in the configurations of stars, the entrails of animals, and most indicators in between. The results, on the whole, have been disappointing. Surprise remains one of the few things one can count on, and very few princes have succeeded in avoiding it, however assiduous the efforts of their respective wizards, medicine men, counselors, advisers, and think tank consultants to ward it off.

Surprise is still very much with us. The abrupt end of the Cold War, an unanticipated hot war in the Persian Gulf, and the sudden disintegration of the Soviet Union astonished almost everyone, whether in government, the academy, the media, or the think tanks. Although there was nothing inherently implausible about these events—the Cold War did have to end sometime, war had always been a possibility in the Middle East, and communism's failures had been obvious for years—the fact that they arose so unexpectedly suggests that deficiencies persist in the means by which contemporary princes and the soothsayers they employ seek to discern the future course of world affairs.

No modern soothsayer, of course, would aspire to total clairvoyance. We have no equivalent of Isaac Asimov's famous character, the mathematician

John Lewis Gaddis is Distinguished Professor of History and Director of the Contemporary History Institute at Ohio University. During the 1992–93 academic year, he is serving as Harmsworth Professor of American History at Oxford University. His most recent book is The United States and the End of the Cold War: Implications, Reconsiderations, Provocations *(Oxford University Press, 1992).*

I would like to acknowledge support, in the preparation of this essay, from the National Research Council's Committee on Contributions of Behavioral and Social Science to the Prevention of Nuclear War. My thanks, for research assistance, to Ed Merta, and for advice and comments to Kennette Benedict, David Broscious, Richard Crockatt, Barbara Gaddis, Michael Gaddis, Alexander George, Samuel P. Huntington, Robert Jervis, Andrew Katz, Ed Merta, Harold Molineu, Philip Nash, Olav Njølstad, Stefan Rossbach, J. David Singer, Paul Stern, and Philip E. Tetlock. I also benefited from an opportunity to present preliminary conclusions from this essay at a conference on "The Transformation of the International System and International Relations Theory," organized by Richard Ned Lebow and Thomas Risse-Kappen at Cornell University in October 1991, as well as from the suggestions of several anonymous reviewers for the National Research Council and *International Security*. The views expressed herein are, of course, my own only.

International Security, Winter 1992/93 (Vol. 17, No. 3)
© 1993 by the President and Fellows of Harvard College and of the Massachusetts Institute of Technology.

Hari Seldon, whose predictive powers were so great that he was able to leave precise holographic instructions for his followers, to be consulted at successive intervals decades after his death.[1] But historians, political scientists, economists, psychologists, and even mathematicians have claimed the power to detect patterns in the behavior of nations and the individuals who lead them; an awareness of these, they have assured us, will better equip statesmen—and states—to deal with the uncertainties that lie ahead.

The end of the Cold War presents an unusual opportunity to test these claims. That event was of such importance that no approach to the study of international relations claiming both foresight and competence should have failed to see it coming. None actually did so, though, and that fact ought to raise questions about the methods we have developed for trying to understand world politics. The following essay suggests some reasons for this failure of modern-day soothsaying; it will also advance a few ideas on how the accuracy of that enterprise might henceforth be improved.

Theory, Forecasting, and the Possibility of Prediction[2]

The claims that those who study world politics have made regarding their ability to forecast the future grow, for the most part, out of efforts to construct theories of international relations. There is a very simple reason for this:

---

1. Isaac Asimov, *Foundation* (New York: Ballantine Books, 1951).
2. My own use of these terms—which is not the usage of everyone cited in this paper—follows the distinctions of John R. Freeman and Brian L. Job: "a *forecast* is a statement about unknown phenomena based upon known or accepted generalizations and uncertain conditions ('partial unknowns'), whereas a *prediction* involves the linkage of known or accepted generalizations with certain conditions (knowns) to yield a statement about unknown phenomena." Freeman and Job, "Scientific Forecasts in International Relations: Problems of Definition and Epistemology," *International Studies Quarterly*, Vol. 23, No. 1 (March 1979), pp. 117–118. It follows from this that forecasts can be neither deterministic—"if A, then (inevitably) B"—nor conditional "if A, then (under specified conditions) B." They are instead probabilistic statements: "if A, then (probably) B." I owe this distinction between deterministic, conditional, and probabilistic statements to a suggestion from Alexander George, although I have fit it within my own differentiation between prediction and forecasting. See also, on these problems of definition, Nazli Choucri, "Key Issues in International Relations Forecasting," in Nazli Choucri and Thomas W. Robinson, eds., *Forecasting in International Relations: Theory, Methods, Problems, Prospects* (San Francisco: W.H. Freeman, 1978), p. 4; and Richard A. Skinner, "Introduction: Research in the Predictive Mode," in Charles W. Kegley, Jr., Gregory A. Raymond, Robert M. Rood, and Richard A. Skinner, eds., *International Events and the Comparative Analysis of Foreign Policy* (Columbia: University of South Carolina Press, 1975), p. 211.

visions of any future have to proceed from the awareness of some kind of past; otherwise there can be no conceptual frame of reference—more than that, there can be no language—with which to express them.[3] Theories provide a way of packaging patterns from the past in such a way as to make them usable in the present as guides to the future.[4] Without them, all attempts at forecasting and prediction would be reduced to random guessing.

Hans J. Morgenthau put forward the first comprehensive modern theory of international relations—and the one from which most subsequent theories in that field have evolved—in his 1948 book, *Politics among Nations: The Struggle for Power and Peace;* his approach came to be known, in a somewhat self-congratulatory way, as "realism."[5] Earlier studies by diplomatic historians, international lawyers, and well-meaning reformers, Morgenthau complained, had failed to identify the "fundamental principles" of world politics, "which are revealed only by the correlation of recent events with the more distant past." Even the most idiosyncratic event—and it is important to stress that Morgenthau never disregarded the importance of such events—reflected "social forces" which were, in turn, "the product of human nature in action. Therefore, under similar conditions, they will manifest themselves in a similar manner." Knowledge of these patterns would allow one to "understand international politics, grasp the meaning of contemporary events, and *foresee and influence the future.*"[6]

---

3. For the centrality to forecasting of theory based on past experience, see Choucri, "Key Issues in International Relations Forecasting," pp. 5–7.
4. Charles A. McClelland, *Theory and the International System* (New York: Macmillan, 1966), pp. 15–16, provides a succinct but comprehensive summary of the uses of theory in the study of international relations. See also J. David Singer, "The Level-of-Analysis Problem in International Relations," *World Politics,* Vol. 14, No. 1 (October 1961), pp. 78–80; and Patrick M. Morgan, *Theories and Approaches to International Politics: What Are We to Think?* 4th ed. (New Brunswick, N.J.: Transaction Books, 1987), pp. 18–19.
5. Hans J. Morgenthau, *Politics Among Nations: The Struggle for Power and Peace* (New York: Knopf, 1948). There have been six editions of Morgenthau's classic, the most recent published in 1985. (My references are to the 1948 edition.) Morgenthau was, of course, hardly the first "realist." The tradition goes back at least as far as Machiavelli, and if one can accept E.H. Carr's succinct definition of "realism"—"the impact of thinking upon wishing"—then the idea is as old as its opposite, which is utopian idealism. Edward Hallett Carr, *The Twenty Years' Crisis, 1919–1939: An Introduction to the Study of International Relations* (New York: St. Martin's Press, 1939), p. 10. For Morgenthau's primacy in the field of post-1945 international relations, see Martin Hollis and Steve Smith, *Explaining and Understanding International Relations* (Oxford: Oxford University Press, 1990), pp. 22–28; and Robert O. Keohane, "Realism, Neorealism and the Study of World Politics," in Robert O. Keohane, ed., *Neorealism and Its Critics* (New York: Columbia University Press, 1986), p. 10.
6. Morgenthau, *Politics Among Nations,* pp. 4–5 (emphases added).

What was new in all of this was not Morgenthau's insistence that the identification and careful examination of past patterns could improve the quality of future statecraft: historians had been saying that all along. Morgenthau's innovation, rather, was the claim to have developed, as he himself put it, "the science of international politics."[7] The principal characteristics of this science were its reductionism—the argument that a drive for power inextricably rooted in human nature animated all politics—and its tough-mindedness—the assertion that a focus on power would free the study of international relations from the sentimentality, legalism, and irrelevant empiricism with which it had been afflicted.[8]

Morgenthau was always careful not to promise too much. "Trustworthy prophecies" in international politics would never be possible, he argued as early as 1948, because "contradictory tendencies" would always be present in every political situation: which of them would prevail was "anybody's guess." What theory could do, though, was to allow scholars to "trace the different tendencies which, as potentialities, are inherent in [the] situation[,]. . . . point out the different conditions which make it more likely for one tendency to prevail than for another, and, finally, assess the probabilities for the different conditions and tendencies to prevail in actuality."[9] It could, therefore,"confront what governments do, and what governments and peoples think, about international relations with independent prudential judgment and with the truth, however dimly perceived and tenuously approximated."[10]

Subsequent theorists of international relations—whether or not they agreed with Morgenthau's insistence on the centrality of power—have nonetheless

---

7. Morgenthau used this as the title of Chapter Two of *Politics among Nations* beginning with its second edition, published in 1954.

8. Although some of Morgenthau's writings appear to be scathing attacks on attempts to construct a "science" of politics—see his *Scientific Man vs. Power Politics* (Chicago: University of Chicago Press, 1945); also "Reflections on the State of Political Science," *Review of Politics*, Vol. 27, No. 3 (October 1955), pp. 431–460; and "Common Sense and Theories of International Relations," *Journal of International Affairs*, Vol. 21 (1967), pp. 207–214—a careful reading suggests that what Morgenthau really objected to in idealist, behavioral, and quantitative approaches was their unwillingness to place "power" in the central position to which he had assigned it. Morgenthau's ambivalence about "scientific" approaches is discussed in Hollis and Smith, *Explaining and Understanding International Relations*, pp. 23, 27.

9. Morgenthau, *Politics among Nations*, pp. 6–7. Raymond Aron had an even more modest conception of the role of theory in statecraft: theory, he wrote, would be scientifically valid "to the extent that it does not provide the equivalent of what noble-hearted people and lightweight minds expect, that is, a simple ideology guaranteeing morality or efficiency." Aron, "What Is a Theory of International Relations?" *Journal of International Affairs*, Vol. 21 (1967), p. 204.

10. Morgenthau, "Common Sense and Theories of International Relations," p. 212.

embraced his assumption that a "scientific" approach enhances the possibility of forecasting. Morton A. Kaplan acknowledged in 1957 that although theory would be of little use in anticipating the specific actions of individuals and nations, it could "predict characteristic or modal behavior within a particular kind of international system" as well as "the conditions under which the characteristic behavior of the international system will remain stable, the conditions under which it will be transformed, and the kind of transformation that will take place."[11] J. David Singer argued several years later that any analytical model should "offer the promise of reliable prediction"—indeed Singer maintained that this task would be less difficult to accomplish than the other two requirements of such models, which were description and explanation.[12] "As our knowledge base expands and is increasingly integrated in the theoretical sense," he added in 1969, "the better our predictions will be, and therefore, the fewer policy disagreements we will have."[13]

Kenneth N. Waltz, whose approach to theory differed sharply from those of Kaplan and Singer, nonetheless shared with them the goal of using theory to forecast the future. Waltz's triple "images" of international relations, set out in *Man, the State, and War* in 1959, had explicitly prescriptive (and thereby implicitly predictive) purposes: "to explain how peace can be more readily achieved requires an understanding of the causes of war."[14] And in his even more influential *Theory of International Politics*, published in 1979, Waltz clarified his claims regarding prediction, in terms that did not differ greatly from those of Morgenthau or Kaplan: "Theory explains regularities of behavior and leads one to expect that the outcomes produced by interacting units will

11. Morton A. Kaplan, *System and Process in International Politics* (New York: John Wiley, 1957), pp. xvii–xviii. See also Kaplan, "Systems Theory and Political Science," *Social Research*, Vol. 35, No. 1 (Spring 1968), especially pp. 33 and 45–46; and Kaplan, "The New Great Debate: Traditionalism vs. Science in International Relations," in Klaus Knorr and James N. Rosenau, ed., *Contending Approaches to International Politics* (Princeton: Princeton University Press, 1969), especially pp. 46–51, 56–57.
12. Singer, "The Level-of-Analysis Problem in International Relations," pp. 79–80. See also J. David Singer, *Models, Methods, and Progress in World Politics: A Peace Research Odyssey* (Boulder, Colo.: Westview Press, 1990), p. 249.
13. J. David Singer, "The Incompleat Theorist: Insight Without Evidence," in Knorr and Rosenau, eds., *Contending Approaches to International Politics*, pp. 66–67. See also Singer, *Models, Methods, and Progress in World Politics*, pp. 62, 261, 269; and Melvin Small and J. David Singer, "Conflict in the International System, 1816–1977: Historical Trends and Policy Futures," in J. David Singer and associates, *Explaining War: Selected Papers from the Correlates of War Project* (Beverly Hills, Calif.: SAGE, 1979), p. 76.
14. Kenneth N. Waltz, *Man, the State, and War: A Theoretical Analysis* (New York: Columbia University Press, 1959), p. 2.

fall within specified ranges. The behavior of states and of statesmen, however, is indeterminate."[15]

The quest for forecasting and prediction has by no means operated exclusively at the level of international systems. The "operational code" technique for studying political leadership evolved from efforts made, during the early Cold War, to forecast the intentions and actions of top Soviet officials.[16] Decision-making theorists set out to produce general propositions—which could be taken as forecasts—regarding behavior of leaders in crises.[17] Deterrence theorists made specific predictions during the 1950s about how the two nuclear superpowers would behave; these in turn directly influenced decisions on the procurement, deployment, and planned use of nuclear weapons in both Washington and Moscow.[18] Political development theory sought to identify patterns in the modernization process that would allow not only an anticipation of events in the Third World, but the formulation of policies aimed at shaping them.[19] Studies of perception and misperception in international relations employed psychological literature to identify recurring patterns in the behavior of individuals, a knowledge of which might improve the conduct of statecraft.[20] And the use of game theory to model international

15. Kenneth N. Waltz, *Theory of International Politics* (New York: Random House, 1979), p. 68. A theory of international politics, Waltz noted, was not the same thing as a theory of foreign policy; from the standpoint of the former, it was only "to the extent that dynamics of a system limit the freedom of its units [that] their behavior and the outcomes of their behavior become predictable." Ibid., p. 72.
16. Nathan Leites, *The Operational Code of the Politburo* (New York: McGraw-Hill, 1951). See also Alexander L. George, "The 'Operational Code': A Neglected Approach to the Study of Political Leaders and Decision-making," *International Studies Quarterly*, Vol. 13, No. 2 (June 1969), pp. 190–222.
17. Richard C. Snyder, H.W. Bruck, and Burton Sapin, eds., *Foreign Policy Decision-Making* (New York: Free Press of Glencoe, 1954). See also Glenn D. Paige, *The Korean Decision: June 24–30, 1950* (New York: Free Press, 1968); and Glenn H. Snyder and Paul Diesing, *Conflict among Nations: Bargaining, Decision Making, and System Structure in International Crises* (Princeton: Princeton University Press, 1977), especially pp. 470–530.
18. See, in particular, Thomas C. Schelling, *The Strategy of Conflict* (Cambridge: Harvard University Press, 1960); and Schelling, *Arms and Influence* (New Haven: Yale University Press, 1966). Lawrence Freedman, *The Evolution of Nuclear Strategy* (New York: St. Martin's, 1981), provides the best overview of the influence deterrence theory had on policy. Non-nuclear deterrence theory also had predictive aspirations. See Alexander L. George and Richard Smoke, *Deterrence in American Foreign Policy: Theory and Practice* (New York: Columbia University Press, 1974), especially p. 512.
19. D. Michael Shafer, *Deadly Paradigms: The Failure of U.S. Counterinsurgency Policy* (Princeton: Princeton University Press, 1988), especially pp. 48–78.
20. Robert Jervis, *Perception and Misperception in International Politics* (Princeton: Princeton University Press, 1976), especially pp. 6, 409.

rivalries had clear implications for attempts to anticipate the future of Soviet-American relations.[21]

My point, then, is that the major theoretical approaches that have shaped the discipline of international relations since Morgenthau have all had in common, as *one* of their principal objectives, the anticipation of the future. Whether in science or politics, whether by the tough standards of prediction or the more relaxed ones of forecasting, the role of theory has always been not just to account for the past or to explain the present but to provide at least a preview of what is to come. It follows, therefore, that one way to confirm the validity of theories is to see how successfully they perform *each* of the tasks expected of them.[22] The failure to accomplish a particular task would not necessarily invalidate an entire theory, but it should raise questions in our minds. It would be a warning signal, suggesting the need to rethink underlying assumptions. That is the kind of test this essay seeks to apply: how well did international relations theory carry out one of the important tasks it set for itself, which was forecasting the future of the Cold War?[23]

---

21. Anatol Rapoport, *Fights, Games, and Debates* (Ann Arbor: University of Michigan, 1960); Robert Axelrod, *The Evolution of Cooperation* (New York: Basic Books, 1984).
22. "A theory is a good theory if it satisfies two requirements: It must accurately describe a large class of observations on the basis of a model that contains only a few arbitrary elements, and it must make definite predictions about the results of future observations." Stephen Hawking, *A Brief History of Time: From the Big Bang to Black Holes* (New York: Bantam, 1988), p. 9. See also, on this point, Heinz R. Pagels, *The Dreams of Reason: The Computer and the Rise of the Sciences of Complexity* (New York: Simon and Schuster, 1988), p. 204; Skinner, "Introduction: Research in the Predictive Mode," pp. 208–209; Charles F. Hermann, Warren R. Phillips, and Stuart J. Thorson, "Validating International Relations Forecasts to Develop Theory," in Choucri and Robinson, eds., *Forecasting in International Relations*, pp. 69–78; M.R. Leavitt, "Computer Simulation in International Relations Forecasting," in ibid., p. 240; Milton Friedman, "The Methodology of Positive Economics," in May Brodbeck, ed., *Readings in the Philosophy of the Social Sciences* (New York: Macmillan, 1968), pp. 508–528; and Waltz, *Theory of International Politics*, p. 69. Singer, conversely, argues that "despite the folklore to the contrary, *prediction* is neither the major purpose nor the acid test of a theory; the goal of all basic scientific research is *explanation*." But he then goes on to make the point that "a strong explanatory theory will—because it is better able to account for and explain the effects of changing conditions—provide a more solid base for predicting than one that rests on observed covariations and postdictions alone." Singer, *Models, Methods, and Progress in World Politics*, p. 74; see also p. 249.
23. For reasons of space, I have limited this analysis to theoretical approaches that attempted, in one way or another, to forecast the workings of the international system as a whole. There are other ways in which one could use the end of the Cold War to test theory: one could, for example, consider the extent to which sub-systemic level theories relating to deterrence, bargaining, alliances, crisis-management, and collective and individual decision-making provided a basis for anticipating what happened; one could also apply the same scrutiny to the specific field of Soviet studies and the theoretical insights that arose from within it. Some preliminary efforts along these lines include Daniel Deudney and G. John Ikenberry, "The International

Approaches to the Future

Before we can apply that test, though, there is an organizational problem to be got out of the way. It has to do with the fact that although international relations theorists have agreed on the importance of prediction and forecasting, they have by no means agreed on how to construct the theories that must be in place prior to performing these tasks.[24] Differences over theory have long impeded efforts to build a "science" of international relations; they have also affected the assumptions behind, the procedures employed in, and the accuracy of the attempts theorists have made to look ahead.

Morgenthau's "realism" provided little practical guidance on how to use theory to foresee the future. It was true enough that statesmen define their interests in terms of power, Stanley Hoffmann pointed out, "but only at a level of generality that is fatuous":[25] after all, if everyone seeks power because they are human, then the value of a forecast stating that humans will seek power is somewhat limited. Other critics noted that Morgenthau had attempted to derive universally-valid propositions about human behavior from a particular set of human characteristics: there was no explanation of why the craving for power should necessarily take precedence over other human desires, or determine all human actions, or remain immutable for all time to come.[26] Still others accused Morgenthau of failing to specify whether power was an end in itself or a means to an end; if it was both, then what he had

---

Sources of Soviet Change," *International Security*, Vol. 16, No. 3 (Winter 1991/92), pp. 74–118; Richard K. Herrmann, "Soviet Behavior in Regional Conflicts: Old Questions, New Strategies, and Important Lessons," *World Politics*, Vol. 44, No. 3 (April 1992), pp. 432–465; and John W.R. Lepingwell, "Soviet Civil-Military Relations and the August Coup," ibid., pp. 539–572; as well as papers prepared by Herrmann and Thomas Risse-Kappen for the October 1991 Cornell University conference on "The Transformation of the International System and International Relations Theory" organized by Richard Ned Lebow and Thomas Risse-Kappen.

24. One recent review of the field has characterized these contending schools of thought as "partisan bands" who seize academic departments, entice graduate students into their camps, and carry on permanent feuds with one another. Yale H. Ferguson and Richard W. Mansbach, *The Elusive Quest: Theory and International Politics* (Columbia: University of South Carolina Press, 1988), p. 18.

25. Stanley Hoffmann, "Notes on the Limits of 'Realism'," *Social Research*, Vol. 48, No. 1 (Winter 1981), p. 655.

26. Waltz, *Man, the State, and War*, pp. 26–41. See also Richard N. Rosecrance, *Action and Reaction in World Politics: International Systems in Perspective* (Boston: Little, Brown, 1963), p. 268; and K.J. Holsti, "Retreat from Utopia: International Relations Theory, 1945–70," *Canadian Journal of Political Science*, Vol. 4, No. 2 (June 1971), p. 169.

achieved was not a theory but a tautology.[27] Finally, Morgenthau's recommendations for policy-makers boiled down to the exercise of prudence and restraint, qualities that seemed at odds with the unchanging characteristics of human nature he had earlier claimed to have identified.[28] Morgenthau's "realism" was a starting point, but clearly much more would be required if international relations theory was to lead to the detection of laws, and hence to any possibility of forecasting and prediction.

Dissatisfaction with Morgenthau's attempt to build a comprehensive theory of international relations has led to a bewildering array of efforts, over the past several decades, to construct viable alternatives. None of these has come close to commanding universal assent, nor is there even any generally accepted way of categorizing them. For the purposes of this essay—but with the caution that these are oversimplifications—I identify them in terms of three distinctive approaches to theory: the "behavioral," the "structural," and the "evolutionary."[29] I then assess what the major practitioners of each of these approaches either said or implied about the end of the Cold War.

THE BEHAVIORAL APPROACH

The behavioral approach bases itself upon a key assumption of classical empiricism: that we can only know what we can directly observe and measure. "History, experience, introspection, common sense, and logic do not in themselves generate *evidence*," one of the leading behavioralists, J. David Singer, wrote in 1969; they are, rather, "ideas which must then be examined in the light of evidence," and that procedure can only take place on the basis of observations that are "systematic, explicit, visible, and replicable by other researchers."[30] A true science of politics would not simply call itself "scien-

---

27. Kaplan, *System and Process in International Politics*, p. 12. See also Keohane, "Neorealism and World Politics," p. 11.

28. Stanley Hoffmann, "International Relations: The Long Road to Theory," in James N. Rosenau, ed., *International Relations and Foreign Policy: A Reader in Research and Theory* (New York: Free Press, 1961), pp. 423–424.

29. For somewhat similar distinctions, see Johan Galtung, "The Social Sciences: An Essay on Polarization and Integration," in Knorr and Rosenau, eds., *Contending Approaches to International Politics*, pp. 243–285; also Hayward R. Alker, Jr., and Thomas J. Biersteker, "The Dialectics of World Order: Notes for a Future Archeologist of International Savoir Faire," *International Studies Quarterly*, Vol. 38, No. 2 (June 1984), pp. 121–142; Daniel Druckman and P. Terrence Hopmann, "Behavioral Aspects of Negotiations on Mutual Security," in Philip E. Tetlock, et al., eds., *Behavior, Society, and Nuclear War: Volume One* (New York: Oxford University Press, 1989), pp. 152–155; and Yosef Lapid, "The Third Debate: On the Prospects of International Theory in a Post-Positivist Era," *International Studies Quarterly*, Vol. 33, No. 3 (September 1989), pp. 239–240.

30. Singer, "The Incompleat Theorist," p. 68.

tific," as Morgenthau had described his theory; rather, it would apply methods of the physical and natural sciences, to the maximum extent possible, in analyzing human and state behavior.[31] Without the rigor such methods provide, behavioralists insist,[32] the study of international relations will always be subject to the very utopianism, emotionalism, bias, confusion, and contradiction from which Morgenthau's "realism" had sought to liberate it.

Behavioralists concentrate, for this reason, upon the careful characterization, and where possible quantification, of observable phenomena: examples have included battlefield casualties, voting returns, trade statistics, newspaper stories, and even patterns of communication.[33] Where direct measurement is not possible, they seek to generate measurable data either through the creation of rules for coding the activities of states, organizations, and individuals,[34] or through the simulation of situations in such a way as to yield calculable "inputs" and "outputs."[35] Considerable emphasis is placed on the use of rigorous mathematical techniques in analyzing information produced by these methods, both as a safeguard against bias and as a means

---

31. James N. Rosenau, "Moral Fervor, Systematic Analysis, and Scientific Consciousness in Foreign Policy Research," in Austin Ranney, ed., *Political Science and Public Policy* (Chicago: Markham, 1968), pp. 197–236; J. David Singer, "The Behavioral Approach to International Relations: Payoff and Prospects," in James N. Rosenau, ed., *International Politics and Foreign Policy: A Reader in Research and Theory*, rev. ed. (New York: Free Press, 1969), pp. 65–69. Singer has always been careful to acknowledge the impossibility of a *pure* science of politics; the behavioralist approach was to be an improvement on, but not a rejection of, more traditional methods like those of Morgenthau and other "realists."
32. For a recent argument to this effect, see Paul Huth and Bruce Russett, "Testing Deterrence Theory: Rigor Makes a Difference," *World Politics*, Vol. 42, No. 4 (July 1990), pp. 466–501.
33. Richard A. Brody, "The Study of International Politics qua Science: The Emphasis on Methods and Techniques," in Knorr and Rosenau, eds., *Contending Approaches to International Politics*, pp. 110–128, provides a good introduction to this kind of analysis. For some representative applications, see Singer and associates, *Explaining War*; Karl Deutsch and others, *Political Community in the North Atlantic Area: International Organization in the Light of Historical Experience* (Princeton: Princeton University Press, 1957); J. David Singer, ed., *Quantitative International Politics: Insights and Evidence* (New York: Free Press, 1968); Bruce M. Russett, ed., *Peace, War, and Numbers* (Beverly Hills, Calif.: SAGE, 1972); Jonathan Wilkenfeld, Gerald W. Hopple, Paul J. Rossa, and Stephen J. Andriole, *Foreign Policy Behavior: The Interstate Behavior Analysis Model* (Beverly Hills, Calif.: SAGE, 1980); and Paul Huth, *Extended Deterrence and the Prevention of War* (New Haven: Yale University Press, 1988).
34. Singer, *Models, Methods, and Progress in World Politics*, pp. 113, 119–120. See also J. David Singer, "The 'Correlates of War' Project: Interim Report and Rationale," *World Politics*, Vol. 14, No. 2 (January 1972), pp. 243–270.
35. Examples include Thomas H. Naylor, et al., *Computer Simulation Techniques* (New York: John Wiley, 1966); Charles F. Hermann, *Crises in Foreign Policy: A Simulation Analysis* (Indianapolis: Bobbs-Merrill, 1969); and Harold Guetzkow, et al., *Simulation in Social and Administrative Science: Overviews and Case-Examples* (Englewood Cliffs, N.J.: Prentice-Hall, 1972).

of ensuring comparability.[36] The behavioralists proceed from a determinedly inductive, "bottom-up" approach, deferring the construction of theory until they have collected, measured, and compared as much observable evidence as possible, and after that cumulated, replicated, and thus verified the resulting findings.[37] Only then, presumably, can forecasting on any "scientific" basis take place.

THE STRUCTURAL APPROACH

The structural approach differs from the behavioral in that it focuses upon unobservable and hence unmeasurable structures that nonetheless shape international relations in observable and measurable ways.[38] Behavioralists have never denied the existence or the importance of such structures;[39] they maintain only that science lacks the means to deal with them. But structuralists point out that some of the most striking accomplishments of twentieth-century science have arisen from the assumption that unobservable structures produce observable effects: theories about the invisible structures of atoms, after all, brought about the all too visible incineration of Hiroshima and Nagasaki.[40] The only truly inductive method, structuralists insist, is that of the blank mind; one has to assume *a priori* and unobservable structures because without them theories themselves could not exist, reality would be uncharacterizable, and certainly forecasting would be impossible.[41] "Collect-

---

36. See, on the use of mathematics, Michael Nicholson, *Formal Theories in International Relations* (New York: Cambridge University Press, 1989), pp. 10–13, 18–21. Nicholson is careful to distinguish between what he calls the "mathematical theory," "the mathematical model," and the "mathematical picture." Behavioralists, following a principally inductive approach, for the most part use the last of these.

37. Singer, "The 'Correlates of War' Project," pp. 249–251. See also Singer and Small, "Conflict in the International System," p. 76; J. David Singer, "The Peace Researcher and Foreign Policy Prediction," Peace Society (International) *Papers*, Vol. 21 (1973), pp. 5–8; and John A. Vasquez, "The Steps to War: Toward a Scientific Explanation of Correlates of War Findings," *World Politics*, Vol. 40, No. 1 (October 1987), pp. 111–114.

38. My definition of structures here follows Alexander Wendt's discussion of "scientific realism" in "The Agent-Structure Problem in International Relations Theory," *International Organization*, Vol. 41, No. 3 (Summer 1987), especially pp. 351–352. See also Waltz, *Theory of International Politics*, pp. 79–101; and John Gerard Ruggie, "Continuity and Transformation in the World Polity: Toward a Neorealist Synthesis," in Keohane, ed., *Neorealism and Its Critics*, pp. 131–136.

39. See, for example, Singer, "The Incompleat Theorist," pp. 65–68; also Vasquez, "The Steps to War," pp. 113–114.

40. Wendt, "The Agent-Structure Problem in International Relations Theory," p. 352.

41. See, for example, Waltz, *Theory of International Politics*, pp. 4–5. Thomas S. Kuhn, *The Structure of Scientific Revolutions*, 2d ed., enl. (Chicago: University of Chicago Press, 1970), makes the most influential argument regarding the impossibility of a pure empiricism.

ing facts is not enough," Stanley Hoffmann has commented; "it is not helpful to gather answers when no questions have been asked first."[42]

International systems are one such structure: no one has ever seen, measured, or even described an international system with any precision; but few would deny that groups of nations in world politics do have characteristics that add up to more than the sum of their parts.[43] Multipolarity and bipolarity are real conditions in international affairs, despite the fact that no state's policies deliberately create them;[44] it makes a difference which of these conditions prevails at any given time.[45] Forms of government provide another example: no absolute standard allows one to distinguish democracies from dictatorships in the way that one can specify the differences between apples and oranges; and yet everyone knows that these two forms of government are not the same, and that the effects they produce—whether in terms of free elections, functioning economies, or respect for human rights—are indeed measurable. Unobservable structures can exist within governments, where they take the form of bureaucratic, organizational, and psychological constraints that do not always reflect what might be apparent on the "observable" surface.[46] And it is very likely that such structures also exist in our minds, producing observable effects in the way in which we perceive reality, respond to it, and even, by means of language, characterize it.[47]

---

42. Hoffmann, "International Relations: The Long Road to Theory," p. 422. See also, for related arguments, David Hackett Fischer, *Historians' Fallacies: Toward a Logic of Historical Thought* (New York: Harper and Row, 1970), pp. 65–68; and Stephen Jay Gould, *Time's Arrow, Time's Cycle: Myth and Metaphor in the Discovery of Geological Time* (Cambridge, Mass.: Harvard University Press, pp. 48–49, 196.

43. See Robert Jervis, "Systems Theories and Diplomatic History," in Paul Gordon Lauren, ed., *Diplomacy: New Approaches in History, Theory, and Policy* (New York: Free Press, 1979), pp. 212–213; also Waltz, *Man, the State, and War*, pp. 159–223; Waltz, *Theory of International Politics*, p. 40.

44. This is not to say that statesmen have not *tried*, at one time or another, to create these structures: witness the efforts of Castlereagh and Metternich at the Congress of Vienna to build a multipolar system in post-Napoleonic Europe, or the attempts of their principal historical chronicler, Henry Kissinger, to follow their example during the Nixon administration. My point is that such efforts cannot work unless the systemic conditions that favor them are already present.

45. I refer here to the long debate over whether bipolarity or multipolarity is the more stable configuration for international systems. The debate can be conveniently sampled in Waltz, "International Structure, National Force, and the Balance of World Power"; and Karl W. Deutsch and J. David Singer, "Multipolar Power Systems and International Stability," both in Rosenau, *International Politics and Foreign Policy* (1969 ed.), pp. 314–324.

46. See Graham T. Allison, *Essence of Decision: Explaining the Cuban Missile Crisis* (Boston: Little, Brown, 1971); Irving L. Janis, *Victims of Groupthink: A Psychological Study of Foreign-Policy Decisions and Fiascoes* (Boston: Houghton Mifflin, 1972); Richard K. Betts, *Soldiers, Statesmen, and Cold War Crises* (Cambridge, Mass.: Harvard University Press, 1977).

47. See Jervis, *Perception and Misperception in International Politics*, passim; Deborah Welch Larson,

Structuralists proceed, then, from a primarily deductive, "top-down" approach that assumes the existence of unobservable phenomena in international relations, uses the collection of empirical evidence—by no means excluding quantitative and simulative techniques—to refine and verify generalizations about them, and then produces forecasts by projecting the resulting patterns into the future.

THE EVOLUTIONARY APPROACH

The evolutionary approach combines elements of the structural and the behavioral approaches, but extends them along a third axis, which is that of time. Both structuralists and behavioralists tend toward a static perspective; they pay relatively little attention to the possibility that structures and behaviors in international relations might evolve.[48] But the geological and biological sciences have preoccupied themselves with evolutionary processes—inanimate and animate—for almost two centuries now; historians, of course, have a much longer tradition of temporal analysis. It should have come as no surprise, therefore, that an evolutionary approach to international relations theory would sooner or later make its appearance.[49] Its adherents have come to see that the passage of time can not only influence both behavior and structure in world politics; it can also obscure the distinction between them.[50]

Theorists have become increasingly interested, for example, in the possibility that periods of war, peace, and political-economic hegemony recur in

Origins of Containment: A Psychological Explanation (Princeton: Princeton University Press, 1985), especially pp. 24–65; Robert Jervis, Richard Ned Lebow, and Janice Gross Stein, *Psychology and Deterrence* (Baltimore: Johns Hopkins University Press, 1985); also for a particular manifestation of this phenomenon, Richard K. Ashley and R.B.J. Walker, eds., "Speaking the Language of Exile: Dissidence in International Studies," *International Studies Quarterly*, Vol. 34, No. 3 (September 1990).

48. Which is not to imply that they ignore this possibility altogether. See, for example, Waltz, *Theory of International Politics*, pp. 199–204; also J. David Singer, "The Global System and its Sub-Systems," in James N. Rosenau, ed., *Linkage Politics: Essays on the Convergence of National and International Systems* (New York: Free Press, 1969), pp. 21–43.

49. Stanley Hoffmann explicitly encouraged such an approach in 1959; see "International Relations: The Long Road to Theory," p. 425. See also George Modelski, "Is World Politics Evolutionary Learning?" *International Organization*, Vol. 44, No. 1 (Winter 1990), pp. 1–24; and discussions of the "rediscovery" of history in Joseph S. Nye, Jr., and Sean M. Lynn-Jones, "International Security Studies: A Report of a Conference on the State of the Field," *International Security*, Vol. 12, No. 4 (Spring 1988), pp. 18–19; and Stephen M. Walt, "The Renaissance of Security Studies," *International Studies Quarterly*, Vol. 35, No. 2 (June 1991), p. 217.

50. See Wendt's summary of "structuration theory" in "The Agent-Structure Problem in International Relations Theory," pp. 355–361.

cyclical patterns extending over several hundred years.[51] This interest, in turn, has spawned a lively concern—extending well beyond the academic community—with the conditions that lead to the rise and decline of great powers.[52] But theorists have also begun to turn their attention to the possibility that irreversible shifts in individual and state behavior can occur on a worldwide scale, and that these can over time modify systemic structures.[53] The assumption here is that human beings and the states they create not only accumulate experience but also learn from it; and that such learning can bring about new ways of doing things, whether at the level of the international system as a whole, aggregations of states within that system, individual states themselves, or groups and individuals within the state.[54] The passage of time itself appears to be the critical requirement in order for this process to take place: if states are to transcend their own natures and evolve techniques of cooperation, then they must have the opportunity to learn from

51. See, for example, Robert Gilpin, *War and Change in World Politics* (New York: Cambridge University Press, 1981); George Modelski, ed., *Exploring Long Cycles* (Boulder, Colo.: Lynne Rienner, 1987); Joshua A. Goldstein, *Long Cycles: Prosperity and War in the Modern Age* (New Haven: Yale University Press, 1988).

52. Here the work of a historian, Paul Kennedy, has had the greatest influence through the national debate generated by the appearance of his book, *The Rise and Fall of the Great Powers: Economic Change and Military Conflict from 1500 to 2000* (New York: Random House, 1987). But see also Mancur Olson, *The Rise and Decline of Nations: Economic Growth, Stagflation, and Social Rigidities* (New Haven: Yale University Press, 1982); Aaron L. Friedberg, *The Weary Titan: Great Britain and the Experience of Relative Decline, 1895–1905* (Princeton: Princeton University Press, 1988); Henry R. Nau, *The Myth of America's Decline: Leading the World Economy into the 1990s* (New York: Oxford University Press, 1990); and Joseph S. Nye, Jr., *Bound to Lead: The Changing Nature of American Power* (New York: Basic Books, 1990).

53. See, for example, Robert O. Keohane and Joseph S. Nye, Jr., *Power and Interdependence: World Politics in Transition* (Boston: Little, Brown, 1977); Richard W. Mansbach and John A. Vasquez, *In Search of Theory: A New Paradigm for Global Politics* (New York: Columbia University Press, 1981); Michael Doyle, "Kant, Liberal Legacies, and Foreign Affairs," *Philosophy and Public Affairs*, Vol. 12, No. 3 and No. 4 (Summer and Fall 1983), pp. 205–235, 323–353; Richard Rosecrance, *The Rise of the Trading State: Commerce and Conquest in the Modern World* (New York: Basic Books, 1986); John Mueller, *Retreat from Doomsday: The Obsolescence of Major War* (New York: Basic Books, 1989); James Lee Ray, "The Abolition of Slavery and the End of International War," *International Organization*, Vol. 43, No. 3 (Summer 1989), pp. 405–439; Francis Fukuyama, "The End of History?" *The National Interest*, No. 16 (Summer 1989), pp. 3–18. Waltz in his recent writings has begun to acknowledge this possibility. See "Reflections on *Theory of International Politics*: A Response to My Critics," in Keohane, ed., *Neorealism and Its Critics*, pp. 327–328, 343.

54. See Stephen D. Krasner, ed., *International Regimes* (Ithaca: Cornell University Press, 1983); Joseph S. Nye, Jr., "Nuclear Learning and U.S.-Soviet Security Regimes," *International Organization*, Vol. 41, No. 3 (Summer 1987), pp. 371–402; Alexander L. George, "Incentives for U.S.-Soviet Security Cooperation and Mutual Adjustment," in Alexander L. George, Philip J. Farley, and Alexander Dallin, eds., *U.S.-Soviet Security Cooperation: Achievements, Failures, Lessons* (New York: Oxford University Press, 1988), pp. 641–654.

experience, together with the confidence that existing conditions will continue at least into the near future.[55]

Behavioral, structural, and evolutionary approaches to the construction of international relations theory each have their weaknesses. The behavioralists tend to focus only on observable, measurable phenomena, thereby excluding from their vision those aspects of international relations that do not fall into that category. The structuralists, by taking the opposite approach, produce impressionistic judgments and unverifiable conclusions. And both behavioralists and structuralists neglect the role of time in world politics, a subject the evolutionists focus on, but only at the expense of blurring the distinction between behavior and structure in the first place. It is hardly surprising, therefore, that no grand theory of international relations has arisen to replace Morgenthau;[56] the absence of such a theory, in turn, greatly complicates efforts to forecast world politics. Still the distinction between behavioral, structural, and evolutionary approaches should serve as an adequate framework within which to evaluate such efforts as have been made, and from which to make suggestions about possible improvements.

Theory, Theorists, and the End of the Cold War

Establishing criteria for success, in forecasting, is no easy thing to do.[57] How much weight should one give, for example, to a vision of the future that turns out to be right, but for the wrong reasons? What if the reasons are right but the timing is wrong? How much precision should one demand, and how much detail can one expect? To what extent should one reward lucky guesses? How does one take into account the possibility that forecasts might make themselves inaccurate by encouraging action to alter existing

---

55. These points are made on the basis of both theoretical and historical evidence in Axelrod, *The Evolution of Cooperation*; and Kenneth A. Oye, ed., *Cooperation Under Anarchy* (Princeton: Princeton University Press, 1986).
56. For the decline of grand theory, see K.J. Holsti, "Retreat from Utopia," pp. 165–177.
57. Some efforts to define criteria for success in forecasting appear in William Ascher, *Forecasting: An Appraisal for Policy-Makers and Planners* (Baltimore: Johns Hopkins University Press, 1978), pp. 2–13; Singer, "The Peace Researcher and Foreign Policy Prediction," p. 5; Choucri, "Key Issues in International Relations Forecasting," p. 4; and Edward E. Azar (drawing on earlier work by Davis Bobrow), "Behavioral Forecasts and Policymaking: An Events Data Approach," in Kegley, et al., eds., *International Events and the Comparative Analysis of Foreign Policy*, pp. 216–217. I have also benefited from an informal seminar on this problem organized by Kennette Benedict and Philip E. Tetlock at the John D. and Catherine T. MacArthur Foundation in October 1990.

trends? The complexities are such that one is tempted to fall back on Justice Potter Stewart's famous rule for recognizing pornography: "I know it when I see it."[58]

For the purposes of this essay, though, let us establish a relatively easy test. Let us say that a successful anticipation of the Cold War's end need not have been a deterministic or a conditional prediction, but only a probabilistic forecast.[59] Let us absolve it of any obligation to have foreseen all or even most of the circumstances that brought about that event. Let us require of it only the specification in advance of at least one of the following as *likely:* (1) the asymmetrical outcome—that is, the fact that only one of the two Cold War superpowers, not both, lost that status; (2) the manner in which this happened—that is, an abrupt but peaceful collapse of Moscow's authority both within and beyond the borders of the former Soviet Union; (3) the trends that caused this loss of authority to occur—that is, the increasing unworkability of command economies, together with the infeasibility of using authoritarian means to rescue them; (4) the approximate timing of these developments—that is, the last half of the 1980s and the early 1990s; or (5) the rough outlines of a world without the Cold War—especially one in which German reunification has taken place, NATO has survived despite the Warsaw Pact's demise, and democratization has revived ancient ethnic, linguistic, and religious rivalries in territories that once lay within, or adjacent to, the Soviet sphere of influence.

What is immediately obvious, on reviewing this list, is that very few of our theoretical approaches to the study of international relations came anywhere close to forecasting *any* of these developments. One might as well have relied upon star-gazers, readers of entrails, and other "pre-scientific" methods for all the good our "scientific" methods did;[60] clearly our theories were not up to the task of anticipating the most significant event in world politics since the end of World War II.[61] The following discussion of inter-

---

58. James B. Simpson, compiler, *Simpson's Contemporary Quotations* (Boston: Houghton Mifflin, 1988), p. 79.
59. For definitions of these terms, see note 2.
60. For evidence that the Reagan administration did at times employ such methods, see Donald T. Regan, *For the Record: From Wall Street to Washington* (New York: St. Martin's Press, 1988), pp. 78–83, 409–412; and Lou Cannon, *President Reagan: The Role of a Lifetime* (New York: Simon and Schuster, 1991), pp. 583–586.
61. They have not been particularly successful in anticipating other major events either. See, on this point, David Easton, "The New Revolution in Political Science," *American Political Science Review,* Vol. 63, No. 4 (December 1969), pp. 1053, 1057; also James N. Rosenau, "Assessment in International Studies: Ego Trip or Feedback," *International Studies Quarterly,* Vol. 43, No. 3

national relations theorists and the end of the Cold War must necessarily concentrate, therefore, on what did not happen rather than on what did. Still, as Sherlock Holmes noted long ago, dogs that do *not* bark in the night have their own important messages to convey.

BEHAVIORAL APPROACHES

The behavioralist research agenda, J. David Singer argued in 1972, was to move from the collection of data through the construction of theory to the generation of forecasts: "The number one task for peace research always turns out to be that of prediction," which, in turn, was "the ability to forecast, with increasing reliability, the outcomes which are most likely to emerge out of a given set of background conditions and behavioral events." Existing methods of forecasting were inadequate: "if we peace researchers are to nudge human history onto a slightly different course—and we can strive for nothing less—we must radically revise the style and method of social forecasting as we know it today."[62]

Nine years earlier, Singer and his colleagues had founded the Correlates of War Project at the University of Michigan, a careful effort to catalog the causes and nature of modern wars that must now be the most frequently-cited of all data-collection enterprises in the field of international relations. The research program he laid out in 1972 is of special interest, therefore, not simply for its clarity but also for the central position its author has occupied in the study of war and peace over the past three decades. It provides a standard against which to measure what the behavioralist approach has achieved.

Dismissing such familiar—or fashionable—forecasting techniques as simple extrapolation, "seat of the pants" guessing, Delphi methods,[63] and simulations, Singer called first for work to identify relationships between variables that were likely to influence conditions of war or peace. These correlations could be tested against the historical record; if they held up—and if one could reasonably assume their continuation into the future—then they might

(September 1974), p. 344; and Michael D. Wallace, "Early Warning Indicators from the Correlates of War Project," in J. David Singer and Michael D. Wallace, eds., *To Augur Well: Early Warning Indicators in World Politics* (Beverly Hills, Calif.: SAGE, 1979), p. 17.
62. Singer, "The Peace Researcher and Foreign Policy Prediction" pp. 1–2.
63. Popularized by the RAND Corporation in the 1950s, the Delphi method involved eliciting successively more specific predictions on a particular problem from a group of experts who were in touch with one another only to the extent that they reviewed each other's predictions.

provide a means of forecasting what was to come. What would be needed if one were to accomplish this, though, Singer insisted, was "theory-based prediction."[64]

Singer defined theory as "a reproducible and compelling explanation of a given class of events." Theories were superior to correlations because they could not only identify patterns, but also explain why, when, and under what circumstances patterns occurred. They could describe the dynamics of systems as well as their static characteristics. "In sum," Singer concluded, "correlational knowledge can carry us part way, but until we have built and empirically tested a theory which offers a compelling explanation of the changing as well as the constant associations in the past, we make predictions of less than desirable solidity."[65]

The construction of such a theory would require, first, "a reasonably extensive and accurate data base." Computer modeling could then allow the manipulation of variables at different magnitudes, after which the results could be checked—and refined—by reference back to historical experience. This technique would allow one, in effect, to "reproduce" diplomatic history, while at the same time projecting it into various futures as specified by the researcher. Out of these efforts would come, first, "the most feasible way of ascertaining when, and in what fashion, the theoretical dynamics of the international system change"; second, "the factors that most strongly account for those changing relationships"; and third, the ultimate identification of "the mechanisms which account for and produce such systemic dynamics."[66]

In the years that have followed the appearance of Singer's article, behavioralists have indeed made heroic efforts to collect and analyze data, not just on the causes and nature of war but on the workings of the international system generally.[67] They have done this in a manner consistent with their determination to build theory only on a base of observable and measurable

64. Singer, "The Peace Researcher and Foreign Policy Prediction," pp. 2–5.
65. Ibid., pp. 5–6.
66. Ibid., pp. 7–8.
67. I refer here, not just to the Correlates of War Project, but also to such other data collection enterprises as the Dimensionality of Nations Project, the World Event Interaction Survey, the Conflict and Peace Data Bank, the Cooperative Research on the Events of Nations Project, and the Foreign Relations Indicator Project, all of which have operated according to different rules and for different purposes. I have chosen to focus this analysis on the Correlates of War Project because I believe its influence on the field of international relations has been, and remains, greater than that of the other data collection efforts; it is also the case that its principal founder, Singer, has made the most explicit claims regarding the utility of such data collection efforts in forecasting.

phenomena. They have identified key variables from this body of data; they have established correlations among them using an ingenious array of statistical and computer techniques; they have checked and rechecked these findings against the historical record; they have communicated the results honestly and openly; and they have trained an entire generation of students to carry on this research agenda into the future.

Unfortunately, though, the behavioralist approach has produced neither theory, nor forecasts, nor usable policy recommendations.[68] At the time the Cold War ended it was still gathering and correlating data, a process from which few firm conclusions of any kind have emerged. The behavioralists themselves have often commented on this phenomenon: "Regardless of the theoretical interpretation, the empirical investigations led once more to inconsistent results."[69] "Although the goal of a social scientific perspective on negotiations is cumulation, the development of the literature in this field to date suggests that the results fall well short of this goal."[70] "Unquestionably, one of the greatest disappointments experienced by early [comparative foreign policy] proponents has been their perceived failure to generate intellectual products even roughly commensurate with early expectations."[71]

There are, to be sure, good reasons why the behavioral study of world politics has yielded such inconclusive results. For one thing, fewer directly measurable entities exist at the level of international relations than at other levels of human activity. It is not all that difficult to accumulate data from questionnaires documenting the habits and preferences of individuals, or from votes cast in national elections, or from statistics on national economic performance, but how does one translate concepts like "polarity," or "hostility," or "deterrence"—fundamental as they are to an understanding of global systems—into calculable expressions?[72] It is also worth remembering

68. See, on this point, Ferguson and Mansbach, *The Elusive Quest*, pp. 29–30; John A. Vasquez, "Statistical Findings in International Politics: A Data-Based Assessment," *International Studies Quarterly*, Vol. 20, No. 2 (June 1976), pp. 171–218; and Charles F. Hermann and Gregory Peacock, "The Evolution and Future of Theoretical Research in the Comparative Study of Foreign Policy," in Charles F. Hermann, Charles W. Kegley, Jr., and James N. Rosenau, eds., *New Directions in the Study of Foreign Policy* (Boston: Allen and Unwin, 1987), pp. 13–32.
69. J. David Singer, "Accounting for International War: The State of the Discipline," *Journal of Peace Research*, Vol. 28 (1981), p. 9.
70. Druckman and Hopmann, "Behavioral Aspects of Negotiations on Mutual Security," p. 96.
71. Hermann and Peacock, "The Evolution and Future of Theoretical Research in the Comparative Study of Foreign Policy," p. 16.
72. David Dessler, "Beyond Correlations: Toward a Causal Theory of War," *International Studies Quarterly*, Vol. 35, No. 3 (September 1991), pp. 340–342, discusses the problems heterogenous variables have posed for the Correlates of War Project.

that behavioralism began as a young science,[73] and that the behavioralists never claimed the ability to forecast anything with authority until theories derived from scientifically valid evidence were solidly in place, however long this took. From these perspectives, then, it is unfair to criticize behaviorialist scholarship for not having anticipated the end of the Cold War.

Still, the protracted delay in producing what was promised cannot help but create doubts as to the ultimate viability of the behavioralist enterprise. It makes one wonder whether the approach may not be stuck in a permanent condition of adolescence. Certainly it raises question as to whether theory has not become, for the behavioralists, something like what the classless society once was for Marxist-Leninists: a goal to which one pays deference and toward which one works, but without ever getting there. The behavioral approach to international relations theory remains just that—an approach: it has never gotten beyond the generation of correlational knowledge that Singer specified as the first step toward theory construction. The absence of theory is a major reason, therefore, as well as an excuse, for why the behavioralist literature has given so little attention to forecasting, and hence to the end of the Cold War.

What insights, though, has behavioralism produced? Behavioralists have put forward *some* generalizations relating to present conditions and future prospects in world politics, but these tend to be highly tentative, imperfectly integrated, and drawn almost entirely from statistically demonstrated correlations.[74] I have tried to summarize the most important of these below, with a view to determining what forecasting utility, if any, they might have had:

WARS ARE BECOMING LESS FREQUENT, BUT MORE DANGEROUS. The Correlates of War Project has shown that the frequency of both international and civil wars has been declining—when measured against the increasing number of states in the international system—and that it has done so dramatically since 1945.[75] But behavioralists have not concluded from this, as have other scholars,[76] that great power war is becoming obsolete; on the contrary, they have

---

73. See, on this point, Bruce M. Russett, "The Young Science of International Politics," *World Politics*, Vol. 12, No. 1 (October 1969), pp. 87–94.
74. Dessler, "Beyond Correlations," passim.
75. Small and Singer, "Conflict in the International System," pp. 61–74. See also Jack S. Levy, *War in the Modern Great Power System, 1495–1975* (Lexington: University Press of Kentucky, 1983), pp. 144–149, which argues that wars among great powers have been declining in frequency over the past five hundred years, but that they have been increasing in their severity.
76. For example, Mueller, *Retreat from Doomsday*; Ray, "The Abolition of Slavery and the End of International War."

stressed the increasing severity of the wars that do occur, together with the persistence of arms races, the dangers of nuclear and conventional weapons proliferation, and the absence of safeguards that would keep wars from breaking out. They have tended to conclude, as Singer and Melvin Small did in 1979, that the international system remains "fundamentally as war-prone as it has been since the Congress of Vienna."[77]

ALLIANCES RARELY BRING SECURITY. One generally forms alliances for the purpose of making one's nation more secure, but the behavioralist literature suggests strongly that one ought not to count on this. Past efforts to bolster security by aligning against potential adversaries have more often than not set off arms races, thereby diminishing security in the long run.[78] Except during the nineteenth century, most participants in alliances over the past five centuries—and all great power participants—have found themselves at war within five years after the alliance was formed.[79] One cannot rely on alliance partners to meet their obligations if war breaks out; alliances also tend to expand wars once they have begun.[80] "In sum," Michael D. Wallace concluded in 1979, "most of the evidence seems to be against those who see military alliances as necessary to peace, and on the side of those who see them as a danger."[81]

PREPARATION FOR WAR RARELY ENSURES PEACE. The dictum "Let him who desires peace prepare for war" has long been used to justify the existence and expansion of large military establishments. But Correlates of War Project statistics suggest that preparation for war has most often caused arms races, with all their attendant risks, rather than the peace this ancient maxim promises. The "far safer course of action," Wallace noted in 1981, "is to maintain unilateral restraint in acquiring new weapons systems while seeking every opportunity to negotiate bilateral and multilateral agreements to limit development and deployment."[82] Subsequent research in this area has shown a close correspondence between increases in military spending and involvement in military conflict: excuses tend to be found to use the weapons one

---

77. Small and Singer, "Conflict in the International System," p. 80.
78. Singer, *Models, Methods, and Progress in World Politics*, pp. 194–195.
79. Jack Levy, "Alliance Formation and War Behavior: An Analysis of the Great Powers, 1495–1975," *Journal of Conflict Resolution*, Vol. 25, No. 4 (December 1981), pp. 581–613.
80. Vasquez, "The Steps to War," pp. 120–123.
81. Michael D. Wallace, "Early Warning Indicators from the Correlates of War Project," in Singer and Wallace, *To Augur Well*, p. 97.
82. Michael D. Wallace, "Old Nails in New Coffins: The Para Bellum Hypothesis Revisited," *Journal of Peace Research*, Vol. 28 (1981), pp. 94–95.

develops.[83] Meanwhile, quantitative studies of deterrence successes and failures have revealed little correlation between military superiority, on the one hand, and success in deterring adversaries, on the other.[84]

POWER DISPARITIES PROMOTE PEACE. Behavioralists have also argued, though, that in the twentieth century at least, a well-defined international system—that is, one in which each state clearly understands the intentions and capabilities of the others—makes the events that take place within that system more predictable; war, which tends to arise from the inability of statesmen to foresee consequences, therefore becomes less likely.[85] It would appear to follow from this that a hierarchical system of international relations—a situation in which a few great powers dominate a much larger number of weaker states—encourages stability. Great powers are more likely than smaller ones to be cautious in their dealings with one another, while smaller powers, whether cautious or not, lack the means and the inclination to challenge larger ones.[86]

BIPOLARITY MAY, OR MAY NOT, PROMOTE PEACE. Behavioralists have long sought to settle, by scientific means, the important question of whether bipolar or multipolar systems are more stable. But as one recent review of this literature has noted, the findings have been "exceedingly complicated and sometimes inconsistent."[87] Some evidence suggests that war is more likely under conditions of extreme bipolarity and extreme multipolarity, but less likely if the situation falls between these extremes.[88] Other research concludes—even less helpfully—that the increasing "tightness" of bipolar alignments tends to lead to war, but that an expansion of "poles" within the international system is likely to have the same result: shifts toward either

---

83. Singer, "Research, Policy, and the Correlates of War," pp. 54–55.

84. Jack S. Levy, "Quantitative Studies of Deterrence Success and Failure," in Paul Stern, Robert Axelrod, Robert Jervis, and Roy Radner, eds., *Perspectives on Deterrence* (New York: Oxford University Press, 1989), pp. 117–118, 120.

85. J. David Singer, "Research, Policy, and the Correlates of War," in Øvind Østerud, ed., *Studies of War and Peace* (Oslo: Norwegian University Press, 1986), pp. 51–52; Singer, *Models, Methods, and Progress in World Politics*, pp. 242–244. It is important to note, however, that Singer's evidence suggests the opposite to have been the case during the nineteenth century. For his non-quantitative speculation as to the reasons for this, see ibid., pp. 252–255.

86. See Manus I. Midlarsky, "A Hierarchical Equilibrium Theory of Systemic War," *International Studies Quarterly*, Vol. 30 (1986), especially pp. 85–87; also Manus I. Midlarsky, *The Onset of World War* (Boston: Unwin Hyman, 1988).

87. Vasquez, "The Steps to War," p. 123.

88. Michael D. Wallace, "Alliance Polarization, Cross-Cutting, and International War, 1815–1964: A Measurement Procedure and Some Preliminary Evidence," in Singer and associates, *Explaining War*, p. 105.

bipolarity or multipolarity, it appears, are dangerous.[89] One can only conclude from all of this, as Singer himself does, that "depending on the variables used, the ways in which they were measured, the spatial-temporal
domain covered, and the statistical models that were applied to the data, we
obtain appreciably different results."[90]

This brief summary of behavioralist findings on the problem of war and
peace fails to do justice to the complexities and nuances of the research that
produced them. But the above propositions will serve, I think, as a fair
approximation of what a policy-maker interested in applying behavioral research to world politics would have drawn from this body of work. They
also suggest the difficulties such a policy-maker would have in seeking to
base any reasonably coherent course of action on them.

What is one to make, for example, of the observation that wars are becoming less frequent but more dangerous? Is this insight likely to have escaped
the attention of policy-makers unfamiliar with behavioralist research? How
is one to reconcile the arguments (a) that alliances rarely achieve security
and (b) that preparation for war provides no protection against it, with the
assertion (c) that disparities in power correlate with peace? How have power
differentials developed in the past, after all, if not largely through the accumulation of the military strength that alliances and armaments provide? And
what policy implications would behavioralist findings on the respective merits of bipolarity and multipolarity suggest, given the uncertainty of the behavioralists themselves as to what those findings are? In short, the major
"policy-relevant" conclusions behavioralist research has produced are either
self-evident, self-contradictory, or self-confusing.

Nor, if the fading of Soviet-American competition can serve as a test, do
these findings provide any very good basis for forecasting. The declining
incidence of war would have been a good indicator of what was to happen,
but behaviorialists chose not to make the forecast one might have expected
from such data; instead they concluded that the danger of a great power
conflict would be at least as high during the 1980s as it had been in the past.
The Western military buildup during the early part of that decade—together
with the strengthening of the NATO alliance that accompanied it—does not
appear to have delayed the end of the Cold War; on the contrary, these

---

89. Bruce Bueno de Mesquita, "Systemic Polarization and the Occurrence and Duration of War,"
in Singer and associates, *Explaining War*, pp. 129–32.
90. Singer, *Models, Methods, and Progress in World Politics*, p. 255.

initiatives may have hastened it.[91] The behavioralists' point about power disparities does help to explain the relative stability of the Cold War international system, but it would have provided no warning of that system's impending collapse. Nor—given their uncertainty on the effects of bipolarity and multipolarity—are the behavioralists able to make any coherent forecasts of what might replace it.

It is not my purpose here to question the competency of those scholars who have embraced behavioralism in the study of international relations. They have often been their own toughest critics; few of the criticisms I have made above have not also been made by behavioralists themselves in assessing their own work or that of their colleagues.[92] But if we are to determine why behavioralism's performance with respect to forecasting has fallen so far short of what was promised, we must consider certain difficulties that have affected the approach as a whole:

THE TYRANNY OF METHOD OVER SUBJECT. Despite the self-chosen association of many behavioralists with the field of "peace studies," the data bases they have assembled have concerned themselves, to a striking degree, with the subject of war. Their focus has been on conflict, escalation, deterrence, crisis management, and crisis decision-making. They have shown more interest in the circumstances that cause peace to break down than with those that cause it to break out. This has happened, I think, for two reasons.

---

91. This point is a controversial one, and the evidence necessary to confirm it is not yet available. It is clear that the initial response by the Brezhnev-Andropov leadership was a dangerous war scare, best discussed in Christopher Andrew and Oleg Gordievsky, *KGB: The Inside Story of its Foreign Operations from Lenin to Gorbachev* (New York: HarperCollins, 1990), pp. 581–605. But it also seems clear that President Reagan's announcement of the Strategic Defense Initiative in March 1983, together with the Soviet government's failure to prevent the NATO intermediate-range nuclear forces deployment later that year, did set off a fundamental reassessment of foreign and military policy inside the Kremlin. See Jerry Hough, *Russia and the West: Gorbachev and the Politics of Reform*, 2d ed. (New York: Simon and Schuster, 1990), pp. 118–121; also Michael MccGwire, *Perestroika and Soviet National Security Policy* (Washington, D.C.: Brookings, 1991), pp. 115–173. The key question is what influence this reassessment had on Mikhail Gorbachev when he came to power in 1985: did the Soviet Union's failures in these areas push him into *perestroika*, or would he have gone in that direction in any event? Preliminary attempts to answer this question include Deudney and Ikenberry, "The International Sources of Soviet Change," passim; Thomas Risse-Kappen, "Did 'Peace Through Strength' End the Cold War? Lessons from INF," *International Security*, Vol. 16, No. 1 (Summer 1991), pp. 162–188; Daniel Deudney and G. John Ikenberry, "Who Won the Cold War?" *Foreign Policy*, No. 87 (Summer 1992), pp. 123–138; and the account of a well-informed journalist, Don Oberdorfer, *The Turn: From the Cold War to a New Era: The United States and the Soviet Union, 1983–1990* (New York: Poseidon, 1991).

92. This is especially true of Singer, whose recent collection of essays, *Models, Methods, and Progress in World Politics*, repeatedly reflects his willingness to submit behavioralist research to critical scrutiny. See also, in particular, Hermann and Peacock, "The Evolution and Future of Theoretical Research in the Comparative Study of Foreign Policy," passim.

First, these projects all began at the height of the Cold War, when the prospects of a hot war were uppermost in people's minds. Given the massive character of these projects, and especially their emphasis on reproducible cumulative research, it has not been easy to redirect priorities as circumstances have changed. There is a considerable irony in the fact that it proved easier to modify the official policies of the United States and the Soviet Union toward one another than to shift the focus of the major behavioralist data-collection projects that were supposed to provide insights into how those governments' policies might be modified.

Second, the behavioralists' concentration on the causes and manifestations of conflict reflect what the historical logician David Hackett Fischer has called the "quantitative fallacy": this is the assumption that "facts are important in proportion to their susceptibility to quantification."[93] It was simply easier to count events related to war than to peace. War is an exceptional event in international relations; despite the frequency with which it has occurred, it is always a departure from the normal state of affairs, and departures from the norm are always less difficult to measure than the norm itself.

There was nothing inherent in behavioralism that required its practitioners to proceed in this manner. One of the few even partially successful anticipations of the Cold War's end came from a pioneer in the behavioral approach to international relations, Karl Deutsch, in a 1966 article entitled "The Future of World Politics." In it, Deutsch focused not so much on the causes of conflict or the nature of the global system as on its impending transformation, a process he saw taking place because of the growth of literacy and urbanization, diminishing income inequalities, and the increasing involvement of the masses in politics. From these trends, he forecast that autocracies would find it more and more difficult to govern, that the costs of intervention in foreign countries would mount, that threats would carry less and less credibility, that nationalism would erode ideological blocs, that economic influence would become more important than military force and that, in the end, a more mature condition of international society would develop than the one that had existed throughout most of the twentieth century.[94]

If a pioneer in the behavioralist movement could come up with these prescient observations a quarter of a century prior to the end of the Cold

---

93. Fischer, *Historians' Fallacies*, p. 90. For related criticisms, see Waltz, *Theory of International Politics*, p. 64; and Hoffmann, "The Long Road to Theory," pp. 427–429.
94. Karl W. Deutsch, "The Future of World Politics," *Political Quarterly*, Vol. 37, No. 1 (January–March 1966), pp. 9–32.

War, one has to wonder why the field as a whole was unable to accomplish anything like this. The answer would appear to be that Deutsch was prepared to depart from quantitative analysis when that technique was inappropriate: for him, subject determined method, rather than the other way around. Too many other behavioralists let method determine subject,[95] with the consequences one might expect in any situation in which means are allowed to overshadow avowed ends.

PROBLEMS OF DATA COLLECTION AND ANALYSIS. Any behavioralist would acknowledge, in principle, that one can never be totally atheoretical, otherwise one could never define research priorities. But Singer has made a point, in the Correlates of War Project, of deferring a commitment to any single theory until as much evidence as possible has been gathered. This procedure allows the testing of theories without preconceptions; presumably it would also make the endorsement of a particular theory, were that to occur, more convincing than it otherwise would have been.[96] The difficulty here is that such a deferral also vastly increases the task of data collection, because one thereby loses a major function that theories serve, which is to provide a basis for distinguishing between significant and trivial information. The amount of potentially useful but still unassimilated evidence does not noticeably diminish, in an atheoretical research enterprise, with the passage of time.[97] Or, to paraphrase a famous law of administrative science, data expands to fill the vacuum left by the absence of theory, and one never gets past the first step in one's research agenda.

A related difficulty has to do with the kind of data one collects. Behavioralists limit themselves to measuring directly observable phenomena. They by no means ignore unobservable influences, but they count them only when they manifest themselves in some quantifiable form. That approach may work in fields like politics, economics, or academia, where a single universally accepted unit of measure—votes, for example, or money, or ponderous publications—exists. But there is no such unit in the field of international relations;[98] one must choose, instead, between two alternatives, neither of them completely satisfactory: One can confine one's analysis to that limited

---

95. Waltz, *Theory of International Politics*, p. 13; Ferguson and Mansbach, *The Elusive Quest*, pp. 28–30.
96. See, on these points, Singer, "The 'Correlates of War' Project," pp. 248, 251.
97. Waltz, *Theory of International Politics*, p. 5. The behavioralists have fallen victim, I believe, to the fallacy of "holism." For more on this, see Fischer, *Historians' Fallacies*, pp. 65–68.
98. See Hoffmann, "The Long Road to Theory," p. 428.

sphere of world politics in which quantifiable entities do exist—war casualties, arms races, trade statistics, population movements, and the like—but this can lead to the quantitative fallacy, and hence to the danger of missing the kind of non-quantifiable information Deutsch focused on in his 1966 article. Or one can artificially create quantifiable entities, a procedure that has been the basis for the "events data" movement, an important part of the behavioral approach to theory construction over the past several decades.

But this latter course raises other difficulties, which have to do with the way in which one interprets the data one collects. Because information gathered has to be coded if it is to be quantified—and because coding is inescapably dependent on the subjective perceptions of those doing the coding—"events data" tends to fall short of scientific standards for objectivity and reproducibility.[99] Comparisons of data bases covering the same subject have shown an unsettling lack of correspondence, as have efforts to replicate coding procedures.[100] One is left with the suspicion that our supposedly objective data-collection efforts may not be much freer from impressionistic and arbitrary judgments than are the old-fashioned historical narratives they sought to replace.

MODELING REALITY. Even if methods were subordinated to subjects and problems of data collection and analysis had been solved, the behavioralist approach to theory and forecasting would confront a remaining difficulty: it has to do with relating the generalizations that emerge from correlations to the real world. When Singer composed his 1972 research agenda, he envisaged constructing "the most plausible and parsimonious model" one could devise that would explain the recurrence of war and peace; one would then "examine how closely that model fits the historical patterns which have been

---

99. "No matter how detailed and thorough an historical inquiry may be, it certainly cannot leave us with a unique correlation between the various empirical variables which will force all observers to make identical inferences and conclusions." Olav Njølstad, "Learning from History? Case Studies and the Limits to Theory-Building," in Nils Petter Gleditsch and Olav Njølstad, eds., *Arms Races: Political and Technological Dynamics* (London: SAGE, 1990), p. 223.
100. See Llewellyn D. Howell, "A Comparative Study of the WEIS and COPDAB Data Sets," *International Studies Quarterly*, Vol. 27 (1983), pp. 149–159; Jack E. Vincent, "WEIS vs. COPDAB: Correspondence Problems," ibid., pp. 161–168; Charles A. McClelland, "Let the User Beware," ibid., pp. 169–177; Charles H. Anderton, "Arms Race Modeling: Problems and Prospects," *Journal of Conflict Resolution*, Vol. 33, No. 3 (June 1989), pp. 350–353; Gary King, "Event Count Models for International Relations: Generalizations and Applications," *International Studies Quarterly*, Vol. 33, No. 2 (June 1989), pp. 125–128; and Richard Ned Lebow and Janice Gross Stein, "Deterrence: The Elusive Dependent Variable," *World Politics*, Vol. 42, No. 3 (April 1990), pp. 336–369.

observed and recorded earlier." Adjustments in the model would bring it progressively closer to historical experience; computer simulation would then allow movement "from runs of the past to runs of the future," without committing "the sin of mechanical extrapolation from past into future."[101]

There have always been doubts about the possibility of accomplishing this kind of thing. Gabriel Almond and Stephen Genco summarized them well in 1977 when, borrowing from Karl Popper, they pointed out that reality comprises a range of phenomena extending from the determinate to the indeterminate—from predictable clocks to unpredictable clouds, to use Popper's metaphor—and that "models, procedures, and methodologies created to explore a world in which clocklike and cloudlike characteristics predominate will capture only a part of the much richer world of social and political interaction." In their determination to be "scientific," social scientists had "overlooked the fact that much of social and political change has to be explained . . . by accidental conjunctions—by events that had a low probability of occurring." The implication of all of this, Almond and Genco insisted, was that "the explanatory strategy of the hard sciences has only a limited application to the social sciences."[102]

This argument made little impact at the time, given the conviction of behavioralists that a scientific approach, even to the study of apparently unpredictable phenomena, was indeed possible: all that was necessary was to get the proper "fit" between models and reality. But even as the social scientists were insisting on the need to apply "hard" scientific techniques to their field if it was ever to succeed at forecasting, the "hard" scientists themselves were backing away from the view that all phenomena could be modeled and their future behavior therefore predicted. What is even more ironic, in the light of Almond and Genco's critique, is that this shift away from scientific certainty began, quite literally, with the study of clouds.

Why, meteorologists had long asked, could one not build a computer simulation of the atmosphere that would allow reliable long-range weather forecasting? In what has now become a famous experiment, Edward Lorenz, a mathematically-inclined meteorologist, sought to construct such a model on a primitive computer at the Massachusetts Institute of Technology in 1961. Lorenz had his computer calculate certain meteorological correlations, based

---

101. Singer, "The Peace Researcher and Foreign Policy Prediction," pp. 7–8.
102. Gabriel A. Almond and Stephen J. Genco, "Clouds, Clocks, and the Study of Politics," *World Politics*, Vol. 20, No. 4 (July 1977), pp. 493, 496–497.

on known variables and a single starting point. But he quickly found that tiny variations in his parameters—the rounding of a number from six decimal points to three, for example—produced startling effects on his computer screen: patterns that should have corresponded in fact diverged dramatically, and did so on the basis of statistical variations so minute that no real-world measuring device could possibly compensate for them. What this suggested, Lorenz noted in another cloud-related metaphor, was that something as unpredictable as the fluttering of a butterfly's wings over Beijing could produce a hurricane over New York. Thus was born the principle of "sensitive dependence on initial conditions," the "butterfly effect," that makes long-term weather forecasting—the transformation of clouds into clocks, if you will—impossible.[103]

Not all phenomena, to be sure, are subject to the butterfly effect. The motions of planets, and of spacecraft traveling between them, do proceed like clockwork, and the familiar principles of Newtonian physics provide an entirely adequate method of forecasting their behavior for, if necessary, centuries to come. But these are systems in which only a few critical and easily calculable variables are at work. Equally reliable weather forecasting over a time scale extending only into next week would require calculating an infinite number of variables with infinite precision, a task well beyond the abilities of even the most sophisticated computer today, or in the foreseeable future. As a consequence, scientists have had to learn to live with the fact that some phenomena can be predicted with great accuracy, but that other phenomena can never be. Regularity and apparent randomness co-exist quite easily in a real world, which does not require their measurement, if not always in our minds, which do.[104]

Surely human affairs, and the history they produce, come closer to falling into the unpredictable rather than the predictable category: not only are the potentially relevant variables virtually infinite, but there is the added complication—not found in either clouds or clocks—of self-awareness, which means that the "variables" themselves can often foresee the consequences of contemplated actions, and reconsider them accordingly. The behavioralist enterprise of attempting to theorize about, and then to forecast, the actions

---

103. The story is well told in James Gleick, *Chaos: Making a New Science* (New York: Viking, 1987), pp. 11–21. Dessler, "Beyond Correlations," pp. 342–344, employs a similar meteorological metaphor to critique Correlates of War Project methodology.
104. See also, on the limited possibilities of prediction in the physical sciences, Kaplan, *System and Process in International Politics*, p. xvii.

of individuals, societies, nations, and groups of nations on the basis only of observable, calculable evidence and without taking into account the critical variable of self-awareness is, ultimately, an attempt to transform clouds into clocks. It is an incomplete, misleading, and washed-out representation of reality; no wonder, therefore, that it was so unsuccessful in forecasting the end of the Cold War.

STRUCTURAL APPROACHES

What about the structuralists? Did an approach to theory construction that incorporated the role of unobservable—and unquantifiable—phenomena in world politics do any better than the behavioralists in anticipating recent developments?

Morton A. Kaplan's 1957 book, *System and Process in International Politics,* was the first major attempt at a structural analysis of world politics. In it, Kaplan identified six distinctive international systems, only two of which had actually existed in modern history.[105] He described the characteristics of these systems in considerable detail, as well as the processes operating within them that would contribute to systemic perpetuation or disintegration. Kaplan claimed no ability to forecast what particular states within any of these systems might do in specific situations. He pointed out, though, that although physical scientists had no means of mapping in advance the paths of individual gas molecules, they could reliably predict how an aggregation of such molecules would behave under known pressures and temperatures. Theories of international politics, Kaplan thought, ought to work in much the same way: they should allow one to detect patterns of behavior within international systems, and they should be capable of specifying the conditions under which those systems would remain stable, or be transformed into something else.[106]

The two historical systems Kaplan identified were the familiar "balance of power" system, which had lasted throughout the eighteenth, nineteenth, and early twentieth centuries, and the "loose bipolar" system, which had

---

105. Ibid., pp. 21–53. For an even more elaborate typology, based on actual historical experience, see Rosecrance, *Action and Reaction in World Politics*, pp. 219–275. As Waltz has pointed out, however, Rosecrance's typology is not a structural theory. Waltz, *Theory of International Politics*, pp. 41–43.

106. Kaplan, *System and Process in International Politics*, pp. xvii–xviii. It is worth noting that Kaplan's claims regarding the structuralist approach to forecasting did not differ significantly from those Singer had made from a behavioralist perspective. See especially Singer, "The Peace Researcher and Foreign Policy Prediction," p. 8.

been functioning since 1945. As its name implied, the balance of power system had operated without a dominant power or combination of powers; instead each major state sought to counter bids for dominance on the part of other states. The loose bipolar system, in contrast, evolved from the fact that two predominant states had emerged from World War II capable of incorporating less powerful states into coalitions they controlled; the configuration was "loose" because some other states remained apart from these alignments, and because a few significant actors within the system—the United Nations, in particular—were not states.[107] Kaplan was able to draw upon historical evidence in describing these two systems, and in explaining how the first of them had evolved into the second. No historical evidence was available in 1957, though, to illustrate the breakup of a loose bipolar system, or to answer the question of what might replace it. Kaplan's theoretical description of this process is of interest, therefore, as an early attempt to forecast, solely by deductive means, how the end of the Cold War might come about.

Total war in a loose bipolar system, Kaplan anticipated, would bring about a unipolar international system if one side won, or chaos if both sides were exhausted. A stalemate, he thought, would produce a "tight bipolar" system, in which both antagonistic coalitions would become hierarchical. But what if these blocs should begin to disintegrate without war taking place? Here Kaplan argued that the greater the amount of hierarchy within a bloc, the more resistant to fragmentation it would be: coalitions that had come together freely would tend to fly apart more easily than those that had been forged, and sustained, by tight central control. Instability within voluntary coalitions would probably push the system as a whole toward unipolarity; in the unlikely event that involuntary coalitions should break up, the international system would revert to a balance of power configuration, or toward some form of international organization. A simultaneous weakening of both coalitions would also probably revive the balance of power system or encourage movement toward some form of central world government.

Loose bipolarity, Kaplan noted, contained "a considerable degree of inherent instability," because so much depended upon the kind of relationship

---

107. Kaplan, *System and Process in International Politics*, pp. 22–25, 36–38. Loose bipolarity did not require equivalent behavior by each pole: Kaplan made a point of stressing that the coalitions within such a system could be organized either hierarchically or non-hierarchically, so that integration within them could come about by coercion or by choice.

that existed between the two dominant states. There would be, on the one hand, a strong temptation for each of them to seek to eliminate its rival, if for no other reason than to avoid the danger of being eliminated itself. But, on the other hand, if "the destructive power of weapons increases to an inordinate degree, this fact may raise the costs of military action so greatly that the blocs arrive at some form of accommodation." And if such weapons should become relatively cheap, yet another kind of international system might evolve: a "unit veto" arrangement in which "each actor responded to the negative golden rule of natural law by not doing to others what he would not have them do to him." In short, all of the above options were possible: "Depending upon conditions, the loose bipolar system can be transformed . . . into a tight bipolar system, into a hierarchical international system, a universal international system, a 'balance of power' system, or a unit veto system."[108]

Kaplan's book was a remarkable feat of theoretical imagination, but that was also its problem. Critics found his discussion of four systems that had never existed to be puzzling: how could one know, Hedley Bull asked, that these were the *only* four possible systems and that, even if they were, all of the relevant variables that might shape their character had been included?[109] Kaplan's terminology was confusing—he used the term "subsystem dominant," for example, to suggest that the international system dominated units within it, and he applied the adjective "hierarchical" both to systems and to blocs within systems.[110] His structuralist approach did generate forecasts, but these tended to be so abstract and indecisive—so inclined toward "all of the above" conclusions—that they were of little greater use to policy-makers than those of the behavioralists would be. And in those few instances in which Kaplan did make specific predictions—for example, his assertion that tightly controlled coalitions would be more durable than those that functioned by mutual consent—they have not held up particularly well.

The principal criticism of Kaplan's method, though, was that he had failed to distinguish the structure of his respective international systems from the behavior of states within them. In an effort to explain how systems can become unstable and evolve into something else, he fell into the argument

---

108. Ibid., pp. 40–43, 50.
109. Hedley Bull, "International Theory: The Case for a Classical Approach," in Knorr and Rosenau, eds., *Contending Approaches to International Politics*, pp. 32–33.
110. See Kaplan, *System and Process in International Politics*, pp. 17, 40–41, 48–50.

that *processes within states* could shape systemic structures. The point would have been unexceptionable had Kaplan not also insisted that *international systems* determine the behavior of states. But since Kaplan had made that assertion, the logic of his analysis, and hence its capacity for forecasting, was questionable.[111]

That, at least, that was the argument that Kenneth N. Waltz, Kaplan's chief critic and the most influential "structuralist" in contemporary international relations theory, made in 1979. In his book, *Theory of International Politics,* Waltz sought to rescue the structuralist approach by making a sharp distinction between what he called "systems level" and "unit level" phenomena. Any theory that sought to account for or to anticipate the workings of an international system, he insisted, had to concern itself only with the characteristics of that system; it could not confuse the issue by introducing the behavior of individual states within it. The reason for this was that international systems imposed their own limits upon state action. Even the most revolutionary state would not revolutionize world politics if systemic influences resisted that objective; even the most conservative nation would fail to stabilize an international order if the systemic prerequisites for stability were not present. The internal character of states—whether democratic or autocratic, capitalist or communist, peace-loving or aggressive—made no difference; what defined an international system was the anarchic environment in which it operated, together with the distribution of capabilities across the states that existed within it. Changes in this distribution produced shifts in systemic structure.[112]

Waltz agreed with Kaplan that there had been only two international systemic structures in modern history: the multipolar system that had characterized interstate relations from approximately the time of the Treaty of Westphalia through the end of World War II, and the bipolar system that had replaced it. But Waltz went well beyond Kaplan in insisting, on both theoretical and historical grounds, that bipolar systems were inherently more "stable" than their multipolar counterparts. From a theoretical perspective, the existence of only two major adversaries minimized the possibilities of misperception, confusion, and unpredictable interaction: as any physicist could explain, two-body problems are far easier to solve than those involving

---

111. Waltz, *Theory of International Politics,* pp. 54–59.
112. Ibid., pp. 97–98.

three or more.[113] From a historical perspective, Waltz could point to the success of the United States and the Soviet Union in managing crises and maintaining alliances without resort to war over three and a half decades, a record that compared favorably with what the pre-1945 great powers had accomplished in a multipolar international environment.[114]

What did all of this imply about the future of the Cold War? A superficial reading of Waltz would suggest that, because he described bipolarity as more stable than multipolarity and because he defined "stability" as simply the capacity of the system to endure,[115] he had been quite wrong in 1979: multipolarity, after all, lasted for three hundred years; bipolarity would survive only for another ten. But Waltz had been careful to point out that the principal actors in the pre–World War II multipolar system had changed frequently: of some seven great powers in 1700, only France and Great Britain continued to enjoy that status in 1939. Turkey, Sweden, Spain, Austria, and the Netherlands had all lost their preeminence by the time World War II broke out; Germany, Italy, Japan, the Soviet Union, and the United States had arisen to take their place. Soviet-American bipolarity seemed robust forty years later because no third power had developed capabilities comparable to those commanded by Moscow and Washington, but the system was "unlikely to last as long as its predecessor."[116]

Common threats, Waltz believed, could transform enemies into allies. The emergence of the Soviet Union and the United States as adversaries after World War II had had the paradoxical effect of reconciling once antagonistic states in Western Europe. Conditions of insecurity that had caused Europeans to distrust one another for so long disappeared in the face of greater danger; long-term cooperation became possible, even as the Cold War itself intensified.[117] Even if no third state seemed likely to threaten Russians and Americans in a way that might cause them to settle their differences, Waltz came to see that a common technological threat might have the same result. Waltz had minimized the effects of nuclear weapons in *Theory of International Politics*—"in shaping the behavior of nations, the perennial forces of politics are

---

113. Ibid., p. 192. See also Waltz, "The Stability of a Bipolar World," *Daedalus*, Vol. 93, No. 3 (Summer 1964), pp. 881–909. A succinct explanation of why three-body problems defy solution appears in Peter Coveney and Roger Highfield, *The Arrow of Time: A Voyage Through Science to Solve Time's Greatest Mystery* (New York: Fawcett Columbine, 1990), p. 267.
114. Waltz, *Theory of International Politics*, pp. 163–176.
115. Ibid., pp. 132n, 161–162.
116. Ibid., p. 162.
117. Ibid., pp. 70–71.

more important than the new military technology"[118]—but he soon reconsidered this position, so much so, indeed, that by 1981 he was advocating the proliferation of nuclear capabilities to smaller powers as a sure way to guarantee peace among them. The possibility of an all-out nuclear war might well serve as the functional equivalent of a third party threat in driving the United States and the Soviet Union toward the discovery of common ground; certainly concentration on the destructive capabilities of nuclear weapons "has obscured the important benefits they promise to states trying to coexist in a self-help world."[119]

It was also the case that the very character of bipolar confrontation carried within it the causes of its own eventual demise. Citing conclusions drawn from the study of oligopolistic competition among corporations, Waltz pointed out that the passage of time makes it easier for rivals to cooperate: "The increasing similarity of competitors' attitudes, as well as their experience with one another, eases the adjustment of their relations." Bipolar situations, in particular, encouraged this process: "Tension in the system is high because each can do so much for and to the other. But because no appeal can be made to third parties, pressure to moderate behavior is heavy. . . . The simplicity of relations in a bipolar world and the strong pressures that are generated make the two great powers conservative."[120] By this logic, the bipolar structure of the post-1945 international system suggested an eventual moderation of Soviet-American hostility, if not an end to it altogether.

Waltz was not at all certain, therefore, that the Cold War would continue: indeed *Theory of International Politics* holds up rather well in its anticipation of several influences that would bring that conflict to an end. He did maintain, however, that bipolarity would survive: "The barriers to entering the superpower club have never been higher and more numerous. The club will long remain the world's most exclusive one."[121] The maturation of a bipolar relationship did not necessarily mean its passing: "American and Russian behavior has changed somewhat over time, but it has changed in the direc-

---

118. Ibid., p. 173.
119. Kenneth N. Waltz, "Toward Nuclear Peace," in Robert J. Art and Kenneth N. Waltz, eds., *The Use of Force: Military Power and International Politics*, 3d ed. (Lanham, Md.: University Press of America, 1988), p. 689. This essay originally appeared as *The Spread of Nuclear Weapons: More May Be Better*, Adelphi Paper No. 171 (London: International Institute of Strategic Studies, 1981). See also Kenneth N. Waltz, "Nuclear Myths and Political Realities," *American Political Science Review*, Vol. 84, No. 3 (September 1990), pp. 733–734.
120. Waltz, *Theory of International Politics*, pp. 173–174.
121. Ibid., p. 183.

tion one may expect it to take so long as the world remains bipolar."[122] This is where Waltz went wrong: he allowed for the possibility that Soviet and American behavior within a bipolar structure might evolve from confrontation to cooperation; but he made no allowance for the possibility that the structure itself might shift, or that changes in the policies of nations within it might contribute to that process.

The failure to account for structural change has always been the weakest point in Waltz's theory.[123] For if systemic structures do in fact reflect the distribution of capabilities across units, and if shifts in this distribution can in fact alter such structures, then it is difficult to see where those shifts might come from except from changes in the capabilities of states within the system. Those changes may arise, in turn, from a decision to make peace with rivals, or from a recognition that one can no longer keep up with rivals, or from both—the two perspectives are not incompatible, as Soviet policy after 1985 showed. But in either case they result from actions taken *within units,* and yet because they shape capabilities they also *affect structures.* Waltz himself acknowledged that structure does not account for everything that happens in world politics: "To explain outcomes one must look at the capabilities, the actions, and the interactions of states, as well as at the structure of their systems. . . . Causes at both the national and the international level make the world more or less peaceful and stable."[124]

If unit-level behavior as well as system-level constraints can cause cooperation to evolve, though, it is difficult to see what is gained by insisting that students of world politics emphasize the latter at the expense of the former. Waltz had concentrated on the systemic level, he explained near the end of *Theory of International Politics,* "because the effects of structure are usually overlooked or misunderstood and because I am writing a theory of international politics, not foreign policy."[125] But this was only to make the same error the behavioralists had made, which was to let the method of one's

---

122. Ibid., p. 204.
123. See Ruggie, "Continuity and Transformation in the World Polity," pp. 142–152; Robert O. Keohane, "Theory of World Politics: Structural Realism and Beyond," pp. 169–173; Robert W. Cox, "Social Forces, States and World Orders: Beyond International Relations Theory," p. 243; and Richard K. Ashley, "The Poverty of Neorealism," p. 288, all in Keohane, ed., *Neorealism and Its Critics.*
124. Waltz, *Theory of International Politics,* pp. 174–175. See also Waltz, "Reflections on *Theory of International Politics:* A Response to My Critics," pp. 327–329, 343.
125. Ibid., p. 175.

inquiry shape its conclusions. It was also to imply that the behavior of states as well as systems is critical to an understanding of international relations—precisely what Waltz had criticized Kaplan for having asserted. In the end, then, the rigid separation of systems from units provided no firmer basis for theory—or for forecasting—than had an approach that had taken both of them into account.

Apart from these early and highly theoretical efforts by Kaplan and Waltz, structuralism produced few significant insights as to how the Cold War might end until the publication of Stephen Rock's *Why Peace Breaks Out* in 1989, literally on the eve of that event.[126] This book deserves special emphasis, not just because it is the only explicitly structural analysis we have of the circumstances that have caused cold wars in the past to disappear, but also because Rock sought to use the resulting hypotheses to specify what it would take would bring our own Cold War to a peaceful conclusion. Rarely does history provide so rapid an opportunity to test theory against experience.

Rock began by arguing that traditional balance of power theory fails to account for several important historical instances of great power rapprochement. Why, for example, did the unification of Germany in 1871, the most significant challenge to European equilibrium since the Napoleonic wars, produce more than four decades of European peace? Why did Great Britain in the 1890s suddenly stop trying to counter the rising power of an old antagonist whose rapidly increasing capabilities posed the greatest of all potential threats to British global hegemony—the United States? In neither of these cases, Rock maintains, did the emergence of any common threat force former adversaries to cooperate;[127] considerations other than those of pure power were obviously involved. Complementary economies and ideologies muffled geopolitical conflicts: there were times when appeasing an ascending rival was likely to be less costly and more beneficial, from the standpoint of national priorities, than the path of resistance that strict adherence to balance of power principles would require. The causes of peace,

---

126. Stephen R. Rock, *Why Peace Breaks Out: Great Power Rapprochement in Historical Perspective* (Chapel Hill: University of North Carolina Press, 1989). As Rock notes (pp. 3–4), the only previous modern effort to build a theoretical explanation of how peace evolves was Deutsch, *Political Community in the North Atlantic Area*, the first stage of a research design that was never completed.
127. Not all diplomatic historians would agree with Rock's assertion that growing concern about Germany did little to influence Britain's determination to improve relations with the United States.

therefore, lay not just in the configurations of international systems, but also in the internal structures of the states that make them up.[128]

A careful analysis of these causes, Rock argued, would not reveal in advance exactly when two previously antagonistic states might reconcile their differences, but it would nonetheless have "predictive value." It could, in particular, "provide us with clues as to whether or not a [Soviet-American] reconciliation is probable, and to the kinds of developments that would make one more (or less) likely in the future."[129] Rock extracted, from his study of great power rapprochements in the past, four specific hypotheses that could be used to evaluate the prospects for an end to the Cold War:

1. "A state of peace is most likely to emerge among states that are heterogenous in the exercise of national power." By this somewhat murky formulation, Rock meant simply that states whose geopolitical interests do not clash tend not to clash militarily.

2. "A state of peace is most likely to emerge among states that are heterogenous in their economic activities." Here Rock was making the useful point that the complementarity of economies, not the volume of transactions between them, encourages peace: states whose economies are not directly competitive with one another—whose exports do not displace the other's domestic producers—will maintain more friendly relations than states in which similar commodities are produced and competitive efforts to market them therefore ensue.

3. "A state of peace is most likely to emerge among states that are homogenous in their societal attributes." This proposition was straightforward enough: states that resemble one another tend not to fight.

4. "Even if the exercise of power, economic activities, and societal attributes favor pacific relations, some catalytic event may be required to set the process of reconciliation in motion. The most probable candidate for this role is an acute crisis between the two states." Or, the imminence of military conflict may force greater attention to economic and ideological complementarities.[130]

The Soviet-American relationship, Rock noted, had never come close to meeting these standards. It was—and had been since 1945—one involving "intense geopolitical competition, a keen sense of ideological estrangement and mistrust, [and] potentially strong but actually weak economic connec-

---

128. Rock, *Why Peace Breaks Out*, pp. 8–12.
129. Ibid., p. 149.
130. Ibid., pp. 12–18.

tions." Not even a crisis like the one over Cuba in 1962 had been sufficient to overcome these unpromising conditions and produce anything approaching a lasting reconciliation between Moscow and Washington. It was hardly surprising, therefore, that the Cold War had gone on for so long; "nor does any fundamental improvement in Soviet-American relations seem likely without some alteration in these conditions." In the light of these structural impediments, it would be "naive," Rock argued, to claim "that changes conducive to a far-reaching transformation of the Soviet-American relationship are probable, or that a rapprochement could be easily effected."[131]

The situation was not, however, entirely hopeless. The rise of a third power like China could cause Washington and Moscow to develop common geopolitical interests. A "long-term decline in Soviet and/or American military capabilities could force a strategic retrenchment on the part of one or both superpowers, reducing the extent to which their interests overlap"; the experiences of Vietnam and Afghanistan had already shown that the superpowers' capacity for intervention in the Third World was not what it once had been. Both the Soviet Union and the United States faced potentially serious internal economic difficulties, and "although the correlation between a nation's economic strength and its military capabilities is not perfect, there is clearly a relationship between the two factors." There was no immediate prospect of ideological reconciliation: the United States was not about to relinquish its democratic principles; "nor can one expect the Soviet Union to renounce socialism, particularly since Marxist-Leninist doctrine serves to legitimize the existing Soviet regime." Historical, linguistic, and cultural traditions were vastly different, "and will surely remain so." But the economies of the two countries were potentially compatible, and there were some indications that Mikhail Gorbachev was seeking to jettison ideological orthodoxies, although by no means to the same extent that the Chinese government was doing.[132]

For the immediate future, Rock concluded, "perhaps the best for which we can hope is an end to . . . shrill ideological rhetoric." More fundamental changes might be possible over the long run as domestic politics in the United States swung back toward liberalism and as Gorbachev's reforms took hold.[133] The existence of nuclear weapons had had "a considerable and even

---

131. Ibid., p. 151.
132. Ibid., pp. 151–154.
133. Ibid., p. 153.

profound impact on the relations between states," even if they had not removed "the need to analyze and to understand other, more fundamental, sources of states' attitudes and behaviors toward one another." Effective statesmanship could certainly make a difference at the margins once the structural prerequisites for a reconciliation were in place.[134] But nothing in Rock's book would have led a reader to expect the Cold War to end clearly and decisively within months of its publication. Nor did *Why Peace Breaks Out* come anywhere close to explaining how—or why—that event took place.

What actually happened, after all, was the abrupt and asymmetrical collapse of one superpower, not the gradual and symmetrical decline of both. The government of the Soviet Union did give up Marxism-Leninism, despite the fact that its own authority derived from that ideology. The Cold War ended without any significant increase in Soviet or Eastern European economic contacts with the West; indeed one could argue that it was precisely the absence of such contacts that hastened the Cold War's demise. No obvious third party threat existed: far from forcing cooperation between Moscow and Washington to counter the growing influence of China in the world, Beijing's aging gerontocracy aborted a once-thriving reform movement and turned that nation inward upon itself. Nor was any catalytic crisis required to shock Soviet and American leaderships into recognizing their mutual dependence upon one another; instead the crises that developed in Eastern Europe in the fall of 1989 shocked Marxist governments throughout that region by demonstrating that they could no longer depend upon Moscow to prop them up. In short, the most serious structuralist effort to forecast the end of the Cold War failed, and failed thoroughly.

I say this not to demean Stephen Rock's attempt. After all, he alone among structuralists (and behavioralists as well) had the courage to venture clear theory-based forecasts of how the Cold War might end.[135] It is a daunting thing to freeze one's vision of the future in the highly-visible and unforgiving medium of cold type; perhaps that is why so many theorists—however confident they may be about the validity of their theories—avoid that exercise altogether. It is also the case that failed forecasts can provide insights into the causes of failure: in that sense, they can be just as valuable as forecasts

---

134. Ibid., pp. 155–159.
135. Sean M. Lynn-Jones did collaborate with Rock on an essay, "From Confrontation to Cooperation: Transforming the U.S.-Soviet Relationship," in Joseph S. Nye, Jr., Graham T. Allison, and Albert Carnesale, eds., *Fateful Visions: Avoiding Nuclear Catastrophe* (Cambridge, Mass.: Ballinger, 1988), pp. 111–131, the conclusions of which roughly parallel those of Rock's book.

that succeed. Rock's inability to foresee what turned out to be a very near future reflects, not so much his own shortcomings as an analyst of international politics, but rather a more general weakness in the structuralist approach to theory as a whole, and thus to whatever forecasts might be based upon it.

This weakness is the tendency to treat time as a dimension—like length, width, and depth—but not as a process. Structuralists see time as a scale against which to measure events, but they pay little attention to the fact that the passage of time, in and of itself, also shapes events. In this respect, they resemble those pre-Darwinian paleontologists who believed in the immutability of species: despite being surrounded by evidence showing that animals, plants, and even land forms had evolved over time, these scientists simply assumed the absence or the unimportance of evolution and therefore lacked the means to understand, account for, and anticipate structural change.[136] Like pre-Darwinian paleontologists, structural theorists of international relations have produced firm and at times startling conclusions; these go well beyond the range of behavioralist analysis, which normally extends from the cautious confirmation of the obvious to the inability to confirm anything at all. But the static character of the structuralists' conclusions—the failure to account for change—left that approach little better equipped than behavioralism to forecast the quite dramatic changes that brought about the Cold War's end.

EVOLUTIONARY APPROACHES

"Evolutionists" assume the interaction of behavior and structure in world politics, and incorporate observable and unobservable phenomena into their explanations of how that happens. But their chief distinguishing characteristic—the one that differentiates evolutionists most sharply from other theorists—is the attention they give to changes in behaviors and structures over time. Evolutionists see time itself as influencing what happens, even as it provides the chronological framework we use to make sense of what has happened. A static representation of behavior and structure may work reasonably well when the objects being described are inanimate, or when the organisms being cataloged are incapable of learning from experience.[137] But

---

136. See Gould, *Time's Arrow, Time's Cycle*, pp. 146–149.
137. Although not perfectly well: as Darwin pointed out long ago, natural selection provides a way for even the most primitive organism to "learn" at least indirectly from experiences of the past.

human beings do learn from the past: history allows for the inheritance of acquired characteristics, even if biology does not.[138] For this reason, the passage of time, which is the process through which experience accumulates, affects behavior and structure in observable and unobservable ways: it constitutes a third axis along which the search for a theory of international relations must proceed.

Evolutionists disagree, though, on how time produces its effects. Linear evolutionists tend to see historical processes as irreversible: like time itself, history flows in one direction only; a return to prior conditions is as improbable as it would be for an arrow to reverse its course in mid-flight. The future, from this perspective, will not resemble the past; one can nonetheless foresee certain aspects of it by calculating the trajectories of historical trends—or arrows—that seem likely to continue. Cyclical evolutionists believe that although time does indeed move forward and not backward, historical processes may do both: they can reverse themselves even as time proceeds; cycles rather than arrows provide the appropriate metaphor. From this angle of vision, the future will at times resemble, even if it does not precisely replicate, the past; one can foresee certain aspects of it by understanding the frequency, amplitude, and implications of historical cycles.

To be sure, distinctions between linear and cyclical views of history are rarely this sharply drawn in practice. For if the future were completely unlike the past, then we would have no categories with which to characterize it: each morning—indeed each moment—would be totally novel,[139] and forecasting of any kind would be impossible. Conversely, if the future always resembled the past, nothing would be unexpected and there would be no need for forecasting in the first place.[140] Still, evolutionists do tend to work within linear or cyclical frames of reference when they generalize about the past; the choice they make, in turn, affects how they see the future.

LINEAR EVOLUTION. The conviction that historical processes operate in a linear manner goes back as far as the ancient Hebrews;[141] but it was Karl

---

138. See E.H. Carr, *What Is History?* (New York: Vintage Books, 1961), pp. 150–151; also Ernest Gellner, *Plough, Sword and Book: The Structure of Human History* (Chicago: University of Chicago Press, 1988), p. 14.
139. For a poignant clinical analogy, see Oliver Sacks, *The Man Who Mistook His Wife for a Hat, and Other Clinical Tales* (New York: Harper and Row, 1987), pp. 23–42.
140. The above discussion of cycles and arrows has been very much influenced by Gould, *Time's Arrow, Time's Cycle*, a book that shows brilliantly how insights drawn from geology, biology, and paleontology can sharpen one's understanding of history.
141. See Herbert Butterfield, *The Origins of History* (New York: Basic Books, 1981), pp. 80–117.

Marx who created the most influential theory of irreversible historical change by inverting the Hegelian dialectic to insist that deeply-rooted economic forces—shifts in the "means of production," to use Marx's term—determine the structure of societies and the behavior of states, driving them forward in time in ways that are inexorable and, therefore, largely predictable.[142] The progression from feudalism through capitalism to socialism and ultimately communism was as certain as was the Darwinian process of natural selection, Marx's collaborator Friedrich Engels insisted; individuals could harness these forces only by aligning their own objectives with them.[143] Subsequent history—not least the end of the Cold War—has shown Marx and Engels to have been wrong about the *direction* in which history was moving: it certainly did not bring about the death of capitalism, the triumph of communism, and the consequent disappearance of the state. Marxism's botched forecasts have by no means disproven the Marxist assumption that underlying historical processes do exist, though, and that they function rather in the way we now know tectonic forces move continents around on the surface of the earth. These processes may operate very slowly, with no visible consequences for long periods of time. But when their effects do appear, they can be as dramatic as the earthquakes that result from the buildup of strains along geologic fault lines. And once such upheavals happen, they cannot be undone.[144]

Evolutionists have devised no general theory of linear change in world politics, but they have advanced specific theories based on the workings of irreversible processes in several areas that relate to the problem of how the Cold War would end:

Development. The dismantling of European colonialism in Africa, the Middle East, and Southeast Asia during the 1950s and 1960s created a strong demand for explanations that would not only account for what was happening within

---

142. Ernst Breisach, *Historiography: Ancient, Medieval, and Modern* (Chicago, Ill.: University of Chicago Press), pp. 293–297. Marx did not, however, completely deny the possibility of individual autonomy in history: "Men make their own history, but they do not make it just as they please; they do not make it under circumstances chosen by themselves, but under circumstances directly found, given, and transmitted from the past." Karl Marx, "The Eighteenth Brumaire of Louis Bonaparte" (1852), in Robert C. Tucker, ed., *The Marx-Engels Reader*, 2d ed. (New York: Norton, 1978), p. 595.

143. Friedrich Engels, "Socialism: Utopian and Scientific" (1892), in Tucker, *The Marx-Engels Reader*, pp. 696–697, 712.

144. For more on this "tectonic" metaphor, see John Lewis Gaddis, *The United States and the End of the Cold War: Implications, Reconsiderations, Provocations* (New York: Oxford University Press, 1992), pp. 155–167.

a bewildering array of newly-independent states, but also provide a basis for future policies toward them. There emerged, in response, a theory of "development" that purported to show how economic and social evolution shape politics. Based on the assumption that stages of modernization exist, much like Marx's stages of production, this literature sought to identify corresponding political structures; it even attempted to forecast points at which "developing" countries would be most vulnerable to communism's seductive claim that it could accelerate what Walt Rostow liked to call the "takeoff" to mass production and consumption. It was no accident—as the Marxists themselves would have said—that Rostow chose for his influential 1960 book, *The Stages of Economic Growth*, the sub-title *A Non-Communist Manifesto*.[145]

Development theory proved to be of little use in anticipating events in the Third World: it overestimated the appeal of communism and underrated that of nationalism; it failed to foresee the durability of markets as against command economies; and it encouraged a hyperactive interventionism on the part of the United States, which found it necessary to try to "guide" new nations along the path to social stability and geopolitical reliability, at times with disastrous results.[146] Particularities of events taking place on several different continents and within dozens of different cultures overwhelmed the capacity of theorists to advance valid generalizations about them. But attempts to link stages of economic growth with political evolution have worked much better when applied to the narrower task of evaluating what was happening within the Soviet Union, Eastern Europe, and China.

As early as 1960 Rostow and other development theorists were predicting that economic modernization without political democratization—the path Marxist-Leninist states were following at the time—was certain to fail. The reason had to do with what Lenin had added to Marx: a rigidly centralized political structure superimposed upon what was supposed to have been a largely spontaneous process of economic development. Authoritarian gov-

---

145. W.W. Rostow, *The Stages of Economic Growth: A Non-Communist Manifesto* (Cambridge; Cambridge University Press, 1960), especially pp. 1–3, 145–167. For other examples of applied modernization and development theory, see Max Franklin Millikan and Donald L.M. Blackmer, eds., *The Emerging Nations: Their Growth and United States Policy* (Boston: Little, Brown, 1961); Edward Shils, *Political Development in the New States* (The Hague: Mouton, 1962); Cyril E. Black, *The Dynamics of Modernization: A Study in Comparative History* (New York: Harper and Row, 1966); Samuel P. Huntington, *Political Order in Changing Societies* (New Haven: Yale University Press, 1968); and Edward L. Morse, *Modernization and the Transformation of International Relations* (New York: Free Press, 1976).
146. See Shafer, *Deadly Paradigms*, especially pp. 276–290.

ernment might indeed set industrialization in motion, as the Soviet Union's experience under Stalin had shown. But the effective management of an industrial economy would require mass education; peasants do not automatically become technocrats. Education, though, would raise political consciousness, thereby creating the risk that a politically aware population would not indefinitely accept political repression. The choice Marxism-Leninism would eventually face, then, would be a bleak one: either dismantle authoritarianism in order to save the economy, or ruin the economy in order to save authoritarianism. Marx had the process right but the outcome wrong: it turned out to be communism, not capitalism, that carried within it the seeds of its own destruction.[147]

Interdependence. Modern industrial economies make their requirements felt within capitalist societies as well; by the mid-1970s these had elicited, in the rise of "interdependence" studies, a second linear evolutionist approach to international relations theory. The emergence of this field reflected widespread dissatisfaction with the "realist" tendency to reduce all of world politics to a simple struggle for power. Such reductionism, critics argued, overlooked the post–World War II expansion in commerce and communications that had already altered the nature of traditional geopolitical competition. No single nation, or group of nations, had set this trend in motion; instead it was the product of something Marx himself might have recognized—a fundamental shift in the means of production with both structural and behavioral consequences. Relationships based on integration and cooperation were becoming at least as important as those conducted according to old-fashioned balance of power rules; collaborative international "regimes" were emerging in certain areas, even as competitive international rivalries continued in others.[148]

---

147. Rostow, *The Stages of Economic Growth*, pp. 159–162. See also Seymour Martin Lipset, "Some Social Requisites of Democracy: Economic Development and Political Legitimacy," *American Political Science Review*, Vol. 53, No. 1 (March 1959), especially pp. 75–85; Zbigniew Brzezinski, *Between Two Ages: America's Role in the Technetronic Era* (New York: Viking Press, 1970), pp. 154–176; and Morse, *Modernization and the Transformation of International Relations*, pp. 191–192. For excellent retrospective descriptions of this process, see Theodore S. Hamerow, *From the Finland Station: The Graying of Revolution in the Twentieth Century* (New York: Basic Books, 1990), pp. 210–225, 302–309; also William H. McNeill, "Winds of Change," in Nicholas X. Rizopoulos, ed., *Sea-Changes: American Foreign Policy in a World Transformed* (New York: Council on Foreign Relations Press, 1990), pp. 168–171. Rostow applied his own analysis to the future of Soviet-American relations in "On Ending the Cold War," *Foreign Affairs*, Vol. 65, No. 3 (Spring 1987), pp. 831–851.
148. Keohane and Nye, *Power and Interdependence*, especially pp. 3–22, provides the best intro-

Perhaps because the end of the Cold War seemed so distant during the late 1970s and early 1980s, regime theorists were slow to apply their findings to the study of that conflict.[149] But the fact that several previously-established patterns of Soviet-American cooperation survived the "era of stagnation" in Moscow and the first Reagan administration in the United States, together with the rapid decline in Cold War tensions that followed the advent of Mikhail Gorbachev in 1985, left little doubt that mutual suspicion was no longer the only force driving the superpower relationship.[150] Meanwhile, new developments in game theory and in the study of corporate behavior were revealing that competitors might well reciprocate cooperative intiatives if they had reason to believe that their competition would continue.[151] Historical and theoretical developments converged, therefore, to show how the passage of time could make possible the evolution of cooperation—which is to say, the emergence of regimes—even under conditions of anarchy. For the first time there appeared to be both a practical and a conceptual way out of the "prisoner's dilemma" that had for so long confounded those seeking a model for how the Cold War might end.[152]

There was one difficulty, though, in extending interdependence from economics into geopolitics. If in fact the requirements of modern industrial economies linked nations more closely than ever before, then the likelihood of war among them should have diminished: classical liberalism had long argued that nations who traded with one another would have few incentives

---

duction to this line of argument. See also Krasner, *International Regimes*; and, for a longer historical perspective, Rosecrance, *The Rise of the Trading State*, passim. Waltz anticipated many of the basic elements of regime theory in *Theory of International Politics*, especially pp. 173–174.

149. See Robert Jervis, "Security Regimes," in Krasner, ed., *International Regimes*, pp. 173–194.

150. See John Lewis Gaddis, "The Long Peace: Elements of Stability in the Postwar International System," *International Security*, Vol. 10, No. 4 (Spring 1986), pp. 99–142; also the case studies in Dallin, George, and Farley, *U.S.-Soviet Security Cooperation*.

151. These developments are discussed in Axelrod, *The Evolution of Cooperation*; and in Oye, *Cooperation under Anarchy*.

152. "Prisoner's dilemma" games have figured so prominently in the theoretical literature on international relations over the past three decades that it hardly seems necessary to describe them here. Those in need of elucidation may find it in Axelrod, *The Evolution of Cooperation*, pp. 7–12. I cannot refrain, however, from calling attention to Robert Jervis's observation that: "It is not a good sign [when] prisoners confronted by a District Attorney do not behave as the [prisoners' dilemma] model would lead us to expect." Jervis, "Realism, Game Theory, and Cooperation," *World Politics*, Vol. 40, No. 3 (April 1988), p. 319. Jervis is citing here the work of Brian Forst and Judith Lucianovic, "The Prisoner's Dilemma: Theory and Reality," *Journal of Criminal Justice*, Vol. 5 (Spring 1977), pp. 55–64.

to fight one another.[153] But security regimes, if understood in the context of the Cold War, grew out of a security dilemma:[154] it was the fear of war, not the desire for profit, that induced cooperation, and if war was improbable, then it was not clear why the Soviet Union and the United States should cooperate, given the infrequency of economic contacts between them. The improvement in Soviet-American relations that was so obviously taking place in the 1980s seemed to require more than the purely economic explanation that development and interdependence theories had provided.

The obsolescence of war. If large-scale and long-term processes were so important in the economic realm, some linear evolutionists wondered, why should comparable mechanisms not also shape social institutions and the actions that take place within them? Historians had long understood that societies can change over time: despite the fact that the keeping of slaves, the denial of education to women, and even the abandonment of children were all ancient traditions that had been socially acceptable for centuries, they were so no longer. Once attitudes shifted against each one of these practices, its future differed quite dramatically from its past.[155] Three different linear evolutionist arguments arose, during the 1980s, suggesting that something like this might be happening to the institution of war itself.

The first of these had to do with the nuclear revolution. The quantum jump in destructive capabilities that had suddenly become available in 1945, many experts argued, revolutionized statecraft as well as warfare by virtually ruling out the use of military force in relations between great powers. Technological innovation had produced a geopolitical shock of the most fundamental proportions, and as a result "nuclear learning" had taken place, so that the world's most powerful nations were far less inclined than ever before to risk war with one another.[156] Evolution had worked, in this instance, not

---

153. The argument is clearly made in Rosecrance, *The Rise of the Trading State.*
154. Alexander L. George, "Factors Influencing Security Cooperation," in George, Farley, and Dallin, *U.S.-Soviet Security Cooperation*, pp. 655–678.
155. See, on these points, David Brion Davis, *The Problem of Slavery in Western Culture* (Ithaca: Cornell University Press, 1966); Lawrence Stone, *The Family, Sex and Marriage in England, 1500–1800* (New York: Harper and Row, 1979); and John Boswell, *The Kindness of Strangers: The Abandonment of Children in Western Europe from Late Antiquity to the Renaissance* (New York: Pantheon, 1989).
156. Nye, "Nuclear Learning and U.S.-Soviet Security Regimes," passim. See also McGeorge Bundy, *Danger and Survival: Choices About the Bomb in the First Fifty Years* (New York: Random House, 1988), pp. 463–516; and Michael Mandelbaum, *The Nuclear Revolution: International Politics Before and After Hiroshima* (Cambridge: Cambridge University Press, 1981).

through the slow accumulation of desirable adaptations, but rather through an abrupt "punctuation" that instantly and irrevocably altered the international environment and the requirements for survival within it.[157]

A second evolutionist argument came to the same conclusion by a different route. War had been well on the way to becoming obsolete before nuclear weapons had been invented, John Mueller insisted in his 1989 book *Retreat from Doomsday;* even without the bomb, the escalating costs of military operations—because of the increasing lethality of weapons and vulnerability of targets—would have made a war among great powers no more likely in the last half of the twentieth century than it would have been for statesmen from those countries to try to settle their differences through the nineteenth-century expedient of fighting a duel.[158] By this logic, industrialization and modernization, even as they produced instruments of war, became forces for peace.

A third argument for the evolving obsolescence of war stressed the influence of democratization. Building on a suggestion made by Immanuel Kant in 1795, Michael Doyle argued that liberal democracies have strong ideological and psychological inhibitions about fighting one another, quite apart from the quantity and character of the arms they possess. Through careful historical research, Doyle documented an accelerating trend toward democratic forms of government over the past two centuries; he also pointed out that there has never been a war between two liberal democracies.[159] Wars between democracies and non-democratic states were still possible, Doyle acknowledged, but as the former became more numerous and the latter less—a proportion significantly shifted in democracy's favor by the end of the Cold War—his findings appeared to reinforce what Mueller and the "nuclear learning" theorists have suggested about the diminishing likelihood of great power war.

From these linear evolutionist perspectives, then, a Soviet-American reconciliation should have been an entirely predictable development. The end

---

157. My analogy here is to the concept of "punctuated equilibria" in evolution. See Niles Eldredge, *Time Frames: The Evolution of Punctuated Equilibria* (Princeton: Princeton University Press, 1985).

158. Mueller, *Retreat from Doomsday,* pp. 3–13.

159. Michael Doyle, "Liberalism and World Politics," *American Political Science Review,* Vol. 80, No. 4 (December 1986), pp. 1151–1163. See also Doyle, "Kant, Liberal Legacies, and Foreign Affairs," passim; also Melvin Small and J. David Singer, "The War-Proneness of Democratic Regimes, 1816–1965," *Jerusalem Journal of International Relations,* Vol. 1, No. 3 (Summer 1976), pp. 50–68, a Correlates of War Project study which anticipated Doyle's findings, but expressed pessimism about "the continuing democratization of the world" (p. 68).

of the Cold War was "over-determined," in that several separate historical processes—the invention of nuclear weapons, the steadily-mounting costs of conventional war, and progress toward democratization, as well as the development dilemma of Marxism-Leninism, the trend toward interdependence, and the emergence of regimes—all pointed toward the same outcome. These processes became apparent only along a temporal axis of analysis: the passage of time was required for their effects to appear, but once they did they were as irreversible as time itself. History was like Humpty-Dumpty: old ways of doing things, once broken up, could never be put back together again.

But linear evolutionists in fact came no closer than behavioralists or structuralists to forecasting the actual circumstances that brought the Cold War to an end. One reason, I suspect, is that long-term historical processes are indeed, as Marx suggested, subterranean phenomena. One discovers their existence from the consequences they produce; it often requires an earthquake to determine where a fault line really is.[160] A second explanation has to do with the familiar problem of compartmentalization: theorists may well identify a particular process and even forecast its consequences, but few if any theories are built on the *convergence* or *intersection* of complementary processes or, for that matter, on the potential fratricide of contradictory ones.[161] Finally, linear evolutionists tend to commit what I would call the "Fukuyama fallacy," named after the political scientist Francis Fukuyama, who chose the summer of 1989 to publish an article arguing that because Western liberal democracy had triumphed over Marxism-Leninism, Hegel's old vision of an end to history had finally come to pass. "Centuries of boredom" affording minimal opportunities for "daring, courage, imagination, and idealism" lay ahead, Fukuyama lamented,[162] six months before the Berlin Wall came down, a year before an unprecedented international effort to

---

160. Or, as Alexander L. George has put it: "I believe that theory does better in explaining what has happened than in predicting it." George, "The Transition in U.S.-Soviet Relations, 1985–1990: An Interpretation from the Perspective of International Relations Theory and Political Psychology," *Political Psychology*, Vol. 12, No. 3 (September 1991), p. 469.

161. I have tried to elaborate on this problem in *The United States and the End of the Cold War*, pp. 168–192. The only forecast I have seen that argued explicitly for the possibility of a *near-term* end to the Cold War is Eric A. Nordlinger, "Prospects and Policies for Soviet-American Reconciliation," *Political Science Quarterly*, Vol. 103, No. 3 (Summer 1988), pp. 197–222. But, interestingly, this forecast was a projection of several converging historical trends. In this sense, it resembles the 1966 Karl Deutsch article cited in note 94.

162. Francis Fukuyama, "The End of History?" *The National Interest*, No. 16 (Summer 1989), p. 18.

liberate Kuwait began, and two years before Boris Yeltsin and a few of his supporters, through the sheer force of their moral and political authority, so thoroughly humiliated the KGB, the Soviet government, and the Communist Party of the Soviet Union as to call into question the very survival of those institutions.

The Fukuyama fallacy is the tendency for those who advance propositions about irreversible forces in history to conclude that history will stop with them. Hegel, for a time, believed that history had ended with Napoleon. Marx committed a similar error when he made the proletarian revolution the final stage in historical development;[163] and so too, although to a less egregious extent, have more recent linear evolutionists. Certain that they have exposed *an* engine that drives history forward, they never seem to ask whether there might be others, or whether the one they have focused on might also operate in reverse. Confident that they have identified *a* direction in which history is proceeding, they rarely tell us how they have determined what the ultimate destination actually is. A flea creeping along the inside of a hula hoop might well see its progress as linear, purposeful, and irreversible: curved surfaces often appear flat to those with limited horizons. Or, as Mark Twain once warned: "The past does not repeat itself, but it rhymes."[164]

CYCLICAL EVOLUTION. Cyclical evolutionism is a useful corrective to the Fukuyama fallacy. Its antecedents go back at least to the ancient Greeks; certainly they were implicit in Thucydides's hope that "these words of mine [will be] judged useful by those who want to understand clearly the events which happened in the past and which (human nature being what it is) will, at some time or other and in much the same ways, be repeated in the future."[165] Modern interest in historical cycles has grown largely out of the field of economics, where recurring patterns exist at several different levels of analysis.[166] Evolutionary theorists of international relations have used cyclical approaches to explain—and make forecasts about—the course of

---

163. Breisach, *Historiography*, pp. 231–232, 297.

164. Quoted in David Pratt, "The Functions of Teaching History," in Stephen Vaughn, ed., *The Vital Past: Writings on the Uses of History* (Athens: University of Georgia Press, 1985), p. 208.

165. Thucydides, *History of the Peloponnesian War*, trans. by Rex Warner (New York: Penguin Books, 1954), p. 48. See also Butterfield, *The Origins of History*, pp. 121–126; and a classic book on this subject, Mircea Eliade, *The Myth of the Eternal Return*, trans. by Willard R. Trask (New York: Pantheon, 1954).

166. See Edward R. Dewey and Edwin F. Dakin, *Cycles: The Science of Prediction* (New York: Henry Holt, 1947); also W.W. Rostow, *The World Economy: History and Prospect* (Austin: University of Texas Press, 1978).

revolutions, alternations between democratic and authoritarian forms of government and, most extensively, the relationship between war, peace, and national power over extended periods of time.[167]

Revolutions. One of the most fruitful efforts to employ historical cycles in forecasting has had to do with the phenomenon of revolution, and why it has so rarely produced the results Marx anticipated. Marx himself, along with Lenin, Trotsky, and the other architects of the 1917 upheaval in Russia, recalled very vividly how the French Revolution of 1789 had fallen into an autocratic "Bonapartist" phase; they worried that a similar gap between intentions and consequences might arise as socialism supplanted capitalism.[168] That concern did not prevent the rise of Stalin, but his totalitarian rule did provoke a good deal of thought during the 1930s and 1940s about what causes revolutions to go astray. Trotsky made significant contributions to this analysis prior to his assassination; so too did his biographer, Isaac Deutscher.[169] But it was the historian Crane Brinton who provided the most durable explanation of how revolutions originate, evolve, and eventually degenerate in his 1938 book, *The Anatomy of Revolution.*

Basing his findings on a comparative study of the English civil war and the American, French, and Russian Revolutions, Brinton identified a cycle through which such disruptions tend to proceed: the collapse of the old regime, the euphoria of revolution itself, the failure of moderates to match ideals with accomplishments, the rise of extremists, their use of—but ultimately consumption by—terror, and finally the reassertion of a central authority whose oppressiveness might well exceed anything that existed under the old regime in the first place.[170] Brinton claimed no scientific rigor for this model, and refused to regard it as a basis for theory.[171] But as another

---

167. Strictly speaking, a cyclical view of history would appear to rule out evolution: if everything repeats, how can anything change? But as the Mark Twain quotation in the text suggests, the argument is not that *everything* repeats but that *some things do.* Once certain processes are set in motion—like revolutions, reforms, wars, and the building of empires—certain patterns tend to recur, even as time (as always) moves on.
168. Richard Pipes, *The Russian Revolution* (New York: Knopf, 1990), pp. 468–469.
169. Leon Trotsky, *Stalin: An Appraisal of the Man and His Influence* (New York: Harper, 1946); Isaac Deutscher, *Stalin: A Political Biography* (New York: Oxford University Press, 1949). George Orwell's caustic novels, *Animal Farm* (New York: Harcourt, Brace, 1946) and *1984* (New York: Harcourt, Brace, 1949), of course fit into this tradition as well.
170. Crane Brinton, *The Anatomy of Revolution,* rev. ed. (New York: Prentice Hall, 1952), passim. Brinton's inclusion of the American Revolution has always struck critics as having strained his argument, which would have held up just as well without this peculiar case.
171. Ibid., p. 18. However, Brinton did see himself as following "scientific methods" in his study.

historian, Theodore S. Hamerow, showed half a century later, Brinton's cycles of revolutionary evolution came remarkably close to anticipating what would happen to Marxism-Leninism, not just inside the Soviet Union, but also in Eastern Europe, China, Vietnam, and Cuba during the Cold War: they explain how once vigorous revolutions lose their momentum, ossify, and eventually turn into old regimes themselves, vulnerable to new revolutionary challenges.[172]

Brinton's work parallels—and in terms of predictive potential holds up considerably better than—Marx's own use of linear evolutionist analysis to forecast the overthrow of capitalism a century earlier.[173] From Brinton's vantage point one might well have foreseen, in a way that no behavioralist, structuralist, or Marxist perspective would have allowed one to foresee, the otherwise unexpected combination of petrification and fragility that has come to characterize once-revolutionary regimes in our time, and that accounts, to a large degree, for the asymmetrical manner in which the Cold War ended.[174]

Liberalism and authoritarianism.[175] One should not assume, though, that democracies are exempt from the kind of cyclical evolution that afflicts revolutionary regimes. Our understanding of how democratic governments rise and decline has not advanced as far as our knowledge of how revolutions evolve; but we have more than enough historical evidence to know that democratization is by no means an irreversible process. Athens lost its democracy and Rome its republic; fascism and communism originated, during and after World War I, in states that had appeared to be well on the way to representative constitutional government. The second half of this century has indeed seen a remarkable expansion of democracy throughout the world; certainly that ideology has proven to be more durable than its Marxist-Leninist alternative. But there is no clear guarantee that this process will

---

172. Hamerow, *From the Finland Station,* passim.

173. See also, on Marx's failures as a forecaster, Theda Skocpol, *States and Social Revolutions: A Comparative Analysis of France, Russia, and China* (Cambridge: Cambridge University Press, 1979), especially pp. 284–293; and Zbigniew Brzezinski, *The Grand Failure: The Birth and Death of Communism in the Twentieth Century* (New York: Scribner's, 1989).

174. "The *ideas,* the *promises* of orthodox Marxism as now embodied in Stalin's Russia," Brinton wrote in the revised edition of *The Anatomy of Revolution* in 1952, "may well prove in the next few years almost as embarrassing in Russian internal politics as useful in Russian external politics. The Marxist heaven on earth will do as a mere promise in Indonesia or Iran, for a while, but in Moscow, it has got pretty soon to become in part visible—or the whole doctrine must undergo a still unpredictable transformation" (p. 248.)

175. I am using the term "liberalism" here in its original sense, that is, one that emphasizes the value of individual liberties and seeks to minimize government control.

continue;[176] hence the importance of attempting to determine whether the present movement toward liberalism really is irreversible, or whether it simply alternates, over long periods of time, with authoritarianism.

Recent work by the sociologist John A. Hall provides a starting point for such an undertaking. Hall accepts the linear evolutionist view that democratization is necessary to sustain economic development; but he does not conclude from this that liberalism is necessarily the wave of the future.[177] For one thing, governments may conclude that the danger of losing their authority exceeds the costs of political repression and of resulting economic regression: presumably this is what happened in China in 1989. More significant in the long run, though, is the possibility that Marx may have been partially right after all: that capitalism and the liberalism it generates do carry within them the seeds of their own periodic decline, if not destruction altogether. Societies do not determine qualities of life solely by calculating economic advantage. Spiritual, psychological, and emotional needs have to be satisfied as well, and liberalism—depending as it does upon rationality—is often ill-equipped for that task.[178] Where did fascism and communism come from, after all, if not from the disillusionment their followers felt with late nineteenth-century liberal capitalism?

Threats to contemporary liberalism are already becoming apparent, even as that ideology consolidates its victory in the Cold War. Religious, linguistic, and ethnic tensions have risen dramatically in Central and Eastern Europe and even within the former Soviet Union itself as the heavy hand of Moscow's authority has disappeared: these provide infertile ground for the growth of democratic institutions. The resurgence of religious fundamentalism in the Middle East has already shown that the creation of wealth and indulgence in consumption do not always ensure democratic politics. The lowering of barriers to trade and immigration within the European Community and North America is causing protectionist and restrictionist pressures to build in those parts of the world; improvements in transportation have also facilitated the spread of illicit drugs and AIDS; economic devel-

---

176. See John J. Mearsheimer, "Back to the Future: Instability in Europe After the Cold War," *International Security*, Vol. 15, No. 1 (Summer 1990), pp. 48–51.

177. John A. Hall, *Powers and Liberties: The Causes and Consequences of the Rise of the West* (Berkeley: University of California Press, 1985), pp. 197–209.

178. John A. Hall, *Liberalism: Politics, Ideology, and the Market* (Chapel Hill: University of North Carolina Press, 1987), especially pp. 71–100. For a critique of "rational actor" models, see Hollis and Smith, *Explaining and Understanding International Relations*, pp. 144–146.

opment, we now understand, can bring about ecological dangers not just in the form of pollution but also ozone holes, disappearing rain forests, and rising ocean levels. And in the United States, an uneasy compromise tolerates the existence of an economic and social "underclass," a deteriorating physical and educational infrastructure, corporate greed, ballooning deficits, and vapid politics in return for the short-term gratifications of minimally-intrusive government and low taxes.[179]

From these perspectives, it is not all that difficult to see how late twentieth-century *laissez-faire* liberalism could give rise to a collective alienation comparable to that induced by its late nineteenth-century counterpart. It may be, then, that neither liberalism nor authoritarianism is foreordained, but rather that a dialectical relationship exists between them in which the excesses of one create opportunities for the other. The end of the Cold War could turn out to be the precursor of something worse.

War and peace. Theories of cyclical evolution are most fully developed with respect to the issue of war and peace, where there has been a major effort over the past two decades to determine whether conflict in the international system really is like earthquakes along fault lines: a recurring phenomenon brought about by the accumulating pressures of underlying economic, social, and geopolitical forces.[180] Proponents of "long cycle" or "power transition" theory accept Marx's view that uneven rates of economic and technological development cause shifts from one phase in history to another.[181] But where Marx saw these phases as linear progressions in forms of economic organization, scholars in this field have seen them as part of a cyclical process—extending over periods of anywhere from 100 to 150 years—by which rising powers challenge dominant "hegemons" for control of the international system.

---

179. For an elaboration of this screed, see Gaddis, *The United States and the End of the Cold War*, pp. 202–208. Arthur M. Schlesinger, Jr.'s cyclical theory of American politics suggests that a shift toward more active government and a greater concern for public as opposed to private interests is on the way. See Schlesinger, *The Cycles of American History* (Boston: Houghton Mifflin, 1986), pp. 23–48.

180. The best review of this literature is Jack S. Levy, "Long Cycles, Hegemonic Transitions, and the Long Peace," in Charles W. Kegley, Jr., ed., *The Long Postwar Peace: Contending Explanations and Projections* (New York: HarperCollins, 1991), pp. 147–176. But see also George Modelski and Patrick M. Morgan, "Understanding Global War," *Journal of Conflict Resolution*, Vol. 29, No. 3 (September 1985), pp. 391–417; Nathaniel Beck, "The Illusion of Cycles in International Relations," *International Studies Quarterly*, Vol. 25, No. 4 (December 1991), pp. 455–476; and Joshua S. Goldstein, "The Possibility of Cycles in International Relations," ibid., pp. 477–480.

181. Gilpin, *War and Change in World Politics*, p. 93; Goldstein, *Long Cycles*, p. 282. See also Kennedy, *The Rise and Fall of the Great Powers*, pp. 436–437.

Such challenges, according to the theory, produce a "hegemonic" war from which a single superpower emerges: the most recent examples have been Great Britain after the Napoleonic Wars and the United States after World War II. The new hegemon need not have initiated the challenge that over-threw its predecessor; it does not even have to be the strongest nation in the postwar international arena. It is, however, the state best positioned to establish and maintain a worldwide system of international economic and political relationships, and it does this as much by eliciting the cooperation of other nations as by intimidating them. The resulting hegemonic manage-ment produces, for a time, a long peace. Eventually, though, the rise of other states that have chosen to follow the hegemon's example—together with the hegemon's own exhaustion, bureaucratization, and consequent loss of imag-ination—creates instabilities that lead to major war and to the emergence of a new hegemon, thereby starting the cycle all over again.[182]

The Cold War, from this angle of vision, was a brief, unsuccessful, and not even particularly interesting challenge by the Soviet Union to the hege-monic position the United States established for itself in world politics after 1945.[183] Predictably, the challenge failed, not just because of the economic and technological backwardness of the USSR, but also because international systemic conditions themselves worked against a successful challenge to the dominant hegemon at such an early point in a historical long cycle. Wash-ington wrote the "rules" for the international "game" that emerged from World War II: it was hardly surprising that the deck was stacked against Moscow.[184]

---

182. I have attempted to summarize here: Gilpin, *War and Change in World Politics*, pp. 9–15; Goldstein, *Long Cycles*, pp. 15–17; Olson, *The Rise and Decline of Nations*, p. 45; and A.F.K. Organski and Jacek Kugler, *The War Ledger* (Chicago: University of Chicago Press, 1980), pp. 13–63; as well as a paragraph from my own essay, "Great Illusions, the Long Peace, and the Future of the International System," in Gaddis, *The United States and the End of the Cold War*, p. 187.

183. Witness the extent to which some theorists of hegemonic stability neglect Cold War history altogether. For more on this, see Gaddis, ibid., pp. 175–176.

184. Adherents to the "world system" approach to international affairs would argue that it is not just the United States but capitalism in general that has "stacked the deck" against both the Second and Third Worlds, severely inhibiting progress toward social and economic development in those regions. See, for example, Immanuel Wallerstein, *The Capitalist World-Economy* (New York: Cambridge University Press, 1979); and Wallerstein, *The Politics of the World-Economy: The States, the Movements, and the Civilizations* (New York: Cambridge University Press, 1984); also the discussion in Ole R. Holsti, "Models of International Relations and Foreign Policy," *Diplomatic History*, Vol. 12, No. 1 (Winter 1989), pp. 27–29. But this approach is a crude form of static structuralism which allows no role whatever for particularities of history, personality, politics, or culture. Change can occur, presumably, only when the worldwide Marxist revolution finally comes, which now looks to be a while.

Long cycle theorists have had less to say about the end of the Cold War than about the possibility that the United States may have already begun the gradual decline in power that eventually afflicts all hegemons, and that more serious challenges than the one the Soviet Union posed are likely to arise in the twenty-first century. Future historians may find it odd that this concern over "decline" should have intensified during the late 1980s, the very point at which the United States was emerging as the world's sole surviving superpower. But long cycle theory never saw the Soviet Union as a credible competitor with the United States in anything other than brute military strength, and that capability, the theorists would argue, is of relatively little importance in maintaining hegemonic control. The real threat to American predominance lies, they believe, in what the United States is doing to itself by failing to maintain its competitive edge in the global economy, together with what new competitors like Japan and the European Community are doing to exploit the opportunities thereby handed them.[185]

No cyclical theorist would claim that cycles—long-term, short-term, or in between—repeat themselves precisely. Some linear evolution always takes place: cycles may operate but time pushes them forward as they do, thereby subjecting them to modification by non-cyclical forces.[186] Robert Gilpin has explicitly raised the possibility, for example, that a linear development—the invention of nuclear weapons—may have broken the old cycle of recurring hegemonic wars; Mueller and Doyle have implicitly suggested a similar effect as the result of shifting social consciousness and growing political awareness.[187] But this is what makes forecasting from a cyclical evolutionist perspective difficult. Long cycle theory provides no very good way of determining the extent to which linear progression has modified cyclical patterns, and the longer the cycles are, the harder it is to resolve this question: it is frustrating to lack the means of verifying one's vision of the future other than by awaiting completion of the next historical cycle. Only history, by this logic, can confirm theory, and that may take a while.

---

185. The argument is most thoroughly laid out in Robert Gilpin, *The Political Economy of International Relations* (Princeton: Princeton University Press, 1987). But see also David P. Calleo, *Beyond American Hegemony: The Future of the Western Alliance* (New York: Basic Books, 1987); and Kennedy's *The Rise and Fall of the Great Powers*, discussed below.
186. If the term did not already have specific connotations in deterrence theory, a "spiral" model would be a good way of illustrating how cyclical processes actually work.
187. Gilpin, *War and Change in World Politics*, pp. 213–219. For Mueller and Doyle, see notes 158 and 159, above.

Decline. Late in 1987, a surprise best-seller brought the implications of long cycle theory to the attention of a mass audience in a way that the theorists themselves could never have managed; indeed Paul Kennedy's *The Rise and Fall of the Great Powers* may well have had as great an impact on American society during the final stages of the Cold War as did Edward Gibbon's *The Decline and Fall of the Roman Empire* at the time of its publication in Great Britain during the War for American Independence.[188] The condition of being a great power is in fact transitory, Kennedy argued; the United States can no more exempt itself from the historical cycle of ascendency and enfeeblement than any other powerful state has ever been able to do. "It simply has not been given to any one society to remain *permanently* ahead of all the others, because that would imply a freezing of the differentiated pattern of growth rates, technological advance, and military developments which has existed since time immemorial."[189]

The resulting uproar—for it was nothing short of that[190]—over Kennedy's thesis reflected the transition to the post–Cold War world that was already beginning to develop within the American public consciousness. Previous outbreaks of anxiety over national inadequacies, most notably the one that occurred in the wake of the *Sputnik* launch in 1957, had focused on what the United States had to do to keep up with the Russians. But the Soviet Union hardly figured in the "declinism" debate of the late 1980s: Kennedy himself had seen its power as eroding even more rapidly than that of the United States,[191] and most of his readers no doubt worried more about Japan as a potential challenger to the American position in the world than they did about the Soviet Union.

Kennedy did warn, though, along with many others,[192] that the disintegration of Soviet authority would be a dangerous thing. His argument is worth quoting in full, because it reflects views that were almost universally held prior to the revolutionary year 1989:

---

188. See Roy Porter, *Gibbon: Making History* (New York: St. Martin's Press, 1988), p. 161.
189. Kennedy, *The Rise and Fall of the Great Powers*, p. 533.
190. For the debate, see Peter Schmeisser, "Taking Stock: Is America in Decline?" *New York Times Magazine*, April 17, 1988, pp. 24–27, 66–68, 96; Joseph S. Nye, Jr., "Understating U.S. Strength," *Foreign Policy*, No. 72 (Fall 1988), pp. 105–129; Samuel P. Huntington, "The U.S.—Decline or Renewal?" *Foreign Affairs*, Vol. 67, No. 4 (Winter 1988/89), pp. 76–96; and Paul Kennedy, "Can the U.S. Remain Number One?" *New York Review of Books*, March 16, 1989, pp. 36–42.
191. Kennedy, *The Rise and Fall of the Great Powers*, pp. 488–514.
192. Including John Lewis Gaddis, "How the Cold War Might End," *The Atlantic*, Vol. 260 (November 1987), pp. 88–100. My own retrospective critique of this mostly unsuccessful effort at forecasting appears in Gaddis, *The United States and the End of the Cold War*, pp. 132–154.

There is nothing in the character or tradition of the Russian state to suggest that it could ever accept imperial decline gracefully. Indeed, historically, *none* of the overextended, multinational empires which have been dealt with in this survey—the Ottoman, the Spanish, the Napoleonic, the British—ever retreated to their own ethnic base until they had been defeated in a Great Power war, or (as with Britain after 1945), were so weakened by war that an imperial withdrawal was politically unavoidable. Those who rejoice at the present-day difficulties of the Soviet Union and who look forward to the collapse of that empire might wish to recall that such transformations normally occur at very great cost, and not always in a predictable manner.[193]

Whatever the accuracy of Kennedy's views on American "decline," it is clear now that he was quite wrong—as was almost everyone else—in failing to foresee how suddenly, how thoroughly, and how *peacefully* the Soviet Union would relinquish its position as a superpower, indeed its own existence as a state. History contains no precedent for so striking an example of abrupt but amicable collapse. Either the world has been extraordinarily lucky, or linear evolution has pushed familiar cycles of war, peace, and decline into a new and wholly unfamiliar environment. How does one account for—and how might one have anticipated—this development?

One obvious answer is that we give too little thought to how cyclical and linear patterns interact with one another. Some attention to what development and interdependence theorists were saying about the Soviet economy, combined with what the "nuclear learning" theorists, Mueller, and Doyle were suggesting about shifts in collective social consciousness, might have hinted that old habits of using force to repress change would no longer work. Certainly Kennedy's materialist analysis of the nature of power did not give sufficient weight to the role immaterial forces have played in this situation: the Cold War ended as much because of what people believed as because of what they possessed. As one of Kennedy's most thoughtful critics, Joseph S. Nye, Jr., has pointed out, new "soft" forms of power are emerging, especially in the form of culture, education, and mass communications, the nature of which cannot be calculated according to traditional geopolitical equations.[194]

It is also the case that we tend to bias our historical and our theoretical analyses too much toward continuity. Despite our awareness that abrupt

193. Kennedy, *The Rise and Fall of the Great Powers*, p. 514.
194. See Joseph S. Nye, Jr., "Soft Power," *Foreign Policy*, No. 80 (Fall 1990), pp. 153–171; also Nye, *Bound to Lead*, passim.

change occurs frequently in history and in personal experience, despite our understanding that intellectual breakthroughs more often result from sudden flashes of insight than from the diligent piling up of evidence,[195] we rarely find a way to introduce discontinuities into theory, or to attempt to determine what causes them to happen. This is another area in which social scientists could learn from recent developments in mathematics and the "hard" sciences, where a new understanding of complexity, chaos and catastrophe is providing ways to anticipate otherwise unexpected shifts in what had seemed to be gradual evolutionary processes. The circumstances surrounding the end of the Cold War may not be all that different, at least by way of analogy, from the sudden die-offs that occur among animal species under certain conditions, or the unexpected collapse of bridges due to metal fatigue, or wild fluctuations in markets, or even the transition from regular to turbulent flow that happens every time we turn on a water tap.[196]

The geological and biological sciences, from which the idea of evolution arose in the first place, have always allowed for the integration of linear, cyclical, and even catastrophic phenomena: landforms rise up and collapse but never in exactly the same way; ontogeny recapitulates phylogeny but genetically-unique individuals (almost) always result from the process; violent eruptions and abrupt extinctions periodically occur. It is odd that the evolutionary approach to international relations theory—which will have to incorporate both pattern and particularity if it is ever to provide a basis for forecasting—seems to find these kinds of juxtapositions so difficult to manage.

---

195. Kuhn, *The Structure of Scientific Revolutions*, has become the classic text on this subject.
196. See Gleick, *Chaos*, pp. 59–86, 262–267. In addition to Gleick, helpful guides to these new developments—at least for laypeople—include Pagels, *The Dreams of Reason*; Coveney and Highfield, *The Arrow of Time*; Nicholson, *Formal Theories in International Relations*; and (now somewhat out of date), Alexander Woodcock and Monte Davis, *Catastrophe Theory* (New York: Dutton, 1978). Preliminary efforts to apply these techniques to the study of history and international relations include Alan D. Beyerchen, "Nonlinear Science and the Unfolding of a New Intellectual Vision," *Papers in Comparative Studies*, Vol. 6 (1988/89), pp. 25–49; Beyerchen, "Clausewitz, Nonlinearity, and the Unpredictability of War," *International Security*, Vol. 17, No. 3 (Winter 1992/93), pp. 59–90; C. Dyke, "Strange Attraction, Curious Liaison: Clio Meets Chaos," *The Philosophical Forum*, Vol. 21 (Summer 1990), pp. 369–392; George A. Reisch, "Chaos, History, and Narrative," *History and Theory*, Vol. 30 (1991), pp. 1–20; Donald N. McCloskey, "History, Differential Equations, and the Problem of Narration," ibid., pp. 21–36; and, interestingly, James N. Rosenau, *Turbulence in World Politics: A Theory of Continuity and Change* (Princeton: Princeton University Press, 1990). I have also benefited a great deal from having read several unpublished papers on this subject by Stefan Rossbach which grew out of his work as a Social Science Research Council/MacArthur Foundation Fellow at the Ohio University Contemporary History Institute and the Department of War Studies at King's College, London.

Conclusion[197]

"If you are a student, switch from political science to history." Such was the blunt reply of Robert Conquest, the distinguished Anglo-American historian of the Soviet Union, when asked to draw lessons from the abortive coup against Mikhail Gorbachev in August 1991.[198] Conquest is hardly a neutral observer, but he does have a point. The efforts theorists have made to create a "science" of politics that would forecast the future course of world events have produced strikingly unimpressive results: none of the three general approaches to theory that have evolved since 1945 came anywhere close to anticipating how the Cold War would end.

It will not do to claim that forecasting was never an objective of these theories in the first place, because the theorists repeatedly set that task for themselves. Nor was the "case" in question an insignificant one: the end of the Cold War brought about nothing less than the collapse of an international system, something that has happened in modern history only once before—if one accepts structuralism's emphasis on the shift from multipolarity to bipolarity at the end of World War II.[199] Nor is the test at issue here an unfair one: after all, more than one generation of theorists made the Cold War their central preoccupation. If their forecasts failed so completely to anticipate so large an event as that conflict's termination, then one has to wonder about the theories upon which they were based. Either those theories were themselves artifacts of the Cold War, in which case they lacked the universal applicability so often claimed for them; or they were universally applicable, in which case they were simply wrong.

This failure of international relations theory arose primarily, I believe, because of a methodological passing of ships in the night. The social sciences, seeking objectivity, legitimacy, and predictability, set out to embrace the traditional methods of the physical and natural sciences. But they did so at a time when physicists, biologists, and mathematicians, concerned about disparities between their theories and the reality they were supposed to characterize, were abandoning old methods in favor of new ones that accommodated indeterminacy, irregularity, and unpredictability—precisely the

---

197. Portions of this section appeared, in a somewhat different form, as a "Point of View" essay in the *The Chronicle of Higher Education*, July 22, 1992, p. A44.
198. Quoted in the *Wall Street Journal*, August 22, 1991, editorial page.
199. One ought not to judge theories by how well they perform with respect to a single case—unless it is a very big one.

qualities the social sciences were trying to leave behind. To put it another way, the "soft" sciences became "harder" just as the "hard" sciences were becoming "softer."

The old Newtonian vision of a totally deterministic science—one that could not only account for but predict all phenomena—had begun to fade as early as the beginning of the twentieth century: "He could not affirm with confidence, even to himself," a worried Henry Adams wrote of himself at the time, "that his 'largest synthesis' would turn out to be chaos, since he would be equally obliged to deny the chaos."[200] And yet, Einstein's physics was already making time, like space, a relative concept; another element of certainty dropped away with Heisenberg's unsettling discovery, in 1927, that the very act of *observing* certain particles altered them, so that the precise measurement of one characteristic obscured others.[201] By the 1960s, it was becoming apparent that this entanglement of observation with reality extended across a very broad spectrum indeed: two whole classes of phenomena existed, one of which lent itself to prediction, and one that did not. Prediction was possible where one or two variables interacted under known or controlled conditions. But if the number of variables increased even slightly, or if the conditions under which they operated changed even a little, all bets were off. One was into Adams's feared realm of chaos, and although there is much that one can say about the boundaries and behavior of chaotic systems, one cannot predict the specific actions of their specific parts at any specific time.[202]

The classical scientific method had been to generate laws, and hence predictions, from experiments that limited the number of variables involved and that controlled—sometimes quite arbitrarily—the conditions within which they operated. Newton's laws of motion, for example, assumed perfectly smooth balls rolling down frictionless inclines with no air resistance, a condition never actually encountered in the real world. Generations of students were taught that feathers and stones fall to earth at the same speed, despite the fact that they never really do. Predictability was achieved by removing

---

200. *The Education of Henry Adams: An Autobiography* (Boston: Houghton Mifflin, 1961 [first published in 1918]), p. 408. Adams followed carefully the pioneering work of the French mathematician Henri Poincaré, whose early demonstration of how complexity persists regardless of scale, Adams wrote, "promised eternal bliss to the mathematician, but turned the historian green with horror" (p. 455). Newtonian determinism is well summarized in Coveney and Highfield, *The Arrow of Time*, pp. 64–69.
201. Ibid., pp. 125–26.
202. Gleick, *Chaos*, pp. 48, 145.

the object being studied from its origins and its surroundings: one gained a vision of the future by shutting one's eyes to the past and the present. But the more one observed past and present, the more Heisenberg's principle came into play, and the less confidence one could have in the forecasts one made.

Theorists of international relations are using the methods of classical science when they conduct their investigations exclusively along a behaviorial, structural, or—within the evolutionary approach—a linear or cyclical axis of analysis. They are excluding other variables and controlling conditions in order to produce theories from which they can forecast events. They know that if they do not impose such exclusions and controls, complications will quickly overwhelm their calculations, and predictability will suffer. Exercises of this kind can yield useful insights: so too can simple experiments in freshman physics. But generalizations of this kind perform badly when applied to the real world, which functions along behaviorial, structural, and evolutionary axes *simultaneously*.[203] The generation of theory—at least in the traditional scientific method—requires departures from reality; if forecasts derived from theory are to succeed, however, they must also account for reality. That is the paradox that theorists of international relations have been struggling, with such lack of success, to resolve. Theorists in the "hard" sciences gave up on resolving it some time ago.

The "predictability paradox" is not the only difficulty that confronts theorists of international relations, though: they face another that no physicist in a laboratory has ever had to worry about. It has to do with the fact, as Stanley Hoffmann once reminded his colleagues, that human beings are not "gases or pistons."[204] They are conscious entities capable of reacting to, and often modifying, the variables and conditions they encounter. They can at times see the future taking shape; they can devise, within limits, measures to hasten, retard, or even reverse trends. If molecules had minds of their own, chemists would be much less successful in predicting their behavior.[205] It is

---

203. For more on this point, see Robert Jervis, "The Future of World Politics: Will It Resemble the Past?" *International Security*, Vol. 16, No. 3 (Winter 1991/92), especially pp. 39–46.

204. Hoffmann, "The Long Road to Theory," p. 429.

205. Recent evidence suggests that inorganic molecules can have a surprising capacity for self-organization under certain conditions. See, on this point, Coveney and Highfield, *The Arrow of Time*, pp. 35–37, 159–168; also Roger Penrose, *The Emperor's New Mind: Concerning Computers, Minds, and the Laws of Physics* (New York: Penguin Books, 1991).

no wonder that the effort to devise a "molecular" approach to the study of politics did not work out.[206]

The simple persistence of *values* in politics ought to be another clue that one is dealing here with objects more complicated than billiard balls. Not only does this kind of "input" into political behavior resist expression in scientific terms; it also means that the "scientists" themselves—because they are human—can never be totally objective about what they are studying.[207] A biological scientist must view battles between viruses and antigens with strict impartiality; otherwise his or her career will suffer.[208] Political scientists who fail to achieve that standard survive quite comfortably, which suggests that the science they do is of a rather different character.

One might—at least as a thought experiment—construct a model capable of simulating human behavior in all of its complexity, but it would have to be of such complexity itself as to render it indistinguishable from the object being modeled.[209] Even then it might not predict behavior: identical twins do not have identical personalities, and there is no reason to expect that clones would either. In practice, therefore, we "model" human actions by falling back upon the only known simulative technique that successfully integrates the general and the specific, the regular and the irregular, the predictable and the unpredictable: we construct narratives.[210] But that is also what novelists and historians do.

We come, therefore, full circle: the "scientific" approach to the study of international relations appears to work no better, in forecasting the future, than do the old-fashioned methods it set out long ago to replace.[211] Novelists

---

206. See John Lewis Gaddis, "Expanding the Data Base: Historians, Political Scientists, and the Enrichment of Security Studies," *International Security*, Vol. 12, No. 1 (Summer 1987), especially pp. 5–8.
207. For a good discussion of this point, Ferguson and Mansbach, *The Elusive Quest*, pp. 32–48; also Njølstad, "Learning from History?" pp. 222–225.
208. This is a point that several prominent biological scientists have recently discovered.
209. Pagels, *The Dreams of Reason*, p. 229.
210. Reisch, "Chaos, History, and Narrative," pp. 17–18. A fine commentary on the value of narratives appears in Richard E. Neustadt and Ernest R. May, *Thinking in Time: The Uses of History for Decision-Makers* (New York: Free Press, 1986), pp. 247–70.
211. "We are arguing for a new research agenda that will explore the evolution, overlapping, and interaction of authority patterns and attendant human loyalties from past to present. Such analysis will necessarily identify dominant and competing patterns, as well as continuities and changes over time, and attempt to explain both the reasons for the patterns observed and the important consequences that have flowed from them." Yale H. Ferguson and Richard W. Mansbach, "Between Celebration and Despair: Constructive Suggestions for Future International

and historians make forecasts all the time, but they do so more by analogy than by scientific theory. They assume, in what seems to social scientists a distressingly imprecise way, that if a particular occurrence is "like" something that has already happened, and if the surrounding circumstances are much the same, then the chances are it will produce a similar result. But then again it may not.[212] The track record for this kind of forecasting is, as one might expect, mixed. For all of its insights into the nature of authoritarianism, George Orwell's 1948 vision of 1984 could hardly have been less accurate; and the historiographical landscape is now littered with the failed predictions of historians, my own included,[213] who thought that the Soviet Union would never peacefully tolerate its own collapse. "Stranger things have happened," George F. Kennan commented years ago when discussing this possibility, "though not much stranger."[214]

But novelists and historians never advertised their forecasting abilities with the frequency and self-confidence once common among political scientists. Their chief concern was rather to make sense out of the past and, if possible, the present; if in the process they shed a little light in the direction of the future, then so much the better. This does sometimes happen: insights derived from careful narration and thoughtful analogy—not from an excessive deference to a now outmoded scientific method—can illuminate even quite distant futures. Brinton's cycles of revolution were one such example; Kennedy's cycles of great power rise and fall may yet turn out to be another. And consider, as a third example, this observation from the historian James Billington, buried on page 594 of his 1966 book, *The Icon and the Axe:*

That the phantasmagoria of Soviet construction seems to us the most real thing about Soviet history may only be a reflection of our own essentially

Relations Theory," *International Studies Quarterly,* Vol. 35, No. 4 (December 1991), p. 382. Perhaps a historian might be pardoned for asking: isn't that what we have been doing all along?

212. Neustadt and May, *Thinking in Time,* provides the best guide to how to do forecasting by analogy responsibly, but also to how easily things can go wrong. See also Ernest R. May, "Lessons" of the Past: The Use and Misuse of History in American Foreign Policy (New York: Oxford University Press, 1973); and Yuen Foong Khong, *Analogies at War: Korea, Munich, Dien Bien Phu, and the Vietnam Decisions of 1965* (Princeton: Princeton University Press, 1992), especially pp. 255–257, which is more pessimistic than Neustadt and May about the possibility of training policymakers to use analogies wisely.

213. See note 192; also a particularly short-sighted commentary of mine in Robert K. German, ed., *The Future of U.S.-USSR Relations: Lessons from Forty Years without World War* (Austin, Tex.: Lyndon B. Johnson School of Public Affairs, 1986), pp. 163–166.

214. George F. Kennan, "America and the Russian Future," *Foreign Affairs,* Vol. 29 (April 1951), p. 368.

materialist conception of reality. The Russians, on the other hand, have always been a visionary and ideological people, uniquely appreciative of the ironic perspectives on reality offered in such works as . . . Shakespeare's *Tempest*. It may be that only those who have lived through the tempest of Stalinism will be able, like Prospero, to look on it as "the baseless fabric of a vision"; to see in "the cloud-capped towers, the gorgeous palaces, the solemn temples" only an "insubstantial pageant faded," and to find fresh meaning in Prospero's final affirmation that man is, indeed, "such stuff as dreams are made on."[215]

Or, for that matter, an even earlier insight, also drawn from a literary analogy, that occurs in the most basic of all Cold War texts, Kennan's 1947 article on "The Sources of Soviet Conduct":

Observing that human institutions often show the greatest outward brilliance at a moment when inner decay is in reality farthest advanced, [Thomas Mann] compared the Buddenbrook family, in the days of its greatest glamor, to one of those stars whose light shines most brightly on this world when in reality it has long since ceased to exist. And who can say with assurance that the strong light still cast by the Kremlin on the dissatisfied peoples of the western world is not the powerful afterglow of a constellation which is in actuality on the wane?[216]

These observations hardly qualify as forecasts. They were vague, impressionistic, and would certainly have been maddeningly elusive for anyone trying to pin down exactly what they were anticipating or when it would occur. Still, it is not at all clear that Conquest's student would have been any less well off, in seeking to foresee the events of 1989–91, had she or he avoided the reading of theory altogether, and concentrated instead on the admittedly imprecise and necessarily intuitive insights that can be drawn from well-constructed narratives.

My point, though, is not to suggest that we jettison the scientific approach to the study of international relations; only that we bring it up to date by recognizing that good scientists, like good novelists and good historians, make use of *all* the tools at their disposal in trying to anticipate the future. That includes not just theory, observation, and rigorous calculation, but also narrative, analogy, paradox, irony, intuition, imagination, and—not least in

---

215. James H. Billington, *The Icon and the Axe: An Intrepretive History of Russian Culture* (New York: Knopf, 1966), p. 594.
216. "X" [George F. Kennan], "The Sources of Soviet Conduct," *Foreign Affairs*, Vol. 25, No. 2 (July 1947), p. 580.

importance—style.[217] If today's physical and natural sciences can benefit from, and even enrich themselves by, a recognition of how imperfectly the old scientific method "modeled" the real world, then surely the social sciences can do the same. We may not gain greater clairvoyance as a result. But we will learn more about the limits of our vision, and hence more about ourselves.

---

217. It is interesting to note that some of our best literary stylists these days are "hard" scientists: the names of Stephen Jay Gould, Stephen W. Hawking, Lewis Thomas, Philip Morrison, and the late Heinz Pagels come to mind. How many social scientists write as well, or have as many readers?

Suggestions for Further Reading

There is a vast literature on the causes of war, the role of nuclear weapons, U.S.-Soviet relations during the Cold War, and prospects for peace. This bibliography is organized around some of the most important questions raised by the essays in this book. Of necessity, it omits many significant works. In deciding what to list, we have tried to include more recent works on general questions, while leaving out older studies and those that examine particular historical cases of war. Additional references on these topics can be found in the footnotes of each article in this collection, as well as in some of the works listed below. To avoid repetition, all the works listed appear only once, even if they belong in several categories.

The Causes of War: General Works

Blainey, Geoffrey, *The Causes of War*, 3rd ed. (New York: Free Press, 1988). A readable and comprehensive overview and analysis of many of the most important theories of war.

Brodie, Bernard, *War and Politics* (New York: Macmillan, 1973), chap. 7. Explicates and assesses economic, psychological, and political theories of war, finding all deficient, in varying degrees.

Brown, Seyom, *The Causes and Prevention of War* (New York: St. Martin's, 1987). A useful introductory survey.

Levy, Jack S., "The Causes of War: A Review of Theories and Evidence," in Philip E. Tetlock, Jo L. Husbands, Robert Jervis, Paul C. Stern, and Charles Tilly, eds., *Behavior, Society, and Nuclear War*, Vol. 1 (New York: Oxford University Press, 1989), pp. 209–333. An extremely useful and up-to-date survey of most important theories of war. Includes a comprehensive bibliography.

Rotberg, Robert I., and Theodore K. Rabb, eds., *The Origin and Prevention of Major Wars* (Cambridge: Cambridge University Press, 1989). Originally a special issue of the *Journal of Interdisciplinary History*, this book offers brief chapters on various theories of war and reconsiderations of the outbreak of the Thirty Years' War, World War I, World War II, and other conflicts.

Waltz, Kenneth N., *Man, the State, and War: A Theoretical Analysis* (New York: Columbia University Press, 1959). A classic work that examines the causes of war at the level of the individual, the state, and the international system.

Wright, Quincy, *A Study of War*, 2nd ed. (Chicago: University of Chicago Press, 1965). Although somewhat dated, this book still offers a remarkable and comprehensive overview of war and its causes.

The International System and War

Craig, Gordon A., and Alexander L. George, *Force and Statecraft: Diplomatic Problems of Our Time*, 2nd ed. (New York: Oxford University Press, 1990). Examines the evolution of international systems and international relations from the seventeenth century to the present. A useful introductory text.

Deutsch, Karl W., and J. David Singer, "Multipolar Power Systems and International Stability," *World Politics*, Vol. 16, No. 3 (April 1964), pp. 390–406. Employs a formal, semi-quantitative method of analysis to show that multipolar systems are more stable than bipolar ones. The authors suggest that in the long run multipolarity may become less stable.

Gilpin, Robert, *War and Change in World Politics* (New York: Cambridge University Press, 1981). Analyzes major wars as the result of the rise and decline of successive hegemonic states in the international system.

Keohane, Robert O., ed., *Neorealism and Its Critics* (New York: Columbia University Press, 1986). Includes major portions of Kenneth Waltz, *Theory of International Politics*, critiques of neorealism, and replies from Robert Gilpin and Waltz.

Morgenthau, Hans J., *Politics Among Nations: The Struggle for Power and Peace*, 5th ed., revised (New York: Knopf, 1978). A classic work in the realist tradition of international politics. Argues that international politics is dominated by a struggle for power that makes war inevitable.

Rosecrance, Richard N., "Bipolarity, Multipolarity, and the Future," *Journal of Conflict Resolution*, Vol. 10, No. 3 (September 1966), pp. 314–327. Assesses the case for the peacefulness of bipolar and multipolar systems. Finds flaws in each, and proposes an intermediate system instead.

Waltz, Kenneth N., "The Stability of a Bipolar World," *Daedalus*, Vol. 93, No. 3 (Summer 1964), pp. 881–909. Introduces many arguments for why a bipolar world may have more intense competition, but fewer wars than a multipolar one.

Waltz, Kenneth N., *Theory of International Politics* (Reading, Mass.: Addison-Wesley, 1979). An elegant statement of Waltz's neorealist theory that the distribution of power provides the key to understanding the major patterns of behavior and the probability of war in an international system. Includes a rigorous formulation of balance-of-power theory and an extended argument for why bipolar systems are relatively peaceful.

Nuclear Weapons and International Stability

Allison, Graham, Ashton B. Carter, Steven E. Miller, and Philip Zelikow, eds., *Cooperative Denuclearization: From Pledges to Deeds*, CSIA Studies in International Security No. 2 (Cambridge, Mass.: Center for Science and International Affairs, Harvard University, January 1993). Detailed analysis of the problem of coping with

Cold War nuclear arsenals in the post–Cold War era. Particular emphasis on the safe consolidation and contraction of the Soviet nuclear legacy.

Betts, Richard K., *Nuclear Blackmail and Nuclear Balance* (Washington, D.C.: Brookings, 1987). An examination of the role of nuclear weapons in Cold War crises.

Brodie, Bernard, ed., *The Absolute Weapon: Atomic Power and World Order* (New York: Harcourt Brace, 1946). Includes Brodie's classic statement that nuclear weapons have revolutionized warfare and that weapons will henceforth be intended to prevent wars, not fight them.

Bundy, McGeorge, *Danger and Survival: Choices about the Bomb in the First Fifty Years* (New York: Random House, 1988). A detailed review of U.S. policy toward nuclear weapons and the evolution of a tradition of nonuse. Particularly strong on the policies of the Truman, Eisenhower, and Kennedy administrations. Explores the likely outcomes of policies not chosen.

Campbell, Kurt, Ashton B. Carter, Steven E. Miller, and Charles A. Zraket, *Soviet Nuclear Fission: Control of the Nuclear Arsenal in a Disintegrating Soviet Union*, CSIA Studies in International Security No. 1 (Cambridge, Mass.: Center for Science and International Affairs, Harvard University, November 1991). Assesses nuclear risks associated with the demise of the Soviet Union, and possible policy responses.

Feldman, Shai, *Israeli Nuclear Deterrence: A Strategy for the 1980s* (New York: Columbia University Press, 1982). Includes a statement of why nuclear weapons are fundamentally defensive weapons.

George, Alexander L., and Richard Smoke, *Deterrence in American Foreign Policy: Theory and Practice* (New York: Columbia University Press, 1974). Although somewhat dated now that many more documents have been declassified, this book remains an important study of how the United States attempted to exploit its nuclear forces for political purposes during the Cold War.

Iklé, Fred C., "Can Nuclear Deterrence Last Out the Century?" *Foreign Affairs*, Vol. 62, No. 4 (January 1973), pp. 267–285. A pessimistic account of how nuclear deterrence might eventually fail.

Jervis, Robert, *The Meaning of the Nuclear Revolution: Statecraft and the Prospect of Armageddon* (Ithaca: Cornell University Press, 1989). A comprehensive statement of the arguments for why nuclear weapons have made wars and crises less likely.

Mandelbaum, Michael, *The Nuclear Revolution: International Politics Before and After Hiroshima* (New York: Cambridge University Press, 1981). Examines how nuclear weapons have affected international politics, with comparisons to earlier international systems and weapons technologies.

Nye, Joseph S., Jr., "Nuclear Learning and U.S.-Soviet Security Regimes," *International Organization*, Vol. 41, No. 3 (Summer 1987), pp. 371–402. Uses the concept of learning to explore the evolution of U.S.-Soviet attitudes and cooperation on nuclear weapons.

Waltz, Kenneth N., *The Spread of Nuclear Weapons: More May Be Better*, Adelphi Paper No. 171 (London: International Institute for Strategic Studies, 1981). Takes the argument that nuclear weapons preserve peace to its logical extreme and suggests that proliferation may be stabilizing.

Wohlstetter, Albert, "The Delicate Balance of Terror," *Foreign Affairs*, Vol. 27, No. 2 (January 1959), pp. 211–234. A classic statement of the view that nuclear deterrence is fragile and must be scrupulously maintained lest war break out. Emphasizes the need for secure retaliatory forces to reduce preemptive incentives.

Offense, Defense, and War

Jervis, Robert, "Cooperation Under the Security Dilemma," *World Politics*, Vol. 30, No. 2 (January 1978), pp. 167–214. A seminal explication of how offensive and defensive advantages affect the prospects for war.

Quester, George, *Offense and Defense in the International System* (New York: Wiley, 1977). Traces the evolution and consequences of the shifting offense/defense balance in the history of world politics.

Sagan, Scott D., "1914 Revisited: Allies, Offense, and Instability," *International Security*, Vol. 11, No. 2 (Fall 1986), pp. 151–176. (Reprinted in *Military Strategy and the Origins of the First World War*, rev. ed. [Princeton, N.J.: Princeton University Press, 1991].) Argues that states may sometimes require offensive doctrines to prevent war.

Van Evera, Stephen, "The Cult of the Offensive and the Origins of the First World War," *International Security*, Vol. 9, No. 4 (Summer 1984), pp. 58–107. (Reprinted in *Military Strategy and the Origins of the First World War* [Princeton, N.J.: Princeton University Press, 1985 and rev. ed., 1991].) Traces in detail how the widespread belief in the efficacy of offensive military action contributed to the outbreak of World War I.

Economic Interdependence, International Institutions, and Peace

Baldwin, David, ed., *Neorealism and Neoliberalism: The Contemporary Debate* (New York: Columbia University Press, 1993). A collection of important recent articles on liberal and realist theories of cooperation.

Buzan, Barry, "Economic Structure and International Security: The Limits of the Liberal Case," *International Organization*, Vol. 38, No. 4 (Autumn 1984), pp. 597–624. Offers an explication and critique of liberal theories that claim that an open international economic system contributes to peace.

Grieco, Joseph M., "Anarchy and the Limits of Cooperation: A Realist Critique of the Newest Liberal Institutionalism," *International Organization*, Vol. 42, No. 3 (Summer 1988), pp. 485–507. Argues that states are unlikely to cooperate because they fear that potential adversaries may gain more from cooperation, even if both parties gain compared to not cooperating at all.

Keohane, Robert O., *After Hegemony: Cooperation and Discord in the World Political Economy* (Princeton: Princeton University Press, 1984. Attempts to build a theory of international institutions and their implications for cooperation.

Keohane, Robert O., and Joseph S. Nye, Jr., *Power and Interdependence: World Politics in Transition*, 2nd ed. (Boston: Little, Brown, 1977). A classic statement of how interdependence and international institutions can influence state behavior in ways not predicted by a realist approach.

Keohane, Robert O., and Joseph S. Nye, Jr., "Power and Interdependence Revisited," *International Organization*, Vol. 41, No. 4 (Autumn 1987), pp. 725–753. The authors of *Power and Interdependence* review their conclusions, respond to their critics, and suggest directions for further research.

Mitrany, David, *A Working Peace System* (Chicago: Quadrangle Press, 1966). An important presentation of the functionalist theory of how international institutions can promote integration and peace.

Nye, Joseph S., Jr., "Neorealism and Neoliberalism," *World Politics*, Vol. 40, No. 2 (January 1988), pp. 235–251. Reviews *Neorealism and its Critics* and *The Rise of the Trading State*. Explicates theories of economic liberalism and critically assesses neorealism.

Rosecrance, Richard N., *The Rise of the Trading State: Commerce and Conquest in the Modern World* (New York: Basic Books, 1986). Argues that trading states that emphasize commerce (e.g., Japan) are more successful in the present international system than those that rely excessively on military power.

Domestic Structure and War

Andreski, Stanislav, "On the Peaceful Disposition of Military Dictatorships," *Journal of Strategic Studies*, Vol. 3, No. 3 (December 1980), pp. 3–10. Points out that military regimes are rarely able to go to war because their armed forces are preoccupied with repressing dissent at home.

Chan, Steve, "Mirror, Mirror on the Wall . . . Are the Freer Countries More Pacific?" *Journal of Conflict Resolution*, Vol. 28, No. 4 (December 1984), pp. 617–648. Finds that democratic countries are not notably more peace-loving than other types.

Doyle, Michael W., "Kant, Liberal Legacies, and Foreign Affairs," *Philosophy and Public Affairs*, Vol. 12, Nos. 3 and 4 (Summer and Fall, 1983), pp. 205–235; pp. 323–353. This two-part article combines old theories and modern evidence to support the argument that liberal democracies do not fight one another, even if they sometimes go to war against non-democracies.

Doyle, Michael W., "Liberalism and World Politics," *American Political Science Review*, Vol. 80, No. 4 (December 1986), pp. 1151–1169. Develops the themes of Doyle's earlier article.

Russett, Bruce, *Controlling the Sword: The Democratic Governance of National Security* (Cambridge, Mass.: Harvard University Press, 1990), chap. 5. A general argument for why democratic states do not fight one another.

Small, Melvin, and J. David Singer, "The War-Proneness of Democratic Regimes, 1816–1965," *The Jerusalem Journal of International Relations*, Vol. 1, No. 4 (Summer 1976), pp. 50–69. Examines the empirical record and finds that democracies are as prone to war as other types of states, and that democracies tend to fight longer wars with fewer casualties. Also concludes that democracies have not fought one another, but that this may be due to geographical separation.

Snyder, Jack, *Myths of Empire: Domestic Politics and Strategic Ideology* (Ithaca: Cornell University Press, 1991). Argues that aggressive states seek to expand because their governments are captured by narrow elites who do not reflect the national interest.

Weede, Erich W., "Democracy and War Involvement," *Journal of Conflict Resolution*, Vol. 28, No. 4 (December 1984), pp. 649–664. A useful empirical study.

Militarism and War

Berghahn, Volker R., *Militarism: The History of an International Debate 1861–1979* (New York: St. Martin's, 1982). A useful overview.

Betts, Richard K., *Soldiers, Statesmen and Cold War Crises* (Cambridge, Mass.: Harvard University Press, 1977). An important study of military advice in U.S.-Soviet crises. Concludes that military leaders rarely recommend the use of force, although they may support escalation once war has begun.

Craig, Gordon A., *The Politics of the Prussian Army, 1640–1945* (New York: Oxford University Press, 1955). A comprehensive survey of the perils of militarism in German history.

Ienaga, Saburo, *The Pacific War, 1931 1945*, trans. Frank Baldwin (New York: Pantheon, 1978), chap. 7. Examines Japanese military thinking and the role of the military in Japanese politics and foreign policy in the 1930s.

Kitchen, Martin, *The German Officer Corps, 1890–1914* (Oxford: Clarendon Press, 1968). Discusses German militarism and the events leading to the First World War.

Snyder, Jack, *The Ideology of the Offensive: Military Decision Making and the Disasters of 1914* (Ithaca: Cornell University Press, 1984). Examines French, Russian, and German military planning on the eve of World War I and shows why organizational factors led each country to adopt a offensive posture that proved to be disastrous.

Nationalism and War

Herwig, Holger H., "Clio Deceived: Patriotic Self-Censorship in Germany After the Great War," *International Security*, Vol. 12, No. 2 (Fall 1987), pp. 5–44. An excellent account of how Germans rewrote the history of the outbreak of World War 1, creating myths that helped lead to the next great war.

Kennedy, Paul M., "The Decline of Nationalistic History in the West, 1900–1970," *Journal of Contemporary History*, Vol. 8, No. 1 (January 1973), pp. 77–100. A useful discussion of the evolution of this issue.

Shafer, Boyd C., *Faces of Nationalism: New Realities and Old Myths* (New York: Harcourt Brace Jovanovich, 1972). A useful general survey.

Snyder, Louis L., *Encyclopedia of Nationalism* (New York: Paragon House, 1990). A good overview with a comprehensive bibliography.

Snyder, Louis L., *German Nationalism: The Tragedy of a People: Extremism contra Liberalism in Modern German History* (Port Washington, N.Y.: Kennikat Press, 1969). An overview of the evolution and problems of German nationalism in its political and cultural forms.

"Ethnic Conflict and International Security." *Survival*, Vol. 35, No. 1 (Spring 1993); (special issue of *Survival* devoted to the issue of nationalism, ethnic conflict, and international security).

Why the Cold War was a Long Peace

Deporte, Anton W., *Europe Between the Superpowers: The Enduring Balance*, 2nd ed. (New Haven: Yale University Press, 1986). An excellent account of alliance relations in divided Europe.

Gaddis, John Lewis, *The Long Peace: Inquiries into the History of the Cold War* (New York: Oxford University Press, 1987). Considers the evolution of U.S.-Soviet attitudes toward subjects such as satellite reconnaissance, regional conflicts, and nuclear weapons.

George, Alexander L., *Managing U.S.-Soviet Rivalry: Problems of Crisis Prevention* (Boulder, Colo.: Westview, 1983). Examines how the superpowers have attempted to develop rules of the game to prevent crises, especially over regional conflicts.

George, Alexander L., Philip J. Farley, and Alexander Dallin, eds., *U.S.-Soviet Security Cooperation: Achievements, Lessons, Failures* (New York: Oxford University Press, 1988). A comprehensive examination of areas in which U.S.-Soviet cooperation has been successful, as well some conclusions about the conditions for cooperation.

Gowa, Joanne, and Nils Wessell, *Ground Rules: Soviet and American Involvement in Regional Conflicts* (Philadelphia: Foreign Policy Research Institute, 1982). Discusses the evolution of superpower rules of conduct.

The New Europe

It is difficult to keep abreast of the literature on international politics in Europe after the Cold War. New books and important articles will appear frequently in the next few months and years. The works listed here are representative samples of background reading for the Snyder, Mearsheimer, and Van Evera contributions to this volume.

Brenner, Michael, "The EC in Yugoslavia: A Debut Performance," *Security Studies*, Vol. 1, No. 4 (Summer 1992), pp. 586–609. Discusses the EC's relatively unsuccessful performance in the Yugoslav crisis, arguing that its emergence as a player in European politics may be as important as the fact of failure in this particular case.

Brzezinski, Zbigniew, "Post-Communist Nationalism," *Foreign Affairs*, Vol. 68, No. 5 (Winter 1989–90), pp. 1–25. A timely and insightful discussion of the likely consequences of the end of the Soviet Empire.

Bunce, Valerie, "Rising Above the Past: The Struggle for Liberal Democracy in Eastern Europe," *World Policy Journal*, Vol. 7, No. 3 (Summer 1990), pp. 395–430. A thoughtful assessment of the problems of building democracy in the formerly communist countries of Eastern and Central Europe.

Garton Ash, Timothy, *The Magic Lantern: The Revolution of '89 Witnessed in Warsaw, Budapest, Berlin, and Prague* (New York: Random House, 1990). A fascinating inside look at how communism collapsed in East Central Europe. The chapters on Czechoslovakia and Poland are particularly good.

Hoffmann, Stanley, "The Case for Leadership," *Foreign Policy*, No. 81 (Winter 1990–91). An extended rebuttal to Mearsheimer's essay, as well as a set of predictions and policies for the new Europe.

Joffe, Josef, "Collective Security and the Future of Europe: Failed Dreams and Dead Ends," *Survival*, Vol. 34, No. 1 (Spring 1992), pp. 36–50. A skeptical view of the prospects for collective security in post–Cold War Europe.

Larrabee, F. Stephen, "Long Memories and Short Fuses: Change and Instability in the Balkans," *International Security*, Vol. 15, No. 3 (Winter 1990/91), pp. 58–91. Offers a detailed analysis of the ethnic conflicts and boundary disputes that may emerge in the Balkans.

Mortimer, Edward, *European Security after the Cold War*, Adelphi Paper No. 271 (London: Brassey's for IISS, 1992). A survey of post–Cold War Europe which identifies dangers and proposes remedies.

Ramet, Sabrina Petra, "War in the Balkans," *Foreign Affairs*, Vol. 71, No. 4 (Fall 1992), pp. 79–98. Explains how Yugoslavia's troubles became a European crisis.

Stares, Paul B., ed., *The New Germany and the New Europe* (Washington D.C.: The Brookings Institution, 1992). A substantial collection of essays that comprehensively assess the implications of German unification.

Van Evera, Stephen, "Managing the Eastern Crisis: Preventing War in the Former Soviet Empire," *Security Studies*, Vol. 1, No. 3 (Spring 1992), pp. 361–381. Provides an argument about how to avoid war in the conflict-prone former Soviet empire.

Zelikow, Philip, "The New Concert of Europe," *Survival*, Vol. 34, No. 2 (Summer 1992), pp. 12–30. Assesses Europe's institutions in light of post–Cold War challenges.

Zielonka, Jan, *Security in Central Europe*, Adelphi Paper No. 272 (London: Brassey's for IISS, 1992). Analyzes sources of instability in Hungary, Poland, and the Czech and Slovak republics.

The Future of War and the Changing International System

Fukuyama, Francis, "The End of History?" *The National Interest*, No. 16 (Summer 1989), pp. 3–18. Argues that the liberal democratic ideal has triumphed over its ideological adversaries, ushering in an era devoid of great international conflicts over political ideas.

Gaddis, John Lewis, *The United States and the End of the Cold War: Implications, Reconsiderations, Provocations* (New York: Oxford University Press, 1992). Thoughtful collection of essays on the causes and consequences of the end of the Cold War, by one of America's most insightful scholars.

Huntington, Samuel P., "The U.S.—Decline or Renewal?" *Foreign Affairs*, Vol. 67, No. 2 (Winter 1988–89), pp. 76–96. An excellent critique of arguments that the United States is in inexorable decline.

Kennedy, Paul M., *The Rise and Fall of the Great Powers: Economic Change and Military Conflict from 1500–2000* (New York: Random House, 1987). Argues, with an impressive range of historical examples, that great powers must be sensitive to the economic underpinnings of their power. Suggests that the United States must pay particular heed to this problem if it is to avoid an impending decline.

Krauthammer, Charles, "The Unipolar Moment," *Foreign Affairs: America and the World*, Vol. 70, No. 1 (1990/91), pp. 23–34. Argues that, for now, claims of a multipolar world are incorrect, and sketches the international challenges for the United States at its moment of predominance.

Mueller, John, *Retreat from Doomsday: The Obsolescence of Major War* (New York: Basic Books, 1989). Argues that major war among industrialized countries is becoming unthinkable, like dueling and slavery.

Nye, Joseph S., Jr., *Bound to Lead: The Changing Nature of American Power* (New York: Basic Books, 1990). A comprehensive response to Paul Kennedy's argument. Concludes that the United States will retain a leadership role in all spheres of world politics.

International Security
Center for Science and International Affairs
John F. Kennedy School of Government
Harvard University

The articles in this reader were previously published in **International Security**, a quarterly journal sponsored and edited by the Center for Science and International Affairs at the John F. Kennedy School of Government at Harvard University, and published by The MIT Press. To receive subscription information about the journal or find out more about other readers in our series, please contact MIT Press Journals at 55 Hayward Street, Cambridge, MA, 02142.